DEVON AND CORNWALL RECORD SOCIETY

New Series, Vol. 40

General Editor: Mrs Margery Rowe BA, DAA

To the memory of Peter Newton
an enthusiastic and valued member of
The Uffculme Archive Group

DEVON AND CORNWALL RECORD SOCIETY

New Series, Vol. 40

THE UFFCULME WILLS AND INVENTORIES

16th to 18th Centuries

Edited on behalf of **THE UFFCULME ARCHIVE GROUP** by

PETER WYATT

B Sc, Ph D, C Chem, FRSC, FRSE

Professor Emeritus of the University of St Andrews

With an Introduction by

ROBIN STANES

MA, *Part-time Tutor*,

Department of Continuing and Adult Education, University of Exeter

1997

ISBN 0901853 40 2

Typeset for the Society by
Peter Wyatt
and printed and bound for the Society by
Short Run Press Ltd, Exeter
United Kingdom

CONTENTS

LIST OF ILLUSTRATIONS

TEXT FIGURES

PLATES

Between pages xxxii and xxxiii

PREFACE

The Uffculme Archive Group was formed from the members of a course promoted by the Department of Continuing and Adult Education of the University of Exeter, with Robin Stanes as tutor, and the resulting work was very much a joint effort by the members of that group, whose names are appended below. Uffculme was chosen for special study because of its peculiar status in the jurisdiction of the Diocese of Salisbury, which saved its probate records from the wartime destruction suffered by those for other Devon parishes;[1] and the original intention was to transcribe a sample of the inventories held at the Wiltshire Record Office at Trowbridge to see what light they could throw upon farming and cloth-making activities and village life in general in Uffculme, mainly during the 17th century. As the project developed however, it became clear that a much fuller and more accurate picture would be obtained by transcribing *all* the Uffculme inventories held at Trowbridge, and then by examining all the wills over the period, with or without inventories, both at Trowbridge and at the Public Record Office in London. Much of our work had already been done on the inventories before the other documents were abstracted and this explains the somewhat arbitrary division of the archive material into sections. The essays generated by our study of these documents are printed in a companion volume, *Uffculme: a Peculiar Parish.*[2]

Though stray documents may emerge from time to time, transcriptions of all the known Uffculme inventories are collected here, together with abstracts of all the Uffculme wills at Trowbridge up to 1800 (and a few beyond that date, which happened to be indexed in the list of the Dean of Salisbury). However, since our material exceeded the bounds of the present volume, the only probate documents submitted to the Prerogative Court of Canterbury included here are the seventeen at the Public Record Office in London which were found to have accompanying inventories (distinguished by a number with the prefix L for London). The remaining London wills and letters of administration without accompanying inventories, 166 in all up to the year 1700, are printed in the other volume along with the essays,[2] where they are distinguished by the prefix LW, for London Will. (After 1700 the wills in London are much harder to find, being indexed by name and not by parish.)

While the group as a whole were involved in the transcriptions of the inventories and in the many discussions thereafter, Mary Fraser supplied the bulk of the death and marriage records from the parish registers and did all the work at the Public Record Office in London on the Prerogative Court of Canterbury documents. Almost all the other wills were abstracted by Peter Wyatt, who also prepared the indexes. As this book is being prepared for the press, it is sad to have to report the death of one of our group, Peter

---

[1] Margaret Cash, *Devon Inventories of the 16th and 17th Centuries*, Devon & Cornwall Record Society, New Series, Vol.11, 1966.

[2] *Uffculme: a Peculiar Parish*, ed Peter Wyatt and Robin Stanes, published by the Uffculme Archive Group and printed by the Short Run Press at Exeter, 1997.

Newton. He compiled the glossary and worked tirelessly as our business manager in promoting *Uffculme: a Peculiar Parish.* His enthusiasm and forthright manner will be greatly missed by us and by many others in several fields of local activity.

Robin Stanes was the originator of this project and acted as historical advisor throughout, but I should be held to account for shortcomings in the general lay-out and detailed editorial work.

Peter Wyatt
Sidmouth
July 1997

THE UFFCULME ARCHIVE GROUP

R Priscilla Flower-Smith, BA, PhD, historian.
Mary Fraser, MA, wife of former Vicar of Uffculme; genealogist.
Peggy Knowlman, born at Northcott Farm, Uffculme, and lived there for many years and then at Culmstock and Hemyock; local historian.
Peter H. Newton, CEng., FICE; an engineer in Africa and England; resident in Kentisbeare and Uffculme since 1954; founder-chairman of the Uffculme Society.
Robin G.F. Stanes, MA, part-time tutor in the Department of Continuing and Adult Education, University of Exeter; farmed at Slapton 1957-65; author of *A History of Devon* and *The Old Farm.*
Margaret C.M.Tucker, BA, holder of Certificate in Local and Regional History, Univ. of Exeter; retired schoolteacher; a Devonian resident in Uffculme since 1986.
Peter A.H. Wyatt, BSc, PhD, CChem, FRSC, FRSE, Professor Emeritus of the University of St. Andrews; an incomer with Devon roots.

Enquiries concerning the companion volume, *Uffculme: a Peculiar Parish*, may be addressed to:

Robin Stanes, Culver House, Payhembury, East Devon, EX14 0HR.

ACKNOWLEDGEMENTS

Thanks are due to Professor Nicholas Orme for his initial encouragement to publish the material in this form, to Steven Hobbs and other members of the Wiltshire Record Office, to Margery Rowe, the Devon County Archivist at the time (and now our DCRS editor), and other members of the Devon Record Office, for invaluable help during the course of this work. We are also grateful to the Record Offices for permission to publish the documents and to the Public Record Office in London for permission to use Crown Copyright material. We thank Geoffrey Fraser for the photograph of the Uffculme Prebendal Stall in Salisbury Cathedral and the National Portrait Gallery, London, for permission to reproduce the portrait of Edward Seymour. We are also indebted to the Uffculme Local History Group for a grant towards the cost of the photocopies and to the Short Run Press for helpful cooperation in the final stages of this book's production.

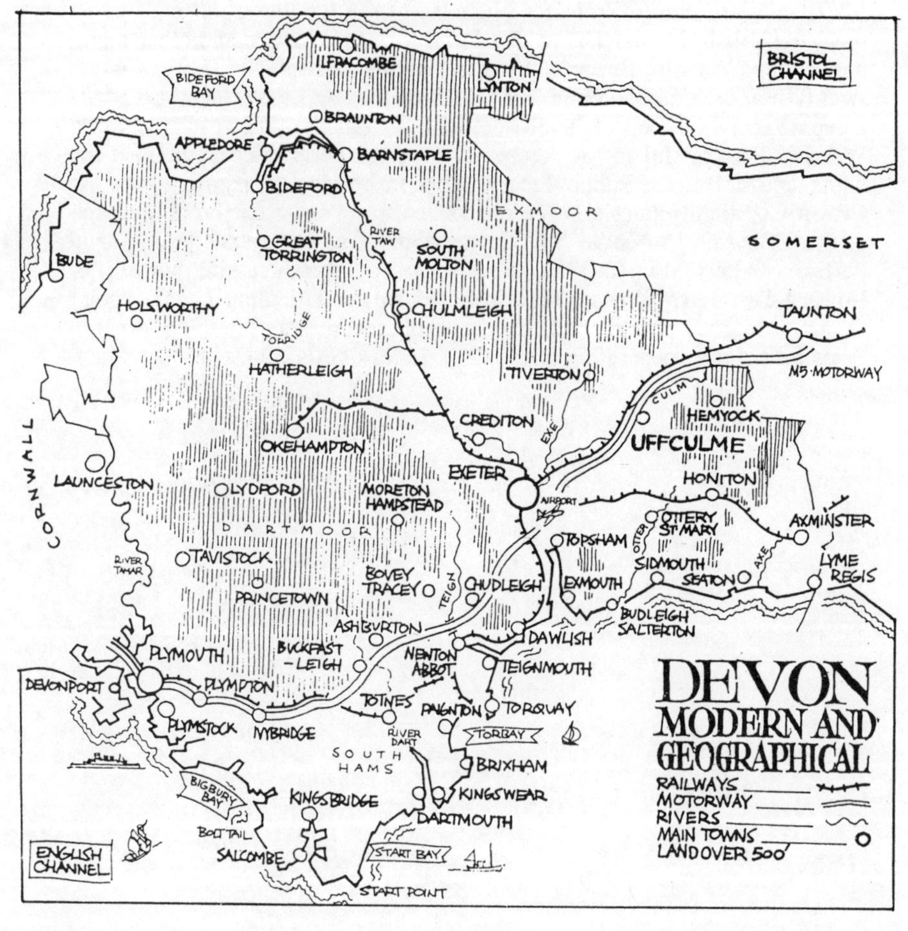

Map showing the location of Uffculme in Devon
(J R Stanes)

INTRODUCTION

by Robin Stanes

In her editorial introduction to *Devon Inventories* published by this society in 1966,[1] Margaret Cash explains the reason for adding to the collections of inventories already published: "For Devon the reason is simple; all but a very few of these documents were destroyed when the Exeter Probate Registry was bombed in 1942."

For this collection the reason for publication is much but not quite the same. This volume contains abstracts of numerous wills as well as inventories, and most Devonshire wills were burnt in 1942. Secondly the wills and inventories included here, principally dating from the seventeenth century, all relate to the parish of Uffculme. They thus offer an opportunity, denied almost entirely from such sources elsewhere in Devon, to shed some light on the cloth making and farming and other activities of what was then a not untypical small industrial town set in a large pastoral parish.

Inventories have been much studied. A bibliography[2] published in 1983 lists some 500 publications relating to inventories and more have been produced since then. One result of these studies has been to identify the limitations of the inventory.[3] Among other matters, freehold land and property owned, and debts owed, by the deceased are excluded from inventories normally, thus limiting any accurate assessment of total wealth. A number of such inventory studies have been used in the writing of this and the companion volume,[4] namely those relating to Cleethorpes,[5] Ipswich,[6] Mid-Essex,[7] and Dore and Totley,[8] in addition to those for Devon as a whole, referred to above.[1]

Other probate documents do survive for Devon. Those of the villages of Stockland and Dalwood, once in the Archdeaconry of Dorset, are at the Dorset Record Office in Dorchester; those of the village of Chardstock, also once in Dorset, are at Trowbridge. One hundred and forty wills and inventories for Cockington,[9] proved in the Manor Court between 1540 and 1623, are at the Devon Record Office, as are 216 inventories and 75 wills of

---

1 Margaret Cash, *Devon Inventories of the 16th and 17th Centuries,* Devon and Cornwall Record Society, New Series Vol 11, 1966.

2 Mark Overton, *Bibliography of British Probate Inventories*, University of Newcastle, 1983.

3 Margaret Spufford, "The limitations of the probate inventory", in J. Chartres and D. Hey, ed., *English Rural Society 1500-1800; Essays in honour of Joan Thirsk.*

4 The Uffculme Archive Group, (ed. Peter Wyatt and Robin Stanes), *Uffculme: a Peculiar Parish*, 1977: referred to elsewhere in this book as "the companion volume".

5 R.W. Ambler & B & L Watkinson, *Farmers and Fishermen: The Probate Inventories of the Ancient Parish of Clee, South Humberside 1536-1742*, University of Hull, 1987.

6 Michael Read, *Ipswich Inventories*, Suffolk Record Society, 1981.

7 Francis W. Steer, *Farm and Cottage Inventories in Mid-Essex 1635-1749*, Essex Record Office Publications No. 8, Chelmsford, 1950.

8 David Hey, *Seke in Body but Hole in Mynd: a selection of Wills and Inventories of Dore and Totley 1539-1747*, Dore Village Society, 1990.

9 Margery Rowe, "Cockington Manor Wills", *Devon and Cornwall Notes and Queries*, 33, No. 4, pp 109-113; Mallock Papers, Cockington, DRO 48/13.

Exeter people whose children came under the care of the Exeter Orphans' Court between 1555 and 1721.[10]

The Uffculme inventories begin in 1575 and become very scarce after 1720. The intervening century and a half was a period of great change politically, economically, and socially. To reflect these changes fully would require the existence of many more inventories than survive. Some calculations and conclusions have necessarily therefore been based to some extent on inadequate evidence with too wide a chronological spread. Change over time has however been examined where possible. The findings suggested in this Introduction are based, with their permission and help, on the work of the Uffculme Archive Group (see page x), whose contributions appear in fuller form under their own names in the companion volume, *Uffculme: a Peculiar Parish*, referred to above.

The probate documents for Uffculme were for reasons explained below in Salisbury in 1942 and thus escaped the Exeter bomb. Included in this volume are, firstly, two hundred and forty nine inventories preserved at the Wiltshire Record Office at Trowbridge. One hundred and thirty-four of these are attached to wills, and abstracts of these follow the inventory in the text. These are in turn followed by three hundred and twenty two Uffculme wills without inventories attached, also preserved at Trowbridge, and then by seventeen Uffculme inventories and wills proved at the Prerogative Court of Canterbury at Lambeth and preserved at the Public Record Office in London.

A further one hundred and sixty-six wills from before 1701, proved at the Prerogative Court but without inventories attached, survive in the Public Record Office in London. For reasons of space abstracts of these appear in the companion volume. The later PCC wills are less easily accessed by the London indexes and have not been included; but, apart from those, probate documents of some sort thus survive for 754 inhabitants of Uffculme.

THE PECULIAR OF UFFCULME

From *circa* 1543 to 1833 the parish was a "peculiar" jurisdiction of the diocese of Salisbury. Previously it had been within the diocese of Exeter and two at least of its Rectors had been Prebendaries of Exeter Cathedral.[11] By 1534 the patronage of Uffculme, which had belonged to Bath Abbey and the living of Uffculme, had passed into the hands of Edward Seymour, then Earl of Hertford and later Duke of Somerset, brother to Queen Jane Seymour.[12] The seat of the Seymours was at Wolf Hall in Savernake Forest in Wiltshire near the village of Great Bedwyn. At the same time as he acquired the patronage of Uffculme, Seymour also acquired for himself the

---

[10] Exeter Orphans' Court Inventories, DRO.

[11] G.L. Henessey, MS: *Institutions of Incumbents in Devon and Cornwall,* c 1700, West Country Studies Library, Exeter; and G.R. Dunstan, ed., *The Register of Edmund Lacy, Bishop of Exeter, 1420-1455,* Vol I, p 308, Devon and Cornwall Record Society, New Series Vol 7, 1963.

[12] Letters and Papers, Henry VIII 25 and 33-35.

Prebend of Great Bedwyn with its property. To compensate the Diocese of Salisbury, the Prebend of Uffculme was transferred to that diocese by Act of Parliament in 1543.[13] The Prebendary of Uffculme still occupies a stall in the choir of Salisbury Cathedral, bearing the inscription UFCOMB OLIM BEDWIN.

Uffculme thus became a Peculiar of the diocese of Salisbury, geographically within the diocese of Exeter. Until 1833 Uffculme wills had to be proved and administrations granted by the Salisbury courts rather than those of Exeter. The Prebendary of Uffculme appointed the Vicar of Uffculme and held courts there and might reside there, perhaps originally at Parsonage House. Wills could be presented and proved and administrations granted at the Prebendal court in Uffculme, or in Salisbury itself, and sometimes elsewhere in the diocese of Salisbury as the documents show. The Dean of Salisbury - with a superior jurisdiction - or his surrogate, also made a triennial visitation to Uffculme and held a court. The documents resulting from all these courts were returned to Salisbury.

The location of the Peculiar of Uffculme within the Exeter diocese created problems probably common to all parishes lying close to a diocesan boundary. Church law laid down that, generally, the wills of those with land in more than one diocese, principally the larger landowners, had to be proved at the Prerogative Court of Canterbury at Lambeth. It cannot have been unusual in Uffculme for relatively poor men to hold land in two dioceses and this must account for some of the probate documents at the Public Record Office. A footnote to Francis Taylor's inventory [62] reveals what may have been the rule in such cases. His goods were worth £12 7s 0d, of which £10 worth lay in Hemyock, outside the Peculiar, although he died within it at Uffculme. Administrators of wills in Uffculme had to swear that no more than £5 worth of property lay "out of the peculiar" and this Francis Taylor's administrators could not do. Advice was sought from the Prerogative Court Clerk, who stated that "it belonged not to them" and that "administration ought to be taken there where the party died". A further note indicates that if the goods to the value of £5 lay both "within and without the jurisdiction" then Canterbury would be involved. Francis Taylor died in Uffculme but his property there was only worth £2 7s, so probate lay with Salisbury not Canterbury.

THE INVENTORIES AND WILLS

The two hundred and forty nine inventories and their accompanying wills surviving at Trowbridge are listed there either in the register of the "Dean of Sarum" or in that of the "Prebendal Peculiar Court of Uffculme", and are designated DS or PU in the text. This distinction arises from the Dean's duty of supervision of the Prebendary and his Prebend, and involved the triennial visit of the Dean or his surrogate mentioned above. Such visitations were made in 1613, 1625, 1628, 1631, 1635, 1641, 1662, 1665, and 1682 at least. In the eighteenth century the Vicar of Uffculme seems to

[13] 34 Henry VIII; and *Fasti Ecclesiae Sarisbriensis*, ed. Jones, 1879; *Victoria County History of Wiltshire*, Vol 3, p 185.

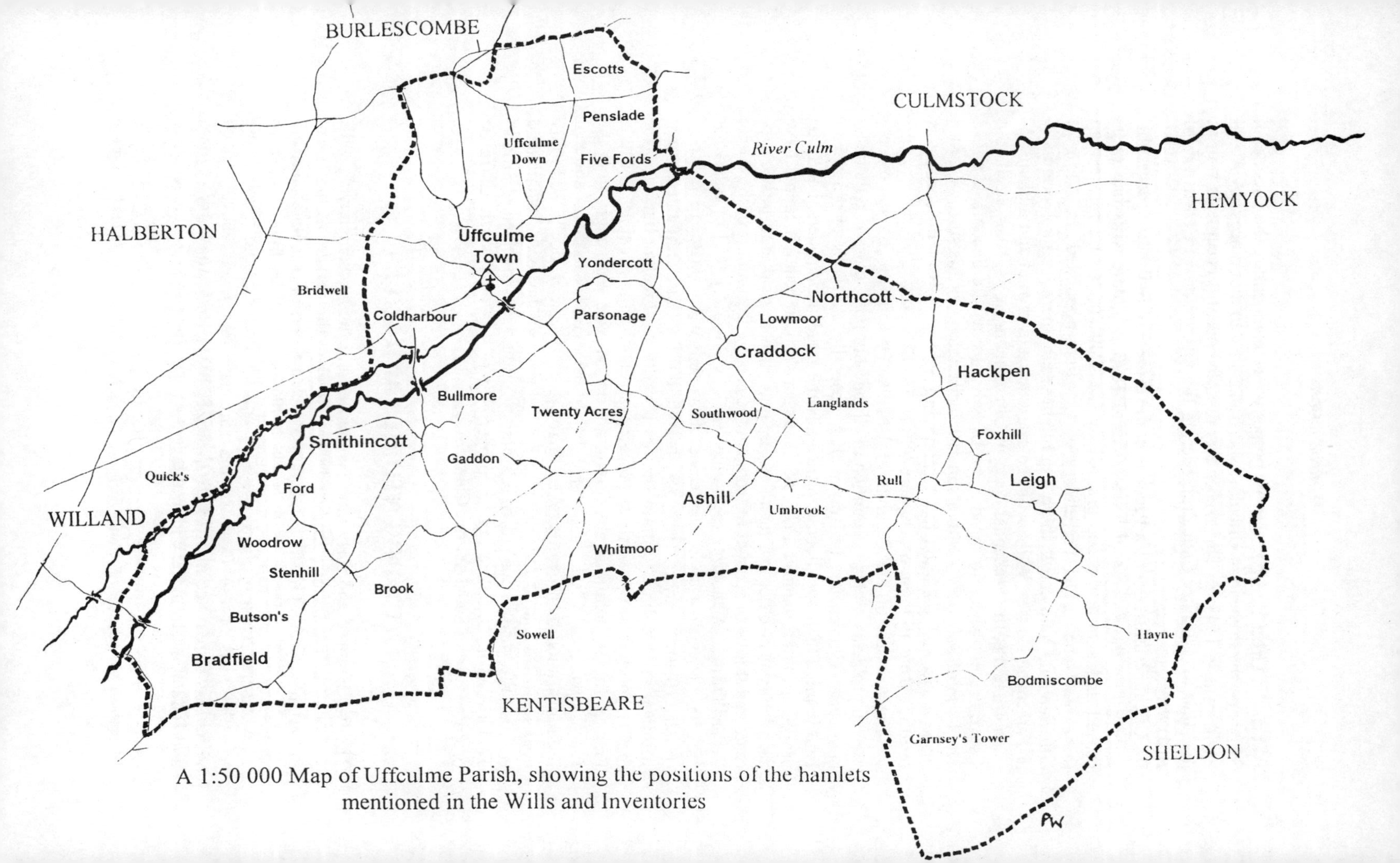

A 1:50 000 Map of Uffculme Parish, showing the positions of the hamlets mentioned in the Wills and Inventories

have acted as the Dean's surrogate. Normally the probate administration is shared equitably between Dean and Prebendary, but very few Prebendal documents survive from between 1553 and 1623 and none after 1800. Changes of regime do not seem to have affected the overall style or content of the documents.

The inventories and wills are listed and numbered chronologically here, with prefixes before the assigned number as appropriate, [and referred to in square brackets below]. Inventories from Trowbridge have a number only; wills from Trowbridge have the prefix W; Prerogative Court inventories from the Public Record Office in London have the prefix L, and Prerogative Court wills (in the companion volume) the prefix LW.

Also included immediately below the name and number of the will or inventory are the burial and marriage entries from the Parish Register which seem to correspond most closely to the deceased.

From 1529 the law demanded that, "to safeguard the administrators of the will and protect the heir from fraud", an inventory should be made of the goods and chattels of the deceased before a will could be proved or an administration granted.[14] This should be done even where there was no will. Thus, shortly after the death of a man, a widow, or a spinster, three or four neighbours or relatives visited the house and buildings, made a more or less systematic list of the contents and property and put a value to each item. No tax was paid on the estate, but probate values are generally thought to be on the low side. Cattle and sheep valuations are generally less than the market price; (see the *Uffculme Husbandry* chapter in the companion volume). All moveable goods had to be included, furniture, kitchen equipment, food that was not perishable, ready money, livestock, corn in the barn and in the ground, hay in the barn or rick, firewood, dungheaps, and farm implements. Debts owed to the deceased were included - they were his - as were leases of land or property, "chattel" leases. Debts owed by the deceased were not normally included as they were the creditors' property. Freehold real property, houses, and land were also excluded, as were growing trees and growing grass, as being part of the freehold, one with the land.[15] This absence of debts and freehold from the inventories limits the use of such documents to establish total wealth.

It seems likely that, as the law demanded, every will was once accompanied by an inventory. This is suggested by references in administrations to inventories that have not survived and by the function ascribed to the inventory. Once the estate was settled and the goods were distributed, the inventory could presumably be discarded. Chance alone however does not seem to determine the inventories' survival. None survive for Uffculme from after 1754 and very few from after 1720. The vast majority (78%) date from between 1600 and 1700, though wills begin in 1528 and end in the Dean's list in 1845. In the absence of any known change in the law, the determining factor in the survival of inventories must be changing use and

---

14 21 Hen VIII c.5

15 See the *Inventory* entries in *The Law Dictionary* by Sir Thos Edlyne Tomlins, 3rd Ed., London, 1820, and *A New Law Dictionary* by Giles Jacob, corrected & enlarged by O Ruffhead & J Morgan, London, 1772.

custom. Burn's *Ecclesiastical Law*,[16] written in 1809 (but revised in 1842), states that the practice of providing inventories "had fallen into desuetude" and that the Court would "no longer call for one *ex officio*".

Between 1576 and 1733 the Uffculme parish registers record the burials of 4362 men, women, and children. During that period probate documents of some sort survive for 507 individuals. Normally only men of full age, widows, and spinsters made wills. Wives did not do so normally as their property was by law their husbands', and children were not "of age". The registers consistently indicate relationships, "wife of", "son of", "daughter of", "widow", and "spinster" normally occurring after the burial entry. Using these descriptions, 2033 burials in Uffculme were found to be those of men of full age, widows, or spinsters, who would be likely to make wills. Thus for one in four of those eligible to make a will some sort of probate document survives.

One group that was unlikely to make wills, though eligible to do so, were the young unmarried, the apprentices and journeymen, working perhaps away from home and family, living with their masters or in lodgings at their death. It is clear from the inventories, and from the estimated population figures and other sources, that the cloth trade was booming in Uffculme in the late seventeenth century and was likely to draw in such labour. The population may have trebled in the seventeenth century.

The poor too were unlikely to make wills or perhaps have anything to bequeath. Administration accounts suggest that it cost at least £3 to make a will [73]. For some of those for whom inventories survive, £3 was a large proportion of their total estate. A note in a legal directory suggests that before 1751 the poor did not prove wills unless there was a dispute. A contemporary jingle runs:

For whoso will prove testament that is not worth ten pound
He shall pay for the parchment the third of the money all round.

In 1674 over half the recorded population of Uffculme was exempted from paying the Hearth Tax on grounds of poverty.

Men's wills and inventories form 80% of the collection. Only 154 women's wills and inventories survive from a total of 754 and twenty-six are those of spinsters and seven those of wives. The rest are widows' wills, apart from a few where the status is uncertain.

At first sight these figures suggest that, unlike today, most husbands outlived their wives. The wills show otherwise, so widows' wills should be more numerous. However widows, particularly those with property, were likely to remarry; and if they then married younger men, who survived them, the preponderance of men's wills can be better explained.

The will of Joane Smeath [177] is one of seven exceptions that "prove the rule" that wives did not make wills. Her will states that it had been made with the agreement of her second husband "at her intermarriage with him". He survived her and in her will she makes bequests to her son by her first marriage. Three of the seven wives' wills were made after second marriages, two more refer to previous settlements, and another [W254] states that her estate was "not for her husband's use".

---

16 R. Burn, *Ecclesiastical Law*, 1809, Phillimore; 9th ed., 1842, Sweet and Stevens, Vol 4, p 405.

THE TOWN OF UFFCULME

Documents suggest that from the seventeenth century at least Uffculme was a small industrial town. Its urban history must be older than that however. Though there is no evidence that it was ever a "borough", Lysons[17] refers to a market and fairs for three days each at the feasts of St Peter and St Paul (June 29th) and of St Peter ad Vincula (August 1st), and for one day each on Good Friday and the middle Wednesday in September. At least one of these seemingly mediaeval fairs was still being held in 1676 when the carpenter Richard Patch [174] "kept the poles for it". The old Shambles in the Square at Uffculme is a small vestige of this urban past.

The town lies beside the Culm and the parish extends up and down the valley of that river to include the manors and hamlets of Gaddon, Craddock, Ashill, Leigh, Bradfield, Smithincott, and Bodmiscombe. The land rises to the south east to the 800 ft moory ridge of the Blackdown Hills. To the north the old road from Taunton to Exeter runs close to the town, a route to be followed later by both the Great Western Canal and the railway. The market and cloth making towns of Tiverton, Wellington, and Cullompton were easily accessible, and further up the Culm were the populous cloth-making villages of Culmstock and Hemyock.

The parish was largely pastoral; fertile meadow by the Culm, arable and pasture, alternating according to the West Country practice, on the valley sides; and rough moory grazing on Blackdown and its outliers.

Uffculme folk made a living principally from farming and from the making of woollen cloth. There was a paper mill in the town in 1683[18] and the nearby Blackdown Hills were dug for whetstones from the seventeenth century on some scale. "Bog" iron was also dug and smelted on the Blackdowns from Roman times and clay extracted on a large scale in the fourteenth century at Clayhidon. Cloth making was however the principal and growing activity in the Culm Valley in the seventeenth century. Figures from the registers and the Protestation returns and the Hearth Tax suggest that the population grew from around 800 in 1600 to nearly 2000 in 1700.

The inventories reveal that, like most small towns, Uffculme was largely self-sufficient. All the skills and crafts needed to provide for the more ordinary simple needs of seventeenth century country people were followed within the parish. Similarly all the basic foodstuffs, building materials, and simpler materials for clothing could be produced locally. Only more specialised fabrics and more exotic foodstuffs had to be brought in from outside and bought locally.

There was a range of economic activities dependent on farming and cloth making. The seventeen millers or mill owners, who can be identified from the wills and inventories, either fulled Uffculme cloth or ground Uffculme corn; the six butchers, seven tanners, and nineteen saddlers, shoemakers, cordwainers, tallow chandlers, and soap boilers processed the cattle and sheep of Uffculme's husbandmen. For maltsters local oats and barley were available to supply the needs both of the local inns, the Fountain, the

---

[17] Daniel & Samuel Lysons, *Magna Britannia, Devon*, Vol 2.

[18] Somerset Record Office, Q/SR/153-157.

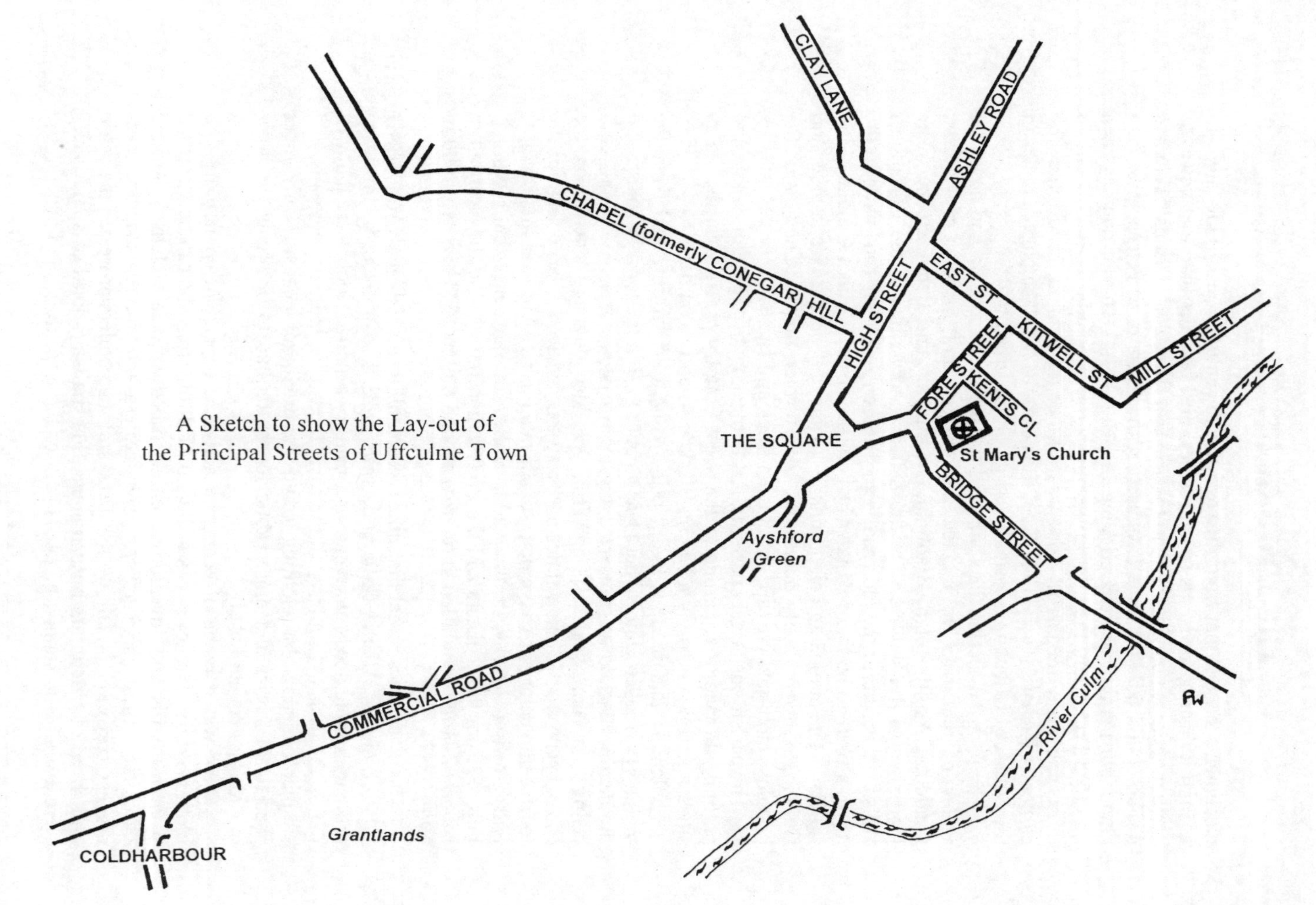

A Sketch to show the Lay-out of
the Principal Streets of Uffculme Town

George, the Half Moon, the Lamb, or the London, and of the great many households where beer was commonly made.

The names of one hundred and eight weavers, thirty six woolcombers, and forty fullers, mercers, and clothiers, and of two woolbrokers can be identified and these attest to the importance of the cloth trade in the town. The ten recorded tailors made up local cloth in the main. Blacksmiths and carpenters could make cards, combs, shears, looms, and spinning wheels for the cloth trade, just as they could meet the needs of farmers for ploughs, harrows, hand tools, and packsaddles.

The growing population, attracted by work in cloth making, had to be housed. There is evidence of the building of houses on the waste [242] - the commons - of both Uffculme and Culmstock,[19] many probably built as squatters' cob and thatch cottages by those who occupied them. Older houses and cottages surviving in the town are almost entirely cob and slate. Some are clearly "industrial", built to house workers in the cloth industry in the last century or so. The documents identify twelve masons and thatchers and carpenters to build in stone or cob and lay roofs of local rye or wheat reed, and joiners and glaziers and blacksmiths to fit and furnish the houses. The absence of slaters and helliers suggests the predominance of thatch.

Uffculme had shops from at least the early seventeenth century. These sold exotic and foreign goods, tobacco, sugar, raisins, prunes, cloves, saffron, and paper, and a large range of haberdashery, ribbons, inkle, lace, tapes, buttons, and foreign cloths, but almost nothing in the way of basic foodstuffs. Samuel James's detailed inventory [187], dated 1683, is the best of four shopkeepers' inventories to survive [81, 129, 188].

By the eighteenth century rather more sophisticated skills appear. There were gunsmiths [W196, W275] and clockmakers [W273] working in Uffculme by 1749, and "white bakers" were baking wheaten bread to supplement the more usual home-baked rye or barley from the late seventeenth century [140, W264].

THE LAND

Landowners

Not uncommonly in Devon, Uffculme parish contained no less than seven manors. Two of these, Hackpen and Bodmiscombe, had been monastic and these passed at the Dissolution to men with influence at Court,[20] the Earl of Bath, of Tawstock Court in North Devon, and jointly to Alexander Popham and William Portman, both Somerset men. The Earl of Bath also acquired the manor of Uffculme itself. None of these men were resident in the parish, but as landlords they issued leases and managed their estates. Leases were commonly chattel leases for three lives or ninety nine years. These occur frequently in the inventories and demanded the payment of a large "fine" at commencement and only small, often nominal, annual rents,

---

19 *Culmstock: a Devon Village*, Culmstock Local History Group, 1981.

20 Joyce Youings, *Devon Monastic Lands: Calendar of Particulars for Grants 1536-1558*, Devon and Cornwall Record Society, New Series Vol 1, 1955.

with sometimes little active supervision by the landlord, so that holders of long leases, particularly where the landlord was an absentee, acquired what could amount to a freehold.[21] Lessees could add to the lives on payment of a further fine. Some of the debts recorded in the wills and inventories were incurred to pay the fine on a lease.

The Walronds of Bradfield were the principal resident gentry family in Uffculme. They had been at Bradfield from the fourteenth century and were sufficiently wealthy to rebuild their great house there in the sixteenth century and again in the nineteenth. In the Hearth Tax lists of 1674,[22] Bradfield was assessed at fifteen hearths: Powderham Castle, the seat of the Earl of Devon, was assessed at twenty two. The Walronds had no hereditary title, but in 1674 William Walrond was knighted and they were invariably granted the honorific title "esq". In the last century they were ennobled and took the title Lord Waleran.[23] [See LW118, W193, LW150, and 178, 201].

They acquired Stenhill, one of the other Uffculme manors, and in the early nineteenth century they owned - perhaps as demesne - more than five hundred acres of Uffculme land at least; and their contributions to the seventeenth century lay subsidies are far and away the largest in the parish. They had land outside the parish as well and, though no direct connection with cloth making has been found, Bradfield Mill was a tucking mill for part of its existence. It seems likely that the wealth needed to maintain Bradfield came from that source rather than land alone. They, doubtless, exercised all the potent influence in the parish usual to resident country gentry. A glimpse of this can be obtained from the account of a dispute about the funds of an important local charity on which the poor were dependent. It was stated that the deeds of the charity were always kept at Bradfield and not at the church and Major Walrond took charge of the charity's capital prior to new investment.[24]

Like many gentry families they attended University and the Inns of Court. Their tombs and monuments embellish Uffculme parish church and they had their own chapel at Bradfield.

Another resident family of gentry were the Holways of Leigh or Goodleigh. Lysons describes them as "the ancient family of Holway" and they paid hearth tax for twenty two hearths. This, in the Holways' case, was almost certainly paid on two houses, the other being the Parsonage house, leased from the Prebend of Uffculme. This, probably with the right to collect the Rectorial Tithe, seems to have been leased from at least the late sixteenth century: [see the last line in LW34].

In the parish church is a memorial to James Holway, clothier, who with other members of his family left considerable sums to the poor [LW102]. The link between this well-off landowning family and the cloth trade is

---

[21] W.G. Hoskins, "The Occupation of Land in Devonshire", *Devon & Cornwall Notes & Queries*, 21, 1940, pp 2-12.

[22] Mary Fraser, *The Hearth Tax of 1674*, [PRO: E: 179 245/17/2], pp 188-9 in the companion volume; see also T.L. Stoate, *Devon Hearth Tax 1674*, publ. Stoate, Almondsbury, Bristol, 1982.

[23] Charlotte Walrond, *The Walrond Papers*, Arthur L. Humphreys, London, 1913.

[24] Uffculme Charity Money, DRO 1926B/W/P3/10; see Priscilla Flower-Smith, *The Uffculme Landowners* in the companion volume, pp 21-22.

thus well established. In his will James refers to the "mansion house in which I live". His descendant, Peter Holway, was one of the two influential men in Uffculme listed by Blome in 1673.[25] Some of the clothiers whose wills and inventories survive had land. Alexander Melhuish of Five Fords, where there was a tucking mill, left an estate of £1000, was described as a clothier, and had other mills and land and property both in and out of Uffculme [L8].

The estates of the absentee landlords seem to have been dispersed towards the beginning of the eighteenth century. The appearance of a number of freeholders in the parish at the same date is probably not a coincidence. Churleys, Marshalls, Bishops, Garnseys all appear as such, some distinguished with "esq" or "gent" or "Mr". They added to other existing parish gentry, the Moultons, the Champneys, the Salkelds. The Dowdneys of Gaddon, of Leigh, of Craddock, of Stenhill, of Foxhill, were a prominent yeoman family with many branches and lands in all parts of the parish.

Husbandry

Nearly three quarters of the inventories contain references to farming goods of some sort, while others refer to land and leases. For about a quarter of all these, farming goods account for less than a tenth of the inventory total, but for the rest husbandry of some sort provided at least part of their livelihood: it was part of the normal life of most country people, even of those with other clearly defined trades. Gentlemen, clothiers, millers, bakers, carpenters might all have land or crops or stock.

Uffculme farming was largely pastoral. Only in one fifth of the inventories was corn growing of more value than the keeping of stock. It was also by today's standards small scale. Rather more than four fifths (84/101) of the recorded herds were of fewer than ten cattle, and the average size of herd of those with more than half their wealth in farm goods varied only between six and eight at quite different dates. Overall the average size of herd was six and the largest recorded was twenty seven. The average size of a sheep flock was thirty three and the largest was 160 strong.

The principal farming activity in Uffculme seems to have been dairying. Most of those with cattle (68%) had the gear or the space - milk rooms or cheese rooms - to make cheese or butter. One of the most common items recorded in the inventories, particularly after 1650, is the cheese press or wring of which sixty occur. In contrast there are no certain references to butter churns [but see 43 and 16]. Indeed the Vicar of Uffculme stated that the churn only came into use in Uffculme in the late eighteenth century.[26] As was the case with the Tavistock Abbey dairies,[27] butter was made first by separating the cream by scalding and then "by hand", by stirring the scalded cream until butter was formed. Scalding the cream pasteurised, and thereby preserved, both it and the resulting butter and cheese. This

---

[25] R. Blome, *Britannia*, 1673.

[26] The Reverend James Windsor, MS, DRO 1920A PI 16, pp 2-11.

[27] H.P.R. Finberg, *Tavistock Abbey*, CUP, 1969, p 138.

would be advantageous if there were distant markets, as there certainly were in the next century. What was left after raising and scalding the cream was "scald milk", and from this cheese with a rather poor reputation was made - Devon had no distinct named cheese. It is however likely, from a cheese dealer's accounts,[28] that whole-milk cheese was also made in Uffculme.

Cattle were commonly used for ploughing. They are recorded frequently in yokes, multiples of two; in only three cases is a full plough team of eight oxen suggested. One hundred and eleven inventories record the growing of corn but only twenty seven ploughs are recorded and the rest of the corn growers had no means of ploughing, though some had harrows. Ploughs were not expensive objects (1s to 2s), so the limiting factor in the number of ploughs was probably not the implement but the oxen or horses available to pull it. Most corn growers must have either shared with their neighbours the labour of ploughing with what cattle or horses they had or relied entirely on their neighbours to plough for them. That plough gear was shared is borne out by the will of Giles Bishop [231].

Sheep were less commonly kept than cattle. Sixty inventories record them, compared with a hundred for cattle. Flocks were small. Thirty two were of twenty or less and a quarter of all the sheep were in flocks of less than thirty. Another quarter were in only seven flocks belonging mainly to the richer folk who proved their wills in London. Only in very few cases were sheep of more value than cattle, where both were kept. Only one early will suggests that sheep were kept to provide wool from which clothes were made for the family [LW9]. No fleece weights can be calculated and nothing can be learnt of the quality of the local wool.

Pigs were the most commonly kept animal but only in ones or twos shared with a neighbour, to feed the family.

Corn is recorded in one hundred and eleven inventories. Wheat, oats, barley, rye, maslin, peas, and beans were all grown. Wheat and barley were much more commonly grown after 1650, taking the place of oats and rye. Barley had replaced oats as the grain for malting after 1650. In accordance with later West Country practice, there are no references to fallow land and a full year's fallow forms no part of later covenants in local leases.[29]

Acreages of corn are only recorded in twenty two inventories, and in nineteen of these the acreage is less than ten; the largest acreage is 25½. Later leases stipulated that only a quarter or a fifth of the land of a farm should be in corn. The rest would have been in temporary ley grass or meadow or rough pasture, all but the meadow to take its turn to be ploughed. Using this proportion as a rough guide, the sizes of the farms growing corn can be crudely calculated. They averaged twenty five acres; the twelve growing the smallest acreage of corn averaged twelve acres only. The largest acreage of corn, 25½ acres, would have been grown, on this basis, on a farm of 100 acres. This was that of Henry Gill [131] whose total estate was worth £365. Winter and spring corn were recorded together in many inventories. Three or four crops of corn followed by ley grass was

---

28 Account book of Francis Broom; privately owned.

29 R. Stanes, "Landlord and tenant and husbandry covenants in eighteenth century Devon", *Exeter Papers in Economic History*, No. 14, 1981.

normal in the West Country and such crop combinations do not imply any "open field" rotation. Uffculme was almost entirely enclosed. The Blackdown tops were common pasture and the hay meadows of the Culm, the hams, were often "common", subdivided and unenclosed, but the rest of Uffculme was hedged and enclosed.

Beer was commonly made on the farm; malt and malt hutches and malt mills and malt chambers are recorded in just over a quarter of the inventories. Hops are recorded only once and were said to be new to the parish in 1604.[30] Oaten malt occurs in four early inventories and it was with this that Devon's notoriously disgusting beer was made, reported in 1600 "to make to strangers vomit".[31] Cider was being made by 1594 but apple orchards were rare in the parish at the beginning of that century.[30] Cider wrings and presses occur commonly and by 1691 reference was made to a "cider ingen", perhaps an apple crusher. Stills recorded in the inventories suggest that "still liquor", apple brandy, was made.

Carriage on the farm was almost entirely done on horseback, using pack saddles. These with their various fittings, crooks and panniers and dung pots, occur in forty four inventories. In contrast wheeled farm carts were rare. Wains or putts (butts) or "pairs of wheels" are recorded only nine times. Side saddles and hackney saddles and heavy leather riding boots - gambadoes - are recorded, but no carriages or coaches or traps of any sort.

There is some evidence of innovation. By 1604 irrigated water meadows were being "made" by digging furrows and damming and diverting water to encourage the growth of grass in the early spring - the hungry gap - and again in the summer drought. The growing of clover, red clover, was being encouraged by farming writers in 1650[32] as a new crop; and this occurs in three inventories in Uffculme after 1676, as ricks of clover. Turnips and potatoes get no mention - potatoes were grown in the parish as a garden crop only until the end of the eighteenth century.[33] Lime is mentioned only once, but in East Devon marl had been used to sweeten acid land for centuries. Barn machinery, malt mills, and "mills to cleanse corn", perhaps winnowing machines, occur towards the end of the seventeenth century.

CLOTH

At the west end of Uffculme, close to the Culm, is the settlement of Coldharbour, marked by a prominent mill chimney. This is Coldharbour Mill, bought by the Quaker clothier, Samuel Fox of Wellington, in 1797. It was still spinning yarn in 1981, its steam engine and water wheel in working order. Higher up on a Culm tributary at Dunkeswell, the Abbey Mill was fulling or tucking cloth by 1238, one of the earliest of such mills in the

---

30 Tithe Dispute, DRO, Uffculme, 56/4/7/1, 1604.

31 William J. Blake, "Hooker's Synopsis Chorographical of Devonshire", *Transactions of the Devonshire Association*, 47, 1915, pp 334-348; see p 345.

32 *Agrarian History of England and Wales*, ed. J. Thirsk, CUP, 1985, Vol 5/2, pp 547-554.

33 Windsor, MS, *op. cit.*

country.[34] The Culm in 1086 powered twelve mills in twenty five miles, with two in Uffculme itself. Later there were five mills in the parish, all but one with adjoining "rack fields", where cloth was stretched after fulling. Cloth making has ancient roots in Uffculme.

It is unlikely that much of the wool was locally produced. Devon traditionally imported wool and yarn from Ireland and Spain and finer wool from the Midlands. Sixty six inventories record sheep but of these only twenty record gear for making cloth as well. Thirty six record stocks of wool, but of these eleven record no sheep. Flock sizes averaged thirty three and in only four cases were sheep the principal farming activity. In only one case [LW9] is there a clear link between the keeping of sheep and the making of clothes: John Edwards left twenty six fleeces to five children for clothing in 1569. In 1691 James Batt, a rich clothier, grew corn and kept cattle but had no sheep [L10].

The names of one hundred and five weavers, thirty eight fullers or tuckers or clothiers, and thirty six wool combers, dating from 1546 to 1800, can be identified from the wills and inventories or from insurance policies issued by the Sun Fire Office between 1726 and 1770.[35] Similarly, inventories refer to every tool or implement or apparatus commonly used in the domestic making of cloth: broad and narrow looms, quill turns, spinning turns, warping frames and bars, loom weights, swifts, raths, sleas, shears and leads, cloth presses, dyeing furnaces, dyehouses, racks, fulling mills, combs, and cards. The precise way in which cloth was made before the introduction of powered machinery is described by Peter Newton in the companion volume (pp 40-66).

Cloth itself occurs in the inventories as serges, kerseys, broadcloths, worsteds, and druggets. The papers of the Fox family[36] add other types of cloth locally produced, such as dozens, duroys, bays, perpetuanos, long ells, stamens, shalloons, and sagathies. (See Glossary.)

There were two main cloth types and processes. The "woollen" industry used *carded* short stapled wool for both weft and warp on the loom and produced broadcloths, kerseys, druggets, and dozens. The worsted industry used long stapled *combed* wool for both warp and weft, while the "new draperies" used combed wool for the warp only and produced serges, bays, perpetuanos, and duroys. The change from mainly heavy broadcloths using carded wool to lighter worsteds or serges using combed wool is fundamental to the industry, and seems to have occurred in Uffculme in the last quarter of the seventeenth century. In 1682 the inventory of the clothier John Starke [185] lists a combing shop and worsted combs - the first reference to combs. Three other inventories list combs, all after 1680. Thirty six wool combers can be identified, all from between 1680 and 1800.

---

34 Henry Summerson, *Crown Pleas of the Devon Eyre of 1238*, Devon and Cornwall Record Society, New Series, Vol 28, 1985.

35 Stanley D. Chapman, *The Devon Cloth Industry in the 18th Century Sun Fire Office Inventories 1726-1770*, Devon and Cornwall Record Society, New Series, Vol 23, 1978.

36 Fox & Co, "History of the Firm of Thomas Were & Sons 1737 - 1812", folio 40, transcribed by Prof W.G. Hoskins and presented to the Devon and Exeter Institution, 1973 (unpublished).

Sun policies were insuring the combing shops of well-to-do sergemakers by 1724.

Clothiers/fullers were the industry's leaders. Latterly clothiers were merchants dealing in rather than making cloth, but earlier they were fullers as well, either buying cloth in the open market or buying from weavers to whom they had supplied the yarn. John Campeny is recorded in a will as a clothier in 1546, but nothing more is known of him.

The earlier inventories provide examples of independent spinners and weavers, the basic workers in the industry. John Mill [7], Philip Havell [9], and John Hodge [10] were all small farmers with turns and cards and sometimes wool and yarn. William Norton [22] seems to have relied on weaving only; he had no farming goods but had a loom in use at his death in 1594. Thomas Rudge was a farmer and weaver with a pair of shears, a loom, and turns and cards in 1602. Humphrey Holwell who died in 1613 [51] was a weaver on a larger scale employing some labour probably. He had quilturns, three looms, warping gear, four kerseys in stock, and wool worth £8, and yarn worth £2 10s. He had two cows, a pig, and a horse - but no sheep - and made butter and cheese. Barnard Tucker [52] was also a substantial farmer/weaver with corn in the ground and in the barn, five cattle and 52 sheep, two looms, turns, and one piece of coarse cloth.

Rather better-off and representing the next step in the industry were the Hurley family who were fullers. Four of their inventories, those of Thomas [73] and Alice Hurley [84], their son Thomas [78], and their son-in-law Edward Marshall [143] survive. Between them they owned the necessary equipment of a fuller and dyer, five racks, three presses, a furnace, three pairs of shears, sheer boards, cottning boxes, a mill wheel and shaft, and the lease of a fulling mill. They had no looms or turns. The first three all died in 1627-8 in an epidemic. Edward Marshall died forty years later, leaving an estate, nearly three times the value of that of his in-laws, that included twenty two pairs of shears and leads. He lived in a house of ten rooms with "shopp" attached, apart from the millhouse, and he had an "estate" in Craddock. He must have been a considerable employer. None of the above had cloth in stock of any kind. Their business was strictly fulling and dyeing.

In contrast John Starke [185] was a clothier with £40 worth of serges, £1 7s worth of broadcloth, £29 worth of yarn, and wool and worsted (combed) wool, a dyeing furnace, worsted combs and a combing shop, oil and dyestuff, and £5 worth of debts in an estate of £122. Henry Gay [192] was another clothier, leaving an estate of £194 at his death in 1686. He had 20 serges and druggets worth £35, worsted yarn, drugget wool, a press, a furnace, and worsted and wool "in the spinsters hands" worth £6, clear evidence of contracting out. He was a fuller rather than a true clothier.

Alexander Melhuish [L8] and James Batt [L10] were much richer contemporaries of the above. The former was described as a clothier and he had a lease of a fulling mill at Five Fords, but no cloth or gear at his death. He had leases on seven other chattel estates and cattle and sheep and debts owing to him of £100. He died worth £937, perhaps in retirement from the cloth business. James Batt, in contrast, was fully active in that business when he died in 1691. He was owed £541 by London, Bristol, and Tiverton merchants for cloth, and had 5 packs of cloth on the way to Flanders worth

£120, and wool of all sorts: serges, broads, kerseys, druggets, yarn, and white and dyed wool waiting to be spun. He was truly a clothier; he had no cloth-making gear of his own but wool and yarn ready to put out to spinners and weavers. He clearly did not specialise in one type of cloth. Cloth made up 90% of his total estate of £1182. He farmed in a small way as well. His is the only inventory that can in any way match that of Elizabeth Hellings of Culmstock,[37] whose estate in 1669 was worth £1275 with debts owing from all over the country, cloths waiting to be sold in London, perhaps thirty employees, with much wool and cloth put out for processing "in the burlers' and shearmen's and spinners' hands".

Defoe suggests that in 1724[38] cloth making in the Culm Valley was in the hands of the Tiverton clothiers. This seems to be borne out by the absence of clothiers and fullers from Uffculme records after 1714. In contrast weavers and sergemakers and combers continue to appear in the records until the 1780s. Thomas, Barnard (who had married Alexander Melhuish's daughter), and William Byrd were sergemakers between 1742 and 1763. William's insurance inventory in 1763 was valued at £2600.[39]

These men were employers. Their employees, the journeymen, apprentices, and wage-earning workmen, have left no wills or inventories. They were paid 9s a week as combers, fullers, and hot pressmen, rather above the 7s of the farm labourer.[40] They do not however entirely escape notice and at times made their presence felt. In 1810 the then Vicar, James Windsor, wrote a brief account of the history of Uffculme over the previous ninety years.[41] Both his father and grandfather had been Vicars of the parish. He wrote:

> *The woolcombers and weavers who were very numerous formed themselves into societies and clubs and were governed by laws of their own making - of all others the most arbitrary - and if any shopkeeper or innkeeper was accused by them of unfair practices they levied a fine on him at their discretion, which if he refused to pay they and their families were prohibited all further dealings with him until it was paid, when it was invariably spent on liquor. On all occasions they behaved with insolence to their employers and occasionally when any matter of dispute arose between them they seized their persons and dragged or carried them by force to their club house or any other place they chose. But a baker named William Hucker who had frequently suffered by their attentions (unawed by their threats) indicted them at Exeter in consequence of which they were severely punished and never afterwards attempted to levy a fine on anyone. This happened between 1760 and 1770 and gave the death blow to their power. Previous to this the inhabitants stood in awe of them and their numbers rendered them truly formidable.*

---

37 Margaret Cash, *Devon Inventories*, No. 217 (Elizabeth Hellings).

38 Daniel Defoe, *A Tour through the Whole Island of Great Britain by a Gentleman, 1724*, Frank Cass & Co. (with Heinemann), 1968, pp 264-5.

39 Stanley D. Chapman, *Devon Cloth Industry*, p 148.

40 W.G. Hoskins, *Devonshire Studies: The Farm Labourer through Four Centuries*, Cape, 1952.

41 Windsor, MS, *op. cit*; see also Margaret Tucker, pp 134-5 in the companion volume.

The account then describes "a general" battle in the streets of Culmstock between the "societies" of Bradninch, Silverton, Cullompton, and Thorverton on the one hand and the "societies" of Culmstock, Uffculme, and Hemyock on the other, in which one man was "hewn asunder" by a scythe and the husbandmen joined in with their flails. Prisoners were taken and lodged in the church tower. The cause of this dispute between what seem to have been incipient local unions is not stated and remains unknown.

The Vicar continues:

The population of the parish and its trade were at their highest about the year 1745 and from that time they have been regularly decreasing and all the females belonging to the labourers of every description were employed in spinning, but at the present moment [1810] *there is not a comber or weaver under the age of thirty five nor has there been one bred as such for the last twenty years ....*

Between 1780 and 1790 machinery worked by water was first introduced into the woollen manufactory which produced a most sudden change. Those whose capital consisted of but a few hundred pounds - who though not rich were independent and happy - were suddenly reduced to poverty as they could not render their goods sufficiently low to ensure a sale and afford them any profit. The manufacturers, combers, weavers, etc were thrown out of employ in the lines in which they had been respectively bred and a most melancholic scene ensued as numbers of them in old age were obliged to engage in new employment and to handle tools they had never before used to prevent starving. Many of them were employed ... on the highway or digging gravel.

DEBT AND INVESTMENT

Of Uffculme's 266 inventories 107 record debt of some sort. Almost all these were debts owed to the deceased as they were his property. What he owed belonged to his creditors and rarely appears in his inventory but does so occasionally in administrations.

It is clear that lending and borrowing money in the seventeenth century was usual. There were no local banks. Instead the inventories show that those in need of a loan were able to borrow from their neighbours or relatives and probably from well-to-do yeomen or clothiers who had accumulated funds that they needed to "put to use". Cash in hand was "idle money" and amounted to only 2% of the sum of the Trowbridge inventories and even less, 1.2%, of the inventories in London.. Profits and savings need to be invested and put to use and lending locally, where the risk might be assessed best, was probably commonplace.

The need to borrow more than a few pounds probably arose when the entry fine on an estate had to be paid. By the seventeenth century the three-life lease, the "chattel lease", was the usual way of holding land in Devon. This demanded a large entry fine, often ten or more times the nominal annual rent, and was based on the "lives" of three named living persons. These lives could be added to by payment of another proportional "fine". Finding this fine almost certainly required borrowing. In Uffculme few men had much cash in hand (see below), but there is a record for Farway of £250 of a fine of £570 being paid in gold. The fine on a large farm in North Devon valued at £80 p.a. was £778.[42] In Uffculme John Dyer [L11] was owed £785 on his death in "bills and securities", but no other comparably large sums occur in the inventories or administrations. Lesser but still substantial sums occur often. Among others John Rawlins [161] was owed £146, the spinster Joane Dowdney [208] had £223 of "good debts and money in purse". Uffculme's smaller farms and cottages would not attract such large "fines" and the documents suggest the possibility that larger sums were most prudently and easily raised through a number of smaller loans. So, Matthew Cadbury [72] borrowed £155 from fourteen men, and John Oland [64] £79 from nine people. All these sums could have been used to raise a "fine".

The percentage of inventories with debts recorded nearly doubles from 23% pre-1600 to 42% post-1658, and is matched very nearly by the percentage with chattel leases recorded, which rise from 28% to 46%. This suggests a link. In one inventory the link is specific: John Peppreel [16] lent his son £23 "to pay the fee of his bargain with the Earl of Bath" - the entry fine on his lease.

Another obvious need to borrow was for ready money at the end of the season before the harvest was won or stock sold. A third of the debts owed were for less than £5 and this may represent this sort of need, though a chattel lease on a cottage was often valued at no more than that, decreasing, perhaps, as the "lives" died. Three quarters of all recorded debts were for less than £25.

These sums were large if seen in perspective. Towards the end of the period a labourer's annual wage was £12-£15, a craftsman's £20. The sums borrowed were often more than the total of the borrower's inventory: Richard Waldron [178] owed debts of £170 with an inventory total of £108, Mathew Cadbury [72] owed £155 with one of £124, and William Cape [119] owed £94 with one of £74. They all may, however, have had freehold property as well, normally never included in an inventory.

There seems to have been a neighbourhood web of borrowing and lending. Mathew Cadbury and John Oland were just two who had numerous creditors. Uffculme men went as far as Tawstock, where the Lord of the Manor, the Earl of Bath, lived to borrow as well as to all the nearby parishes. Lenders with money to put out to use were doubtless known locally. John Dyer [L11] lent on a large scale, perhaps using bills of exchange. He had £70 in his chest at his death as well as the large sum owed to him. One such lender with wide contacts was George Good of Stoke Canon, whose inventory was abstracted by Margaret Cash.[43] In 1696 he was owed £424, in sums ranging from 12s 6d to £100, by fifty six debtors of all sorts - husbandmen, tailors, gentlemen, clerks, fullers, carpenters - from thirty one places in all parts of Devon: Plymouth, Barnstaple, Tiverton, Bampton, Honiton, Dawlish, Totnes, Chulmleigh, and Newton Abbot. Many of the sums owed him were for double the original loan. Women seem to have lent rather more readily than men: 45% of their inventories

---

42 W.G. Hoskins, *Devon*, Collins, 1954, p 91.

43 Margaret Cash, *Devon Inventories*, No. 260.

record debts owing to them compared to 35% for men, though some of this difference might be accounted for if many were retired elderly widows of moderately well-off farmers with savings to invest.

In many cases the debts owed formed the largest item in the inventory. Augustine Tawton [70] was owed £50 in a total of £65 and Mary Gill [41] £38 in a total of £44. Again there are many other examples. These debts, if they attracted interest, were of course investments, money "put to use".

There were various degrees of security. Debt might be "sperate", "desperate", "good", "bad", "doubtful", "on specialty", "without specialty", "on bond", "if recoverable", "chaste". George Starke [58] had £9 of debt with "no specialty" and £3 of "bad debt"; John Cornish [103] had £23 "due upon bond", of which £16 2s was "desperate". Humfry Henson [128] was owed £26 "on specialty" and £9 of "desperate debt". The distinctions are not clear. Desperate, bad, and doubtful debt amounted to 11% of total debts.

What was not lent out at interest might be invested in other ways. Chattel leases could be bought and the land could then be sublet on an annual basis or rack rented at so much an acre to bring in an income. Margaret Dowdney [127], a widow, left an estate of £218, of which £200 was chattel and another widow, Bridget Baker [135], had chattel leases worth £300 in an estate of £405. These women had invested in leases. Agnes Cotterell [149] similarly had bought an annuity of £20. In the same way the money belonging to the Uffculme Charities for the poor was invested and was expected to produce 4½% interest. There was alarm amongst the poor when such an investment could not be safely found and the money had to be lodged with the Walronds at Bradfield. By that time the poor were "clamorous" for their money.[44]

What was not lent or invested was "idle money", "cash in hand". Only five inventories show substantial amounts of this. The Vicar Richard Matthew [191] had £48 in cash at his death, the yeoman Robert Mill [112] had £42 in cash in an inventory total of £99, John Dyer [L11] had £70 in his chest, Jane Welsh [222], a widow, had £25 in her purse in 1698; but almost all the rest record cash below £20, and half record cash of less than £1. The architypical image of money hoarded beneath the floor boards seems to be a myth.[45]

Before 1648 only eleven inventories (9%) record money in hand. After 1648, 67 (48%) do so. Such an abrupt change may perhaps reflect the amount of coin in circulation or a change in the appraisers' methods. In the eighteenth century Portuguese moidores were in circulation in Uffculme [L17], perhaps for lack of "coin of the realm". Some wills stipulated that legacies should be paid in English money. Early wills sometimes left single sheep as bequests, perhaps as an "investment" or for lack of coin [LW15, LW16, LW30].

The inventories divide equally and conveniently in 1648. For the period before that date the average value of the inventories at Trowbridge is £40. After 1648 the figure nearly doubles to £79. Inventories do not accurately

---

44 Uffculme Charity Money; see ref. 24 above.

45 B.A. Holderness, "Credit in English Rural Society", *Agricultural History Review*, xxiv, pp 97-109.

record total wealth: freehold land and debts owed by the deceased are omitted. Nevertheless it seems unlikely that this doubling of wealth in Uffculme in the seventeenth century is an illusion.

HOUSES AND THEIR CONTENTS

Twenty nine buildings in Uffculme are included in the list of historic buildings made by the Department of the Environment in 1987.[46] Of these, two, Bridwell and Bradfield are great houses, two, St Mary's Church and the Spiceland Quaker meeting-house are ecclesiastical, one was a school, and one was a mill. The rest are houses dating mostly from the sixteenth or seventeenth century. There are probably others of this date not on the Department of the Environment's list. Three of the houses have smoke-blackened roof timbers and so were once hall houses, open to the roof, with a hole for the smoke. This was the earliest house, a single room with a central fire in which the family lived and slept and ate, with sometimes a parlour or solar at one end and, sometimes, a jettied room above one end, leaving the main room open to the roof. Later the fire was moved to a fire-place in the side or end wall and ceilings could be inserted to make a full two-storey house. These first floor rooms were "chambers" and were distinguished from each other by the room below, and so became the hall chamber, the parlour chamber, the kitchen chamber, and so on. This great domestic change began in the sixteenth century in the main, and can be observed in the inventories.

One hundred and twelve of the Uffculme inventories mention separate, named rooms. Some of the rest may have had such rooms unremarked on by the appraisers because they contained nothing of value, or perhaps were hall houses with one room only. The most common room is the Hall which is referred to eighty four times. Five inventories refer to the Hall and to no other room and are likely also to be hall houses. Furthermore the Hearth Tax of 1674[47] records thirty two taxpayers with one hearth only and one hundred and eight poor who paid no tax, also with only one hearth. One hearth could well be combined with a number of unheated rooms, but it is likely that many of the poor had only a single room with a hearth in a cob house with a thatched roof.

The next most common room referred to in the inventories is the Hall Chamber, the room above the Hall. This does not get a mention till 1627 [72] and occurs in all sixty three times. Chambers of one sort or another, almost always upstairs rooms, are mentioned first, as the "inner" and "utter" (outer) chamber, in 1602 [37], forty five times between 1604 and 1658, and one hundred and sixty six times after 1660.[48] This suggest that the insertion of ceilings ("sealings") in hall houses, or the new building of houses with two floors, was only fully under way in Uffculme in the latter half of the seventeenth century.

---

46 *Register of Historic Houses in Uffculme*: Department of the Environment List of Buildings of Special Architectural or Historic Interest, 1987, (at Mid-Devon District Council Offices).

47 *Hearth Tax*; see ref. 22.

48 For further details see Margaret Tucker, companion volume, chapter 6.

V View southwards from Leigh towards Bodmiscombe

VI Cottages in Mill Street, Uffculme Town

VII The town seen to the east from Grantlands

VIII Gill's Cottage, Craddock

Two of the places still bearing the names of earlier inhabitants of the parish (PW).

I The Uffculme Prebendal Stall in Salisbury Cathedral. The brass plate is inscribed UFCOMB OLIM BEDWIN (Photography by Geoffrey Fraser)

II Edward Seymour, whose exchange of Uffculme for Great Bedwyn led to Uffculme's "peculiar" status. (Reproduced by courtesy of the National Portrait Gallery, London.)

III Ashill

IV Rull

Some places mentioned in the documents, as they are today (PW)

Slightly less commonly recorded is the parlour. This was a ground-floor room next to the hall - occasionally with a bed - which afforded some privacy. It is first recorded in John Welch's inventory in 1603 [38] and occurs forty times in all. The same inventory refers to a "room within the hall" and contains the first reference to the kitchen. Above the parlour was the parlour chamber, mentioned twenty eight times. Chambers were often storerooms as well as bedrooms. More frequent than the parlour chamber was the kitchen, mentioned thirty one times in all but only three times before 1660, food being originally cooked and eaten in the hall. By 1713, in one case at least, the kitchen had become the main living room. In Richard Gill's kitchen [233] meals were prepared, cooked over the fire, and eaten at the table; there was a settle, a chair, a side board, and shelves, and pork and bacon were stored, perhaps in the settle or hung from the roof. This house had no parlour but still had a hall - now perhaps the best room - containing a fireplace but no cooking gear, a table, a settle, three joint stools, and a pair of virginals.

Entries and entry chambers occur occasionally after 1660. These may be the familiar porch with a room over it, a fairly commonplace conspicuous addition to a house. Many specialised rooms appear after 1660 too, as "milk", "malt", "cider", "drink", "bake", "dye", "wring" houses or chambers. John Mills's inventory of 1670 [L2] records a "men's chamber", where living-in farm servants were housed, and a study with a clock. Rooms were mentioned when what they contained could be appraised. This may explain the absence of the "jakes", "privy", or "garderobe" from the inventories. Such rooms certainly existed, both inside and upstairs in houses of this date.

The most common size of house in the inventories is one of four rooms, mentioned twenty times in the one hundred and twelve inventories where the rooms were clearly specified. Eight houses had more than ten recorded rooms, another forty one had five or more, and sixty two had four or less. John Mills, yeoman, had a house of nineteen rooms in 1670, nine of them store or service rooms. His estate of £1481 is the highest recorded [L2].

The Hearth Tax of 1674 shows two thirds of the taxed houses having one or two hearths and only six houses with five hearths or more. Bradfield was taxed on fifteen hearths and the Holways of Leigh on twenty two. No one house of such a size is known to have existed at Leigh.

Conventional equipment for the hearth with its open fire, on which all food was cooked, occupies a lot of space in the inventories. These are well illustrated and described by Margaret Tucker in the companion volume. One object, the cotterell, used to hang a pot over the fire, occurs only in early inventories in what appear to be hall houses and may form part of a central hearth.

Furniture in the early inventories was very sparse and basic and it is evidence of increasing wealth that in the later inventories houses were much better equipped. Beds were "performed" - with posts and curtains and bedding - or "truckle", or "trundle", small and moveable. "Dousebeds" and "flock beds" were no more than mattress covers stuffed with chaff or wool remnants. Feather beds were the softest. Sheets were of rough "dowlas" or finer "Holland". the table was most often a "table board" with "forms" to sit on, though "round" and "square" and "side" and "livery" tables also occur. A settle is first recorded in 1627 [73]. Chairs were not common; most households with any chairs had only one. For storage there were chests, coffers, hutches, aumbries, presses, trunks, and "caiges" (as in "dishcaiges") - perhaps slatted cupboards - for glass or trenchers or cloam or dishes. A desk is first mentioned in 1622 [56], a dresser (on which, originally, food was dressed) in 1700 [225], a chest of drawers in 1690 [208].

A clock, first recorded in 1688 as belonging to Elizabeth Bishop [194], may appear in two subsequent inventories of the Bishop family [231 and 238] in 1709 and 1719. Henry Walrond [LW118] had a pocket watch in 1650 and Elizabeth Walrond had a gold watch a hundred years later [W193].

Thirty two inventories record bibles or prayer books. Other religious works were those of St Augustine of Hippo [237], John Flavel and Bishop Burkit [W153]. Mary Coombe had, in 1762, a cookery book and a book of jests by the satirist Tom Brown [L17]. A lute, a cithern, pairs of virginals, playing tables for chess or draughts are recorded, and one inventory refers to cockfighting equipment [237].

Twenty one inventories, all from before 1637, list armour and military arms. A number of others list what appear to be sporting guns. All men between sixteen and sixty five had, if need be, to bear arms. In 1539 thirty four Uffculme men were mustered, none of them with firearms.[49] Thirty years later in 1569, a very dangerous year in the contest with Spain, Uffculme paraded forty five archers, forty seven "gonners", twenty four pikemen, and fifty three billmen, 169 able men in all. Forty six parishioners were required to supply arms according to their wealth. The least contribution was a bow, a sheaf of arrows, a steel cap and a black bill. Other arms recorded were corslets, "almen rivets" (armour), pikes, "arquebuts", and "murrions" (helmets). The 1638 muster lists only sixteen names for Uffculme. The arms supplied were often kept in the church; all the rest were stored in private houses.

CLOTHES

With a few notable exceptions inventories have little to say about clothes. One of the earliest, that of Bennet Fryer, a miller [5], listed his wardrobe in 1581 as: a cloak, four doublets of cloth, canvas, and leather, a pair of hose, five jerkins, two hats, three shirts, a petticoat, a girdle, four pairs of stockings, leather breeches, a waistcoat, a pair of boots with spurs, and two pairs of shoes.[50] These were worth 35% of the total of his inventory and are exceptional in their detailed listing and in their proportional value. For the most part apparel and "money in his purse" are lumped together at the beginning of the inventory and clothes form no more than 7% of the value.

The inventory of Richard Matthew the Vicar [191] is another exception.

---

49 See Malcolm Flower-Smith, companion volume, chapter 8, and the Muster Rolls, PRO E101/61/35 & SP 12/57, and SRO DD/WO 53/1/115 & 53/1/121.

50 See Mary Fraser, companion volume, chapter 7, and the glossary for descriptions of clothes and fabrics.

It lists his clothes in detail: cassocks, riding clothes, "trowses", red and white waistcoats, black and white stockings, drawers, shirts, riding hoods, satten caps, bands, cuffs, and his Master of Arts gown. Some of his late wife's clothes are also recorded: a silk gown, silk scarves, and green and shot silk petticoats. These are the exceptions. In general no detail is given. The appraisers were always men, intent only on fixing a value.

The average value of clothing in the inventories rose by a third from £2 in the sixteenth to £3 in the seventeenth century and was £5 in the London inventories after 1660. This conceals an enormous range of values: John Horne's [48] clothes were worth 5s, Richard Matthew's [191] £14. As might be expected richer folk's were worth more in total, but often form a smaller proportion of their estates. The rich clothier Alexander Melhuish [L8] whose inventory was valued at £937 had clothes worth 11s only, and James Batt's [L10] clothes were worth £10 out of a total of £1182. The percentage of wealth represented by clothes in the inventories fell from 7% to 4% during the seventeenth century.

Wills are more informative on clothes and often specify bequests of clothes or jewelry. Commonly clothes were left to one person, but Dunes Dowdney [97], for instance, left her daughter Johan "my best segard, my old workedays petecott, one dubble kercher, one grograyn Apren, one smocke and one partlet"; and to Wilmot she left "one Apren & one kercher"; and to Agnes "two pieces of cloth to make a petecott & a wast cott" and "one Holland kercher". Clothes were referred to as "market" or "best" or "third best" or "workaday".

Rings were the most common item of jewelry left in wills. Sarah Garnsey had nine of these [W190] and richer folk had *memento mori* mourning rings to be worn at the funeral [LW19, W158]. Other jewelry items were silver girdles [1], sleeve buttons, shoe buttons of silver, diamond earrings belonging to Anna Windsor [W234], the Vicar's widow, and a gold watch belonging to Elizabeth Walrond [W193].

All sorts of items of costume occur as well as those already mentioned: for men gowns, frocks, suits, drawers, shifts, caps, night caps, and neck cloths; and for women mantles, smocks, kirtles, undercoats, partlets, waistcoats, and whittels. There is no mention of a ruff for either sex, nor of a wig. Available fabrics were numerous and fitted to all sorts of uses: fustian, dimity, morchadue, worsted ("usterd"), kersey, broadcloth, frieze, serge, grograyne, plush, stammel, stuff, dowlas, calico, shagg, perpetuano, lawn, duroy, poplin, callamanco, lutestring, muslin, linen, barraty, hamborough, druggets, cambric, barrass, and hemp.

Samuel James's detailed inventory lists many of these [187] in his shop in 1681, along with haberdashery of all sorts. He had no ready-made clothes to sell and was clearly catering for the housewives who made clothes at home. Much of the cloth they used was probably made locally (see above).

There are inventories or references to seven Uffculme tailors all from the end of the seventeenth century or later. None of these men owned cloth, so it is likely that they made up what their customers had actually bought from Samuel James or from local clothiers.

There were also local chapmen or pedlars, who travelled the countryside on foot or horseback to sell their lengths of cloth, lace, ribbons, and brooches, ballads, gloves, perfumes, and pins. Several local chapmen, from Broadclyst, Halberton, Bampton, and Cullompton, were licensed by an act of 1696/7.[51]

CHURCH, CHAPEL, AND CHARITY

Unlike many other parishes in Devon Uffculme saw few changes of parson in the seventeenth century. Humphrey Steare [LW143] became Vicar in 1620 and died in Uffculme in 1660, and his successor Richard Matthew [191] was Vicar until 1685. This was at a time, during and after the Civil War, when clergy were regularly and commonly ejected from their livings for their beliefs. In fact more clergy were ejected in Devon after the Restoration in 1660 than in any other county. Three of Uffculme's adjoining parishes experienced such ejections.[52]

The Walronds of Bradfield and the Clarkes of Bridwell may have been influential in creating a tolerant religious climate in the town. William Walrond was regarded by the Bishop of Exeter as a dangerous Presbyterian and was included in the Bishop's list of corrupt Presbyterian justices.[53] William's uncle was himself ejected from a family living for Nonconformity. The Clarkes gave the land for a Presbyterian meeting-house in Uffculme in 1720. Nonconformity was well established in Uffculme by then, partly because there were a number of ejected ministers who still lived locally and were ready to lead services and congregations.[54] There were Presbyterian, Baptist, and Quaker congregations in or near the parish and Presbyterians numbered at least 250 in 1715.[55] The "Clarendon Code", designed to suppress Nonconformity, may not have been too strictly enforced by the local JPs.

Just at this period Uffculme's cloth industry was flourishing. Cloth workers tended at this time to be strong supporters of Nonconformity just as they tend to support the Parliamentary cause.[56] Recent work has shown that the cloth-making communities of the Culm Valley were strongly for Parliament,[57] as was the principal landowner William Walrond.

The presence of Nonconformists in some numbers made the Vicar's task more difficult. Whatever their own sympathies they had to obey the law

---

51 PRO AO 3/370.

52 P.W. Jackson, *Nonconformists and Society in Devon, 1660-1689* (Exeter PhD, 1986); James Haddridge, John Balster, and Richard Saunders were ejected from Halberton, Sampford Peverell, and Kentisbeare.

53 J. Simmons, "Some Letters from Bishop Ward of Exeter", DCNQ, xxi (1940-41), p.282-7.

54 F. Bate, *The Declaration of Indulgence, 1672* (Liverpool, 1908), pp xxii and lxv.

55 A. Gordon, *Freedom after Ejection* (Manchester, 1917), p.346.

56 M. Watts, *The Dissenters* (Oxford 1978, p.b. 1985), pp. 270-1.

57 M. Stoyle, *Loyalty and Locality: Popular Allegiance in Devon during the Civil War*, Exeter University Press, 1994, pp 51, 230; Hemyock and Uffculme were "well affected to Parliament", PRO SP/19/157/27-28.

and take action against Nonconformity if need be. Humphrey Steare actively looked after the interests of his parishioners at the Salisbury probate courts, was often involved in the preparation of inventories, and had galleries added to the church to cope perhaps with a rising population. There were complaints in 1642 about a parishioner, John Bolster an excommunicant, who ran an unlicensed school and lived with Susan Bowden "as his wife" and had a supposedly unbaptised child.[58] Steare took no action apparently. Bolster later became a dissenting minister and in 1665 preached to a congregation of 300 at the house of Humphrey Bowden, who kept "a constant conventicle". Bowden owned fulling mills and was at one stage a churchwarden but was excommunicated for Nonconformity during Richard Matthew's incumbency. He obtained a licence for a "meeting" at his house in 1672.[59] Edward Marshall [143] was another onetime churchwarden with cloth-making interests and Nonconformist leanings. John Marshall, probably his son, married Humphrey Bowden's daughter and had a licence for a meeting at his house at Gaddon, once held in the open on Gaddon Down.

The Quakers of the Spiceland meeting, founded in 1672, were also involved in cloth making. William Rawlins [LW166], a sergemaker. was brought before Quarter Sessions for attending a Quaker meeting and was gaoled for refusing to swear the oath of allegiance.[60] His daughter married Peter Were and the Weres founded the Wellington woollen mills eventually taken over by the Foxes of Wellington, also Quakers, with whom the Weres intermarried. The Fox family later bought and developed the Coldharbour spinning mill in Uffculme. Many other Quakers and Baptists and Presbyterians are listed in the companion volume.

Nonconformity may have been one reason for the great change in charitable giving to the church and the poor revealed by Uffculme wills. The earliest Pre-Reformation wills reveal Catholic practice. They make donations to the rood light and for wax candles and for prayers to be offered for the dead. Post-Reformation wills regularly and commonly leave bequests to the church and the poor, often in sums of 12d or 3s 4d but sometimes in food, "20 pecks of rye to 20 poor" in 1566 [LW5]. By the seventeenth century bequests were more commonly invested for the employment of the poor, or "invested in the parish Stocke" [LW133] or on behalf of the poor [LW67, LW70] and were sometimes specific. The "aged poor" or the "aged and impotent poor", or "those who have great charge but no pay from the poor book", become targeted objects of charity. There were some large bequests. The Walronds and Holways gave £220 to the poor between 1640 and 1669, and Wilmot Burrough [LW71], who died in 1618, gave the poor of Uffculme £100 during her lifetime. This formed the basis of the present-day charitable fund that bears her name still.

Such giving was commonplace before 1660; 65% of wills record such donations. In the forty years after 1660 only 22% make such gifts and four fifths of them come from the wills proved in London, largely those of the better-off or more prominent. Amongst the Trowbridge wills between 1660

---

58 See churchwarden's Presentment in companion volume, p 126.

59 DRO 71/13/1/37.

60 John Slate is thanked for this information.

and 1700 only four of sixty four made bequests, whereas before that date exactly half did so. After 1700 only one Trowbridge will [W112], made in 1709, contains such a bequest. The London wills after 1700 have not been summarised here, but up to that date half still record charitable bequests.

There is nothing in the Uffculme records to explain this decline in charitable giving. Nationally the Elizabethan Poor Law had been codified in 1601, and after that date property owners had to contribute to the poor rate willy nilly. There were changes in the Poor Law after 1661 but none that might account for the decline. Uffculme's population was growing fast in the last half of the century, the expanding cloth trade provided work but also, probably, periods of unemployment in recession. The poor were probably numerous. Simon Welch left money to 80 poor in 1683 [189], and Thomas Jarman [L1] left 20 gns in bread for the poor in 1661; and the Hearth Tax of 1674 records 128 names exempt on grounds of poverty, out of a total of 234. In 1717 the Uffculme Church House seems to have been converted to a workhouse for the poor. All the above point to an increase in need rather than otherwise. Charitable bequests however were presumably administered by the churchwardens and overseers of the established church and this may not have been acceptable to new Nonconformist congregations, who might have preferred to look after their own poor with their own funds.

EDUCATION

Ayshford School was founded in 1701 by Nicholas Ayshford of Taunton. Uffculme, like almost every other town in Devon, thus acquired a grammar school, a necessary part of urban life. The school building survives as Ayshford House, now flats and apartments. The original specifications and plans for it are printed in the companion volume.[61]

Education had however been available before 1701. The Vicar, Richard Matthew, had kept a school; his inventory [191] refers to a school house. Before that John Bolster had evidently kept an unlicensed school (see previous section) and there is an inventory [116], including books and a lute, for Edward Branch, "schoolmaster", dated 1641, though it is not clear that he kept a school in Uffculme. Permission was obtained by Samuel Godfrey to establish a Quaker school in Uffculme in 1706, but nothing more is known.

The wills make it possible to make a rough assessment of literacy in Uffculme at different dates. The testator of the will and all the witnesses to it had either to sign or make a mark. Whatever degree of literacy is implied by the ability to make a signature to a will increased in Uffculme from about half in the seventeenth century to about four fifths in the eighteenth.

---

[61] For more detailed references on this and other topics see the chapters by Priscilla Flower-Smith, Malcolm Flower-Smith, Mary Fraser, Peggy Knowlman, Peter Newton, Robin Stanes, Margaret Tucker, and Peter Wyatt in the companion volume, *Uffculme: a Peculiar Parish*, the Uffculme Archive Group, 1997.

EDITORIAL CONVENTIONS

Of the 249 Uffculme inventories found at the Wiltshire Record Office at Trowbridge, 126 (marked DS) were exhibited at the visitations of the Dean of Salisbury and the remainder (PU) were in the list of the Uffculme Prebendary. They have been arranged chronologically as far as could be ascertained (apart from the appendix [249]) and have been transcribed with as much retention of their original character as possible. Thus the original spelling has been retained, as has the "y" symbol for "th", though "ff" occurring at the beginning of a word has been read throughout as capital "F". Bars over letters to indicate abbreviations are represented by the ~ sign, either over the letter or following it; and, as in the written documents themselves, the underlined letter "p" shows that "er" or "ar" has been omitted: thus "p" stands for "per" and "pish" for "parish", and so on. The evolution of the pound sign from *lî* to something approaching £ has been simulated at the column heads. Similarly, the gradual transition to arabic numerals in the columns themselves can be traced from 1622 onwards.

Until well into the 17th century the valuations were not usually gathered into columns on the right but each item carried separate indications of *lî*, *s*, or *d*, often as superscripts. For clarity we have departed here from the original form in this respect and all figures are collected into columns. Where our additions do not agree with those of the assessors we have made a tentative correction in square brackets, though sometimes the differences may be due to a misreading (despite our care to track such errors down) since considerable practice with these sums led us to the conclusion that their arithmetic was usually at least as good as ours.

Though most of the people involved would have farmed to some extent, the descriptions "yeoman" and "husbandman", and specifications of other trades, are only included in the initial summaries when they occur explicitly in any of the documents.

Abstracts of surviving wills have been added to the transcripts, as have the marriage and burial dates from the Parish Registers which appeared to give the closest match to the deceased.. These and all other added comments, not in the original inventories, are enclosed in square brackets. Some dates (e.g. 30 Jan 1575/6) show both the year of the register (beginning March 25th for most of this period) and the modern form.

The 249 Trowbridge inventories (in the jurisdiction of Salisbury) are followed by 17, labelled L for London, submitted to the Prerogative Court of Canterbury and now located at the Public Record Office.

The Uffculme wills at Trowbridge surviving without inventories are then summarised separately and have reference numbers preceded by W. Abstracts of the corresponding London wills without inventories, with reference numbers preceded by LW (for London Will), are printed in the companion volume, *Uffculme: a Peculiar Parish*. Although all the names referred to and most of the items in the wills are mentioned, in some cases it may be necessary to go back to the source for details of special interest.

The Illustrations in this Section

A few copies of the original documents are interspersed throughout the text to give an impression of their lay-out and of the changes in style of handwriting throughout the period. They have been much reduced from sheets approaching foolscap in size and may not be easily legible without a magnifying glass, but they have been chosen from the shorter documents which could conveniently fit onto one page.

Abbreviations used in the abstracts

admin	adminstratrator, -trix
admon	(letters of) administration
alš	alias
bro	brother
bur	burial
ch	child
chn	children
dr	daughter
ea	each
exec	executor, executrix
grch	grandchild
grdr	granddaughter
grson	grandson
k	kinsman/woman
mar	marriage
ovsr	overseer
pr	proved/probate granted to *or* pair
s	son
Sr	Sir [= "Rev" in the 16th century]
witn	witness(ed)

THE INVENTORIES

(a) Salisbury Jurisdiction

The original documents are held at the Wiltshire Record Office at Trowbridge, but copies of most of those marked (PU) can be found on the Uffculme microfilm MF 75 at the Devon Record Office at Exeter.

Editorial policy and abbreviations are explained on pp xxxi-xxxii **[?]**.

1 ELLIN DOWDENY 1576 (DS)

[Bur: "Helen Dowdney, widdow" 31 Dec 1575. Stock, corn, rents, & cloth but no clothmaking gear; value c £28.]

The Inventory of the goods of ellin Dowdeny late widoe of the parishe of ufcolm made and presed the second Day of January and in the year of our lord god [an..*md*?] *lxxv*[1575/6] By John norhamton Robert mill John vale william leman

	lî	*s*	*d*
Imprimis too keye too bullockes & oñ calf	*vj*		
It the peggs		*xxxiij*	*iiij*
It the shepe		*xx*	
It powtry		*iiij*	
It thre croakes		*xiij*	*iiij*
It too pannes		*xxvj*	*viij*
It poyt~ vessell		*iij*	*iiij*
It a cubbord a bord and a form		*x*	
It treing vessell		*xx*	
It a broche a brandies a pere axces and all other yron stuf		*xl*	
It a pear of splintes and a sallet		*vj*	
It a bed pformed		*xij*	
It her apparrell		*xvj*	
It her lining		*iij*	
It an old chitell a chafin dish too candelstickes		*x*	
It corne and otes in the barn		*xl*	
It hay		*xiij*	*iiij*
It malt		*ij*	*vj*
It larder		*xx*	
It corn in ground		*x*	
It thre quarters of rent at Salsbury	*iij*		
It Rent at Langford		*iiij*	*ij*
It of austin Dowdeny		*vij*	
It a girdell and a litell crooke		*x*	
It thre Coffers		*v*	
It foure [fowe?] pere of shares		*xx*	
It yarn and gresse[?] & too yeardes of cors clothe		*vj*	
It a pear of harrowes		*viij*	
It wood and other trashe		*xiij*	*iiij*

Sum total xxix^{li} $xiiij^{s}$
[£1 17s too much?]

[Exhibited by John Dowdeney, exec, 10 Jan 1575(/6): Latin endorsement signed by W Blacke.

Will pr 10 Jan 1575/6: residue to s John Dowdney, exec; 4 sheep &c to s Thomas; silver girdle conditionally to dr Jone; 6s 8d to s Austine via Jone; clothes to Alse Monke & Mary Dowdney & Jone Dowdney; 4d each to godchn Jone [--], John Pringe, Ellin Marshall, & Ellin Cheek; "too hogg sheep to too of John Dowdenies dafters of fivebriggs"; witn: John Segar vicar of Uffculme, Richard Lindon, William Loaman, Austin Dowdeny.]

2 FLORENCE PEARSIE 1576 (DS)

[Bur: "Florence Persye, widdow" 30 Jan 1575/6. Kersey & wool but no clothmaking gear; value c £16.]

Inventorie Indented of the goods Cattells and Detts of Florence Pearsie of Uffecolome in the Countie of Devon weddoe deceassed made and praysed the fyftenth daie of Februarie a° dm 1575. and in the Eightenth yeare of the Rayne of our Sov'aigne ladie Elizabeth by the grace of god Quene of England France and Irelande Defender of the Faithe &c by John Cheke John Rawlyns & Robte Butstone As heareafter follow-eth -

	lî	*s*	*d*
Imp'mis three keyne	*v*		

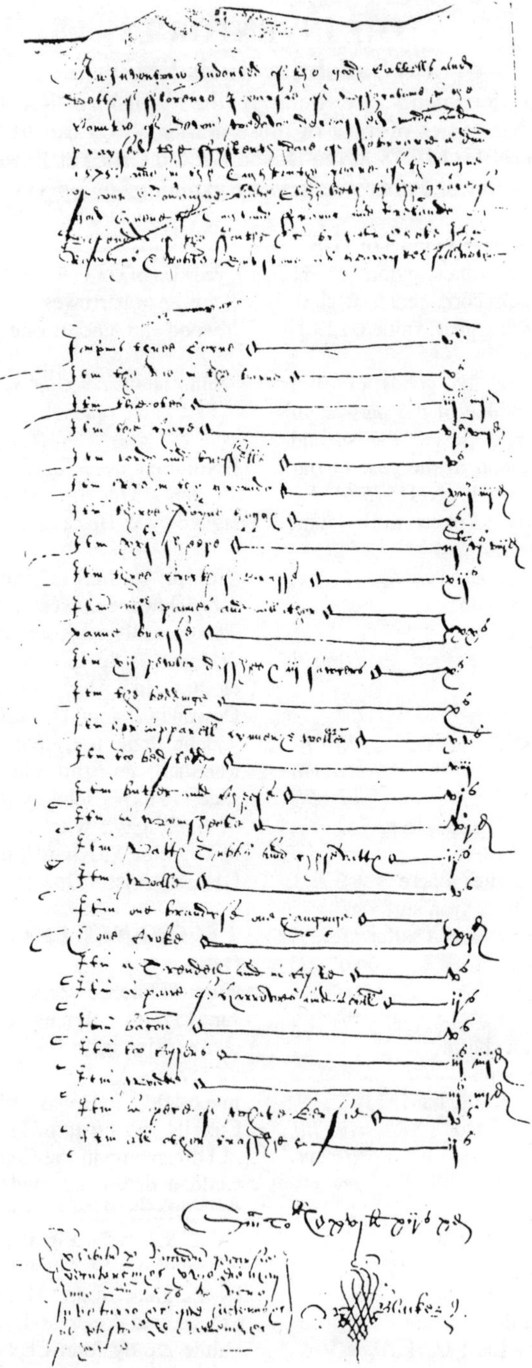

The inventory of Florence Pearsie 1576 [2]

	lî	*s*	*d*
Itm the Rie in the barne		*x*	
Itm the otes		*iij*	*iiij*
Itm the haye		*vj*	*viij*
Itm bords and tressells		*v*	
Itm Rye in the grounde		*xiij*	*iiij*
Itm three swyne hoggs		*x*	
Itm xxj[ti] sheepe	*iij*	*vj*	*viij*
Itm three Crockes of Brasse		*xij*	
Itm iiij[or] pannes and all other panne brasse		*xx*	
Itm xij pewter disshes and iij sawcers		*x*	
Itm the beddinge		*x*	
Itm her apparrell Lynen and wollen		*xv*	
Itm too bedstedds		*viij*	
Itm butter and Cheese		*vj*	
Itm a Wymsheete			*vj*
Itm Vatts Tubbs and chese vatts		*ij*	
Itm Woolle		*v*	
Itm one brandyse one hanginge & one Croke			*xij*
Itm a Trendell and a Coste		*v*	
Itm a pare of Harrowes and a byll		*ij*	
Itm bacon		*v*	
Itm too Coffers		*iij*	*iiij*
Itm Woodde		*iij*	*iiij*
Itm a pece of white Kersie		*v*	
Itm all other trasshe		*ij*	

Sma Totš *xvj[li] xij[s] x[d]* [2s 8d too much?]

[Exhibited by Richard Pearsie, exec, 16 May 1576: Latin endorsement signed by W Blacke.

Will pr 16 May 1576: residue to Richard Pearsy, exec; £6 13s 4d to dr Mary; several itemised dishes, clothes, &c to drs Mary & Ann; "greatest crocke of brasse" to Peter Pearsy, s of Richard; sacks of rye & malt & 6 elm boards to s-in-law John Starck & 6 wether sheep to his 6 chn; 6d each to all godchn; witn: Robt Butstone, William Facy, Richard Pearsy.]

3 WILLIAM READ 1576 (DS)

[Bur: "Wm. Read, of Gaddon" 30 Jan 1575/6. Stock, corn, plough, & some clothmaking gear; c £96]

The Inventory of the goods of William Read late of the perish of Ufcolm made and presed by Thomas Corton John Davy Humfry Tawton wth others the xx[th] daye of Februarie and in the year of our lord god 1575

	lî	*s*	*d*
Imprimis Sixe Oxen	*xv*		
It eight keye a heaffer and a calff	*xix*[?]		
It sheep wth their lames	*v*		
It the widgh beasts	*iiij*	*vj*	*viij*
It Swyne and Pigges		*xxx*	
It the Poultry		*vj*	*viij*
It the Rye in the ground	*xij*		
It Corne in the house	*iiij*		
It Oats in the house		*lvj*	*viij*
It the malt		*ix*	
It For haye	*iiij*		
It Plowestuffe		*xxvj*	*viij*
It harroes		*iiij*	
It ladders and heardels		*lvj*	*viij*
It the Dunge		*iij*	*iiij*
It Crookes and Pannes		*l*	
It the Peoyt vessell		*x*	
It Candelsticks bills and booes[?]		*v*	
It a broch pothangings a gridiron and brandirones		*v*	
It a Gooespane			*iiij*
It Tobbes vates and other treing vessell		*xxx*	
It A chisewringe and chiserakes		*ij*	
It Tornes cardes and skeners		*x*	
It Erthinge vessells		*iij*	*iiij*
It Tabelbords forms chears & stoolles		*vj*	*viij*
It One grindingstone		*iij*	
It a Packsadell tresses Ropps and tings		*viij*	*viij*
It a Sellope and butts			*xij*
It For Chiese and Butter		*vj*	*viij*
It Bacon		*xvj*	
It a wemshite wth bagges and Sakks		*v*	
It For wood		*vj*	*viij*
It bordclothes wth a brushe		*iiij*	
It a bed pformed		*xlvj*	*viij*
It the beddinge	*iij*		
It koffers and bedsteeds		*x*	
It the shepshares and a peare of sissers			*xiiij*
It For Seame		*xvj*	
It For woolle and yearn	*iiij*		

	lî	s	d
It For Reewd		*xij*	
It corn Pecks donge Pecks Tresseles Racks and Seves		*iiij*	*viij*
It all other trashe		*xxvj*	*viij*

Sm tot $xciiij^{li}\ x^{s}\ ij^{d}$

[Exhibited by Agnes Reade & Thomas Reade, admins, 16 May 1576: Latin endorsement signed by W Blacke.

Will pr 16 May 1576: residue to wife Agnes & s Thomas, exec^{s}; £6 13s 4d each to ss John & William and drs Mary, Jane, Agnes, Jone, Ellyn, Thamsine, & Alce; 20s to dr Elizabeth Cudbord & 6s 8d each to her 3 chn; payment within 2 years to 5 chn already of age & provision for sharing out if any of the others die before 21; 1s each to ovsrs John Segar, vicar, & David Tucker; witn: John Segar, David Tucker, Richard Lindon.]

4 WYLLIAM READ 1576 (DS)

[Bur: "Wm. Read, of Ashell" 19 Dec 1576. Stock, poultry, no clothmaking gear; £21]

The Inventorie of the goods of Wyllm~ Read of the pishe of ufcolm made and preased by John Baker John marshall and John cole the xxjth daie of December and in the yeare of our lord god <u>1576</u>

	lî	s	d
Imp^{mis} three kee and one yearlinge	*v*	*xvj*	*viij*
Itm a mare		*xxvj*	*viij*
Itm three sheepe		*x*	
Itm three Piggs		*xv*	
Itm Pultrie		*ij*	
Itm ij croks		*xiij*	*iiij*
Itm pane brasse and a skillett		*x*	
Itm a chafer and a candelsticke		*iij*	*iiij*
Itm brandyse goosepane cotterell and a broche		*v*	
Itm Poyt and a saltseller		*iij*	*iiij*
Itm a trendell vatts & treinge vessell		*xiij*	*iiij*
Itm [bords and] formes		*vj*	*viij*
Itm chesses		*xx*	
Itm morte and gresse		*v*	
Itm coffers		*iiij*	
Itm his aparrell		*x*	
Itm his beddinge		*x*	
Itm a byll			*xx*
Itm a stayned clothe & a tester		*iij*	*iiij*
Itm butter		*xvj*	
Itm bacon		*xvj*	
Itm corne in barn	*iij*		
Itm haye		*xvj*	
Itm corne in ground		*xl*	
Itm mattocks & peecks		*ij*	*vj*
Itm all other trashe		*iij*	

Smtot $xxj^{li}\ xj^{s}\ x^{d}$ [1s short?]

[Exhibited by Humfrey Woodroff for the exec, 8 Jan 1576, i.e. 1576/7: Latin endorsement signed by W Blacke.

Will pr 8 Jan 1576/7: residue to dr Agnes, exec; 12d to church; 10s & 1 sheep each to ss Robert & John and dr Margarett Hodge and 12d each to their chn; 10s & "the great coffer" to Lyonerd Gredye; 2s to servant Katheren Landman; witn: John Segar, vicar, Robert & John Read, Lyonerd Gredie.]

5 BENNETT FRYER 1581 (DS)

[Bur: "Bennet Fryer" 17 Jul 1581. Chattel lease for mill, otherwise only clothing and domestic items and poultry; value c £17.]

The Inventorye of the goods of Bennett Fryer late of Uffcolume Decessed in the Countie of Devñ myller made and prysed by John Baker John Cole John Marshall Robert Reade and John Peperell the xxixth Daie of Julie A^{o} dm <u>1581</u>.

	lî	s	d
Impmis one cloake		*xvj*	
Itm one Cloth Dublett		*x*	
Itm one Dublett of Canvas		*iij*	*iiij*
Itm one peyre of hose		*iiij*	
Itm ij Jerkins		*ij*	*vj*
Itm ij hatts		*v*	
Itm a napkyn			*vj*
Itm thre shirts wth a peticote		*vij*	
Itm one girdell			*iiij*
Itm iiijor peyre of stockyns		*iij*	

	lî	s	d
Itm one peace of Cloth		iiij	
Itm thre Jerkyns more		vj	
Itm two Dubletts of leather		ij	
Itm a peyre of breches of leather		ij	vj
Itm a wast coate			xij
Itm iij peecs of clowtinge leather		ij	
Itm in money the summe of	iij	iij	iij
Itm his beddinge		xiiij	
Itm a fryinge pan			viij
Itm iiij^{or} pottingers one salte one sawcer a cuppe of tynne and one Candlesticke		iij	iiij
Itm one Cawdren			xx
Itm two gallons of butter		v	
Itm bacon and beefe		ij	vj
Itm a spitt a gridiron a brandyron two peyre of pothooks a pothanginge and a hatchett		ij	
Itm woodd		xvj	
Itm a peyre of boots a peyre of spurres & two peyre of shoes		ij	viij
Itm a staff			vj
Itm one cheste and one Coffer		x	
Itm viij seaves wth a semott[?]			xvj
Itm powltrye		iij	
Itm ij^{o} borryers[?] and a handsawe			x
Itm a brush			vj
Itm bords			xij
Itm a pipe one hoggeshed and a barrell wth two Coostes		iij	
Itm a Cheatell lease for the mill	vij		
Itm coggs and Ranges[?]		iij	iiij
Itm all other trashe			xij

Sma tolis.....*xvij^{li} iiij^{s} ix^{d}*

[Exhibited by Henry Gyrde, 10 Oct 1581: Latin endorsement signed by Egidius (=Giles) Hutchens.

Admon 20 Jul 1581 names Mary Mayor alš Fryer as admin & "natural" sister of Bennet Fryer of Uffculme, & also Gregory Clarke of Salisbury, hosier, & Henry Gerde of Cullompton, clothier; signed by Gregory Clarke & Harry Gyrd.]

6 WYLLYAM TOSER 1582 (DS)

[Bur: "William Toser" 8 Jan 1581/2. Stock, corn, brewing. Inventory partly damaged at top; value c £36.]

The Inventory of the goods of Wyllyã Toser of Ufc[ombe?] made & praysed by John Helyar John Rawlyngs and Robert Toser the xjxth day of January And~ 1581

	lî	s	d
Inpmis a horse & a mare		xl	
It kie & calfes	vj	xiij	iiij
It shepe	v		
It peggs		v	
It pultry			viij
It corne in the barne		xliij	iiij
It [corne in] the grounde	iij	vj	viij
It hay		xx	
It his apparell		xx	
It sylver spounes		xvj	
It pane & crok brasse		xlvj	viij
It pewter		xx	
It beadyng and beadsteds		xlv	
It tabelbords and a cupboard		xl	
It butter and chess		xiij	iiij
It candysteks and a chafer		iiij	
It larder		iij	iiij
It wolle		v	
It armur		x	
It selyng yn ye hall		v	
It coffers & putts[?]		v	
It broche & hanging for ye croks		vj	viij
It bruyng vessel and a trye[?]		xx	
It hogheds and a barell		ij	
It stened clothes		ij	
It harrows		iij	iiij
It matoxs & dunge pots			xvj
It dunge		v	
It Rede			vj
It a goosepan & others[?]			xviij
It wood		ij	
It cus[?]ps			viij
It horsharness		x	
It all other trashe		ij	

Sm *xxxiiij^{li} xix^{s} iiij^{d}*

detts

Wyllyã pococke for a cowe *xxxiij^{s}*

Sm tot' *xxxvj^{li} xij^{s} iiij^{d}*

[Exhibited by Agnes Toser, exec, 6 Sep 1582. Latin endorsement signed by Egidius (= Giles) Hutchens.

Admon 6 Sep 1582 names Agnes Toser as widow & admin, & also Robert Toser of Uffculme, husbandman.]

7 JOHN MYLL 1582 (DS)

[Bur: "John Mill" 22 Aug 1582. Mar: "John Mill & Jone Halse" 31 Aug 1550? (but cf W34). Cow, mare, pig, oats, clothmaking gear; value c £11.]

The Inventory of the goods of Johñ Myll of the parish of Ufcolm made & praysed by Wyllyã Lymã & Johñ Lyman ye xxviij^th^ day of August & yn the yer of o^r^ Lord 1582°.

	s	d
first a cowe	*xxxiij*	*iiij*
It' an old mare	*iij*	*iiij*
It' a pegge	*jx*	
It' otts	*xl*	
It' hay	*xvj*	
It' crok brasse	*xx*	
It' panne brasse	*xxviij*	
It' hangyns for the crok,		*viij*
It' treyng vessell	*x*	
It' borde & plankes	*v*	
It' hys apparell	*x*	
It' his beade & bedsteeds	*xiij*	*iiij*
It' woll	*x*	
It' harrows	*v*	
It' peewter vessell	*jx*	
It' a coffer		*xx*
It' turns & cards		*xvj*
It' woode	*v*	
It' a peke & workyn toyulls	*iiij*	
It' all other trashe		*xx*

Sm totalš *xj^li^ vj^s^ iiij^d^*

[Exhibited by Johanna Myll the widow admin, 6 Sep 1582: "Robt Rede of Ulfcolme", weaver, "bound in £20".

Admon 6 Sep 1582 names Johan Myll as widow & admin, & also Robert Rede of Uffculme, weaver.]

8 JOHN SANDER 1582 (DS)

[Bur: "John Saunder" 7 Sep 1582. Stock, corn, looms; value £49.]

The inventory of John Sander taken & praysed by John Chyck John Colyford & Thomas Cotterell theleventh daye of September anno dmi 1582

	lî	s	d
Imprimis fower key	*vj*	*xiij*	*iiij*
.... heffers		*xl*	
Itm three Calves		*xx*	
Itm his shepe	*vj*		
Itm two geldings & one mare	*v*	*xiij*	*iiij*
Itm his Corne	*x*		
Itm Haye		*liij*	*iiij*
Itm hoggs		*xx*	
Itm woodde		*xxvj*	*viij*
Itm pannes & brasse potts		*xl*	
Itm pewter vessell		*x*	
Itm one Cubbord		*xiij*	*iiij*
Itm a pear of lumbs		*xiij*	*iiij*
Itm bedds & bedsteds		*liij*	*iiij*
Itm Coffers		*vj*	*viij*
Itm vatts & tubbes		*xx*	
Itm his apparell		*xl*	
Itm his Armore		*x*	
Itm wooll		*xx*	
Itm Butter & Chesse		*xx*	
Itm Bords planks & formes		*vj*	*viij*
Itm packesaddels w^t^ their furnyture		*vj*	*viij*
Itm iron & other trashe		*v*	
Itm his dunge		*iiij*	
Itm pultry		*ij*	

Sma tot *xljx^li^ xvij^s^ viij^d^*

[Latin endorsement dated 8 Jan 1583.

Admon 8 Sep 1582 names John Sander of Uffculme, husbandman, & Marie Sander as admin^s^ of the goods &c of (their father?) John Sander the elder, & also Richard Broke of Uffculme, yeoman.]

9 PHILLIPP HAVELL 1585 (DS)

[Bur: "Phillipp Havell" 1 Nov 1585. Mar: "Phillip Havell & Mary Aplynge" 13 Apr 1581. Inventory exhibited 1594. Mare, colt, sheep, pigs; butter & cheese but no cows mentioned; clothmaking gear; value quoted £19, but figures make about £12 as they stand.]

The Inventorie of the goods and Cattells of Phillipp Havell of the pishe of Ulfcombe in the Countie of Devon made and praised by Richard London John Starke and Richard Persey the second day of November A^{o} dmi <u>1585</u>.

	lî	*s*	*d*
Imprlmls vij pole uf pewtcr vessell		*v*	
Itm iij^{e} Candelsticks			*xij*
Itm iiij^{or} pannes of brasse and a cawdren		*xx*	
Itm one Crock of brasse			*xx*
Itm one Cubard		*iij*	*iiij*
Itm one bedd and bedsteede		*iij*	
Itm iij^{e} tubbs a paile & a annige[?]		*iiij*	
Itm one turne a brandise a paire of hangings & a paire of cotterells			*xx*
Itm vij pole of pewter vessell one salt & ij^{o} Candlesticks		*iij*	*iiij*
Itm one pann of brasse one brasse Crocke one skillett & a Cawdren		*viij*	
Itm one brasse Crock more		*iij*	*iiij*
Itm tryen vessell			*xx*
Itm one vate		*iij*	
Itm a Colte		*xxxiij*	*iiij*
Itm one Mare		*xiij*	*iiij*
Itm xxx^{tie} sheepe	*iiij*	*vj*	*viij*
Itm strawe & hay & reede		*xiiij*	
Itm ij^{o} piggs		*xij*	
Itm the dunge		*iij*	
Itm the beddinge		*viij*	
Itm his wearing apparrell		*v*	
Itm iiij^{or} Coffers		*v*	
Itm shop stuff			*xij*
Itm Iron stuff		*ij*	
Itm butter and Cheese		*v*	
Itm turnes and Cards			*xviij*
Itm bords and formes		*ij*	*vj*
Itm ij^{o} whelebarrowes			*xvj*
Itm ij^{o} paire of Crooks			*viij*
Itm one Chaire and all other trashe			*xij*

Suma tolis *xix^{li} xv^{s} viij^{d}* [£7 1s 4d too much?]

[Exhibited by Clement Sunter husband & procurer of Mary Sunter alias Havell, dr & exec, 24 Jul 1594.

Will 28 Aug 1585 of Phillip Havell of Uffculme, pr at Uffculme before Mr Wm Wilkinson 24 Jul 1594: residue to dr Marie Havell, exec; 12d to poor; 6d to church; to dr Elizabeth Havell 1 cow, 14 sheep, bed, &c; to wife Mary what she owned before marriage plus 1 ewe, 1 pig, & 3 hens, & 1 ewe each to her 2 drs Jone & Florence, conditionally upon wife's paying 20s of debts to ovsrs; 12d to goddr Grace Will-iams; linen divided between drs Mary & Elizabeth; 2s 6d each to ovsrs John Rawlyns & Thomas Branford; debts owed to Mary Goodridge 20s, Phillipp(?) Pullinge of Sampford Peverell £4, John Rawlinges 12s, Robert & John Reed 3s, Thomas Milton of Willand 4s; witn: John Rawlynges, Thomas Branford, & Willm Facie.]

10 JOHN HODGE 1588 (DS)

[Bur: "John Hodge" 19 Nov 1588. Stock, corn; clothmaking gear; value £28.]

An Inventorye of the goods and Cattells of John Hodge of Uffcollumbe in the Countye of Devon made and praised by John Baker John Dune and Roborte Baker the xxvth Daye of november anno dm <u>1588</u>

	lî	*s*	*d*
Imprimis ij Kyne and ij heyffers	*vj*	*vj*	*viij*
Itm Sheppe		*xxviij*	
Itm Pigges		*xx*	
Itm Corne in the house and in mowes	*vj*	*xiij*	*iiij*
Itm Corne in the grounde		*l*	
Itm Haye		*xl*	
Itm Crock Brasse		*xij*	
Itm Pan Brasse		*xvj*	
Itm Puyter vessell		*vij*	
Itm Beeds and Bedsteeds		*xvj*	*viij*
Itm a Cov~lett			*xvj*
Itm his wearinge apparrell		*xxxiij*	*iiij*
Itm iij Coffers		*v*	
Itm Treeyinge vessell		*xiij*	*iiij*
Itm Bords and planckes		*viij*	
Itm matockes shouldes and peicks		*ij*	
Itm a Tabell Borde and a Forme		*x*	

	lî	s	d
Itm Turnes and Cardes			xx
Itm Brandisses and hangeinges		v	
Itm Butter and Cheese		v	
Itm Ladders and Crockes			xvj
Itm a Cheesewringe and ij brakinge stockes			viij
Itm steminge Clothes and shellfes		ij	
Itm Armore		x	
Itm a Broche and andiers		ij	
Itm Pultrey			xij
Itm woulle and yearne		v	iiij
Itm Bordes and Justes		vij	
Itm Candelstickes and all other trashe		iij	

Sma total~ *xxviij*^{li} *vij*^{s} *viij*^{d} [1s too much?]

[Exhibited by John Davye, procurer of Magarete Hodge, widow & exec, at Salisbury Wednesday 16 April 1589.

Will - Nov 1588 of John Hodge of Uffculme, pr 16 Apr 1589: residue to wife Margerete, exec; 1 lamb each to 2 chn of s Willm; witn: John Seager, cleric, Robert Reede, *et al.*]

11 RICHARD MANDER 1591 (DS)

[Bur: "Richard Maunder" 10 Oct 1591. Corn, pigs, 1 cow & heifer; value £15.]

The Inventorye of all the goodes and Cattelles of Richard Mander of the prishe of Uffcolmbe in the Countie of Devon Praysed by John Mander John Rawlinges and Richard London the xxijth day of October in the xxxiijth yeare of the Raigne of our Sov~ayne Ladie Elizabeth by the grace of God of England Fraunce and Irelande Queene Defender of the Faithe &c //

	lî	s	d
In primis one Cowe and a heypher	iij	xiij	iiij
Itm three Piggs		xvj	
Itm Corne in the Barne	iij	x	
Itm Corne in the Feilld		xxx	
Itm Haye		xiij	iiij
Itm Reed		iij	
Itm Fowre pannes of brase		xvj	
Itm two Crockes of brase & a posnett		vj	viij
Itm thre brasen Candelstickes			vj
Itm Pewter vessell		vj	viij
Itm his Apparrell		xiij	iiij
Itm Beddinge		xx	
Itm Bedsteedes		ij	viij
Itm two Cophers		ij	vj
Itm one Cubborde		viij	
Itm treen vessells		v	
Itm butter and Cheese		v	
Itm woode			xx
Itm one Barrell and three Costes		v	
Itm Boordes and plancks		viij	
Itm Firevote [or Frewte?]		ij	vj
Itm his woorkinge toolles		ij	vj
Itm a paire of Harrows		ij	vj
Itm pothangings and other yron stuffe			xx
Itm formes and other things forgotten			xx

Sma *xv*^{li} *xvij*^{s} *vj*^{d}

[Exhibited at Uffculme for the widow by John Mander and John Rawlyns, yeoman of Uffculme, 24 Jul 1594.

Admon 24 Jul 1594 names Jone Mander as widow & admin, & also John Rawlinges of Uffculme, yeoman; signed by Johan Mander & John Rawlynges.]

12 JOHN DOWDNEY 1592 (DS)

[Bur: "John Dowdney of Sowell" 18 Nov 1592. 10 cattle, 50 sheep, pigs, hay, & corn; £35.]

The trewe Inventorye of all the goods & Cattells of John Dowdney of Sowell in the prishe of Uffcollumbe in the Countye of Devon decessed made and prised by Thomas Cotterell & Davye Tucker the xxth Daye of november A^{o}:1592

	lî	s	d
Imprimis for Fyftye Sheepe	x		
Itm for ij Keyne	iij	xiij	iiij
Itm for iiij younge Bullockes	iiij		
Itm for iij Caulves		xxx	

	lî	*s*	*d*
Itm for Pygges		*xxvj*	*viij*
Itm for his Apparrell		*xl*	
Itm for Howsholde stufe and Toolles	*vj*		
Itm for Haye		*xxvj*	*viij*
Itm for Corne	*vj*		

Sum *xxxv^li^ xvj^s^ viij^d^*

[Exhibited at Salisbury by William Facy for Robt Dowdney, s & exec, 11 Jan 1592(/3).

Will 24 Feb 1591(/2) of John Dowdney of Sowell in Uffculme, pr at Salisbury 11 Jan 1592(/3) before Mr William Wilkinson: residue to s Roborte, exec; 3s 4d to church; 3s 4d to poor; £11 to dr Ane; &20 to dr Marye; £10 to s Henrye; 6d each to ss Thomas, William, & Nicholas; 40s to s Humfrye; 2s each to ovsrs John Seagarre, vicar, Roborte Reede; witn: Roborte Reede, Nicholas Dowdney, Willm Facye, Humfrye Howe, & Henrye Dowdney.

Admon 11 Jan 1592(/3) names Robt Dowdney as exec & William Facye, "shewmaker"; witn: John Symons not^y^ pub.]

13 RICHARDE MARSHALL 1592 (DS)

[Bur: "Richard Marshall of Norcote," 21 Dec 1592. Husbandman with some land, corn, stock, armour & weapons; value £47.]

The Inventorye of all & singuler of the goods chattells cattells and detts of Richarde Marshall of Uffcolumbe in the Countie of Devon Husbandman decessed /made & praysed by Robarte Reedd Richarde Baker Junr Robarte Marshall & Alexander Goodridgie /in the xxix^th^ Daye of December Anno dm 1592 as Here Followith

	lî	*s*	*d*
Inprimis acrees of wheett in grounde	*iiij*		
Item Corne in the Barne & in a mowe		*xlviij*	
It Otts in the Barne		*xxxiij*	*iiij*
It ij busshells of malte		*iiij*	
It seven Keen	*xiiij*		
It fyve Bullocks of one years agie & the vantaige	*vj*	*xiij*	*iiij*
It three yearlinge Cauvnes [calves]		*xlv*	
It one maar		*xxiiij*	
It sixe sheepe		*xxx*	
It one sowe & one peegg		*xiij*	*iiij*
It to sokinge Cauvnes		*x*	
It powltrye		*ij*	
It seven acrees of Haye	*iij*	*x*	
It one pear of wood Crooks one pear of Corne Hooks to saddells wth harnes therunto belongginge		*iij*	*iiij*
It armur for our ma^ties^ servis		*v*	
It one sorde & a dagger		*ij*	*vj*
It His apparrell		*xxvj*	*viij*
It one Fether bed pformed		*xxvj*	*viij*
It one Table borde & one Cobbarde		*xx*	
It one Trindell Thre fatts one Couste one pipe and one Litell Tubbe		*x*	
It fower pogers one sawser one salte siller one Teninge Couppe wth other Cupps		*ij*	
It to Crockes of brasse		*x*	
It one brassen pan one potthokes and a brandice		*ij*	
It thre pekes one Hooke one Hatchett & a shooll		*ij*	
It woodde		*iij*	*iiij*
It a Ladder sheed			*vj*
It Halfe a Hundred of Rued		*ij*	*vj*
It Butter & Chees		*xxx*	
It Larder & Baken		*x*	
It thre Coffers		*v*	
It peells Boolls dishes wth other tember stuffe			*xij*
It fyve pecks of wheett thre busshells of Rie		*x*	
It detts owed to him: Walter Buffett of offett		*vj*	*viij*
It Roberte Marshall		*iij*	*iiij*

It one peace of meaddow Called Braddemeade Contyvninge by estima~ iij acres be it mor or leesst for & dueringe the terme of xxij years or more yff one Nicholas Waddam awing [?] Margarett Waddam & Johãn

Waddam gen[er]osae shall so Longe happen to Leyve is praised & valued in thirtie iij shillings & iiij^d yearlye Dueringe the naturall Lyves of them *xxxiij^s iiij^d*

The forsaid Nicholas Margarett & Johãm so [say?] yt may amount to the som of xxxvj^{li} that we Refer to your opinnyon to sett yt ydown as you List & thinks yt best /

Toto somma *xlvij^{li} xviij^s vj^d* [2s too much?]

besides [not counting] the meaddow

[Exhibited at Salisbury by Mr. John Sec.r.(?) for the exec, 22 Mar 1592/93: Latin endorsement signed by Egid^s Hutchens Reg^r.

Will 19 Dec 1592 of Richarde Marshall of Uffculme, husbandman, pr at Salisbury 22 Mar 1592/3: exec wife Anne Marshall or, if she refuses, s John; 12d to church; 3s 4d to poor; 4d each to godchn; residue to ss John & Edwarde at age 21, wife to care for them till then; ovsrs Richarde Baker junr, & bros John & Robarte Marshall; witn: John Norhampton, Nicholas Bishopp, Richarde Baker jun^r, Robarte Marshall sen^r, & John Foweracres.]

14 THOMAS BUTSTONE 1593 (DS)

[Bur: "Thomas Butston" 12 Jan 1592/3. Corn, oats, rye, 1mare, 1pig, & 31 sheep; wool but no clothmaking gear; £39.]

The trewe Inventorye of all the gods Cattells & Detts of Thomas Butstone of the pishe of Uffcollumbe in the Countye of Devon decessed made and prised by Roborte Reede Anthonye James and Richarde Pearse the xvjth Daye of January Anno dm 1592[/3].

	lî	s	d
Imprimis three keyne	*v*	*xiij*	*iiij*
Itm. one Pygge		*xv*	
Itm. a Bedde and a Bolster		*x*	
Itm. one Cov^{r}lette		*vij*	
Itm. xxxj Sheipe	*v*	*xiij*	
Itm. Haye		*xl*	
Itm. Corne and otts in the Barne	*vj*	*xiij*	*iiij*
Itm. vij akers of Rye in grounde	*x*		
Itm. one mare		*xviij*	*vj*
Itm. his Wearinge Apparell		*vij*	
Itm. Woulle		*vj*	
Itm. one Crocke of Brasse		*xiiij*	
Itm. one Caudren		*iiij*	
Itm. Irone stufe and a peare of Corne Crockes		*vj*	*viij*
Sum	*xxxiiij^{li}*	*vij^s*	*x^d*

Detts Oweynge unto the foresaied Thomas

Imprimis Willmotte Skyner widowe	*v*		
Sum totalis	*xxxix^{li}*	*vij^s*	*x^d*

[Exhibited by Silvester Game 8 Aug 1593.

Admon 21 Jan 1592/3 names Mathew Butstone as bro & admin, & also John Cadbury & John Cornyshe, all being described as husbandmen of Uffculme; witn: Robart Marshall, who makes his mark.]

15 ELIZABETH RUDGE 1593 (DS)

[Bur: "Elizabeth Rudge, widdow" 17 Jan 1592/3. Domestic items only, including a spinning turn; value £5.]

The Inventorie of the goods of Elizabeth Rudge late of the pishe of Ulfcombe in the Countie of Devon widdoe deceased taken by John Leyman A^o dmi 1592°

	s	d
Imprmis one bedd pformed	*xx*	
Itm one Cobard	*xvj*	
It brasse and pewter	*xv*	
Itm one silver [spoon? (*v* will)]	*ij*	
It wooll	*vij*	
It tymber vessell	*vij*	
Itm a turne		*vj*
It ij^o Iron wedges and hangings	*iij*	
It Corne	*vj*	*viij*
It bacon	*v*	
Itm butter		*xx*
It beefe	*vj*	*viij*

	s	*d*
It a coffer wth other trashe	*iij*	
It her apparrell and lynnen	*xx*	

Sma total *v*^{li} *iij*^{s} *vj*^{d} [10s short?]

[Exhibited by Silvester Game for Thomas Rudge, exec, 8 Aug 1593.

Will pr 8 Aug 1593: residue to s Thomas Rudge, exec; 33s 4d to s Robert; 2 pewter dishes to Leonard Credy's 2 drs; ditto to Henry Dunsford's 2 chn; a silver spoon to Thomas Rudge's s; 1 pewter dish to Robert Rudge's s & 1 candlestick to his dr; apparel divided between drs Alice & Mary; 16d to Nicholas Knight; witn: Leonard Credye, Roborte Rudge, Nicholas Knighte.]

16 JOHN PEPPREELL senior 1593 (DS)

[Bur: "John Peperell of Ashell" 12 Mar 1592/3. Husbandman with 9 cattle, 59 sheep, oats, wheat, beans; clothmaking gear; c £68.]

An Inventory of all & singuler of the goods chattells cattells and detts of John Peppreell señ des.ss.. in the prishe of Uffcolumbe in the Countie of Devon Husbandman made and praysed by John Marshall señ John Marshall of Umbrooke Robarte Reed Willm Marshall John Crodgie & John Norhampton in the xvjth daye of Marche anno dm 1592 / as followethe

	lî	*s*	*d*
Impmis fower acres and halfe of Rie in grounde & to acres & halfe of wheatt & beans	*x*	*viij*	*iiij*
Itm fyve acres of ottes in grounde	*iij*	*vj*	*viij*
Itm wheatt & Rie in the Barne		*xl*	
Itm aighte busshells of otts		*xvj*	
Itm sixe Busshells of malte		*xiiij*	
Itm Haye in House		*xxxiij*	*iiij*
Itm fyve Kee to Heaffers & to yearlings	*xiiij*	*xiiij*	*viij*
Itm to maars [mares]	*ij*	*xiij*	*iiij*
Itm xxxiij sheepe wethers & Hoggs	*viij*	*v*	
Itm twellve Cuppell of yeawes & Lammes & to yolde yeawes	*iiij*	*xij*	
Itm thre peggs		*xxj*	
Itm thre bedds pformed	*iij*		
Itm to bedd sheets & one borde clothe		*xiij*	*iiij*
Itm all his apparrell		*xl*	
Itm brassen pannes & one Cawdren & a Chaffer of brass	*xl*^{s}[?]	*vj*	*viij*
Itm to crocks one posnett & 1 fryen pan		*xxiij*	*iiij*
Itm pewter vessells & iij salte sillers		*xxiij*	*vj*
Itm one bason & iij Candelsticks of brasse		*ij*	
Itm one broche ij brandies ij pear of Iren Hanggings & one of Cottrells		*iiij*	
Itm ij matticks ij pekes one exe one shoull one bilhouke wth one Iren Wadge		*iiij*	*iiij*
Itm one Table borde & a forme		*xx*	
Itm to Coffers one Chear yeinche bords and plongs [planks?]		*vj*	*viij*
Itm armur for our ma^{ties} servis videlzt [viz] one sowrde one lange Bowe & a sheve of arroes & a still Cape[?]		*viij*	*iiij*
Itm one saargie[?]			*xij*
Itm fower Cousts & one barrell		*iiij*	
Itm one Tryndell sixe faetts iij hogsides wth other tubbs		*xxiij*	
Itm a pear of Harroes		*vj*	*viij*
Itm a pear of woodcroks one Candellmolde & pear of doungepotts		*ij*	
Itm one sie[?]			*xij*
Itm woode		*iiij*	
Itm one hundred of Rued		*v*	
Itm Dounge		*xiij*	*iiij*
Itm Bakon		*xx*	
Itm one que[.]ne of butter & a Chees		*ij*	
Itm Che[ese]faetts			*xij*
Itm [eart]hen vessels			*vj*
Itm packesaddell wth his Harness		*ij*	
Itm to bolls iij peells xij hoolldisshes		*ij*	

	lî	s	d
Itm to sacke baggs			*xvj*
Itm pultre			*xx*
Itm one Turne & a sellop[?] wth other tymber stuffe and trashe			*xij*
Itm iij Turnes ij peare of woullen Cards		*ij*	*vj*

Toto soma *lxviij*^{li} *viij*^{s} *x*^{d} [2s 8d short?]

[Exhibited by John Symons for Joan Pepprell, relict & exec, 3 May 1593.

Will 9 Mar 1592(/3) of John Pepprell sen^{r}, husbandman, pr Thursday 3 May 1593: residue to Johan Pepperell, wife & exec; 12d to church; 12d to poor; 12d to godson John Marshall & 4d each to other godchn; to ss John & Edward & drs Johan, Agnes, Mary, & Margery Pepprell £6 13s 4d each, out of which £23 is to be lent to their bro Robarte to pay the "feu of his bargain" to W^{m}, Earl of Bath; 20d each to ovsrs John Marshall senr & Henry Godfre of "Ayeishell"; 20d to John Norhampton; witn: John Norhampton, John Marshall sen^{r}, & Henry Godfre.]

17 HENRYE GODFFRAYE 1593 (DS)

[Bur: "Henry Godfrye" 2 Apr 1593. Mar: "Henry Godfry & Jone Dunne" 24 Nov 1571. Stock, no grain; value £16.]

The trewe Inventorye of the goods and Cattells of Henrye Godffraye of the prishe of Uffcollombe in the County of Devon Decessed made and prised by John Baker Mathewe Butstone John Dune thelder John Salter and Willm M[a]^{r}shall the xxviijth Daye of Aprille Anno dm 1593.

	lî	s	d
Imprimis one Heiffer and a Caulfe		*l*	
Itm. one Horse	*iij*		
Itm. Fyvfe Lambes		*xiij*	*iiij*
Itm. towe Pigges		*xx*	
Itm. a Tabell Borde and a forme		*v*	
Itm. a Coubborde		*xx*	
Itm. Fower Panes of Brasse		*xv*	
Itm. towe Crokes of Brasse and a posnette		*xiij*	*iiij*
Itm. a Skillett and a Cawdren		*ij*	
Itm. towe Chafendiches of Brasse			*xx*
Itm. towe Candelstyckes			*vj*
Itm. Pueter Vessell		*viij*	
Itm. three Stoninge [stoneware?] Cuppes			*vj*
Itm. three Beeds pformed wth Beedesteeds		*xxx*	
Itm. his wearinge Apparell		*xviij*	
Itm. one Coffer one olde Trunke and a hamp[er]		*iij*	
Itm. A Cheese Racke and a Sarge			*xviij*
Itm. one Trendell to Costes wth all other wodden vessell		*x*	
Itm. one Borde Clothe			*xij*
Itm. one stayened Clothe			*xij*
Itm. Bordes and Plankes		*ij*	
Itm. Wodde		*xx*	
Itm. Dunge		*iij*	*iiij*
Itm. Haye		*iiij*	
Itm. one tongeinge Exe ackauntinge Knyfe wth all his other Slaufter Towlls		*ij*	
Itm. one Exe a hatchett wth all his husbandarie towls			*xij*
Itm. one peare of weyttes			*xij*
Itm. ij Potthangeinges one peare of Cotterells towe Brandices and a gredirone		*iij*	*iiij*
Itm. one Irone Barre and ij Irone wadges			*xvj*
Itm. a Saddell a peare of paynniers a Tynge & a gerse		*v*	
Itm. three Caulfe Skynes			*xviij*
Itm. ij Turnes a peare of Cards wth all other Trashe		*ij*	*vj*

Sum *xvj*^{li} *x*^{d}

[Exhibited at Salisbury by John Symons, notary public, for Joan Godfry, widow & admin, 3 May 1593.

Amongst the conditions mentioned in the (undated) grant of administration by Dr Bridges, Dean of Salisbury, the widow Jone is required to raise and educate the chn, John, Mary, & Alice, until lawful age or marriage.]

18 JOHN HOWE 1594 (DS)

[Bur: "John Howe alš Tanner, son of Anstice" 6 Feb 1593/4. Small shop (?); 2 acres of wheat, few stock; value £11.]

The trewe Inventorye of all the goods Cattells and Dettes of John Howe of the prishe of Uffcollm in the Countye of Devon Decessed made & prised by Anthonye James, Roborte Dowdney & Roborte Wealshe the xxviijth daye of Februarie an^{o} dm <u>1593</u>

	lî	*s*	*d*
Imprimis. Corne in house	*iij*	*x*	
Itm toe acres of wheat in grounde		*xliij*	
Itm his shopestufe		*vj*	*viij*
Itm his wearinge apparrell		*xxx*	
Itm one Earlen		*x*	
Itm one Sowe		*x*	
Itm one Ewe shepe		*iiij*	
Itm one Caudren		*ij*	*vj*
Itm one Beede tye		*iiij*	

Sum *ix^{li} ij^{d}*

Dettes oweinge hime
Petter Chas.e[?] *xl^{s}*. Willm middeldõ *iij^{s}*
Sum *xliij^{s}*

Sum totalš *xj^{li} iij^{s} ij^{d}*

[Exhibited at Uffculme by Humfrey Howe, bro & exec, 24 Jul 1594.

Will 3 Feb 1593(/4) of John Howe of Uffculme, pr Wednesday 24 Jul 1594: residue to Humfrye Howe, bro & exec; 6s to the poor & 12d to the church; to wife Grace all her apparel & household goods brought with her at marriage or given by friends of hers since; to s George £3; best cloak to mother Anstice Howe; debts owed (by John Howe) to sisters Johan & Elizabethe Howe £10 each, to Roger Bysshope £5, to Willm Kepper 37s, to Thomas Morrel 6s, to Isette Hagley 8s, to Thomas Kepper 6s, to Willm Starke 12d; debts owed (to John Howe) by Petter Chance of Bucklande, Somerset, 40s, by Willm Middledone 3s, by Willm Kepper for 4 pairs of spoons & 15 bushels of wheat; witn: Humfrye Saunders, Humfrye Howe, & Willm Facy.]

19 JOHN COLLIFORD the elder 1594 (DS)

[Bur: "John Colliford thelder" 5 Mar 1593/4. Mar: "John Colliford & John Dumnett" 11 May 1579. Husbandman; mostly arable but also cider & cloth-making gear; value £88.]

Inp----
Itm -----
Itm th-----
Itm one M--- [Top of inventory missing]
Itm Cleome C---
Itm Fower Hogg---
Itm fyve ackers of wh---
Itm Gannies[?] Capons and---
Itm fyve sacks of ottes
Itm Maltte
Itm Haye
Itm Reed
Itm a wrynge to make Cedar and other things therto belonginge
Itm the dounge
Itm wood and Furses
Itm tubbs trendels and Cowells
Itm barrells and Costes
Itm three Trowes of timber

	lî	*s*	*d*
Itm three Hoggeshedds of Cedar and their vessels	*xx-*	---	
Itm a dozen of Hoopes			*vj*
Itm two Turnes			*xvj*
Itm two Chesewringes			*xvj*
Itm a Range Seves semmets a sellope a pecke and a sarge		*iij*	*x*
Itm Baggs sacks and wynowshets		*vj*	*iiij*
Itm a packe saddle a hacney saddell and a side saddle		*v*	*vj*
Itm pangers a tyinge gerses & Crooks		*ij*	
Itm Harrowes and Harowinge stuffe		*xj*	
Itm a brydell and Roppes			*xx*
Itm mattocks shewells and doung forks		*iij*	*iiij*

	lî	s	d
Itm Corne picks		*ij*	*iiij*
Itm pells trenchers and other treen vessele		*v*	
Itm bords and plancks		*xvij*	
Itm Sallte		*ij*	
Itm brasen pannes	*iiij*	*vij*	*viij*
Itm one kettell		*xiij*	*iiij*
Itm brasen Crocks & ij° fryinge pannes		*xlij*	
Itm two Chaffinge disshes a morter and brasen Candelsticks		*ix*	*vj*
Itm broches and other Iron stuffe		*xxij*	*viij*
Itm six stone Cuppes			*xij*
Itm Sallts and pewter		*xxx*	
Itm Larder		*xl*	
Itm Butter and Chesses		*xviij*	
Itm a mustard Mill & a bottell		*ij*	
Itm Armor		*xxvj*	*viij*
Itm two tablebords one Rounde borde three Formes and Sylinge	*iij*		
Itm Cophers and Chests		*xvj*	
Itm one steell bowe		*vj*	*viij*
Itm one presse		*ij*	
Itm borde clothes Shetts table napkins and towells		*xlij*	
Itm bedds and bedsteds	*vj*	*vj*	*viij*
Itm Appells		*v*	
Itm his apparrell	*v*	*xij*	
Itm Russett kerseye		*x*	*vj*
Itm Cusshions		*ij*	*vj*
Itm one standard			*xij*
Itm in monie		*x*	
Itm two Cheres Erthen vessell and other things Forgotten		*iij*	*iiij*

Sma total~ *lxxxviij*[li] *xviij*[s] *x*[d]

[Exhibited at Uffculme by Mary Coliford, dr & exec 24 Jul 1594.

Will 11 May 1593 of John Colliforde of Uffculme, husbandman, pr Wednesday 24 Jul 1594: residue to wife Johan & dr Mary, exec; 3s 4d to poor of Uffculme & 3s 4d to church; £4 to s Humfye Colliforde; 2s each to grandchn; 4d each to godchn; 20d each to Willm Mille, Willm Dunnette, & Humfrye Meere, ovsrs of will; witn: Willm Facye & Magdalene Facye.]

20 JOHN SEAGAR 1594 (DS)

[Bur: "John Segar vicar of Uffculme" 27 Mar 1594. Vicar; household goods, £10 in books; £45.]

An Invithory of the goods of John Seagar late viccar of Uffcolm~ deceassed taken and prised by Thomas Cole John Stark Robt Reade and Lionard Gredy the xxvij[th] daie of m[r]che 1594.

	lî	s	d
Inp[mis] ij Bedsteedes		*xxvj*	*viij*
Itm. ij Feather Beddes	*iij*	*vj*	*viij*
Itm. ij Flock beddes		*xxvj*	*viij*
Itm. ij bolsters ij pollowes of feathers		*xiij*	*iiij*
Itm. ij peare of blanketts		*xvj*	
Itm. ij Cov[r]letts		*xlvj*	*viij*
Itm. iij peare of sheets		*xliij*	*iiij*
Itm. iij pillowe tyes		*iij*	*iiij*
Itm. ij bord Clothes		*xv*	
Itm. one surples w[th] his lynning teaster		*xxiij*	*iiij*
Itm. ij other teaster		*vj*	*viij*
Itm. his appoll w[th] his lynning	*iij*		
Itm. his Bookes	*x*		
Itm. ij dusson and fyve spoones of silv[r]	*vj*		
Itm. poyter vessell		*xiij*	*iiij*
Itm. pann Brasse	*iiij*	*x*	
Itm. pott Brasse		*xxx*	
Itm. a morter iij Candelsticks of brasse		*viij*	
Itm. one Cheast		*xiij*	*iiij*
Itm. one folding bord & ij formes		*xx*	
Itm. one Cubbord & square table		*xiij*	*iiij*
Itm. plancks wth other Tymber		*xvj*	
Itm. Treeing Vessell		*xj*	
Itm. ij Cheares and a stoole		*ij*	
Itm. one pigg and Bakon		*x*	
Itm. Iron stuffe		*iiij*	
Itm. j Cofer wth all other trashe		*v*	

Sm~ tot~ *xlv*[li] *iij*[s] *ij*[d] [6d short?]

[Exhibited by John & Robert Reade before Egid~ Hutchens Reg^{r} 2 Apr 1594.

Will 14 Jun 1587 of John Seagar, vicar of Uffculme, pr before Willm~ Wilkenson 2 Apr 1594; residue to Agnes Reade, exec; 40s to sister's dr Margarett Hake; 12d each to godchn; bur^{d} in chancel; witn: Robt Reade sen^{r}, John Reade, Leonard Gredy, Richard London, & Robt Reade.]

21 THOMAS CORTONE the elder 1594 (DS)

[Bur: "Thomas Courton thelder" 25 Jun 1594. Mar: "Thomas Courton & Elizabeth Wills" 23 May 1594. Few stock, some corn; value £17, including £8 owed to him.]

The trewe Inventorye of all the goods Cattells and detts of Thomas Cortone thelder of the prishe of Uffcollum in the Countye of Devon Decessed made and prised by Willm Olande Davye Tucker and Humphrye Woddroffe the xxvth daye of June Anno dm 1594

	s	*d*
Imprimis one Coubborde	*x*	
Itm one Table Borde	*x*	
Itm one borde more & a beynche		*xvj*
Itm iij panes of brase one Cawdre[n] & a skillet	*xj*	
Itm one Crocke of brase	*vj*	
Itm ij Candelstickes		*iiij*
Itm one Puyter vessell	*iij*	
Itm one brandice a pothaneinges wth other Irone stuffe	*iij*	
Itm Butter and Cheese	*vj*	*viij*
Itm wodden vessell & ij bedsteds	*viij*	
Itm Beeddinge	*iij*	*iiij*
Itm wearinge apparrell	*xx*	
Itm a Ladder		*xij*
Itm Corne in the grounde	*lvij*	*vj*
Itm one Cowe	*xxx*	
Itm ij pigges	*vj*	
Itm viij Geyes wth other pultrey	*iiij*	*viij*
Itm wodde	*ij*	*vj*
Itm Reede		*xviij*
Itm one Forme with all other Trashe		*xij*

Sum *ix^{li} vj^{s} x^{d}*

Detts Oweinge to the foresaied Thomas Corton

Imprimis Willm Wills of Poltimore *viij^{li}*

Sum totalš *xvij^{li} vj^{s} x^{d}*

[No Latin endorsement to show when this inventory was exhibited.

Will 23 Jun 1594 of Thomas Cortone the elder of Uffculme, pr 29 Jan 1594/5: residue to two drs Johan Cortone the younger & Frances Cortone, exec^{s}; 12d to the poor & 12d to the church of Uffculme; to wife Elizabeth 4 bushels each of wheat & oats, a table, & the bed she brought with her; 40s to s Marke, 20s to s John, 40s to s Thomas, & 10s to dr Margerye Lange; 20d each to Willm Olande alš Tayller & Gerome Lange, ovsrs of will; witn: John Hardinge, pastor ecclesiae, Willm Oland, & Willm Facye.]

22 WILLIAM NORTON 1594 (DS)

[Bur: "William Norton" 12 May 1594. Mar: "Wm Norton & Florence Rewe" 19 Sep 1586. Weaver [?] with one kersey in stock, loom & harness; bees & 2 pigs but no other farmstock; value £11.]

An Inventhorie of the goodes & Ch[attels]of William Norton late of Uffcolm deceased made and praysed by John Rawlings & John P[er]dye the xviijth daie of July 1594.

	s	*d*
Imp^{mis} his app[ar]ell	*xlj*	
Itm one mare	*xxx*	
Itm one kersey	*xxxiij*	
Itm his Bedding	*xx*	
Itm one peare of Loomes wth one slaye and harnes	*xx*	
Itm wolle	*x*	

	s	d
Itm one brasse pott	*v*	
Itm pan brasse	*vj*	
Itm puyter vessell	*x*	
Itm ij piggs	*viij*	
Itm ij Buttes of Bees	*vj*	*viij*
Itm woode	*vj*	*viij*
Itm one Fliche of Bakon	*v*	
Itm ij presses	*vj*	*viij*
Itm iiij Coffers	*iiij*	
Itm one Butt of strawe		*xij*
Itm earthing pottes		*vj*
Itm Bordes		*viij*
Itm Treeing vessells	*iij*	*iiij*
Itm j [ij?] borde Clothe		*xij*
Itm potte hangings		*xij*
Itm one Candelstick		*vj*
Itm stooles & all other trashe		*xij*

Sum^a totš *xj*^{li} *xij*^{d}

[Exhibited at Uffculm by the widow & exec 24 Jul 1594.

Will 8 May 1594 of William Norton of Uffculme, pr Wednesday, 24 Jul 1594: residue to Florance, wife & exec; 1 mare, 1 kersey "now in the looms", 1 butt of bees, & a pig to s Robte Norton; a pewter platter each to Anthony & Robte P̲dye (Perdye), ss of John P̲dye; bro John Norton as ovsr; witn: John Lane & John P̲dye.]

23 HENRYE SKINNER 1594 (DS)

[Bur: "Henry Skinner of Brodfield" 26 Oct 1594. Domestic items only; £3.]

The trewe Inventori of all the goods of Henrye Skinner of the p̲rishe of Uffcollum in the Countye of Devon decessed made and prysed by Thomas Cotterell Roborte Wealshe and Humfrye mille the thirteythe Daye of november A^o dm 1594

	s	d
Imprimis Peyter vessell	*viij*	
Itm ij Candelstyckes		*xviij*
Itm one brase Crocke ij littell brasse panes and a skellett	*x*	
Itm one Beede p̲formed	*vj*	*viij*
Itm his wearinge apparrell	*vj*	*viij*
Itm one Broche one pottehanginge a gredirone a peere of Cotterells and iij Irone wagges	*v*	
Itm towe Coffers	*vj*	*viij*
Itm for Tember vessell	*x*	
Itm one Borde and ij Tressells	*ij*	
Itm one Packe saddell		*xij*
Itm one Coubbourde	*ij*	
Itm one Irone showlle		*xvj*
Itm ij mattockes iij peyckes a hatchett and a bylhocke	*ij*	*viij*
Itm one fryeinge pane & ij Cupes wth the Tranchers		*xij*
Itm one peare of dungepotts wth stowells and all other thinges forgotten		*xij*

Sum^a totalš *iij*^{li} *v*^{s} *vj*^{d}

[Exhibited by John Symons, notary public, for widow & admin, 29 Jan 1594/5]

24 JOHANE OSMONDE 1594 (DS)

[Bur: "Jone Osmonde, widdow" 9 Dec 1594. Mar: "Henry Osmonte & - Burrowe"? 26 Nov 1549; see LW37. Mostly domestic items, no livestock but saddles, bees, & a spinning turn; value £16.]

The trewe Inventorye of all the goods moveabell of Johane Osmonnde widowe latelye deceessed at brodfeyld wthin the prishe of Uffcollum in the Countye of Devone made and praysed by Thomas Cotterell Roborte Combe thelder and Roborte Walshe the Twenteythe daye of December Anno dm 1594

	lî	s	d
Imprimis all her wearinge apparrell	*iij*		
Itm one Tabell Borde one Forme the beinche and the seelinge		*xx*	
Itm three Crockes of brasse		*xxv*	
Itm one Kettell one fryeinge pane one goosepane sixe panes of brasse ij skellets & a Chaffendishe		*l*	
Itm one Teyninge potte			

	lî	s	d
one Cupe one salte wth the Peyter disshes		*xl*	
Itm Beddes and Bedsteedes wth their furniture	*iij*		
Itm one Chest wth towe Coffers		*v*	
Itm all the wodden vessell one sacke three bagges and a spininge Turne		*xxiij*	*iiij*
Itm one spitte towe andiers one pediron[?] ij hangeinges towe pothombes one brandice one peycke and a peere of Tonges		*vj*	*viij*
Itm one side saddell a packe saddell a peere of Corne Crockes a peere of muxpottes[?] wth Tynges and gersses		*v*	
Itm ij houckes a mattycke a shoulle & one Exe		*ij*	
Itm Bees		*iij*	*iiij*
Itm a Costlette furnished		*xx*	
Itm Erthen vessell			*vj*
Itm planckes bordes and other Tymber		*ij*	
Itm one Carprett towe bordeclothes one Toowell and a Coubborde Clothe		*vj*	*viij*
Itm for all other thinges not put downe			*xij*

Sum totalš *xvj*^{li} *x*^{s} *vj*^{d}

[Exhibited at Salisbury by John Symons, notary public, for Thomas Bussell, exec 29 Jan 1594/5.

Will 6 Nov 1594 of Johane Osmonde of Uffculme, widow, pr 29 Jan 1594/5: residue to Thomas Bussell, exec; 2s to poor; 3s 4d each to Goweyne, Elizabethe, Margarette, John, Dowritie, & Johane Kelley; 6s 8d each to Ellyes, Roborte the younger, & Susanna Combe; one pan(e) to Henrye Osmonde; witn: Roborte Combe the elder & Roborte Walshe.]

25 JOHN BUSSELL 1595 (DS)

[Bur: "John Bussell" 9 Aug 1595. Mar: "John Bussell & Thamsyn Grantlange" 19 Jul 1593. Yeoman; modest stock & corn; £36.]

The trewe Inventorye of all the goods Cattells and Dettes of John Bussell of the prishe of Uffcollum in the Countye of Devon yeoman decessed made and prayssed by Thomas Bussell John Snowe & Willm Grantlande the Sixteynthe Daye of Auguste An^{o} 1595

	lî	s	d
Imprimis three Heyphers and Fyvfe yearlenes	*xiij*		
Itm towe Colltes		*liij*	*iiij*
Itm one Pigge		*x*	
Itm for Cleane Corne in grounde	*vij*		
Itm for Ottes in grownde	*iij*	*xvj*	
Itm for Haye		*xxx*	
Itm one pakesaddell and a pere of Panniers		*iiij*	
Itm towe platters		*ij*	
Itm towe pottengers towe sawcers & a tunne[?]		*iij*	*iiij*
Itm one pane and towe skylletes		*vj*	*viij*
Itm towe brasse Crockes		*xiij*	*iiij*
Itm one Frame borde and a Forme		*v*	
Itm one yowteinge Fatte		*vj*	*viij*
Itm one broche and towe Andiers		*ij*	
Itm towe Coffers		*v*	
Itm one Truncke		*v*	
Itm one flocke Beede one bolster and a peare of sheittes		*xx*	
Itm three dublettes		*xxvj*	*viij*
Itm one Cotte [coat here?]		*xij*	
Itm towe Clockes [cloaks?]		*xx*	
Itm towe Hattes		*v*	
Itm three peare of breches wth towe shertes		*xv*	
Itm one peare of boutes and spures wth stockeinges		*x*	
Itm for thinges forgotten yf anye be			*xij*

Smo totalis *xxxvj*^{li} *xij*^{s}

[Exhibited at Uffculme by Thomasine Bussell, widow & exec 22 Sep 1597. Latin endorsement signed by Egidius Hutchens Reg^{r}.

Will 19 Apr 1595 of John Bussell of Uffculme, pr at Uffculme 22 Sep 1597 before Mr Wm Wilkinson; residue conditionally upon no remarriage to wife Thomasyne, exec, including "halfe deall" of her mother's living given at marriage according to covenants held by Wm Walronds, squire of Bradfield, but if she sells her part of the living she pays 5 marks to bro Thomas Bussell; 2s to poor; 3s 4d to godchn; from £4 16s due from Henry Chase & wife Marione of Kentisbeare, £3 to bro Thomas Bussell, plus a coat & 2 doublets; a grey mare colt to friend John Heyball; witn: John Heyball, Thomas Bussell, *et al*; debts due from Richard Longe 12s, George Crosse 20s, Christopher Smithe 40s.]

26 JOHN COLLE alias KERSWILL 1595 (DS)

[Bur: "John Cole" 28 Dec 1595. Mar: "John Cole & Jone Jarvice" 15 Jun 1562. Stock, poultry, wheat, rye, barley, oats; no clothmaking gear; £45.]

The Inventorie of all the goods Cattells & Detts of John Colle alš Kerswill of Ufcolum decessed made and prised by John Turner Edwarde Andrewe John Beere & Roborte Marshalle the xxx^{ti} of December Anno Dm 1595

	lî	*s*	*d*
Imprimis iij Keyne one heyffer & one yearlen	*viij*	*xiij*	*iiij*
Itm viij sheepe ij pigges & pultrey		*liij*	*iiij*
Itm all the Haye		*xxx*	
Itm wheatt Rye barlye Otts & malte	*vij*		
Itm A Tabell borde formes chaires stowles & coushens		*x*	
Itm one fether beede ij flockebeeds iij playne beedsteeds wth Cov^{r}letts blanketts bolsters sheetts & his wearinge apparell	*vj*	*xiij*	*iiij*
Itm v litell Coffers		*viij*	
Itm vj silfer spones		*xxvj*	*viij*
Itm woulle & yearne		*xxvj*	*viij*
Itm vj littell panes iij Crokes astell [a steel?] pane wth an olde brase pane		*xlvj*	*viij*
Itm Payter vessell iij Candelstickes & ij Chanfendishes		*xiij*	*iiij*
Itm all wodden vessell as Trendells fatts &c		*xl*	
Itm one broche ij potthangeinges iij peere of Cotterolls wth the Reste of the Iron stufe		*vj*	*viij*
Itm v acres & halfe of Corne in grownde	*vij*		
Itm a milke borde wth other plankes & bordes		*v*	
Itm all the woode		*viij*	
Itm one peare of harrowes wth ij Tries[?]		*v*	
Itm Baken		*xviij*	
Itm a matocke a peyke & earthen vessell wth all other thinges not praysed		*x*	
Itm Butter & Cheese		*xiij*	*iiij*

Sum *xlv^{li} vij^{s} viij^{d}* [4d too much?]

[Exhibited at Salisbury by Silvester Game for the widow & admin 12 Feb 1595(/6).

Admon 25 Jan 1595(/6) names Jone Colle "alias Cassher" as widow & admin, & also John Beere, yeoman, & Robert Boorowe, blacksmith, both of Uffculme; marked by Jone Colle & Robt Boorowe & signed by John Bear in presence of Robt Marshall & Willm Facye. Delivered to Silvester Game for the Dean of Salisbury.]

27 ROBERT MYDELTON 1596 (DS)

[Bur: "Robart Middleton of Rill" 21 Apr 1596. Corn & oats, 7 sheep; £12.]

The Inventory of all and singuler the goods Cattalls and detts of Robert Mydelton of Ulfcombe in the County of Devon deceased taken and praysd the xxvjth of Auguste A^{o} Dm 1596° by John Goodridge and John Leyman/

	lî	*s*	*d*
Imprimis vij sheep		*xxx*	
Itm in mault and otes		*xx*	
Itm tymber		*x*	

	lî	s	d
Itm iiijor pannes		*xxiij*	*iiij*
Itm one Crock and a posnett		*vj*	
Itm in pewter vessell		*iij*	*viij*
Itm in Corne	*v*	*xj*	*viij*
Itm treene vessell		*vj*	*viij*
Itm in beddinge and his appell		*xxxiij*	*iiij*
Itm a brandiron a grediron and a toster			*xx*
Itm a borde a forme and a Chaire			*xx*
Itm the dung hill		*vj*	*viij*

Sma totalis xij^{li} $xiiij^{s}$ $viij^{d}$

[Exhibited at Uffcombe by William Mydeldon, admin 22 Sep 1597. Latin endorsement signed by Egidius (Giles) Hutchins Reg^{r}.

Nuncupative will 20 Apr 1596 of Robert Mydelton of Uffculme,proved 22 Sep 1597: no exec named; 4 ewes & lambs to dr Elizabeth Mydelton; a ewe hog to s Thomas Mydelton; residue equally divided between chn William, Elizabeth, Alice, & Jone (all Mydelton, but s Thomas not included in this list). Admon 22 Sep 1597 names Wm Mydelton of Uffculme, weaver, as s & admin, & also Robert Reade of Uffculme, yeoman; marked by Wm Mydelton & Robt Reade in presence of John Symons, not^{y} pub.]

28 MARY SAUNDER 1596 (DS)

[Bur: immediately after the Thomas Cottrell entry on 24 July 1596 occurs "The _ day of _ was Mary Saunder widdow buryed", with the blank spaces as shown. The day and month were clearly uncertain and the entry should evidently have been made shortly before 4th June to be consistent with the date of the inventory. (It would then have come just before that of Thomas Cottrell.) Cattle, sheep, pigs, poultry, wheat, oats, & barley; £40.]

An Inventory of all the goods & Chattells of Mary Saunder of the pishe of Uffecolume widow w[ith]in the peculyer Jurisdiccon of Newbury taken by Richard Brooke Nicholas Dowdnay Robt Walshe & Mathew Facye the fourth daye of June Ann Dm 1596

	lî	s	d
Imp[ri]mis six kyne one steer & heffer	*xiiij*	*x*	
Itm tow yearlings		*xxvj*	*viij*
Itm xxix^{tie} weathers & hogge sheep	*vj*	*xv*	
Itm seven Ewes & lambs & tow Calves		*lviij*	*iiij*
Itm one mare & tow Colts	*iij*	*vj*	*viij*
Itm Tow piggs & pultry		*xiij*	
Itm Three akars of Ry & wheat	*iiij*		
Itm Fower akars of Otts & barly	*iij*		
Itm wood		*x*	
Itm apparell		*l*	
Itm dunge		*ij*	
Itm one kytle butter & Cheese		*ix*	*vj*
Itm five flyses of woull & tow brasse panns		*x*	
Itm one syd saddle & things forgotten		*ij*	

Sma totalš xl^{li} v^{s} x^{d} [7s 4d short?]

[Exhibited at Salisbury by John Saunder, s & exec, 11 Jan 1596/7. Latin endorsement signed by Egid's Hutchins Reg^{r}.

Will 9 May 1596 of Marye Saunder of Uffculme, widow: residue to s John Saunder, exec; 12d to poor; 12d to church; £6 13s 4d to s Henrye Saunder, plus 2 lambs (valued at £1 6s 8d) his father left him; 6s 8d to Johan Saunder, goddr & dr of s Humfrye; 1 sheep to godson Edwarde Webber; to dr Christine her best "Comme" (comb?), a brass pan, the best of her "middell" pans, 13s 4d, & 1 bushel of corn; 30s to Johan Wealsh, dr of Robt Wealsh; 3 sheep to Willm Wealsh, s of Robt Wealsh; to dr Agnes her best petticote, a pair of sleeves, 1 brass pan, the lesser of the "middell" pans, & 5s; to dr Darytie Wealsh her second best gown; to other grandchn 12d each; 1 sheep to John Saunder, s of s Henrye;

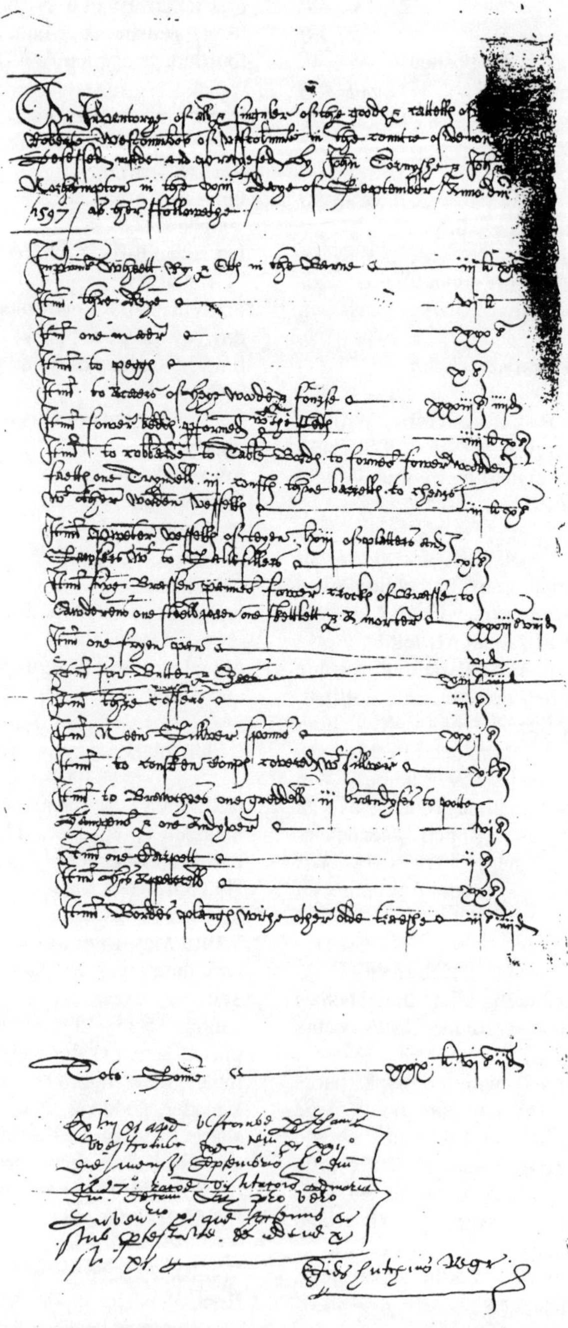

The inventory of Robert Wescombe 1597 [30]

4d each to godchn; 12d each to ovsrs Nicholas Dowdney & Mathewe Facye; witn: Nicholas Dowdney, Mathewe Facye, & Willm Facye.]

29 THOMAS COTTERELL 1596 (DS)

[Bur: "Thomas Cottrell" 24 July 1596. Mar: "Thomas Cotterell & Joan Curwood" 23 Nov 1579. Yeoman with cattle, sheep, pigs, poultry, corn, barley, & oats; value £45.]

The trewe Inventorye of all the goods & Cattells of Thomas Cotterell of the prishe of Uffcollum in the Countye of Devon decessed made & prised by Willm Cowroode [= Curwood?] Willm Newtone Nicholas Dowdney and Henrye Dowdney the laste daye of Julye Anno Dm 1596

	lî	*s*	*d*
Imprimis towe Keyne & a Heyffer	*vij*		
Itm ij yearlens		*l*	
Itm ij weaninge Caulves		*xxij*	
Itm one mare		*xx*	
Itm xv sheepe & fyvfe Lambes	*iiij*		
Itm ij Pigges		*xvj*	
Itm Cleene Corne in grounde	*v*	*vj*	*viij*
Itm Barley & otts in grounde	*iiij*		
Itm Haye		*xxx*	
Itm Beedes & beedsteedes	*vj*	*xiij*	*iiij*
Itm his wearinge Apparrell		*xl*	
Itm one Croke of Brasse		*viij*	
Itm Pane Brasse		*x*	
Itm one Cawdren		*x*	
Itm Payter vessell		*x*	
Itm ij Candelstyckes			*xij*
Itm a Table Borde & a forme		*x*	
Itm a Cubborde		*ij*	
Itm woodden vessell		*xxx*	
Itm woodd and Furse		*xxx*	
Itm Bordes and Plankes		*xj*	
Itm woulle		*vj*	*viij*
Itm Butter & Cheese		*xxiij*	
Itm iij Coffers		*x*	
Itm pothangeringes Cotterells & other Iron stufe		*v*	
Itm Dunge		*v*	
Itm Reyde			*xij*
Itm a Saddell wth Croukes tinges & gerses		*v*	
Itm a peare of Harrowes		*iij*	*iiij*
Itm Pultrey			*xij*
Itm naperye wth all other thinges forgotten		*iij*	*iiij*

Sum totalš *xlv*^{li} *ij*^{s} *iiij*^{d}
[1s short?]

[Exhibited at Salisbury 11 Jan 1596/7. Latin endorsement signed by Egids Hutchins Reg^{r}.

Will 5 Jul 1596 of Thomas Cotterell of Uffculme, yeoman, pr at Salisbury 11 Jan 1596/7 before Mr. Wm Wilkinson Ll D (for the Dean of Salisbury) by Johan Cotterell, widow & exec, & by John Sander on behalf of William & John Cotterell, underage ss: residue to joint exec^{s}, wife Johan & 2 youngest ss, William & John; 12d to church & 12d to the poor; £6 13s 4d to dr Alice; £5 to dr Mary; £3 to John, "youngest s of first wife's chn"; coffer, apparel, & 10s to s John; 4d each to grand- & godchn; 20s each to ss Thomas & Ambrosse; ovsrs Nicholas Dowdney & Wm Newton; witn: Nicholas Dowdney, Wm Newton, & Wm Facie *et al.*]

30 ROBERTE WESCOUMBE 1597 (DS)

[Bur: "Robarte Westcombe of Cradocke" 17 Jul 1594. Husbandman; 3 cows, 1 mare, 2 pigs; wheat, rye, oats,hay; household goods; £30.]

An Inventorye of all & singuler of the goods & cattells of Roberte Wescoumbe[s?] of Uffcolumbe in the countie of Devon husbandeman Desessed made and prayesed By John Cornyshe & John Norhampton in the xiijth Daye of September Anno dm~ /1597/ as her~ Followethe/

	lî	*s*	*d*
Inprimis wheett Ry & Otts in the Barne	*iij*	*x*	
Itm~ thre Keye	*vj*		

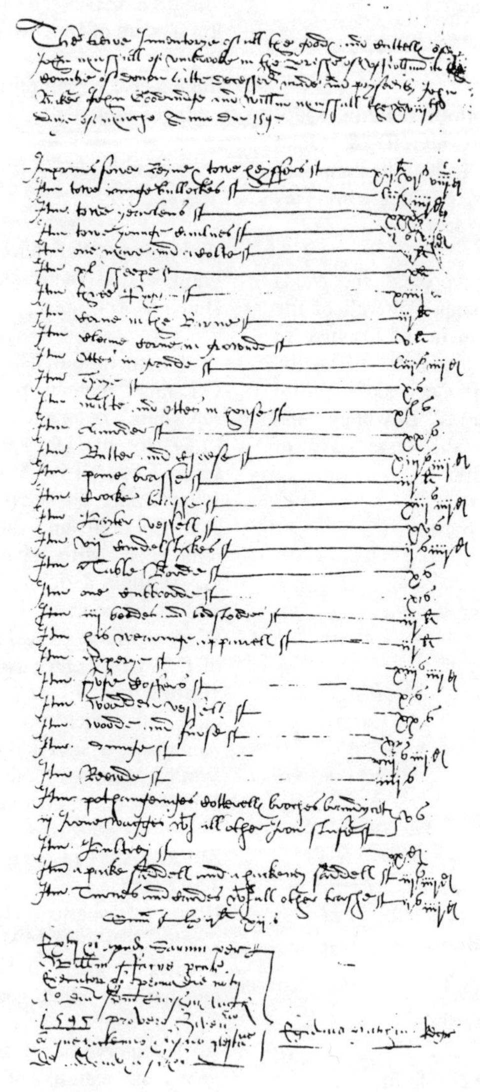

The inventory of John Marshall of Umbrook 1598 [32]

	lî	s	d
Itm~ one maer		xxx	
Itm~ to peggs		x	
Itm~ to acaers of heye woode & fourse		xxxiij	iiij
Itm~ fowere~ bedds pformed w^{t} the steds	iiij	x	
Itm~ to cobbarde to Table Bords to formes fower~ woodden faetts one Tryndell iij cousts[?] thre barrells to chears w^{t} other wooden vessells	iij	x	
Itm~ pweter vessells of teyen lxiij of platters and Sawsers w^{t} to Saltesillers		xl	
Itm~ sixe Brassen pannes fower~ crocks of Brasse to Cawderens one steellpaen one skettlett & a morter		xxxiij	viij
Itm~ one fryen~ pan~			vj
Itm~ for Butter & Chees		xiij	iiij
Itm~ three coffers		iij	
Itm~ Neen Sillver spouns		xxj	
Itm~ to cousken[?] Coups covered w^{t} sillver		xl	
Itm~ to Brawchees one greddell iij brandyses to potte Hanggens & one Andyver		vj	
Itm~ one Carpett		ij	
Itm~ his Apparrell		xx	
Itm~ Bordes plangs withe other~ olde traeshe		iij	iiij

Toto Som~e *xxx^{li} vj^{s} ij^{d}*

[Exhibited at Uffculme by John Westcombe, exec, before Egid^{s} Hutchins Reg^{r}, 22 Sep 1597.

Will 13 Jul 1597 of Roberte Wescoumbe of Uffculme, husbandman, pr before Willm~ Wilkinson 22 Sep 1597: goods she had before marriage & residue to wife Johane exec; 12d to church maintenance; to drs Johane & Mary Wescoumbe the goods he had before present marriage, in his house at Collumpton or at Craddock, except 1 brass pan for s Marck Wescoumbe; ovsrs/witn: John Cornishe & Roberte Wescoumbe, s.]

31 ALICE WOODE 1597 (DS)

[Bur: "Alice Wood, widdow" 25 Nov 1597. Cattle, sheep, pigs, poultry, corn, & a cider press; value £19.]

The trewe Inventorye of all the goodes and Cattells of Alice Woode vid. of the prishe of Uffcollm in the Countye of Devon decessed made and prysed by Robt Dowdney Thomas Newtone Henrye Dowdney the xiiijth daye of December Anno Dmi 1597

	lî	s	d
Imprimis towe keyne and iij heyffers	vj	xiij	iiij
Itm. iiij sheepe		x	iiij
Itm. A mare & a Colte		xxxiij	iiij
Itm. one sowe & ij younge pigges		x	
Itm. the Corne in the barne and in the grounde groweinge	iiij	xiij	iiij
Itm. Haye		x	
Itm. her wearinge apparrell		xl	
Itm. one beedsteed & ij beedes		x	[-?]
Itm. Fower pannes and iij Crockes		xiij	iiij
Itm. Peyter dishes		ij	
Itm. iij Candelstyckes		vj	
Itm. bordes Coffers and formes		v	
Itm. Fattes Costes and hoggesydes		vj	viij
Itm. a Cheese Wrynge bordes & tressells			xx
Itm. Laurder		vj	viij
Itm. butter & Cheese		v	
Itm. one Appell Wringe		iij	iiij
Itm. Pultrey			xij
Itm. a grediron a spitt one andier & potte hangeinges			xx
Itm. Woolle			xviij
Itm. Woode		ij	
Itm. a bill hooke wth other Irone tooles			iiij
Itm. iij borde Clothes			xij
Itm. Treeinge Vessell			viij
Itm. bagges & Sackes wth all other Trashe		ij	vj

Sum *xix^{li} xix^{s} x^{d}* [10d short?]

[Exhibited at Salisbury by Willm Facye for the exec 1 Mar 1598/9.

Latin endorsement signed by Egidius Hutchins Reg[r].

Will 1 Apr 1594 of Alice Wodde of Uffculme, widow, pr at Salisbury before Ven. Wm Wilkinson 1 Mar 1598/9: residue to dr & exec Agnes Woode; 12d to poor; 12d to church maintenance; 10s each to ss Thomas, William, Humfrye, & George, & to dr Alice Dowdney; also to s George his bed & 20s owed to him; 12d to Hughe Grigorye; 4d each to Marye Lamprye & her chn John, Temperance, & Anstyce; 4d each to godchn; witn include Thomas Cotterell, Rob[t] Dowdney, Thomas Facye, & George Wodde.]

32 JOHN MARSHALL of Umbrooke 1598 (DS)

[Bur: "John Marshall of Umbrooke" 12 Mar 1597/8. Mar: "John Marshall & Helen Dowdney" 26 Jan 1552/3. Husbandman; 12 cattle, mare & colt, 40 sheep, 3 pigs; corn, oats, malt, hay; household goods; £62.]

The trewe Inventorye of all the goods and Cattells of John Marshall of Umbrooke in the prishe of Uffcollm~ in the Countye of Devon latte decessed made and prysed by John Baker John Goodridge and Willm~ Marshall the xviij[th] daye of marche Anno dni 1597[/8]

	lî	s	d
Imprimis fower keyne & towe heyffers	*xij*	*vj*	*viij*
Itm~.towe younge bullockes		*liij*	*iiij*
Itm~.towe yearlens		*xxx*	
Itm~.towe younge Caulves		*[vj viij]j?*	
Itm~.one mare and a Colte[*ii*]*ij*?			
Itm~.xl sheepe	*x*[?]		
Itm~.three Pygges		*xiiij*	
Itm~.Corne in the Barne	*iij*		
Itm~.Cleane Corne in grownde	*v*		
Itm~.Ottes in gronde		*liij*	*iiij*
Itm~.Haye		*x*	
Itm~.malte and ottes in house		*xl*	
Itm~.Laurder		*xx*	
Itm~.Butter and Cheese		*xiij*	*iiij*
Itm~.pane brasse	*iij*		
Itm~.Crocke brasse		*xiij*	*iiij*
Itm~.Payter vessell		*xv*	
Itm~.vij Candelstyckes		*ij*	*iiij*
Itm~.a Table Borde		*x*	
Itm~.one Cubboorde		*x*	
Itm~.iiij beedes and bedsteedes	*iij*		
Itm~.his wearinge apparrell	*iij*		
Itm~.naperye		*xiij*	*iiij*
Itm~.fyvfe Coffers		*x*	
Itm~.woodden vessell		*xx*	
Itm~.woode and furse		*xx*[?]	
Itm~.dunge		*xiij*	*iiij*
Itm~.Reeude		*iiij*	
Itm~.pothangeinges Cotterells broches brandyce iij Irone wagges wth all other Iron stufe		*v*	
Itm~.Pultrey			*xx*
Itm~.a packe saddell and a hackeney saddell		*ij*	*iiij*
Itm~.Turnes and Cardes wth all other trashe		*ij*	*iiij*
Sum~ *lxij[li]* *xij[s]*			

[Exhibited at Salisbury by Willm Facye for exec before Egidius Hutchens Reg[r], 1 Mar 1598/9.

Will 10 Mar 1597/8 of John Marshall of Umbrooke, husbandman, pr at Salisbury before W[m] Wilkinson, 1 Mar 1598/9: residue to wife Ellyne & s John Marshall; 12d to church maintenance; 12d to poor; £20 each to drs Margerett, Elizabethe, & Johan Marshall; to dr Ellyne Marshall £6 13s 4d & the right to remain with the exec[s]; 1 ewe between Marye & Grace Marshall, drs of s John; 1 ewe between cousins Christopher & Richarde Marshall; 4s each to ovsrs, John Baker sen[r] of Ashill, John Goodridge of Rull, & William Marshall; witn: ovsrs & John Northamtone.]

33 WILLIAM READ 1599 (DS)

[Domestic items & loans; value £27.]

The Inventory of the goods of William Read of Laine in the pishe of Uffcullumbe in the County of Devon taken and prassed by Roberd Read and

Memorandum that about the first daye of marche last past
in the yere of our Lord god 1597 John Davie the elder
of [illegible] in the countie of Wilton husbandman
beinge sick in bodye but of good and perfect memorie
thankes be to god did declare his last will nuncupative
or by word of mouthe in manner and forme as
followethe viz. he did give and bequethe all his goode
and cattelle moveable and unmoveable whatsoever unto
Edithe his wife And further his will was that
the [illegible] of his [illegible] goode as should remaine
at the time of her decease not [illegible] should be devided
[illegible] her discretion amongest his daughters the[illegible]
[illegible] which wordes were uttered and spoken in the
presence and hearinge of John [illegible]

xxiiijo die Julij Anno domini 1600 [illegible]
[illegible]
[illegible] Edithe Davie [illegible]
[illegible]
[illegible]
[illegible] in debita [illegible]
forma iurat[illegible]

An example of a nuncupative will: John Davie the elder 1600 [34]

John Cadberye of Uffculumb aforesayd the thurd daye of October in the yeare of our lord god 1599/

	lî	*s*	*d*
Imprmis we pryse a gould pyne by Judgement or estemation in	*xvj*		
Itê twoe kyne in seven nobles a pece that is in	*iiij*	*xiij*	*iiij*
Itê a brase Crock in		*vj*	
Itê twoe selver spons in		*ix*	
Itê a beed and bedsted in		*l*	
Itê a Carpet or Tablecloth in		*xv*	
Itê an horse or nage in		*xxx*	
Itê his aparell	*iij*		
Itê in the hands of Mr Hugh Chechester is		*xx*	
Itê in the hands of Mr Edmond Marvine is		*x*	
Itê in the hands of Mr Richard Eevelye the yunger of Lazane Clist is	*vj*	*xiij*	*iiij*
Itê in the hands of Richard Crodon of Budelscom in the County of Devon	*iiij*		
Itê in the hands of Thomas Goodsoule		*xx*	
Itê in the hands of Thomas Read of Uffculmb		*x*	

The Sume is *xxvij*^{li} *xij*^{s} *viij*^{d}

[Exhibited at Salisbury by John Read, exec, 17 Apr 1602.

Will 1 Mar 1598(/9) of Willm Read of Uffculme, pr at Salisbury 17 Apr 1602: residue to John Read, father & exec, who also claims the debts of 20s from Mr Hugh Chechester, 10s from Mr Edmond Marvine, £4 from Richard Crodon, & 20 nobles from Mr Richard Eveleye; to Mrs Katren Couke 20s due from Mr Thomas Godsoule; a gold pin to Alice Couke; 2 kine to sisters Johan & Elizabeth; signed Wylliam Read; witn: Roberd Elringeton "dwellinge in the longe woolstaple in Westimt" (?) & John Cadberye.]

34 JOHN DAVY the elder 1600 (DS)

[Bur: "John --- the elder" 11 Mar 1597/8? Mar: "John Davy & Edith Lowe" 24 Jan 1551. Husbandman; domestic items only; value £4.]

The trewe Inventory of the goods and Cattells of John Davy thelder of Uffcollm in the countye of Devon decessed made & prised by Nicholas Dowdney and John Colliforde the xxth day of July Anno di 1600

	s	*d*
Imprimis ij flocke beeds pformed	*xxvj*	*viij*
Itm his wearinge apparrell	*xx*	
Itm vij Payter disshes & v Candelstyckes	*xij*	
Itm ij littell Cawdrens & a skillett	*iij*	
Itm one Croke of brase a broche a gredirone & a brandyce	*iiij*	
Itm a Cubborde	*vj*	*viij*
Itm for bordes & formes	*x*	
Itm ij Coffers	*ij*	
Itm iiij littell Tubes		*xx*

Suma *iiij*^{li} *vj*^{s}

[Exhibited at Uffculme by the admin 23 Jul 1600.

Nuncupative will 1 Mar 1597/8 of John Davie the elder of Uffculme, husbandman: all to wife Edithe and thereafter to surviving drs; uttered in presence of John Culliford. Admon 23 Jul 1600 names Edithe Davie as widow & admin & also John Culliford of Uffculme, yeoman; both mark.]

35 DAVYE TUCKER 1601 (DS)

[Bur: "Davyd Tucker of Smithencote" 13 Dec 1601. Mar: "David Tucker & Mary Toser" 20 Oct 1566. Cows, sheep, pigs, poultry, bees, & corn; armour; no clothmaking gear; £56.]

The trewe Inventorye of all the goods and Cattells of Davye Tucker of Uffcollum in the countye of Devon decessed made and praysed by John Wealshe John Rawlings Willm Seagar and Humfrye Crosse the xvth daye of December 1601

	lî	*s*	*d*
Imprimis his wearinge apparrell	*iij*	*x*	
Itm iij Beeds as they are furnished wth ij peare of sheetts		*xlvj*	*viij*
Itm Payter vessell		*vj*	*viij*
Itm brasen vessell as Crockes panes &c		*liij*	*iiij*
Itm Cheese and butter		*xl*	
Itm Coffers		*iij*	*iiij*
Itm A Tabell Borde Forme & Carprett		*x*	
Itm Tubbes Vatts and other wodden vessell		*xiij*	*iiij*
Itm Baken and Lawrder		*x*	
Itm napre		*vj*	*vj*
Itm Woulle		*v*	
Itm iiij pounde of yearne		*v*	
Itm Corne in house	*v*		
Itm vj keyne & iij heafers	*xx*		
Itm wigge beasts	*iij*	*xiij*	*iiij*
Itm iiij Pigges		*xxvj*	*viij*
Itm Woode		*xij*	
Itm xx sheepe	*vj*	*xiij*	*iiij*
Itm pothucks Crockhangeings & other Irone stufe		*iij*	*iiij*
Itm pultrey			*xx*
Itm bordes planckes and sheelfes		*x*	
Itm Armore		*x*	
Itm Corne in grounde		*xx*	
Itm Haye	*iij*		
Itm all furniture for a horse			*xx*
Itm Rewde [reed]			*xij*
Itm ij Sillver spones		*v*	
Itm Husbandrye tolles			*xij*
Itm Honye			*xviij*
Itm ij Stockes of bees		*ij*	
Itm one Harrowe			*xij*
Itm one Ladder			*xij*
Itm wodden disshes wth all other trashe		*ij*	

Sum totall *lvj*^{li} *xvj*^{s} *iiij*^{d}

[Exhibited at Salisbury by Silvester Game for the exec, 4 May 1602: Latin endorsement signed by Egidius Hutchins Reg^{r}.

Will 24 Feb 1600(/1) of David Tucker of Uffculme, pr 4 May 1602: residue to wife Mary, exec; £3 to Margerye Dowdney, sister; 6s 8d to k Thomasine Hiltone; 3s 4d to the church & 6s 8d to the poor; to k Johane Membrey £5 at her marriage; 4d each to godchn; 12d each to ovsrs Humfrye Crosse & John Wealshe; witn: Humfrye Crosse & Margerye Dowdney *et al.*]

36 ROGER LOMONE 1602 (DS)

[Bur: "Roger Loman" 3 Apr 1602. Mar: "Roger Loman & Margret Hodge widow" 10 Nov 1589. Husbandman with cattle, sheep, oats, rye, & corn; some clothmaking gear; value £40.]

The trewe Inventorye of all the goods and Cattells of Roger Lomone of the prishe of Uffcollum in the countye of Devon decessed made and praysed by John Cornishe Robt Reed John Leyman and Willm Marshall the seaventh Day of Aprill Anno Dm 1602/

	lî	*s*	*d*
Imprimis ij Keyne and ij Caulves	*v*	*vj*	*viij*
Itm one eylde Cowe		*xl*	
Itm one Steere		*xxx*	
Itm two yearleins		*xl*	
Itm one mare		*xl*	
Itm viij couple of Eweys and lambes wth xij other sheepe	*v*	*vj*	*viij*
Itm iiij acres of Rye in grounde	*vj*	*xiij*	*iiij*
Itm iiij acres of otts in grounde		*liij*	*iiij*
Itm Corne in the barne		*xl*	
Itm malte		*vj*	
Itm Haye and Reyde		*iiij*	
Itm one Cheeste: one Coffer & all that ys in hime wth his wearinge apparrell	*vij*	*xij*	
Itm Pane brasse		*x*	
Itm one Croke of brasse & a Cawdren		*iij*	*iiij*
Itm Puyter vessell		*v*	
Itm ij Candelstyckes			*iiij*
Itm ij beeds and iij beedsteeds		*xx*	
Itm one broche one andier a brandice wth other Irone stufe		*ij*	
Itm one Table Borde & a forme		*vj*	*viij*

	lî	*s*	*d*
Itm vij other bordes		*ij*	
Itm woodden vessell		*iij*	
Itm Dunge		*vj*	*viij*
Itm Laurder		*ij*	
Itm one Turne & Cardes wth all other Trashe			*xij*

Sum *xl*li *xiiij*s

[Exhibited at Salisbury by John Reade for the exec, 17 Apr 1602.

Will 2 Apr 1602 of Roger Lomone of Uffculme, husbandman, pr at Salisbury 17 Apr 1602: residue to wife Margerett, exec; to s Edwarde Lomone best apparel (best cloak, hat, jerkin, breeches, & doublet), coffer, beds, sheets, coverlet, &c, & one chest in the solar; to s-in-law George Woode 20s towards the education & upbringing of his chn & better maintenance of his wife; ovsr John Cornishe; witn: John Cornishe, Robt Reede, Simone Sheylde, & Willm Hodge.]

37 THOMAS RUDGE 1602 (DS)

[Bur: "Thomas Rudge of Rill" 10 Sep 1602. 2 cows, 1 heiffer, 1 pig, 1 lamb, corn, & clothmaking gear; value £22.]

The Inventarie of the goods debtes and chattels of Thomas Rudge of Uffocolumb within the dioces of Salisburie lately decessed apprised and made by Robte Beare John Osmond Robte Dowdney and John Leyma[n] apprisers in his behalf the xxijth daye of September A° dm 1602 with a protestacon to adde to his same Inventorie according to the rules of the Law./

	lî	*s*	*d*
Imp~is in the Halle one tablebord and one forme		*vj*	
Itm two coffers		*ix*[?]	
Itm one Cubbord		*xxv*	
Itm his pewter		*viij*	
Itm one brasse candlesticke			*x*
Itm one sardge			*xviij*
Itm two brasse crockes		*x*	
Itm two brasse pannes		*xxvij*	
Itm one cawdron one little panne and a skillett of brasse		*vj*	*viij*
Itm two bordes			*vj*
Itm two crockehanginges and two payr of cottrels		*ij*	
Itm one broch and one drippinge panne		*ij*	
Itm one brandise & one gridiron			*xx*
Itm one paire of sheres			*ij*
Itm in the Inner chamber one coffer		*ij*	
Itm one trendle		*iiij*	
Itm fower cheesefatts			*xx*
Itm two tubbes and one pecke		*ij*	*viij*
Itm his butter		*xj*	*viij*
Itm earthen pannes			*viij*
Itm one baskett			*viij*
Itm honey			*xij*
Itm one Cheesewringe		*ij*	
Itm one butt for wotemeale [oatmeal]			*vj*
Itm two costes and two steanes for good ale		*iiij*	
Itm two bordes, two formes, one planck and a snappe [trap?] for a mowse			*xij*
Itm two burriers			*xij*
Itm two iron wedges			*xij*
Itm old Iron			*xx*
Itm one skayner			*vj*
Itm three buttes for bees			*viij*
Itm one milkinge payle			*x*
Itm doungeforcks pytcheforcks and other instrumts for husbandry			*xx*
Itm an addse			*viij*
Itm xvij cheeses		*vj*	
Itm disshes bolles and trenchers			*xij*
Itm two seeves			*vj*
Itm two spyninge turnes and two paire of cardes		*ij*	*viij*
Itm in the Utter chamber one bedsteede one flockebed, one paire of blancketts one coverlett a fether bolster, and two pilloes of fethers		*xxiiij*	*iiij*
Itm one bedsteed and flockbed		*viij*	
Itm one coffer		*ij*	
Itm his corne		*xxxiij*	*iiij*
Itm two milch keen & one hefer yerlinge	*v*		

	lî	*s*	*d*
Itm a sowe and one lambe		*xvj*	
Itm woode at home and in the feild		*xiij*	*iiij*
Itm Haye		*xiij*	*iiij*
Itm dounge		*v*	
Itm one paire of lumbes a quilturne and a rath			*xxj*
Itm pulterie		*ij*	
Itm his wearinge apparell		*xl*	
Itm bagges sacks and things forgotten		*iij*	

Suma totlis *xxij*^{li} *xj*^{s} *8*^{d}
[£1 18s 3d too much?]

[Exhibited at Salisbury by Robert Rudge for ovsr & admin 25 Sep 1602: Latin endorsement signed by Egidius Hutchins Reg^{r}.

Will 11 Sep 1602 of Thomas Rudge of Uffculme, pr 25 Sep 1602: everything to be equally divided between the joint exec^{s}, ss John & Nicholas and dr Elizabethe Rudge, with reversion to the survivors if any should die before age 21; 12d each to ovsrs, bro John Rudge & Leonard Credie; witn: Robarte Rudge, Nicholas Bisshoppe, & Nicholas Knighte.]

38 JOHN WELSHE 1603 (DS)

[Bur: "John Welche" 1 Apr 1603. A second, rougher, copy of this incomplete inventory was helpful in making out some words, but they both end at the same point. Estate at Rooke; cattle & corn; c £33.]

The Inventorey of the goods and Chattells of John Welshe late of Ufculme deceassed taken the fifth day of Aprill A^{o} Dm 1603 & praised by John Rawlings Robt Welshe and Humfrey Crosse and Christopher Aland as followeth

	lî	*s*	*d*
Inprimis his Corne in the grounde	*iiij*		
It his Heye		*xiiij*	
Itim a peece of a dung potte worthe			*xvj*
Itim one packe sadle		*vj*	*viij*
Itim corne crooks woode Croockes Rackes shaves and peeckes			*xvj*
Itim on peire of Harrowes		*iij*	*iiij*
Itim one showell			*xviij*
Itim two kyne	*iiij*	*x*	
Itim one heyfer		*xxxvj*	
Itim one Mare worthe		*xxiij*	*iiij*
Itim two iron wedges			*xiiij*
Itim one hacney sadle			*xij*
Itim one fryinge panne			*iiij*
Itim his apparell	*iij*	*vj*	*viij*
Itim his napery		*xv*	
Itim his bedding	*iij*		
Itim a bedsteede		*xxxiij*	*iiij*
Itim botes and shoes		*iiij*	
Itim his pewter		*viij*	
Itim his potte brasse		*xxij*	
Itim his kittle and panne brasse		*vj*	
Itim one furnisse		*xx*	
Itim one Table bord in the Hall		*xx*	
Itim two side bordes		*iiij*	
Itim ioyned formes		*iiij*	*vj*
It one ioyned stoole & one cheire			*xviij*
Itim one iron Barre		*ij*	*vj*
It on spit two potcroocks and other iron stuffe		*iiij*	*vj*
Itim one bitte			*xij*
Itim one Coffer		*ij*	
It on Coliñ[?] wth his furniture		*xiij*	*iiij*
It five barrelles and one Coste		*xxij*	
Itim one Bottle			*iiij*
Itim one Bilhoocke			*vj*
It on yeating vate		*x*	
It two other vates in the kytchinge		*iiij*	
Itm one table Borde in the p[ar]lor		*xx*	
Itim one viniger Bottle			*vj*
Itim one Trendle		*iij*	*iiij*
Itim two spinning turnes		*ij*	
It one brackestocke and chesering and all suche stuf as [is] in the chamber wthin the Hall		*iiij*	
It five Curtines		*v*	
Itim wood		*x*	
Itim dung		*vij*	
Itim timber and planckes shelfes and suche like implementes		*x*	

	lî	s	d
It another trendle and fowre other tubbs		vj	viij
Itim fowre cheese vates		ij	
Itim one pecke, seve, cheseracke and suche like implementes		ij	
Itim two bagges		ij	
Itim eleven pecke of moult		v	

....

[Value so far, £33 4s 8d, agrees well enough with that quoted in the margin of the will, viz. £33 8s 8d, to show that the inventory is virtually complete.

Will - 1603 of John Welshe of Uffculme, pr 28 Jul 1603: residue to Florance, dr & exec, who also inherits the Rooke estate; to dr Katherynne a round table & form, 20s, & maintenance from the sale of 2 cattle by ovsrs, & £5 within 4 years after death of Katherinne, late wife of deceased bro Humfrye Welshe, or 4 years after redemption of her estate; 20s to dr Mary; £5 to s-in-law John Cotterell on similar conditions; 40s at age 21 or marriage to Anne Coterell, dr's dr, or if Anne should die 20s of this money to go to her mother "when she shall accomplishe the said age" (!); 3s 4d to church maintenance; 3s 4d to poor; 12d each to grandchn; 6d each to godchn; 2s each to ovsrs John Rawlinges, Robert Welshe (brother), & Humfry Crosse, who also witn. In a codicil the time limit above is extended to 6 years & goods to the value of £6 13s 4d are given to s-in-law Robert Oland.]

39 WILLIAM RAWLINGS 1604 (DS)

[Bur: "William Rawlings" 23 Jan 1603/4. Yeoman with 43 ewes & 10 (?) hogs; £17.]

The Inventory of the goods and Cattels of Willm Rawlings late of Ufcome in the County of Devon Yeoman deceased p'sed by John Rawlings and Humfrye Crasse the xxvij^th^ January [no year given] as foloweth

	lî	s	d
Imprimis his apparell	iij		
Item one flocke bed furnished		l	
Item one kittell and skillet		iij	iiij
Item one trylett [tryvett?] and a sawser		iiij	
Item his boots [book?]		xx	
Item two Coffers		iij	iiij
Item husbandry tools and other implements of howst [hews?]		iiij	
Item xliij^tie^ ewes and Tenne[?] hoggs price	viij		
Item two acres of Rye in grounde price		xlv	

Sm total *xvij^li^ ix^s^ viij^d^*

[Signed] by me John Rawlings Humfrye Crasse

[Will 22 Jan 1603(/4) of Willm Rawlings of Uffculme, pr at Uffculme - July 1604: residue to (bro?) Bartholomew Rawlings, exec; 3s 4d to church; 6s 8d to poor; 1 ewe to goddr Christian Sander; 1 lamb to godson Willm Palfrey; 1 ewe to Ambrose Crasse; 1 ewe to John Starke, s of Christopher Starke; 12d each to Christopher Starke, his wife, his s Willm, his dr Joan, James Stabback, & Roger Copp; ovsrs father John Rawlings & Humphrey Crasse; witn: John Rawlings & Humfrey Hoowe.]

40 JANE DOWDNEY 1606 (DS)

[Bur: "Jane Dowdney, widdow, of Lee" 7 Aug? 1606. Mar: "John Dowdney & Jane Hurley" 7 Oct 1566. Widow with 13 cattle, 1 horse, 10 sheep, 6 pigs, wheat, rye, oats, & barley; 6 silver spoons & other household items; no plough, but 2 turns; total £73.]

[The Inventory of Jane Dowdney of the parish of] Uffcolum in the county [of Devon .....] decessed made and prised by Robt Hurley Robt Dowdney and Nicholas Tucker wth others the fyfteynth daye of Auguste in Anno Dm 1606

	lî	s	d
Imprimis fyve keyne	x		
Itm fyve yearlynge bullockes	vij		

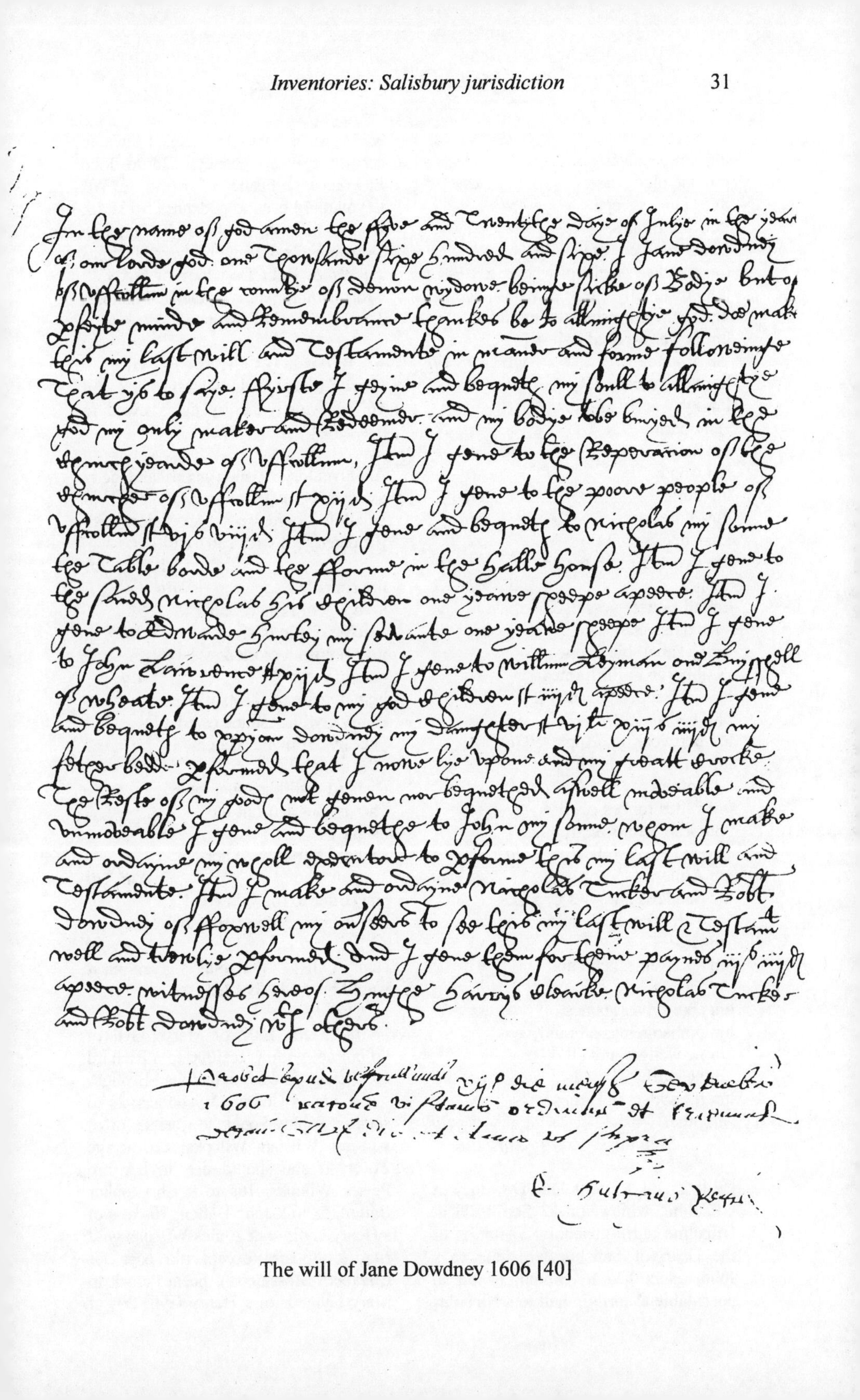

The will of Jane Dowdney 1606 [40]

	lî	*s*	*d*
Itm three Calves		*xl*	
Itm one olde horse		*xx*	
Itm Tenne sheepe	*iij*		
Itm sixe Pigges		*xl*	
Itm nyne flyces of woulle		*xv*	
Itm sixe Buysshells of wheat		*xxiiij*	
Itm Fower Buysshells of Rye		*xij*	
Itm Tenne Buysshells of malte		*xx*	
Itm Fower acres of [wheat] in grounde	*vj*[?]	*xiij*	*iiij*
Itm three acres of Rye	*iij*		
Itm Fyve acres of ottes and barley	*vj*		
Itm haye	*iiij*	*x*	
Itm woode		*x*	
Itm dunge		*xvj*	
Itm Butter		*xviij*	
Itm Cheese		*xl*	
Itm Crockes of brasse and panes	*iij*	*vj*	*viij*
Itm all Pewter vessell & Candelstyckes		*xiij*	*iiij*
Itm ij Tabell bords one Cubborde & iiij formes		*xl*	
Itm iiij Beddes p̱formed & iiij bedstedes	*iiij*		
Itm her wearinge Apparrell	*iij*		
Itm one maltewhitche & ij Coffers		*xv*	
Itm vattes tubbes plankes bordes barrells & all other woodden vessell	*iij*		
Itm Armore		*vj*	*viij*
Itm Saddells haroows Crookes and all other husbandrye towles		*xl*	
Itm one wemeshette and bagges		*iij*	*iiij*
Itm sixe sylver spones		*xx*	
Itm pothangeings a brandyce Irone wedges and all other Irone stuffe		*iij*	*iiij*
Itm ij Ladders ij Turnes wth all other Trashe		*vj*	*viij*
Sum totall	*lxxiij*^{li}	*xiij*^{s}	*iiij*^{d}

[Will 25 Jul 1605 of Jane Dowdney of Uffculme, widow, pr 12 Sep 1606 at Uffculme during triennial visitation of the Dean of Salisbury: residue to s John, exec; 12d to church; 6s 8d to poor; table & form in hall to s Nicholas & 1 ewe each to his chn; 1 ewe to servant Edward Hurley; 12d to John Lawrence; 1 bushel of wheat to Wm Leyman; 4d each to godchn; £6 13s 4d, feather bed, & crock to dr Christian Dowdney; 3s 4d each to ovsrs Nicholas Tucker & Robt Dowdney of Foxwell; witn: Hughe Harrys, clerk, Nicholas Tucker, & Robt Dowdney.]

41 MARY GYLL 1607 (PU)

[Bur: "Mary Gill, widdow" 28 Jul 1607. Mostly family debts owed to her; £44.]

An Inventory of such goods and detts as dyd belonge unto Mary Gyll of Ufculme widowe Late decessed/ [Undated, but with 1607 will.]

	lî	*s*	*d*
Imprimis her apparrell	*iiij*	*x*	
Item a goold ringe, and taches & pin of silver		*xiij*	
Item a posnet crock & teening-cup		*iiij*	
Item a peare of sheets worth		*v*	
Henry Gyll her sonne owed her by her owne account the some of	*xv*		
Richard Gyll her sonne owed her by her account the some of	*xx*		
Richard Perin owed her uppon a bond	*ij*	*xiij*	*iiij*
one coffer to the valawe of			*xij*
Her daughtr Johan Brougton		*xvij*	

Henry Gill [No total is given but it would be £44 3s 4d]

[Will 27 Jul 1607 of Marye Gyll of Uffculme, widow: residue to s Richard Gyll, exec; 5s each to dr Johan Broughton & her ss Charels & Thomas; 2s to servant Sobley Soper; to Caritas, dr of s-in-law William Wilcoks, £20 at age 21 or, if she should die, to her bro Peeter Wilcoks; 16s to k Christopher Batten; 5s to k John Batten; 10s to s of s Henry Gyll; to dr Agnes Wilcoks gold ring & apparel except old coat for Elizabeth Mosseter(?); posnet crock to Mary Gyll, dr of s Henry Gyll; 20s at age 21 to Peter Wilcoks, s of William Wilcoks; 10s to k Doraty Batten; 5s to poor; ovsrs s Henry Gyll & s-in-law Wm Wilcoks; marked by Mary Gyll in presence of Henry Gyll (signed) & Agnes (A mark?) Extroll(?).]

42 ALEXANDER GOODRIDGE 1610 (DS) & 1613 (PCC)

[Bur: "Alexander Goodridge" 23 Feb 1609/10. Mar: "Alexander Goodridge & Jone Facy" 18 Jun 1598, or "Alexander Goodridge & Jone Washbear" 7 Oct 1576. Yeoman with cattle, sheep, pigs, & corn; lent & borrowed money; value without debt balance £83.]

An Inventorie of the goodes & chattels of Alexander Goodridge of Uffculme in the countie of Devon wthin the iurisdiction of the right w^{ll} the Deane of the Cathedrall churche of Sarum yeaman deceased, taken and prised by Nicholas Tooker, Richard Baker, John Baker, Robert Marshall &.others [on the].vth of March 1609[/10]/

	lî	*s*	*d*
Imprimis Sheepe			
Threescore & five sheepe	*xviij*	*x*	
Cattell			
It Fower keyne	*xiij*	*xiij*	*viij*
two steares	*v*	*vj*	*viij*
three heafers	*v*	*vj*	*viij*
three calves	*iij*	*vj*	*viij*
on mare		*xlvj*	*viij*
Fower pigges		*xxx*	
Bacon		*xlij*	*viij*
Corne			
wheat & Rie	*iiij*	*x*	
nine sackes of Oaten malt	*iij*	*xij*	
Corne in ground			
on acre & halfe		*l*	
an acre in Huchings close		*xx*	
two bussels of pease		*iiij*	
Three gallons of butter		*xiij*	
meat salted		*ij*	
beanes			*vj*
thirteen cheeses		*xvj*	*viij*
tallow			*xiiij*
hops			*xxj*

	lî	*s*	*d*
eighteene flesses woll		*xxvj*	*viij*
yarne		*ij*	*vj*
His wearing apparel	*iij*		
Sixe silver spoones		*xx*	
A bedsteede a Bedtie, sixe coverlets, fower blankets, & two beds	*iiij*		
Brasen pans & pots	*iiij*		
Pewter disshes		*xiiij*	
A chafen dishe & a candlesticke		*ij*	
on coubberd		*xiij*	*iiij*
a greate Vate		*xiij*	*iiij*
two coffers		*vj*	*viij*
Three lesser vates on trendell two silters		*xiij*	*iiij*
three barrels & a milkin payle		*v*	
a shovell 2 mattockes & an Axe		*ij*	
a brichandize[?] pothanginge		*ij*	
for furse		*iij*	*iiij*
for dunge		*xiij*	*iiij*
	83^{l}	10^{s}	11^{d}

Suma totalis *lxxxiij*^{l} *x*^{s} *xj*^{d} [8d short?]

	lî	*s*	*d*
Item three paire of silver taches & a silver pinn		*xx*	
a pillobere a towell & a tableclothe		*iiij*	
a peece of freeze		*v*	

Debts due by Alexander G to others

	lî	*s*	*d*
to Webber		*xl*	
for the use [interest?]		*iiij*	
to marian		*xl*	
&		*x*[*ix*?]	
&	*iij*		
to John Cudbert	*iij*		
to Richard Baker		*v*	
John Baker		*xij*	
&		*xv*	
to Robart Baker		*iiij*	
to Mr Auerie [Averie?]		*iij*	*iiij*
to Goodwife Pepprell		*ij*	*vj*
to the widow Gregorie		*viij*	
to Searle		*viij*	
to Edward Bryar			*xviij*
for the maydes wages		*ij*	*iiij*
for Willia~ Newton	*iiij*	*xix*[?]	

lî s d

Suma *xij*[l] *ix*[s]

besides Marians *iij*[l] [& possibly other (faded) exclusions]

Debtes due to Alex Goodridge deceased

from Robt Brockwell *xlij*

From Tho Lynscombe of Cullombstoke *x viij*

Fro~ Edward Smeathe of Cullomstucke *vij*

For Edward Eastbrooke of Ulfcumbe *xl*

It covere[?] from him *iiij*

Suma *v*[l]

besides Eastbrookes *iiij*[l]

I owe my brother *xxviij*[s]

& [si?]ster for cloth *xxxij*[s]

[Will 1 Oct 1609 of Alexander Goodridge of Uffculme, yeoman, pr before Ven. Wm Wilkinson 12 Jun 1610: residue to ss & execs John & Richard Goodridge; 13s 4d invested for the poor; £5 to sister Florence Bryar; 10s each to nieces Daratie & Marie, drs of Anthonie Oland; 12d each to godchn; £6 13s 4d per year, if the investments yield sufficiently, to wife Johane, part to be reckoned as the "halfendeale" of a piece of ground called the Hele, & after her to eldest s John, who also has interest in Coganse Parke; marked by Alexander Goodridge in the presence of John Baker & Robert Baker, who both make marks.
A copy was referred to the PCC, where a further probate was granted to the same execs in London on 16 May 1613. This copy was slightly different in the spelling of names and in other detail, such as: £6 13s 4d invested for poor; piece of ground called "Olde Heale"; wife also to have 40s a year interest *from her share of 1/3 parte of "Saganisse parke" late in my possession in fee simple*; John to pay Joan 20s a year; also £3 to Joan from sale of goods if enough; also to Joan 1 brass pot, 2 brass pans, 1 chest & 2 coffers (emptied except for her apparel) bed, bolster, 2 blankets, 1 coverlet, one bedstead *with a ticke thereunto appertayninge*.]

43 HUMFREY TAWTON 1610 (DS)

[Bur: "Hu~fry Tawton" 2 Apr 1610. Yeoman with cattle, pigs, poultry, & corn; no clothmaking gear; £56.]

An Inventory of all the goodes & Cattells of Humfre[y] Tawton Late of Ufculme in the County of Devon yeoman deceased taken the xvij[th] daie of Aprill A° domini 1610 prysed by Humfrey Cross Robte Oland Henry Tawton and Henry Fowler as followeth [A repeated symbol before each valuation is interpreted as "at". In the first line "psed @" then makes sense as "prysed at", with "prysed" being omitted but understood thereafter.]

	lî	*s*	*d*
Imprimis iij Keinde [kine] & ij Calves p[ry]sed @	*viij*		
Item one mare and one Calfe @	*iiij*		
Item all Corne in grounde @	*xvj*		
Item ij piggs @		*xiij*	*iiij*
Item all woode and fuell [furze?] @	*iij*		
Item all Corne in house @	*iiij*		
Item Heye and Rude @		*x*	
Item Dunge @		*vj*	*viij*
Item all kende of furniture for a packe horse @		*vj*	*viij*
Item one peare of harows[?] @		*iiij*	
Item all such furniture as he hadd for a plowe @		*xvij*	
Item one lytle table borde & all tymbr in house & about the house unwrought as yeat to any use @		*viij*	
Item all his peawter @		*xl*	
Item all brasen pots brasen pannes & all other brasse mettle		*xl*	
Item all husbandry towles @		*vj*	*viij*
Item one Cubborde @		*xxiij*	*iiij*
Item his apparell @	*iij*	*vj*	*viij*
Item all his naprye @		*xx*	
Item one fether bedd bolster & one Covlett @		*xl*	

	lî	*s*	*d*
Item ij Duste bedds wth there furneture @		*xx*	
Item one peare of pleing [?] tables @		*ij*	
Item one bedd pte fethers & pte flocks wth his furnyture		*xvj*	
Item one Cheste & ij bedsteds @ [?]		*x*	
Item one musket mirryon [?] flaske & tuchcock @		*xvj*	
Item bacon & Larde @		*viij*	
Item vats barrels & woden vessel @		*xxiij*	*iiij*
Item tryvets potcroks fryen panne and such iron stuffe @		*iij*	*iiij*
Item pultrey @		*iiij*	
Item Ladders Formes woden dishes erthen vessell & all other trashe about the house unprised @		*v*	*vj*
Item one waye tu waye Curnes [churns?] @			*xij*
Item Desperate Debtes @		*xxxv*	*ij*
Item baggs sacks & windshets @		*iiij*	

Sum total..*lvj*^{li} *v*^{s} *viij*^{d} [£1 5s short?]

[Exhibited by Elizabeth Tawton, exec, 26 Apr 1610: Latin endorsement signed by Egid^{s} Hutchins Reg^{r}.

Will 30 Mar 1610 of Humfrey Tawton of Uffculme, pr 25 Apr 1610: residue to dr & exec Elizabeth Tawton; 20s to poor; 12d each to godchn & to Nicholas & Thomasine, chn of s Henrie Tawton, & to 2 chn of s John, who receives best fustian doublet & breeches; ovsrs Robert Oland & s Henry Tawton; witn: Richard London & Robart Oland.]

44 THOMAS TUCKER 1610 (DS)

[Bur: "Thomas Tucker" 22 Apr 1610. Husbandman with stock but no corn; looms; £12.]

An Inventory of all & singuler of all the Goods & cattells of Thomas Tucker of Uffcholume in the Countty of Devon husbandman decesed made & prayssed by Henry Tawtton Willyame Peacoke John Cheecke of Cradoke & Barnard Tucker in the xxiiijth Day of Aprill Anno domi 1610 as here Followeth

	s	*d*
Impmis one Cowe fifty three shillings---iiijd	[*liij*	*iiij*]
Item Seven Coppells of Ewes & Lames v^{s} iiij^{d} a peece	[*xxxvij*	*iiij*]
Item sixe hogde sheep iiij^{s} a peece	[*xxiiij*]	
Item one halfe pige	*ij*	
Item a paer of lommes	*xiij*	*iiij*
Item one Colte	*ij*	
Item two Caldrens of brasse one brassen pan & one Crocke of brasse	*xvj*	
Item peawter vessell of teen		*xij*
Item one Iron goos pan five branises one gridron with all husbandry tooles & all other instroments of Iron belonging to the house	*iij*	*iiij*
Item two Beads pformed with the steeds	*xiij*	*iiij*
Item all his apparrell	*xxv*	
Item two Coffer iiij tobes & all other impellments of timber belonging to the house	*x*	
Item wooll & yearn	*v*	
Item beanes in ground & halfe the Gardden hearbs	*ij*	*iiij*

Toto Sume *x*^{li} *viij*^{s}

Signe of Henry HT Tawton Willyame W[? mark] Peacocke John Cheeke Barnard Tucker [both signed]

45 AGNES STONE 1610 (DS)

[Bur: "Agnes Stone widdow" 24 Oct 1609. Few household items; £1.]

The Inventorie of all the goodes of Agnes Stone late of Uffcolombe deceased praised by John Rawlings Richard London and others the iiijth daie of May anno dm 1610.

	s	*d*
In primis her Apparell	*xiij*	*iiij*
Itm one peece of howsolde clothe	*vj*	
Itm three Cophers	*iiij*	
Itm one olde Borde		*xij*

Som *xxiiij*^{s} *iiij*^{d}

Test Richard London John Rawlings

46 WILLIAM RUGGE 1610 (DS)

[Bur: "William Rugge alš Cutbert" 30 Apr 1610. Yeoman; some weaving gear & 2 sheep & lambs, but most items involve moneylending; £57.]

An Inventorie of all and singular goodes Chattells Cattells and Debts of Willm Rugge of Uffcolumbe in the Countie of Devone yeoman deceased made and praised by Robt M[a]^{r}shalle Richard Baker and Henry Gill in the first day of June Anno Dm 1610 as here followeth

	lî	s	d
Imprimis his waringe apparell	*l*		
Item two Eawes and lams		*xij*	
Item one pare of Lommes and queltorne		*xvij*	
Item due debts wthout specialltie	*xij*	*j*	*viij*
Item due debts of legese	*x*		
Item due debts by specialtie	*xx*		
Item two bookes			*xx*
Item one selver sponne		*ij*	
Iotem one beed performed in the Costatie of John Beare and one table borde	*iij*	*x*	
Item more debte wthout specialtie		*l*	
Item debte by specialtie due from Henry Gill one yeare after the death of Johane Beare wiffe of John Beare of Uffcom	*v*		

Sma *lvij*^{li} *iiij*^{s} *iiij*^{d}

[Exhibited by Henry Rugg, admin, 2 Jun (1601, corrected to) 1610: Latin endorsement by Rob: White no^{t} pub.

Admon 20 Jul 1610 names Henrie Rugg of Uffculme, yeoman, as bro & admin & also William Burnett, cleric, & Leonard Creedie, weaver, all of Uffculme; signed by Henry Rugg & Willm Burnett & marked by Leonard Creedy in presence of Wm Hutchins.]

47 WILLIAM MARSHALL 1612 (DS)

[Bur: "Willm Marshall of Ashell" 27 May 1612. Mar: "Wm Marshall & Elizabeth Dunne" 11 Jun 1574. Husbandman; mare, colt, 9 cattle, sheep, pigs, poultry; corn, malt; household goods; £74.]

The Inventorye of all & singuler the goods and Chattells of Williã Marshall latte of Uffcolmbe decessed prised by Thomas Densham John Beare & Roberte Marshall the thirde of June Anõ Dm~ 1612/

	lî	s	d
Inprimis wee prise all his apparrell	*iij*		
It~ fowre beds: fowre beds steds wth the furniture	*v*		
It~ one table borde one Cubborde & two formes		*xiij*	*iiij*
It~ seaven brasse pannes, two Cawdrons & fowre brasse potts	*iij*		
It~ 17:platters & podinggers 4 Candelstecks & one salt		*xl*	
It~ one Chest & fyve Coffers		*xx*	
It~ seaven barrells, fyve tubs, two pips,& one greate vatt		*xxx*	
It~ two trendells & one Cowle		*v*	
It~ plancks & other tember		*xv*	
It~ all the wood		*xxx*	
It~ all the Irone towlls wth Irone wadges		*vj*	*viij*
It~ butter, Chesse & bacoñ		*xx*	
It~ Corne in the barne	*iij*		
It~ malt		*xl*	
It~ Corne in gronde	*xiij*		
It~ one mare wth saddell & furniture		*l*	
It~ one Colt		*xl*	
It~ two kine Chosen for heriott	*vij*		
It~ one other Cowe	*iij*		
It~ fowre younge bullucks & two Callves	*vj*	*xiij*	*iiij*
Itm~ shepp & Lambs	*xiij*	*vj*	*viij*
It~ piggs & pulterye		*x*	
It~ Ladders,& all other implements of smalle valewe		*xx*	

Sum Totall *lxxiiij*^{li}

[Will 24 May 1612 of William Marshall of Uffculme, husbandman: residue to wife Elyzabeth Marshall, exec; 3s 4d to church maintenance; 4d each to 20 poor; £20 to dr Anne Marshall; 20s a year for life to bro John Marshall; 20s to be invested until age 21 for John Marshall, s's s; a sheep each to Thomas Densham's chn & dr's chn; ovsrs & witn: Thomas Densham & John Beare. (An oath was sworn before Egidius Hutchins on 23 Feb 1612/3 that William Marshall did not possess more than £5 outside the jurisdiction of the Dean of Salisbury.)]

48 JOHN HORNE 1612 (1613?) (DS)

[Bur: "John Horne" 7 Dec 1612: will dated Nov 1612 but inventory, erroneously, Dec 1613. A few household items only; £1.]

The Inventorie of all the goodes and Cattels of John Horne, late of Uff-colombe deceased Made and praised By Richard London, John London wth others, the thertinthe daie of December, in the yeres of the Raigne of our Sovraigne Lord James, by the grace of god of England, Fraunce and Ireland Kinge, Defender of the Faithe &c the Eleventhe, and of Scotland the xlvijth

	s	*d*
Inprmis, one Tie of a bed wth his furniture	*vj*	*viij*
Itm two Coffers	*v*	
Itm one litell Crocke of bras	*iij*	*iiij*
Itm his Apparell	*v*	
Itm one platter of pewter		*viij*
Itm one Fryinge pan		*vj*
Itm one Bedsteed & bords	*ij*	*vj*
Sm *xxiij^{s} viij^{d}*		

[Will 24 Nov 1612 of John Horne of Uffculme, pr at Uffculme before Willm Wilkinson 9 Sep 1613: residue to John Norton exec; coffer & platter to Darothie & Johane Norton respectively, drs of John Norton; witn: Richard London & Barnard London.]

49 NICHOLAS TOOKER 1613 (DS)

[Mostly household items with some weaving gear; value £16.]

A True & pfict Inventory of all the goods Chattels & Cattels moveable & unmoveable of Nicholas Tooker late of Ufculme in the Countie of Devon deceased Taken the viijth day of February 1612[/13] And prised by Indifferent men viz John Prynge John Leeman Robert Myles & John Broadley as followeth &c

	lî	*s*	*d*
Inp^{r}is all his wearinge Apparrell		*xxvj*	*viij*
Item iij Coffers a Foslett & A joyne stoole		*vj*	
Item a Standinge Beadstead a feether Bead & Bolster A duste bolster A pellitye Two Blanckets A coverlett & A Tester	*iiij*		
Item A Cheste		*xiij*	*iiij*
Item A Borden Beadstead A CheeseRacke A payre of Tables A Copcase & Two Chargers		*iij*	
Item Two Tableboords & Two formes		*xx*	
Item A Coboord Chayre one Frame stoole And a Brakenstocke		*xvj*	
Item all his pewter Vessell eight platters fyve Podgers syx pewter poridge dishes, fower sawcers Two whyte Candlestickes, a Bottell Two brasse Candlestickes & a Chaffer		*xxx*	
Item iij Brasse pannes & a Brakestocke		*x*	
Item syx costes		*viij*	
Item A Trendell fyve Vates Two standerds A Tube wth Cards Two old Hogsydes		*xij*	
Item A wymbe sheett			*xij*
Item a Breache An Andiron, a payre of weights wth An Iron beame		*iij*	
Item A payre of Harrowes A Grediron A Trivett & Two Pothangines		*ix*	

	lî	*s*	*d*
Item halfe a payre of Lumbes warpinge Pynes And a Slia		*xiij*	*iiij*
Item A Ladder, An Almerye A cheese wrynge		*v*	
Item Planncks Boords Matockes showels & other Implements		*v*	
Item Uppon Bands & bylles	*iij*		

Somma totalis *xvj*^{li} *xvj*^{d}

[Admon 4 Mar 1612 names Nicholas Looman/Leeman, husbandman, as s-in-law & admin, & also Richard Denninge of Bath, husbandman, & William Toogood of Chute (Shute?) in Devon, weaver; signed by Nicolas Lomon & Richard Denning & marked by Willm Toogood in presence of Wm Huchins.]

50 NICHOLAS DOWDENY 1613 (DS)

[Bur: "Nicholas Dowdney of Sowell" 8 Apr 1613. "Nicholas Dowdney & Dewnes Herringe" 23 Nov 1579; see 97. Prosperous; stock, corn, plough, armour, & clothmaking gear; chattel leases; £391.]

The Inventory of all & singuler the goods and Chattells of Nicholas Dowdeny late of Sowell in the prishe of Uffcolmbe & County of Devon decessed prised by John Sander, Mathewe Cadbery, John Beare, & Mathewe Herryñ[?] the xiiijth day of Aprill Año Dm 1613 /

	lî	*s*	*d*
Imprimis wee prise All his apparrell	*v*		
It fowre oxen, six Kine, one heffer & three yerlyngs	*xl*		
It three score & nyne shepp	*xxj*		
It two mares & one Colte	*vj*	*xiij*	*iiij*
It fowre piggs & all the pultery	*xl*		
It one Chattell Lease of Sowell tenement	*CC*		
It one Chattell Lease of Bromparcks alîs Bromcloses	*xxij*		
It dry Corne in the barne & howse	*iij*		
It malte	*x*		
It rye & wheate in the grownd	*xx*		
It otts in the grownde	*xv*		
It one wene, wheles, yron ropps, & all the rest of the plowe gere	*iiij*		
It one peare of Harrows		*x*	
It Saddels, Crocks, & all the furniture		*xiij*	*iiij*
It three standynge bedsteds wth beds & furniture	*xiij*		
It two other bedsteds wth beds & furniture	*iij*	*vj*	*viij*
It one Chest & fowre Coffers	*xxv*		
It wooll		*x*	
It two table bords, fowre formes, two Joyned stoles, one Chere, & one Cubbord		*liij*	*iiij*
It Cusshens		*ij*	*vj*
It all the tynnynge vessell, & Cupps		*xxvj*	*viij*
It three brasse potts, one skillett one Chaffer, & one morter		*xl*	
It eight brasse pannes, & three Cawdrens	*iij*	*vj*	*viij*
It bacon, butter, & Chese	*iij*		
It two yowten fatts, one trendell nyne tubs & two standerds	*iij*		
It two hodgheds, fyve Cossts, fowre payles & other wooden vessell		*xiiij*	
It one Chesse wrynge, & one Chesse racke		*vj*	*viij*
It one broche, one onIron, two peare of pott hocks, two peare of Crocks, one fryenpan & one gredIron		*iij*	*iiij*
It one muskett furnessed		*xiij*	*iiij*
It plancks, bords, & tember		*xiij*	*iiij*
It wood		*xx*	
It dunge		*xiij*	*iiij*
It two spinynge tornes		*ij*	
It matyckes, showles, pycks, hocks And all the other workynge tolls		*v*	
It one wemshett & baggs		*iij*	*iiij*
It Ladders, one grinyng stone & all other thingks not prysed		*xx*	
It --p~wy[?unclear] goods		*xl*	

Suma totalš *CCClxxxxj*^{li} *xxij*^{d}

[Exhibited at Salisbury by the admin, 21 Apr 1613. Latin endorsement signed by Egidius Hutchins Reg^{r}.

Admon 21 Apr 1613 names Dionicia, or Denis (Dunes?) Dowdney as widow & admin, & also John Sanders & Nicholas Dowdney, yeoman, both of Uffculme; marked by Dionica Dowdney & John Sanders & signed by Nicholas Dowdney in presence of Will Hutchins & Willm Colet, both not^{y} pub.]

51 HUMFRY HOLWILL 1613 (DS)

[Bur: "Humfry Holwell" 8 (or 13?) Jul 1613. Mar: "Humfry Clarke alš Holwill of Holcombe & Florence Norton" 29 Jan 1594; see 63. Largely clothmaking gear & cloth, apart from household items; also a hog, 2 cows, a gelding, & bees; £46.]

The Inventorie of All the goodes and Cattels of Humfry Holwill, late of Uffcolombe deceased, Made and praised by Willm Pococke Richard Wooddroffe and John Norton the twelfth daie of Julij in the yere of the Raigne of our Sovraigne Lorde James, by the grace of god of England. Fraunce. and Ireland. kinge, defender of the faith &c the Eleventhe and of Scotland the xlvijth

	lî	*s*	*d*
In pmis his Sleas		*xx*	
Itm three Quiltorns. warpinge barrs & frarme and Lister		*vj*	
Itm Fowar kerseis	*iiij*	*xvj*	
Itm of yarne - lx^{li}	*iiij*	*x*	
Itm three paire of Lumbes	*iiij*		
Itm one Rathe			*vj*
Itm Lime[?] waightis and Shuttels			*xviij*
Itm one yarne bag and thrumbs		*ij*	
Itm his Apparell		*l*	
Itm one Cubborde. one framed Tabelbord and a forme		*xviij*	*iiij*
Itm Pewter		*xiij*	*iiij*
Itm three Brasen Crockes		*xviij*	
Itm brasen pannes. A cawdren and Candelsticks		*xj*	
Itm one Standinge bed pformed		*xl*	
Itm one Trokelbed pformed		*xiij*	*iiij*
Itm two other Beddes pformed		*xxvj*	*viij*
Itm two Chestes and Coffers		*xx*	
Itm Haie		*v*	
Itm woode		*liij*	*iiij*
Itm one Hog		*x*	
Itm one Geldinge		*liij*	*iiij*
Itm troen vessell & bords		*xiij*	*iiij*
Itm two kee	*v*	*vj*	*viij*
Itm woole	*viij*		
Itm Butter and Cheeses		*vij*	
Itm one broche a fryinge pan pothangins and other yron stuffe		*iij*	*iiij*
Itm Earthen panns			*iij*
Itm Bees		*iij*	*iiij*

Sm *xlvj*^{li} *ij*^{s} *iij*^{d}

[Exhibited at Uffculme during visitation, 9 Sep 1613: Latin endorsement signed by Egidius Hutchins Reg^{r}.

Will 9 Jul 1613 of Humfry Holwill of Uffculme, pr at Uffculme before Willm Wilkinson 9 Sep 1613: residue to wife Florence & s-in-law Robartt Norton, execs; market suit to bro [*sic*] John Clarke & 5s to his dr Elsabeth Clarke; 12d to godson Humfry Furber; witn: Willm Pococke & Richard Woodroffe.]

52 BARNARD TUCKER 1613 (DS)

[Bur: "Barnard Tocker" 29 Oct 1613. Mar: "Barnard Tucker & Joan Darke" Feb-Mar 1610/11. Weaver with cattle, 52 sheep, poultry, 1 pig, wheat, rye, & oats; looms, slays, turns; hall, chambers, & buttery in house; fowling piece, playing tables & "tablemen"; £72.]

An Inventory Indented of all the goods Chattels and debts of Barnard Tucker late of Ufecolume in the Countye of Devon Weaver deceassed made the Eighth daye of November in the year of o^{r} lord God One Thowzand Syxe hundred and Thirteene, Taken & prysed by John Leyman & Robert Baker as followith

	lî	*s*	*d*
In the Hall			
Imprimis Two table bords one Cubbord & one Forme		*xxvj*	*viij*

	lî	*s*	*d*
Itm one Chest, one Cheare			
& one Framed stoole		*vj*	
Itm Eight pewter platters fowre			
Sawcers, fowre poddish dishes			
of pewter fowre Candlesticks			
two salts & spones		*xxvj*	*viij*
Itm one tynnen bottle two Stone			
Cuppes & pepper querns			*xij*
Itm fowre brasse pannes &			
two brass Crocks		*xlvj*	*viij*
Itm one posnett & one skellett		*iij*	
Itm one sydborde & Certen			
other bords about the howse			*xij*
Itm two Flittches of Bacon		*xvj*	
Itm one Fowlinge peece		*vj*	*viij*
Itm one Andyron two doggs			
one Brandice & one			
pothangings of yron		*iij*	
In the Chambers			
Itm one standing bedstedde one			
Fether bedd wth all the Furnyture			
to the same belonginge	*iij*	*vj*	*viij*
Itm one truckle bedstedd one			
dustbedd wth his Furnyture		*xxvj*	*viij*
Itm one lowe bedstedd & one			
dustbedde wth furnyture		*xvj*	
Itm one peece of Course			
newe Cloath		*xvj*	
Itm two Coffers & one forslett		*vj*	*viij*
Itm one Trunke two little			
Coffers and one badd bord		*viij*	
Itm his Apparell		*liij*	*iiij*
Itm his Cheeses		*viij*	
Itm one payre of playeinge			
tables & table men			*xij*
Itm his woolle		*xl*	
In the Buttery			
Itm Fowre litle vats and			
two standers		*vij*	
Itm three Coasts & Certen			
other treen vessell		*xv*	
Itm two yotinge vats & one			
olde hogshead		*vj*	*viij*
Itm one Treendle		*viij*	
Itm two Weavers lommes			
Sleas & quyll turnes	*iij*		
Itm one spinninge turne			*viij*
Itm one payre of Harrows		*viij*	
Itm one shovell a mattocke			
& other yron tooles		*iij*	
Itm one packsadle one payre of			
pannyars one payre of dung potts			

	lî	*s*	*d*
Crooks tings & gyrses		*ix*	
Itm one Ladder		*ij*	
Itm his Wheate & Rye			
in the barne & mowe	*vij*		
Itm his Otes	*iiij*		
Itm his Wheate in ground		*l*	
Itm his Haye		*xxx*	
Itm one Mare	*iij*		
Itm two kyne	*vj*		
Itm three Heyffers	*vj*		
Itm two & fiftye sheepe	*xiij*		
Itm one pigge & pultrye		*xiij*	*iiij*
Itm all other trashe in &			
aboute the howse		*ij*	

Sma *lxviij*^{li} *xiij*^{s} *viij*^{d}

Debts owyd to the said Barnard
Imprimis Nicholas Loman of Lovepitt [Luppitt] owith *iij*^{li}
Itm Thomas Myddleton owith *xj*^{s}
Sma totals *lxxij*^{li} *iiij*^{s} *viij*^{d}

[Will 18 Oct 1613 of Barnard Tucker of Uffculme, weaver: residue to wife Johane, exec; 3s 4d to poor; £13 6s 8d each to be invested for s Nicholas Tucker & for wife's unborn ch till age 21; 12d each to ovsrs Robert Myll & Robert Baker; witn: Thomas Wilson, cleric, who signs, & Andrew Tucker, Robert Baker, & Robert Woodrowff, who all make their marks. On 24 Mar 1613 the exec had to swear that assets outside the Dean's peculiar jurisdiction did not exceed £5.]

53 JOHN READE 1616 (DS)

[Bur: "John Read of Gaddon Downe" 21 Aug 1616. "Groom" in will; few cattle, plough; £19.]

An Inventorye made the Eighteenthe day of September in the yeare of o^{r} lord god (accordinge to the Computacōn of the Churche of England) One Thousand Sixe hundred & Sixteene, of all the goods & Chattels of John Reade late of Gaddon in the pishe of Ufculme & County of Devon deceassed Taken and prised by Leonard Pococke Willm Reade & Cutbert Rugge as followith./

	lî	*s*	*d*
Inprimis two Oxen	*vj*	*xiij*	*iiij*
Itm two Kyne	*v*	*xiij*	*iiij*
Itm one Mare	*iiij*		
Itm his apparell		*xx*	
Itm one Carme[Carine?], one payre of wheeles & other plowgh stuffe		*xl*	
Itm one Axe & one addice [adze?]			*xij*

Sma *xix^{li} vij^{s} viij^{d}*

[Will 18 Aug 1616 of John Read of Gaddon in Uffculme, groom, pr 13 Nov 1616: residue to exec & sister Jane Evans; 40s each to bros Thomas & Willm Reade, & to sisters Thomazin & Joane Reade ; 1 mare, cart, wheels, & plough gear to sister Jane Read; ovsrs bro William Reade & nephew Cutberte Rugge. In Nov 1616 the exec had to swear that her bro's assets outside the Dean's peculiar jurisdiction did not exceed £5.]

54 ROBERT MAUNDER 1617 (DS)

[Bur: "Robt. Mãnder" 30[?] Sep 1616. Mar: "Robt Mawnder & Julyan Brooke" 14 Jan 1605/6. Largely debts owed; £24.]

An inventory of all the goods & Chatt[els of] Robert Maunder dessesed wthin the pishe of Ufculme psed by Richard [ ] Henry Rugg Edward Andro and John Cheeke the seaventh daye of Feabuary 1616[/7]

	lî	*s*	*d*
Imprims~ his Aparell		*xx*	
Itm~ debts owed [wth speciallty *two and*] *twenty^{li}*			
Itm~ debts owed wthout speciallty		*xiij*	*iiij*
Itm~ his beddinge		*iiij*	
Itm~ fower Coffers		*viij*	
Itm~ one Crocke and one Chillet		*v*	
Itm~ one tourne		*j*	*iiij*
Itm~ three littell baggs		*j*	
Itm~ one Corne picke and a matocke		*j*	
Itm~ other smale Implements		*iij*	

Some *xxiiij^{li} xvj^{s} viij^{d}*

Edward Andro Henry Rugge [both sign]
John Cheeke [+ mark]

[Admon 12 Jun 1617 names Julian Maunder as relict & admin & also Robert Marshall of Uffculme, yeoman; marked by Julian Maunder & Robert Marshall & signed by Henry Rugge in presence of Richard Woodde, clerk, & William Woodde (both sign). An oath was sworn that not more than £5 lay outside the jurisdiction of the Dean.]

55 THOMAS READE 1617 (DS)

[At Gaddon; rye, oats, & few animals; musket; £24.]

An Inventorye indentyd made the Sixth daye of September in the yeare of o^{r} lord god, (accordinge to the Computacõn of the Churche of England One Thowzand Sixe hundred and Seaventeene, of all the goods & Chattles of Thomas Reade late of Gaddon in the pishe of Ufecolme in the Countye of Devon Yeoman deceassed, Taken & prysed by Leonard Pococke & Cutbert Rugge as Followithe

	lî	*s*	*d*
Inprimis the Rye in the barne	*viij*		
Itm his Ots in the barne	*v*	*vj*	*viij*
Itm Two kyne	*iiij*	*vj*	*viij*
Itm Three stoore piggs		*xx*	
Itm one mans armor, viz a muskett pformed		*xxvj*	*viij*
Itm his haye in the Tallet		*xx*	
Itm all his Fyre woodd		*xiij*	*iiij*
Itm one Brasse panne		*xiij*	*iiij*
Itm one Brasse Crocke a payre of pothanginges & a gryddle		*v*	
Itm one bedde & bedstedde		*xx*	
Itm his apparell		*xx*	
Itm Three podingers one Sawcer & one Candlesticke		*iij*	
Itm Two Coasts		*ij*	
Itm Two Ladders		*ij*	

Sma *xxiiij^{li} xviij^{s} viij^{d}*

[Admon 6 Dec 1617 names Jane Read as sister & exec (though no will attached) of Thomas Read of Gaddon.]

56 WALTER KEEPER 1622 (DS)

[Bur: "Walter Keeper" 17 Mar 1621/2. Some corn & oats; sword; £11.]

The Inventary of the goods and Chattles of Walter Keeper of the pish of Ufculme in the county of Devon deceased taken by John Champnies gent and Thomas Hellier yeoman the sixth day of Aprill 1622

	lî	*s*	*d*
Inprimis his appell two coffers & other trifeling things in the coffers	2	10	
Item two old hatts		1	6
Item two shirts two bandes and a paire of cuffes		6	
Item one deske		2	6
Itm one sworde		5	
Itm Corne in the barne	1	6	8
Itm oates in the ground	1	6	8
Itm bordes poles & tressels		5	
Itm one cupbord and a table bord	1	13	4
Itm one prayer booke		1	6
Itm one paire of bootes		4	
Itm one trunck		1	
Itm monie due unto him	2	14	
Itm monie in his purse		4	
Sum tot 11^{li} 1^{s} 2^{d}			

[Admon 10 May 1622 names Willm Keeper of Uffculme, husbandman, as bro & admin, & also Humphry Steare, vicar. Both sign in presence of Will Hutchins & Tho: Belle.]

57 BEATEN RUDGE 1622 (DS)

[Bur: "Beaten Rudge, widowe" 5 May 1622. Household items only; value, including chattel lease, £37.]

The Inventory of all & singular the goods cattles & chattles of Beaten Rudg[e] late of Ufculme in the County of Devon wid deceased praised by Humphry Butson John Hurly & Edmond Byshop the sixt day of May anno dm 1622 as followeth

	lî	*s*	*d*
Imprimis wee prize all her appell		*l*	
Itm one dust bed bedsteed and all the furniture	*xxx*		
Itm 2 little brazen panns	*x*		
Itm one little brased crock	*vj*	*viij*	
Itm 7 pewter dishes	*vij*		
Itm 2 candlesticks		*xvj*	
Itm one table bord 2 formes	*xiiij*		
Itm one side bord & j brack	*ij*		
Itm 3 plancks		*xviij*	
Itm 4 coffers	*x*		
Itm one barrell		*xx*	
Itm one frying pan one broch one pothangings and one picke	*ij*	*vj*	
Itm one Chattle lease	*xxx*		
Itm one pips[?] corne one p[air]e of shooes and all other things not prized	*iij*	*iiij*	
Suma *xxxvij*^{li}			

[Exhibited at Salisbury by the exec, 9 Jan 1622/3.

Will 2 May 1622 of Beaten Rudge of Uffculme, widow, pr 9 Jan 1622/3: residue to s Robert Rudge, exec; clothes, bedding, & brass pan to dr Mary Lake; bolster & coffer to dr Thomasin Rodden & brass crock to her dr Elizabeth Rodden; 2s 6d each to Nicholas & Susanna Lake & 7s 6d to John Lake, all chn of Thomas Lake; table, pan, & pewter dishes to Rbreichta (Rebecca?) & John Rudge, chn of Robert Rudge; 40s each to s Walter Rudge & to Thomas Lake; ovsrs ("rulers") Humphry Butson & Edmond Byshop; marked by Beaten Rudge in the presence of John Beare & Humphry Butson.]

58 GEORGE STARKE 1623 (PU)

[Bur: "George Starke" 30 Jan 1622/23. Mar: George Starke & Judith Bidgood" 3 Feb 1612/3. 6 sheep, household goods & £12 in debts owed to him; value £3, or £15 with debts.]

Primo die Februarij ./ Anno Dom- ./ 1622[/3]

In the name of god Amen in the xxvjth of January in the yeare of o' Lord god one thousand six hundred twenty fowr I Anthony Brooke als Butstone of the parish of Ufculme in the County of Devon yeoman being sicke of bodye but thankes bee to Almighty god perfect of remembrance doe make this my last will and testament in manner and forme followinge that is to say first I bequeth my soule to almighty god my maker and redeemer and my bodye to be buryed in the churchyard of Ufculme Item I geve to the church of Uffculme iiis iiijd It I geve to the poore of Uffculme iiis iiijd It I geve to my brother Humfry my best pan of brasse and three of my best silver spoones that have a letter in the end of them and also all my plowe stuffe belonginge one chire and culter and three iron roped(?) three payre of crookes three staples and three yorkes It I geve to my brother Humfrye daughter Elizabeth the wife of Samuell Bishop my best crocke of brasse and one silver spoone Itt my second best pann of brasse and my fowerth best pan of brasse my best candlesticke and my best charger of peuter one platter one porer(?) and one sauser It I geve to my brother John his daughter mary the wife of John Chaffcott fower pound and my bed one bolster one payre of blankets two coverlets and one peale(?) It I geve to my brother John his daughter Jane fower pounde It I geve to my brother John his daughter Emmot fower pounde It I geve to Humfry Turke his two children one silver spoone a peece It I geve to Agnes Lawrance fower shillings It I geve to Elizabeth Rogers twelve pence It I geve to every one of my god children twelve pence a peece All the rest of my goods ungeven and not bequethed my debtes payed and funerall expences discharged I doe geve and bequeth to my brother John and I doe ordayne and make the sayd John my sole executor also I doe ordayne and make Thomas Hurley of Burscombe and William Cooper to be my overseers to see this my will performed and doe geve them for their paynes five shillings a peece these beinge witnesses Humfry Butson Thomas Hurley William Cooper and others

the signe of Antony B Butstone

the signe of Samuell B Bishop

The will of Anthony Brooke *alias* Butstone 1624 [59]

The Invitorie of the goods of George Starke of Ufculme late deceased and prised by Bartholomewe Rawlins and Rycharde Trasey /

	lî	*s*	*d*
Imprisus all his apparrell	0	10	0
all his bedding and bedsteedes		5	0
one Chest & two Coffers		5	0
all the pewter and brasse		10	0
all the woddne vessells		5	0
all his husbandrye tooles		4	0
for bordes and planckes		2	0
for six sheepe	1	1	0
and allsoe there is owed of desperate debte wch is uncertaine whether or noe it wille ever be payed having noe specialtye for the sayed debt the some of	9	0	0
and allso theire owed unto [o?]ne of badd dette more uppon bills the some of	3	0	0
Som is	15	2s./	

[Exhibited at Uffculme by Judith, widow, 22 Aug 1623; sworn by Mr. Sharpe.

Admon: 22 Aug 1623 names Judith Starke as widow & admin, & Alexander Starke of Uffculme, fuller (son?). Judith made her mark & Alex^r^ signed.]

59 ANTHONY BROOKE alias BUTSON 1623 (DS) & 1624 (PCC)

[Bur: "Anthonie Butson" 13 Feb 1622/3. Yeoman; plough & household goods; debts owed to him £35 10s; value including debts £49.]

An Inventorie of the Goods of Anthony Brooke alš Butson of Rill w^th^in the pish of Ufculme deceased takne and praysed by Nicholay Dowdny of Leigh Simon Hidon Robert Bishop, and Humphry Tucke, the thirteenth daye of February 1622

	lî	*s*	*d*
Imp^r^s his wearinge appell	*ij*	*x*	*oo*
It his bedinge	*ij*	*x*	*oo*
It five silver spoones	*j*	*iiij*	*oo*
It Seaven brasse pans	*iiij*	*oo*	*oo*
It two brasse Crocks	*j*	*iij*	*iiij*
It Five brasse Candlesticks	*oo*	*x*	*oo*
It pewter dishes	*j*	*j*	*oo*
It his plowe stuffe	*j*	*oo*	*oo*
It One Showvle of yron wth other workinge tooles	*oo*	*vj*	*viij*
It Money due upon bond	*xxiiij*	*v*	*oo*
It More due unto him	*xj*	*oo*	*oo*
Sum	49^l^	10^s^	00

[Will 26 Jan 1622/3 of Anthony Brooke alš Butstone of Uffculme, yeoman, sworn to by the exec 10 Mar 1622/3, no more than £5 lying outside the peculiar jurisdiction: residue to bro John, exec; 3s 4d to church; 3s 4d to the poor; to bro Humfry a brass pan, 3 silver spoons, & plough gear, &c; to Elizabeth, dr of bro Humfrye & wife of Samuell Bishop, brass, pewter, & 1 silver spoon; to Mary, dr of bro John & wife of John Hatswill, £4 & bedding; £4 each to Jane & Emmel, drs of bro John; a silver spoon each to the 2 chn of Humfry Tucke; 4s to Agnes Laurance; 12d to Elizabeth Rogers; 12d each to godchn; 5s each to ovsrs Thomas Hurley of Banscombe & William Keeper; witn named as Humfry Butson, Thomas Hurley, William Keeper, & others, but only Antoni Butstone (B) & Samuell Byshope (SB) mark.

Despite the assertion that property outside Uffculme did not exceed £5, a copy was referred to the PCC & a further probate was granted to the same exec in London on 12 Jun 1624.]

60 JOHN DUNE the younger 1624 (PU)

[Bur: "John Dunne, son of Robert" 29 Jan 1623/4. This inventory, made on 10 Feb, untypically records the death on 27 Jan. 7 sheep & clothing; value, including debts owed to him, £24.]

A true Invitare of all the goods and Cattells of John Dune of Ufculme the younger late deceased the Seaven and twenteth day of January Anno Dom:1623[/4]

	lî	s	d
Imprimis owed Unto the said John Duñe late deceased by John Cheeke thelder of Gadden in Ufculme aforsaid Uppon A bond the sume of Sixteene pounds and tenne shillings	*xvj*	*x*	
Owed Unto the said John Duñe by one John Cheeke the younger Uppon a bonde the some of fowre and fortie shillins	*ij*	*iiij*	
All his wearing apparrell apprysed in the some of three pounds and fifteene shillings	*iij*	*xv*	
The Seaven sheepe were apprysed in the some of three and thirtie shillings and fowre pence	*j*	*xiij*	*iiij*

Suma in toto *xxiiij*^{li} [2s 4d short]

this goods was apraysed the tenthe day of Februari by John Wodruffe and Bartholomewe Rawlins
Signed John [W mark] Wodruffe and Bartho Rawlins [signed]

[Exhibited before Mr. Humfrey Steare at Uffculme: date not given.

Nuncupative will 26 Jan 1623/4 "by John Donne of Smedingcot in the parish of Uffculme"; to every ch a sheep & a goat; residue to Robert Donne, father & exec; witn: Jhoane (J mark) Woodrowe, wife of Bartholomewe Woodrowe, & Agnes (F mark?) Foxe; pr at Uffculme 11 Aug 1624 before Mr. Humfrey Steare.]

61 MARYE LEYMAN 1624 (DS)

[Bur: "Mary Leman" 1 Jan 1623/4. Spinster owning lease of mill & lending money; 2 cows & a pig; value including all assets £60.]

The Inventory of All and singuler the goods and Cattells of Marye Leyman Latt of Uffculmbe in the County of Devon spinster decessed presed by Mathewe Cadbery John Norris & John Beare the seaventh day of Aprill Año Dm 1624 as Followeth

	lî	s	d
Imprimis wee prease all her Apparrell		*v*	
It one Fether bed		*xxx*	
It two Kine	*v*		
It one Lytle pigg		*v*	
It beafe and baken		*xiij*	*iiij*
It Butter Chese		*x*	
It one brasse pan		*iiij*	
It mony in and uppon specialtyes	*xxxvj*		
It one pece of wollen Cloth		*vj*	*viij*
It one silver pinn & silver tayches		*iij*	
It two Coffers, & one box		*iiij*	
It tallow			*xij*
It woll		*iij*	
It Lytle pewter disshes			*xviij*
It detts owed wthout specialty by Anne Welch vid		*xl*	
It Elizabeth Newton oweth		*xx*	
It George Currum of Culmbestocke oweth		*xx*	
It Henry Manninge oweth one quarters rent for her mill	*iij*		
It Fraunces Leman oweth	*iij*		
It one Lytle skillet one milcken payle: & all other thinges not presed		*iij*	*iiij*
It Mary Oland oweth		*vj*	

Summa totalis *lx*^{li} *x*^{s} *x*^{d}

[Exhibited at Salisbury by admin, 10 Jul 1624.

Nuncupative will 27 Dec 1623 of Mary Leyman of Uffculme, spinster: £20 & a piece of white cloth to bro Robert Leyman; £20 to sister Agnes Leyman, part to be taken in clothes, butter, cheese, &c; 4d each to 20 poor people; 3s each to 2 goddrs, chn of Aunt Mary Oland, from the 6s owed to her by her aunt; 12d each to other godchn; 2s 6d to Joane Anstice; exec bro Francis Leyman; witn: Francis & Agnes Leyman. Admon 10 Jun 1624 names Francis Leyman of Uffculme, yeoman, as admin, & also William Keeper, husbandman, who both sign & seal in presence of James Hill, not^y^ pub.]

62 FRANCIS TAYLOR alš OLAND 1624 (DS)

[Intestate; few items (47s), but the £10 chattel lease in another parish raised a problem; total value £12.]

An Inventorie of the goods and Chattels of Francis Taylor alš Oland of Ufculme deceased, takne and prised by Humfry Butson Robert Oland and Thomas Hurley the sixe and twentith daye of Aprill 1624.

	lî	*s*	*d*
Imp^{ris} his weareinge apparell	2	00	00
It one silver spoone	00	05	00
It one Chattell Lease the te[ne]ment lyeinge wthin the pish of Hemiocke [Margin note: *This is in another parish out of the Jurisdiction*]	10	00	00
It one Coffer	00	02	00
Robert Oland Suma	12^{li}	7^{s}	

Humfry Butson
Thomas Hurley

There is a Clause in the oath that the administratrixe shall sweare that the intestate has noe goods to the value of v^{li} out of the peculiar iurisdiction. But as our case is that oaths cannot be taken for the Inventary beinge but 12^{li} 7^{s} in all (as above), 10^{li} thereof lyeth out of the Jurisdiction and but 47^{s} within, yet I was advised the last Tearme by one of the Clearks of the prerogative office that it belonged not to them But in reguard that there were not sev^{r}all Five pounds wthin and wthout, that the administracoñ ought to be taken there where the p[ar]tye dyed, and the rest though it were above 5^{li} should be drawne thither, And soe this [c]annot stand wth the oath / Jõ quere de hoc [?] /
George Wood /

4^{d} ci________ 8^{d}
4^{d} ext________ *xiij*^{d}
12^{d} ab^{o}________ *xviij*^{d}
4^{d} cerns______ *ix*^{d}
act______ *viij*^{d}
shdd______ 4^{d}
12^{d} examo______ *xviij*^{d}
20^{d} art______ *iij*^{s} *iiij*^{d}
4^{d} Jurat______ 4^{d}
4^{d} ordo______ *xvj*^{d}
6^{d} dio______ *x*^{d}

5^{s} 10^{d} Sma
/xsutors [executors?]_ 3^{s}
15^{s} 4^{d}

[This looks like an account of legal charges. The left column sums to 5s 10d and the right (including the extra 3s) to 15s 4d, but the connexion between the two is not clear.]

63 FLORENCE HOLWILL 1624 (PU)

[Bur: "Florence Holwill, widowe" 4 May 1624. Widow of Humfry 51; clothmaking gear; chattel lease & debt but no farming items; £17.]

The Inventorie of all the goods and Chattels of Florence Holwill late of Ufculme deceased, made and praysed by John Norton Willm Keeper and George Fursdon the eightteenth daye of Maye in the yeare of o^{r} Lord God 1624.

	lî	*s*	*d*
Imprs her weareinge apparell		*xx*	
It one peece of newe cloth		*j*	4
It one standinge bed pformed		*xx*	
It twoe other beds		*xiij*	*iiij*
It twoe chests and a coffer		*xiij*	
It one Cubbord, and one table bord and forme		*xv*	
It pewter		*xij*	
It three brassen Crocks		*xx*	
It brassen pans & twoe Caldrons		*x*	
It twoe payre of lumbes [looms], one spininge turne and on quillturne		*xl*	
It timber vessels		*xiij*	*iiij*
It twoe broches a Fryinge pan pothangings and other iron stuffe		*iiij*	
It twoe tree platters and other such like stuffe			*vj*

	lî	*s*	*d*
It one iron shovell one Rake, twoe piks		*ij*	
It wooll and yarnes		*ij*	*iiij*
It one Chattell lease	*iiij*		
It in money owinge unto her	*iiij*		
It one Ringe			*rviij*

[Two totals are crossed out but the above list comes to £17 8s 4d. Exhibited before Mr. Steare at Uffculme: date not given.

Will dated 3 May 1624, pr 11 Aug 1624 at Uffculme before Mr. Steare: residue to s Robert Norton (sic), exec; detailed items of clothing to Mary Norton, dr of s Robert, & Ingrett Ware; also 40s to Mary Norton, 10s & twine & cards to Ingrett; 5s & 4s respectively to ks Dorothie & Johan Norton; ovsrs George Fursdon & John Norton; witn: Hum: Steare, Dorothy (D mark) Norton, Johan (+ mark) Cornie.]

64 JOHN OLAND 1624 (PU)

[Administration account by widow Mary Oland. Bur: "John Oland" 1 Feb 1621/22. Debts of £90 paid though assetts only £84.]

The accompt of Mary Oland widow the Relict and Adm[x] of the goods of John Oland her husband late of Ufculme deceased made & ex[ted] before Mr Humfry Steere clarke vicar of Ufculme the tenth of August 1624 as followeth viz-

The Charge

First this accomp[r] chargeth herself wth the sum of fower score & fower pounds & one shilling eight pence Lawfull english money comprised and set downe in an Inven[ry] of the goods of the sd deceased as by the same appeth

Soma patet [Total not entered but presumably £84 1s 8d]

Discharge	*lî*	*s*	*d*
Item for the funerall charges in interring the sd deceased	*viij*	*x*	
Item pd to Mr Steare for a mortuary		*x*	
Item for a funerall sermon to him [no charge quoted]			
Item pd to Wm Grant of Ufculme due by bond	*x*		
Item pd to Samuell Byshop of Ufculme due by bond	*xij*		
Item p[d] to Thomas Moore of Hemiocke due by bond	*xij*		
Item p[d] to John Wealand of Ufculme due by bond	*viij*		
Item p[d] to Humfry Butson of Ufculme due by bond	*x*		
Item p[d] to George Osmond of Kentesbeare due by bond	*viij*		
Item p[d] to John Thorne of Hemiocke due by bond	*xiiij*		
Item p[d] to Edward Butson due by bond		*xxvj*	
Item p[d] to Florence Franck widow of Ufculme a debt of the deceaseds	*v*		
Item p[d] for the ltres of Adm[on] & ex[ting] the Inventaryes		*viij*	
Item for drawing this accompt & ingrossing the same the quietus est theruppon & other charges incident to the same		*xxxiiij*	*iiij*

Soma exonerat [Total not quoted but comes to £91 8s 4d]

65 NICHOLAS LANGBRIDGE 1625 (DS)

[Bur? Mar: "Nicholas Langbridge & Elizabeth Canne" 1 Nov 1606, Witheridge; see 118. Clothmaking gear; 1 cow, 1 calf, 1 mare; corn; £13.]

An Inventary of the goods and chattles of Nicholas Langridg of ufculme deceased taken and praised the xxj[th] day of January Anno dm <u>1624</u>[/5] by Peeter Cape Peeter Weare and Thomas Langridg

	lî	*s*	*d*
Imprimis his weareing appell	*x*		
Itm his beding	*x*		
Itm 2 bedsteeds		*iij*	*iiij*
Itm 2 coffers		*iiij*	
Itm one shouell one hooke			

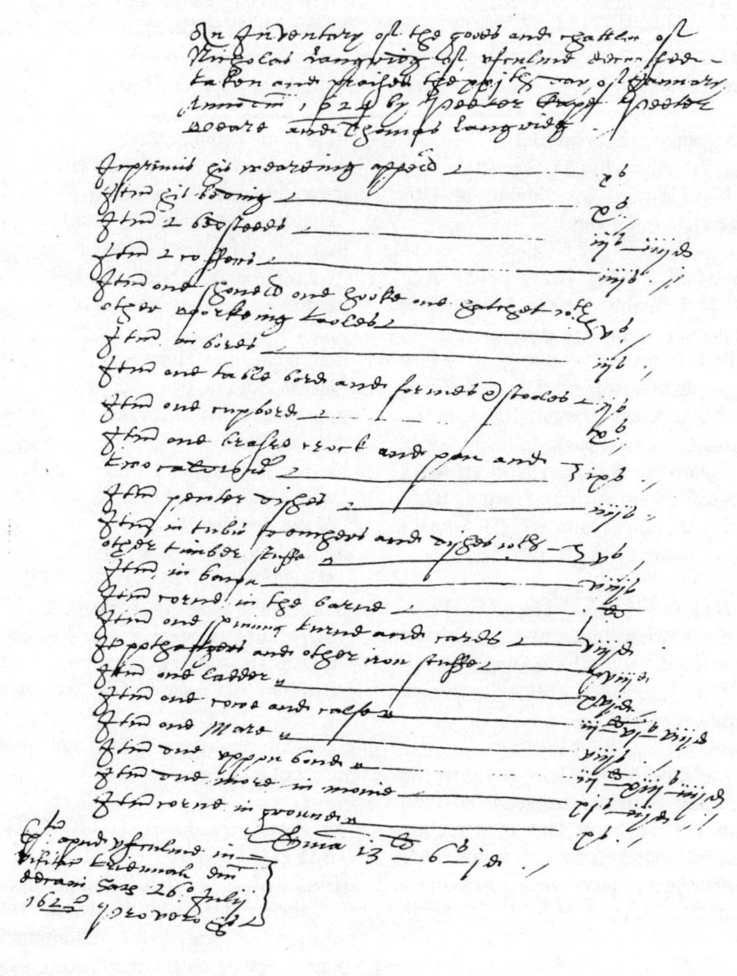

The inventory of Nicholas Langridge 1624 [65]

	lî	*s*	*d*
one hatchet wth other workeing tooles		*v*	
Itm in bords		*iij*	
Itm one table bord and formes & stooles		*ij*	
Itm one cupbord		*x*	
Itm one brasse crock and pan and two caldrons		*ix*	
Itm pewter dishes		*iiij*	
Itm in tubs trenchers and dishes wth other timber stuffe		*v*	
Itm in bacon		*viij*	
Itm corne in the barne	*j*		
Itm one spinning turne and cards			*viij*
It~ pothangers and other iron stuffe			*xviij*
Itm one ladder			*xvj*
Itm one cowe and calfe	*iij*	*vj*	*viij*
Itm one Mare		*viij*	
Itm due uppon bond	*iij*	*xiij*	*iiij*
Itm due more in monie		*xj*	*iij*
Itm corne in ground		*x*	

Sma 13^{li} 6^{s} *j*^{d}

[Exhibited at the triennial visitation of the Dean of Salisbury 26 Jul 1625.

Admon 26 Jul 1625 names Elizabeth Langbridge as widow & admin & also Thomas Baker of Uffculme, husbandman; marked by them & signed by witn James Hills.]

66 CHRISTOPHER MARSHALL 1625 (DS)

[Bur: "Christopher Marshall" 7 Mar 1624/5. Mar: "Christopher Marshall & Joan Tooker" 29 Nov 1615. Corn, oats, 10 cattle, several sheep, & 1 pig; sidesaddle & packsaddle; £5 debts owing; wool & yarn but no clothmaking gear; £61.]

An Inventary of the goods and chat[tels] of xpofer marshall late of the pish of Ufculme taken and praised the xjth day of March 1624 by Robert Mill Robert Marshall and James Butson as followeth

	lî	*s*	*d*
Inprimis his weareing appell	*ij*	*x*	
Itm 3 bedsteeds 3 beds and other things therunto belonging	*iiij*		
Itm one chest 2 coffers 2 chaires one stoole one little bord in the chamber ov^{r} the entry		*xiij*	*iiij*
Itm 2 coffers 2 bords in the chamber ov^{r} the milke house		*ij*	
Itm white wooll and yarne	iij	*x*	
Itm 7 cheeses		*x*	
Itm oates in the chamber oate meale and malt		*xxv*	
Itm one sidesaddle and packsaddle		*vj*	
Itm one cupbord one tablebord j chest and one forme in the hall	*j*	*xiij*	*iiij*
Itm 2 brasse crocks one posnet		*xv*	
Itm 4 brasse pans one caldron and one skillet	*j*		
Itm pewter dishes, salts, sawcers, and candlesticks	*j*		
Itm one trendle 4 barrels one cheese wringe & other timber vessels		*xiij*	*iiij*
Itm 5 flitches of bacon	*j*	*v*	
Itm corne in the barne	*j*		
Itm corne in ground	*ij*		
Itm one mare and colt	*iiij*		
Itm 4 kine 3 calves	*xij*		
Itm 2 heyfers one yearling	*iiij*		
Itm sheepe	*xij*		
Itm one pigg		*vj*	
Itm haye		*vj*	*viij*
Itm one paire of harrowes		*iij*	*iiij*
Itm one axe one hooke one shovell & other workeing tooles		*ij*	
Itm 2 spitts one grediron and other iron implem^{ts}		*ij*	*vj*
Itm due uppon specialty	*v*	*xvj*	*viij*

Smã

[No total given but the figures add up to £61 0s 2d.]

[Exhibited at Uffculme at the triennial visitation of the Dean of Salisbury 26 Jul 1625.

Admon 26 Jul 1625 names Joane Marshall as widow & admin of Christopher Marshall of Uffculme, & also Robert Marshall & Mathew Cadbury,

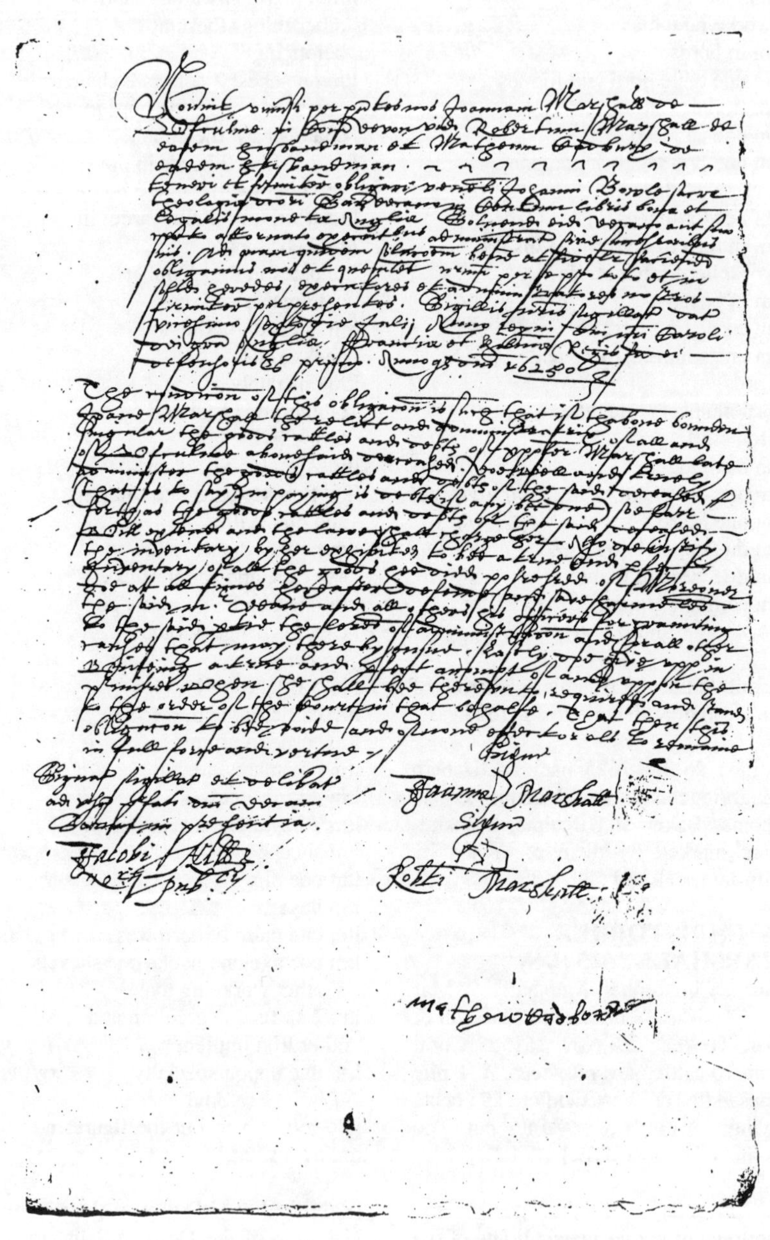

The admon for the goods of Christopher Marshall 1625 [66]

both husbandmen of Uffculme; marked by Joane & Robt Marshall in presence of James Hill, not^{y} pub.]

67 RICHARD BROOKE 1625 (DS)

[Bur: "Richard Brooke" 2 Jun 1625. Yeoman, with rye & oats, few sheep, 1 cow; half-acre meadow; body armour; £24.]

Nono die Julij <u>1625</u>

A true Inventary of all the goods of Richard Brooke of Ufculme in the County of Devon yeoman late deceased taken and prized by Humphrey Steare Clarke of the same ꝑish and Bartho: Rawlins and John Trickher

	lî	*s*	*d*
Imprimis 5 acres of Rye	*viij*		
Itm 2 acres of oates	*ij*		
Itm one milch Cowe	*ij*	*x*	
Itm one mare	*ij*		
Itm 4 sheepe 5 lambs	*ij*		
Itm one cosslet furnished	*j*	*vj*	*viij*
Itm one p[ar]cell of meadowe contayning by estimacoñ halfe an acre	*vj*	*xiij*	*iiij*
Itm for all other implements unprized		*iij*	*iiij*

Summa *xxiiij*^{li} *xiii*^{s} *iiij*^{d}

[Exhibited at Uffculme at the triennial visitation of the Dean of Salisbury 26 Jul 1625.

Admon 26 Jul 1625 names John Brooke of Uffculme, yeoman, as s & admin, & also Bartho: Rawlins, husbandman, both of whom sign in the presence of James Hill, not^{y} pub.]

68 JOHN CULLIFORD 1626 (PU)

[Bur: "John Culliford" 16 Dec 1625. Mar: "John Collyford & Susan Hellier" 15 Sep 1600, Colyton. Household items & side saddle; £14.]

An Inventory of the goods of John Culliford Late decessed of Uffculme./

	lî	*s*	*d*
Imprimis for one table boord and two formes		*xx*	
for one levery Cubberd & two Chaires and for two frame stooles & one frame		*x*	
for Siling in the hall		*x*	
for one Croke of Brasse		*xiij*	*iiij*
for one pan of brasse one Caldron		*xij*	
for two beds ꝑformed ij bedsteads and one Coverlet beside	*vj*	*xiij*	*iiij*
for one press and fower Chests xxx			
for two Trunkes		*vj*	*viij*
for one side sadle wth his furniture		*xiij*	*iiij*
for one Carpet iiij kushings		*v*	
for xij peater dishes iij saucers		*xiij*	*iiij*
for ij barrells and iiij Tubes		*x*	
for j friing pan ij andires and one pothanging		*ij*	*vj*
for one pessell and morter		*j*	*vj*
for one boaell ij wooding platers and other Trash		*ij*	

Some *xiiij*^{li} *iij*^{s}./

Praised by Williã Keeꝑ[er] and Thomas Balliman

[Exhibited at Uffculme 12 Sep 1626.

Nuncupative will pr at Uffculme 12 Sep 1626: goods that were his own before his marriage to his wife Susan to go to his drs Agnis & Alice; rest to the said Susan; witn: John (JB mark) Ballyman, Thomas Ballyman (signed).]

69 ELIZABETH COURTON [COURTNEY] 1626 (PU)

[Bur: "Elizabeth Courton, widowe" 31 Aug 1626. Corn & 3 cattle; no clothmaking gear; £19.]

An Inventory of the goods and Chattelles of Elizabeth Courton of the ꝑish of Ufculme in the County of Devon widdowe deceased taken and praised the first daye of September Anno Dm- 1626 By Thomas Moulton Gent and John Woodroffe as Followeth viz -

	lî	*s*	*d*
Imprim her wearinge apparell	*j*	*x*	

	lî	*s*	*d*
It one bedsteed twoe beds wth Cov^rletts Blankets and sheetes		*xiij*	*iiij*
It brasse pannes and Caldron two skillets and two Crockes	*j*	*xv*	*x*
It pewter dishes		*ix*	*oo*
It one candellstick and one sallt			*vj*
It one frying pan one gridyon wth other iron stuffe		*ij*	
It one Table borde one Cubord one Chayre two stooles one forme 2 Coffers		*xvij*	*viij*
It three Barrells wth other timber vessels one payre of harrowes and a ladder		*xvij*	*iiij*
It Butter and Cheese	*j*	*xj*	2
It twoe kine and one Calfe	*vj*	*vj*	*viij*
It Corne in the feilde	*iij*	*x*	*oo*
It haye and Reed	*j*	*xiij*	*iiij*
It wood		*vj*	*viij*
It one Ringe and a payre of silver taches		*ij*	*o*
xix^li xv^s vj^d			

[Exhibited at Uffculme 12 Sep 1626.

Will of Elizabeth Courtney (sic) of Uffculme, widow, dated 19 Oct 1625, pr at Uffculme 12 Sep 1626: residue to Robert Facie, cousin & exec; 5 groats to poor; clothing & bedding to Alice Facy, sister; £4 to Mary Sachell "to be employed to best use" till her age 21; 5s, ring, & coffer to Phebe Facie; 5s each to Robert Facie "the youngest", Meller Facie, & Richard Lee, cousin; ovsrs & witn: John Wooderough (W mark) of Uffculme, & Richard Streete of Pinhon. Marked by Elizabeth Courtney.]

70 AUGUSTEN TAWTON 1626 (PU)

[Bur: "Augustine Tawton" 7 Sep 1626: date of death given in inventory as 5 Sep 1626. Mar: "Austin Tawton & Mary Slader" 25 Apr 1625, Otterton. Only household items apart from debts owed to him of £50; value including debt £65, but £15 quoted below.]

A True menistration of al ye goods of Augusten Tawton, of Uffculumbe in ye county of Devon woe deceassed, ye 5th day of September, in the yeare of our Lord 1626.

	lî	*s*	*d*
In primus, his waring A parill,	3		
and in his purse A		11	
A II peater deshes, & seven sausseres and on touñe & saltseller, on brase candelsteck, and on peatter; on dessen of tening spounes		20	
on brase pan, & on crok & on posnett & on Caudron, & on skyllet		22	
on bead & bead steed and furnurtue belonging to it	3	v	
on Chest, & to couffers and to foslets		16	
4 toubes and on pail,		10	
A peare of tables		4	
on gridireron, on pot hiner & on pothoukes to brand ises, & on frieing pan		5	
on Baring, shet, to boord Cloothes & 9 table nackpkings		24	
As moni oniones as are worte 3s		3	
for houpes & fessell timber unwrogt 5 noebles:	[1	13	4]
the toules,		16	
to oulld Chelfes wth othere things forgoten, 10 grates:		[3	4]
A grining ston		4	
Deates owed to hime upon tow bandes	50		
on selver, spone		6	

The wo^ull Som, is 15^ll & ii^s & 8^d

[The shortfall in the total, £50, corresponds to the £50 for debts.]

This goods being preased by Edmont Coulle and Christofer Starke

[Admon: 12 Sep 1626, naming Mary Tawton as admin, & Robert Slader of Otterton; sworn before Francis Roberts, notary public.]

71 ANNE WELSHE 1626 (PU)

[Bur: "Anne Welch, widowe" 6 Oct 1626. Household items & a debt; £7.]

The Inventorie of the goods of Anne Welshe late deceased apprysed by Bartho Rawlins and John Norton the nynth day of October: Anno Dom: <u>1626</u>

	lî	*s*	*d*
Imprimis her wearing apparrell	1	10	0
Itê all the rest of her liñing	0	13	4
Itê all her bedding and all that belongin thereunto	0	13	4
Itê one paire of Briches and dublett wch were her late husbands	0	6	8
Itê one skillett one pare of Crocke haingins two lattiñe Candle-sticks & two sawcers	0	2	0
Itê one Coffer one box and one duzen of Cheese trenchers	0	2	0
Itê all other Implements and other smale goods unprysed	0	4	6
Itê one obligation of Seaven pounds for the payment of three poundes & seaventeene shillings of desperatt debte	3	17	0
Suma in totš	7^{li}	8^{s}	10^{d}

[Exhibited by John How, admin, 13 Dec 1626.

Admon 13 Dec 1626 names John How of Uffculme, farmer, as bro to Anne Welsh, widow, & William How of the same, farmer; sworn before Thomas Clarke, prebendary of Uffculme.]

72 MATHEW CADBURY 1627 (PU)

[Bur: "Mathewe Cadbury" 15 Apr 1627; died intestate. Mar: "Mathew Cadbery & Jone Leaman" 13 Jan 1605. Prosperous; books, oats, wheat, rye, peas, horses, cattle, pigs, & poultry, but no sheep or clothmaking gear. The buildings include a hall, wringehouse, & milkhouse, all with chambers over; but the enterprise was apparently financed by debts which approximated to the total value of the inventory, £124.]

An Inventory of the goods and Chattles of Mathew Cadbury late of the p̱ish of Ufculme deceased taken and praysed the Twentith daye of Aprill 1627 by Thomas Moulton gent John Ballima~[n] Robert Leyman and John Dowdney as Followeth /

	lî	*s*	*d*
Imp^{rs} his weareinge apparrell	*v*	*oo*	*oo*
It one bed p̱formed and one bed-teed in the Chamber ov^{r} the wringe house wth one Chest and one Coffer there	*v*	*oo*	*oo*
It one bed p̱formed and bedsteed in the Chamber ov^{r} the hall & one truckle bed, p̱formed	*vij*	*oo*	*oo*
It one table bord standinge in the sayd Chamber ov^{r} the hall one Carpett three ioine stooles, one Chayre, five Cushens, and one boxe	*j*	*iij*	*iiij*
It one bible, one booke of Comõ prayer and one other little booke		*xvj*	
It one bed p̱formed standinge in the Chamber ov^{r} the milkhouse and one little Coffer there		*xiij*	*iiij*
It one Chest, one Coffer, one forme, and one board standinge at the stayre head		*xiij*	*iiij*
It butter and Cheese	*j*	*iij*	*oo*
It one table board standinge in the hall, one liv^{r}y table, one forme one Chayre, and seeleinge about the same	*j*	*vj*	*viij*
It one little Amery in the hall		*iiij*	*oo*
It Bacoñ	*ij*	*x*	*oo*
It pewter dishes and other pewter stuffe	*ij*	*oo*	*oo*
It two brasse candlesticks one morter, and one payre of brasse weights		*xij*	*oo*
It brasse pañs, Caldroñs and a skillett	*iij*		
It three brasse Crocks	*j*	*iij*	*iiij*
It barrles and other timber stuffe in the buttery	*j*	*vj*	*viij*
It tubs and Fates and suchlike timber stuffe in brewhouse	*j*	*xij*	*oo*
It bags and wiñowinge sheet and a haye Cloath for the drie	*j*		

	lî	*s*	*d*
It malte, and thresht Corne	*iiij*		
It one Cheese wringe and other timber stufe without the entrie	*j*	*oo*	*oo*
It yron tooles and other old yron	*j*	*x*	*oo*
It broaches pott hangings and other yron things about the hall		*xiij*	*iiij*
It one side saddle, three boards Cheese fats, and other timber stuffe in a little Chamber		*xvij*	*oo*
It silver spoones and other spoones	*ij*	*ij*	*oo*
It table Cloathes and table napkins		*x*	*oo*
It Cups, glaces & trenchers and glasse bottle		*iij*	*iiij*
It Saddles, dunge potts tings guisses and such like stuff	*j*	*iij*	*iiij*
It one payre of harrowes and harrowinge stuffe		*x*	*oo*
It Corne in the barne	*v*	*oo*	*oo*
It one sider wringe	*j*	*oo*	*oo*
It Reed		*iij*	*oo*
It seaven stocks of beefe	*j*	*oo*	*oo*
It Rie in ground	*v*	*oo*	*oo*
It oats in ground and halfe an acre of winter wheate	*x*	*oo*	*oo*
It pease in ground	*j*	*vj*	*viij*
It haye	*j*	*xiij*	*iiij*
It Five kine and one bull	*xix*	*oo*	*oo*
It two mares and one nag	*vij*	*oo*	*oo*
It twoe pigs	*j*	*x*	*oo*
It seame [lard]		*jx*	*oo*
It one grindinge stone		*iiij*	*oo*
It Furze and wood	*j*	*oo*	*oo*
It dunge		*vj*	*oo*
It Five bullocks of twoe yeare old, and Five of one yeare old	*xx*	*oo*	*oo*
It For pultrie		*iiij*	
It one hutch wth other old stuffe not seene and forgotten		*v*	*oo*

[End missing: no total is given but the figures sum to £123 13s 8d, thus approaching fairly satisfactorily the total of £124 12s 8d mentioned at the beginning of the widow's account below. The agreement is close enough for the inventory to be virtually complete.]

Th[e]Accompt of Joan Cadbury Adm^x of the goods of Matthew Cadbury her husband late of the pish of Ufculme intestate deceased made the xiij^th of September 1627, as followeth -

	lî	*s*	*d*
Th[e] Inventary	*Cxxiiij*	*xij*	*viij*
Discharg^es			
The Funerall	*iij*		
Item due by bond to Allexander Clarke of halberton	*v*	*x*	
Item p^d to John Courten due by bond	*iiij*		
Item p^d due by bond to Eliz: Facy	*x*	*xvj*	
Item p^d to henry Rowland due by bond	*viij*	*xij*	
Item p^d to Bridget Baker due by bond	*xj*		
Item p^d due by bond to John Ballyman	*x*	*xvj*	
Item p^d due by bond to George Welsh of Tawstock	*xx*		
Item p^d due by bond to Eliz: Butson alš Brooke	*x*	*xvj*	
Item p^d due by bond to the sd Georg^e Welsh	*x*		
Item for th[e] adm^on		*xiij*	*iiij*
Item for the com^on [?commission]		*viij*	
Item p^d to John Chicke due from the deceased		*xl*	
Item more due to the said Bridget Baker	*xij*	*xij*	
Item p^d due by bond to Richard Tracy	*iiij*	*xvj*	
Item to Ames Holway due from the sd decd	*xj*		
Item to Henry Manning	*xij*		
Item pd to Mr Champnies	*v*		
Item the Fees of the accompt		*xxxiij*	*iiij*
Sum tot	*Cxxxix*	*xij*	*viij*
	[£5 short?]		

discharged more than the Inventary xv^li

[Admon: [20] Apr 1627, naming Joan Cadbury widow & admin, & John Leman of Clehidon, yeoman, & Robert

Leman of Hemiocke, yeoman. Signed by Hum: Steare, William Key, & John Leman; marked R by Robert Leman.]

73 THOMAS HURLEY the elder 1627 (PU)

[Bur: "Thomas Hurley thelder" 12 Nov 1626: intestate. Mar: "Thomas Hurley & Alice Petter" 3 Aug 1578. Household items & 3 pigs; a £50 chattel lease accounts for most of inventory total; £71.]

An Inventorie of the goods and Chatls of Thomas Hurley thelder late of the pish of Ufculme deceased taken and praysed the xth daye of Maye Anno Dm[i] 1627 by Humfry Steare, Thomas Hurley and John Mill as Followeth -

	lî	*s*	*d*
Imp[r]s his weareinge apparell	*ij*	*oo*	*oo*
It Foure bedsteeds and Foure beds pformed	*iij*	*xiij*	*iiij*
It one Chest and twoe old Coffers		*xij*	
It one table board standinge in hall one forme and twoe table Cloathes	*j*	*oo*	*oo*
It one Cubboard standinge in the hall one settle, and twoe Chayres	*j*		
It one Cubboard standinge in the pler [parlour], one table board and one forme		*xx*	*oo*
It three presses wth things there unto belonginge	*j*	*x*	*oo*
It timber vessells	*j*		
It timber		*x*	*oo*
It pewter dishes and one candlesticke		*xviij*	
It one Furnace, twoe brasse pans, and one Caldron		*xxvj*	*viij*
It Foure Crocks	*j*	*x*	
It Five Racks	*iij*	*vj*	*viij*
It three payre of shayres		*xij*	*oo*
It one gridyre one Frying pan, and a broach [spit]		*ij*	*vj*
It one ladder, and other old implements		*v*	*oo*
It three pigs	*j*	*iij*	*iiij*
It bacon		*iij*	*iiij*
It one Chattle lease of one dwellinge house in Ufculme aforesayd, one garden, one acre of ground or thereabouts, and one Fallinge in lue for the term of Certaine yeares determynable upon three lives	*l*	*oo*	*oo*

[No total given here but the above numbers sum to £71 12s 10d if the £50 chattel lease at the end is included. This agrees with the total quoted in the widow's account below.]

The Accompt of Alice [apparently substituted for Thomas] Hurley Adm of all & singular the goods chattles & credits of Thomas Hurley thelder her husband lately decd made the iiij[th] day of September 1627: as followeth vezt. First this Accompt chargeth herself wth the Sum of *lxxj[li] xij[s] x[d]* being the true Value of all & singular the goods chattles & credits of the decd according *lxxj[li] xij[s] x[d]* as they were valued & praised in an Inventry herew[th] made & ex[ted] whereunto she refereth herself

The discharge	*lî*	*s*	*d*
The Funerall		*xx*	
for a mortuary		*x*	
for a sermon at the Funerall		*x*	
for a com[r] to take her oath		*viij*	
charges in fetching therof		*xij*	
The adm[on]		*xiij*	*iiij*
Accompt & quietus		*xxxj*	*iiij*
Som is	*v[li]*	*iiij[s]*	*viij[d]*

[Admon 13 Nov 1627, signed by Hum: Steare & Thomas Hurley, names Alice Hurley, widow, as admin, & also Thomas Hurley (son?), described as a fuller of Uffculme.

Alice Hurley, Thomas's widow, was required to sign an oath stating that Thomas died intestate and that she would discharge his debts &c and make an inventory. Marmaduke Lynne, a lawyer, seems to have acted on behalf of Thomas Clarke, the prebendary of Uffculme, and Humphrey Steare & Mr. Curnet are referred to as the vicars of Uffculme & Culmstock respectively.]

74 SIMOND SHILDS / SYMON SHEILD 1627 (PU)

[Bur: "Simon Childs" 11 May 1627. Mar: "Simon Sheeles & Marye Searle" 9 Nov 1626, Culmstock. Poultry & 1 pig; house with chamber over hall; clothmaking gear & part of musket; value £26.]

The Inventorye of All & singuler the goods & Cattels of Simond Shilds Late of Uffculme in the County of Devon Decessed, prised by Robert Marshall, John Beare, & William Hodge the twelveth Daye of Maye Año Dm~ 1627 as Followeth:

	lî	*s*	*d*
In primis wee prise all his Apparrell		*xx*	
It one bed, bedsted; & furniture		*xl*	
It one Chest, & 3 Coffers		*xviij*	
It 3 Costs, 2 plancks, a forme, & Cheese vatts		*vj*	
It one Cubbord		*x*	
It 4:Candelsticks, & one Chaffer		*viij*	
It pewter vessel, & 2 salts		*xvj*	
It 2 Crokes, & one possionet of brasse wth one branyron, & Crocks		*xxj*	
It 4 pannes; & 2 Cawdrens of brasse, And one Litle Skillett		*xxx*	
It Corne in grownd	*x*	*xiij*	*iiij*
It Corne in the barne		*xxxv*	
It earthen vessell			*xij*
It one fryinge pan & A grediron			*viij*
It one table borde, 2 bord Clothes, 2 formes; 2 Cheares wth bords, stolls, & shelfes in the hall		*xiij*	*iiij*
It 2 bedsteds, one bed & furniture, And all othere Implements in the Chamber over the hall		*v*	
It one spynninge torne & Cards			*xij*
It one halfe parte of A muskett furnished		*xiij*	*iiij*
It one Chesewringe, one trendle, tubbs, & other wooden vessel		*xiij*	*iiij*
It 4 baggs		*iij*	*iiij*
It one mattocke & showell			*x*
It one peare of Harrowes, one peare of Corne Crocks, dunck potts, & one peare of panniers		*viij*	
It one Ladder, & redd sheves		*ij*	*viij*
It one pigg		*vj*	*viij*
It Dunge		*vj*	*viij*
It Peter Furson, alîs Furshay, oweth		*xx*	
It one Cock, henes, & Cheekens			*xviij*
It wood & all other thinges not prised		*xx*	

Soma totalis *xxvj*^{li} *xiiij*^{s} *viij*^{d}

[Exhibited 12 Sep 1627: no other information in Latin endorsement.

Will of Symon Sheild dated 2 Apr 1627, pr 12 Sep 1627: residue to Mary Sheild, widow & exec; £4 to sister's dr Thomasine; £4 to John Alwaie (Holway?) the s of yeoman Alwaie; marked + by Symon Sheild; witn: marks of Bo(?)lwynt Sheild, Petter Flue, & Wm Hodge.]

75 ROBERT & CATEREN RIDGE [=RUDGE] 1627 (PU)

[Bur: "Robert Rudge" 7 Jan 1626/7, "Katherine Rudge, widow" 17 Jan 1626/7. Mar: "Robart Rudge & (blank) Husseye" 23 Nov 1608; but see LW73. Evidently a tragedy: Robert & Katherine died in quick succession through accident or illness and their chn, John & Beaten Rudge, were left orphans, as the admon shows. Apart from the £8 chattel lease, household items only to value £4.]

A Inventarie made the xiij daie of September in the Third yeare of the Raine of o^r^ Soveraine Lord Charles by the grace of god King of England Scotland France and Iearland defender of the Faith according to the Computation of the Cathedrale Churche of England of all the goods and Chattels of the saide Robert Ridge and Cateren Ridge his wyfe latly decessed within the pishe of Ufcullme praysed by John Hurley Edmund Bishop and James Callowe and Nicholas Ridge

	lî	*s*	*d*
Im primis wee doe praise			

	lî	s	d
one Chattell lease in	viij		
Item wee doe praise tow bedstedes with the furneture ther unto belonging in		xx	
Item wee doe praise three Coffers Three tubes one littell boule and a Trendell		vj	viij
Item wee doe praise one sideborde Tow plankes one forme		vj	vj
Item wee doe praise tow brasen Crockes one littell stele panne one little Catheren		xij	
Item wee doe praise ix puter disshes one sacer one Tennen boule one salte		viij	
Item we doe praise all her apparrell in		xxx	
Item all other Implements [erasures] belonging to the house wee doe praise in		v	
Suma tot. xij^{li} $viij^{s}$ ij^{d}			

[Admon, 13 Sep 1627, states that Robert & Katherine Rudge died intestate and binds Edmund Bishop, John Hurley, & James Callowe to administer their affairs and to present an account of their administration when the chn, John & Beaten Rudge, come of age. Sworn before Francis Roberts, notary public.]

76 HUMFRY LUTLEY 1628, the elder & the younger (DS)

[Bur: "Humfrey Lutley" 30 Mar 1628. Inventory for the elder: Few cattle, 15 sheep, 2 pigs; plough & spinning gear; £27.]

An Inventory of the goods and Chattles of Humfry Lutley deceased taken and praysed the xxviijth of March 1628 by Denis Lutley, John Osmonde and John Lampey as Followeth.

	lî	s	d
Imprs his weareinge apparell	xxviij		
It three kine	viij	oo	
It one horse	j	oo	
It one colte, and a calfe	j	oo	
It Fifteene sheepe	iij	xv	
It 2 piges	oo	xij	
It Corne in the barne	j	oo	
It 3 flitches of bacon	j	x	
It 3 crockes & one posnet	j	oo	
It brasse pañes	oo	xij	oo
It pewter	oo	viij	oo
It a cubboard one borde and a Forme	oo	x	oo
It 2 turnes	oo	ij	oo
It horse tacklinge	oo	v	oo
It timber vessels	oo	xiij	iiij
It one Ringe a silver spoone a silver piñ and a payre of taches	oo	v	oo
It 2 beds pformed	j	x	oo
It other apparell	j	x	oo
It Coffers	oo	viij	oo
It wooll	oo	viij	oo
It malt	oo	vj	iiij
It a payre of waights and a skaimer	oo	oo	vj
It a gridyrõ and a brandize	oo	j	oo
It one broach and a bell[?]	oo	j	oo
It 2 ladders	oo	j	oo
It dunge	oo	iij	oo
It a sowle and culter	oo	ij	oo
It one while barrowe	oo	ij	oo
It bords and plancks	oo	iij	oo
It Corne in ground	j	oo	oo
It other trash	oo	v	oo
Suma tot $xxviij^{li}$ iij^{s} ij^{d} [2s too much?]			

[Exhibited at Salisbury 16 Apr 1628.

Admon 16 Apr 1628 names Nicholas Lutley, farmer (agric) as admin of the goods &c of both "Humfry Lutley his father & Humfry Lutley his bro late of Uffculme deceased", & also mentions John Lutley, farmer of Sampford Peverell; Nicholas Lutley signs & John makes a mark in the presence of Richard Page, not^{y} pub. The inventory is that for Humfry the elder.]

77 THOMAS CROSSE 1628 (DS)

[Bur: "Thomas Crosse" 3 Apr 1628. Mar: "Thomas Crosse & Elizabeth Pearce wid." 27 Sep 1613. Household items only, apart from £12 in debts owed to him; total £ 15.]

An Inventory of the goods of Thomas Crosse deceased take~ and praysed the xijth of Aprill 1628 by John Stephens & Willm Pearcse

	lî	*s*	*d*
Imprs his weareing apparell		*xx*	*o*
It his bedinge		*xx*	*o*
It 3 Coffers		*iiij*	*o*
It one bedsteed		*iij*	*iiij*
It 2 barels		*ij*	*oo*
It tubes		*j*	*vj*
It pewter		*j*	*o*
It 2 brasse pans		*x*	*o*
It 2 brasse Crockes		*x*	*o*
It one showle		*ij*	*o*
It one payre of pot hangings wth other implem^{ts}		*iij*	*o*
It money due unto him upon bond	*iiij*	*oo*	*oo*
It more, being desperate debt	*viij*	*oo*	*oo*
Sum tot *xv^{li} xvj^{s} x^{d}*			

[Exhibited at Salisbury 10 May 1628.

Nuncupative will 2 Apr 1628 of Thomas Crosse of Uffculme: residue to wife Elizabeth exec; 12d each to chn of bro Robert Crosse; 5s to k Mary Crosse; 10s to John Pearse; 55s to Willm Pearse the younger; sworn to by exec 16 Apr 1628.]

78 THOMAS HURLEY 1628 (DS)

[Bur: "Thomas Hurley" 8 May 1628. Fuller (cf. 68) with 5 pigs & cloth-handling gear; fowling piece & 2 bows & arrows; £28.]

An Inventory of the goods of Thomas Hurley of the pish of Ufculme in the County of Devon Fuller deceased taken and praysed the xxjth daye of Maye in the yeare of our lord God 1628. By Humfry Steare Clearke, Thomas Hurley, John Trickey and Jo: Welland o~-

	lî	*s*	*d*
Imprs his weareinge Appell	*iij*	*oo*	*oo*
It twoe standinge beds and one truckle bed; wth the beddinge unto them belonginge	*iij*	*oo*	*oo*
It pewter dishes	*ij*	*iiij*	*oo*
It stoneinge iugs	*oo*	*ij*	*vj*
It brassen vessells	*ij*	*oo*	*oo*
It one table bord, twoe Carpetts twoe bord Clothes, sixe ioyne stooles, and one forme	*j*	*xiiij*	*oo*
It one truncke, coffers, and one deske	*oo*	*x*	*oo*
It other bords and formes	*j*	*oo*	*oo*
It one Cubbord	*j*	*oo*	*oo*
It one mustard mill	*oo*	*j*	*oo*
It one seeleinge	*oo*	*xiij*	*iiij*
It one glasse boxe	*oo*	*oo*	*viij*
It one fowleinge peece	*oo*	*xiij*	*iiij*
It one Citherne	*oo*	*iij*	*iiij*
It one bible	*oo*	*v*	*oo*
It twoe bowes and a quiver of arrowes	*oo*	*vj*	*viij*
It one layer nett	*oo*	*x*	*oo*
It timber vissels	*oo*	*xviij*	*oo*
It one showle wth other tooles		*vj*	*viij*
It Five payre of sheeres	*ij*	*oo*	*oo*
It twoe skranes, sheere bords, cottninge bords and other timber a payre of brushes and handles[haulles?]	*j*	*oo*	*oo*
It Five pigs	*ij*	*x*	*oo*
It one longe Racke standinge in the upper end	*j*	*x*	*oo*
It one mare	*j*	*oo*	*oo*
It the pale standinge before the westside of the house	*j*	*oo*	*oo*
It one grindinge stone	*oo*	*j*	*vj*
It one sword and hanginge	*oo*	*x*	*oo*
It one gridyron wth other implem^{ts} wth glasse in the shop windowe, and in the chamber over the entry	*oo*	*vj*	*viij*

xxviij^{li} vj^{s} iiij^{d} [4d short?]

Itm a mill wheele and a shafte *vj^{s} viij^{d}*

[Exhibited at Uffculme at the triennial visitation of the Dean of Salisbury 9 Jul 1628.

Admon 9 Jul 1628 names Elizabeth as widow & admin, & also Edward Andro; marked by her & signed by him in the presence of James Hill, not^{y} pub.]

79 JOANE CHEEKE 1628 (DS)

[Bur: "Johan Cheeke" 26 Sep 1627. Spinster with a silver spoon; total, including £4 owed to her, £7.]

An Inventary of all and singular the goods cattles, and debts of Joane Cheeke of Uffculme spinster deceased taken and apprized the ninth day of July 1628 By those whose names are subscribed. /

	s	d
Inprimis her weareing appell	*xl*	
Item one bed furnished	*xx*	
Itme two sheepe	*x*	
Item one silver spoone	*iiij*	
Item one Coffer	*j*	*vj*
Item one pewtr dish		*vj*
Item due unto the deceased from one Richard Pring a Butcher	*xl*	
Item due more from Joane Cadbury widdowe wch is since receaved	*xl*	
Sma *vij*^{li} *xvj*^{s}		

Praisers/ Henry Gill/ Atwell Wheadon/ Edward Andro/ Wm Starke.

[Exhibited at Uffculme at the triennial visitation of the Dean of Salisbury 9 Jul 1628.

Nuncupative will Oct 1627 of Joane Cheeke, spinster of Uffculme: residue to sister Mary Merson, wife of Simon Merson; a silver spoon to Margeret Facy; a sheep to ... Greene. Admon 9 Jul 1628 names Mary Merson, wife of Simon Merson of Uffculme, fuller, as sister & admin, & also George Osmond of Culmstock, husbandman; signed by Simon Merson & marked by Geo: Osmond in presence of James Hill, not^{y} pub.]

80 JOHN NORTON 1628 (PU)

[Bur: "John Norton" 1 Aug 1628. Mar: "John Norton & Dorothy London" 17 Jan 1599/60. Brewer(?): room over kitchen mentioned in will; brewhouse & furnace, vats, measures, hogsheads, & barrells; 1 sow; total, including £10 lease, £32.]

An Inventory of the goods and Chattles of John Norton of the pish of Ufculme deceased: taken and praysed the First daye of Septe^{r}: Anno dm 1628: By Humfry Steare Clearke: Barth: Rawlins and Christopher Palfry as Followeth:

	lî	s	d
Imp^{r}s his weareinge appell	*ij*	*oo*	
It bedsteeds and beds pformd	*vij*	*oo*	
It one table bord standinge in the Chamber, wth formes there		*x*	
It one Chest, and three coffers		*xiij*	*iiij*
It one table bord wth benches and formes standinge in the sumer house		*x*	*oo*
It one table bord one cubbord standinge in the hall; with formes stooles and Chayre		*xiij*	*iiij*
It three Fates, three trendelles, one Cowle[bowle?], twoe buckets, twoe tubes and a Jeb wth other small impleme[n]ts in the brewehouse		*xx*	
It Fowre hogsheads one barrell wth other timber stuffe in the buttery		*xx*	
It three brasse Crockes one Caldrõ, three skillets one fryinge pañ, one gurse pañ one gridyrõ wth potthangings, and pothooks wth andyrons	*ij*	*oo*	
It one brewinge Furnace	*ij*		
It three malt sackes, and twoe little bagges		*iiij*	*oo*
It twelve pewter dishes eight sawcers, three salts, one chamber pott, one houpes[?] quart, one halfe pynte twoe Candlestickes		*xxv*	
It table cloathes, and table napkins		*x*	
It wood, and Furze		*xxx*	
It one varinge [farrowing?] sowe		*xx*	
It one Chattle lease for her [sic] life in the house	*x*	*oo*	

	lî	s	d
It other implem^{ts} not seene nor praysed		*v*	*oo*
Suma total~ *xxxij^{li} oo viij^{d}*			

Hu~: Steare: Barth: Rawlins: Chrisr: Palfry

[Exhibited 29 May 1629.

Will 18 Jul 1628, pr at Uffculme 29 May 1629 before Mr Humfrey Steare, surrogate &c: residue to wife Dorothy, exec; to dr Dorothy the house "& backside" after the death of her mother, a bed "standinge by the windowe in the chamber ovr the kitchen", coffer, crock, & 3 pewter dishes; to dr Joan £5 after death of her mother, crock, & 2 pewter dishes; 1s each to little Humfry Steare, Elizabeth Steare, & the church.]

81 EDMUND COLE 1628 (DS)

[Bur: "Edmund Coale" 5 Oct 1628. Shopkeeper with hall & chamber over shop; woollen cloth, linen, haberdashery, candles, soap, tobacco, sugar, currants, & raisins; 1 horse; total, including £20 chattel lease, £61.]

An Inventory of the goods and chattles of Edmund Cole of the pish of Ufculme deceased: taken and praysed the xvijth daye of October Anno dm^{i} 1628: By Humfry Steare Clearke: Edward Androwe: Thomas Hurley: and Tho: Batteñ as Followeth: -

	lî	s	d
Imp^{r}s his wearinge apparell	*ij*	*oo*	*oo*
It one standinge bed, and one truckle bed wth their furniture	*ij*	*oo*	*oo*
It one table bord in the chamber ov^{r} the shoppe, wth twoe formes	*oo*	*x*	*oo*
It twoe Coffers	*oo*	*v*	*oo*
It wood		*jx*	*oo*
It Haye		*iij*	*iiij*
It one table board standinge in the hall wth bench, and formes		*vj*	*viij*
It pewter dishes		*jx*	*iiij*
It brasse Crockes, and caldrons	*j*	*vj*	*oo*
It timber, and timber vessels	*j*	*vj*	*oo*
It one Fry inge pañ, potthooks and one broach		*ij*	*vj*
It woollen cloath in the shoppe	*v*	*j*	*oo*
It stockings	*ij*	*iij*	*oo*
It Sarge wth other such like stuffes	*v*	*v*	*ij*
It Lineñ cloath, and stuffe	*vj*	*xvj*	*vij*
It Tobacco	*oo*	*ij*	*oo*
It Candles and sope	*oo*	*xij*	*oo*
It other things as Reasons, Curents sugar girdles, poynts, piñs &c	*v*	*oo*	*viij*
It one horse	*j*	*oo*	*oo*
It one Chattle lease	*xx*	*oo*	*oo*
It money lyinge by him	*iiij*	*xiiij*	*oo*
Suma totals *lxj^{li} xvij^{s} iij^{d}*			

[£2 5s too much?]

82 PHILLIP PARSONS 1628 (PU)

[Bur: "Phillippe Parsons" 6 Oct 1628. Mar: "Phillipe Parsons & Helen Foweracre" 5 Nov 1600. Weaver (retired?); looms, poultry & 2 pigs; £7.]

A True inventori of the goodes of Phillip Parsons taken &[ ] by William Dunne and Adrian Ashellford in the yeare of our lord 1628

	s	d
in primis 2 piges ["sixteen shillings" crossed out]	*x6*	
one vine[-?] of woode	*x*	
one hen and chicken	*j*	
2 beads blanckets and Couerlets	*xxj*	
his waringe apparrell	xxxiij	vj
five[face?] towells	*j*	*viij*
his trining[tinning?] toolles	*j*	
4 Croockes one posnet and a scillet	*viij*	
2 katherins	*vj*	
one frying pan one brandis 2 payre of pot hangers	2	
the Pewter dishes	4	
4 littell tubes one hogside 2 littell barrells	12	
3 chayres	1	
3 slleaces	3	
one shuttell	1	

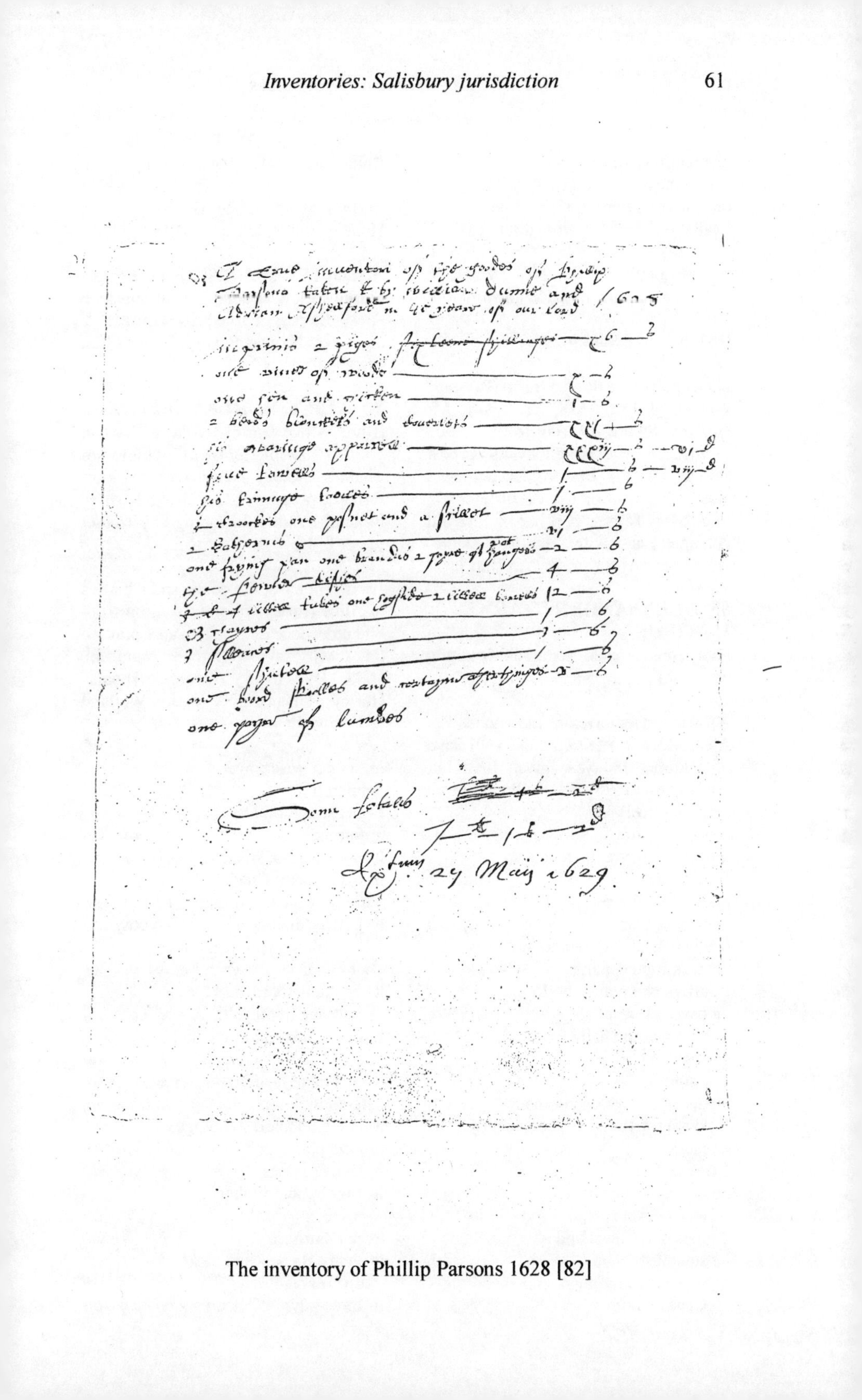

The inventory of Phillip Parsons 1628 [82]

	s	d
one boord stoolles[?] and certayne other thinges	v	
one payre of lumbes [looms: no value on copy, but from total 15]		

Som totalis 7li 1s 2d [Arabic & Roman numerals mixed as shown.]

[Exhibited 27 May 1629.

Nuncupative will of Phillip Parsons, weaver, 4 Oct 1628, pr before Mr Humfrey Steare, 27 May 1629: residue to wife Ellen, exec; all looms & best suit to s Henry Parsons; second best suit to 2 drs; to dr Dina a little crock; to dr Mary "a posnet if her mother did not spend it"; witn: Humfrey Steare, vicar, Thomas Baker, & Wm Dun.]

83 ALEXSANDER STARKE 1628 (PU)

[Household items, some clothmaking gear; £7.]

A true inventori of the goods of Alexsander Starke taken the xviij daye of ocktober [no year given here but presumably 1628] by William Starke and Thomas Baker

	s	d
Inprimis 3 payre of shares and leades	xxxij	
one Cubberd 4 pewter dishes and 3 saysers	xxij	viij
one bedstead and beddinge	xx	
his wearinge apparrell	xx	
2 caffers one planck and a payre of tresells	iiij	viij
one bord in the halle	iiij	
one brasse Crocke and a katherin	vj	
2 payr of hanger one brandis wth other trifells	ij	8
on ladder	i	vj
2 turnes	2	
one press 4 barrells and 2 buckets	xx	
2 tubes one Cowle and a standard	vj	viij
on plancke one Chayre and a Cheese fatte	j	

Som totalis 7li 3s 2d [Arabic & Roman numerals mixed as shown.]

[Exhibited at Uffculme before Mr. Humfry Steare 27 May 1629.

Admon 27 May 1629 names Bridget Starke widow & admin of the intestate Alex. Starke; marked by Bridget & signed by Thomas Baker in presence of Francis Roberts.]

84 ALICE HURLEY 1628 (DS)

[Bur: "Allice Hurley, widowe" 26 Oct 1628. Comfortably-off widow of Thomas No.68; house with parlour, furnace, presses, shears, 1 pig & share in another; total, including £50 chattel lease, £74.]

An Inventory of the goods and Chattles of Alice Hurley widowe, of the pish of Ufculme deceased: taken and praysed the xxvijth daye of October Anno dmi 1628. By Humfry Steare Thomas Hurley of Banscumbe & Jo: Welland as Followeth -

	lî	s	d
Imprs her weareinge apparell	iij	oo	oo
It- bedsteeds and beds pformed	v	iiij	oo
It- one payre of silver taches	oo	ij	oo
It- Five brasse Crockes 2 pans one caldron & a skillett	iij	xv	oo
It- pewter dishes		xvij	oo
It- one frieing pan, pothookes pot hangi~gs and gridyron	oo	v	vj
It- one table bord, and forme standinge in the hall	oo	xiij	iiij
It- one Cubboard in the hall one settle and a chayre	j	v	oo
It- one table board, and forme standinge in the p[ar]lor	oo	vj	viij
It- one Cubboard standinge in the p[ar]lour	oo	viij	oo
It- three presses	j	xiij	iiij
It- timber, and timber vessels	j	x	oo
It- one Furnace	j	vj	viij
It- Foure Rackes and racke tarrowes	ij	iij	iiij
It- three payre of sheeres	oo	xij	oo

	lî	*s*	*d*
It- one pig and p[ar]te in another	*j*	*oo*	*oo*
It- one ladder wth other old implem^ts^	*oo*	*v*	*oo*
It- one chattle lease of one dwellinge house in Ufculme aforesayd, one garden one acre of ground or thereabouts, and one fullinge mill for the terme of Certaine yeares determinable upon three lives	*l*	*oo*	*oo*

Sum totalš 74^li^ 6^s^ 10^d^

[Exhibited at Salisbury by the exec 9 Dec 1628 before Mr. Thornbury.

Will 6 Jul 1628 of Allice Hurley of Uffculme, widow, pr at Salisbury 9 Dec 1628: residue to s-in-law Edward Marshall, exec; £20, £10, £5, & £5 to ks Willm, Edward, & Bartholomewe Hurley, & Bartholomewe Williams, respectively; £5 to dr Elizabeth Cole & 20s each to her 4 chn; 20s each to kinsfolk Anne Marshall, Jo: Marshall, & Thomas & Mary Williams, & to Rebekah & Richard Marshall, chn of dr Tacy Marshall, & to Jo: & Jane, chn of dr Jane Welland; 6s 8d each to James Welland, & to drs Jane & Tacy, & to dr-in-law Elizabeth Hurley; 12d each to godchn; 10s each to ks Henry Welland & Richard Marshall; specified articles of clothing, bedding, furniture, &c to the named drs & ks; s-in-law John (?) Welland also mentioned; marked by Allice Hurley in the presence of Hum: Steare, cleric, & Thomas Hurley, who both sign.]

85 JOHN CHAMPNEYS 1629 (DS)

[Bur: "John Champneyes" 27 Sep 1629. Described as "gent", but only household items, apart from books, oats, & 4 fowls; £15.]

An Inventorie of the goods and Chattles of Jo: Champneys gent of the pish of Ufculme deceased taken and praysed the xvj^th^ daye of November 1629 : By Hu~: Steare Jo: Woodroffe and Barth: Rawlins as followeth &c

	lî	*s*	*d*
Imprs his weareinge appell	*ij*	*x*	*oo*
It bedsteeds, wth beds and the cloathes thereunto belonginge	*iiij*	*x*	*oo*
It one bord, and stooles in the chamber ov^r^ the p[ar]lour	*oo*	*v*	*oo*
It one presse, twoe trunks, one chest and a little bord	*j*	*v*	
It books	*oo*	3	*iiij*
It one table bord wth the benches, and seilinge standinge in the p[ar]lour	*ij*	*oo*	*oo*
It one carpet, and Foure chuses[?]	*oo*	*ij*	*oo*
It bord cloathes and napkins	*oo*	*iij*	*iiij*
It one table board twoe formes, seilinge and bench in the hall ioyne stooles and one chayre	*j*	*x*	*oo*
It brasse and pewter	*j*	*x*	*oo*
It one spitt, turninge yrons, and one brandize	*oo*	*iij*	*iiij*
It twoe old trendles, twoe tubbes wth other old timber stuffe in the kitchin	*oo*	*vj*	*viij*
It barrels	*oo*	*iij*	*iiij*
It twoe cocks and twoe hens	*oo*	*j*	*iiij*
It one gridyron and pot hangings	*oo*	*j*	*viij*
It oats, and oat malt	*oo*	*x*	*oo*
It haye	*oo*	*j*	*oo*
It wood and Furse	*oo*	*iij*	*iiij*
It all implem^ts^ not seen nor prased	*oo*	*ij*	*vj*
	15	11	10

Hum: Steare & Bartho Rawling [sign]
Jo: Woodroffe [marks]

86 JOHN SANDER 1629 (PU)

[Bur: "John Sander" 23 Oct 1629. Mar: "John Saunder & Jone Aplyne" 11 Oct 1596; see 92. Yeoman with corn, 1 pig, 1 hen; total, including £15 debts owed to him, £35.]

An Inventorie of the goods and Chattles of John Sander of the pish of Ufculme deceased: taken and praysed the xvj^th^ daye of November 1629: By

Hum: Steare John Woodroffe and Barth: Rawlins as Followeth &c:

	lî	s	d
Imp^rs his weareinge appell	iij	oo	oo
It twoe bedsteeds pformed	iiij	oó	oo
It timber stuffe in the twoe chambers	j	oo	oo
It one table board, one chest, one forme, one chayre, and a stoolle	ij	oo	oo
It brass Crocks, a brass pan, a caldron wth other brasse things	j	xj	vj
It one broach [spit]	oo	ij	oo
It pte in one brasse pan	j	iij	iiij
It pewter dishes, wth a salt and candlesticks	oo	x	oo
It pte in one side saddle	oo	iiij	oo
It twoe chushens	oo	j	vj
It one board cloath and Five napkins		vij	oo
It one hogside wth twoe hanginge bords	oo	iiij	oo
It twoe corne piks and one lunge pike	oo	j	iiij
It meate in salte	j	x	oo
It one pig, and one henne	oo	x	oo
It corne in the barne	ij	xiij	iiij
It Corne thresht and malte	oo	vij	oo
It due upon specialty beinge good debts	vj	oo	oo
It one bond beinge desperate debt	jx	9[!]	oo
It other small implem^ts not seene, nor praysed		ij	iiij
It wood	oo	xiij	iiij

Som 35^li 10^s 8^d

Hum: Steare & Bartho Rawlins [sign]
John Woodroffe [marks]

[On 4 May 1630 Joan Sander, named as John Sander's widow, swore on oath that a certain schedule contained John's last will & testament and that she would administer it. At the same time a similar undertaking was made by Edward Clarke with repect to a will of Robert Welch (No. 83).

Will 22 Feb 1627(/8) of John Sander, yeoman of Uffculme, pr 17 Nov 1630: residue to wife Joan, exec; 4d each to 20 poor of the parish & to all godchn; best brass pan to grandch John Londewell, s of William Londewell; brass crock to grandch Alce Herman, dr of Thomas Herman; 12d each to rulers (ovsrs) John Woodruffe & Bartholomewe Rawlins, yeomen of Uffculme, who also witness the will; marked "JS" by John Sander. A further admon, dated 31 May 1639, enables Mary Sander alias Jarman, dr of decd yeoman John Sander to complete the administration of her father's will, left uncompleted by Joan, her mother: signed in the presence of Hum: Steare by Thomas Jarman & Amb: Cottrell (C mark) & Michael Greene (MG mark).

There was another John Sander(s), described as a weaver, for whom there is no inventory. He was presumably the one buried 17 Oct 1628 since his nuncupative will ("wife to have all") was made before John Ballyman "sometime" in October 1628 and was pr on 27 May 1629, i.e. 5 months before 23 Oct 1629.]

87 DOROTHY NORTON 1630 (DS)

[Bur: "Dorothy Norton, widowe" 7 Jul 1630. Widow of John No. 75; some pigs; mostly domestic items; 2/3 room house, summer house; brewing, table cloth & napkins; £20.]

An Inventorie of the goods and Chattles of Dorothy Norton widowe taken and praysed the xix^th day of July 1630 By Hum: Steare Dañ: Berryma~ and Edward Marshall as Followeth &c

	lî	s	d
Imp^rs her weareing appell	ij	x	oo
It bedsteeds and beds pformed		v	oo
It one table bord standinge in the chamber ov^r the hall & twoe formes	oo	x	oo
It one chest & twoe coffers		vj	viij
It one table bord wth benches and formes in the sumer house		x	oo
It one table bord, one cupbord in the hall wth formes			

	lî	*s*	*d*
stoules and a chayre	*oo*	*xiij*	*iiij*
It trendels, buckets wth other implem^{ts} in the brewhouse		*xiij*	*iiij*
It 3 hogseads, one barrell wth other timber stuffe in the buttery	*oo*	*xvj*	*oo*
It 2 brasse crockes one caldrõ, one fryinge pan, one dripping pan, pothangings, pothookes, and yron dogs	*j*	*vj*	*viij*
It one brewinge Furnace	*j*	*xiij*	*iiij*
It malt sackes	*oo*	*iij*	*iiij*
It pewter	*j*	*oo*	*oo*
It table cloathes and table napkins	*oo*	*x*	*oo*
It wood and furse	*j*	*xviij*	*iiij*
It sowe, and pigs	*j*	*xv*	*oo*
It the other small things not seen nor praysed		*v*	*oo*

Smã 19^{li} 13^{s} 4^{d} [2s 4d too much?]

[Exhibited at Uffculme at the triennial visitation of the Dean of Salisbury 23 Jun 1631. Latin inscription signed by Jo: Johnson Reg^{r}.

Will 18 Jan 1629/30 of Dorothy Norton of Uffculme, widow: residue to dr Dorothy Lutley, exec; 12d to church; 6s 8d to the poor; 10s & bedding at stairhead to mother; 20s each to Elizabeth & Humfry Steare; 5s to bro John London; 12d each to sister Margery's chn & to cousin Anne London & her bro; 2s 6d to Allice Rawlins; 12d to godson; ovsrs Humfry Steare, clerk, & Tho: Hurley; marked by Dorothy Norton & witn by Hum: Steare.]

88 ROBERT WELSH 1630 (PU)

[Bur: "Robert Welch" 20 Dec 1629. Yeoman with stock & corn; top of inventory missing but total £26.]

	lî	*s*	*d*
Itm won heffer [illegible	*ij*		?]
Itm won stear earling ["	*j*		?]
Itm won hogge ["		*x*	?]
Itm won other hogge ["		*x*	?]
Itm for Corne thrisht and wonthrisht ["	*j*	*xv*	?]
Itm his haye	*ij*	*iij*	*iiij*
Itm all his peater		*x*	*ij*
Itm won bras poot		*vij*	*vj*
Itm won scillet on Candilstick		*j*	*iiij*
Itm won poothings on brandis on gridirn		*iij*	*vj*
Itm won bilhock			*iiij*
Itm won tabell bord		*xviij*	
Itm won forme		*j*	*iiij*
Itm won Chest		*vij*	
Itm too barrils too tubs		*iiij*	
Itm won trendell wth other empelments		*viij*	
Itm too flichhes of baken	*j*		
Itm won milking payle on beam on bigge[?]		*ij*	
Itm won bedstead wth his beding		*xiiij*	
Itm won scheare			*vj*
Itm won pick			*iij*
Itm won plinck		*j*	*vj*
Itm won draftror[?], wth other things		*iij*	
Itm three Cheeses		*j*	*vj*
Itm the doung and too pigstroos		*iiij*	*vj*
Itm won sarg on ringe on seasie[?]			*jx*
Itm other things not praysed		*j*	*vj*

Som 26^{li} 1^{s} 0^{d}

praised by Robert Maiger and Thomas Heller

[Exhibited 12 Nov 1630. On 4 May 1630 Edward Clarke swore on oath that a certain schedule contained the last will & testament of Robert Welch and that he would administer it. A similar undertaking was made at the same time by Joan Sander in respect of the will of her husband John (No. 86).

Will 3 Apr 1621 of Robert Welch, yeoman, pr 12 Nov 1630: residue to s-in-law Edward Clarke, exec; to s George Welche "my Cubett board"; to s Arture Welche 3s 4d & to each of his chn 3s 4d; to s Humfry Welche apparel, £6 owed by s George & £15, or the "moitye or halfendett" of all goods & chattels, & £1 to each of his chn; £2 to each of Edward Clarke's chn at age 21, amounting to £8 owed by s George; £2 to dr Anne; 4d to goddr Johaine Lange; 12d to church; Mathew Cadbery & s George Welche ovsrs;

John Beare & Mathew Cadberye witn; Robert Welche marked.]

89 ROBERT READ 1631 (DS)

[Bur: "Robert Read" 3 Mar 1630/1. Corn, 3 cattle, 1 nag, 2 pigs, & 6 fowls; no spinning gear; £38.]

[Top missing....] of Robert Read of the pish of Ufculme deceased taken & praysed the jxth day of March Anno dm 1630[/1] by Robert Bishoppe and Richard Woodroffe as Followeth &c:

	lî	*s*	*d*
Imp^{r}s his weareinge apparell	*ij*	*x*	*oo*
It twoe bedsteeds, and beds pformed	*ij*	*x*	*oo*
It one Chest standinge in the hall and one forme	*oo*	*x*	*oo*
It twoe brasse pañs, & one caldron	*oo*	*xvj*	*oo*
It twoe brasse crockes and pott hookes & hangings	*oo*	*xvj*	*oo*
It Three coffers	*oo*	*x*	*oo*
It Three tubs & one Trendleoo		*x*	*oo*
It Twoe bords and one chayre		*ij*	*oo*
It workeinge Tooles	*oo*	*vj*	*viij*
It one gridyron brandizes and other yron stuffe	*oo*	*ij*	*vj*
It Twoe packe saddles twoe ges[?]es, and one payre of Crookes	*oo*	*vij*	*oo*
It pewter deshes	*oo*	*v*	*oo*
It Three flitches of bacoñ	*j*	*vj*	*viij*
It cheeces	*oo*	*vj*	*oo*
It Corne in barne	*x*	*oo*	*oo*
It Corne in ground	*v*	*oo*	*oo*
It haye	*j*	*vj*	*viij*
It wood	*oo*	*x*	*oo*
It Three kine	*viij*	*oo*	*oo*
It one nagge	*ij*	*oo*	*oo*
It one cocke Five hens		*v*	*oo*
It Twoe pigs	*oo*	*x*	*oo*
It other things not seene nor praysed		*ij*	*vj*
Sum tot	38^{li}	12^{s}	0

[marks of] Robert Bishoppe & Richard Woodroffe

["Jurat" is the only Latin endorsement. Nuncupative will 24 Feb 1630/1 of Robert Read of Uffculme, pr at Uffculme 23 Jun 1632: residue to wife, exec; £3 to John Read, s of bro Willm, or if he should die before age 21 to his bro & sister Hugh & Mary Read (with interest accrued); marked by witn Robert Bishoppe & Richard Woodroffe.]

90 JOHN CORAM 1631 (DS)

[Bur: "John Coram" 7 May 1631. Mar: "John Coram & Joane Burman" 12 Feb 1615; but see LW109. Husbandman with corn & clothmaking gear; £11.]

An Inventory of all and singuler the goods & Cattels of John Coram Late of Uffculme in the County of Devone, husbandman decessed prised by Robert Bysshopp, John Beare & peter peperell the six & twenty day of May in the yere of o^{r} Lord god one thousand six hundred thirty one as Followeth.

	lî	*s*	*d*
Inprimis wee prise all his Apparrell		*xx*	
It his bed, bedsted, & furniture		*xxvj*	*viij*
It seven pewter disses & one Sauser		*jx*	
It one Litle pan of brasse		*vij*	
It one old Coffer			*xij*
It three tubbs, & one milkinge payle		*vj*	
It two Lytles barrels		*ij*	*vj*
It one hand picke			*vj*
It one Welch hocke, & one old sawe			*xij*
It one Iron Crucke, Cotterels, & brandirons		*iij*	
It two spinnynge tornes, & one peare of Cards		*iij*	
It Baken		*v*	
It Hay and hay Crucks		*iij*	
It wood		*ij*	
It wooll		*vij*	
It one peare of pannyers			*xx*
It Corne in grownd	*vj*		
It dunge, & worth		*v*	
It two puntery [poultry?]			*viij*
It two formes, one stole, two Ladders and all other things not presed		*v*	

Sma *xj*[li] *jx*[s]

[Exhibited at Uffculme before the Ven[l] Edmund Mason, Dean of Salisbury, by Joan(na) Coram, exec, 23 Jun 1631. Latin endorsement signed by Jo: Johnson Reg[r].

Will 5 May 1631 of John Coram of Uffculme, pr at Uffculme before Ven. Edward Mason 23 Jun 1631: residue to wife Joan Coram, exec; 3s 4d to poor; 40s to dr Joan Coram; marked by Jo: Coram & witn by Hum: Steare & Thomas Baker, who both sign.]

91 JOHN RAWLINS the elder 1631 (DS)

[Bur: "John Rawlins, thelder" 18 Jul 1631. Mar: "John Rawlings & Grace Bidgood" 26 Oct 1601. Prosperous yeoman; house with chamber over hall & bakehouse; corn (£15), sheep, 3 cattle, 3 pigs, 1 mare; no clothmaking gear; musket; £86.]

An Inventorie of the goods of John Rawliñs thelder of the pish of Uffculme: taken and praysed the xxij[th] day of July 1631 - By Humfry Butston, John Balliman, John Leyman, and George Fursdon as Followeth -

	lî	*s*	*d*
Imp[s] his weareinge apparell	*v*	*oo*	*oo*
It Three bedsteeds, and Featherbeds pformed	*xv*	*oo*	*oo*
It one flocke bed, and one dust-bed and twoe bedsteeds	*j*	*xiij*	*iiij*
It one carpett, Four tablecloaths and Five table napkins	*j*	*oo*	*oo*
It one trunke, twoe chests and one coffer in the chamber ov[r] the hall	*j*	*v*	*oo*
It one bord in the chamber ov[r] the hall, one forme, three ioynt stooles, and one chayre	*oo*	*x*	*oo*
It wooll	*ij*	*oo*	*oo*
It one cuppbord and amery standinge in the hall	*j*	*xiij*	*iiij*
It pewter, w[t] tindinge salts	*j*	*xiij*	*iiij*
It Foure brasse candlestickes	*oo*	*iij*	*oo*
It brasse pañs, and twoe caldrons	*iij*	*oo*	*oo*
It Foure brasse crockes	*j*	*oo*	*oo*
It yron implements	*oo*	*xiij*	*iiij*
It one Furnace	*iij*	*oo*	*oo*
It one table bord in the hall & one forme	*j*	*oo*	*oo*
It silv[r] spoones	*j*	*vj*	*viij*
It one muskett pformd	*j*	*vj*	*viij*
It bacoñ	*oo*	*xv*	*oo*
It butter, and cheese	*j*	*oo*	*oo*
It tubs, and barrells, and other timber stuffe	*ij*	*vj*	*viij*
It one payre of harrowes	*oo*	*viij*	*oo*
It one wheele barrowe	*oo*	*ij*	*oo*
It one bord in ye bake house and one coffer there	*oo*	*iiij*	*oo*
It wood	*j*	*viij*	*oo*
It hay	*ij*	*oo*	*oo*
It bords, tressells, planckes and ladders	*ij*	*oo*	*oo*
It dunge	*oo*	*xiij*	*iiij*
It one mare wth a saddle	*ij*	*x*	*oo*
It one Cowe, and twoe calfes	*iiij*	*x*	*oo*
It three piggs	*ij*	*vj*	*viij*
It sheepe	*jx*	*oo*	*oo*
It Corne in ground	*xv*	*oo*	*oo*
It one malt hutch	*oo*	*x*	*oo*
It pikes, and Rakes, wth other implem[ts] nor seene nor prised	*j*	*oo*	*oo*

Sum 86 - 18 - 4d

[Will 1 Dec 1628 of John Rawlins the elder of Uffculme, yeoman, pr 8 Sep 1631: residue to wife Grace, exec; 10s to poor; £40 to dr Allice & bed, brass, & pewter, provided that she marries with the approval of her mother & the ovsrs, but £20 at age 23 otherwise; 40s to s John; 40s & a lamb conditionally to k William Rawlins; 20s & a lamb to Frances Rawlins at age 12; 3s 4d to s Bartholomewe; 3s 4d to ovsrs Humfry Steare & Humfry Butson, who both sign as witnesses the will marked by John Rawlins. On 2 Sep 1631 the exec swore that John Rawlins held no more than £5 outside the peculiar jurisdiction.]

92 JOANE SANDER 1631 (DS)

[Bur: "Joan Sander, widdowe" 25 Dec 1631; see 86. Widow with corn & malt; value, including £22 owed to her, £44.]

An Inventary of the goods & Chattles of Joane Sander of the pish of Uffculme deceased taken & praysed the thirtith day of December 1631 by John Woodroffe Leonard Ashelford & Francis Ellis as Followeth vizc

	lî	*s*	*d*
Imprimis her wearinge apparrell	*vi*		
Ite ij bedsteeds pformed	3	*xiij*	*iiij*
Ite tymber stuffe in the two chambers	*i*		
Ite one table boarde one chest one forme one chaire & a stoole	*ij*		
Ite brasse crocks a brasse panne a caldron with other brasse things	*i*	*vj*	*viij*
Ite on broache		*i*	*vj*
Ite parte in one brasse panne	*i*	3	*iiij*
Ite pewter dishes with a salt and candlesticks		*x*	
Ite parte in one side saddle		*ij*	
Ite two cushions			*xvj*
Ite one board cloth & five napkins		*vi*	
Ite one hogshead with ij hanginge bordes		*ij*	*vi*
Ite ij corne pikes & one dunge pike		*j*	*iiij*
Ite ij fliches of bakon	*i*	*vi*	*viij*
Ite one henne			*vi*
Ite corne in the barne	*ij*		
Ite corne threst & malt		*iij*	
Ite due uppon specialty being good debts	*xi*		
Ite due uppon one bond being desperat debte	*ix*		
Ite wood		*vi*	*viii*
Ite for fower bushels of woats		*xij*	
Ite money in her purse	*i*	*iiij*	*vj*
Ite one ringe		*i*	*vj*
Ite a quarters Rent due	[*ij*	*vj*	*viij*?]
Ite other smale implements not seene nor praysed		3	*iiij*

Som tot *xliiij*^{li} *xi*^{s} *i*^{d} [21d short?]

[Exhibited at Salisbury 1 Mar 1631/2. Latin endorsement signed by Jo: Johnson Reg^{r}. In the inventory i and j are both used for a final digit and some Arabic numerals also intrude.

Admon 25 Jan 1631/2 names Mary German, wife of Thomas German of Uffculme, yeoman, as only dr & admin, & also George Walrond of Uffculme, gent; signed by Thomas Jarman (sic) & George Walrond in the presence of Hum: Steare & Mary Ellis, who makes her mark.]

93 HENRY RUGG 1632 (DS)

[Bur: "Henry Rugge" 22 Jan 1631/2. Very prosperous yeoman owning leases at Craddock(£60) & Northcott(£40) and with £39 in debts owed to him; house has hall & parlour & rooms over both, & buttery; "water" house and "fourth" house mentioned; wheat, rye, cattle, pigs, 1 mare, & a plough; shot-guns, long & crossbows & arrows; bible & other books; £273.]

The Inventory of All and singuler the goods Chattles & Cattels of Henry Rugg latt of Uffculme in the County of Devon yeoman decessed prised by Nicholas Hollway Henry Gill Simoñ Merson & John Beare the seven & twenteeth day of January Año Dm 1631 As Followeth.

	lî	*s*	*d*
Inprimis wee prise all his Apparrell	*x*		
It one bedsted, bed & all the furniture that belongeth to the same in the parler	*v*		
It one Table borde one forme, one foslett & one Trockell bedsted in the parler		*xx*	
It one byble & all the rest of his books		*xiij*	*iiij*
It one Quiver of Arrowes and his bowes		*xx*	
It one Lytle presse of bords & 3 Coffers		*viij*	
It five old wooden vessels & one old forme		*vj*	*viij*

It 3 wooden vessels in the

	lî	*s*	*d*
water house		*v*	
It one Try, one Amery, fyve barrels & other smale tryvels in the buttery		*xx*	
It all the pewter vessell		*xl*	
It three silver spones		*xv*	
It all the brasse vessels, & Ireronds, belonginge to the same	*iij*		
It one Table borde, one forme, Chers, stoles, & the Sylinge in the hall		*l*	
It baken		*xx*	
It one fowlynge pece, one burdynge pece one Crosbowe, and benders, one Clooke & one Lytle Cage in the hall	*iij*		
It two bedsteds; 3 beds & all the furniture in the Chamber over the hall	*iiij*		
It wooll, & other & other smale Implements in the Chamber over the parler		*v*	
It one musterd bowll			*xx*
It 2 Coffers; 3 planks, & one skemer		*iiij*	
It 2 bedsteds, one bed, & furniture		*xxx*	
It one Cage, bells, & all other Implements in the fourth house		*x*	
It all his workeynge tools		*xx*	
It one geldynge, & two oxen for heriotts	*xviij*		
It foure oxen & 2 Lytle steres	*xx*		
It six kine	*xviij*		
It foure yerlyngs	*iiij*		
It one mare, Saddels, & all other furniture	*v*		
It foure piggs	*iiij*		
It all the corne in the house	*x*		
It hay	*iiij*		
It on peare of wheels, weene, & all the plowe stoufe, that belongeth to the plowe	*iiij*		
It wheat & Rye in the grownd	*viij*		
It one Chattell beynge part of A tenement Lyinge in Cradocke in the pishe aforesaid	*lx*		
It one other Chattell, in Northcott in the same pishe after the death of two p[er]sons	*xl*		
(torne over)			
Itm Richard Rugg oweth uppon specialty	*iij*	*vj*	
It John Marshall oweth uppon specialty	*iij*	*x*	
It Richard Rugg oweth uppon specialty	*x*		
It Richard Rugg oweth uppon one other specialty	*xx*		
It Alexander Starke & Elizabeth his Daughter oweth uppon specialty		*xxxj*	
It Reed, Dounge, plancks, Ladders, Tember, & all other thinges not prised		*xx*	
Sma tot~	*CClxxiij*^{li}	*xv*^{s}	*viij*^{d}

[Exhibited at Salisbury before the Dean 31 Jan 1631/2. Latin endorsement signed by Jo: Johnson Reg^{r}.]

94 JOHN BAKER 1632 (DS)

[Bur: "John Baker" 15 Apr 1632. Bachelor: yeoman with wheat, oats, & barley; £33.]

The Inventory of All & Singuler the good of John Baker Lat[e] of Uffculme in the County of Devon batcheler decessed p[rised by] Richard Newbery Edmund Gellard & John Beare the [torn paper] three & twenteith day of Aprill Año Dmi.1632./ as Followeth

	lî	*s*	*d*
Inprimis we prise all his Apparrell	*vj*	*xiij*	*iiij*
It one fether bed, bedsted, & furniture	*x*		
It wheat in grownd	*viij*		
It otts, & barly in grownd	*v*		
It for A Heriote	*iij*		
It all other things forgotten and not presed		*x*	
Suma totalš	*xxxiij*^{li}	*iij*^{s}	*iiij*^{d}
	33^{li}	3^{s}	4^{d}

[Exhibited at Salisbury 28 Jun 1632.

Will 28 Apr 1628 of John Baker of Uffculme, yeoman, pr 28 Jun 1632:

residue to sister Bridgett Baker, exec; 3s 4d to church maintenance; 10s to poor; £30 to godson John Baker after a year; signed by witn Richard Newberie & John Beare. On 7 Jun 1632 the exec swore that assets outside the peculiar jurisdiction did not exceed £5.]

95 ELIZABETH CROSSE 1635 (DS)

[Bur: "Elizabeth Crosse, widdowe" 9 Dec 1634. Household items; total, including £4 bond, £6.]

An Inventorie of the goods of Elizabeth Crosse widdowe taken & prised First of Aprill 1635 - By John Steephens & Richard Woodroffe as Followeth

	lî	*s*	*d*
Imp^r^s her weareinge apparell	*oo*	*xvj*	*oo*
It one bedsteed & beddinge	*oo*	*viij*	*oo*
It brasse & pewter	*oo*	*xvj*	*vj*
It one coffer & one barrell	*oo*	*iiij*	*oo*
It due upon bond	*iiij*	*x*	*oo*
Suma tot *vj^li^ xiiij^s^ vj^d^*			

[Exhibited by the admin before Mr. John Gandy, cleric, at Uffculme at the visitation of the Dean of Salisbury, 18 Sep 1635. Latin endorsement signed by Jo: Johnson Reg^r^.

Admon 18 Sep 1835 names Wm Pearce of Uffculme, gardener, as k & admin, & also John Cole of Uffculme, farmer ("agricola"); marked by both in the presence of Hen: Coles & Thomas Aden, who both sign.]

96 MARY CHAMPNEYES 1635 (DS)

[Bur: "Mary Champneyes, widdowe" 4 Mar 1634/35. Corn, rye, & oats; house has hall & parlour & rooms over both; clothmaking gear; £19.]

An Inventory of the goods of Mary Champneyes of the pish of Uffculme in the County of Devon taken and prised the sixth day of March 1634 by Humfry Steare John Woodroffe Thomas Balliman & Humfry Welch as followeth &c.

	lî	*s*	*d*
Imp^s^ her weareinge apparell	*ij*	*oo*	*oo*
It beds and bedcloathes	*ij*	*x*	*oo*
It three bedsteeds & one truckle bed	*j*	*xv*	*oo*
It one standinge presse in the chamber ov^r^ ye hall	*j*	*oo*	*oo*
It one chest standinge in the chamber at ye stayre head	*oo*	*vj*	*viij*
It one little square board in the chamber ov^r^ the p[ar]lour		*vj*	*viij*
It twoe old Trunckes	*oo*	*iij*	*iiij*
It one payre of sheets & 2 pillowe ties		*vij*	*viij*
It one table cloath & sixe napkins		*viij*	*iiij*
It the seeleinge and bench in the plour & seelinge in the hall	*ij*	*oo*	*oo*
It one table board in the plour		*xiij*	*iiij*
It Five stooles one chayre & forme in the hall	*oo*	*vj*	*viij*
It one old side bord in ye hall	*oo*	*j*	*oo*
It twoe trendells: three barrells one tubbe one old amery one timber boll & one fate	*j*	*iij*	*oo*
It a thinge in the buttery to sett barrells ov^r^ and shillfs about the house	*oo*	*v*	*iiij*
It Foure brasse pañs	*j*	*x*	*oo*
It pewter candlestickes and salt	*oo*	*xj*	*vj*
It one brasse Crocke a posselett & skillett	*oo*	*viij*	*viij*
It one spitt wth other yron stuffe	*oo*	*iiij*	*oo*
It one spininge turne	*oo*	*oo*	*viij*
It one flitch of bacon	*oo*	*vj*	*viij*
It Corne thresht & unthresht	*oo*	*vj*	*oo*
It hay	*oo*	*v*	*oo*
It wood & furse	*oo*	*x*	*oo*
It rye & oates in ground	*ij*	*vj*	*viij*
It old implem^ts^ not seene nor prised	*oo*	*j*	*iiij*
	19	17	6d

[Exhibited at the Uffculme visitation of 18 Sep 1635 before Mr. Jo: Gandy, clerk. Latin endorsement signed by Jo: Johnson Reg^{r}.

Will 13 Nov 1632 of Mary Champneyes of Uffculme: residue to cousin Maud Bryañ, exec; to drs Margret & Jane specified items of furniture in the parlour, the parlour chamber, the hall chamber, & the stairhead chamber; to k Robert Champneyes a truckle bed & 2 sheep; marked by Mary Champneyes in the presence of Hum: Steare, who signs, & Hum: Welch, who marks.]

97 DUNES DOWDNEY 1635 (DS)

[Bur: "Dunes Dowdney, widdowe" 11 Mar 1634/5; see 50. Household items only; cloth but no clothmaking gear; total, including £34 in annuities, £62.]

The Inventory of all & singuler the goods of Dunes Dowdney Latt of Uffculme in the County of Devon widowe decessed prised by William Harte John Wood and John Beare the fyve & twenteeth day of March in the yeere of o^{r} Lord god - one thousand sixe hundred thirty fyve as Followeth.

	lî	*s*	*d*
Inprimis wee prise all her Apparrell	*iiij*	*x*	
Itm one bed.bedsted.& furniture		*v*	
It one other bedsted.two beds foure Coverlets.one peare of blanckets. two boulsters.three Litle pillows, & one bed shett	*iiij*		
It three Coffers.& two Litle Fosletts		*xj*	
It foure yeards of newe Cloth .one elle of newe stamen Cloth .and one Apron & Cloth		*xxxiiij*	
It two tabell bords. two borde Clothes And two formes		*xxxij*	
It fourteene platers,three podingers. fyve sausers.two salts,two Candelsticks one mortis.& spones		*xl*	
It one Cubbord		*v*	
It one great Crocke		*xxx*	
It two Lesser Crocks.& one skillett		*xx*	
It one brasse pan in the Custody of William Butler		*jx*	
It one other brasse pan in the Custody of Ambros Cotterell		*iij*	
It fyve other brasse panes & two Cauldrens		*iiij*	*ij*
It all the wooden vessels		*xx*	
It one Anuity of eight pounds ten shillyngs for one quarters rent due alredy	[8	10	00]
It one other Anuity of twenty fyve pounds.ten shillyngs to be payd quarterly by even portions videliz. at Midsumer Michelmas & Chrismas next: yf Matthew Dowdney, or John Dowdney or ether of them Lyve soe Longe	[25	10	00]
It one Chere,two Cusyngs, two stonynge Cupps,one spitt, & other yron implements, one Sarge,two seaves,three stenes.& all other things not presed		*xij*	
Suma *lxij*^{li} *viij*^{s}			

[Exhibited at Uffculme by the exec at the Dean's visitation before Mr. John Gandy, clerk, 18 Sep 1635. Latin endorsement signed Jo: Johnson Reg^{r}.

Will 27 Aug 1632 of Dunes Dowdney of Uffculme, widow, pr at Uffculme 18 Sep 1635: residue to s-in-law John Coll, exec; 6s 8d to church maintenance; 10s to poor; to Nicholas Dowdney s of Mathew Dowdney, s, brass cauldron & crock, coffer, a pewter platter, & a coverlet, Mathew to retain the use of these for life; to Ellin Coll, dr of John Coll, table, cupboard, brass pan, & trendle, the use to remain with her mother for life; to Dunes Dowdney, dr of John Dowdney, table, forms, brass pan, bench, & coverlet, the use to remain with her father for life; to Agnes Dowdney, dr of John Dowdney, a bed & brass crock, the use to remain to her father for life; to dr's drs & s, Johañ, Christian, & William Cotterell, brass pans & pewter; to Johan Baker, dr's dr, bed, bedding, & coffer; to dr Johan brewing vat, hogshead, bench, form, coverlet, tub, & specified clothing; brass crock to dr's dr Agnes Baker, from John Coll at 21 or, if she should die before then, to her sister Dunes Baker, who also inherits the best candlestick; brass pan & pewter dish to dr's dr Tamsen Butler; 3 pewter dishes to Johan Baker, dr's dr; specified clothing to drs Wilmoth, Agnes, & Ellen, & to Elizabeth the wife of John Dowdney; ovsrs William Hart & s John Dowdney, who act as witn together with John Beare; marked by Dunes & John Dowdney, but signed by the other two.]

98 RICHARD BAKER 1635 (DS)

[Bur: "Richard Baker" 23 Mar 1634/5. Husbandman; household items & 2 acres of wheat; no clothmaking gear; £12.]

The Inventorye of All & singuler the goods of Richard Baker Latt of Norcott in the pishe of Uffculme & County of Devon husbandman decessed presed by Robert Bysshopp & John Beare. the seventh day of Aprill in Año Dmi one thousand sixe hundred thirty fyve: as Followeth:/.

	lî	*s*	*d*
Inprimis wee prise all his Apparrell		*xl*	
It one bed.bedsted,& all the furniture	*iiij*		
It two pannes. two Crocks. two platers.& one skillett		*xxxv*	
It two tubs		*v*	
It two Coffers		*vj*	*viij*
It two Acres of Whete in grownd		*xl*	
It in mony		*xv*	
It one hodghed.& one barrell		*iij*	*iiij*
It one Cubbord		*xx*	
It wood		*ij*	*iiij*
It yroñ implements & all other things not presed		*iij*	*iiij*

12^{l}.10^{s}.8^{d}.

[Exhibited at Uffculme before Mr. Jo: Gandy, "clico Com^{rio}", at the visitation of the Dean, 18 Sep 1635. Latin endorsement signed Jo: Johnson Reg^{r}.

Admon 18 Sep 1635 names Joane Rugge, widow, as dr & admin, & also Richard Rugge, yeoman; marked by Joane & signed by Richard Rugge in the presence of Hen: Coles & Thomas Aden, who both sign.]

99 DOROTHY PEARSEY 1635 (DS)

[Bur: "Dorothy Pearsey, widdowe" 31 Mar 1635. House has hall & parlour & "shop"; mostly domestic items, plus barrow, pitchfork, & harrows; no clothmaking gear; £14.]

An Inventory of the goods of Dorothy Pearsey deceased taken and prised the seaventh day of Aprill Anno dm^{i} 1635 - By Humfry Steare Edward Marshall & John Rawlins as followeth &c:

	lî	*s*	*d*
Imprs her weareinge apparell	*iiij*	*iij*	*vj*
It three pillowties & one payre of sheets	*oo*	*xij*	*oo*
It bord cloathes & napkins	*oo*	*vj*	*oo*
It twoe brasse crockes and one possnett	*j*	*v*	*oo*
It one brasse morltell & pessell	*oo*	*j*	*vj*
It pewter dishes	*oo*	*xviij*	*oo*
It three formes one little side board & a ioyne stoole in the plour	*oo*	*xij*	*oo*
It one glasse boxe	*oo*	*j*	*oo*
It seelenige & bench in the plour	*oo*	*vj*	*viij*
It one board in the chamber	*oo*	*v*	*oo*
It one corne pike	*oo*	*oo*	*viij*
It two tressells & one forme	*oo*	*j*	*oo*
It one payre of harrowes	*oo*	*x*	*oo*
It one bord in the shoppe	*oo*	*j*	*oo*
It three barrells & one Jibb	*oo*	*vj*	*vj*
It one bench in the hall and the bord behinde the same	*oo*	*ij*	*vj*
It timber vessels	*oo*	*xij*	*oo*
It one spitt & other yron implem^{t}s	*oo*	*vij*	*oo*
It one wheele barrowe	*oo*	*j*	*oo*
It wood	*ij*	*xv*	*oo*

	lî	*s*	*d*
It boards poles & tressells	*j*	*viij*	*oo*
It things not seene nor prised	*oo*	*j*	*oo*
Sum tot	13	15	4

[21s short?]

[Exhibited at Uffculme by the exec before Mr. Jo: Gandy, "clico Com^{rio}", at the visitation of the Dean of Salisbury, 18 Sep 1635. Latin endorsement signed by Jo: Johnson Reg^{r}.

Will 6 Mar 1634/5 of Dorothie Persey of Uffculme, widow, pr 18 Sep 1635: residue to s Peter Persey, exec; 10s to Mr Steare; 3s 4d to s John Pearsey & 1s to his s John; 12d each to dr Joan Pagie(?) & her chn, & to s Richard & his chn; to dr Anne Persey 2 boards, a forme, & a brass crocke in the parlour & chamber, & the pewter dishes "standing on the amerie in the parlour"; marked by Dorothie Persey in the presence of Hum: Steare, who signs, & John Persey, who marks.]

100 ELIZABETH BLACKMOORE 1635 (DS)

[Bur: "Elizabeth Blackmore, widdowe" 10 May 1635. Household items; £3.]

Uffculme./
The goods of Elizabeth Blackmoore widdow praised by John Doudnie and Edward Andrewe

	lîb	*s*	*d*
Imprimis her wearinge apparell	*ooo*	*vj*	*o6*
Item her beddinge and bedsteed	*ooo*	*xiiij*	*oo*
Item one iron posnet and other implements	*ooo*	[?]	*xij*
Item one crocke and cubbord twelve pounde of wool and other implements	*ooi*	*oo*	*oo*
Item two platters of tinne			
Item a saucer of tinne bords and other implements	*ooo*	*ov*	*oo*
Item a platter more of tinne a hutt apron and other implements	*ooo*	*xj*	*oo*
Suma tot	*lib*	*s*	*d*
	002	18	02

[8d too much?]

[Exhibited at Uffculme by the admin before Mr. Jo: Gandy, "clico Com^{rio}", at the visitation of the Dean of Salisbury, 18 Sep 1635. Latin endorsement signed by Jo: Johnson Reg^{r}.

Admon 18 Sep 1635 names Wm How alš Tanner of Uffculme, farmer, as s-in-law & admin, & also George Hancocke; marked by them in the presence of Hen: Coles & Thomas Aden.]

101 JAMES OLAND alš TAYLOR 1635 (DS)

[Bur: "James Oland" 16 Aug 1635. Bachelor with wheat & oats, 4 pigs, & 2 horses; no clothmaking gear; total, including £4 owed to him, £57.]

The Inventory of all and singuler the goods Chattels and Cattels of James Oland alis Tayler Late of Uffculme in the County of Devon Batchler decessed prised by Thomas Hurly Henry Manninge and Christopher Bysshopp the seven & twenteeth day of August Año Dmi 1635: as Followeth./.

	lî	*s*	*d*
Inprimis we prise all his Apparrell	*viij*		
It one peare of newe blanckets		*xxvj*	*viij*
It one Chattle Lease	*xiiij*	*vj*	*viij*
It wooll		*vij*	
It Marke Crosse of Shilden oweth uppon specialty	*iij*	*x*	
It one blacke nagg.wth saddell & furniture	*v*	*vj*	*viij*
It one other poore nagge		*xiij*	*iiij*
It foure Kine	*xij*		
It two Acres & halfe of wheat & foure Acres of Otts	*xj*		
It John Summeries of Clehiden oweth		*x*	
It one burding pece		*x*	
It one Cupp & Candelsticke			*vj*
It wood		*viij*	
It Johan Levermore oweth		*xj*	
It all his workeynge tules,& all other things not presed		*viij*	

Suma 51^{li} 11^{s} 10^{d} [£6 6s short?]

[Exhibited at Uffculme by the exec before Mr. John Gandy MA, clerk, "Com^{rio}" at the visitation of the Dean of Salisbury, 18 Sep 1635. Latin endorsement signed Jo: Johnson Reg^{r}.

Nuncupative will 13 Aug 1635 of James Oland alš Taylor of Uffculme, bachelor, pr at Uffculme 18 Sep 1635: all to mother Mary Oland alš Taylor, exec; marked by Margarett Hurley & Mary Simons as witn.]

102 EDMUND SATCHELL 1636 (PU)

[Bur: "Edmund Satchell" 19 Apr 1636. Corn, 1 heriot, poultry, & clothmaking gear; £23.]

The Inventary of all and singuler ye goods of Edmund Satchell late of Ufculme in the county of devon husbandmã deceased praysed the last day of Aprill 1636.by Robert Bishop Willm Hodge and Robert Gill as followeth

	lî	*s*	*d*
Imprimis wee praise all his appell		*xl*	
It 1 bedsteed & ye furniture	*iij*		
It 1 other bed bedsteed & the furniture		*xx*	
It 1 old trunke		*v*	
It iij coffers		*vj*	*viij*
It 1 dishe & ij Fosletts		*vj*	*viij*
It ij Formes in the chamber		*v*	
It 1 herryot		*iij*	*iiij*
It Corne in Ground		*xl*	
It vj ioyned stooles		*viij*	
It 1 table bord carpett & two bord clothes		*xl*	
It 1 chayre & other stooles			*xvj*
It 1 cubbord		*xxx*	
It all the pewter & vessell		*xl*	
It iij candlesticks 1 morter & one chaffer		*viij*	
It 1 cupp			*xij*
It ij crocks of brasse 1 posnet 1 skillet & the implements that belong to the same		*xxvj*	*viij*
It iiij pans of brasse & one Caldron		*xxx*	
It 1 musterd mill			*xij*
It bacon		*xx*	
It all ye woodden vessell		*xxx*	
It ij singing [spinning?] turnes & cards		*x*	
It all his tooles		*x*	
It wood		*vj*	*viij*
It ij broaches 1 brandiron & frying pann		*v*	
It earthen vessell & all other things not praised		*iij*	*iiij*
It posses & timber that the mow did stand upon		*ij*	*vj*
It poultry			*xviij*

Sum is 23^{li} 1^{s} 6^{d} [2d short]

[Admon dated 22 Sep 1636 names Elizabeth Satchell as widow & admin, & also Edward Androe, who signs "Edward Androw".]

103 JOHN CORNISH 1636 (DS)

[Bur: "John Cornish" 6 Oct 1636. Yeoman: mostly household & (blacksmith's?) shop items; total, including £21 owed to him, £52.]

An Inventorie of the goods of John Cornish late of Uffculme deceased, taken and prysed the xvth day of October 1636 By Humfry Steare, Thomas Harte, Thomas Weare, and Samuel Bishoppe as Followeth &c:

	lî	*s*	*d*
Imp^{r}s his weareinge apparell	*ij*	*oo*	*oo*
It one Bedsteed and bed pformed standinge in ye plour	*iij*	*x*	*oo*
It one table board twoe formes and twoe ioyne stooles in the plour	*oo*	*xiij*	*iiij*
It one Cubbord in the plour	*oo*	*xiij*	*iiij*
It pewter dishes beinge twoe and twentie in number: eight sawcers three salts one tine bottle & one chamber potte	*j*	*x*	*oo*
It one bedsteed in the chamber over the plour wth bed and bed Cloathes to the same, and one new bed Cord	*j*	*oo*	*oo*
It one Carpett	*oo*	*iij*	*iiij*
It one Chest, three Coffers			

Twoe boxes, & one forme	*oo*	*x*	*oo*
It nine brasse pans, three Caldrons, Twoe Skillets & Foure brasse candlestickes	*iij*	*vj*	*viij*
It Three Crockes and one Chaffendish	*j*	*xiij*	*iiij*
It one bedsteed in the chamber ov^{r} the buttery & twoe bolsters	*oo*	*vj*	*viij*
It Twoe board clothes Twoe pillow ties, one towell, and one table napkin	*oo*	*x*	*oo*
It one fryinge pañ and one dripinge pan	*oo*	*j*	*oo*
It barrells, hogsheds and other timber vessells	*oo*	*xvj*	*oo*
It one Cheese wringe	*oo*	*j*	*vj*
It one garden Rake and winowinge sheete	*oo*	*ij*	*oo*
It Twoe andyrons, one gridyron, one toster, twoe longe Crookes, one brandise and a payre of pottehookes	*oo*	*v*	*oo*
It One Spitte	*oo*	*j*	*oo*
It Foure basketts & a little boord	*oo*	*ij*	*vj*
It Three corne pikes & one staffehooke	*oo*	*ij*	*oo*
It one glasse Cage twoe glasse bottles, and one Jugge	*oo*	*ij*	*oo*
It one old table board and forme in the hall	*oo*	*ij*	*vj*
It one Anvill[?], twoe sledges, one vice, Foure payre of Tongs three viles, harñess, pincers, wth other shoppe tooles	*iij*	*oo*	*oo*
It pte of an armes	*oo*	*vj*	*viij*
It one yron barre	*oo*	*iij*	*iiij*
It weights	*oo*	*iij*	*oo*
It things not seene nor prysed	*oo*	*x*	*oo*
It due upon bonds [including the following £16 18s]	*xxj*	*xij*	*oo*
Of wch there is desperate debt	*xvj*	*xviij*	*oo*
It money owinge and in his purse	*viij*	*xiij*	*vj*

Sum totalš 52 oo^{s} 8^{d}

[signed] Hum: Steare, Thomas Harte, Thomas Weere
[mark of] Samuell Bishopp

[Will 22 Jan 1627/8 of John Cornish of Uffculme, yeoman, sworn to by the exec^{s} 27 Oct 1636: residue to Jo(h)an Crosse of Burlesc(ombe) & John Mill alš Gudderidge of Uffculme, exec^{s}; 6s 8d to poor, to be distributed by Robert Mill & Johan Crosse on day of burial; table in the parlour to Robert Mill: 2nd best cloak to k Atewill Blake; coffer to Dorothy Crosse; 12d each to godchn; marked by two named John Cornish & by Richard Baker, & signed by Hum: Steare, John Crosse, & Attewell Wheddon. A memorandum, signed by Attewill Wheddon & John Crosse on 22 April 1635,states that the will had to be newly signed, sealed, & delivered because one of the original signatories, Richard Baker, had died.]

104 FRANCIS LEYMAN 1637 (DS) & 1639 & 1641 (PCC)

[Bur: "Francis Leyman" 20 Dec 1637. Corn, plough, 6 cattle, 20 sheep, 3 pigs; room over hall; bible & other books; sword; £86. See also LW130]

The true and pfect Inventory of the goods and chattels & debts of Francis Leyman of of [sic] Ufculme and County of Devon decesed Taken and pised the 27th of this December 1637 By Richard Goodridg, John Myll Simon Merson Thomas Midelton of the pishe and County aforesayd.

	lî	*s*	*d*
Inprimis his wearing apparell	06	13	04
Item on table bord and 2 formes 3 chairs & a settell on cupbord & presse	02	10	00
Item 20 peater dishes or thear abouts	02	00	00
Item brasse bason and Uure	03	00	00
Item 3 brasse potts	01	00	00
Item 2 paire of Andians 4 spitts on frying pann on paire of pott hangings	00	13	04
Item on birding pice	00	06	00
Item on byble and other bookes	00	10	00
Item on handbowe and an ould sword	00	02	00

	lî	s	d
Item on featherbead and on dust bead over the hale pformed	05	00	00
Item coffers and chests in the chamber over the hale	01	13	04
Item on board and tressels & shilfe	00	02	00
Item parte of a costlet	00	06	00
Item fagots and hard wood	02	00	00
Item on beadstead and bead pformed within the chamber over the hale	02	00	00
Item 2 trendels tobbs and barrels and other wooden vessels	02	10	00
Item 5 beadsteads cloathes and on bead & on cheese rack	01	16	00
Item on morter and pestell	00	04	00
Item Plow stuffe & ould Iron			
Item corne in ground	06	00	00
Item corne in the barne & Mowe	10	00	00
Item 6 kyne	16	13	04
Item on cheese wringe	00	03	04
Item 20 sheepe	07	00	00
Item 3 piggs	02	05	00
Item 2 table cloathes & other liñing	00	10	00
Item haye and reede	01	06	08
Item on packe sadell & crookes hackney saddell & gambadaws & bridell	00	06	08
Item mony in his purse	07	00	05
Item debts owinge	02	10	00
Item triffels unprized	00	06	00
Suma total	[£86	07	05]

[Exhibited at Salisbury before Dr. Henchman 27 Feb 1637/8. Latin endorsement signed Jo: Johnson Reg^r^.

Admon 13 Dec 1637 (*sic*: but cf bur & inv dates) names Robert Leyman of Uffculme, yeoman, as bro & admin, & also Robert Byshopp of Uffculme, yeoman; marked by them in the presence of Willm London, clerk, & Hen: Coles.

Referred to the PCC in London where a commission, 5 Jan 1638/9, granted admin^n^ of the goods of Francis Leaman of Uffculme to his sister Agnes Weare alš Leaman, wife of John Weare of Culmstock, yeoman. A case brought by Agnes against Robert was eventually decided at St Paul's Cathedral by Mr.Basil Wood by sentence, 16 Jul 1641, apparently in favour of Agnes, though difficult to read.]

105 SAMUELL JAMES alš SLADE 1638 (PU)

[Bur: "Samuel James alš Slade" 28 Jan 1637/8. Mar: "Samuell James & Anne Keep" 14 Feb 1616. Weaver; house with at least hall & "shop" (cf. No. 162, 1682) & rooms over both; corn, hay; 12 cattle, 2 "labour beasts", 1 colt, 1 sow & 6 piglets; broad & narrow looms; household & farm implements; no books; £100, including £12 house & garden chattel.]

The Inventarie of the goods [& chattels of Samuell James] alias Slade of the pish of Uffcolume t[aken] & praysed the ix^th^ day of February 1637[/8] [by] Humphry Prescot Zachary Endicott [..] as followeth

	lî	s	d
Imprimis his wearinge apparell	4	[0	0]
Itm one house & garden being a Chattle	12	0[	0]
Itm one bedsteed & fetherbedd pformed	2	0[	0]
Itm two bedsteedds & two dowst bedds pformed in the chamber ov^r^ the hall	2	10	[0]
Itm one Cheest & two Coffers	0	13	4
Itm one table bord in the chamber ov^r^ the hall	0	8	0
Itm three bedsteedds & three Dowst bedds pformed in the chamber ov^r^ the shope	3	0	0
Itm one truncke One Coffer & one box	0	7	6
Itm one table bord in the hall & one forme	0	10	0
Itm one Cubbord in the hall	0	10	0
Itm one Coffer & one forme in the hall	0	5	0
Itm one chayre two hanginge bords & two stooles	0	5	0
Itm pewter & one tinen bowle			

	lî	*s*	*d*
& one tinen Candlesticke	1	12	0
Itm two brasse Crockes & five brasse pans	5	0	0
Itm one kittle & one brasse Skillett	0	6	0
Itm bakon & other salt meat	3	10	0
Itm three payre of broad lumbes & part of two narrow lumbes with theire furniture	6	10	0
Itm one little malt hutch	0	1	6
Itm tubbs & barrels and other timber vessells	1	7	0
Itm fyve kine	17	0	0
Itm two heaffers & fyve yearlinges	10	0	0
Itm two labour beasts & one Colt	9	0	0
Itm two pack Saddles with theire furniture	0	10	0
Itm Corne in the barne	7	0	0
Itm Corne in the ground	6	0	0
Itm haye	3	0	0
Itm one Sowe & six little piggs	1	10	0
Itm one silv^r^ spoone		3	0
Itm Iron Implements	1	0	0
Itm pikes & rakes with other implements not seene nor prised	1	0	0
	lî	*s*	*d*
Sume is	100	18	4

The Accompt of Anne James alš Slade the Relict & Administratrix of all & Singler the goods & chattles & credits of Samuell James alš Slade late of Uffculme dec^{d} made there the second day of September Año dmi 1640

The Charge	*lî*	*s*	*d*
Imprimis the whole sum of the Inventary being	*C*	*xviij*	*iiij*
Soma oñis patet [?]			
The discharge	*lî*	*s*	*d*
Imprimis for the funeralle charge of the deceased in the whole	*iij*		
It pd since the deceaseds death as debt due to sev^{r}alle p[ar]tyes the sum of	*xxij*		
It For the mortuary upon the decd death		*x*	
It For the Fees of administracõn in grossing the Inventaryes & ex[hib]iting them		*xviij*	
It she hath given bond for ye payment of v^{li} a peece to ev^{r}y of hers & her s^{d} deceaseds children beinge seaven in the whole, at their sev^{r}all ages of one & twenty yeares in tot	*xxxv*		
It for the Fees of passing this accompt in toto &c		*xxxiij*	*iiij*
Som exoñ	*Lxiij*	*j*	*iiij*
Sic rem[ane]t in mañ suis compts	*xxx[v?]ij^{li}*	*xvij^{s}*	

[Admon 20 Mar 1637[/8] names Anne James alš Slade as widow & admin, who subscribes an A mark; also names John Rawlins, yeoman, who signs.]

106 ELIZABETH EASTBROOKE 1638 (DS)

[Household items & £1 owed to her; £7.]

Jurat

A trew Inventory of the goods and Chattles of Elizabeth Eastbrooke late of Uffculme in the County of Devon deceased taken & apprised by Edward Eastbrooke Robert Wiett & Henry Wiett the 25th day of May Anno Dmi 1638 as followeth; viz

	lî	*s*	*d*
Inprimis her appell lynnen & wollen	*iij*	*vj*	*viij*
Item the pewter in house	*oo*	*vj*	*iiij*
Item on brasse pot three Cauldrons & on skillet	*oo*	*xiiij*	*vj*
Item on fryinge panne on paire of pothinges the Crookes & rings	*oo*	*ij*	*viij*
Item three Coffers	*oo*	*iiij*	*oo*
Item Two Bedsteeds & the Bedinge	*j*	*oo*	*oo*
Item on Chest	*oo*	*vj*	*viij*
Item the tymber vessels in house	*oo*	*iiij*	*oo*
Item on Ammery	*oo*	*iij*	*oo*
Item the wood stooles & all other things out memory			

	lî	s	d
& not prized	*oo*	*ij*	*vj*
Item debt owed to the deceased by Nicholas Weare	*j*	*oo*	*oo*
Summa totalis *vij*[li] *x*[s] *iiij*[d]			

[Exhibited at Uffculme 9 Jul 1638.

Nuncupative will 14 May 1638 of Elizabeth Eastbrooke of Uffculme, pr 9 Jul 1638: residue to sister Alice Wiett, exec; chest, "podinger", & platter to k Grace Wiett; pillow to k Susanne Palfrey; bed & coverlet to Alice, wife of Henry Wiett, & to his drs Susanne & Grace Wiett a feather pillow & aprons; coat, blanket, & blue undergarments to Anne, wife of John Wiett, & to his dr Rebecca a red waistcoat; red petticoat & waistcoat to k Dewnes Eastbrooke; 2 smocks to Bridgett, wife of Humfry Webber of Uffculme, & to his middle dr a grey petticoat & 2 napkins; 12d each to bro Edward Eastbrooke & sister Johan Giles, & to Robert & Stukeley, ss of Henry Wiett, & John & Johane, chn of Robert Wiett; marked by Johane Rew(?), Bridgett Webber, & Henry Wiett.]

107 THOMAS KEEPER 1638 (DS)

[Bur: "Thomas Keeper" 8 Jun 1638. Corn, 1 cow, 1 pig, & £10 owed to him; total £26.]

An Inventory of the goods of Thomas Keeper taken and prysed July y[e] 5[th] 1638 - by Humfry Steare: George Fursdon and John Colle as Followeth

	lî	s	d
Imp[r]s his weareinge apparell	*ij*	*oo*	*oo*
It twoe bedsteeds and beds pformed	*iij*	*oo*	*oo*
It one Coffer	*oo*	*j*	*oo*
It workeinge tooles	*oo*	*viij*	*oo*
It brasse pans and Caldrons	*j*	*xvij*	*oo*
It brasse Crockes	*oo*	*xv*	*oo*
It pewter dishes and candlestickes	*j*	*oo*	*oo*
It one Cubboard and other timber vessells	*oo*	*vj*	*viij*
It one Cowe	*iiij*	*oo*	*oo*
It Corne in grounde	*j*	*oo*	*oo*
It due upon speciallty	*x*	*oo*	*oo*
It one pigge	*j*	*oo*	*oo*
It wood & Furse	*oo*	*x*	*oo*
It haye	*oo*	*x*	*oo*
It things unprysed & not seene	*oo*	*j*	*oo*
Sum tot	26	8[s]	8d

[Exhibited at Uffculme by the exec before Mr. Gandy, surrogate clerk, 9 Jul 1638. Latin endorsement signed by Jo: Johnson Reg[r].

Will 5 Jun 1638 of Thomas Keeper of Uffculme, pr 9 Jul 1638: residue to wife, exec; 40s, brass pot & pan, & 2 pewter dishes to grandch Mary Grove; marked by Thomas Keeper in the presence of Hum: Steare.]

108 JAMES POOKE 1639 (PU)

[Bur: "James Pooke" 27 Feb 1638/9. Mar: "James Pooke & Dorothie Lutley" 26 Jun 1634. Prosperous brewer with pigs & 2 horses; new & summer houses; rooms over hall & kitchen; buttery; brewhouse; total, including £20 chattel lease & £47 owed to him, £120.]

An Inventory of the goods Chattles and Credits of James Pooke of the pish of Uffculme in the county of Devon deceased: taken and praysed the 22[th] day of March Anno Dm 1638: by Hum: Steare Edw: Marshall and John Rawlins as followeth &c

	lî	s	d
Imp[r]s his weareinge Apparell	4	00	00
It bedsteeds and beds pformed	6	15	00
It one table bord one bench and one forme standinge in the newhouse	00	8	00
It one table bord standinge in the chamber ov[r] the hall and 2 formes	00	*x*	00
It one chest and 3 coffers and one boxe	00	*x*	00

	lî	*s*	*d*
It one table bord standinge in the chamber ov^r the kitchinge	00	3	4
It one table bord wth benches and formes in the sumer house	00	10	00
It one table bord and Cupbord in the hall wth formes stooles and a chayre	00	13	4
It trendles bucketts vates wth other implem[en]ts in the brewehouse	*i*	6	00
It Five hogheads 3 barrells other timber stuffe in ye buttery	*i*	6	00
It 5 brasse potts one caldron 2 fryinge pans, one dripinge pan, potthookes & 2 yron dogs & other yron things	2	6	8
It one skillett	00	*i*	6
It one brewinge Furnace	2	00	00
It 3 old[erased?] brasse pans	*i*	15	00
It pewter	*i*	5	00
It table cloathes and table napkins	00	13	4
It malt sackes	00	6	00
It wood and other fewell	4	5	00
It 2 naggs and one colt wth saddles and other Furniture of horses	11	00	00
It pegges	05	00	00
It one Chattle lease	20	00	00
It due upon specialty	22	6	00
It due wthout specialty	25	00	00
It other stuffe at the mill	00	10	00
It money in his purse	5	00	00
It other things not seene nor prised	00	5	00
It bacon & other victualls	2	10	00
	120^li	16^s	2^d
	[11s too much?]		

[Will of James Pooke of Uffculme, 25 Feb 1638(/9), pr at Uffculme before Mr Steare 3 Sep 1640: residue to wife Dorothy, sole exec; £20 to s James Pooke; £10 to dr Wilmotte Pooke; £5 to dr-in-law (step-dr) Dorothy Lutley; £5 to wife's unborn ch; £3 to his mother; to sister Allice & her husband Henry Ball the £5 10s they owe him; 10s to Edward Pooke, s of bro Edward; 12d each to rest of godchn; 20s to Humfry Steare, vicar, & 5s to his s Humfry; after wife's death, her dr Dorothy Lutley to have the present house & dr Wilmotte Pooke to have the new house; 5s to servant Roberte; 2s to Mary Toler; 3s 4d to poor; witn: Hum: Steare & Peter Palfry.]

109 LUCE HEATHFEILD 1639 (PU)

[Bur: "Luce Heithfeild, widdow" 12 Mar 1638/9. Household items, cloth-making gear, & £5 owed to her; £11.]

An Inventorye of the goods of Luce Heathfeild of Uffcolume deceased taken & prised the 18th day of March Anno Dom 1638[/9] by John Rawlins John Bidgood & Willyam Sheppiard as followeth./

	lî	*s*	*d*
Imprimis her wearinge apparrell	2	0	0
Itm one bed & bedstead pformed	0	5	0
Itm two brasse Crocks & one Caldron	1	6	0
Itm one scillett	0	1	6
Itm one Cheest & one Coffer	0	12	0
Itm one table board one furme one planke one tub one buckett & other timber Implements	0	5	0
Itm one brasse chayffing dish one brasse morter & pessell	0	6	0
Itm two pewter dishes & other pewter stufe	0	6	0
Itm one spinninge turne & Cardes	0	1	6
Itm two pound of wooll	0	2	0
Itm one frine pann & other Ire stufe	0	1	0
Itm money due upon specialty	5	16	0
Itm other Implements not seene nor prised	0	1	0
	lî	*s*	*d*
Sume is	11	3	0

[Exhibited 1 Sep 1640.

Nuncupative will of Lucy Heathfeild, widow of Uffculme, made in hearing of Katherine White when taken ill a year before death & pr at Uffculme before Mr Steare 1 Sep 1640: 40s to s Michaell Heathfeild (then abroad); rest to dr Mary Heathfeild, exec.]

110 EDWARD BRYAR 1639 (PU)

[Bur: "Edward Bryer" 6 Jul 1639. Weaver; household items & queel turn; total, including £5 owed to him, £10.]

An Inventory of the goods of Edward Bryar of Uffcolmne deceassed taken & praised the 8th day of July Anno Dom 1639 by John Steven & John Anstice as followeth-

	lî	*s*	*d*
Imprimis his wearinge Apparell	0	i3	4
Itm one bedstead & bed pformed	*i*	4	0
Itm two Cauldrons one scillet & one frine panne	0	8	0
Itm three Coffers	0	8	0
Itm two pewter dishes & one sawser	0	3	0
Itm one fate & one tubb	0	5	0
Itm one brasse Crocke	0	2	0
Itm one table board one barrell with other things which are in the house of Robert Bryar	0	8	0
Itm two Iron Wadges one shovell & one Iron Rake one brand Iron with other Ire stufe	0	4	0
Itm two furmes with other timber stufe	0	*i*	0
Itm one queele turne & one leather bottell	0	*i*	0
Itm his lininge	0	*i*	0
Itm money due upon specialty	5	0	0
Itm money in his purse besides	0	4	0
Itm other Implements nor seene nor prised	0	*i*	6
Itm one brasse panne	*i*	0	0
Itm money due without specialty	0	3	3
	10	7	1

[Exhibited 26 Aug 1639.

Will of Edward Bryar of Uffculme, weaver, 23 Jan 1639, pr before Mr Steare 26 Aug 1639: residue to John Rawlins, exec; 10s to Mr Steare; 10s to Nicholas Holway; 5s each to Nicholas Holway's 2 eldest drs; 2s to s Robert Bryar; 2s 6d to Robert Leaman's s of Hacpin; 2s to Rebecka Pringe; witn: John Anstice & John Stephen.]

111 BEATEN RUDGE 1639 (PU)

[Spinster, dr of Robert & Caterin No. 70. Apparel & debts owed to her; £9.]

An Intary of the goods of Beaten Rudge late of Uffculme deceased taken and prized by Jo: Hurley Edmond Bishoppe and James Callow [...] the xxixth of September 1639 - as followeth

	lî	*s*	*d*
Imp^{rs} her wearinge apparell		13	4
It due upon specialty	5	00	00
It due without specialty	4	00	00
Suma tot	9	13	4

[Note attached to this inventory:]
20 10^{bris} 1639
Sent downe this adm^{on} & Inventary wthe the bond & this note of Fies vdt [viz.]

	s	*d*
The admon & bond of ye goods of John Sanders [..] administ[rati]ons	*xiij*	*iiij*
The will of Edward Bryar	*viij*	*iiij*
The copying		*xviij*
Thadm^{on} of Beaten Rudge	*x*	*iiij*
	xxxiij^{s}	*vj^{d}*

112 ROBERT MILL 1639 (DS)

[Bur: "Robert Mills" 19 Nov 1639. Yeoman (retired?); apparel & £42 in purse; total, with £50 tenement, £99.]

A true Inventorie of the goods and Chattles of Robert Mill of Ufculme in the County of Devon yeomã deceased made and approved by Humfry Steere Humfry Mill George Welch and John Cross the Twoe and Twentieth day of November in the fifteenth yeare of the Raygne of o[r] Sov[r]aigne Lord Kinge Charles &c. Anno Dm[i] 1639

	lî	*s*	*d*
In primis his weareinge apparrell	*vj*	*xiij*	*iiij*
Item his right in one Tenement which he Claymeth to hold by virtue of a graunt to him made from Edward Earle of Bath beareinge date the the 18[th] day of June in the 22[th] yeare of Late Kinge James	*l*		
Item mony in purse	*xlij*	*xvj*	*vj*
Item things not seene & omitted		*iij*	*vj*
Suma tot	99	13	4

apprised p nos Hum: Steere Humfery Mill
signed George Welch [mark] John Cross

[Exhibited 26 Nov 1639 before Dr. Henchman by John Mill alias Goodridge, admin, (during the minority of the exec). Latin endorsement signed by Jo: Johnson.

Will 10 Sep 1634 of Robert Mill of Uffculme, yeoman, pr 26 Nov 1639 before Ven. Humfrey Henchman: residue to Robert Mill alš Goodridge, exec, with his father, John Mill alš Goodridge, named as his guardian until age 21, or, if he should die, to Frances Mill alš Goodridge, exec; 20s to poor; 40s to servant Johane Woode; 20s each to other covenanted servants; 12d each to godchn at age 21; to s John Mill alš Goodridge all beasts, household goods, & furniture; to Robert, s of John Mill alš Goodridge, the remainder (conditional in some way upon the lives of John Mill, James Holway, & John Tucke) of the 99-year lease on the messuage & tenement of "Foorde House alš Foorde Lande", occupied by George Osmond; £10 each at age 21 to Frances & Ann, drs of John Mill alš Goodridge; 16s a year for life to father-in-law, John Cornishe; ovsrs John Mill alš Goodridge & John Crosse, s of John Crosse, late of Burlescombe; witn: Arthur Hill, Humfrey Henson, & Dorytye Hill; marked by Robert Mill. Admon 26 Nov 1639 names John Mill alš Goodridge of Uffculme, yeoman, as admin, & also Roger Michell of Uffculme; signed by John Mill & marked by Roger Michell in the presence of Jo: Johnson, not[y] pub.]

113 HUMFREY BRAY 1640 (PU)

[Bur: "Humfry Bray" 23 Feb 1639/40. Weaver with broad & narrow looms & a spinning turn; £29.]

An Inventory of the goods and Chattles of Humfrey Bray of Uffcolume in the County of Devon Weaver deceased taken & praysed the 27th day of February Anno Dom 1639[/40] by Robert Mayor George Fursdon & Michael Greene as Followeth -/

	lî	*s*	*d*
Imprimis his wearinge apparrell	2	6	8
Itm 2 halfe headded bedsteads pformed	3	o	o
Itm one bedstead one Covlid [coverlet?] & blancket with a blankette Cloth	2	*i*	o
Itm brasse pannes	*i*	*i*9	o
Itm 3 crocks a posnet & a skillet	*i*	*i*6	8
Itm 3 Cauldrons	o	*i*6	o
Itm pewter dishes & saucers	o	*i*7	4
Itm a Candelsticke saultseller & two tunnes of pewter	o	2	6
Itm one table board one furme one Round table board one brakinge board & bench	o	*i*3	8
Itm two brewinge tubbs two trendles & a payle with 3 other tubbs	*i*	*i*8	4
Itm beere vessels & a Corne vessell	*i*	*i*	6
Itm 3 Coffers & one old truncke	o	*ii*	o
Itm 3 Cheese fates	o	2	o

	lî	*s*	*d*
Itm earthen Cupps & potts	o	2	6
Itm 2 sives	o	o	8
Itm a steele & one tinnin bottle	o	*i*	8
Itm a sarge & Range	o	*i*	4
Itm one broade loome with the furniture	3	*i*o	o
Itm one narrow loome with the furniture	*i*	*i*o	6
Itm bacon	*i*	5	o
Itm haye	o	*i*5	o
Itm timber under the haye	o	*i*4	8
Itm wood & freith	*i*	*i*5	o
Itm Iron Implements of divers sorts	o	6	4
Itm 3 ladders	o	4	o
Itm a Cheese wringe	o	io	o
Itm a wimbsheete & 3 baggs	o	6	*i*
Itm 4 wedges	o	*i*	4
Itm Cloath in the loombs	*i*	o	o
Itm a spinninge turne	o	*i*	6
Itm old Implements not seene nor praysed	o	6	8
	lî	*s*	*d*
Sume is	29	*i*7	*ii*

[Exhibited at Uffculme 16 Mar 1639/40.

Will of Humfry Bray, weaver of Uffculme, 20 Jan 1639/40, pr before Mr Steare 16 Mar 1639/40: residue to s John Bray, exec; 1s to poor; to s Christopher Bray 20s & "all the glasse of the windowes of the house which I now dwell in"; 2s 6d to Grace Rawlins, dr of John Rawlins of Uffculme; marked HB by Humfry Bray & witn by John Rawlins, James Symons (J mark), Michael Greene (MG mark), & Grace Rawlins (GR mark).]

114 JOHN OSMOND the elder 1641 (DS)

[Bur: "John Ossmond" 23 May 1641. Husbandman with mare, colt, 8 cattle, 2 pigs, wheat, barley, oats, & peas; total, including £10 chattel lease, £38.]

A true and pfett Inventory of All the goods & Chattles of John Osmond the elder late of Ufcolume husbandman deceased made & prised the three and twenteth daie of June 1641 by John Osmond Robert Coleman William Hentton & Nicholas Were as followeth

	lî	*s*	*d*
Imp^r^imis his wearinge Appell	*ij*		
Itm one bedd & besteed wth the furniture to him belonginge	*ij*		
Itm one Cubbord & settle	*j*		
Itm one table board two Coffers two trunckes one forme & one trendle		*x*	
Itm three Kyne one Calfe	*x*		
Itm one mare & Colt	*iij*		
Itm one Chattle lease bearinge date the twenteth daie of December in the fifteeneth yeare of Kynge Charles	*x*		
Itm fower acres of Wheat barlye Woates & pease	*v*		
Itm one packsaddle & one pare of harrowes		*x*	
Itm for peater		*vj*	*viij*
Itm for Brazen stuffe	*ij*		
Itm two pigges		*x*	
Itm two fleches of Bacon		*xx*	
Itm for Butter & Cheese		*xiiij*	
Itm for Corne in the barne		*x*	
Itm all other Imployments not seen & forgotten		*x*	

Sume is *xxxviij*^{li} *j*^{s} *viij*^{d} [29s short?]

[Exhibited by the admin before Mr. Humfrey Steare at Uffculme 9 Nov 1641: sworn by Joan(na), relict. Latin endorsement signed Jo: Johnson Reg^r^.

Admon 9 Nov 1641 names Joane Osmond of Uffculme, "spinster", as "relict" & admin, & also John Osmond of Uffculme, husbandman; marked by both in the presence of William Kerle & Robt Aden.]

115 BARTHOMEW RAWLINS 1641 (PU)

[Bur: "Bartholomew Rawlins" 28 Sep 1641. Yeoman; mostly corn, 1 mare & 2 pigs; cider-making but no cloth-making gear; hall & parlour & milk-house with room above; 1 bible; £54.]

An Inventory of the goods & Chattells of Bartholomew Rawlins of Uffcolume in the County of Devon yeoman deceased taken & prised the last day of September Anno Dom 1641 by John Wooddrow John Stephen & Edward Marshall as followeth./

	lî	*s*	*d*
Imprimis his waringe apparrell	4	*i*o	o
Itm two beds & bedsteads pformed in the chamber over the hale	3	*i*2	o
Itm one bed & bedstead pformed in the Parler	3	*i*o	o
Itm one bed & bedstead pformed in the chamber ov^r the milkhowse	*i*	4	o
Itm table boards & Ioyne stooles	*i*	*i*2	o
Itm two cheares & other stooles	o	5	o
Itm one Cubberd in the Parler	*i*	*i*3	4
Itm one glasse keadge	o	3	o
Itm Pewter	*i*	*i*o	o
Itm one warminge pann	o	2	6
Itm two Caldrons one brasse pann & one brasse Candlesticke	o	*i*5	o
Itm two brasse Crockes two Posnetts & two Iron Crockes	*i*	*i*o	o
Itm one Furnace	o	*i*3	4
Itm Fates & barrels & other timber Vessels	3	2	o
Itm two Corne hutches with other timber stufe	3	*i*o	o
Itm Apples	*i*	6	8
Itm one Apple wringe	o	*i*2	o
Itm Corne in the barne	9	o	o
Itm haye	3	o	o
Itm wood	*i*	6	8
Itm one Mare two Saddles with other furniture	3	o	o
Itm two pigges	3	o	o
Itm two spitts two AnnIres with other Ire stufe	*i*	o	o
Itm bakon	o	6	o
Itm two board Clothes six table napkins with other lininge	o	*i*o	o
Itm one Bible	o	8	o

	lî	*s*	*d*
Itm one chist & three Coffers	o	*i*6	o
Itm other Implements not seene nor prised	o	5	o
Itm money due without specialty	2	2	o
	lî	*s*	*d*
Sume is	54	4	6

[Admon 11 Oct 1641 names William Cape, s-in-law of the intestate Barholomew Rawlins, as admin, & also John Rawlins (son?), both yeomen of Uffculme; signed Hum: Steare, Wm Cape (inverted W mark), & John Rawlins.]

116 EDWARD BRANCH 1641 (DS)

[Bur: "Edward Branch, schoolmaster" 28 Aug 1641. Domestic items, books, & lute; clothmaking gear; inner room & room over hall; total, including £10 chattel lease, £26.]

An Inventory of the goods and Chattles of Edward Branch late of the pish of Uffculme deceased taken and prized by Humfry Steare George Fursdon & Edward Marshall the sixth day of November 1641 as Followeth: &c:

	lî	*s*	*d*
Imp^rs his weareinge apparell	6	oo	oo
It one bedsteed & bed pformed in the iñer chamber	*i*	6	8
It one bedsteed & bed pformed in the chamber ov^r the hall	*oo*	16	oo
It one taruckle bed wth cloathes belonging to the same	oo	*i*o	oo
It one deske tuoe boxes	oo	6	8
It one Chest & one coffer	oo	*i*o	oo
It one Lute and lute case	oo	*i*o	oo
It one table bord in the hall a carpett & stooles	oo	15	oo
It one chayre & three cushens	oo	o3	6
It one cubbord in the hall	oo	o5	oo
It pewter	*i*	oo	oo
It a brasse crocke & other brasen vessells	*i*	*i*o	oo
It one bord & spining turns			

	lî	s	d
wth other implemts	oo	5	oo
It bookes	i	oo	oo
It one chattle lease	io	oo	oo
It linen	oo	5	oo
It yron implemts	oo	5	oo
It wood	oo	16	oo
It things not seene nor prised	oo	5	oo
	26	8	10

[Exhibited at Uffculme before Mr. Humfrey Steare by the admin at the visitation of the Dean of Salisbury, 9 Nov 1641. Latin endorsement signed Jo: Johnson Regr.

Admon 9 Nov 1641 names Anstice Branch as widow & admin, & also Edward Marshall of Uffculme, fuller: marked by Anstice Branch & signed "EM" by Edward Marshall in the presence of Will: Kerle & Robt Aden.]

117 AGNES DOWDNEY 1642 (PU)

[Bur: "Agnes Dowdney, daughter of John" 9 Apr 1642; described as a "spinster" in her will. Almost all in £8 annuities, total £10.]

A true Inventory of the goods & chattles of Agnes Dowdney of Uffculme taken & prased by Abra: Endicott & Richard Woodrow xxxth of May - 1642.

	lî	s	d
Imprs her weareinge apparell	1	15	0
It one bedsteed bed & bolster	00	13	4
It one Crocke	00	6	0
It one anuity of xxs a yeare in possessiõ[n] for terme of ye lives of Mathew Dowdney & John Dowdney: & one annuity of 40s in Revrsioñ for & dureinge the lives of the sayd Mathew & John	8	00	0
It other implemts	00	1	0
Sum tot	10	14	4 [1s short?]

[Will 8 Apr 1642, pr 28 Sep 1647: residue to John Dowdney, father & exec; 1 pair of "bodyes" to sister Mary Dowdney & rest of apparel to sister Dunes Scoyer; 10s each to bro-in-law Barth Scoyer & to sister Dunes Scoyer; 20s, bedstead, flock bed, bolster, & brass crock to their dr Dunes; 2s to goddr Thomasin Hollwell; the two annuities mentioned in the inventory to sister Mary Dowdney. Witn: Richard Woodrow, Debora Tozer.]

118 ELLIZABETH LANGBRIDGE 1644 (PU)

[Bur: "Elizabeth Langbridge, widdow" 18 Mar 1642/3; see 65. All in debts owed to her; £16.]

An Inventory of ye goods of Ellizabeth Langbridge of Uffculme in the County of Devon taken and prised the xxijth of March Anno dm 1643[/4] by Willm~ Tolly & John Blackmore alš Thorne as Followeth &c

	lî	s	d
Imps due upon specialty as appeareth	12	00	
due without specialty	4	00	
All the rest of her goods shee delivred wth her owne hands before her death			
	lî	s	d
Sum tot	16	00	00

[Exhibited 18 May 1647.]

119 WILLIAM CAPE 1644 (PU)

[Oats, cattle, & 22 sheep; hall, entry, & parlour with rooms above, kitchen, & a brewing house; £71.]

An Inventory of the goods Cattles & Chattles of William Cape late of Uffcolmne taken & prysed the xith of December Anno Dom 1644 by Edward Marshall Thomas Baberstocke & Robert Baker

	lî	s	d
Impr his wearing apparrell	2	0	0
Itm one trundle bedstead & bed with other bed cloathes in the plour	1	15	0

	lî	*s*	*d*
It ii pewter dishes one bowle two pottag dishes two Candlesticks one flaggon one tune one Chaffen Dish pestle & morter & one warminge pan	1	6	8
It Joyne stooles	0	4	0
It one Coffer	0	3	0
in the Chamber ov^{r} the hall			
It one bedstead 2 beds 2 bolsters one blankett i board & a Coffer	4	5	0
Itm 3 bedsteads & a bed in the chamber ov^{r} the entrie	1	5	0
It 3 Hogsheads a Cradle a chaire & a pillyan	0	13	0
It wooll	2	0	0
It in the chamber ov^{r} the parler one bedstead 2 beds 2 boulsters 2 pillows 1 rugge 1 blankett	2	0	0
Ite 3 Chests & 3 Coffers	1	0	0
Ite 1 Trendle 3 Tubbs & 1 Hogshead	0	16	0
Ite in the kitching 8 Tubbs	1	6	0
Ite 4 barrels & 1 Traye	0	13	0
Ite 2 Andirons	0	3	0
Ite Crocks & pans & 1 Fring pan	3	10	0
Ite Iron stuffe belonging to the halle	0	6	8
Ite in the Bruing howse 1 Furnace & one old Furnace	2	0	0
Ite 1 board 1 Forme 1 Trendle	0	7	0
Ite 2 ladders 2 laddersheeds & 1 paire of harrows	0	16	0
Ite 22 sheep	7	0	0
Ite haye Recke	2	10	0
Ite 4 Bullucks	12	0	0
Ite haye at gadden	4	0	0
Ite Implements in & about the howse not seene nor prysed	1	10	0
Ite oats in a Recke	5	0	0
Ite mony found due uppon specialty	4	13	4
Ite 1 bill of fortie shillings	2	0	0
Ite Henery Tozer for a Cow the mony to bee paide the 3 of Maye	3	10	0
Ite one Cow in the Custodie of Ames Franke 2^{li}-6^{s}-8^{d}	2	6	8
Ite one Farsse Recke in high parke	0	13	4
Ite 1 yewting Vate 1 Chest	0	18	0
	71	11	8
			[19s short?]

[Exhibited by Joseph Cape, admin, 27 Sep 1647.]

lî s d

The Accompt of Joseph Cape & Edward Allen Admrs of all & singler the goods chattles & credits of Wm Cape late of Ufculme in the countie of Devon intestate deceased made the xxvijth daie of Septem 1647. As followeth vizt./

The charge

Imprmis theis Accompts doe charge themselves wth the sum of threescore & eleven pounds eleven shillings & eight pence being the true value of all & singler the said decds goods chattles & debts according as they were valued & prised in an Inventorie thereof made & exhibited into the court by wch it doth more plainlie ap̲p[ear]e & whereto theis Accompts refer themselves *lxxj xj viij*

Suma omis patet

Out of wch theis Acompts praie allowance of theis sums following by them paid & disbursed vizt./

The Discharge

Imprmis paid by theis Accompts to Richard Culm of Canonleigh in the countie of Devonshyr the sum of threescore pounds due by the said dec^{d} upon a bill obligaterie as by the same ap̲p[ear]eth *lx*

Item p^{d} by theis Accompts unto John Woodroffe of Uffculme abovesaid the sum of Fifteene pounds two shillings & Fower pence for a debt due by the s^{d} deceased unto him the s^{d} John Woodroffe upon a bill obligatori *xv ij iiij*

Item p^{d} by theis Accompts unto Peeter Alling of Kentisbere in the countie of Devon Joyner the sum of seven pounds Five shillings & seven pence a debt due from the said dec^{d} upon a bill obligatori as by the same ap̲peth *vij v vij*

lî s d

Item p[d] by theis Accompts unto Richard Clarke of the pish of Halberton in the county of Devon yeoman the sum of seven pounds & eight shillings a debt due from the s[d] deceased unto the s[d] Richard upon a bill obligatorie *vij viij*

Item paid by theis Accompts unto Willm Pearse of Ufculme aforesaid Fuller the sum of Five pounds & eight shillings a debt due from the sd deceased unto him the s[d] Willm upon a bill obligatorie *v viij*

Item theis Accompts praie allowance for the Fees of the [l?]res of Administracon ingrossing the Inventaries & charges in travelling about the same the
Sum of *xx*

Item they praie allowance for their charges necessarilie layd out and expended at the praysing the said goods & at sev[r]all tymes attending the sale & doeing them the
Sum of *xx*

Item they praie allowance for the Fees of passing this accompt vizt for drawing ingrossing registring thereof w[th] thee Quietus est thereupon & other charges incident thereunto the
Sum of *xxxiij iiij*

Soma exondaconis[?] *lxxxxviij xvij iiij*
Sm remt nil
Sed[?] expt ultra recept *xxvij v vij*

[Admon 30 Aug 1647 names Joseph Cape of Buckland, Somerset, weaver, & Edward Allen of Uffculme as admin[s] of goods &c of William Cape of Uffculme, dec[d] intestate: signed in presence of Hum: Steare by Joseph Cape & Adrian Ayshelford (A mark).]

120 NICHOLAS DOWDNEY 1645 (PU)

[Bur: "Nicholas Dowdeney, of Foxwell" 24 Jan 1643/4. Wheat, oats, & rye; bible; total, including £20 chattel lease, £30.]

An Inventory indented of the goods & chattles of Nicholas Dowdney late of Foxwell within the pish of Uffculme in the Countye of Devon taken and praysed by John Osmond and James Osmond the xj[th] Daye of January Año Dm 1644[/5]

lî s d

Imp[s]: his wearinge apparell *iij*
Itm three acres and three rodds of ground of wheate and Rye *iij*
Itm oates in Barne *xl*
Itm one Byble *vj*
Itm Wood in and about the house *xxx*
Itm one chattle lease *xx*
Itm for all things omitted *vj viij*
Suma Inventorij 30[li] 2[s] 8[d]
Itm in doubtfull & desp[er]ate debts *xl[s]*
Sume *xl[s]*

[Exhibited by Hen: Dowdney, s & admin, 7 Jan 1646/7.

The Admon 8 Jan 1646/7 binds Henry Dowdney to administer the effects of his father Nicholas Dowdney, who died intestate. Witn: Hum Steare, Hen Howe, Mary Willms, Willam Howe, only Humphrey Steare signing & the rest making their marks.]

121 AMBROSE COTTERELL 1645 (PU)

[Bur: "Ambrose Cotterell" 25 May 1645. Mar: "Ambrose Cotterill & Agnes Dowdney" 13 Feb 1616. Weaver; 99-yr lease on Broomparks estate mentioned in will but not in inventory; corn, cattle, & sheep; clothmaking gear; £78.]

An Envytarye made and taken the 26th of June 1645 of all the goods and Chattells of Ambrose Cottrell of the pish of Uffcombe in the County of Devon weaver latly Decessed by William Hart Thomas Jarman and John Colle

	lî	*s*	*d*
Impr mes his wearinge Appell	*v*	*o*	
Itm iiij bedsteds & beds pformed	*v*	*o*	
Itm v kine one heffer & on Earlen [yearling]	*xviij*	*o*	
Itm vij shepe	*ij*	*o*	
Itm ij peggs	*ij*	*o*	
Itm Cor[n] in ground	*x*		
Itm Corn in barn	*j*	*x*	
Itm In woode	*j*	*x*	
Itm on tabell bord and on Chest	*o*	*xiij*	
Itm iiij tobes on trendell	*o*	*xij*	
Itm iiij barell iiij bukets	*o*	*xij*	
Itm on form on chaire ij stulls	*o*	*iij*	
Itm tow par of lumbs ij well-turns w th harnes & slease	*iij*		
Itm for wooll & yearne	*iij*	*o*	
Itm on spining turne	*o*	*ij*	
Itm v brase pans ij Cadrons iij brase Croks on skellet	*iij*	*x*	
Itm viij peottar deshes ij Candellsteks on tynen bolle iiij sassers	*j*	*o*	
Itm for Earthen vessels	*o*	*ij*	
Itm on pack sadell on par of Cruks on par of paners w th gesses & tinges	*o*	*xij*	
Itm on Chese wringe on pare of harros on whill brarow	*j*	*o*	
Itm ij ladars iij planks	*o*	*xij*	
Itm ij matocks j showell iiij Corn picks ij pot hangins	*o*	*x*	
Itm on billhuck iij Rephuks on Ex on hatchett	*o*	*v*	
Itm for Rene meat	*o*	*xiij*	
Itm buttar & Cheese	*o*	*vij*	
Itm mony owing & mony in Cash	*xx*	*o*	
Itm for things onsen & not praysed		*j*[?]	

Som is 78 li 14 s 0 d [£3 short?]
Lxxviij li xiiij s

William Hart Thoms Jarman sign
[JC mark] John Colle

[Will 1 Mar 1644(/5) of Ambrose Cotterell of Uffculme, weaver, pr at Uffculme before Mr Humf: Steare, 27 Sep 1647: residue, including estate on 99-yr lease, called Broomparks, to wife Agnes, exec; 5s to poor; 3s 4d to godson John Cotterell; to dr Johane Cotterell £20 & 2 kine; to dr Christian Cotterell £20 at age 21 plus the 20s owed to her; to s William Cotterell the Broomparks estate on wife's death or remarriage, plus all shop stuff & linen & woollen apparel; mention of proportionate sharing of losses in case of taxes, robbery, or billeting of soldiers *in these cruell tymes* signed with an A mark.]

122 BARTHOLOMEW DOWDNEY 1645 (PU)

[Bur: "Bartholomew Dowdney" 7 Dec 1645. Mar: "Bartholomew Dowdney & Elizabeth Dunell" 25 Jun 1607, Willand. Corn & a few cattle, pigs; owned 3 acres; £33.]

An Inventory of the goods and chattels of Bartholomew Dowdney in the parrish of Uphcullumbe late deceased, December the 15th

(1645)

	lî	*s*	*d*
Imprimis, his waringe Apparrell	02	00	00
Item, one Cow two Heifer yerlings two weaninge calfes	06	10	00
Item, the Corne in the barne, and one little mow seven poundes	07	00	00
Item, two akers and halfe of Corne in grounde	02	10	00
Item, one peice of ground called bowee of three akers holden off Atewell Whedon which In money is allredy paide For	03	00	00
Item, three beds two bedsteds with the Furniture thereto belonginge	04	06	08
Item, seven brasse panns	01	16	00
Item, two brasse potts and one brasse possnet	00	16	00
Item, nine Pewter dishes	00	12	00
Item, two tabellbordes on cupboard on paire off sealinge and two formes	02	00	00

	lî	*s*	*d*
Item, one chest	00	06	00
Item, on chare, one settle	00	03	04
Item, on Fat fower barrels and two tubbs	01	00	00
Item, two Piggs	01	00	00
Item, all other small implements besides	00	18	00
Som is	33	18	00

Viewed and Praised by us
Teste me [?] Peter Hollway
Nicholas NH Hollway his marke
Simon Merson Attewell Wheddon

[Admon 28 Sep 1647, binds Elizabeth to administer the effects of her husband Bartholomew Dowdney & describes their s Edward (or Edmund?) as a "sherman"(?). Elizabeth & her s do not sign but make their marks.]

123 ELIZABETH ANDREW 1647 (PU)

[Bur: "Elizabeth Androw" 25 Mar 1647. Widow; a few household items & a £4 bond; £8.]

Ane Inventory of the goods and Chattiels of Elizabeth Androw wid of Ufculme de[cea]ssed the 20 Daie of March AnnD 1646[/7] praysed by Symoñ Marson and Attewell Whiddon the 27: Daie of September 1647:

	lî	*s*	*d*
Imprimis her waerring Aparell	*ij*		
Itm one bond	*iiij*		
Itm one beedstead and beed pformed	*j*	*xiij*	*iiij*
Itm one Amerry		*iij*	*iiij*
Itm tow Coeffers		*v*	*iiij*
Itm other Impielments of howsell [household?] stufe		*vj*	*iiij*
Somme is /	8^{li}	8^{s}	4^{d}

[Admon 28 Sep 1647 names Edward Andrew of Uffculme, baker, & William Andrew, fuller, as admin^{s} of the goods &c of their mother Elizabeth; signed by Wm Andrew(e) in presence of Fran: Roberts n^{y} pub.]

124 SYMON DAVY 1648 (PU)

[Household items, clothmaking gear, & £6 10s chattel (lease); £10.]

A true and perfitt Inventory of all the goods and Chattles of Symon Davy of Uffculme deceassed taken the first day of May 1648: by Humfrey Mill and John Hunt as Followeth.//

	lî	*s*	*d*
Inprimis a table bord two old amaryes & a stoole	0	8	0
It two brasse crockes and a caldron	0	15	0
It a skyllett and a frying-pann	0	1	6
It an old cheire and a paile	0	2	0
It earthen vessells and other small implem^{ts}	0	3	6
It a halfehead:beedsteed a dust beed and the cloathes belonginge to the same	1	5	0
It a cupbord	0	5	0
It Fower barrells and two brewinge tubbs	0	10	0
It two other tubbes	0	3	4
It a trindle	0	5	6
It one Chattle	6	10	0
It a turne and cardes and all other implemt^{s} not before praysed	0	3	0
	lî	*s*	*d*
Sum tot Invent	10	11	10

125 JOHN CHEEKE 1657 (DS)

[Bur: "John Cheeke" 12 Jul 1657. Carpenter; household items & working tools; 1 pig; £12.]

An Inventory of all & singuler the goods & Chattells of John Cheeke of Whitmore in the pish of Uffcolmne in the County of Devon Carpenter deceased taken & prised the 18th day of July Anno Domi 1657 by John Cheeke senr Francis Pratt Willyam Hollway & John Rawlins as followeth

	lî	*s*	*d*
Imp^{r} his wearinge apparrell	*i*	*io*	o
Item one table board & one furme	o	*io*	o
Item one Cheest	o	*io*	o
Item 3 Coffers & one box	o	7	o

	lî	*s*	*d*
Item one Amery	o	6	o
Item 2 tymber barrells & one verkin	o	3	6
Item one standinge bedstead & flocke bed pformed	*i*	*i*5	o
Item one standerd	o	*i*	6
Item one halfe head bedstead & bed pformed	*i*	o	o
Item one other bed & bed Cloathes	o	2	6
Item 3 tubbs	o	5	o
Item 8 pewter dishes	o	*i*o	o
Item 2 Iron Crocks & one brasse Crocke	o	*i*6	o
Item 2 Caldrons & one skillett	o	8	o
Item one grinding stone spill [spitt?] & turner	o	5	o
Item backcrooke & potthoocke	o	3	4
Item 2 Cheares & one sideboard	o	3	o
Item wood poles & other fuell	*i*	o	o
Item one pigg	o	*i*5	o
Item one ladder	o	*i*	o
Item 2 Arme zaws & 2 thurt zaws	o	*i*8	o
Item other workinge tooles	o	8	o
Item one Iron barr one battell & 6 wadges	o	8	o
Item other Implem^{t}s not seene nor prised	o	3	4
Sume is	*i*2	9	2

126 JOHN TRICKEY 1658 (DS)

[Bur: "John Trickey" 17 Feb 1657/8. Weaver with broadlooms & turns, a horse, a bible, a gun, £17 in cash & £18 owed to him; total £62.]

An Inventory of all & singuler the goods Chattles & debtes of John Trickey late of Uffcolume in the County of devon Weaver deceased taken & prised the nyneteenth day of March in the yeare of our Lord god 1657[/8] By Henry Gibbs John Rawlins & Humfrey Woodroffe as followeth./

	lî	*s*	*d*
Imp^{r} his wearing apparrell	2	o	o
Item one halfe head bedstead one dowstbed two blancketts & one Cov^{r}lett & one boulster	3	o	o
Item two other halfe head bedsteads two dowstbeds 3 blancketts 2 sheets with boulsters	3	*i*o	o
Item 9 platter dishes of pewter with other pewter	o	*i*5	o
Item 2 brasse Crocks	*i*	*i*3	o
Item one brasse pann one Caldron & 2 skilletts	*i*	*i*o	o
Item one table board & one furme	o	*i*6	o
Item 2 Cheestes two Coffers & one box	*i*	6	o
Item 3 tubbs 3 barrells & one buckett	o	*i*4	o
Item one glass Caige	o	*i*	6
Item 2 payre of broad lumbs slease & harnis & 2 queelturnes & shuttles	6	o	o
Item one pigg	*i*	6	8
Item one nagg one packsaddle with other furnyture	2	*i*3	4
Item wood	o	*i*4	o
Item 2 back Crooks one payre of potthookes & one Cradell	o	3	o
Item one bible	o	2	o
Item one fowlinge peece	*i*	o	o
Item one payre of warpin barrs & three baggs		6	o
Item money in his purse	*i*7	o	o
Item oweinge upon specialty	*i*8	o	o
Item other Implem^{t}s not seene nor prised	o	2	o
Sume is	62	*i*2	6

[Exhibited at Uffculme by Hannah Trickey, exec, at the visitation of the Dean of Salisbury, 10 Oct 1662. Latin endorsement signed Jo: Johnson Reg^{r}.

Nuncupative will 15 Feb 1657/8 of John Trickey of Uffculme, weaver, pr 10 Oct 1662 at Uffculme before Mr Richard Kent: residue to wife Hannah & s Willyam Trickey, exec^{s}; £20 & best coverlet to wife; to s Willyam a fowling-piece, bible, & any proceeds from his executorship for his late bro

George Trickey; marked by John Knight, Mary Rowland, Mary Sheppyard, & Bartho: Bond.]

127 MARGERETT DOWDNEY 1660 (DS)

[Bur: "Margeret Dowdney of Lee, widdo" 15 Oct 1660. Mar: "Nicholas Dowdney & Margret Holcumbe" 30 Apr 1629. Prosperous widow with hall, chamber, kitchen, & "bakes" (outbuildings?); no clothmaking gear; total, including £200 chattels (leases), £218.]

An Inventory of all the goods and Chattles of Margerett Dowdney of Ufculme in the Countie of Devon widd late decessed taken and praised by Francis Pratt and Samuell Bishopp the twentyeth Day of December in the Twelfth yeare of the Raigne of our soveraigne lord Charls by the grace of god Kinge of England Scotland France & Ierland Defender of the fayth &c 1660

	lî	*s*	*d*
Inprimis her apparrell	04	00	00
In the hale			
Ite one Table borde three firmes and one Cupbord	01	11	08
Ite one Chest and one Chare	00	06	08
In the hale Chamber			
Ite one feather bed bedsted and furniture	02	15	00
Ite two other beds in the said house and furniture	00	10	00
Ite three Coffers	00	05	00
Ite one Trendle and three tubs	00	06	08
Ite six barrells and two Jeebs	00	13	04
Ite one Table borde two firmes and one settle in the kitchen	00	06	09
In the bakes			
Ite one bruinge furnise one Cheese wringe one vate a Jeeb and a dryhorll[?]	00	13	00
Ite two brasse pots two Caldrons and one skillete	00	15	00
Ite eight puter dishes three sasers two candelsticks and one salt	01	00	00
Ite for pvision in the house	00	11	00
Ite three spits pott hangings and Crooks	00	05	00
Ite for Corne in the barne	04	00	00
Ite one silver spoone	00	02	04
Ite one paire of Harrowes a greninge stone and three yron wadgs	00	06	04
Ite her Chattles	200	00	00
Ite puntry wth goods seene and unseene not alredy valeued	00	11	00
Somme totalis	218	18	09

[Exhibited at Uffculme by the exec before Mr. Ric. Kent, surr^o^, at the visitation of the Dean of Salisbury, 10 Oct 1662. Latin endorsement signed by Jo: Johnson Reg^r^.

Will 7 Oct 1660 of Margerett Dowdney of Uffculme, widow, pr at Uffculme before Mr Richard Kent, surr, 10 Oct 1662: residue to ss Nicholas & Robert Dowdney, exec^s^; 20s each to bro Nicholas Holcombe & to s Nicholas Dowdney's ch if living; 10s to Elizabeth Steare; marked MD by Margerett Dowdney; witn: Henry Burdhill & Ane Dowdney (A mark).]

128 HUMFRY HENSON 1661 (DS)

[Bur: "Humfry Henson" 9 Jan 1660/1. Bachelor, probably a weaver; broad & narrow looms; total, including £35 owed to him, £44.]

An Inventory of all & singuler the goods Chattels and debts of Humfry Henson late of Uffculme batcheler deceased taken and prised the tenth daye of January in the yeere of our lord god one thousand six hundred and sixtie by Anthoney Henson thelder Simon Welch and John Lowdwill as followeth: /

	lî	*s*	*d*
Imprimis his wearing Apparrell	5	0	0
Itm one Chest	0	8	0
Itm one paire of narrow			

	lî	*s*	*d*
loombs and pte of a paire of broade loombs	2	10	0
Itm monney due upon specialtie	26	00	00
Itm desp[er]ate debts	09	13	06
Itm monney in purse	01	05	00
Itm all such other goods as are not heretofore menc̃oned in this inventory	00	01	04
Sume is	44	17	10

[Exhibited at Uffculme by the exec at the visitation of the Dean of Salisbury, 10 Oct 1662. Latin endorsement signed J J R (probably Jo: Johnson Reg^{r}.)

Will 20 Nov 1660 of Humfry Henson of Uffculme: residue to Thomas Lee & John Butson, exec^{s}; 40s each to Johan, Sarah, & Mary, drs of Anthony Henson; 45s each to John, Ames, Jane, & Amie, chn of John Butson; £4 each to Anthony & Amie, chn of Thomas Lee, & £3 to his unborn ch & a chest to Grace, his wife; marked by Humfry Henson, & signed by Edward Joyce & marked by John Loudwell as witn.]

129 THOMASINE CARTER 1663 (PU)

[Bur: "Thomasin Carter" 2 May 1663. This is quite a long inventory but much of the beginning is missing. Prosperous shopkeeper; candles, glue, starch, salt, butter, prunes, cloves, rice?; 1 mare; virginals; bible; rings; household items; £75.]

	lî	*s*	*d*
It Candles glue and other...			
It Fruit Tracle & Starch......			
It Salt and Butter & prunes...			
It Two shealfs cloves Rice & other things....................			
It Teeck [?] Rise [?] & cloves	00	08	
It other things	00	06	00
In the hall & Litle Roome by & ye Chamber over			
Inp^{s} one Payre of virginalls	03	10	00
It in bedsteeds bedinge & Furniture	08	00	00
It boxes bonds & barrels	00	08	00
It one glasse cage & Amery	00	08	00
It Six Joynted Stooles & one Chayre	00	07	00
It Thirteen Pewter dishes	01	06	00
It eight Tyninge dishes 3 salts & flagons	00	12	06
It Three brasse crocks	01	00	00
It Two brasse Cauldrons & one pan	01	05	00
It one Chafen dish candlesticke pessell morter and Scoomer [skimmer]	00	11	00
It one Scillett box style & 2 paire of Scales	00	05	00
It Too styles a byble 4 plates one dozen of Tranchers	00	05	10
It one payre of Andires 2 fryinge pans 2 hangings one payre of bellowes	00	07	06
It Two pot crooks & one Tininge bason	00	03	00
It one table board & furm one flaskett and Chest & one Syde Sadle	02	00	00
It one Trunke one coffer & 4 barrells	00	05	00
It Shealfs in ye shop	00	03	00
It one Litle gray Mare	02	10	00
It one gold Ringe one Silver Ringe one bodkin & Thimble	01	00	00
It Things not seen nor apprised	00	03	04
It debts doubtfull upon her booke	02	10	00
Sum is	75	13	08

Sigñ : Thomas Carter [T mark]
Gwyn[?] Rowland

[Exhibited by Elizabeth Carter & Mary Carter, admins, 19 May 1663.

Admon 19 May 1663 names drs Elizabeth & Mary Carter, both spinsters of Uffculme; marked C by both in the presence of Rich. Mathew, John Rowcliffe, John Burrowe, & Henry Osmond.]

130 JOHN CHEEKE 1663 (DS)

[Bur: "John Cheeke" 25 Jun 1663. Yeoman (retired?); household items only, but house has parlour, buttery, & other rooms; £11.]

An Inventory of all & singuler the goods & Chattles of John Cheeke late of Uffcolmne in the County of Devon yeoman deceased taken & prised the twentysixth day of June 1663 by Elias Lang Thomas Ballyman & John Rawlins as followeth./

	lî	*s*	*d*
Imps his wearinge apparrell	1	10	0
Item one standinge bedstead & bed pformed standinge in the parler	2	10	0
Item one table board one lyvery tabell & one furme & one Cheare standinge in the parler	1	5	0
Item one bedstead & bed pformed standinge in the parler chamber	1	0	0
Item one other bedstead in the sayd chamber	0	6	8
Item 2 Coffers in the sayd parler chamber	0	5	0
Item one bedstead & one Coffer in the buttery chamber	0	4	6
Item 3 barrels one trindell & 2 tubbs	0	12	0
Item 2 furmes in the buttery	0	2	0
Item 2 Cubbords in the hall one tabell boards & one furme	1	2	6
Item 9 pewter platters	0	10	0
Itme one brasse Crocke & one Caldron	0	16	0
Item one skillett	0	0	10
Item 2 Iron spitts 2 back crookes & 2 Iron doggs	0	6	8
Item one Cheese wringe one trindle one hutch & one spinning turne	0	6	4
Item bookes	0	7	0
Item his workinge tooles	0	5	0
Item implem^{ts} not seene nor prised	0	3	4
Sume is	11	12	10

the marke of
Elias [L mark] Longe
Tho: Balliman John Rawlins [both sign]

[Exhibited at Uffculme by the admin during the minority of Elizabethe & Margaret Cheeke, drs of the deceased, before Mr. Rico. Kent, surr^{o}, at the visitation of the Dean of Salisbury, 28 Jun 1665. Latin endorsement signed by Wa Johnson Reg^{r}.]

131 HENRY GILL 1663 (PU)

[Bur: "Henry Gill sen^{r}" 22 Jun 1663. Mar: "Henry Gill & Mary Leyman" 2 May 1638. Prosperous yeoman with wheat, barley, oats, peas, 7 pigs, 4 mares, 23 cattle, 75 sheep; plough; gun; hall, kitchen, & other rooms; no spinning gear; total, including his £200 home tenement "The Bushes", £365.]

An Inventory of all & singuler the goods & Chattles of Henry Gill late of Uffcolmne in the County of devon yeoman deceased taken & prised the 30th day of June 1663 by Robert Gill Richard Gill & Francis Haszell as followeth -

	lî	*s*	*d*
Imp^{s} his wearing apparrell & money in his purse & one Remlett of Carsey	5	0	0
It the home tenem^{t} being a Chattle & one peece of ground called the bushes	200	0	0
It two halfehead bedsteads & beds pformed in the hall chamber	2	10	0
It one Malt hutch	1	6	8
It one Chest one Coffer & one box	0	11	0
It one bedstead & feather bed pformed in the kittchin chamber	3	0	0
It one bedstead & Flock bed pformed	1	0	0
It one Coffer two tableboards & one furme	1	8	4
It one brewing pann 2 Caldrons & three brasse panns	1	12	0
It 2 brasse Crocks one skillett & Chafin dish	0	18	0
It all the pewter	1	0	0
It one Cubbord & one settle	1	2	4
It one board furme & Mowldinge board	0	5	6

	lî	*s*	*d*
It six tubbs a cheesewring & cheese vates	1	11	10
It one pipe & one hoggshead	0	11	0
It fyve barrells one standerd 3 boules & two firkins & 4 payles	1	4	0
It all the bords & shillfs in & about the howse	0	9	0
It one fowlinge peece	0	12	0
It 2 back crooks 2 potthangings 2 griddells one frynpan one payre of andIres & brandis	0	8	0
It a bittle & five Iron Wadges	0	2	11
It all the working tooles	0	13	6
It beefe & bakon	1	10	0
It butter & Cheese	1	6	0
It a payre of wheeles butt & one payre of harrows	1	16	0
It one hackney saddle 2 pack saddles with their furniture & tacklin	1	4	0
It one Soole 2 plow Ropes & other plowstufe	0	10	0
It two wheele barrowes	0	2	6
It all the wood & Wallett [?] & 2 Ladders	1	19	4
It Corne & Malt in howse	1	3	0
It seaven Swynes	4	10	0
It fower Mares	13	0	0
It 5 kine two heaffers & Calves	23	6	8
It two Steares	5	10	0
It seaven yearlings	11	13	4
It fyve Calves	4	10	0
It three score sheepe	20	0	0
It fifteene Lambes	2	5	0
It six akers & halfe of wheat	16	5	0
It Nine akers & halfe of barley	14	5	0
It Nine akers & halfe of pease & oates	14	5	0
It all the Lininge	1	6	8
It Implem^{ts} not seene nor prised	0	5	0
Sume is	365	18	7

Richard Gill Robert Gill Frances Hazell

[Exhibited 11 Oct 1663 by Mary Gill. Admon 11 Oct 1663 names Mary Gill as widow & admin, & also Henry Gill (son?), yeoman of Uffculme; + marked & sealed by Marie Gill & signed & sealed by Henry Gill in presence of Rich. Mathew.]

132 RICHARD GOODRIDGE 1663 (PU)

[Bur: "Richard Goodrodge" 26 Sep 1663. Prosperous yeoman; hall, kitchen, & rooms over, buttery, apple-, malt-, cider-, dye-, & milk-houses; 6 horses, 12 cattle, 42 sheep, plough; wheat, oats, barley, peas, & beans; clothmaking gear; £197.]

An Inventory of ye goods Chatles & catles of Richard Goodridge Late of Uffculme yeamon deceased seen and aprized ye 25th day of Septemb^{r} 1663: by Jo: Stephens Willyam Holway Richard Ragge & Hen: Osmond as followeth

	lî	*s*	*d*
Imprs his wearinge Apparell	5	0	0
It in ye Chamb^{r} over ye milkhouse one presse one standinge bedsteed with bedinge pformed	3	6	0
It one halfe head bedsteed & one Trendle Bedsteed pformed in ye same	1	5	0
It one Byble 2 coffers & a Chayre	0	16	0
It In ye Chamb^{r} over ye Hall Too old bedsteeds & bedinge pformed	1	13	4
It one Coffer a Cheese Racke & other things	0	8	0
It Pikes Staves And other such Implements	0	3	4
It one Tyninge Still & other Iron Commodityes	0	15	0
It In ye aple Chamb^{r} a Cheese Racke 2 planks And other Litle things	0	5	0
It In ye Kitchinge Chamb^{r} Two Tester bedsteeds with bedinge pformed	10	0	0
It a Table board six Joynted Stooles a Chest a Coffer a box And 2 chayres	1	3	6

	lî	*s*	*d*
It In ye hall one Table Board & furm one Carpett a Setle & 2 shelfs	2	1	0
It one Cubbord & glasse cage	0	10	0
It one birding peice	0	2	6
It one and Twenty Pewter dishes	2	5	0
It Six Silver Spoones	0	18	0
It one pessell & morter 2 old candlesticks on flagon a butt^{r} plate a salt 2 old saucers an old Bason And Ten Spoones	0	10	6
It In ye buttery 4 Litle Barrells & 3 firkins	0	11	4
It one Brakestocke 3 shelfs & a gibbe	0	4	6
It one dish Racke dishes & Trenchers	0	2	0
It Fowre Brasse crocks	3	0	0
It one Iron pott 2 Fryinge pans & a driping pan	0	9	0
It Two Broaches 3 payre of pot-hangings & Crookes a Brandice a gridiron a Toster a Savinge Iron & fire Tongs	0	17	6
It In ye milke house Ten Brasse pans	3	4	0
It Two Standerds a boall 9 cheese vates & a cubbord	0	9	6
It Two old caldrons	0	12	0
It In ye kitchin one payre of Andires & a firepan	0	5	4
It one great vate a bruinge vate & five Litle tubs	1	12	6
It one Table board & 2 shelfs	0	9	0
It a fire pike Cole rake & Shovell	0	2	6
It A Bruinge Furnace & 5 Bucketts	1	1	6
It In ye Buttery against ye garden on hogshead Six Barrells & a Standerd	1	2	6
It one Trendle 2 old barrells a buckett & Turner	0	6	8
It Two gibs 2 shelfs & a posnett	0	4	6
It In ye Malt house one mill for ye clenseinge of corn	0	5	0
It one Trendle 2 old Tubs a standerd & Spining Turn	0	6	0

	lî	*s*	*d*
It In hoops & vessel Timb^{r}	1	0	0
It In ye Syder house six pipes & three hogsheads	2	0	0
It Two vates	0	10	0
	49	17	6

[The top right-hand part of this next sheet is torn away.]

	lî	*s*	*d*
It a malt hutch and.....			
It a payre of harrows and.....			
It all ye other things in y^{e}.....			
It In ye orchard eighteen pla[nks?]...			
It one peese Reek..................			
It wheat in moowes & in ye barn...			
It woats & barly....................			
It wood Facketts...................			
It In ye Lee house a fan a payre of panyers................ of corn crooks 2 payre of hardwood c... and other Things			
It In ye Stable 4 pack sadles 3 girts Tings and Dung potts			
It In ye entry one bitle 7 Iron Wedges hooks hatchetts mattocks axes & other Tooles	1	1	..
It one Hackney Sadle & gambadoes	0	4	..
It Hay in ye Stalls	11	10	..
It In ye Court Seaven Pigs	8	1?	..
It Two Swynes Trowes	0	1?	..
It one bull 2 heifers & a steer	8	0	0
It In ye Cruft five yerelings	5	0	0
It Att Cogans Park one waynebody & wheels	5	0	0
It a karin draught a putt & 2 earthing puts	0	13	0
It fower Ladd^{r}s	0	6	0
It In ye Stall 4 yokes & bowes a plowsoole a wheellbarrow & Shovell	0	11	6
It Hanyburrows harnes plow chaynes and Tresses	0	5	6
It in ye Chamb^{r} a Sledge & 2 plow chaynes	0	5	6
It old Timb^{r} Stuffe	0	1	6
It in ye dye house old plow stuffe	0	8	6
It in park ground 2 colts	6	0	0
It one Nagge & Three mares	14	0	0
It Three milch Cowes	10	0	0
It Two & forty sheep	10	0	0

	lî	*s*	*d*
It one dragge plow stuffe & Tacklinge	1	0	0
It Dunge & Lyme in ye Court	1	5	0
It Too wheele barrows	0	5	0
It one akre of beanes	2	0	0
It debts desperate from Richard Locke	1	1	8
It Things Seen or nott Seene nor aprized	0	6	8
Sum is	197	11	02

John Stephen William Holway
Richard Rugg Hen: Osmond

	49	17	[6]
	147	13	[8]

[Exhibited by Mr. Philip Syne (?), notary public, for exec, 2 Nov 1663.

Nuncupative will of Richard Goodridge of Uffculme 15 Sep 1663, pr 7 Oct 1663 before Mr Richard Mathew, surr. for Thomas Clark, prebendary; residue to s Alexander Goodridge, exec; £20 to s John Goodridge; 5s each to rest of chn; witn: John Stephen, Mary Radford (M mark), & John Rowe (R mark).]

133 GEORGE FURSDON 1664 (PU)

[Bur: "George Fursden" 31 Mar 1664. Mar: "George Forsdon & Elizabeth Bicknell" 23 Oct 1620. Prosperous yeoman; corn, 2 horses, 6 cattle, sheep, 7 pigs, plough, & brewing tubs; no clothmaking gear; £68.]

An Inventory of all the goods of George Fursdon of Ufculme in the County of Devon Yeoman late deceased made and prised by John Balliman John Palmer John Grantland the sixteenth day of April in the sixteenth yeare of the Raigne of King Charles the second Annoq~ domini 1664 as followeth

	lî	*s*	*d*
Imprimis his wearing appell	02	10	00
Item one bedsted bed and furniture	04	00	00
Item one board one Furme one chest and two joine stooles	01	00	00
Item one Carpett and 4 Cushions	00	05	00
Item one other table board and Furme and one chaire	00	05	06
Item one Cupboard	00	13	04
Item wool	02	06	08
Item beef and bacon	02	00	00
Item one high bed and truckell bed with bedding	01	10	00
Item three Coffers and one chaire more	00	05	00
Item six brasse pans	01	00	00
Item two brasse Caldrons	00	14	00
Item two brasse pots and one skillet	00	12	00
Item one paire of brasse scales	00	01	00
Item one Cheesewring	00	05	00
Item one Andirons one spit one brandise one gridiron three jron wedges two iron crooks three pothangings one dripingpan one frying pan	00	08	00
Item in pewter	00	13	00
Item five barrels two brewing tubs one trendle two other tubs	01	01	04
Item one packsaddle one paire of Crooks and other furniture for a horse	00	05	00
Item harrows and plow stuffe	00	05	00
Item Corne in barne	03	00	00
Item Corne in ground	08	00	00
Item one horse and one mare	06	00	00
Item weathers ewes and lambs	12	06	04
Item one oxe three kine one heifer and one yeirling	16	00	00
Item one sow with foure young and two other pigs	02	10	00
Lastly other implem^{t}s unseen and unminded	00	10	00
Sum totalš	68	06	02

John Ballyman Jo: Palmer [P? mark]
signum Johannis [G? mark] Grantland

[Exhibited by Elizabeth Fursdon, relict & exec, 14 Jun 1664.

Will of George Fursdon, yeoman of Uffculme 26 Dec 1651; residue to wife, exec; 6s 8d to church; 20s to poor; 2s 6d to ovsrs, Thomas Balliman & k John Fursdon; signed & sealed by George Fursdon & witn Tho: Balliman, John Balliman, & Mary Balliman.]

134 FRANCIS FRYER 1664 (PU)

[Bur: "Francis Friar" 3 Jul 1664. Husbandman (retired?); mostly household items; no clothmaking gear; total, including £58 owed to him, £79.]

An Inventory of all & singuler the goods & debts of Francis Fryer late of Uffcolmne in the County of Devon husbandman deceased taken & prised the six & twentyeth day of July 1664./ By John Dune George Tapscott & John Grantland as followeth./

	lî	*s*	*d*
Imprimis his wearinge apparrell	8	0	0
Item three Bedsteads & beds pformed	6	0	0
Item two Coffers three boxes & one Chaire	0	10	0
Item sixteene pewter dishes three sawsers two salt sellers & one teeninge Candlestick	1	10	0
Item three brasse potts & one Cauldron	2	0	0
Item one Cubboard one table board one furme fower Joyne stooles one chaire two barrells & one tubb	2	0	0
Item Iron Implements	0	6	0
Item two silver spoones	0	8	0
Item money oweinge him	58	15	6
Item other goods & Implem[ts] not seene nor prised	0	5	0
Sume is	79	14	6

[Exhibited by Isett(Isola?) Fryer, relict & exec, 20 Dec 1664.

Nuncupative will 2 Jul 1664 of Francis Fryer of Uffculme, husbandman, pr at Uffculme 20 Dec 1664 before Mr Richard Mathew; residue to wife Isett, exec; £5 to dr-in-law (step-dr?) Isett Brooke; £5 to be divided equally among ss-in-law Giles Brooke & John Brooke & dr-in-law Frances Brooke; stockings & shoes to John Grantland the younger; witn: John Grantland the elder (J mark) & Richard Tapscott (RT mark).]

135 BRIDGETT BAKER 1664 (DS)

[Bur: "Bridget Baker widow" 15 Jul 1664. Mar: "Robert Baker weaver & Bridgett Gillard" 21 Sep 1613, Exeter All Hallows. Very prosperous widow; hall & porch with rooms over, parlour, kitchen, & room off hall; no clothmaking gear; 1 horse; total, including £300 chattel lease £70 debts to her, £405.]

An Inventory of all & singuler the goods Chattles & debtes of Bridgett Baker late of Uffcolume in the County of devon Widdow deceased taken & prised the sixteenth day of July 1664 By Richard Gill John Row & Robert Baker as followeth

	lî	*s*	*d*
Imprimis her wearinge apparrell	4	0	0
Item one bedstead & bed pformd standing in the Chamber over the hall	5	0	0
Item one tabell board one Chest & three Coffers in the same chamber	1	13	4
Item one trendle bedstead & bed with some boards in the same Roome	0	10	0
Item one bedstead & bed pformd standing in the chamber within the hall	0	15	0
Item one Coffer one box with one vate in the same Roome	0	6	0
Item one table board one furme & one Coffer standing in the parler	0	14	0
Item one table board one furme one Cubboard two Joyne stooles & one Chaire standing in the hall	2	0	0
Item one bedstead & bed			

	lî	s	d
pformd standing in the chamber over the porch	5	0	0
Item three tubbs one standerd & two trendles in the Kittchinge	1	10	0
Item pewter & brasse vessells	7	0	0
Item one nagg with his tacklinge	1	0	0
Item two hoggsheads & fower barrells	1	3	8
Item one silver boule	3	0	0
Item money oweinge her upon specialty	70	0	0
Item one tenem^t^ being a Chattle	300	0	0
Item for Implem^ts^ not seene nor prised	1	10	0
Sume is	405	2	0

The (JR) marke of John Row
Richard Gill Robart Baker

[Exhibited 28 Jan 1665/6 by the exec.

Will 30 Sep 1662 of Bridgett Baker of Uffculme, widow, pr at Uffculme 28 Jun 1665: residue to exec, Robertt Newbery of Yarcombe, in trust for grandch John Baker, who inherits the reversion lease on her "whombe Living", plus £30; £5 endowment for yearly payments to the poor; 5s to grandch Robertt Baker; £5 to grandch Nicholas Baker; £20 plus apparel to grandch Bridgett Baker; 10s to goddr Bridgett Bazeligh; 10s each to bro John Gaylord & his chn John Gaylord & Agnes Spiller; petticoat, waistcoat, & apron to Joane Tooze & 5s to Elizabeth Harres, drs of deceased bro Edmond Gaylord & 10s to his s Edmond; apron to Elizabeth Hook; coats to Joane R[ow?], widow, & to Katherine Rugg; marked by Bridgett Baker & signed by witn John Baker & Joseph Newbery.]

136 AMES FRANCKE 1664 (PU)

[Bur: "Ames Franck" 7 Aug 1664. Mar: "Ames Franke & Agnes Brooke" 23 Apr 1635. Prosperous yeoman; tenement of Rocke mentioned in will but not in inventory; clothmaking gear; 1 mare, 2 cattle, 14 sheep, 4 hogs, & corn; total, including £80 chattel lease, £196.]

An Inventorie taken ye 13th day of August 1664 of ye goods & Chattles of Ames Francke late deceased of ye pish of Uffculme prised by John Salkeld gent Thomas Balliman & Humphery Woodrow as followeth

	lî	s	d
Inprimis his weareing Appell	8	0	0
It 2 Feather beads & bedsteads pformed	9	5	0
It 2 flock beds & bedsteeds pformed	6	13	4
It 2 dust beds & bedsteeds pformed	2	10	0
It 1 Chest 4 Coffers	1	10	0
It 1 trunke 3 boxes	0	13	4
It 1 other bedsteed & bed pformed	1	10	0
It Woole	2	14	6
It 2 table boards 2 formes & 5 joine stooles	1	18	4
It 4 chaires	0	8	6
It 2 Carpets	0	11	0
It Wooll cloath	1	16	0
Item Lining	3	16	0
Item 17 pewter dishes	3	6	8
Item 2 Flaggons 2 Candlesticks) Item 6 tining dishes & a) Chamberpot	0	13	4
Item 2 trendles a yeating vate 7 tubbs 4 standerds	5	6	8
Item 4 barrles 2 verkings	1	3	4
It 2 hogheads	0	13	0
It 2 hutches	2	0	0
It 1 Cheese wring	1	3	4
It 3 paire of lumbes & slees	6	5	0
It 1 mare & furniture belonging	4	0	0
It 1 side saddle	0	10	0
It 1 Cowe & yeareling	4	13	4
It 14 sheepe	4	4	0
It 4 hogges	4	0	0
It 1 Chattle lease	80	0	0
It Corne in barne	20	0	0
It hay	3	0	0
It wood	4	0	0
It reed	0	6	8

	lî	s	d
It 1 paire of harrowes & other Iron stuffe	1	0	0
It bords	0	13	4
It other implements about ye house	0	10	0
Suma totalis	196	9	8

[£7 15s too much?]

[Exhibited 20 Dec 1664 by Agnes, exec.

Will 3 Apr 1663 of Ames Frank of Uffculme, yeoman, pr 20 Dec 1664 before Mr Richard Mathew: residue & "Ann's house & chamber over" for life to wife Agnes, exec; to s William Frank the tenement of Rocke in Uffculme; £6 each to dr Elizabeth, ss Ames & Joseph, drs Agnes & Jane, & ss Robt, John, Baptist, & Humfry; friend Thomas Balliman & k John Garnesey ovsrs; marked A by Ames Franke in presence of Tho: Balliman & Eliner Cotterell (C mark).]

137 WILLIAM HITCHCOCKE 1665 (DS)

[Bur: "William Hitchcock" 5 Apr 1665. Fuller with 1 mare, 1 cow, & 1 pig; brewing vat; total, including £8 owed to him, £35.]

An Inventory of all the goods Cattles & Cred[its] of William Hitchcocke late of Uffculme in the County of Devon Fuller taken and appraysed by Bartholamew Dowdney Richard Cole & John Marshall the sixth day of Aprill in the seveenteenth year of the Raygne of o^r gratious Soueragne lord Kinge Charles the second by the grace of god of England Scotland France Ireland Kinge defender of the Fayth annoq. dom 1665

	lî	s	d
Imprimis his wearinge apparrell		xx	
Item one bedsteed one Feather bed & bolster & Furniture		xxx	
Item one truckelbedsteed & bedd pformed		x	
Item three Coffers one Chest one table bord one little table board & forme		xxiij	
Item one brewinge Fatt two trendells three tubbs & two payles		xiv	
Item seven braze panns two Kittles two skilletts one skimer one Flesh peike two Candellsticks & two pottage potts of braze		xxxxv	
It one dozen of Pewter dishes Five sawcers three Pewter pottage dishes and one salt		xx	
It two pott crocks two brandlirons one payre of pott hangers & one gredliron & one spitt		iiij	
It in bakon and Cheese		xxxx	
It one Cow		lxx	
It one mare one packe saddle wth guirts panniers & other Furniture		xl	
It one Swyne hogge		vj	
It one bakon Racke shelves stooles & other lumber omitted		v	
It three beare barrells & gibb		v	
It one Cheeswringe		ij	
It all his tooles & imployments belonge to his trade	x		
It in sperat debts	viij		
It in Reddy money		xv	
Sume is	xxxv^li	ix^s	

Sigñ Richard [R mark] Cole
Bartholomew [D mark] Dowdney
Johannis [M mark] Marshall

[Exhibited at Uffculme by the admin, 28 Jun 1665. Latin endorsement signed by Wa: Johnson Reg^r.]

138 THOMAS MOULTON 1666 (PU)

[Bur: "Thomas Moulton, gent" 1 Mar 1665/6. Mar: "Thomas Molton & Joane Webber" 9 Jul 1618, Plymtree. "Gent" with much accommodation & equipment, but modest stocks of wheat, barley, & oats, 2 pigs & poultry; books; £43.]

An Inventory of all & singular the goods & Chattles of Thomas Moulton late of Ufculme in the County of Devon Gent deceased, taken & prized by John Salkeld, Humphry Woodruff, John How & Joseph Drew the twenty second day of February in y[e] Eighteenth yeare of y[e] raigne of our sov[r]aigne Lord Charles y[e] second by y[e] grace of God of England Scotland France & Ireland kinge defender of y[e] faith &c Annoq~ Dom: 1665 as followeth (viz.)

	lî	*s*	*d*
Inprimis his wearinge apparrell, money in purse, & about 6 yeards of gray kersy	08	00	00
It one silver spoone	00	05	00
In y[e] hall chamber			
It one Chest & a little box	00	08	00
It six yards of Course kersy	00	07	00
It bookes	01	00	00
It 2 deskes one coffer, 2 boxes one standerd & other goods of small value there	01	00	00
In y[e] Cheese chamber			
It one bed pformed & one coffer	01	04	00
In y[e] Parlour Chamber			
It all his linnen & napery	02	00	00
It 3 old Cov[r]lets & one blanket	00	15	00
It one Still, 2 old coffers & other goods of small value there beinge	00	10	04
In the wringe house chamber			
It all his pewter	02	10	00
It one Cubbord, one hogshead, two barrels, one Coffer, one tub one chese racke, white & black wooll & other goods of small value there beinge	01	06	08
In the Parlour			
It 2 table boards, one style, 6 ioint stooles, & two formes, one warminge pan, one pestle & mortar & other goods of small value there beinge	02	00	00
In the milke house			
It 8 brasse pans & other good of small value there beinge	01	10	00
In the wringe house			
It one cheese wringe, one trendle, meat in salte, one barrell, 3 tubs, one standerd, 3 cheese fates, one pecke, one range & other goods of small value there beinge	01	10	00
In the little Chamber			
It one halfe headed bedsted one bed and bolster & 2 blankets	01	03	04
In the little house			
It one dust bed & bedsted & one old Cheeswringe & other goods of small value there beinge	00	11	00
In the hall			
It 3 brasse pots, 3 brasse skillets, one brasse chafinge dish, one posnut one brasse kettle one Jacke, 4 spitts, 2 savinge irons, three payre of Andirons, 3 potcrooks, 2 pothangers, one payre of tongs, 2 dripinge pans, one saw, one Iron barre, 5 iron wedges, one fire pike one fryinge pan one grediron one mustard bowle, one payre of pincers[?], two chayres, two table boards, one forme, one bacon racke & one fletch & halfe of bacon & other goods of small value there beinge	04	13	04
In the entry			
It one chest, one milkinge payle, one pike, one hackney saddle & other goods of small value there beinge	00	06	04
In the Bakehouse			
It one old furnace & two old brasse pans	00	10	00
It 3 barrells, one yewtinge fate, 5 tubs & other goods of small value there beinge	01	06	00
It wheat, barly & oats	02	00	00
It 2 pigs	01	00	00
It one grindinge stone & turner	00	02	04
It hay & dunge	00	10	00
It wheat in ground	03	00	00
It one packe saddle, one payre of crookes, other horse tacklinge & tooles for husbandry	00	05	04
It 3 new gates	00	07	06
It Poultry	00	03	00
It wood	00	10	00

	lî	*s*	*d*
It beere butter & cheese	01	00	00
It boards & other timber	01	00	00
It goods seene & unseene not before in this Inventory valued	00	13	04
Suma totalis	43	07	06

John Salkeld Humfry Woodruff
John Houwe [J H mark] Joseph Drew

[Admon 24 Mar 1665/6 names Walther Hale of Staplegrove, Somerset, as admin of goods &c of Thomas Moulton, his uncle, & also Richard Crosse of Uffculme; signed & sealed by Walther Hale, & marked & sealed by Richard Crosse, in presence of John Rowcliffe & Nicholas Webber.

Thomas Moulton's wife, Joane Moulton, refused to administer the estate of the intestate Thomas & named Walther Hale as admin: document 17 Mar 1665/6 marked by Joane Moulton & witn by Joseph Snow & Mary Webber.]

139 ATTEWILL WHEDDON 1666 (PU)

[Bur: "Atwill Whiddon" 10 Mar 1665/6. Mar: "Atwell Whidon & Anne Smith" 21 Aug 1620. Wheat, peas, & 1 hog; hall, hall-chamber, parlour, & milkhouse but no cows mentioned; no clothmaking gear; £19.]

An Inventory of the goods & Chattles of Attewill Wheddon of Uffculme in the county of Devon deceased taken & prized the seaven & twentieth day of March in the eighteenth yeer of the reigne of o^{r} sovereigne Lord Charles the second by the grace of god now kinge of England &c & in the yeer of o^{r} Lord god 1666 By William Hollway Joseph Drew John Wheddon & Symon Leaman as followeth

	lî	*s*	*d*
Imprimis his wearing apparrell	03	06	08
Item in the parlour one feather bed & feather bedsteed pformed	02	13	04
Item Two table-boards seaven Joyne stooles Two Chaires & one Forme	02	00	00
Item Two old brass-potts, one little Caldron & skillett	00	10	00
Item Two pot-crooks, one paire of fire Tongs & one frying pan	00	02	06
Item in the Hall one Cupboard & table-board	01	00	00
Item five pewter dishes	00	09	00
Item old Pewter	00	04	02
Item in the Milke-house five barrells	00	06	08
Item foure small Tubbs & one Trindle	00	15	00
Item one Cheese-wring	00	02	06
Item in the hall-chamber foure Coffers & one Truckle bed pformed	01	06	08
Item one fatt hogge	02	00	00
Item Corne in ye barne	00	16	00
Item one Acre of Wheate in ground	02	10	00
Item one Acre of pease in ground	01	03	04
Item old Implements seen & not seen	00	06	08
Totall Sum is	19	12	06

Will Holway Joseph Drew John Wheddon
Symon Leaman his [S?] Marke

[Exhibited by Ann Whiddon, relict & admin, 16 May 1666.

Admon 16 May 1666 names Anne Whiddon as widow & admin of the goods &c of Atwell Whiddon, & also John Whiddon of Uffculme, blacksmith; marked by Anne Whiddon & signed by John Whiddon in presence of Nicholas Webber.]

140 EDWARD ANDREW 1666 (PU)

[Bur: "Edward Andrew" 28 Jul 1666. Whitebaker with wheat & 1 hog; entry, hall, & buttery, all with rooms over, & middle room; no clothmaking gear; total, including £3 owed to him, £20.]

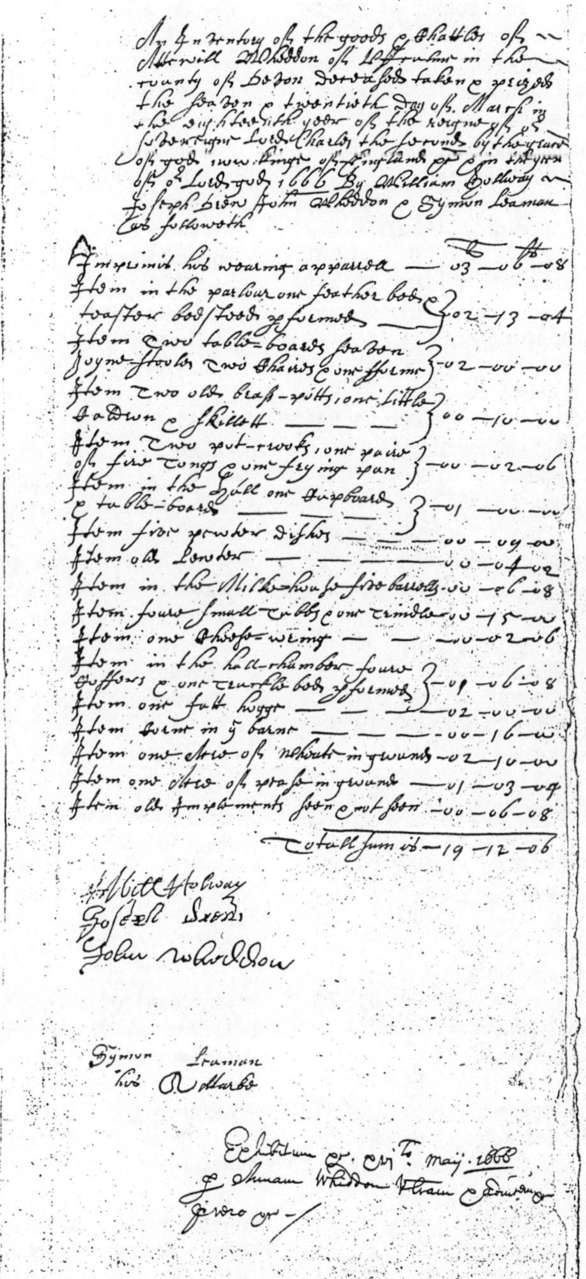

An Inventory of the goods & chattles of Atewill Wheddon of Westrulme in the county of Devon deceased taken & prized the seaven & twentieth day of March in the eighteenth yeare of the reigne of our soveraigne lord Charles the second by the grace of god now kinge of England &c Anno Domini of our Lord god 1666 By William Holway & Joseph Deen John Wheddon & Symon Leaman as followeth

	li	s	d
Imprimis his wearing apparrell	03	06	08
Item in the parlour one feather bed, one tester bedsteed & furniture	02	13	04
Item two table boards seaven joyne stooles two chaires & one forme	02	00	00
Item two old brass potts, one little cauldron & skillett	00	10	00
Item two pot-crooks, one paire of fire tongs & one frying pan	00	02	06
Item in the hall one cupboard & table-board	01	00	00
Item five pewter dishes	00	09	00
Item old lumber	00	04	02
Item in the milkehouse five barrells	00	06	08
Item foure small tubbs & one trendle	00	15	00
Item one cheese-wring	00	02	06
Item in the hall-chamber foure coffers & one truckle bed & furniture	01	06	08
Item one fatt hogge	02	00	00
Item corne in the barne	00	16	00
Item one acre of wheate in ground	02	10	00
Item one acre of pease in ground	01	03	04
Item old implements seen & not seen	00	06	08
Totall sum is	19	12	06

Will Holway
Joseph Deen
John Wheddon

Symon Leaman his mark

Exhibitum … maij 1666 per Annam Wheddon … Jurato …

The inventory of Atewill Wheddon 1666 [139]

An Inventory of All the goods and Chattels of Edward Andrew of the pish of Ufculme in the County of Devon whitebaker late decesd Taken & prised the five & twentyth daye of July in the yeare of our Lord God one Thousand six Hundred sixty six by Richard Rugge William Holway Joseph Drew Thomas Young as Foloweth___

	lî	*s*	*d*
Imprimus His wearing Appill	02	00	00
Item two bras pans	00	12	00
It nine pewter dishes	01	00	00
It two Candelsticks one saltsiller	00	01	00
It one bras Crocke one porstnut	00	05	00
Item in the Hall one tabel bord & forme	00	12	00
It two Chaiers & two stools	00	03	04
It one Glascage & planke	00	01	06
It one Carbine	00	03	04
It one Caldron & one planke	00	08	00
Item in the Midel Roome two vats & a paile	00	07	00
It one Huch & a Ammerry	00	10	06
It one dresingbord & a shilfe	00	02	06
It one brakestocke & a paire of weights	00	02	06
It two sarches & a Range	00	00	08
Item in the buttery two barels	00	02	06
It three shilfs & a Jeb	00	04	00
It one pecke & quarter of pecke	00	01	00
It in the butry chamber one Fether bed & bedsteed pformed	02	10	00
It two Coffers & two boxes & one Joyned stoole	00	06	00
Item in the Hall Chamber one Halfhed bedsteed & a Truckle bed pformed	00	14	00
Item in the Chamber over the Entry one paire of bakers pots & two planks	00	04	00
It Hoops & vesalstaves	00	03	04
It two ould Trendls & a Round tub	00	03	00
Item one Reeck of wood	02	10	00
It wood & Furs	00	08	00
It Reed & spars	00	11	00
It one small Hog	00	05	00
It whete in ground	02	10	00
It one persle & morter & one bras pan	00	08	00
Item ould Implements seen & not seen	00	03	04
Item due from Edward Marshall sen^{r} in Money two pound tenn shillings	02	10	00
Item William Starke sen^{r} for Rent	00	03	00
It Simeon Leamon for Rent	00	05	00
som is	20	10	06

[Exhibited 9 Aug 1666 by Grace Andrew, widow, before Mr Richard Mathew, cleric surr. for prebendary.

Admon 8 Aug 1666 names Grace Andrew as widow & admin, & also Nicholas Halsham of Tiverton, baker; G mark of Grace Andrew & NH mark of Nicholas Halsham witn by Nicholas Webber, who signs.]

141 GEORGE WELCH 1666 (PU)

[Bur: "George Welch" 26 Aug 1666. Mar: "George Welch & Christia Collerett" 20 Sep 1649, Exeter St Sidwell. Weaver; little in inventory, but £100 tenement at Smithincott & £4 cottage at Stenhill; £108.]

An Inventory of the goods & Chattles of George Welch late of Uffcolmne in the County of Devon Weaver deceased taken & prized the 18th day of September 1666./ By Symon Welch Peter Snow & Willyam Cottrell as followeth./

	lî	*s*	*d*
Imp^{s} his wearing apparrell	2	10	0
Item one tenem^{t} in Smethincott within the pish of Uffcolmne aforesayd	100	0	0
Item one Cottage in Stennoll within the sayd pish	4	0	0
Item one Swyne hogg	1	0	0

	lî	*s*	*d*
Item wood & furse	0	10	0
Item money in his purse	0	10	0
Item other Implemts nott seene nor prized	0	2	0
Sume is	108	12	0

[Exhibited by Christian, relict & admin, 31 Oct 1666.

Admon 31 Oct 1666 names Christian Welch as widow & admin, & also William Rawlyns of Uffculme, clothier; marked C by Christian Welch & signed by William Rawlins in presence of Nicholas Webber.]

142 WILLYAM CROSSE 1667 (PU)

[Bur: "William Crosse" 10 Apr 1667. Yeoman with corn, cattle, sheep, & 2 pigs; hall, buttery, & kitchen (& parlour in will); no clothmaking gear; total, including £55 owed to him & a £60 half chattel lease (at Stenhill?), £186.]

An Inventory of all & singuler the goods & Chattells of Willyam Crosse late of the pish of Uffcolmne in the County of Devon yeoman deceased taken & prised the 7th day of October 1667 By Thomas Ballyman Robert Merson Nicholas Tucker & John Rawlins as followeth./

	lî	*s*	*d*
Imprimis his wearing apparrell	5	0	0
Item money oweing upon specialty	50	0	0
It. money oweing without specialty	5	0	0
It. one halfe of a Chattle tenemt	60	0	0
It. one bedstead & feather bed pformed	4	0	0
It. one other bedstead & bed pformed	2	10	0
It. one standing bedstead & trindle bedstead pformed	3	13	4
It. one Chest & 5 Coffers	1	13	4
It. one table board.2.sideboards 3.furmes in the Kitchin	0	13	4
It. tymber vessells standing in the buttery	1	11	0
It. one tablebord.6.Joyne stooles.2.cheares one Cubbord standing in the hall	2	10	0
It. other tymber vessells besides	1	13	4
It. one cheese wring & vates	0	6	8
It. 5.brasse crocks	2	16	0
It. 12.brasse panns	3	15	0
It. 2. Calldrons & one skillett	0	6	6
It. pewter	2	8	0
It. 2.brasse Candlesticks	0	2	8
It. one pessell & morter	0	1	8
It. 2.payre of brandis backcrooks with other Irestuffe	0	10	0
It. kine &.2.heaffers	20	7	0
It. sheepe	1	6	0
It. wooll	0	6	0
It. 2.Swyne hoggs	2	10	0
It. Corne in ground & out of ground	10	0	0
It. wood	1	10	0
It. horse tackling & one payre of harrows	1	0	0
It. other Implemts. not seene nor prised	0	13	4
	186	03	2

[Will 27 Nov 1666 of Willyam Crosse the elder of uffculme, yeoman, pr at Uffculme 10 Oct 1667 before Mr Richard Mathew, cleric surr. for prebendary Mr Thos. Clarke: residue to dr Joane Crosse, exec, & also the bed *which she doth usually lye in now standing in the parlor* & other items; to s Willyam Crosse the tenement at "Stennoll" & share of household goods; to s Thomas Crosse all the corn & share of household goods; marked + by Willyam Crosse in presence of John Rawlins & John Lowdewell (both sign).]

143 EDWARD MARSHALL 1668 (DS)

[Bur: "Edward Marshall sen" 1 Jun 1668. Mar: "Edward Marshall & Dorothy Pooke" 29 Nov 1647. Prosperous fuller with large corn stocks, 1 mare, & 7 pigs; entry, hall, parlour, & shop, all with rooms over; kitchen with room adjoining, buttery, & millhouse; total, including £30 owed to him & £80 chattel lease, £197.]

An Inventory of all & singular the goods Chattles & Credits of Edward Marshall Late of Uffculme in the county of Devon Fuller deceased - Taken and prized the Third day of June in the yeer of o^r Lord god 1668 By John Wills Francis Pratt, Richard Gill, Symon Gill & Edward Marshall as followeth

	lî	*s*	*d*
Imprimis his Wearing apparrell	02	00	00
Item In the Chamber over the Parlour, Two halfe head Bedsteeds, one Truckle Bedsteed, Three Flock-beds, three Boulsters three Coverletts & Two Blanketts	02	10	00
Item in the said chamber over the Parlour, two Coffers, one corne hutch, without a cover, one Little Forme, & two boards.	00	10	00
Item in the chamber over the Hall; one standing Bedsteed; one halfe head Bedsteed; Two Flocke beds wth boulsters, Coverletts & Blanketts, thereunto belonging and one paire of Sheets	03	10	00
Item in the same chamber over the Hall one Chest, one little Table-board, two Chairs & one little Box	00	10	00
Item in the same chamber, two little remnants of Cloath	01	00	00
Item in the chamber over the Entry one halfe head Bedsteed; one Flocke-bed, boulster & Coverlett	00	13	04
Item in the chamber over the Shop one press	00	04	00
Item in the Hall one Table-board, one Forme one old Cupboard, one glass-cage, two little Settles, one Chaire, one Bacon-racke and dishcage	01	02	00
Item in the Hall one paire of doggs	00	01	06
Item in the Parlour one Table-board Six Joyne stooles, one little side boarde & one Carpett-cloath	01	11	00
Item in the Kitchen, three Brass-potts one Porsnett one Pestle & Morter	01	13	04
Item in the Kitchen twelve brass-pannes one Skillett, one Chaffing-dish one Caldron	03	10	00
Item in the Kitchen one paire of Andirons two backe-crookes, two pot crookes one dripping-panne, one Saveing-Iron, two Spitts, one Griddiron & one Fire-panne	00	10	00
Item in the Kitchen one old table-board & one plancke	00	06	08
Item in the Buttery, one Hogshead, two halfe Hogsheads, & three Barrells	01	00	00
Item in the same Buttery one Amery one Gybb, one plancke & foure little Shilfes	00	04	00
Item pewter in the same Buttery	01	07	00
Item in the little roome without ye Kitchen three timber Fatts, three Trundles foure little tubbs, two salting standards & three pailes	01	06	08
Item in the Shoppe the toolles belonging to his Fulling Trade; twenty two paire of Sheeres wth Leads thereunto belonging, two sheer-boards, two dubbing-boards, two Brushes, & handles belonging to the same trade	14	18	00
Item one Spill-press wth papers & other Implem^ts therunto belonging	08	00	00
Item one Racke, & one hanging	06	10	00
Item Corne in the Barne	06	00	00
Item Corne in the ground	20	00	00
Item one Wood-reecke in the court wth other Wood	01	10	00
Item one Mare	03	00	00
Item one Sow, five sucking piggs & one other pigge	01	13	04

Item one Iron-barre, one

	lî	*s*	*d*
Sledge, two Shovells, wth other Husbandry-toolles	00	08	00
Item Horse-tackling	00	10	00
Item one paire of Harrowes & one Wheell-barrow	00	06	08
Item in the Mill-house one halfe head Bedsteed, one old Coffer & a few plancks	00	10	00
Item money due upon specialty	30	00	00
Item one Chattle Lease	80	00	00
Item things omitted & forgotten		[06	08]
The whole Sum is	197	02	02

[Exhibited at Uffculme by Christopher Marshall, exec, at the primary visitation of the Ven. Rodolph Bridebake of Salisbury Cathedral, 13 Jun 1668. Latin endorsement signed Wa: Johnson Reg^{r}.

Will 28 Aug 1666 of Edward Marshall of Uffculme, fuller, pr 13 Jun 1668: residue to s Christopher Marshall, exec; 20s to poor of both Uffculme & Kentisbeare; 20s to wife Dorothy; estate "Andrewes" in Craddock to dr Rebecca, or her chn if she should die, or failing that to John Marshall, s of Christopher Marshall; £20 each at age 21 to 2 chn of s Richard; signed EM by Edward Marshall, & signed by John Ball & marked by Alexander Enery (Endry?) as witn.]

144 ANNE WYATT 1668 (DS)

[Spinster; few household items; no clothmaking gear; total, including £9 owed to her, £13.]

An Inventory of the goods Chattles & Credits of Anne Wyatt Late of Uffculme in the county of Devon spinster deceased taken & prised the Twelveth Day of June in the yeer of o^{r} Lord god 1668 By John Starke John Gay & William Potter as followeth -

	lî	*s*	*d*
Imprimis her purse & apparrell	02	03	04
Item one halfe head Bedsteed one bed one banckett one Coverlett two pillowes & one sheet	00	16	00
Item one Chest one Coffer & one stooll	00	06	08
Item her pewter	00	02	03
Item Two remnants of cloath	00	10	00
Item one old Caldron	00	03	04
Item debt sperate	07	00	00
Item other debt sperate	00	11	06
Item other debt sperate	00	19	00
Item other debt sperate	00	11	00
Item other things omitted & not formerly prized	00	02	04
The Summe is	13	05	05

[Exhibited by Jonas Wyatt, admin, at the primary visitation of the Dean of Salisbury, 13 Jun 1668. Latin endorsement signed by Wa: Johnson Reg^{r}.

Admon 13 Jun 1668 names Jonas Wyatt of Uffculme, dyer, as bro & admin, & also John Whiddon of Uffculme, smith; marked by Jonas Wyatt & signed by John Wheddon, in the presence of Wa: Johnson, not^{y} pub.]

145 WILLIAM GOODRIDGE 1668 (PU)

[Bur: "William Goodridge" 27 Aug 1668. Husbandman (retired?); household items & husbandry tools only, apart from 1 pig; hall & room over; £11.]

The Inventory Indented of all & singuler the goods & Chattles of William Goodridge of Uffculme in the County of Devon husbandman: Deceased made & praysed the 10th day of march in the yeare of o^{r} Lord god 1668[/9] by Humffrey Bishopp Samuell Bishopp & Roger Bishopp

	lî	*s*	*d*
Imprimis his wearinge Apparrell praysed in	03	00	00
Item money in pockett	00	05	00
Item in the Chamber over the hall 2 beeds beedsteads & Furnitude praysed in	03	00	00

	lî	s	d
Item 2 Cheests 2 Cofferrs praysed in	01	00	00
Item 2 pweter dishes 2 flaggons 2 Candlestickes 2 salts one butter plate one boole with other thinges in the said Roome praised in	00	10	00
Item in the hall 3 silt standerds 2 toobes one Fate 2 barrells one virkinge & one payle praysed in	00	12	00
Item one Table boarde & Furme praysed in	00	06	00
Item one bras pot one pann one skillett one Caldron one skimer one Candelsticke & one Iron pot praysed in	01	06	08
Item 2 paire of pot Croocks one pot hanger one Flesh picke & one branIron praysed in	00	02	04
Item one sife one shoule two mattocks with other husbandry twools praysed in	00	05	06
Item one silver spoone praysed in	00	05	00
Item one swine praysed in	00	06	00
Item things about the house seen & not seen nor yet pticulerly praysed: praysed in	00	04	04
Totall Sum is	11	02	10

[Admon 28 Apr 1669 names Anne Goodridge as widow & admin, & also John Daggle of North Werton(?), Dorset, yeoman; marked by Anne Goodridge & signed by John Daggle in presence of Fran: St. Barbe, not[y] pub.]

146 WILLIAM HODGE 1669 (PU)

[Bur: "William Hodge" 9 Mar 1668/9. Prosperous tailor; hall, buttery, kitchen & 2 other rooms mentioned; corn; 2 mares, 1 cow, heiffer, calf, 2 pigs, poultry, & bees; £67.]

The Inventory Indented of all & singuler the goods & Chattles of William Hodge of Uffculme in the County of Devon Taylor Deceased: made & praysed the 16th Day of March in the yeare of o[r] lord God 1668[/9] by Henry Dowdney Robert Gill Richard Waldron & Arther Steevens

[The words "praised in" ending almost every item have been omitted in the transcript.]

	lî	s	d
Imprimis his wearing apparrell praised in	05	00	00
Item two beeds bedsteads & furniture theire unto belongen one Cheest 4 Coffers with other things in the said Roome	05	00	00
Item money in pockett	00	10	00
Item in the Roome within the hall one bead bedsteade & furniture with other things in the Roome	03	00	00
Item in the buttry one Trendle 4 barrells with other things in the Roome	01	10	00
Item in the hall two Table boards one furme one Joyne stoole two Chears one Cubboard & one glas Chaige	02	01	03
Item in the hall three Caldrons two bras poots one posnet eight pewter dishes three Candlesticks two bras panns & one skillett	04	10	00
Item in the hall two poot hangers three paire of poot Crooks one gridiron one braniron one skimer one bras ladle with other things in the Roome	00	10	08
Item bacon butter & Cheese with other pvision in the house	02	05	00
Item in the little Roome within the Kitching three planks & other timber stufe in the Roome	02	02	00
Item in the Kitching one Cheese Wringe one breakeboard with other things in the Roome	00	13	04
Item nine Iron Wagges one battle one shoule with other Husbandry tools	00	12	02
Item Corne in the barne	07	00	00
Item haye in the tallet	01	05	00
Item two mairs	05	00	00
Item one Kine one heafer & one Calfe	06	14	00
Item two hoggs	02	00	00

	lî	*s*	*d*
Item one pack saddle one saydsadle one hacknet sadle one pillion one bridle with other horse tacklen	01	16	08
Item one paire of Harrows	00	03	04
Item wood & Fuel	00	11	06
Item Corne in ground	10	10	00
Item pulltrey	00	02	04
Item two butts of bees	00	05	00
Item one bushell of wheat	00	08	00
Item Desperate Deebt	03	07	04
Item 4 baggs 1 winsheet & other things about the house seen & not seen & not before pticularly praised	00	17	03
Totall Sum is	67	14	10

[Admon 28 Apr 1669 names Jane Hodge as widow & admin, & also Arthur Stevens, farmer of Uffculme; marked by them in presence of F St Barbe, notary public.]

147 EDMONT BISHOPP 1670 (PU)

[Bur: "Edmond Bishop" 30 Mar 1670. Husbandman (retired?); household items only; total, of which he owed £5 & including £8 owed to him, £11.]

The Inventory of all & singuler the goods & Chattles & depts of Edmont Bishopp of Ufculme in the County of Devon Husbandman: deceased made & praysed the 4th of April in the yeare of or Lord god 1670 by John Done & John Lacke

	lî	*s*	*d*
Inprimis his wearing apprell	00	10	00
Item money in pocket	00	03	03
Item his beed & beedsted & Furnitude	00	12	00
Item in the Chamber whare hee lay one old Cheest and other things in the said Roome	00	05	00
Item in the gaarden feestall [?] timber	00	03	00
Item tember & Roten plancks	00	04	09
Item 4 pweter dishes	00	04	00
Item Rowe [raw?] Clooth	00	14	00
Item depts spechall	06	09	08
Item despret debts	02	10	00
Item things not seen nether praysed but forgotten	00	01	00
The Sum is	11	16	08
whareof he owe	05	05	10

[Will 22 Mar 1669/(70) of Edmont Bishopp of Uffculme: residue to "grant Childe" (grandch?) Roger Bishopp; 2s 6d each to Roger Bishopp s of Elizabeth Bishopp & to Catron Bishopp dr of Saml Bishopp, all of Uffculme; brass cauldron & wooden plate to Jone Lacke, wife of John Lacke; 1 pewter dish to William Hodge; marked + by Edmont Bishopp in presence of William Hodge (who signs) & John Done (J mark).]

148 THOMAS CROYDEN 1670 (PU)

[Bur: "Thomas Croydon" 20 May 1670. Mar: "Thomas Croydon & Wilmot Burrow" 9 May 1667. Prosperous yeoman with corn, 2 mares, 1 cow & 2 calves, 21 sheep, 3 pigs, & plough; several rooms, including cider house; 1 bible, 1 other book, & a gun; £77.

The beginning of the inventory is damaged and partly missing.]

......Thomas C...
...[D]evon yeoman deceased...
..Annoqs Dom 1670 by..
......rt Burrough & Leonard
..nd & County aforesd viz.

	lî	*s*	*d*
.....purse	4	0	0
......	2	10	0
	1	0	0
	2	2	0
[half]head bedsted ...[d]ustbe[d]..:1:blancket & 4 bords	0	16	0
It: in ye apple Chamber: 1:Corne huch & 2 planks	0	10	0
It: in ye Inerhouse:2:barrels & 1 trendle	0	10	0
It: in ye Under Roome 1 bedsted 1 Coverlet 1 peece of seeling .....and Coffer	2	15	0

	lî	*s*	*d*
It: in ye hall:1:little tableboard: 1:Cubbrd one bucket or paile & 1 fowlinge peece	1	16	8
It: one flich of bacon	0	15	0
It: in ye forth house:2:hogseds: 2:Coffers	0	13	4
It: 9:peuter dishes:2:peuter Candlesticks 2:Lattine Candelsticks 2:sawsers 1:salt: 1:butter plate	1	10	0
It: one bible & one other booke	0	6	0
It: 2:brass pannes 2 kittles 1: skillet 2:brass pots & one brass Candlesticks	1	12	0
It: 2:sackbags:1:Joyne stoole: 1:Window lid & 2:old tubbs	0	6	8
It: one pothangin 1 potcrook: 1 brandiron:1:gridiron 1:toaster 1 fryingpan 1 spitt & 1 saving iron	0	8	0
It: in ye barne 3:longe peeces & in the bakes 16 plankes	1	0	0
It: in ye poundhouse one siderwringe & other Implim^{ts}	1	10	0
It: in ye stall timber stuff & Implim^{ts}	0	6	0
It: in ye Siderhouse:1:gibb 1 barrell	0	2	0
It: for plowstuff	0	5	0
It: 2:Calves.	1	15	0
It: one Cow:3:swinehoggs: 1:mare & 1:packsadel	8	6	8
It: 12 sheepe & 9 lambes	4	0	0
It: Wood	12	0	0
It: 18:acars of Corne	25	0	0
It: one blinde mare	0	5	0
It: goods seene & not seene of Lumber & Implements	1	0	0
	lî	*s*	*d*
Sum: total	77	0	4

William Holway Leonard Ashelford
Mark Westron Robert Burrow

[Admon 16 Jun 1670 names Andrew Scutt, geñ (gent?) of Cheriton Fitzpayne, Devon, as father-in-law & admin, & also John Lowdwell, farmer, & John Croyden, tanner, both of Uffculme; signed by Andrew Scutt & John Lowdwell & marked by John Croyden in presence of Richard Mathew, John Grantland, & John Dyer (all sign). According to a document of 21 May 1670, the widow Wilmoth Croyden refused to administer & named father-in-law Andrew Scutt.]

149 AGNES COTTERELL 1670 (PU)

[Bur: "Agnis Cotterell, widow" 3 Jun 1670. Comfortably-off widow of Ambrose No. 116, with £20 annuity; hall with room over, & milkhouse; no stock or clothmaking gear; total, including £5 owed to her, £35.

Part of the inventory is missing near the top.]

An inventory of all & singular ye goods & Cattells of Agnes Cotterell latt of Uffcolum in ye County of D[evon.....wi]dow decesed taken & pri[.....] of June in yeare of o[.....] by William Holway [.....P]eetter Snow & [.....as fo]lloweth

	lî	*s*	*d*
Imprimis... waring aparrell	3	0	0
Item in the Chamber over the hall on trukell bedsteed with the furnitur belonging	1	0	0
Item on trunk & to planks	0	5	0
Item on Chest & on ould Bedsted	0	18	0
Item five littell puwter dishes	0	06	8
Item in the milkhouse four brass pans on skillett on Caldron & on brass potte	2	0	0
Item on trundell three barrells three tubs	1	3	0
Item in the halle on tabell borde on settell to Charess on furm on plank	1	2	6
Item on bond du from Henry Hartt	5	0	0
Item on anuaty	20	0	0
Item olde implements seene & nott seene	0	6	8
	35	1	10

Will Holway Leonard Ashelford
Peeter [his mark] Snow William Rawlins

[Will 26 Dec 1655 of Agnes Cotterell of Uffculme, widow : residue & 45s annuity after 5 years to s William Cotterell, exec; apparel &c & 40s annuity after 5 years to drs Joane Snowe & Christian Welch; items to grandchn John & Joan Snowe, & George & Agnes Welch, plus shared £7 10s annuity for 5 years, thereafter 25s yearly; the annuities all to be paid quarterly from the rent of the tenement of Sowell ("which William now liveth in"), conditionally upon the survival of Agnes Cotterell's bro John Dowdeney; 2s 6d each to ovsrs Thomas Balliman & bro John Dowdeney; marked by Agnes Cotterell in presence of Thomas Balliman, Agnes Balliman (A mark), & Mary Palmer (MP mark).]

150 JOHN VOSSE 1670 (PU)

[Bur: "John Fosse" 6 Jun 1670. Mar: "John Fosse & Mary Starke" 14 Dec 1652. Yeoman (retired?); household items & tools only; £7.]

The Inventory of ye goods & Chattles of John Vosse late of Uffculme in ye County of Devon Yeoman deceased made & apprized by John Salkeld gent & Christopher Marshall & George Bakker ye 15th day July 1670

	lî	*s*	*d*
Inprimis in ready money	5	0	0
his Apparell	0	10	0
Item in his beadchameber one halfe headed beadstead & a dustbead one pare of blanckets & a Coverlet & a dustbolster & a feather pillowe	0	13	4
Item 3 pewter dishes one pewter tancket a pewter bowle & a pewter Candlestick	0	6	8
Item one brasse pott one brasse skillet	0	7	0
Item one pare of potthookes & one Irone Crooke	0	1	0
Item one Chest & one box	0	6	0
Item Woorkeing tooles	0	4	0
Item one settle one sidetable-borde one forme one Chare 3 stooles wth other lumber &c	0	10	0
	7	18	0

John Salkeld Christopher Marshall George Baker

[Will 1 Jan 1661/2 of John Forse, husbandman: 1s to wife Mary, best coffer to dr Jane; residue to s Thomas Forse, exec; "ruler" [ovsr] John Ballyman; marked by John Forse; signed by witn Tho Ballyman & Mary Ballyman.]

151 ELIZABETH FURSDON 1670 (PU)

[Bur: "Elizabeth Fursden" 4 Jul 1670. Prosperous widow of George No.133; hall, parlour, 1 other room, & milkhouse; hourglass; corn, 5 cattle, 1 colt, 57 sheep, geese, & poultry; clothmaking gear; £44.]

An Inventory of all the Goods of Elizabeth Fursdon of Uffculme in the County of Devon Widdow late deceased made & taken by John Palmer John Marshall & John Burrow the fifth day of July in the two & twentyth yeare of the reigne of o^r^ soveraigne Lord King Charles the Second over England &c. Annoq~ Domi 1670:

	lî	*s*	*d*
Imp^s^ her Apparrell	02	10	00
Item one bedsteed wth Bedding in the parlour	02	06	08
Item one Tableboard, one furme two Joynt stooles three Cushions, & one Carpett in ye parlour	00	15	00
Item one Cupboard, one Tableboard one furme one Chaire one Glasse-cage in the Hall	00	18	10
Item one bedsteed & truckell bed wth bedding in ye Chamber	01	02	00
Item three Coffers & one Chaire in the Chamber	00	05	00
Item three barrells & shelfes in the Milkehouse	00	05	00
Item three Tubbs	00	04	00
Item one Ladder, one Hurdell one spinning-turne and one wheele of a spinning-turne	00	03	04
Item six brasse panns	00	18	00
Item two Brasse Caldrons	00	12	00

	lî	*s*	*d*
Item two brasse Crocks & one skillett	00	10	00
Item one Paire of Brasse weights	00	01	00
Item one Chest	00	05	00
Item one selting trendle	00	03	04
Item one Plancke & three boards	00	01	04
Item one paire of Andirons one frying pan one Gridiron & one spitt & three wedges	00	04	08
Item three Corne pikes	00	00	08
Item two Crookes & two potthangings	00	02	06
Item one houreglasse	00	00	04
Item butter & Cheese	00	08	00
Item in wooll	02	00	00
Item in Peauter	00	17	00
Item one Cheesewringe	00	04	00
Item in wood	00	07	00
Item Corne & graine in Ground	03	10	00
Item two Cowes	06	00	00
Item one heifer, one yearlyn & one Calfe	05	00	00
Item one Colt	01	06	08
Item in 46 weathers ewes & 11 lambs	12	05	00
Item three Piggs	01	04	00
Item Geese & other pultry	00	03	04
Item other Implem^ts^ in & about the house	00	05	00
Suma total	44	18	08

John Palmer John Marshall John Burrow.

[Admon 18 Jul 1670 names Thomas Ballyman, yeoman, as admin, & also John Ballyman, yeoman, both of Uffculme; signed by both in presence of Nych: Ayshford, Rich: Mathew, & John Grantland.]

152 JOHN GRANTLAND 1670 (PU)

[Bur: "John Grantland sen" 3 Sep 1670. Very prosperous yeoman; 1 mare, 3 colts, 16 cattle, 7 pigs, winnowed corn; no clothmaking gear; no books; £448 in own house & other property; £614.]

An Inventory of all & singuler the goods Chattles & debts of John Grantland late of Uffculme in the County of Devon Yeoman deceased taken & prised the thyrteenth day of September 1670 by Christofer Marshall John Marshall & John Row as followeth./

	[*lî*	*s*	*d*]
Imprimis his wearinge apparrell	003	00	00
Item five bedsteads & beds performed	020	00	00
Item Corne in barne	018	00	00
Item seaven table boards	003	10	00
Item one Cubberd	001	15	00
Item six joyne stoolls	000	06	00
Item one sett of boxes	000	04	00
Item twelve Furms	000	16	00
Item one chest two coffers & two boxes	002	00	00
Item one tryndle	000	06	00
Item butter Cheese & baken	008	00	00
Item three brasse pots & one skillet	002	15	00
Item nyne brasse panns	002	15	00
Item three Caldrons	000	17	00
Item thyrteene puter dishes one salt one butter platt & four saucers	002	00	00
Item seaven hogsheads & six barrills	002	10	00
Item one Furnace	005	10	00
Item six Fatts & six tubbs	002	15	00
Item four jebs	000	08	00
Item two chairs & one Settle	000	13	00
Item twelve quarts & paints	001	10	00
Item five pails	000	05	00
Item two spitts two paire of Andires one frying pan & one brandice	000	13	00
Item two maddiocks one Ax one shovel one billhook & two flesh forks	000	05	00
Item one hayrick	010	00	00
Item two Furssericks	003	00	00
Item one woodrick	000	15	00
Item seaven swinehoggs	006	00	00
Item one cheesewring	000	04	00
Item one glass cage	000	01	00
Item six cheese Fatts	000	04	00

	[*lî*	*s*	*d*]
Item one wheele barrow & one hand barrow	000	07	00
Item two paire of Large crooks	000	04	00
Item one paire of dung potts	000	03	00
Item turffe & Fearnes	001	15	00
Item two butter standerds	000	04	00
Item tenn boards	000	07	00
Item two Carpetts	001	00	00
Item two boardcloths	000	06	00
Item six table Kneptkins	000	05	00
Item one skeemer	000	01	00
Item one hacney saddle	000	05	00
Item one side saddle	000	12	00
Item one pack saddle	000	04	00
Item corne winnowed	000	06	00
Item four sack baggs	000	04	00
Item sixteene Cattle	035	00	00
Item one mare two mare colts and one horse colt	018	00	00
Item five Yeards of Cersey	001	09	00
Item a pessell & morter	000	03	00
Item four shelffs	000	04	00
Item his dwellinge house	036	00	00
Item his revertion in Joane Dowdneys hous	012	00	00
Item his estate in the land called ye rixparks & ye hainsUnder	400	00	00
Item in money oweinge him	010	00	00
Item goods & implements not prised	001	00	00
Y^e^ Sum is	614	16	00
			[£6 short?]

[Will 26 Jul 1670 of John Grantland of Uffculme, yeoman: residue to s John Grantland, exec; to wife Alice £5 a year plus hall & chamber, bed, & household goods unless she should remarry, when all reverts to s John; marked by John Grantland the elder in presence of Walter Leage (W mark) & Mary Hooper (mark).]

153 ROBERT POOKE alias WEEKS 1670 (PU)

[Bur: "Robert Weekes alš Pook" 10 Aug 1670. Husbandman; total, including £6 dwelling (lease?), £7.]

An Inventory of all & singuler ye goods & Chattles of Robert Pooke alš Weeks late of Uffculme in the County of Devon husbandman deceased taken & prised the 14th day of September 1670 by Edward Marshall John Marshall & John Grantland as followeth./

	lî	*s*	*d*
Imp^rs^ his apparrell	00	07	00
Item his bedds	00	06	00
Item one iron pott one fryingpan & one skillet	00	03	00
Item two barrills & one Coffer	00	02	00
Item one board & two Furmes	00	02	00
Item his dwellinge with tapurtinances	06	00	00
	07	00	00

Edward Marshall John Marshall Jno Grantland [all sign]

154 WYLLIAM STARKE 1670 (PU)

[Bur: "William Starke of high-Parks" 14 Sep 1670. Clothier with cloth but no clothmaking gear; 1 horse, 2 cows, 2 pigs; total, including £10 for house, £42.]

[A tru]e & perfect Inventory of all and singuler the goods & Chattells of Wylliam Starke of Uffculme in the County of Devon Clothier deceased taken & prised the 25th day of November j670 by Edward Marshall Arthur Stephens & John Grantland as followeth/

	lî	*s*	*d*
Imprimis his Apparrell	02	00	00
Item three bedds performed	03	00	00
Item two Chests	00	10	00
Item twenty Cheesses	00	10	00
Item six paire of sheers	01	10	00
Item Lidds	00	05	00
Item one Cloth preess & papers thereunto belonginge	02	15	00
Item one Cloth rack	01	10	00
Item three peices of broadcloth	10	00	00
Item two milch Cows	04	00	00
Item one horse	02	00	00
Item two swine hoggs	01	00	00

	lî	s	d
Item one Cubord	00	06	08
Item three brass potts	01	00	00
Item one Caldron two brass panns & one skillet	00	12	00
Item two puter dishes	00	02	00
Item one paire of scalls	00	01	06
Item butter	00	04	00
Item two barrills	00	02	00
Item three tubbs	00	03	00
Item three peices of Cloth	00	06	00
Item one board & one Furme	00	05	00
Item one Chaire	00	01	00
Item his dwellinge house	10	00	00
Item implem^ts not seen & prised	00	05	00
	42	08	02

Edward Marshall Arthur [A mark] Stephens
Jno Grantland

[Admon 30 Dec 1670 names Joan Starke, spinster, as admin, & also John Starke of Uffculme, clothier; marked by both in presence of John Grantland & Hannah Moore (H mark).]

155 JOHN BUTSON 1670 (DS)

[Bur: "John Butson sen" 9 Oct 1670. Husbandman (retired?); mostly household items; spinning turn; total, including £13 part-lease, £28.]

A true Inventory of all the goods Chattles And Creddits of John Butson Husbandman &c: deceased prised at Bradfeild the 17th day of October 1670 by Simon Welch & Robeart Williams & Rich Rose as Followeth &c -

	£	s	d
In Primis for his warring Apparrell	2	00	0
Item for two brasse Caldrons & one skilet	0	16	0
Item for sixe brasse pans & one brase Candelsticke	1	03	0
Item for two brasse pots & two Coffers	1	03	0
Item for sixe puter dishers & one salt	0	08	0
Item for a standing Bead pformed	2	08	0
Item for one trockell Bead pformed	0	16	0
Item for Five tobes one Chare & two standerds	0	13	0
Item for one spitt one firepan two Crookes & one pile	0	02	6
Item for husbandmans tooles	0	06	8
Item for three Barrills	0	05	0
Item for two Bages & one pooledavis winshett	0	03	0
Item for one trendell & spininge turne	0	11	6
Item for one tableboard & one forme	0	10	0
Item for one Amry & one Cheeswringe	0	10	0
Item for one standinge shilfte & three boards	0	03	4
Item for fower Boards two ould hogsheads & one gibe	0	04	0
Item for wood & two plankes	0	12	0
Item for one Ladder	0	01	6
Item for parte of a Cottage which is Chattle	13	06	8
Item mony In purse	2	00	0
Item for all such other goods as are not heretofo^r mencioned In this Inventory	0	03	4
the Sum is	28	06	6

[Exhibited at Uffculme by Francis Buttson, s & exec, before the Dean of Salisbury, 6 May 1671. Latin endorsement signed by Geo: Frome sen^r Reg^r.

Will 21 Aug 1668 of John Butson of Uffculme, husbandman: residue, including houses & gardens for periods of leases, to s Frances Butson, exec; 10s to s John Butson; 5s to dr Jane Welch; 5s each to grandchn John, Jane, & Amie Butson; 20s each to grandchn Ames, Frances, Anne, Henry, & Simon Butson; signed JB by John Butson & marked by Mary Franck & signed by Rich: Rose as witn.]

156 JOHN JORDEN 1670 (PU)

[Bur: "John Jordan" 13 Oct 1670. Mar: "John Jorden & Anne Parker" 11 Jan

1646/7, Culmstock; see No. 183. 1 mare, 3 cows, & 2 pigs; no clothmaking gear; £22.

Much of the heading of the inventory is missing.]

.of John Jorden
....County of Devon
.taken & praised the
..[by] John Dyer
& John Brouncey

	£	s	d
Imp[s] his apparrell	00	13	04
Item three milch Cows	07	10	00
Item two swine hoggs and one mare	03	10	00
Item fower beds performed	02	00	00
Item hay	01	10	00
Item eight puter dishes	00	08	00
Item five brass panns	00	14	00
Item three brass potts	01	00	00
Item two brass Caldrons	00	16	00
[Item] fower table boards [..part missing..] Furme	00	14	00
[Item] one Chest & one Cubbord	00	11	00
Item one chaire & one settle	00	02	00
Item two hogsheads & two barrills	00	12	00
Item tressells & poles	00	05	00
Item one Furnace	01	00	00
Item boards	00	10	00
Item implem[ts] not seen	00	05	00
the Sum is	22	00	04

John Dyer Christofer Marshall
John Brouncey

[Admon 19 Dec 1670 names Ann Jorden as widow & admin, & also John Grantland of Uffculme, "batcheler"; marked in the presence of Rich: Mathew, Hannah Moore (H mark), & John Brouncey (JB mark).]

157 CHRISTOFER PALFRY 1670 (PU)

[Bur: "Christopher Palfrey" 27 Oct 1670. Household items & £16 in *chattles* (leases?: 2 houses mentioned in will); £19.]

An Inventory of all & singuler y[e] goods & Chattells of Christofer Palfry late of Uffculme in County of Devon deceased taken & prised the 20th day of November j670. by John Marshall John Grantland & Walter Leage as followeth -

	£	s	d
Imprimis his Apparrell	00	10	00
Item two beds performed	01	10	00
Item two table boards	00	04	00
Item one Carpet	00	01	00
Item four puter dishes	00	02	00
Item one Caldron & two brass potts	00	12	00
Item one little Cubberd	00	02	00
Item two barrills & two tubbs	00	02	00
Item his Chattells	16	00	00
Item Implem[ts] not seen	00	01	00
	19	04	00

John [M mark] Marshall Jn[o] Grantland
Walter [L mark] Leage

[Exhibited at Uffculme 13 May 1672.

Will of Christopher Palfrey, tailor(?), 25 Aug 1670, pr 13 May 1672 before Mr Richard Mathew: residue to s-in-law Roger Bussell, exec; his present house to dr Joane for life & thereafter to grandch Christopher Bussell; who meanwhile inherits his house called Cookhouse, which later passes to grandchn Joane & Mary Bussell jointly; beds, chests, &c to grandchn Ann, Joane, Mary, & Christopher Bussell, & silver spoon to Ann; marked in presence of John Grantland & Edward Marshall.]

158 HENRY MINIFIE 1670 (PU)

[Bur: "Henry Minifee" 5 Dec 1670. Tailor with hall, shop, rooms over both, & 1 other room; no clothmaking gear; total, including £16 for house, £20.]

An Inventory of y[e] goods and Chattles of Henry Minifie of Uffculme in y[e] County of Devon Tayler taken & apprized by Marke Westerne John Salkeld William Franck & Joseph Lock y[e] therd day of January in y[e] yeare of o[r] Lord god one thousand six hundred & seventy as followeth

	£	s	d
Inprimis in ready monney			
Item In debtes			
Item in plate			

[*No values but the figures as they stand add up correctly.*]

Item his weareing apparle	0	5	0
Item one halfe headed beadstead & the beading thereunto belonging	0	10	0
Item one sidebord & 2 Coffers and one Joynestoole in his chamber	0	8	0
Item one beadstead more & one table bord & Forme in ye Chamber over ye Shopp worth	0	12	0
Item one beadstead more & 3 formes in his Chamber over ye Hall	0	16	0
Item one bord more one Chare & one Forme 2 tubbes & one barrle & 2 shelves in ye Hall	0	14	0
Item Bords	0	10	0
Item 9 Pewter dishes	0	10	0
Item one B[r?]asse Pann one Crock & 2 Skillets	0	6	8
Item one howse	16	0	0
Item other Implements not before Apprized	0	2	2
the wole Sum is	20	13	10

John Salkeld Mark Westron
William Franck Joseph Locke

[Admon 2 Jul 1672 names Humphrey Marsh of Halberton, yeoman, as admin, & also John Grantland of Uffculme, yeoman; signed & sealed by them in presence of Will: Manley & Thomas Young(?). In a document of 18 May 1672 John Minifey of Uffculme, fuller, only s of Henry Minifey late of Uffculme, tailor, declines to administer & names as admin Humphry Marsh, a creditor at the time of his death; marked in the presence of George Bawden & John Howe of Cullompton (H mark).]

159 WILLIAM KENT dyer 1671 (DS)

[Bur: "William Kent sen." 26 Apr 1671. Mar: "Willm Kente & Christen Colle" 24 Jun 1640. Mention of parlour, parlour chamber, & kitchen; 1 pig, but mostly household goods; £12.]

An Inventory of all & singular the goods & Implements of houshold of William Kent late of Uffculme in the county of Devon - Dyer deceased, taked & praysed the First day of May in the yeer of or Lord god 1671 By John Leaman, Richard Coles & John Wheddon as followeth

	lî	s	d
Imprimis his wearing apparrell	01	00	00
Item in the parlour chamber Two bedsteeds & beds ꝑformed	02	10	00
Item the same chamber one chest	00	06	08
Item the chamber over the kitchin one Bedsteed & bed ꝑformed	01	04	00
Item in the same chamber one paire of old weights & Foure paire of old stockcards	00	03	00
Item in the same chamber one ꝑcell of yearne	01	10	00
Item in the buttery Three beer-barrells one Silter & two pailes	00	08	00
Item in the Parlour one Amery one Coffer & one Flaskett	00	04	06
Item in the Kittchin one old brewing kittle	00	16	00
Item in the same roome Two small caldrons	00	16	00
Item in the same roome Two brass-potts	00	18	06
Item in the same roome Two pewter dishes & Two skilletts	00	06	08
Item in the same room Two Fatts & three other small Tubbs	00	10	00
Item one Trundle	00	05	00
Item in the kitchin one old table-board & Two Forms	00	05	00
Item one old Frying panne	00	01	00
Item one old Settle, one Chaire & three Stoolls	00	01	06
Item one hogshead	00	03	06
Item one pigge	00	13	04
Item other Implements seen & unseen & not formerly			

	lî	*s*	*d*
praysed	00	06	08
Sum is	12	09	04

John Leaman his J mark   John Wheddon [signs]   Richard Cool his R mark

For Henry Osmond Ufculme

[Exhibited at Salisbury 5 Oct 1671; signed Geo Frome sen[r] Reg[rius].

Admon 6 May 1671 names Christiana Kent as widow & admin & also Richard Cole of Uffculme; marked by Christiana Kent (+) & Richard Cole (R) in presence of Geo Frome sen[r], not[rio] publiq~.]

160 BERNARD PRINCE 1671 (PU)

[Bur: "Bernard Prince sen." 29 Aug 1671. Weaver with looms & a spinning turn; milkhouse, hall, shop, & room over; wheat, barley, 2 cows, 2 horses, 2 pigs; total, including £8 chattel lease & allowing for £8 debts, £35.]

A true & pfect Inventory of all & singular the goods & Chattles of Bernard Prince late of Uffculme in the county of Devon deceased taken & praysed the second day of September in the yeer of o[r] Lord god One thousand six hundred seaventy & one; by John Baker & Thomas Godfery as followeth: 1671

	lî	*s*	*d*
Imprimis his wearing apparrell	02	00	00
Item in the chamber over the shop one standing bedsteed, & furniture thereunto belonging	03	00	00
Item one halfe-headed bedsteed & bed pformed	01	10	00
Item one Chest	00	10	00
Item two coffers, two boxes, one old hogshead, one little Tubb, & a little Barrell	00	10	00
Item in the Milke-house Foure brass-panns	01	00	00
Item Five Tubbs, one Trundle, & a Cheese-wring	00	18	00
Item in the Shop one paire of broads-lums & the furniture, & tack-ling belonging to them	02	00	00
Item in the Hall one Table board & one form	00	14	00
Item one Cupboard	00	08	00
Item Nine pewter dishes & two Candlesticks	01	00	00
Item one sideboard, three Chayres, one Settle one Joyne-stooll, one payle, one paire of Bellowes, one fire-pan, one paire of brandirons one Griddiron, & one spinning-turne	00	10	00
Item two brass-Crocks, one Kittle, one Settle & one Forme	01	01	00
Item one Chattle Lease	08	00	00
Item one acre & halfe of Wheat & an acre & halfe of barley	07	10	00
Item two Cowes	06	00	00
Item one horse & a colt & the tackling belonging to them	04	00	00
Item one Hay Rick	01	10	00
Item two piggs	01	04	00
Item one little pcell of wood	00	05	00
Item things seen & unseen & not formerly praysed	00	05	00
Sum is	43	15	00

John Baker Thomas Godfry

We crave an allowance as under

	lî	*s*	*d*
First for the crownes Fee	00	13	04
Item for Funerall expences	02	15	00
Item Debts owed by the said Bernard Prince deceased as followeth that is (to say)			
unto Thomas Godfery	02	10	00
unto Mary Prince Grandchild	01	10	00
unto John Maning	01	00	00
unto Richard Pearsey	00	05	00
Sume is	08[li]	13[s]	04[d]

[Exhibited by the exec 13 May 1672.

Nuncupative will 16 Aug 1671 in presence of Bernard Prince & James Prince; all to wife Margarett Prince, exec; & after her death all to be divided amongst his chn; sworn 13 May 1672.]

161 JOHN RAWLINS 1671 (PU)

[Bur: "John Rawlins" 29 Aug 1671. Mar: "Jo. Rowlings & Joan Austine" 22 May 1625. Prosperous yeoman (retired?) with no stock or corn, but £146 owed to him; 1 bible; no clothmaking gear; £177.]

A true & perfect Inventory of all & Singuler the goods & Chattles of John Rawlins late of Uffculme in the County of Devon Yeoman deceased taken and praised the 21th day of September j67j by John Dunn Edward Marshall Christopher Marshall & Arthur Stephens as followeth;

	£	s	d
Imprimis his apparrell	003	15	0
Item money in his Chest	003	07	6
Item money oweing him upon bond	134	00	0
Item in money oweinge without bond	012	00	0
Item three beds performed	012	00	0
Item two brass potts	001	06	8
Item two brass panns	000	16	0
Item three brass Caldrons & one brass Candlestick	000	12	0
Item thirteene puter dishes & one bason	001	04	0
Item one Fatte one trindle & th^r^ee tubbs	001	00	0
Item one Chest & five Coffers	000	19	6
Item two barrills & one tunnell	000	04	0
Item wooll	000	04	0
Item three picks	000	04	0
Item one table bord & three jonye stools	000	10	0
Item two Chairs & one sidebord	000	04	6
Item one settle	000	02	0
Item one paire of Andirons	000	04	0
Item one saveinge Iron one dripinge pann	000	02	0
Item one spitt three paire of potthangings	000	04	0
Item one brandiron one firepan	000	01	6
Item one large bible	000	10	0
Item one glass Cage	000	01	6
Item one paire of harrows	000	12	0
Item wood & Fursse	002	00	0
Item three ladders	000	02	6
Item one pott of butter	000	05	0
Item one Wheelbarrow & hardwood crooks	000	03	0
Item one winnow sheet & two baggs	000	04	6
Item goods of lumber & implem^ts^ not seen	000	06	8
	177	05	10

John [+ mark] Dunn Edward Marshall Christopher Marshall
Arthur [A mark] Stephens

[Exhibited by admin 3 Oct 1671. Latin endorsement signed Hen: Butler Reg^r^.

Admon 3 Oct 1671 names Joane Rawlins as widow & admin, & also William Rawlins, sergemaker, & Wm Cotterell, weaver, all of Uffculme; marked J by Joane Rawlins & signed by William Rawlins & William Cottrell in presence of John Grantland, James Wadham, & Hannah More (H mark).]

162 JOHANE SALTER 1672 (PU)

[Bur: "Joane Salter, widow" 13 Dec 1672. Household goods & £16 annuity; £21.]

A true & pfect Inventory of the Goods of Johane Salter Late of Ufculme in the County of Devon Widdow deceased taken and prized the 11th day of December 1672: by John Grantland Arthur Steevens & Thomas Smyth as Followeth:

	lî	s	d
Imprimis her apparrell	2	0	0
It in money	0	2	0
It two beds & the Furniture thereunto belonging	1	0	0
It two Brasse Potts	1	0	0
It Fower Brasse Panns & one Skellet	0	11	0
It one Chest & one Coffer	0	6	8
It Five Pewter Dishes	0	3	0

	lî	*s*	*d*
It one frying-Pann one Gridiron one brandiron	0	1	0
It one Chaire & one Settle	0	3	0
It her Annuitie	16	0	0
It Implem^{ts} not seene nor prized	0	1	6
	lî	*s*	*d*
The whole Sume is	21	8	2

This is A True Coppie of the Originall as Wittnesse our hands
Joshua:North: Richard Bromfild

[Exhibited by the exec 12 May 1673. Latin endorsement signed by Hen: Butler Reg^{r}.

Will of Johan Salter of Uffculme, widow, 13 Sep 1672 pr 12 May 1673: residue to Willliam James of Church Taunton, exec; 20s each to Alice Toser, wife of Robert Toser, Robert James, & Mary Steevens the elder of Uffculme, & to Jane Shortland of Culmstock; table in hall & 5s to Augustine Steevens of Uffculme; brass pot & pan & pewter to Mary Steevens the younger; chest to Arthur Steevens the younger; 10s each to Henry Steevens, Agnes Toser, Samuell James, Peter James, & Henry James; best coat to Mary James, dr of Wm James of Church Taunton; 2s 6d to Henry James the elder of Uffculme; marked in presence of Tho: Clarke, Faith: Clarke, & Mary Steevens (mark).]

163 WILLIAM FACY 1673 (PU)

[Bur: "William Facy" 18 Dec 1670; (also "Agnis Facy, wife of Wm" buried at Uffculme 11 Sep 1666). Almost only the value of the house; £10.]

A perfect Inventory of the goods & chattles of William Facy late of Uffculme in the County of Devon deceased taken & prized by Marke Westron & John Grantland as followeth

	£	*s*	*d*
Imp^{s} his appell	00	05	00
Item his dwellinge house	10	00	00
Item one shovell	00	02	06
Item one old Coffer	00	01	00
Item old implem^{ts} not seen	00	00	06
ye whole Sum	10	09	00

Jno Grantland Mark Westron

[Nuncupative will Nov 1670 of Willm Facye late of Uffculme: house to dr Grace Facye; witn: John Comens (J mark), Elizabeth Tozer (T mark), wife of Simon Toser; sworn 10 Nov 1673.]

164 JOHN MOORE 1673 (PU)

[Bur: "John Moore" 24 Apr 1673: (also burial of wife Catherine 26 Jan 1672/3). Carpenter with tools & household items & £26 owed to him; total £35.]

The true inventory of ye Goods of John Moore late of Ufculme in ye County of Devon Carpenter deceased taken & praised by Nicholas Rowe Edward Marshall Richard Rose & John Neiles The 24th of April 1673: in Manner & forme Following./.

	lî	*s*	*d*
Imp^{s} His waareing Apparrell	04	01	08
It due upon band	18	00	00
It due from others Depters	08	10	00
It In beadinge and Beadsteeds	00	19	08
It for on Coffer & two boxses	00	04	04
It The brasse	00	16	02
It The puter	00	05	01
It one Ammory on Table borde & on forme	00	08	04
It one Spit two peare of potcrookes & Gridle	00	05	02
It one Chare on ChareStoole & two other Stooles	00	01	00
It Three Tubes two boles one barell & one Peale	00	07	08
It one peare of HarraTings	00	02	07
It for one Rake & one Dish Rake	00	00	09
It for his working tooles	01	06	08
It All Such other Goods of his as are not heretofore Mentioned and unpraised			

	lî	s	d
in this Inventory	00	03	04
The Sum is	35	12	05

Richard Rose Samuell Bonifant
Edward Marshall Nicolas Rowe

[Exhibited at Uffculme 12 May 1673. Latin endorsement signed Hen: Butler Reg^r^.

Nuncupative will 22 Apr 1673 of John Moore of Uffculme, carpenter, pr at Uffculme 12 May 1673: bro-in- law Arthur Stephens named as exec; £12, 6 pewter dishes, brass pot, & sideboard to dr Elizabeth; to drs Hannah & Ursula £6 & £8 10s respectively & equal shares in other household goods & implements; published in presence of Richard Rose & Samuell Bonifant. Admon 12 May 1673 names Arthur Steevens of Uffculme, farmer, admin; marked A by Arthur Steevens in presence of Hen: Butler & Robert Russell.]

165 FRANCIS DOWDNEY 1673 (PU)

[Bur: "Francis Dowdney" 14 Sep 1673. Mar: "Francis Dowdney & Elinore Bale" 4 Aug 1625, Halberton. Yeoman/husbandman with hall, room over, & inner room; plough, corn, 3 horses, 17 sheep, 2 hogs; no clothmaking gear; £39.]

A true & perfect Inventory of all & singuler the goods and Chattles of Francis Dowdney Late deceased of the pish of Uffculme in the County of Devon Yeoman taken the fifteenth day of September j673 by Henry Dowdney John Garnsey John Kitchell & George Ledden

	£	s	d
Imp^s^ his weareinge appell	01	10	00
Item two bedsteads & beds performed in the chamber over the hall	02	00	00
Item two chests with other things belonginge to the same roome over ye hall	00	10	00
Item in the hall two brass potts & three brass panns two Kettells four puter dishes one Cubberd one table board one Forme with other Implem^ts^ in the same roome	01	13	04
Item in the little roome within the hall one trendle two barrells with other implem^ts^	00	06	08
Item one paire of wheels one earthinge butt one plough soole & other horse furniture	03	06	08
Item for Corne in the barne	15	00	00
Item for haye	04	00	00
Item for seaventeene sheep	04	05	00
Item two mares & one Colt	06	00	00
Item for two hoggs	01	00	00
Item for harrows & other things seen & not seene	00	06	08
	39	18	04

Henrey Dowdney John Kitchell
George Leddon John Garnsey

[On 28 Oct 1673 widow Elinor & ss Nicholas & John relinquished the right to admin the goods &c of husbandman Francis Dowdney in favour of his creditor Peter Holway Esq; document marked by Elinor & her ss in presence of William Woodward & Richard Bishop. Admon 12 Nov 1673 names Peter Hollway Esq, armiger, of Uffculme as admin, & also John Daggle of North Wotson(?), Dorset, yeoman; signed by Peter Hollway & John Daggle in presence of Sarah Hollway & Margaret Hodder. A further admon 24 Dec 1673 transfers admin to James Hollway, gent, & also mentions Thomas Mathew of Uffculme, yeoman; signed by James Hollway & marked by Thomas Mathew in presence of Honour Hollway & Margaret Hodder.]

166 GEORGE PRINCE 1674 (PU)

[Bur: "George Prince" 11 Feb 1673/4. Mainly household items & £30 value of house; no clothmaking gear; working tools; hall with room over; £38.]

The Inventory of all & singular of the goods & Chattells [of] George Prince of Uffculme Late deceased seen & apprized ye Twelveth day of February in the yeer of o^r Lord god One thousand six hundred seaventy & three by us whose names are hereunder written as followeth -

	lî	*s*	*d*
Imprimis his Wearing apparrell	01	00	00
Item in the Chamber over ye hall three halfe-head bedsteeds & the furniture thereunto belonging	03	05	00
It in ye same Chamber one Chest, one box, & two Coffers & one trendle	00	18	00
It one board, & one Cubbord, & one Forme	00	12	00
It for two other Formes	00	02	00
It one barrell & one Rack & one shelfe & one tubb	00	02	06
It one washing tubb	00	01	06
It two pewter dishes & one Bole	00	03	00
It two brass crocks & one cauldron & one skillet	01	10	00
It all his working toolls	00	12	00
It the Wood	00	05	00
It his dwelling house	30	00	00
It all ye rest of his goods not seen nor apprized	00	02	00
The Sum is	38	13	00

[No names of appraisers subscribed on the copy.
Exhibited at Uffculme before Mr. Rich: Mathew cleric, 21 Jun 1675. Latin endorsement signed Hen: Butler Reg^r.

Admon 17 Mar 1674 names Pascho Prince (dr?), spinster, as admin, & also Christopher Marshall, yeoman, & William Potter, woolworker, both of Uffculme; marked by Pashcho (sic) Prince & signed by the other two in presence of Jo: Belleme & Mary Salter (M mark).]

167 ANN MERSON 1674 (DS)

[Bur: "Anne Merson, widow" 26 Jul 1674. Prosperous widow with a broad loom, corn, 2 cows, & 4 pigs; £55.]

Devon//.An Inventory of all y^e Goods & Chattles of Ann Merson late of Ufculme vidû deceased taken & apprised the first of August 1674 By John Balliman Davyd Yeaw $Nich^s$ Tucker & Rob^{tt} Merson

	lî	*s*	*d*
Imp^rmis her wearing apparrell	03	00	00
It: In mony in Purse	00	10	00
It: In Pewter dishes &c	00	16	00
It: In Brass Potts & Panns	02	01	00
It: In Iron stuffe belonginge to the Chimney	00	09	00
It: Two Table-Bordes & Joyne stooles	00	10	00
It: One Amery 1 Cupbord 1 Chair	00	10	00
It: One Hutch 4 Tubbs	02	04	00
It: One Furnis & other $implem^{ts}$ there	05	02	06
It: One Mouldinge Bord 1 wringe & other $implem^{ts}$ there	00	19	04
It: In y^e Buttery 8 Barrells and other $implem^{ts}$ there	01	11	05
It: In Chamb 1 Bed pformed	02	15	00
It: Two Beds pformed &c	02	06	08
It: One Chest 5 Coffers & other $implem^{ts}$	01	01	06
It: Butter, Cheese, Bacon, & a Rack	02	12	08
It: One Broade loombe wth app[urtena]n̄ts	02	10	00
It: Two Corne Baggs wth Corne in house	00	15	00
It: One Pair Harrows & a Chaine	00	10	00
It: Wood & Reed about y^e house	01	08	06
It: Hay in house	04	00	00
It: Corne in Ground	10	00	00
Two Cowes & 4 Swine	08	10	00
In Goodes seene & unseene	01	07	02
Some totalis	55	09	09

Rob^{tt} Merson John Ballyman
David Yeawe Nicholes Tucker
his NT marke

[Exhibited at Uffculme before Mr. Rich. Mathew, $surr^o$ &c., under the oath of Simon & Anthony Merson, ss of the deceased, 28 Aug 1674. Latin endorsement signed by Geo: Frome señ Reg[r].

Will 20 Sep 1670 of Ann Merson of Uffculme, widow: residue to ss Simon & Anthony Merson, exec[s]; apparel to dr Ann Cross; £5 to grandch William Cross the younger, s of William & Ann Cross, & 40s plus feather bed to their younger dr Joane Cross, both sums to be invested & paid at age 21 or marriage; 10s to servant Jane Shobrook; 2s 6d to ovsrs Mr John Balliman of Uffculme & Robert Merson of Kentisbeare; marked by Ann Merson & signed by Robtt Merson & marked by Thomasin Heathfeild as witnesses.]

168 WILLYAM TANNER alias HOWE 1675 (PU)

[Bur: "William Tanner alš How" 1 Apr 1675. Yeoman; a few household items & £10 owed to him; hall with room over; £20.]

An Inventory of y[e] goods & debts of Willyam Tanner alius Howe Deceased seen & apprized by John Howe alius Tann[r] & Thomas Lee as Followeth -

	lĩ	*s*	*d*
Imp[s] his weareinge Apparrell & money in pockett	5	10	0
It.in y[e] hall one brasse pott & 3 litle Brasse pans	1	0	0
It.in the Chamb[r] over y[e] hall in bedding & a bedsteed	2	0	0
It.all ye Rest of my [sic] goods seen on not seen nor apprized	1	10	0
It.debt due from Jo: Croydon	2	16	0
It.debt due from Will, Crosse	5	0	0
It.debt due from Anthony Merson	3	0	0
Summis Totalis:	20	16	0

John Tanner alius Howe Tho: Lee

[Will 25 Nov 1670 of William How the elder of Uffculme, yeoman: ss as joint exec[s]; 10s to bro John How; to s Humfry How apparel & half the goods; other half divided between ss John & W[m]; marked (inverted W) in presence of William Crosse & Thomas Crosse.]

169 ADRIAN ASHELFORD 1675 (PU)

[Bur: "Adrian Ayshelford" 7 Apr 1675. Mar: "Adrian Ayshelford & Rachell Holwill" 1 May 1671. Mason of Uffculme: no inventory but inventory value quoted at probate as £8 6s 8d & summary of will included here because of the indication of family connexions & much greater wealth than this value suggests.

Will 28 Jan 1674/5, of Adrian Ashelford of Uffculme, mason, pr before Mr Richd Mathew, 21 Jan 1675/6: house & garden to wife Rachell, exec; to Humphry Ashelford of Uffculme, s of Peter Ashelford, for remainder of lease a house & plot bought of Mrs Ann Vener of Bawdialton (Bathealton?) & the house Austine Dunne(?) now lives in; to Homephery (sic) Ashelford, s of Peter Ashelford of Uffculme, specketmaker, apparel &c; to sister's s, Daniell Clarke of Cullompton, chattel for rest of lease of house & grounds where Peter Baker lives, "made of a barn(?)" & bought of Mrs Ann Venner of Bawdialton in Somerset, widow - legacies to be paid out of this & conditions of bound payments to Ann Venner & John Balle; 20s divided among 4 chn of Thomas Rap...(?) of Cullompton, & 20s divided among 4 chn of Leonard Ashelford, & 20s divided among sister & 3 ss of Holcombe Rogus, all to be paid by daniell Clark out of chattel held by Roger Henner of Wellington for life; 20s to sister's s, John Clarke of Holcombe Rogus; 15s to Wm Southwood's wife of Culmstock & her 2 drs; to sister-in-law Mary Holway, widow, former wife's best red waistcoat in custody of Mrs Clarke of Bridwell, widow; ovsrs Marke Westerne & John Salkeld; marked by Adrian Ashelford in presence of William Holway & Susan Ware (both mark).]

170 THOMAS GEALARD [GILLARD?] 1676 (PU)

[Bur: "Thomas Giliard" 19 Nov 1676. Husbandman: inventory missing but value quoted as £4 7s 2d & summary of will included because of disposal of tenement.

Nuncupative will 10 Nov 1676 of Thomas Gealard of Uffculme, husbandman, sworn at Uffculme before Mr Richd Mathew by Alice Cottrell, dr & legatee, in presence of Grace Osmond & Mary Weekes (both mark), 5 Feb (1677?): all, including house at Northcott Pitt for rest of tenement lease, to dr Alice & her husband John Cotterell.]

171 ROBERTT GILL sen[r] 1676 (DS)

[Bur: "Robert Gill sen[r]" 24 Mar 1675/6. Prosperous yeoman; hall & room over, parlour & a further room, buttery, & milkhouse; 2 mares, 13 cattle, 54 sheep, 4 hogs, & poultry; total, including £70 part of chattel lease, £223.]

The Inventory Indented of all and singular the goods & Chattles of Robertt Gill sen[r], of Uffculme in the County of Devon yeoman Deceased, made & praysed the Fower & twentyeth Day of March in the yeare of o[r] lord god one Thousand six Hundred seventy & Five by Henry Dowdney Simon Gill Samuell Bishopp & Richard Gill

	lî	*s*	*d*
Imprimis his wearing apparrell & money in pockett	07	00	00
Item part of a Chattell Lease	70	00	00
Item in the hall one Cubbord one tableboard one settle one Chaire with other things in the Said Roome	03	06	08
Item in the parlor one feather bed bedstead & Furniture theireunto belonging	05	00	00
Item in the same Roome one table board & Furme one saidetable one Cubbord one Chaire one Chest Fower Joyne stooles with other thinges in the said Roome	03	15	00
Item in the parlor Chamber two beds two bedsteads & Furnitude theireunto belonging & one Chest with other things in the said Roome	05	16	00
Item in the Chamber over the hall two beeds two bedsteads with Furnitude theire unto belonging & one Chest with other things in the said Roome	04	06	08
Item in the buttry six beare barrells with other things in the said Roome	01	03	04
Item in the milke house nine bras panns three Caldrons three bras pottes one warminge pann	09	09	09
Item Fourten puter dishses one flaggon three Candle sticks six sasers Five puter porengers one Salt	03	05	00
Item two Cheese wrings six Cheese vats	01	10	00
Item two trundles two vats Five tubes three payls	02	01	04
Item p[ro]vision in house	05	05	05
Item Corne & malt in house	12	00	00
Item Corne in ground	06	10	00
Item haye	04	00	00
Item plough stufe & horse tacklen	02	00	00
Item six Cowes two maires two sturs three hefers two yearlinges	52	10	00
Item Fifty Fower sheep	20	00	00
Item Fower hooggs	03	10	00
Item pultrey & other things about the house seen & not seen & not before pticularly praysed	00	19	10
Sum is	223	9	0

[Exhibited at Uffculme by the execs before Mr. Richard Kent, 7 Jun 1676.

Will 4 Mar 1675/6 of Robertt Gill sen[r] of Uffculme, yeoman, pr at Uffculme before Mr Richard Kent 7 Jun 1676: residue to ss Robertt & John Gill, exec[s]; detailed partition of land &c, *tenement at Ashell with two parcells of barton land*, to wife Grace (2 closes of pasture land, *Hayland & Umbrooke*, & half of *Hay meadow* with house, garden, & bed, plus £40 if she outlives Richard Woodrowe, *beinge a life upon the said tenement*, or the disposal of the £40 if she does not), to s Robertt (half of *Hayland meadow*, & 5 closes of pasture land, *Arrish Cruft*, *Messerlands*, *Whitemore*, *Triphatch*, & *Twenty Acres*, & after death of his mother the halfendale of the house &c, which he shares until then); £40 & bed to dr Judeth Gill, who may live at home till married; the yearly interest on £30 to dr Mary Lacke, the principal to be employed by execs for benefit of her & her drs; 20s each to Grace Gill, dr of s John, & Richard Lacke, s of dr Mary; 10s to sister Mary Woodrow; marked by Robertt Gill sen[r] in presence of Samuell Bishopp & Richard Saunders, who sign, & Thomsin Gill, who marks.]

172 WILLIAM SMITH 1676 (DS)

[Bur: "William Smith" 5 Jun 1676. Mar: "Willm Smith & Anne Caddy" 2 Dec 1643. Will mentions an estate at Winsford in Somerset; very prosperous husbandman; hall & kitchen with rooms over, parlour, buttery, shop rooms, malthouse; no clothmaking gear; corn, 5 horses, 15 cattle, 32 sheep, 7 pigs, & poultry; total, including £50 owed to him, £195.]

The Inventorie of all the goods and Chattells of William Smith late of Ufculme in the Countie of Devon Deceassed taken and prissed by Henry Dowdney And Thomas Helmore both of the prish of Ufculme and Countie aforsaid The Sixeth day of June in the yeere of our Lord God one [?] one Thousand Sixe hundred Seventie and Sixe - - 1676

	£	s	d
Imprimus his wearinge apparell	05	00	00
Im mony In Pokett	05	00	00
Im In the Pallor one feather Bead pformed one Cubbord one Chest one Coffer one Table Bord with other things belonging to the same roome	08	00	00
Im In the Hall one Table Bord one Cobbord one Chare with other things In the same Roome	02	00	00
Im two Table Bords one great Yeating fatt with other things belonging to the same Roome	02	10	00
Im the Chamber over the Kitching two feather Beeds pformed one Littill table Bord with other things In the same Chamber	06	00	00
Item In the Shope Chambers one Table bord one Coffer with other things In the same Chambers	01	00	00
Item In the Buttry twelfe Barrils wth other things	02	00	00
Itm three flock Beeds and two destbeeds pformed one Sprus Chest one other Chest three Coffers wth other things In the Hall Chamber And old Chare	05	10	00
Itm in the Malt Howse two Yeating fatts two malt Hutches with other Lumber Stufe In the same howse	03	00	00
Im for the Brasse and Putter	12	00	00
Im for Malt in howse	10	00	00
Im for Corne In Barne unthreshed and Corne in howse	10	00	00
Item for the wood & fuell about the howse	08	00	00
Itm for about Seaven Akers of Corne In ground	08	10	00
Itm for eight Cowes And one Bull and two Heffer Yearlings	24	00	00
Itm for three Labour horses with the Tackling thereunto belonging	12	00	00
Item for two Colts and fower Calves	06	00	00
Item Twentie old Shipe and twelfe Lames	08	13	04

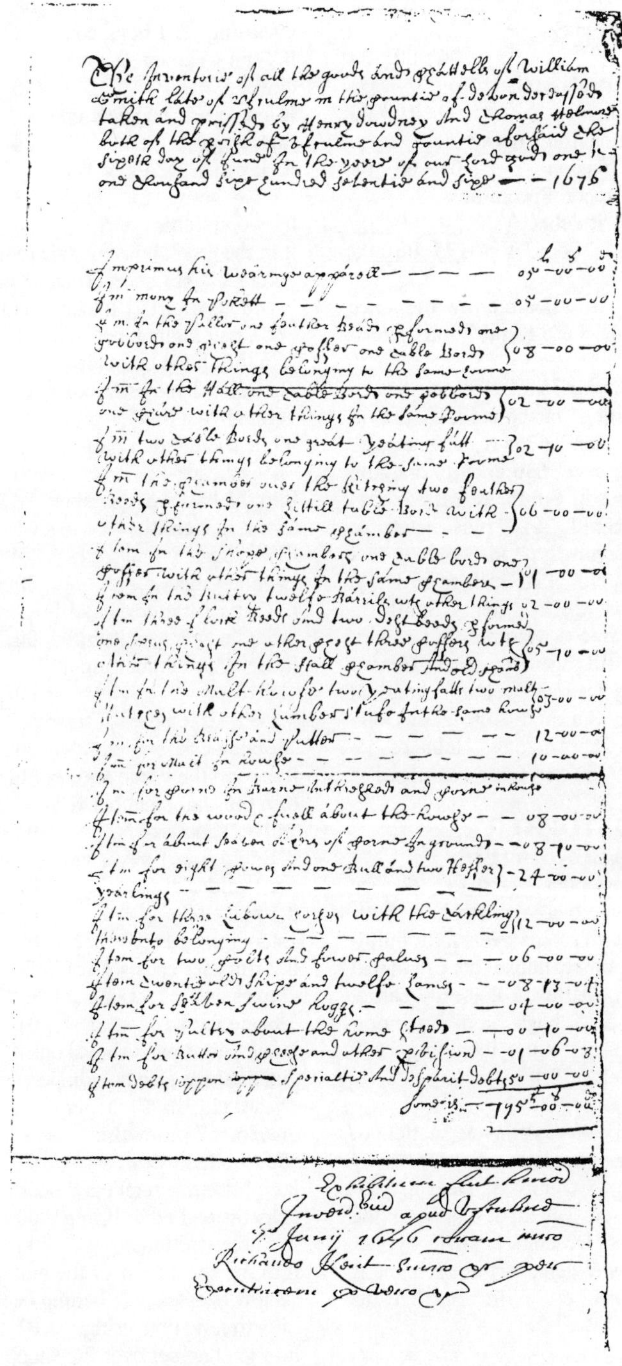

The Inventorie of all the goods and chattells of William Smith late of [illegible] in the countie of [illegible] deceased taken and prised by Henry Dowdney and Thomas Holmes both of the parish of [illegible] and countie aforesaid the sixth day of June in the yeare of our Lord God one thousand six hundred seventie and six — 1676

	l	s	d
Imprimus his wearinge apparell	05	00	00
Item money in pockett	05	00	00
Item in the seller one feather beade & formes one cubbords one chaire one coffer one table borde with other things belonging to the same roome	08	00	00
Item in the Hall one table borde one cobbord one chaire with other things in the same roome	02	00	00
Item two table bords one great [illegible] with other things belonging to the same roome	02	10	00
Item in the chamber over the kitchen two feather beads & formes one little table bord with other things in the same chamber	06	00	00
Item in the [illegible] chamber one table bord one coffer with other things in the same chamber	01	00	00
Item in the buttery twelve barrells with other things	02	00	00
Item three flock beads and two [illegible] beads & formes one [illegible] chaire one other chaire three coffers with other things in the Hall chamber and old chaire	05	10	00
Item in the Malt house two [illegible] vatts two malt [illegible] with other lumber stuffe in the same house	03	00	00
Item in the [illegible] and seller	12	00	00
Item for malt in house	10	00	00
Item for corne in barne [illegible] and corne in house			
Item for the wood & fuell about the house	08	00	00
Item for about seaven acres of corne in grounds	08	10	00
Item for eight cowes and one bull and two heffers yearlings	24	00	00
Item for three labour horses with the tackling thereunto belonging	12	00	00
Item for two colts and fower calves	06	00	00
Item twentie old sheepe and twelve lambes	08	13	04
Item for seaven swine hogges	07	00	00
Item for pultry about the home steede	00	10	00
Item for butter and cheese and other provision	01	06	08
Item debts uppon [illegible] speciallties and desperate debts	50	00	00
Some is	195	00	00

Exhibitum fuit hoc Invent[ari]um apud [illegible] 7o Junij 1676 coram nobis Richardo Kent surrogato per [illegible] Executricem [illegible]

The inventory of William Smith 1676 [172]

	£	s	d
Item for Seaven Swine hoggs	04	00	00
Itm for Pultry about the homesteed	00	10	00
Itm for Butter And Cheese and other pvision	01	06	08
Item debts uppon Specialtie And desparit debts	50	00	00
Some is	195	00	00

[Exhibited at Uffculme by the exec before Mr. Richard Kent, 7 Jun 1676.

Will 31 May 1676 of William Smeth of Uffculme, husbandman, pr at Uffculme 7 Jun 1676: residue to wife Ann Smith, exec; £30 each to drs Ann Maninge, Edith Smith, & (at age 21) Elizabeth Smith; £10 plus house & estate at "Wyndsford" in Somerset to s William Smeith; £20 each to ss Hugh Smeth & (at age 21) Henry Smith; to grandch James Maning 50s, with conditions till age 21; ovsrs Henery Dowdny & Thomas Helmore; marked by William Smith & signed by John Manninge & Thomas Helmore & marked by Abraham Caddy as witn.]

173 CHRISTOPHER MARSHALL 1676 (PU)

[Bur: "Christopher Marshall" 24 Dec 1676. Prosperous yeoman; hall, buttery, shop, with rooms over, farm buildings, & another house at Craddock; plough, corn, barley, 2 horses, 4 cattle, 14 sheep, & 5 hogs; gun; no clothmaking gear; total, including £50 chattel lease, £178.]

An Inventory of ye goods & chattels of Christopher Marshall of ye pish of Ufculme in ye county of Deavon yeoman deceased Taken & apprised the 28th day of December 1676 by Mr James Holway gent. Arthur Steephens Richard Gill & Will: Bartlett as followes

	£	s	d
Imp^{s} his Wearing apparrell & monny by him	14	11	08
It.one nagg two cowes two yearlings & 1 hogg coalt	14	00	00
It.Tenn weathers & four ewes	06	00	00
It.four young hoggs & one fatt hogg	04	03	00
It.Hay in ye meadow Tallett & hay house	03	18	00
It. wood in the court	00	07	00
It.in the crook house 2 pair long crooks 2 pair short crooks 2 pack saddells 4 girts 1 hackney saddle & 1 pair gambadoes	01	08	00
It.in the shopp one pair harrows 2 sooles & other plough tackling	01	05	00
It.one trendle & 3 half hoggsheads	00	10	00
It.in the bakes & chamber over, one chittle	01	10	00
It.six baggs & one winnowsheet	00	12	00
It.2 fatts 1 halfhogshead 1 trendle & 1 cool [tub]	00	16	00
It.barley in the melting burrow	00	12	00
It.1 old table board 5 staves & one peck	00	05	00
It.corn in the barne and reed	13	06	00
It.in the Hall chamber 8 silver spoones	02	10	00
It.1 gold ring 1 silver whistle & 1 gilded ring	00	10	00
It.1 peice of gold & 2 standing beds pformed	07	00	00
It.2 trunks 2 chests 1 coffer 2 boxes one carpet one stoole & one form	01	13	00
It.one pair dowlis sheets one pair canvas sheets 2 diaper board cloaths 10 diaper napkins 7 pillowtyes & 1 holland sheet	01	14	00
It.eight course napkins 2 board cloaths and other lining	00	08	00
It. three whittells	00	05	06
It.in the chamber over the buttery 3 low bedsteads & beding beelonging to it & 1 covering	02	00	00
It.in ye chamber over the shopp 2 malt hutches 1 trendle 1 seedlop & 2 butterstandards	00	08	00
It.Malt: Salt: & 1 parcell of			

	£	s	d
course wooll	01	11	08
It.in the hall; Bacon & pork	04	05	00
It.2 doz: pewter & other small pewter things	02	05	10
It.5 brass potts & three skilletts	03	15	00
It.3 brass cauldrons & 1 warming pann	01	09	00
It.3 spitts 1 dropping pann 1 pair andirons 1 pair doggs 1 firepan 1 pair tongs	00	11	08
It.3 pair pott hangings 2 crooks 1 brass chaffing dish 1 styleing box & Irons	00	05	04
It.1 table board 1 settell 1 chair 2 joynt stooles 1 form 2 litle stooles 1 cuboard 1 glass cage 1 side board 2 skumers 2 fleshpikes 1 chopping kniffe 1 trencher rack & 1 jron candlestick	02	09	07
In the milkhouse 9 brass panns 1 pair weights	03	00	00
It.6 yeartubbs 1 standard 1 cheesewring 1 morter 1 musterd boul 1 jron barr 1 gridiron 1 saveing Iron	00	19	04
It.2 doz: butter 1 doz; ½ sweetmort 10 cheeses and one peice bacon	01	03	04
In the buttery 3 barrells 1 half hogshead 1 dropper 1 great bole 1 ironfoot & 1 fowling peice	00	15	04
It.corn in ground	03	00	00
It.dung & soyl	00	10	00
Att craddiock in the hall chamber 1 standing bedstead	00	13	04
It.in the hall 1 glass cage & 1 gibb	00	01	08
It.in the barn Hay pease & wood	02	01	00
It.in bitterson 1 mow of wheat	08	10	00
It.in Rackclose one mow, part wheat and part barley	04	10	00
It.one reek of cloverseed	02	15	00
It.corn in ground in hills	02	10	00
It.his estate at craddiock being chattell	50	00	00
It.other Implements & lumber stuffe not seen nor praysed	00	10	00
	178	14	3

[30s too much?]

James Hollway
the [A] marke of Arthur Steevens
Richard Gill

[Will 17 Dec 1676 of Christopher Marshall of Uffculme, yeoman: residue to s Edward Marshall, exec, supervised till age 21, or if he dies before 21 half each to go to bro Edward Marshall & James Hollway of Uffculme; to bro Edward Marshall & John Dyer each a grey mare colt; late wife's coats to sister Rebecka, wife of Wm Bartlett, & k Tacey Kent, wife of John Kent; 1 gold ring to Thomasin Gill; ovsrs bro Edward Marshall & John Dyer; marked & sealed by Christopher Marshall in presence of Richard Mathew, Tho: Clarke, & Richard Woodruff.]

174 RICHARD PATCH alias PAGEY 1676 (PU)

[Bur: "Richard Pagie alš Patch" 10 Nov 1676. Carpenter; hall, parlour, & 2 other rooms (?); no clothmaking gear; corn, 1 mare, 5 cattle, 59 sheep, & 1 pig; seems to store some props for the fair; £57.]

A trew and Perfect Inventorÿ of all and singular the goods and Chattells of Richard Patch alš Pageÿ late of Uffculme in the Countÿ of Devon Carpenter dec taken and praised the 11th daÿ of Novembr Anno Dm 1676 bÿ Marke Westron John Dunn & John Grantland as followeth: -

	£	s	d
Impmis His apparrell	2	10	0
Itm one Bed with the furniture thereunto belonging standinge in the parler Chambr	1	15	0
Itm two Beds & Bedsteeds with there furniture standinge in the hall chamber	2	5	0
Itm four & thirtÿ Cheeses	1	5	0
Itm one little Tryndle	0	4	0
Itm two little Chests one old			

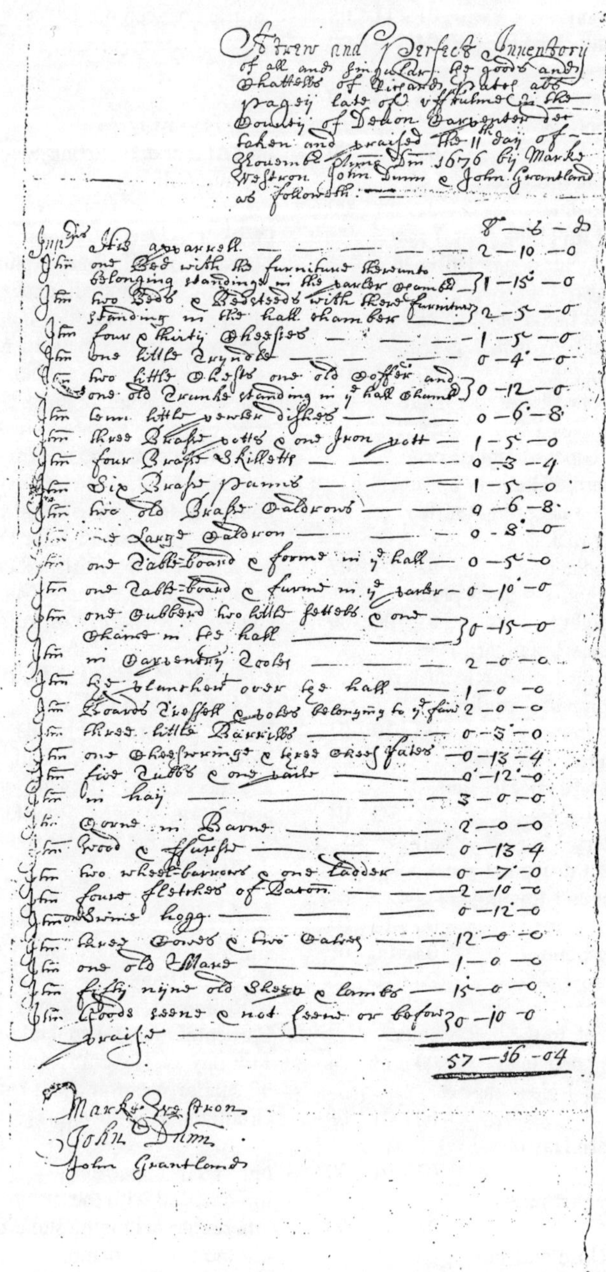

A true and perfect Inventory of all and singular the goods and Chattells of Richard Patch als Pagey late of Uffculme in the County of Devon Carpenter deceased taken and praised the 11th day of November Anno Dm 1676 by Marke Weston John Dunn & John Grantland as followeth:

	li – s – d
Imprimis His apparrell	2 – 10 – 0
Item one bed with the furniture thereunto belonging standing in the parlor chamber	1 – 15 – 0
Item two beds & bedsteeds with there furniture standing in the hall chamber	2 – 5 – 0
Item four & thirty cheeses	1 – 5 – 0
Item one little tryndle	0 – 4 – 0
Item two little chests one old coffer and one old trunke standing in ye hall chamber	0 – 12 – 0
Item some little pewter dishes	0 – 6 – 8
Item three brasse potts & one Iron pott	1 – 5 – 0
Item four brasse skilletts	0 – 3 – 4
Item Six brasse panns	1 – 5 – 0
Item two old brasse caldrons	0 – 6 – 8
Item one large caldron	0 – 8 – 0
Item one table-board & forme in ye hall	0 – 5 – 0
Item one table-board & furme in ye parlor	0 – 10 – 0
Item one cubboard two little settells & one chaire in the hall	0 – 15 – 0
Item in carpentry tooles	2 – 0 – 0
Item the planchen over the hall	1 – 0 – 0
Item boards tressells & poles belonging to ye same	2 – 0 – 0
Item three little barrills	0 – 5 – 0
Item one cheesewringe & three cheese fates	0 – 13 – 4
Item five tubbs & one paile	0 – 12 – 0
Item in hay	3 – 0 – 0
Item corne in barne	2 – 0 – 0
Item wood & ffurse	0 – 13 – 4
Item two wheele-barrows & one ladder	0 – 7 – 0
Item foure flitches of bacon	2 – 10 – 0
Item one swine hogg	0 – 12 – 0
Item three cowes & two calves	12 – 0 – 0
Item one old mare	1 – 0 – 0
Item fifty nine old sheep & lambs	15 – 0 – 0
Item goods seene & not seene or before praised	0 – 10 – 0
	57 – 16 – 04

Marke Weston
John Dunn
John Grantland

The inventory of Richard Patch *alias* Pagey 1676 [174]

	£	s	d
Coffer and one old Trunke standing in ye hall Chamb^r^	0	12	0
Itm tenn little pewter dishes	0	6	8
Itm three Brasse potts & one Iron pott	1	5	0
Itm four Brasse Skilletts	0	3	4
Itm Six Brasse Panns	1	5	0
Itm two old Brasse Caldrons	0	6	8
Itm one Large Caldron	0	8	0
Itm one Table-board & forme in ye hall	0	5	0
Itm one Table-board & furme in ye parler	0	10	0
Itm one Cubberd two little settels & one Chaire in the hall	0	15	0
Itm in Carpentrÿ Tooles	2	0	0
Itm the planchen^t^ [flooring?] over the hall	1	0	0
Itm Boards Tressell & poles belonging to ye fair	2	0	0
Itm three little Barrills	0	3	0
Itm one Cheeswringe & three Cheesfates	0	13	4
Itm five Tubbs & one paile	0	12	0
Itm in haÿ	3	0	0
Itm Corne in Barne	2	0	0
Itm Wood & Fursse	0	13	4
Itm two wheel-barrows & one ladder	0	7	0
Itm foure fletches of Bacoñ	2	10	0
Itm one Swine hogg	0	12	0
Itm three Cowes & two Calves	12	0	0
Itm one old Mare	1	0	0
Itm fiftÿ nÿne old Sheep & lambs	15	0	0
Itm Goods seene & not seene or befor praisd	0	10	0
	57	16	04

Marke Westron John Dunn John Grantland

[Will 20 Oct 1676 of Richard Patch of Uffculme, carpenter: residue to wife, exec, but if she remarries to be divided equally between k Bartholomew Potter & dr-in-law Joane Minifie; 40s to k Bartholomew Potter; signed by Richard Patche in presence of Tho: Donne & Justine Donne (J mark).]

175 SAMUELL BISHOPP 1677 (PU)

[Bur: "Samuel & Elizabeth Bishop, son & daughter of Elizabeth Bishop, widow" 11 Dec 1676: (but perhaps a relative). Yeoman/husbandman with carpenter's tools, clothmaking gear, corn, & 2 cattle; hall with 2 rooms over, kitchen, & shop; £32.]

An Inventory of the goods of Samuell Bishopp of Ufculme in the County of Devon youman Deceased taken & Praised by Robert Batt Roger Bishop & John Garnsey the Twentye thord day of January Año Sav~:1676[/7] as Followeth

	£	s	d
Inpremeces his Apparrell	3	00	00
Itm Two kine	6	00	00
Itm Corne in mow & Barne	2	10	00
Itm Haye in Recke & Tallet	1	00	00
Itm on Bras Pan in the Kitchen with A timberon Croke A botelin [bolekin?]	0	13	04
Itm in the kitchen in Lumber goods	0	03	04
Itm Cerpendors Twoles	2	00	00
Itm on Pare of Narrow Lomes	2	00	00
Itm Husbandtre Toules	0	02	06
Itm Oon Cheswring in the shope & other Lumber Goods	0	05	00
Itm Bearberrels & on Trendall & other timber goods in the butrey	0	13	04
Itm in the hale Two Tabell boards & on Forme & on settle & on Ammrey	1	00	00
Itm Five Lettle Brase Pannes	0	10	00
Itm Two Brase Potts & on hieran Pot	0	13	04
Itm Two Kittles of Brase	1	00	00
Itm Fourtenth Putter Disses one Fligon & two Puter Candellsticke & two Saltsellers	1	03	04
Itm Vettles in house	1	10	00
Itm in the two Lettle Chembers oufer the hale thre Bedes with the furneture thereunto belong en	5	00	00

Itm in the Chembers over the

	£	s	d
hale Two Chests five Cofers & on box	1	10	00
Itm Table Lenen in the house	1	00	00
Itm wood & Fule	0	10	00
Itm for thinges sen & onsen	0	03	04
The Sum is	32	07	06

Rob: Batt The Marke of Roger RB Bishop
John Garnsey

[Will 8 Jun 1669 of Samuell Bishopp of Uffculme, husbandman: residue, unless she remarries, to wife Petronell, exec; to s Gills Bishopp on reaching age 16 part of chattel lease in Ashwell (Ashill) in manor of Hackpen, including Samuell's house, stable, henhouse, weaving shop, Messelands, Goozewill Meadow, &c, beds, household items; if s Gills dies before age 16, all to go to s Samuell, or if he dies to dr Cathren Bishopp; broad loom to s Samuell; other specified household items to drs Cathren & Ann & to s Gills; 2s 6d each to rulers bro Humfry Bishopp & bro-in-law Simon Hidon; signed in presence of Elizabeth Bishopp.]

176 MARY WEEKS 1678 (PU)

[Bur: "Mary Weekes widow" 3 May 1673?. Widow; mostly value of cottage & garden; £5.]

A true and pfect Inventory of all and singuler the goods and Chattles of Mary Weeks Late of Uffculme in the County of Devon Widdow deceased taken and prized the 25th of July 1678 by Jn° Grantland & Edward Marshall as followeth:/

	£	s	d
Imp^r^s her Apparrell	00	03	4
It one little brass pott	00	04	6
It one brass Caldron	00	03	6
It one Cottage house and garden	05	00	00
The whole Sum is	05	11	04

Jn° Grantland Edward Marshall

[Exhibited in the register of the Ven. Thomas Clarke, cleric MA, prebendary of the prebend of Uffculme, before Mr. Richard Mathew, cleric surrogate &c., by Johanna Weekes, admin, 1678. The day and the month were left blank, but the Latin endorsement was still signed by Hen: Butler Reg^r^.]

177 JOANE SMEATH 1678 (DS)

[Bur: "Joane Smeath, wife of Thomas" 14 Sep 1678. Pigs & brewing, but mostly household items & £10 ready money; no clothmaking gear; £29.]

An Inventorie of the goods & Chattells of Joane Smeath Late of Uffculme in the County of Devon Deceased taken & apprised the 17th Day of September 1678 by Thomas Clarke Esq John Ballyman & Nicholas Rowe as Followeth

	£	s	d
Imp^s^ Her Wearing Apparrell	3	0	0
Item A table board in ye hall	0	8	0
Item 2 Chaires	0	2	0
Item 1 Settle	0	4	6
Item 2 Small brass potts	0	13	4
Item 2 Small Brass pans	0	04	0
Item in Peauter Dishes	0	7	0
Item 3 Coffers & 1 Box	0	5	0
Item 2 hogsheads & 6 Barrells	1	10	0
Item Brewing vats trendles & tubbs	1	5	0
Item 3 formes & 2 Joynt Stooles	0	4	0
Item 1 Dripping pan & other Small latten things	0	2	0
Item Potthangers & other Ire Stuffe	0	5	0
Item 1 Dust Bed, Bedstead 1 Rug 1 Coverlett & boulster	1	6	8
Item 1 Carpet & 3 Cushions	0	5	0
Item 2 old Caldrons & skillet	0	3	6
Item 5 old Baggs	0	4	0
Item Earthen ware & glasses	0	3	0
Item in Ready Money	10	0	0
Item in Piggs	5	0	0
Item in Wood	0	15	0

	£	s	d
Item in Furse	1	10	0
Item in Cyder	0	8	0
Item one truckle bed & bedding	1	0	0
Item in lumber & things about the house unseen	0	10	0
Sume tot	29	16	0

[1s too much?]

Tho: Clarke John Ballyman Nicolas Rowe

[Exhibited at Uffculme by the exec before Mr. Richard Kent, cleric surr, 30 Jun 1679. Latin endorsement signed Geo: Frome sen^r Reg^r.

Will 29 Jul 1678 of Johan Smeath, wife of husbandman Thomas Smeath of Uffculme, pr at Uffculme 30 Jun 1679: residue to s Samuell James, exec; disposal in accordance with agreement at "intermarriage" with Thomas Smeath, some effects already having been given to s Henry James: husband Thomas Smeath to have use of house & specified contents for life (except the beer & cider); to s Samuell James the house &c where he lives, passing to his wife Grace if he dies before the term of the lease, & thence successively to their chn Peter & Johan James for the remainder of the term, Samuell having the "liberty of the Lords of the Fee of the premises" to change the named lives accordingly; coats &c to dr-in-law Grace, Mary Steevens, wife of bro-in-law Arthur Steevens, sister-in-law Alice Toser, Dorothy Rice, & k Anstice Swapps; marked by Johan Smeath & signed by John Clarke, Tho: Clarke, & Rich: Mathew as witn.]

178 RICHARD WALDRON 1679 & 1680 (PU)

[At least 2 copies of the inventory survive, with slightly different spellings. Prosperous yeoman, apparently in some debt; entry, hall, parlour, kitchen, & 4 other rooms; milkhouse with milkhouse chamber, malthouse; wheat, 3 horses, 11 cattle, 6 pigs, geese, ducks, & hens; plough gear; cider making; no clothmaking gear; total (less than required to pay the debts listed in his s's account below?) £108.]

An Inventory of all & singler the goods Chatteles & debts of Richard Waldron late of Ufculme in the County of Devon yeoman deceased taken & prised the first day of November 1679: by James Holway Esqr: Richard Waldron John Weslake & Robertt Mills as followeth:/

	£	s	d
Inprimis his Apparell	02	00	00
Itt money in purse	00	05	00
Itt in the Parlor one tabelle board one Chest seven Joyne stooles two Chaires	01	03	4
Itt in the hall one tableboard on side table one forme one Amry one glasecage one tranchercage one chaire one seltter three shelves a baconracke a paire of fire doges	01	00	00
Itt one bench in the hall	00	05	00
Itt nyne puter dishes one putercandelstick halfe a dozen of spoones	01	06	8
Itt three brass panns three brass Caldrons one brasse pott one Iron pott & a brass skillet a skeymer & ladell	02	10	00
Itt a paire of Andirons a spitt three potthangons three pott Croockes three Ironcandelsticks a dripingpan a fleshpike a brandice a saveing Iron & a firepan & tonges	00	14	00
Itt in the kitching a brewing pan a Cheese wring a Trundell ten tubes fowr pailes three Chesevates a pecke with other small thinges there	02	00	00
Itt in the littell Roome adioyneing to the kitching a trundle bedsteed a dust bed a Couerlett & shites	00	10	00
Itt in the milkehouse & milkehouse Chamber & buterey seaventeene hogsheades & barells a butter standard two			

	£	s	d
carnehuches fower Jebbes six hogsheades & halfe of sider & Apples enought to make two hogsheades & halfe of sider more with other small things there	07	10	00
Itt in the kitching Chamber one beadsteed & featherbeed pformed on Chist one cheire	04	03	4
Itt in the Chamber over the Entrey one bedsteed & doust bed pformed & a Coffer	01	10	00
Itt in the hall chamber one standinge bedsteed & feather pformed one other standinge bedsteed & flockbeed pformed one trundell bedsteed & dustbeed pformed a coffer & a huch	05	00	00
Itt the naperie	00	13	4
Itt butter & Cheese	00	13	4
Itt Corne in Barne & in rickes	16	00	00
Itt hay in house & in a Ricke	15	00	00
Itt an woodricke	1	10	00
Itt three acres of wheate in ground in hoamemeades	1	10	00
Itt six steares one Cow one hiffer three earlings Two mares & a Coult	30	00	00
Itt six swines hogges	08	10	00
Itt siderwring & trough	02	00	00
Itt in the maltehouse a greate fate two paire of corne Crookes & paire of panniers a pare of short Croockes w^t othering small things	00	06	06
Itt Two wheele barrowes	00	05	00
Itt in the stable three packsadles three paire of dung-potts with other horse tackling	01	00	00
Itt Two soales two paire of harrowes a plough Chaine with other plough stufe	01	00	00
Itt Geese duckes & other pultrey	00	05	00
Itt goodes seene & unseene & nott before in this Inventory valued	00	05	00
Summa in toto	108	15	6

[1s more quoted in account below.]

[Admon 10 Nov 1679 to the s, Richard Waldron junior, yeoman, by Thomas Clarke the Prebendary of Uffculme, in acceptance of the inventory & the account below. Richard Waldron of Hemyock, yeoman, & Ellinor Lippincott of Culmstock, spinster, were also mentioned & the document was signed by both Richard Waldrons & marked by Ellinor Lippincott in the presence of Richd Mathew, Hen: Moore, (both sign) & Elizabeth Waldron (mark).]

ACCOUNT by RICHARD WALDRON junior 1680

The true & pfecte Accompte of Richard Waldron the younger sonne and Admor of All and singlr the goods Chattles and Creditts of Richard Waldron thelder late of Ufculme in the Countye of Devon and peculiar pbendall ..c.ad Jurisdicon Eccl-[esiast]icall of the p[?] Prebendarie of the Prebend of Ufculme aforesaid Dec^d had made and rendred into the Parish Registrie of the above mentioned Prebendare the sixt day of November in the yeare of o^r Lord God 1680 as followeth/ vizt

	£	s	d
Charge./			
Imprimis this said Accomptant chargeth himself wth the full sume of 108^li 16^s 6^d beinge the true price and value of all and singl^r the goods Chattles and creditts of the said deceased exp^rssed in an Inven^rie thereof had made & taken and into the Registrie abovesaid of the said Prebendall Jurisdicñ exhibited as in and by the said Inven^rie there remayninge on Record whereunto this said Accomptant referreth himselfe./ it doth and may more at large Appeare vizt	108	16	6
Sma oneris patet			

Out of wch this Accomptant Craveth allowances for these sev^rall payments and disbursements following, vizt/

	£	s	d
Discharge			
Imprimis this said Accomptant craveth allowance for the funerall expences of the said deceased ev^{r}ieway	2	0	0
I paid by him for fees of the letters of Adm^{on} of the said deceaseds goods, for the Kings duetye, the bonds, Appisers fees, Charges in expenses in travell and other necessarie expenses about the same	1	3	4
1/ I^{m} paid by this said Accomptant to John Dulinge of Ufculme aforesaid for a debte due to him by the dec^{d} upon bond the sume of	10	0	0
2/ Item To Christopher Baker of Culmestocke for the like debte upon bond	10	0	0
3/ Item paid by this said Accomptant to Willm Sirle of Dunsill the sume of 12^{li} for a debte due to him upon bond by the dec^{d} at his death vizt	12	0	0
4/ Item to Mary Parsons Widowe for a debte due to her upon bond by the dec^{d} at his death, wth interest the sume of	12	14	4
5/ Item to James Pottle of Hemyocke for a debte due to him upon bond by the s^{d} dec^{d} at his death the sume of	11	4	0
6/ Item to Henry Dowdny of Ufculme for a debte due to him upon bond by the said dec^{d} at his death by a Judgm^{t} on the said bond the sume of	25	0	0
7/ Item to Richard Waldron of Hemyocke for a debte due to him upon bond by the said dec^{d} upon bond the sume of	5	0	0
8/ Item to Peter Kerslake for a debte due by the said dec^{d} at his death upon bond wth interest the summe	36	15	0
9/ Item paid by the said Accomptant to James Hollway of Ufculme Esqr for a debte due to him upon bond wth interest by the said dec^{d} at his death the sume of	20	10	0
10/ Item to Nicholas Bennet of Sanford Arundell in Somerst-sheir for a debte likewse due upon bond to him by the dec^{d} at his death wth interest the sume of	12	4	10
11/ Item To Robert Batt of Ufculme for a debt due to him upon bond wth interest by the dec^{d} at his death the sume of	10	10	0
To Abraham Caddy of Ufculme upon a bill of sale for debte due to him by the dec^{d} the summe of	5	0	0
And to Robert Mills for Lords Rent	2	0	8
Item paid by this said Accomptant for the fees of Double Draweing and engrossing this Accompte, the Quietus est under seale, the Judges decree upon the same, for Registring the same and the Appisers fees & other necessarie expenses about the same	1	5	8
Sume total exonerate			

[No total given, but the debts & expenses shown sum to 177 7 10]

179 JOHN HOW alš TANNER 1681 (PU)

[Bur: "John Tanner alš How" 27 Jan 1680/1. Husbandman; hall & 2 other rooms; 2 cows, 23 sheep; no clothmaking gear; total, including £2 cottage chattel lease, £22.]

An Inventory of all & singular ye goods & Chattles of John How otherwise Tanner Late of Uffculme in the county of Devon Husbandman deceased; taken & praysed ye First day of February in ye yeer of o^{r} Lord god 1680 By Symon Gill Baptist Andro & William Potter as followeth

	lî	s	d
Iprimis his purse & apparrell	01	10	00
Item in ye hall chamber one bedsteed & bed pformed	02	00	00
Item in ye same chamber one			

	lî	*s*	*d*
chest one old coffer; one box, & one settell	00	10	8
Item in ye little chamber two old coffers, & one box	00	02	6
Item one Trundell & two barrells	00	07	6
Item in ye hall one little board & one Form	00	05	4
Item two brass pottage potts	00	18	00
Item two old caldrons, two brass pans, & one skillet	00	13	4
Item three pewter dishes nine small pewter dishes & two candlesticks	00	04	0
Item one pewter Flaggon one pewter butter-plate, & one pewter bottle	00	02	2
Item one Cottage house beeing a Chattell	02	00	0
Item two cowes	07	10	00
Item Twenty three sheep	06	00	0
Item his workeing toolls, & other small things not seen nor former praysed	00	05	4
Sum is	22	08	10

Symon Gill Bap Andro William Potter

[Admon 14 Feb 1680(/1) names Mary Tanner alš Howe of Uffculme, widow, as admin, & also Simon Gill of Uffculme, yeoman; marked by Mary How & signed by Symon Gill in presence of Nathaniel(?) Pearse & Mary Salter (both mark).]

180 HENRY PARSONS 1681 (PU)

[Yeoman with corn but no stock apart from fowls; books; no clothmaking gear; total, including £30 chattel lease, £56.]

A true & pfect Inventorie of all the goods & Chattles of Henry Parsons of Uffculme late deceased made Prized & taken the fowreth day of Aprill in the yeare of o^r Lord on thousand six hundred eightie and on by Richard Coocke & John Clist as Followeth

	£	*s*	*d*
Impr his Waringe apparrell	2	0	0
It the Corne in Barn	3	0	0
It the Chattle	30	0	0
It on bed & bedsteed wth the furniture	1	0	0
It two Chaires	0	2	6
It on Tableboard	0	10	0
It on Cheese Wringe	0	2	6
It two Tubbs	0	6	0
It two Coffers	0	2	0
It on Furme	0	1	6
It on beer Barrell	0	1	0
It on Seefe	0	0	2*ob*
It on halfe pecke	0	0	6
It on Wheele Barrow	0	4	0
It two Flitches of Bacon	0	15	0
It on Candlesticke of Brasse	0	1	0
It three Pewter dishes	0	3	0
It on Paire of Billowes	0	1	0
It the bookes	0	12	0
It for hardwood	0	2	0
It on Tymber boole	0	0	6
It fowre brasse pottage potts	1	5	6
It five Brasse Panns	1	11	0
It on teeninge boole [1 tin bowl]	0	0	6
It two glasse bottles	0	0	4
It the foules	0	1	6
It three little boxes	0	1	0
It on Cubboard	0	12	0
It on Chest	0	12	0
It on bedsteed	1	0	0
It on little bedsteed	0	1	6
It on Coffer	0	3	0
It in money	11	9	4
It fowre pickes	0	2	0
It on bill hoocke	0	0	3
It two Cheese fates	0	0	6
It for things not seen & forgotten	0	2	0
The Sume is	56	7	1*ob*

Richard Cooke Jo. Clist

[In the pence column *ob* stands for ½d]

[Will 8 Mar 1680(/1) of Henry Parsons of Uffculme, yeoman: residue to s Peter Parsons, exec; 1s each & apparel to ss Willm & Richard Parsons; 1s each to s Thomas Parsons, dr-in-law (stepdr?) Elinor Churley, & Joan Mullins; to dr Ann Hill £10 & brass pots & pans, bed, &c; to dr Mary Whitenoow the northern part of the house & shop, pots, pans, &c; conditional yearly payments of 40s to s Thomas, & of 20s each to s Richard & to grandch Alice Whitenow; marked by Henry Parsons in presence of Robert Were, John Morden (J mark), & Henry Russell (H? mark).]

181 ARTHUR STEVENS the elder 1681 (PU)

[Bur: "Arthur Steevens sen^{r}" 30 Apr 1681. Mar: "Arthur Stephens & Mary James" 13 Dec 1645; see No. 209. Prosperous yeoman, of Coldharbour & working land at Burrows, Gaddon, & elsewhere(?); entry, hall, parlour, & shop, with rooms (over?), milkhouse, malthouse, & drinkhouse(?); 5 horses, 27 cattle, 52 sheep, & 5 pigs; plough; looms; £220.]

An Inventory of y^{e} goods Catles & Chatles of Arthur Stevens y^{e} elder Late of Ufculme deceased seen & aprizesed the 4th day of May añño dom 1681 by Nicholas Rowe William Rawlins Samuell Bonnifant & Henry Woodrow Followeth =

	£	s	d
Inprimis his wearing apparell & money in purse	7	0	0
Itm In the Hall one Table board & form and one Settle	0	17	0
Itm Three brasse pots & Three Caldrons	2	13	4
And eleaven small pewter dishes & To candlesticks	0	15	8
Itm In y^{e} parler one Tableboard form & Chayre	0	15	0
in y^{e} drinkehouse six Barrells	0	10	0
Itm In ye Milke house seaven Brasse pans and Two Trendles	3	10	0
Itm Two Cheese wrings	0	17	0
In ye Malthouse six Tubs & Vates	1	4	0
Itm In ye Hall Chamber in bedinge & other goods	2	10	0
It, In ye Parler Chamb^{r}, bed & bedinge	3	10	0
It, In ye Entry Chambr, one bed pformed	4	10	0
Itm In beife & Bacon	7	10	0
Itm In Malt	2	0	0
It~ In the Shop Chamber in bedinge &c	3	0	0
Itm In Goods seen or not seen as old Lumbr goods & other things as working Tooles & Implements of Iron or suchlike	0	15	0

A note of ye out doore goodes -

	£	s	d
Itm in out doore goods Fowre oxen & Two steeres	23	0	0
It~ one Mare Colt	5	0	0
It, Sixteen weathers & yeild yewes	6	8	0
It, Fowre heifers & five Rearing Calves	14	0	0
It, Nyne acres of wheat & barly on Burrows Teneñ	13	10	0
It, in Corn upon Gaddon Teneñ	24	0	0
It, one Nagge a Mare & Twentysix Coople of yewes & Lambes	17	10	0
Itm Six Milch Cowes & a bull	23	0	0
It, Two Colts fowre yerelings & a heifer	13	0	0
Itm five swine hogs	4	0	0
Itm Two wheat mowes & one barly mowe	25	15	0
Itm Corn in ye barn & wood	2	10	0
Itm one old Payre of weavers Lumbes	1	0	0
Itm Harrows drags wheelbarow & grinding stone	1	5	0
Itm Plow stuffe & horse Tacklinge	2	5	3
Itm Yoaks & Plow bowes	0	4	6
Itm part of the Cottage house wherein J...[?] then Lived	12	0	0
	£	s	d
	222	2	9

[£8 2s short?]

Nicholas Rowe William Rawlins
Samuell Bomfant Henry Woodraffe

[Will 20 Apr 1681 of Arthur Stevens the elder of Uffculme, yeoman: residue to wife Mary & s Henry Stevens, exec^{s}; £20 to s Agustin Stevens; to s Arthur Stevens, after death of wife

Mary, house & out-buildings &c at Coldharbour on leases formerly granted by the Countess of Bath; £5 to dr Mary Bray & her chn, plus maintenance at discretion of wife Mary; £20 each to all grandchn; 2s 6d each to Ann James & Christian Bishop; 2s to Thomas Beedle; 12d each to John Bishop & John Cumins; marked by Arthur Stevens senr in presence of Samuel James & Henry Osmond.]

182 ELIZABETH RUGG 1681 (PU)

[Bur: "Elizabeth Rugge, widow" 26 Jun 1681. Household items; £6.]

June 24th 81

Account of the vallow of Elizabeth Ruggs goods Latte deceased as followeth

	£	*s*	*d*
Impr's in readie Caush in a trunk	01	09	6
Item one wascoat fowre pitticoats And too flamings	01	10	00
Item on Chist one trunk And one Ammery	00	06	00
Item one beed pformed	02	05	00
Item one bras pott one bras Cittell And one putter dush	00	07	00
Item two Croocks two Andiers And a peare of billes	00	01	06
Item one barrill one tubb	00	01	00
Item one pylling	00	01	06
Item small triffilles not praised	00	00	06
Item one box[?] And the Linning	00	08	06
	06	10	6

[Will 21 Jun 1681 of Elizabeth Rugg of Uffculme, widow: best bed & fittings to grandch Richard Young; residue to grandchn James Rugg, Elizabeth Rugg, & Richard Young, execs; trustees "my truly and well beloved Roger Dinicombe of the Citty of Exeter genl" & John Starke of Uffculme, yeoman; marked by Elizabeth Rugg in presence of Nich: Dowrins (?Rawlins, ?Dowdney), Marke Pomroy(?), & Joan Chub.]

183 ANNE JURDIN/JORDEN 1683 (PU)

[Bur: "Anne Jordan widow" 7 Jan 1683 Widow of John 156; hall, middle chamber, & buttery, & one or more other rooms, & milkhouse; 2 cows; brewing vats; no clothmaking gear; £18.]

An Inventory of the goods and Cattles of Anne Jurdin widdow Late of Ufculme deceased: Seen & Apprized the Fowrteenth day of Aprill in ye yeare of or Lord god 1682[3?] & in the yere of the Raigne of or Soveraigne Lord Charles the Second now of England Scot: France & Ireland Kinge defendr of the fayth, the xxxvth, By Edward Marshall Andrew Aplyn Henry Osmond & Willyam Donne as followeth:

	lî	*s*	*d*
Imprimis her wearinge Apparrell	2	0	0
Itm one old Cowe & one Heifer	6	10	0
Itm In the Hall Chamber one Table board & form	0	6	8
one Livery board one Chayre & one Coffer	0	5	2
Itm & one old bed Tye a bolster 2 pillowes 2 old Blanketts & an old Coverlett	0	6	4
Itm with parcell of Torn Lininge	0	1	6
Itm In the Middle Chamber Two old Halfhead Bedsteeds with old beds old Blanketts Sheets & Bolsters	1	15	0
Itm one other old Bedsteed	0	5	0
Itm In ye Milkhouse one Chest & an old Cupboard	0	16	6
Itm one old Coffer an old board & other things	0	2	6
Itm Nyne Small pewter dishes	0	9	0
Itm In ye Chest 2 old Silver Rings	0	1	0
Itm Three Litle Brasse pans an old Cauldron and a pyre of small weights	0	10	4
Itm In the Hall one old Setle	0	1	0
Itm Two Brasse potts & one			

	lî	*s*	*d*
Iron pott	0	18	6
Itm Two Cauldrons one Brass pan & a skillett	1	2	6
Itm one payre of Andirons one Brandice Two payre of pothooks & one Backe Crooke	0	6	0
Itm In the Buttery Two old halfe Hogsheeds Two small Barrells & one Tub	0	9	6
Itm one litle Trendle Two Brueing Vates one old Tub & a litle eared[?] Tub	1	1	4
Itm in other Lumb^r goods & other things not seen nor Apprized	0	13	4
	18	1	02

Edward Marshall Will: Donne
Andrew Aplin Henry Osmond

[Will 1 Nov 1682 of Anne Jurden of Uffculme, widow: residue to cousin John Brownsey, exec; items of furniture &c to James & John, & Anne Brownsey, ss & dr of John Brownsey; coat to Agnes Freear, widow; 1s each to Frances Culliford & John Pitt; cauldron to Elizabeth, wife of Willm Shepherd & bedstead & brass pan to Thomas Shepherd, his s; 1s each to Katherine Oaton of Plymtree & Duens, sister of John Pitt; pewter dishes to Willm & Anne Shepherd, s & dr of Willm Shepherd; marked by Anne Jurden in presence of John Dyer, Andrew Aplin, John Lugge (mark), & Tho: Holwill.]

184 WILLIAM CROSSE 1682 (PU)

[Bur: "William Crosse" 19 Mar 1681/2. Mar: "William Crosse & Anne Merson" 11 May 1667. Hall, parlour, & kitchen, all with rooms (over?), milkhouse; plough; wheat, barley, peas, 7 cows, 3 hogs; horse tackle; £67.]

An Enventory of ye Goods & Chattels of William Crosse of Ufculme Late deceased taken & Appraysed ye 27th day of March 1682 By Nichlas Rowe John Lowdwell William Marshell Thomas Crosse & Samuell Bonifant

	£	*s*	*d*
Imp^s his waring Apparrell	04	02	06
It his brasse 9 brasse pans 3 potts 1 possenet 2 bottels 1 Chaffen dish 1 pesell & mortar 2 Candelstick one Skulot	6	05	00
It his Putter 13 platters 1 Flagon one Candelstick	1	11	06
Itt in ye Parler one Bedsetede & feather bede performed one Tableborde one Chest one Coffer	6	10	00
Itt in ye Hall one Tabelborde seven Joynstools one Cobord one Chare one Carpet & borde Cloth	5	08	03
Itt in ye ketchen one Tabelborde too forms one Settell one dripenpan too Spits	2	02	10
Itt in ye Parler Chamber too Bedsteds & too Doste Beds Performed one Chests one Coffer one Boxe	3	08	06
Itt in ye Hall Chamber For Feathers in a Tub & Cheseshelfs	01	00	00
Itt in ye Ketchen Chamber one malt Hutch too Old Hodgheds to keep Corn one Hackenie Saddell one paire of Waggets	02	06	00
Itt in ye Buttrey too Hodgheds fower Barels one Brewing fate one Tube	01	12	06
Itt in ye milke House too Trendels fower old Chesefats	00	17	00
Itt for too baggs & a Remnet of Row Cloth	00	07	00
Itt one Chesewreng	00	07	00
Itt For Bakon & Porke	02	05	00
Itt For Barly in ye howse & Barne	02	05	00
Itt For Whete & malte in howse	02	06	00
Itt For Plowstuffe & Harras	01	10	00
Itt For Three Cowes & fower yarlengs	16	10	00
Itt For Three Hoggs	02	04	00
Itt For Whete in ye blade	01	10	00
Itt For Peasen for Seede	00	09	00

	£	s	d
Itt For too Butts & a Wheleborrow	00	14	00
It For ye Horsse Tacklen	00	10	00
It For wood & Lomberstuffe & things not seene & Forgoten	01	00	00
	67	01	01

Nicolas Rowe John Lowdwell
Thomas Crosse Sam Bonifant

[Admon 27 Apr 1683 names Anne Crosse as widow & admin, & also Simon Merson of Uffculme, yeoman; marked by Anne Crosse & signed by Simon Merson in presence of John Daggle & Fran: St Barbe.]

185 JOHN STARKE 1682 (DS)

[Bur: "John Starke" 8 Apr 1682. Prosperous clothier; hall, 2 other rooms, combing shop & dyehouse; £70 stocks of clothing materials; corn, hay, 1 pig; £122.]

A true & perfect Inventory of all & singuler the goods & Chattles of Jno Starke of Uffculme in the County of Devon Clothier Latly deceased taken & prized the 15th day of Aprill 1682 by Marke Westron William Rawlins Edward Marshall Philip Starke & John Gay as followeth

	£	s	d
Imp^s his apparell	02	10	00
It money in his Chest	01	00	00
It money oweinge him	05	00	00
It in Sarges	40	00	00
It in Yearne	21	00	00
It in wooll	05	00	00
It in pinnions	01	05	00
It in Wosterd wooll	03	00	00
It in Fullinge Tooles & implem^ts	04	10	00
It one deyinge Furnace	02	10	00
It tenn puter dishes & other Implem^ts of puter	02	00	00
Item two silver spoons	00	12	00
It four brass potts & one posnett	03	00	00
It five brass panns	01	10	00
It three brass Caldrons	01	00	00
It one warmeinge pann & one dripeinge pann	00	09	00
It two skilletts	00	04	00
It Corne in ground	00	07	00
It in beeffe & baken	02	10	00
It one Cubbord one Table board one Chaire & other implem^ts of Tymber in the hall	01	10	00
It in reasons of the sum	02	00	00
It five barrills & other Impem^ts in the buttry	00	15	00
It three paire of Wosterd Combes & other implem^ts in the Combeinge shope	00	12	00
It one paire of Andirons & other Iron Implemts in the hale	00	15	00
Item in the hall Chamber two bedsteeds & beds pformed	07	00	00
Item in the same Chamber one Chest two old Coffers & one old Truncke	00	18	00
It in the Outer Chamber one bed-steed & bed performed	01	06	08
Item in the same Chamber one tryndle & three old Coffers	00	13	00
It in broade cloth	01	07	00
It in the deyhouse five tubbs two Furmes one barrill & other small Implem^ts	01	05	00
Item in oyle & deystuffe	00	10	00
It one swine hogg	01	00	00
It in wood & Fursse	01	00	00
It Corne Wynnoed & Corne in the barne	02	00	00
It in hay	01	10	00
It two paire of Crooks one wheelbarrow & one paire of panniers	00	07	00
It one pessell & morter	00	04	00
It goods of Lumber & not before seen or prized	00	10	00
	122	09	08

Marke Westron John Gay William Rawlins
Edward Marshall Phillip Starke

Exhibitum... [All that remains of the Latin endorsement.]

186 WALTER RISE 1682 (DS)

[Bur: "Walter Rice sen^{r}" 26 Jan 1681/2. Maltster with 2 sons; mostly household items; total, including £3 owed to him, £6.]

An Inventory of ye goods & Chattles of Walter Rise late of Uffculme in ye County of Devon Malster taken & apprized ye therd day of May Anno Domini one thousand six hundred eighty and two in ye English stile as followeth

	£	s	d
Inprimis in ready monie none	0	0	0
It in debts	3	13	2*ob*
It in plate none	0	0	0
It his weareing apparrle worth	0	12	0
wch he left to his 2 sonnes for monie due to them for works			
It one hog	0	5	0
It one little lowe beadsted wthout a head wth ye beading thereunto belonging worth	0	10	0
It 2 little Barrles & a tunner	0	3	0
It a Coffer wthout a Cover	0	1	6
It 4 tubbes & 2 pailes	0	5	0
It 2 tubbes more & a Butt in ye Maltehowse & a halfe pipe	0	4	10
It a trendle a yeating fate & a bottomeles hogshead in ye yeating howse	0	5	0
It 2 olde pecks a rang a lantherne and an old hackney saddle	0	2	6
It 3 earthen pannes dishes & spoones a pitcher & a earthen pot	0	1	8
It an hower glasse & a brush	0	0	6
It a Gridiron a little Kettle frieing pan a Brandice & 3 old hookes	0	5	6
It 3 baggs & 2 seeves	0	3	0
It one shivit & other things not before apprized	0	3	0
Sumatotalis	6	15	6*ob*
			[2d short?]

John Salkeld senio^{r}
Humphery Woodruff
The [H] mark of Henry Langdon

[Exhibited at Uffculme before Mr. Richard Kent, cleric & (surrogate for?) Dean of Salisbury, by Dorothy Rise, relict & admin, 11 May 1682. Latin endorsement signed by Geo: Frome Reg^{rius} Dep.]

187 SAM: JAMES 1682 (DS)

[Bur: "Samuel James" 29 Apr 1682. Prosperous shopkeeper; hall, kitchen, shop, adjacent rooms(?), cellar, & "little house"; detailed list of haberdashery, cloth, & provisions; books; pigs & 1 mare; £80.]

May 8th 1682
An Inventary of ye goods & Chattles of Sam: James Dec^{d}. taken & valued by us whose names are under written.

	£	s	d
Imp~ Shot in four boxes to ye value of	0	12	0
nayles & boxes to ye value of	0	7	0
3 pounds of twine	0	1	3
1/2 a quart of honey	0	1	4
1 lb of beeswax	0	1	0
for diascordiall & Sev^{r}all Small boxes	0	1	0
for horn bookes & Mattins bookes	0	1	6
for boxes whissells & hookes & eyes	0	1	2
Cord & twine	0	0	6
Sevall remlets of inkles	0	2	8
10 groases of gimp buttons	0	10	0
7 groase of Sattin buttons	0	10	6
5 groase of ye best gimp buttons	0	8	4
½ a dozen of pins number 12	0	1	8
piper & ginger	0	2	6
a quantity of prunes & raisons & Currants	0	3	9
3 dowzen & ½ of Lases	0	0	9
fine threed & nuns threed	0	6	0
for combs points Lases Cards & threed	0	5	0
½ c [cwt?] of ordernary raisons	0	9	0
5 oz of Light Coloured Silk	0	5	10
10 oz of Cloth Coloured Silk	0	6	8

	£	s	d
2 boxes with ribond & other things	0	18	0
4 lb & ½ of Coloured & white threed	0	8	0
tape & inkle	0	19	0
goodloome & Lace	4	0	0
tabby & Stuff & a box	0	12	0
a box of broake buttons	0	8	0
a box of bandstrings	0	2	0
12 y^{ds} of fustin	0	8	0
36 y^{ds} of dowlace at 9^{d} p y^{d}	1	7	0
7 y^{ds} & ½ of dowlace at 7^{d} p y^{d}	0	7	3
37 y^{d} of dowlace at 8^{d} p y^{d}	1	4	8
7/8 of y^{d} of fine Cloth	0	2	2
6 y^{ds} & ¾ of fine Cloth	0	8	0
9 y^{ds} ½ of fine Cloth at 1^{s} 8	0	15	10
1 y^{d} & ¾ at 2^{s} 2^{d}	0	3	9½
2 y^{d} ¾ at 2^{s}	0	5	6
1 y^{d} ¼ of kersy at 1^{s} 8^{d}	0	2	1
3 y^{ds} of Callacow	0	2	0
Sev^{r}all things in ye nest of boxes	0	8	0
nuttmaggs Cloves & Saffron	0	7	0
55 y^{ds} of 2/3 dowlace at 9^{d}	2	1	3
61 y^{ds} & ½ at 7^{d} of	1	18	5¼
7 y^{ds} & ¾ at 10^{d} of	0	6	9¼
9 y^{ds} & ½ of fustin at 10^{d}	0	7	11
43 y^{ds} of Shagg at 8	1	8	4
9 y^{ds} & ¼ of ireish Cloth at 11^{d}	0	8	5 ¾
2 y^{ds} & ¾ of broad buckrom at 9^{d}	0	2	0 ¾
5 y^{ds} & ½ of Coloured fustin at 8^{d}	0	3	8
2 remlets of fustin	0	0	6
20 y^{ds} & ¾ of Coloured Linen at 6^{d} ½	0	11	2½
19 y^{ds} ¾ of Coloured Linen at 6^{d}	0	9	10½
6 y^{ds} of Crokes at 5^{d}	0	2	6
20 y^{ds} of barraty at 1^{s}	1	0	0
7 y^{ds} ¼ of blue at 10^{d}	0	6	0½
remlets of Cloth & 2 pair of Stockens	0	2	0
2 y^{ds} of blue at 9^{d}	0	1	6
6 y^{ds} of ¾ [¾ of] blue at 7^{d}	0	3	6¾
20 y^{ds} ¾ of blue at 9^{d}	0	15	2¼
9 y^{ds} & half of Coloured Linen at 5^{d} ½	0	4	3¼
3 y^{ds} of blue at 7^{d}	0	1	9
4 y^{ds} ¼ of buckrom at 8^{d}	0	2	10

	£	s	d
17 y^{ds} of blue at 7^{d}	0	9	11
7 y^{ds} of hamborough at 7^{d}	0	4	7¾
35 y^{ds} & ¼ of Canvas at 8^{d}	1	4	2¾
12 lb & ¼ of roll tabbacho at 5^{d}	0	5	1
18 lb of Cut tabbacho at 7^{d}	0	10	6
Sand	0	2	0
rosom [resin?]& a whisk	0	1	0
13 quire of paper at 1^{d} ½	0	1	7½
4 lb & ½ of week yarn at 6^{d}	0	2	3
7 dozen & 7 lb [?] of Candles at 4^{s} 2^{d} p dozen	1	9	6
Candy Shugar & a box	0	2	0
Salt & a tub	0	3	0
a quantity of hops	0	10	0
a quantity of Shugar & a Coffer	0	18	0
8 y^{ds} of Cheescloth	0	2	0
a barrell of poweder	0	9	0
Soape & a box	0	1	6
a quantity of water & barrells	1	13	0
Commodities belonging to ye shop	1	0	0
51 lb of glue	1	0	0
4 y^{d} of Cloth	0	3	6
8 pair of Stockens	0	7	0
3 pair of Shears	0	2	0
a Coffer in ye little Chamber	0	2	6
2 bedsheads in ye Shop Chamber	1	5	0
2 ruggs	1	5	0
1 Chest	0	4	6
1 board	0	5	0
2 Joynstools	0	2	0
1 Coffer	0	1	6
1 hogshead	0	2	6
1 Coffer & 1 box	0	5	0
1 pair of Curtaines & valines	0	15	0
wearing apparell	2	0	0
1 featherbead & 2 bolsters & 2 blankets 1 pillow & 1 dustbead	3	5	0
5 Sheets & 4 pillaties & 1 towell	1	5	0
5 table napkens & a board Cloth	0	10	0
Kitchin Chamber			
1 bead 1 blanket 1 bolster 2 ruggs 2 pillows & beadshead & Sheet	1	15	0

	£	s	d
1 Trendle 1 Cradle & Sev^{r}all other things	0	12	0
in hall Chamber			
1 board 1 furm & Joynstools	0	8	0
Celler 2 hogsheads & 2 barrells	1	9	0
1 fletch of bacon	0	6	0
1 range & 1 dripeing pan & tunner	0	3	0
1 glass cage 1 Trencher cage 1 Chair Stoole 1 barrell & 1 pieboard	0	6	0
Kitchin			
3 fates & 5 tubbs & 2 pailes	2	1	0
1 pessell & morter & skeemer	0	3	0
1 Joynstool 1 board 2 seeves	0	7	0
3 pailes & 1 dropper 1 bowl 3 barrells 1 tubb 1 half peck 1 peck & 1 frying pan	0	10	0
2 dishracks 1 Shilf 1 broach 1 Jebb & 1 Saveing iron	0	4	6
2 Crookes 2 pothookes 1 pair of andirons 1 greddle 1 toster & brandiron 2 skillets	0	6	0
hall			
3 potts 57lb½ at 6^{d} p lb	1	8	9
3 brass pans & 2 kittles 25lb at 9^{d} p lb	0	18	9
2 pints 4 flagons & puter dishes 33lb at 7^{d} p lb	0	19	9
1 flagon 1lb½	0	1	0
1 board 1 furm 1 Cubbard & Shilves	1	0	0
in ye little house			
2 Joynstools 1 Chair 1 board & 1 furm	0	9	0
Swines	6	8	0
wood & Furz	6	0	0
one mare	2	0	0
for goods not known or seen	0	5	0
	80	00	3¾

[The values entered do not always quite agree with the pricing details quoted.]

Jno Grantland the [S] marke of
Augustin Stephens John Dyer

[Exhibited at Uffculme before Mr. Richard Kent, cleric & (surrogate for?) Dean of Salisbury, by Robert Tristram & Francis Fouracres, principal creditors of the deceased, 11 May 1682. Latin endorsement signed Geo: Frome Reg^{rius} Dep.]

188 JOHN & ELIZABETH BUTTSON 1682 (PU)

[Bur: "John Butson jun^{r}" 8 Nov 1682; "Elizabeth Butson, widow" 22 Nov 1682. Mar: "John Butson Junr & Elizabeth Rose" 28 Sep 1678. Mostly household items; 1 mare; total, including £6 for cottage & £13 owed to them, £48.]

A True Inventory of all ye goods & Chattles of John Buttson of Uffculme & Ellizabeth his wife deceased - Apprised & taken the three & twenty of November 1682 By Simon Welch Henry Rose & Richard Rose senn^{r} as Followeth

	£	s	d
Inprimus ther Apperrell both Lininge & Woollinge	05	00	00
Item mony in purse	07	00	00
Item on Cotteage howse	06	00	00
Item on Beadsteed & Beadinge	01	10	00
Item on table Bord & on Cheest	00	19	00
Item on Cheere & two stooles	00	02	06
Item on Brasse pott two Caldrons & on skillett & on pan	02	02	00
Item on mare two saddles & hay	05	10	00
Item putter & Iron stuffe	01	04	00
Item two Ferkens two Coffers & three Boxes	00	09	06
Item Lincloth suger Figes & spices	02	04	06
Item dishes spoones & tranches	00	00	10
Item spilles whorres & hopes	00	03	01
Item peeson & Bacon	00	05	00
Item safferon secatreny & dyescordyell	00	04	00
Item nailes & nailes Boxe	00	03	00
Item sturch & threed	00	04	09
Item tapes Enkells & glew	00	18	04

	£	s	d
Item on Coubbord	00	09	00
Item Debtes oweinge	09	10	00
Item disperrett debts	04	05	00
Item Lumber things seen or not seen	00	02	06
Sum is	48	07	00

The [S] marke of Simon Welch
Henry Rose Richard Rose sennr

[Admon 27 Apr 1683 names John Butson of Uffculme, weaver, as father & admin, & also Francis Butson & Francis Butson junr, both farmers of Uffculme; signed by John Butson & Francis Butson but marked by Francis Butson senr in the presence of John Daggle & Fran: St Barbe.]

189 SIMON WELCHE 1683 (PU)

[Mar: "Simon Welch & Jane Butstone" 17 Feb 1643/4; see 222. Inventory undated, but 2 assessors in common with No. 178 (Willm Crosse 1682) & will dated 26 Dec 1682; also acted as assessor for 182. Prosperous yeoman; hall, parlour, & rooms (over?), milkhouse, & wringhouse; corn, 1 horse, & 3 cows; £50 in bonds & cash; total, including £30 tenement, £130.]

An Envertory of ye goods and cattles of Simon Welche of Ufculmbe Late deceased taken and appraised by Nicholuse Row Frances Butsone & Samuel Bonifant as followeth

	£	s	d
Imps: his waring of apparrill	3	0	0
Itt:in money upon bond and in purse	50	0	0
Itt:in ye Inner Cha[m]ber one Beadsteed And Bead prformd One Chast one Trunke one Sealting [Sealling?] Trnddle	1	10	0
One Corn Tobe & foure Boxes	0	15	6
Itt:his plat one silver Boule six sepouns	5	10	4
Itt:his Table lining: three table Clorths & six Napcans	0	12	6
Itt:In ye hale Chamber one beadsteed & bead prformed one truckell beadsteed	1	4	6
one Cofer one malt huch one peare of wights	0	6	2
one Table bord	0	3	4
Itt In ye pa'ler Chember one beadsteed & bead prformd	6	2	6
one old beadsteed & bead	0	15	0
one pruce Cheast	3	0	0
one old Cofer & yeard Cheare	0	2	0
Itt:in paler Chember one Tablebord & forme	0	7	6
one cobord	1	10	0
one peasele & Morter	0	6	8
Tow Brase Candlesteeks	0	2	0
one Brase Chafindish	0	2	6
Two old seattals & Three Joy[n]ingstools	0	7	0
Itt in the hale one Tablebord & one forme	0	6	0
Fouer Brase Cettles	1	10	0
one Warming pane	0	5	0
Fouer Brase pots & one skellets	2	0	0
Eighten puter Dishes	0	18	0
one frinpane & three old Chears	0	2	6
Theree pote Crukes three speets three pothingers one skemmer one basling [basting?] laddle	0	10	0
Itt his box	0	04	0
Itt his Baken	1	10	0
Itt in the Milkhouse nine Braspans	1	19	2
Three Barels	0	08	0
Itt in the wringhouse one Cheswring one Trundele	0	18	0
nine tubs & fats & four old payls	1	09	0
Itt his Quickstofe thee Milch Cows	12	0	0
one old horse	1	10	0
Itt his Corne in house	2	14	0
Itt Appeare of harrows	0	18	0
for a sadle & other tackling for a horse	0	12	0
for bords & shelfs & Lumber stoufe	0	12	0
for tuls for husbantree other things forgotting	1	10	0

	£	s	d
for wood in ye Reike	2	14	0
Itt his Massige ore Tennement y^t he lived in	30	0	0
	130	05	08

[£10 1s 6d short?]

Nich Row y^e [F] marke of Fran: Butson
Sam: Bonifant

[Will 26 Dec 1682 of Simon Welch of Uffculme, yeoman: residue to wife Jane, exec, who retains the house & other household items for life unless she remarries; 6d each to 80 poor; 10s each to Frances Butson, Ann Marshall, Henyry Butson, & Simon Butson, chn of bro-in-law Frances Butson; 10s to sister-in-law Mary Greene, widow; 5s each to Mary Greene's drs, Mary, Jane, & Ann; best suit to Robert Greene, s of Mary Greene; 5s to godsons Richard Rose & Andrew Brient; £5 to k (& housekeeper?) Amy Butson; to Amos, s of John Butson, the pair of looms he already has; to ss & drs of George Welch, lately deceased, fowling gun to George, 2 silver spoons each to Agnes, Jone, & Margeret, & bed & other furniture to George after death of wife Jane; ovsrs Thomas Hill & Samuell Bonifant. (End of will damaged.)]

190 MARY HOW alš TANNER 1684 (PU)

[Bur: "Mary Tanner alš How widow" 7 Sep 1683. Widow of John No.173; hall & 2 other rooms; household items; no clothmaking gear; total, including £2 cottage chattel lease, £8.]

An Inventory of all & singular ye goods & Chattells of Mary How otherwise Tanner late of Uffculme in ye county of Devon Widdow deceased taken and praysed the Fower & twentieth day of March in the yeare of o^r Lord god 1683[/4] by Baptist Andro Symon Merson & William Potter as followeth

	£	s	d
Imprimis her purse & apparrell	01	00	00
Item in ye hall chamber one bedsteed & bed pformed	02	00	00
Item in ye same chamber one chest, one old coffer, one box, & one settell	00	10	08
Item in ye little chamber two old coffers & one box	00	02	06
Item one Trundell, & two barrells	00	07	06
Item in ye hall one little board & one Forme	00	05	04
Item two brass pottage potts	00	18	00
Item two old caldrons one brass pan & one skillett	00	10	10
Item three pewter dishes, nine small pewter dishes & two candlesticks	00	04	00
Item one pewter Flaggon, one pewter butter plate	00	02	02
Item one Cottage house beeing a Chattell	02	00	00
Item other things not seen nor formerly praysed	00	02	04
Sum is	08	03	04

Bap Andro Simon Merson William Potter

[Admon 27 Jun 1684 names Nicholas Hitchcocke of Broadhembury, cordwainer, & Richi Heeper (Hooper?) of Uffculme, farmer, as admins, & Simon Gill of Uffculme, yeoman; marked by Nicholas Hitchcocke & Richi Heeper & signed by Simon Gill in presence of Geo: Woodford, not^y pub.]

191 RICHARD MATTHEW 1686 (PU)

[Bur: "Mr. Richard Matthews, vicar of this pish" 21 Feb 1685/6. Vicar; hall, parlour, kitchen, buttery, with other rooms (over?), stable, woodhouse, & schoolhouse; mostly domestic items; no clothmaking gear; £48 in cash; total, excluding £20 in books, £118.]

An Inventory of the goods of Mr Richard Matthew late Vicar of Ufculme [1686]

	£	s	d
Imprimis in the Parlour 1 Table board with a grey carpet belonging to the same	00	13	00

	£	*s*	*d*
It:One side table with the like carpet	00	05	00
It:One little hanging cupboard	00	02	06
It:One tobacco tongs,One combcase,3 combs,5 small glasse bottles,2 brushes, powderbox,1 knife,1 fork & 1 sheath	00	02	00
It:One looking glasse	00	00	06
It:2 higher, and 1 lower leather chairs	00	05	00
It:1 timber chair with arms	00	02	06
It:2 elbow sedg chairs	00	01	06
It:4 Cushions	00	01	00
It:4 Escutchions	00	02	00
It:1 fire tongs,1 fire shovel, 1 pair of Andogs	00	02	00
It:In the Buttery,5 bigger and five lesser barrels	01	10	00
It:A salting standard and cover	00	01	06
It:One Tub,	00	01	06
It:One lade pail, and one mousetrap	00	00	08
It:2 searces, and 1 range	00	01	06
It:1 glasse cage, and one Urinall,1 cruet, and 9 drinking glasses	00	02	00
It:4 dozen and eight glasse bottles	00	04	08
It:1 Tunner,2 barrell stoopers, 1 pye-board	00	00	08
It:3 baskets,1 bottle brush, 1 pair of pincers	00	00	08
It:2 butter pots, and 1 salting pan	00	01	01
It:3 earthen pans and 1 earthen dish	00	00	03
It:4 jibs, and 1 shelfe	00	01	05
It:In the Hall, 1 Table, and 1 old carpet	00	05	02
It:5 Joynd stoolls	00	03	04
It:1 settle chair, and 1 doore, and 1 board	00	03	00
It:1 still	00	04	00
It:2 sterling boxes and 3 irons, & a rester belonging to em	00	01	03
It:1 dozen of round trenchers, and 2 dozen of square	00	01	06
It:1 bason	00	00	03
It:In the Kitchen 1 furnace	01	10	00

	£	*s*	*d*
It:5 tin pottage dishes, and 1 little mustard dish	00	02	00
It:5 sawcers, 2 butterplates, and 1 tin plate	00	02	06
It:7 tin spoons, and 1 tin salt	00	00	09
It:5 bigger pewter dishes, and 9 lesser pewter dishes	01	04	06
It:1 tinne bason, and 3 tinne candlesticks	00	04	00
It:1 latten Apple roaster,1 latten cheese roaster, 1 latten broyler	00	00	08
It:4 latten plates,3 latten candlesticks,1 latten custard pan,1 latten sawce pan, and 1 latten tunner	00	02	00
It:1 lanthorn	00	00	10
It:1 latten dripping pan	00	00	03
It:1 bell mettall skillet, 1 bell mettall mortar, & 1 iron pestle	00	07	00
It:1 great brasse pot, and 3 lesser brasse pots	02	10	00
[subtotal: 1d short?]	11	06	00
It:In the Kitchen - 1 greater, and 3 lesser brasse Kettles	01	15	00
It:2 brasse skillets,2 brasse dripping ladles,and 1 skumer	00	02	01
It:2 clome jugs, 1 clome bason	00	01	06
It:1 Iron chafing dish,1 frying pan,1 fire shovell,1 fire tongs, 3 pair of pothangers, & 1 beer-warmer	00	03	04
It:2 pair of pot-crooks, 1 gridiron,1 fleshfork	00	02	08
It:1 saving iron,1 pair of Andogs,1 pair of Andirons	00	04	06
It:3 spits, and 1 jack, and weights belonging to it	00	16	00
It:1 fire fork, and 1 pair of bellows	00	01	00
It:1 hourglasse,1 stock,1 little table,1 timber mortar, 1 timber pestle	00	02	00
It:1 Brewing fat,3 tubs, and 1 cowl	00	12	00
It:2 small tubs,2 buckets, 1 timber platter, 1 choppingboard	00	02	02
It:1 Jack cord	00	00	03

	£	s	d
It:1 peck,1 halfe peck, 1 basket,1 sieve	00	01	06
It:In the Parlour chamber- 34 glasse bottles and 2 stone bottles	00	03	00
It:2 warming pans	00	07	00
It:1 feather bed,2 feather bolsters, 1 pair of canmas sheets 1 pair of blankets,1 suit of curtains and vailings, and one coverlet and one standing bedstead	04	10	00
It:1 feather truckle bed,5 feather pillows,3 feather bolsters,2 rugs, the one white and the other red, and 1 truckle bedstead	05	10	00
It:1 side table, and 2 coverings the one linnen, and the other Kiderminster	00	07	00
It:1 pair of bellows, 1 pair of Andogs	00	01	08
It:In the Buttery chamber 1 glasse cage, and 1 trencher cage	00	02	00
It:One standing bedstead, 1 featherbed,1 bolster,2 feather pillows with drawers 1 pair of sheets,3 blankets, and 1 coverlet, and a suit of old curtains	04	10	00
It:3 pewter chamberpots	00	04	00
It:In the Hall chamber One standing bedstead,1 featherbed, 1 suite of old curtains,2 blankets,1 old coverlet, and 1 feather bolster	03	10	00
It:4 blankets	00	13	00
It:1 Winnowing sheet,1 great cushion,3 brushes, and 1 leather chair	00	08	03
It:1 black silk gown,1 green silk petticoat,1 changeable colour silk petticoat	02	00	00
It:1 paper box, with divers sorts of silk,1 necklace,1 needlecase, 1 pin-cushion, three pair of gloves,1 white silk scarfe, and 1 black silk scarfe	00	08	00
It:4 hats,1 tammy,and 1 clothgown, 4 cassocks,1 riding coat,4 doublets, 4 pair of breeches,1 pair of trowses, 2 red wastcoats,2 white wastcoats; 5 pair of drawers, 3 pair of shoes, 9 pair of white stockings,5 pair of black stockings,7 shirts, fine dowlas for 2 shirts,14 handkerchiefes, 2 riding hoods,1 Master of Arts hood, 15 nightcaps,3 neckcloths, 4 satten caps, 14 bands,22 pair of cuffes, 1 pair of golosses	12	03	06
It:22 yeards of broad canmas	01	02	00
It:12 yeards of canmas	00	14	00
It:6 tablecloths,4 dozen and 10 tablenapkins,1 Holland shift, 1 Holland pillowdrawer, 3 tablenapkins more,1 pair of Holland sheets,2 pair of dowlas sheets,6 yeards of of Holland,1 long towell	03	05	00
It:4 pair of sheets,1 long towell,5 pillowdrawers	00	18	00
It:1 Silver cup,9 Silver Spoons	05	18	00
It:1 presse,4 trunks,9 boxes, 1 desk,1 hanger,3 knifes	02	08	00
[subtotal]	53	06	05
It:In the kitchen Chamber,2 snaffle bridles,1 curb bridle 1 hackney saddle and saddlecloth, 1 pair of gambadoes, 2 cloak bags, 1 Portmanteau, 1 maile pillion, 1 succingle, 1 pair of leather stockings, 1 pair of boots and spurs,2 close stooles,7 bags, 1 bucket, 1 pair of weights, 2 baskets, 2 flasks,1 cheeserack, 1 range, 1 pike, and a pike staffe	01	15	09
It:In the stable and hayloft, 1 rack, and a small quantity of hay	00	09	00
It:In the woodhouse 4 bundles of laths,1 hogshead, 1 coop	00	07	00
It:hanging on the woodhouse wall 1 ladder	00	01	00
It:In the court wood uncloven	00	06	08
It:In the Schoole-house 17 boards, and 2 planks	00	15	00
It:1 ladder, It:In the linney 1 ladder	00	04	06
It:1 old wheelbarrow,1 rack	00	01	02
It:In the croft, faggotwood, and hard wood	02	00	00
It:in money	48	03	05
[subtotal]	54	03	06

	£	s	d
It:1 clove [?] basket	00	10	00
It:Books - twenty [?-smudged] pounds			
Sume totall	118	i6	i

[The last 2 items are excluded]

This Inventory was taken by us whose names are hereunto subscribd,
Rog: Grubham Ant: Stocker [Art:?]
John Dyer Edward Marshall
Robert Luscombe

[Will 1 Jul 1685 of Richard Matthew of Uffculme, clerk: £15 to sister Anne, wife of Thomas Aldworth of Reading, Berks, shoemaker; £15 to sister Sarah Druce wherever she lives; £10 to sister(-in-law?) Mary, wife of John Matthew of Staffy in the parish of Sparsholt, Berks, & 10s to her first husband's s, Francis Clifford; £1 to nephew Richard Aldworth, eldest s of Thos Aldworth; £2 to buy each a ring to bro-in-law John Webb of St Mary Hill, London, cheesemaker, & his second wife, Elizabeth, who also inherits a clove basket & cushion if the testator dies unmarried; all books to Roger Grubham of Kentisbeare; £15 to Henry Russell, tailor of Uffculme, (or to wife or ch John), exec; residue to Anne Aldworth, Sarah Druce, Mary Matthew, & Henry Russell; signed by Richard Matthew in presence of J°: Carell of Exoñ(?), Judith Miller (J mark), & John Dyer.]

192 HENRY GAY 1686 (PU)

[Prosperous clothier; household items & clothing materials; no clothmaking gear; £40 owed to him; total, including £30 cottage value, £194.]

A true & perfecte Inventory of all & Singuler the goods Chattles & Creditts of Henry Gay late of Uffculme in the County of Devon Clothier deceased taken & apprized the seventh day of September Annoq~ Dom 1686 by Leonard Poake Jn° Grantland & James Gange as followeth

	£	s	d
Imp^s his appell	04	00	00
It in p^r sent money	03	00	00
It in money due to him in Tiverton	40	00	00
It in wooll	25	00	00
It his estate in the Cottage where he lived	30	00	00
It twenty peices of sarges & drugetts	35	00	00
It in wosterd yearne	06	00	00
It in pynnions	02	10	00
It one deyinge Furnace	04	00	00
It Furss & wood	06	00	00
It one Cloth press racke & Fullinge tooles	05	00	00
It in Charcole	02	00	00
It three beds performed	07	10	00
It two brass potts	02	00	00
It 3 brass caldrons	02	00	00
It 4 brass panns	01	10	00
It 20 puter dishes	02	00	00
It two table boards	00	12	00
It in hogsheads burrills & Tubbs	01	05	00
It in deystuffe & oyle	03	00	00
It one washinge pann	00	15	00
It in mault	01	05	00
It one Cubbard	00	10	00
It two Chests	00	16	00
It two Coffers 2 truncks & two boxes	00	13	04
It in wosterd & wooll in the spinsters hands	06	00	00
Item in drugett wooll	02	13	04
	£194	19	8

the [L] marke of Leonard Poak
Jn° Grantland James Gange

193 JOHN BARNFEILD the elder 1687 (PU)

[Bur: "John Barnfield" 2 Jan 1686/7. Mar: "John Barnfeild & Margaret Chilcott" 19 May 1642, Halberton. Prosperous husbandman; hall, kitchen, & 2 other rooms (1 "new"); corn, 1 horse, 3 pigs; no clothmaking gear; total, including £6 owed to him & £20 estate at Penslade, £45.]

A true & perfecte Inventory of all & singuler the goods & Chattles & Creditts of Jn° Barnfeild thelder Late of Uffculme in the County of Devon husbandman deceased taken & apprized by Jno Grantland Jno Stone & James Stemaker alš Roach the sixteenth day of January <u>1686</u>[/7]

	£	*s*	*d*
Imp^{s} his appell	01	00	0
It p^{r}sent money	02	00	0
It in the Kitchen Chamber, two beds performed	01	10	0
Item in the same chamber five old Coffers	00	05	0
Item one old horse	01	10	0
Item his estate in Penslade	20	00	0
Item three swines	00	12	0
Item in the new chamber one bedsteed & bed pformed	01	05	0
Item in the same chamber one tableboard & one Furme	00	06	8
Item one brewinge Chyttle	02	10	0
Item five brass potts	01	15	0
Item four brass panns	00	16	0
It two Caldrons	00	18	0
It six puter dishes	00	12	0
It one bond or bill of six pounds due from Edward Hitchcocke	06	00	0
It in the Kitchen two boards & one Cubbard & one settle	00	06	8
It in the hall one old Cubboard & one tableboard	00	06	8
It one old Hutch	00	03	0
It three old hogsheads & 3 barrills	01	00	0
It three old Fates & one Tryndell	00	10	0
It two Fletches of baken	01	00	0
It Corne in barne	00	12	0
Item lumber goods not seen or prized	00	05	0
the whole Sum	£45	03	0

Jno Grantland the [S] marke of Jno Stone

the [R] marke James Stemaker alš Roach

[Will 22 Dec 1686 of John Barnfeild the elder of Uffculme, husbandman: residue to wife (Margeret, 211), exec; 1s & a pot to s John Barnefeild; to grandson John Hutchens stable, linhay, & garden after death of wife; dr Mary to live on estate during absence of husband abroad; to dr Elizabeth a brass pot; to s William Barnefeild farm houses & estate after death of wife; marked by John Barnfeild in presence of John Grantland, James Roche (R mark) & Wm Oland (+ mark).]

194 ELIZABETH BISHOPP 1688 (DS)

[Bur: "Elizabeth Bishop" 26 Mar 1688. Prosperous widow; hall, parlour, with other rooms (over?), buttery, shop, apple chamber, milkhouse, draught-house, & bakehouse; no clothmaking gear; farming gear but no stock; bible & other books; £18 owed to her; total, including £13 chattel lease, £79.]

An Inventory of the goods Chattles & debtes of Elizabeth Bishopp late of Ufculme in ye County of Devon wid deceased taken and prised the 27th day of March 1688 by Francis Waldron Robert Mills John Garnsey & Peter Pringe as followeth;

	£	*s*	*d*
Inprimis her Aparell	05	10	00
It money in purse	02	12	00
It in the Parlour one Cupboard one side table six chaires fower ioyned stooles wth other small thinges there	01	10	00
It in the Hall A clock two settles A side table fower cheese boards a glasse cage wth other small thinges there	01	14	06
It in ye Parlour chamber two standinge bedsteeds & one trundle bedsteed wth two featherbeds & furniture A sp^{r}uce chest another chest A truncke two coffers two boxes A littell cupboard & chaire	09	05	06
It in ye Hall chamber A standinge bedsteede A mill to cleanse corne A dust bed two feather bolsters one dust bolster two Coverletts one coffer & cheeseselter two Chairs & A paire of scales & beame A cheese racke with other small things there	01	10	06
It in ye Apple chamber one standard A coffer A forme & two shelves with other small			

	£	s	d
thinges there	00	15	00
It in ye milkehouse five shelves	00	09	00
It in ye butterie two hogsheads two barrells three shelves fower Jebbs one Ammorie and three standers	01	09	06
It in ye shoppe five pailes two tubbs fower hogsheads to keepe corne three drippers wth boards & other things in the said roome	03	10	00
It in ye draughthouse two hutches A brewinge tubb & A trendle with sevrall plankes in the said roome	02	10	00
It in ye Bakehouse A yeotinge fate A brewing fate A cheese tubb A draught tubb A trendle one old fate A mouldinge board A brake board and three barrells	01	15	00
It brasse and Pewter	05	00	00
It three spitts three paire of Andoggs A paire of fire tonges A firepan & A fire pike three paire of pot crookes fower pot hangings one gridiron & two toasters	00	10	00
It A trundle bedsteede	00	02	00
It an Iron barr & seaven Iron wedges	00	08	00
It one bible wth other small books	00	06	06
It A lease for years in A house orchard and garden	13	10	00
It thirtie steeches of wheate	01	05	00
It debt due from John Bishopp	01	03	00
It another debt due from ye sd John Bishopp wch will not be payeable untill ye 24th of June 1689	17	00	00
It two paire of waine wheeles A waine bodie three putts three Iron chaines with other plow tacklinge & horse tacklinge	06	00	00
It goods seen & unseene and not before in this Inventorie valued	01	05	00
Summa totalis Inventorÿ	79	00	06

Mr Rob: Mills of or pish was desirous to have this sent you.

[Will 13 Apr 1683 of Elizabeth Bishop of Uffculme, widow: residue to ss Humfry & Roger Bishop, execs (who renounced this task in favour of s-in-law John Goodridge 30 Apr 1688, the date of an Admon); 20s to elderly poor; 5s & silver spoon to s Giles; £60 & apparel to dr Anne, wife of John Goodridge, but the house where Anne now lives to go to s Roger Bishop though she may continue to occupy the same for life at a rent per year of 20s to Roger & 4s to Giles; after death of Anne grandch Fides, wife of John Evans, to live there; 10s each at age 21 to grandchn; 2s 6d to current maid-servant; ovsrs Mark Westerne & John Garnsey, yeomen of Uffculme; marked E by Elizabeth Bishop.]

195 ARTHUR DOWDNEY the elder 1688 (DS)

[Bur: "Arthur Dowdney" 21 Apr 1688. Tailor; porch, hall, kitchen, buttery, with other rooms; no clothmaking gear; 3 pigs; £17.]

A true & perfecte Inventory of all & singuler the goods Chattles & Creditts of Arthur Dowdney thelder Late of Uffculme in the County of Devon Tayler deceased taken & apprized the 22th day of May 1688 by Edward Marshall & John Lugg as followeth

	£	s	d
Imps his appell	01	00	00
Item one old brewinge Furnace	01	05	00
Item three old Fatts	00	10	00
Item two old Caldrons	00	05	00
Item in the hall chamber one old Coffer one old chest & one standard	00	10	00
Item two bedsteeds & beds performed	03	00	00
Item in the hall chamber one old bed tie & old bolster	00	05	00
Item in the buttery Chamber two tableboardes & two Furmes	01	05	00

	£	s	d
Item in the same chamber one Cubboard	00	10	00
Item in the same chamber seven puter dishes one flagon two paints two candlesticks	00	13	04
Item in the same chamber one old settle	00	03	00
Item in the Kitchen chamber one tableboard & one Coffer	00	10	00
Item in the same chamber five old stooles & one little joyne stoole	00	05	00
Item in the same chamber one old Tubb & one side board	00	02	06
Item in the poarch chamber one table board & one Furme	00	08	00
Item in the same chamber six Chairs	00	06	06
Item three swine hoggs	02	10	00
Item three hogsheads	00	15	00
Item one barrill one Tunnell & one jeb	00	03	04
Item two brass potts	00	18	00
Item two iron potts	00	08	08
Item two skilletts	00	02	00
Item eight old puter dishes	00	08	08
Item five old flagons	00	03	04
Item one old livery table	00	03	06
Item three spitts 2 paire of pottcrooks 4 potthangings & a paire of Andirons & a saveinge iron	00	07	06
Item goods not seen nor befor prized	00	05	06
the whole Sume	17	03	10

[Exhibited at Uffculme before Mr. Richard Kent, cleric, surr. for Dean of Salisbury, by Joan Dowdney, relict & admin, 23 May 1688. Latin endorsement signed Geo: Frome Reg[r] Dp.]

196 JOHN LEAMAN 1688 (PU)

[Bur: "John Leaman" 20 Jun 1688. Yeoman; house with entry, parlour, and other rooms, hall, bakehouse; no clothmaking gear; largely the £70 tenement; £88.]

An Inventory of the goods & Chattles & debts of John Leaman late of Ufculme in the County of Devon deceased taken & prised the tenth day of August 1688: by Robert Mills & Simon Gill as followeth . /

	£	s	d
Inprimis his Apparell	03	00	00
It: money in purse	00	03	10
It: a lease for yeares determinable on one old life in a tenem[t] called Rill	70	00	00
It: brasse & pewter	03	05	00
It: in the parlour Chamber one standinge bedsteede & featherbed pformed one halfehed bedsteede & dustbed pformed a Chest a forme & Cheese sheelves	06	05	00
It: in the Chamber over the entry a trundle bedsteede & dustbed pformed	01	02	06
It: in the bakehouse a brewinge fate & fower tubbs & a barrell	01	02	00
It: in the Hall a tableboard & forme a Cupboard a settle & two chaires wth other smale things there	02	10	00
It: a Cheese wringe a thwart sawe & fower Iron wedges	00	15	06
It: goods seene & unseen beinge of smale value & not before in this Inventory valued	00	04	06
	£	s	d
Summa totalis Inventorij	88	08	04

[Will 3 Jun 1688 of John Leaman of Uffculme, yeoman: residue to s George Leaman, exec; £8 to dr Mary Hole; £6 each to drs Frances & Ann Leaman; oak chest to dr Ann; to 3 drs, Mary, Frances, & Ann, beds, pans, furniture, parlour & hall chamber in his house at Rill for rest of lease, plus garden; 2s 6d each to all grandchn; marked J by John Leaman in presence of Robert Mills, Robert Mills senr, & Henry Sousthwod.]

197 JOHN DUNNE the elder 1688 (PU)

[Bur: "John Dunn" 16 Aug 1688. Very prosperous yeoman ("blacksmith" in will); £300 for Venners & Hales estates; 2 parlours, buttery, with other rooms (over?), kitchen; corn, 1 mare, 8 cattle, 47 sheep, 6 pigs; plough; no clothmaking gear; £421.]

A true & perfecte Inventory of all & singuler the goods Chattles & Creditts of John Dunne the elder late of Uffculme in the County of Devon Yeoman taken & Apprized the 22th day of August 1688 by Marke Westron John Grantland & Thomas Dunne as followeth

	£	s	d
Imps his Apparrill	002	10	00
Item in prsent money	008	00	00
Item his Estate in Venners Tents	140	00	00
Item his Estate in Hales	160	00	00
Item Corne in barne	020	00	00
Item fower Cowes	012	00	00
Item in hay	010	00	00
Item two heffers one bull & one Calfe	007	00	00
Item one old mare	003	00	00
Item seaven & fourty sheepe & lambs	014	00	00
Item in wood	002	00	00
Item 10 puter dishes & one Flagon	001	00	00
Item seaven brass panns	002	00	00
Item five Caldrons	004	00	00
Item six brass potts	004	00	00
Item in ye parler one Cubboard one Furme two joyne stooles one Carpett and three Chaires	003	00	00
Item in the little buttery nyne barrills & one standard	001	10	00
Item in the parler chamber one bed performed	004	00	00
Item in the same chamber one Chest & one Chaire	000	15	00
Item in the buttery Chamber one bed performed	002	00	00
Item in wooll	000	15	00
Item two Sawes	000	05	00
Item in the old parler & in the Chamber over the same three beds performed	006	00	00
Item six swine hoggs	005	00	00
Item in the Kitchinge one Cubboard one table board & one Baken racke	001	00	00
Item in butter & Chesse	002	00	00
Item one Corne Hutch one mill for the cleaneinge of Corne & two chesse presses	002	00	00
Item in old tubbs & Fatts	001	00	00
Item a paire of draggs & Harrow tynes	000	15	00
Item plough stuffe & horse tacklinge	000	10	00
Item in lumber goods not seene or prized	001	05	00
	£421	05	00

Marke Westron Jno Grantland
Tho: Dunne

[Will 5 Mar 1687(/8) of John Dunn of Uffculme, blacksmith: residue to drs, Florence & Dorothy, execs; indoor goods & furniture to wife Justaine, also 2 cows; mention of Hall's tenement in Uffculme manor for 2 years & if lease then unexpired to pass to Robert & Thomas, chn of s Thomas; 5s each to s John & his chn John, Wm, Ann; 5s each to Sarah, Alice, John, & Susanna, chn of s William; 5s each to s Thomas & his chn John, Thomas, Dorothy, Margret, Joane, & Robert; £10 to Mary, dr of deceased s William; £10 to Rebeca, dr of s John; to William, ch of deceased s William, £2 yearly till age 21 & Venner's tenement in Uffculme manor after death of Dorothy; marked + by John Dune in presence of Thomas Pooke, Robert Westron, & John Brodboore.]

198 JOHN SALKELD 1688 (PU)

[Bur: "Mr. John Salkield" 20 Nov 1688. Prosperous gentleman of Smithincott farm (will); parlour, kitchen, & buttery, with rooms over, hall, & outhouse; "library" of books & a clock; no clothmaking gear; 2 horses, 2 heifers; total, including £100 chattel estate, £134.]

A true Inventory of the Goods & Chattles of John Salkeld of the pish of Uffculme in the County of Devon Gent lately deceased taken and apprized the one & Twentieth day of Novembr 1688 by we whose names are hereundr written, as Followeth _ _ _ _

	£	s	d
Imprimis his wearing apparle	03	00	00
Item mony in pocket	07	03	10
It in the kitchen one Tubb and & two old boards	00	03	00
one furnice	01	00	00
It in the kitchen Chamber - a Librarie of books	01	00	00
a hogshead of syd^{r}	00	14	00
Aples	00	05	00
Item in the butt^{r}ie two Hogsheads & Fower burrles	00	15	00
Three gibbs & two hanging boards	00	03	6
It in the pler one Table board one liv^{r}ie Table board one binch two Chaires six Joint stools one Glase Cage	2	15	00
It in the Hall one Table board one side Tableboard one Cubberd two Chaires one shelfe one dishracke one bacon racke three spits one pouring [porrig?] pot one posnet one Crooke on firepan one paire of tongs one warmingpan	01	18	10
It at the head of the stairs one Clock	1	00	00
It in the Chamb^{r} ov^{r} the buttrie one beadstead & bead pformed one Chaire board & Diske [desk?]	2	03	06
It In the pler Chamb^{r} one beadstead one fether bead one fether bolster one fether pillow one Chaire	2	15	00
It In the out house one Malt hutch & hardwood	00	10	10
for Hay	02	00	00
It two Heafer yerlings	02	12	10
It one Maire & Colte	04	00	00
It some Lumb^{r} Goods seene & not seene	00	00	00
It one Chattle Estate	100	00	00
Sumum totall	134	00	04

Hum: Marsh Will Elworthy
John Melhuish

[Will 28 Oct 1688 of John Salkeld of Uffculme, gent: to s Thomas Salkeld the Smithincott farm (lease determining upon the death of Henry Frank), from which conditional annuities to be paid to s Richard, dr Agnes, wife of John Melhuish, & to dr Susan Franke or her chn Ames, Humphry, Robert, & Mary Franke; signed & sealed in presence of Margaret Doone, Humphrey Welch (H mark), & John Welch (J mark).]

199 JOHN DULIN 1689 (PU)

[Bur: "John Duling" 12 May 1689. Fuller; household items; bible & other books; total, including £8 for half cottage lease at Umbrooke, £15.]

An Inventory of All ye Goods & Chattles of John Dulin of ye parrish of Uffculme in ye County of Deavon Fuller Deceased taken & prized the Twentieth day of May 1689 by Robert Mills And Nicholas Tucker as followeth

	£	s	d
Imp^{s} his Wearing Apparrell	01	00	00
Item money & purse	00	06	06
Item in ye Chamber one standing bedsteed And one Trundle bedsteed wth Two flockbeds and furniture	01	10	00
Item one standing bedsteed more	00	04	06
Item Brasse & Putor	02	02	06
Item one Cupboard or Amery	00	04	00
Item one Table-Board Form & Side Board	00	07	06
Item one Chair one Glass Cage And one Dish Cage wth other things of small Vallue	00	04	06
Item in ye Buttery one old hogshead An three Barrels wth other things of small Vallue	00	10	00
Item Two old Coffers And Two small Boxes	00	05	06
Item one Litle Brewing fate And Three old Tubbs	00	04	00
Item one Bible wth other small books	00	05	06
Item A Lease for yeares Determinable on Lives In ye Moiety or halfendeale of A Cottage Lying att Umbrooke	08	00	00
Item Goods seen & Unseen			

	£	s	d
being of small Vallue And not before this Inventory Vallued	00	02	00
Summa Totalis Inventorij	15	06	06

[Will 12 Nov 1687 of John Dulin of Uffculme, fuller, pr at Uffculme 30 May 1690 before Mr Bernard Byrd & George Woodward Reg^r: residue to exec^s, ss William & George Dulin, who also inherit the remainder of the lease of the house, orchard, & garden; 10s to s John; 5s to dr Rebecka Radford; marked J by John Dulin in presence of Nicholas Tucker, Ann Lee, John Hartyn, & Elizabeth Tucker.]

200 WILLIAM KERSLAKE 1689 (PU)

[Yeoman (retired?); household items; virginals; no clothmaking gear; total, including £13 owed to him, £34.]

A true & perfecte Inventory of all and singuler the goods Chattles & Creditts of William Kerslake late of Uffculme in the County of Devon Yeoman deceased taken & apprized the 28th day of October 1689 by James Holway Esqr & Jno Grantland as followeth

	£	s	d
Imp^s his appell	01	00	00
Item in p^rsent money	00	05	00
Item in money oweinge him upon bond	18	10	00
Item four brass panns	00	16	00
Item three brass potts	01	06	08
Item two Caldrons	00	10	00
Item one paire of virginalls	01	10	00
Item two bedsteeds & beds performed	03	05	00
Item two livery table boards	00	08	00
Item two other table boards	00	10	00
Item four Chaires	00	08	00
Item eight large joyne stools	00	08	00
Item three little joyne stooles	00	02	00
Item one Chest	00	09	00
Item two trunkes	00	06	00
Item one Cubboard	00	06	08
Item one pyllion & Coveringe	00	05	00
Item tenn puter dishes	01	05	00
Item two flagons of puter	00	05	00
Item seven silver spoones	01	15	00
Item two puter Candlestickes	00	01	08
Item in barrills & Tubbs	00	06	08
Item two skilletts	00	04	00
Item one Tryndle	00	06	08
Item in goods not seene or prized	00	05	00
	£34	14	4

James Hollway Jno Grantland

[Will 28 Jul 1689 of William Kerslake of Uffculme, yeoman: residue to dr Jane Kerslake, exec; to wife £15, all goods she had before marriage, plus other household items; signed & sealed by William Kerslake in presence of John Grantland, Symon Hamett (SH mark), & Francis Sherbrooke (S mk).]

201 RICHARD WALDRON 1690 (PU)

[Yeoman; virginals; clover, 2 colts, 17 sheep; £18.]

An Inventory of all and singuler the goods and Chattles & debts of Richard Waldron late of Uffculem in the County of Devon Yeoman Deseased tacken and praised the twenty Fowerth day of Aprill 1690 By Robert Gill John Gill And Gilles Bishop And Francis Waldron as folloeth

	£	s	d
Inprimis his apparill	05	00	00
Itt money in purse	01	08	09
Itt to Coults	03	19	00
Itt seventeen sheep	05	00	00
Itt one pare of Virgenalls	01	10	00
Itt on Clover Ricke	01	05	00
Itt three silver spoones	0	15	06
	18	18	03

[Admon 30 May 1690 names Elizabeth Waldren as mother & admin, & also William Waldren of Uffculme, sergemaker: marked E by Elizabeth & signed by Wm Waldren in presence of Geo: Woodford not^y pub.]

202 RICHARD WOODROW 1690 (PU)

[Mar: "Richard Woodrow & Jane Hodge" 29 Jun 1669. Husbandman (retired?); no corn or stock; household items; spinning turn; books; £10.]

A true & pfect Inventorie of all the goods of Richard Woodrow of Uffculme husbandman late deceased made priesed & taken the seventh day of May in the yeare of our Lord 1690 by Stuckly Witte & Thomas Batten as followeth

	£	*s*	*d*
Imp- his waringe apprell	3	0	0
It two bedsteeds & furniture	3	0	0
It one Chest	0	4	0
It one little Coffer	0	2	0
It one Coffer	0	1	6
It one little truncke	0	1	6
It one Coffer	0	1	6
It one box	0	0	6
It a glascage & little barrill	0	1	6
It two beere barrils	0	1	6
It tubs & a paile	0	5	0
It on Jebge [wedge? or jib?]	0	0	6
It on table board & form with on Chare	0	4	0
It on spining torn	0	1	0
It all the brasse	2	0	0
It all the tyn	1	0	0
It on spit & two little hanging crooks	0	2	6
It small clome plats	0	1	0
It for the books	0	1	6
It one Chafing dish of earth	0	0	0f
It one frying payn & gridiron	0	1	0
It on cup of glas	0	0	1
It all other things not seen & forgotten	0	0	9
The Sum totall	10	11	4f

the [B] marke of Thomas Batten
the [S] marke of Stuckly Witte

[Admon 27 May 1689 names Joane Woodrow as widow & admin, & also Thomas Batten of Uffculme, carpenter; marked by Joane Woodrow & Thomas Batten in presence of Bernard Byrd & Geo: Woodford.]

203 JOHN GILL 1691 (PU)

[Prosperous yeoman (retired?); no corn or stock; no clothmaking gear; largely £5 owed to him & £140 for Ashill estate; £165.]

A true & perfecte Inventory of all and Singuler the goods Chattells and Creditts of John Gill late of Uffculme in the County of Devon Yeoman taken and apprized the 5th day of January 1690[/1] by William Palmer Gyles Bishope James Southwood James Gill Richard Gill as followeth

	£	*s*	*d*
Imps his Appell	004	00	00
Item in prsent money	003	00	00
Item in money oweinge him	005	00	00
Item his Estate in Ashell Tenemt	140	00	00
Item two bedsteeds & beds performed	005	00	00
Item one Truckel bedsteed	000	05	00
Item two Chests two Coffers & two boxes	001	03	04
Item two brass potts	001	06	08
Item one old kittle two skilletts & one skemer	000	06	00
Item thyrteene puter dishes	001	10	00
Item eight hogsheads	002	00	00
Item four barrills	000	12	00
Item two table boards	000	13	04
Item one old Amery & three chaires	000	06	08
Item one other board & two tryndles	000	10	00
Item in goods not seen nor befor apprized	000	03	04
	£165	16	04

William Palmer Geailes Bishop
James Southwood Richard Gill
James Gill

[Admon 15 May 1691 names Grace Gill as dr & admin, & also Robert Gill & John Grantland; signed by Grace Gill & John Grantland & marked G by Robert Gill in presence of Bernard Byrd & Geo: Woodford.]

204 HUMFRY WOODRUFFE 1691 (PU)

[Mar: "Humphrey Woodrow & Rebecca Palmer" 26 Jun 1650, Feniton. Prosperous yeoman; entry, hall, kitchen, with other rooms, buttery, cheese chamber, milkhouse, & malt-house; corn, 3 horses, 5 cows, 42 sheep, 8 pigs; plough; gun; no cloth-making gear; no chattel lease; £75.]

An Inventory of all & singuler y[e] goods & Chattles & Creditts of Humfry Woodruffe late of Uffculme in the County of Devon Yeoman deceased taken & apprized the 15th day of January 1690[/1] by Robert Burrow & Thomas Dunne as followeth

	£	s	d
Imp[s] his appell	02	10	00
Item five milch Cowes	10	00	00
Item two & fourtie sheep & lambs	07	00	00
Item one horse & one mare & colt	06	00	00
Item eight swine hoggs	02	00	00
Item Corne in barne	04	10	00
Item in hay	02	00	00
Item in wood	00	15	00
Item in baken butter & Cheese &c	04	00	00
Item three brass pootts & three caldrons	02	05	00
Item nyne brass panns	02	10	00
Item one warmeinge pann one Chaffin dish one skillett & one Candlesticke of brass	00	10	00
Item a Furnace	01	00	00
Item fifteene puter dishes & one pessell & morter	01	00	00
Item in y[e] kitchen one Cubboard one boarde & Furme one dishracke & baken racke	00	12	00
Item one mault mill six Tubbs one Cheese press	01	12	00
Item in the hall one Table board seven joyne stoolls & one little board	01	10	00
Item one Cubboard & glass cage	00	15	00
Item two settles five Chaires & one Carpett	02	00	00
Item in y[e] butterey six barrills & one standard	00	15	00
Item in y[e] milkehouse two hoggsheads & two barrills	00	12	00
Item one Tryndle standerd & Tubb	00	08	00
Item one Tubb standard & Firkin	00	05	00
Item in the kitchen chamber two beds performed	04	10	00
Item one Chest three Coffers & one box	00	16	00
Item in the Entrey Chamber one old bedsteed	00	03	00
Item in wooll	01	05	00
Item in y[e] hall chamber two beds performed	04	00	00
Item one Chest two boxes & little table board	00	13	00
Item in y[e] Cheese chamber one bedsteed one board, Furme, & frame of shelves	00	14	00
Item in the maulthouse 6 Fatts & one mill to cleane corne w[th]all	01	00	00
Item in plough stuffe harrows & horse Tacklinge	02	00	00
Item one saw bittle & wedges	00	10	00
Item Andirons, spitt, dripinge pan & saveinge iron	00	08	00
Item six chaires	00	10	00
Item two tubbs & four bucketts	00	04	00
Item eight Cheese Fatts & four Cushings	00	10	00
Item one Foulinge peece	00	10	00
Item one twobill shovell & madiocke	00	03	00
Item one paire of fire tongs & brandirons	00	02	00
Item two paire of pottcrooks	00	02	00
Item goods not seene or before apprized	01	00	00
	£73	09	00

Robert Burrow Tho: Dunne

[Will 18 Aug 1690 of Humfry Woodruffe of Uffculme, yeoman, pr at Uffculme before Mr Ber: Byrd, cleric: residue to wife Rebecka, exec; £5 to dr Roberta Furwood; £20 to dr Dorothy; signed by Humfry Woodruff in presence of John Grantland, Henry Scoyer (S mark), & Grace Daniel.]

205 BAPTIST DOWDNEY 1691 (PU)

[Prosperous husbandman; corn, 1 horse, cattle, 33 sheep, 1 pig; plough; no clothmaking gear; £64.]

A true & perfecte Inventory of all & singuler the goods Chattells & Creditts of Baptist Dowdney Late of Uffculme in the County of Devon husbandman deceased taken & prized by Thomas Dunne Jno Grantland & John Marshall the 25th day of February Annoq~ Domi 1690/1 as followeth

	£	s	d
Imp^s^ his appell	02	00	00
Item in p^r^sent money	03	00	00
Item thyrteene Cuppells of ewes & lambs	03	10	00
Item seven other sheep	02	00	00
Item one yoake of oxen	07	00	00
Item in other Cattell	06	10	00
Item one horse	03	00	00
Item Corne in barne	07	00	00
Item in hay	04	00	00
Item one swine hogg	00	10	00
Item Corne in the feilds	02	00	00
Item one Ingen & Sider press	02	00	00
Item in Sider	04	00	00
Item one paire of wheels & dunge butt	02	00	00
Item plough Tacklinge	01	05	00
Item in bedinge	02	05	00
Item one Chest & one Coffer	00	10	00
Item in brass & puter	02	00	00
Item one Table board	00	08	00
Item two Corne Hutches	01	00	00
Item in Tubbs & fatts	01	05	00
Item in horse Tacklinge	00	05	00
Item in Fagott wood	01	00	00
Item two Flitches of baken	01	00	00
Item in butter & Cheese	00	10	00
Item one Amry & one settle	00	10	00
Item tenn hogsheads	02	00	00
Item in Tymber & lumber goods of wood & Tymber not before Apprized	02	10	00
	£64	18	00

[Will 4 Jan 1690/1: residue to exec Jane, sister-in-law & wife of bro James Dowdney; £5 each to bro Humfry Dowdney & to James, Humfry's s, on reaching age 21; signed by Baptist Dowdney. Witn: John Grantland, who signs, & John Greene & Mary Taylor, who make their marks.]

206 ELIZABETH KERSLAKE 1691 (PU)

[Widow; inventory undated but will 1691; £12 owed to her, otherwise only household items; virginals; £18.]

A true & perfict Inventory of all ye goods and Chattells of Elizabeth Kerslake of Ufculme Latly Deceased taken and Apprased by John Grantland & William Rawlins as followeth

	lî	s	d
Imp^s^ her apparrill	02	10	00
Itm one pare of old Blankets	00	06	00
Itm 3 joyne stooles	00	03	00
Itm a pare of virgenalls	00	15	00
Itm one Trunke	00	06	08
Itm 4 puter dishes & one plate	00	08	00
Itm 2 Brass potts and one Kittell	00	12	06
Itm one frying-pann & salt box	00	02	06
Itm 2 tinn Candelsticks	00	02	00
Itm one Little Tubbe	00	01	00
Itm one old Fatt & 2 Barrells	00	03	00
Itm one speet driping pann & spoon	00	03	00
Itm 2 Chares and a little joyne stoole	00	02	06
Itm one Table board	00	06	08
Itm one little box	00	01	00
Itm in money upon Bond	12	00	00
Itm Lumber Goods not seen & appraysed	00	02	06
Totall Sume	18	05	4

[Will 26 Dec 1691 of Elizabeth Carslake of Uffculme, widow: residue to k Edward Renolds & k Anne Renolds, exec^s^; gold wedding ring to bro Richard Gardner; 40s to k Edward Renolds; silver spoon to sister Anne Bowden;

marked by Elizabeth Carslake in presence of John Grantland, William Rawlins, & John Pryddis (mark).]

207 WILLIAM COTTRILL 1691 (DS)

[Yeoman; household items only, but halfendeal of an estate mentioned in the will; looms; £2.]

A true & perfitt Inventorie of all the Goods & Chattels of William Cottrill deceased made priased & taken the 3d day of August in the yeare of our Lord one thousand six Hundred ninty & one by John Goard Robertt Tozer & Baptiest Franke as Followeth.

		s	*d*
Imprimus his Waring Apparrill		10	00
Item one paire of Loomes		14	00
Item one Bed performed		10	00
Item 2 hogsheds		04	00
Item 4 Barrills		03	00
Item ye warpingbars		00	10
Item one Coffer		02	00
Item 2 Brewing Vates		03	00
Item one Frine pan & Buckett		01	00
Item one pare of Brandice		00	03
Item one Cubbard		01	06
Item one Great Jebb		00	06
Item one Iron porridg pott		02	00
Item For sleeas & harnises & stay		02	00
Item For ould Iron & bras		00	06
Item For one Appe trough		01	00
Item 3 Reed sheeaves & othr small things not seen & For Gotten		00	07
	£	*s*	*d*
The Sume is	2	16	02

John Goard Robertt Tozer

[Will 12 Feb 1688/9 of William Cottrell of Uffculme, yeoman, pr at Uffculme before Mr Richard Kent 29 Apr 1692: 2s 6d to George Welch, exec, who holds the goods &c & the halfendeal of the estate (so long as sister Christian Welch lives) until settlement of debts &c, then passes residue to Grace & Elizabeth Welch, the 2 drs of Baptiest Franke; 1s to dr Agnes Franke; marked by William Cottrell & by Baptiest Franke, Barbara Phillips, & John Goard as witn.]

208 JOANE DOWDNEY 1691 (DS)

[Wealthy spinster; mostly investments; £300.]

An Inventory of the goods Chattles & debts of Joane Dowdney late of Ufculme in the County of Devon deceased taken and prised the Eighteenth day of November in yeare of our Lord one thousand six hundred nyntie & one by Henry Lyppincott Thomas Helmore & Robert Mills as followeth./

	£	*s*	*d*
Inprimis her Aparell	12	00	00
Item in good debts and money in purse	223	10	00
Item in plate & Jewells	03	10	00
Item an Anuitie of ten pounds p Anñ for one life	60	00	00
It: A Chest of Drawers & a Coffer	01	06	08
	£	*s*	*d*
Summa totalis Inventorij	300	06	08

[Will 28 Sep 1691 of Joane Dowdney of Uffculme, spinster, pr 29 Apr 1692: residue to mother Ann Dowdney, exec; 20s ea to cousins Alice Waldron & James Crosse; 20s gold ring ea to bros-in-law Francis Waldron & Edward Crosse; a gold ring ea to 6 bearers; signed by Joane Dowdney & by Robert Mills & Rebeckah Leppincott (Peppincott?) & marked by Elizabeth Radford as witns.]

209 MARY STEPHENS 1692 (DS)

[See No. 181. Widow; corn, 7 cattle, 1 mare, 24 sheep, 2 pigs; no clothmaking gear; £27.]

Devon/ A true & perfecte Inventory of all & singuler the goods Chattles & Creditt of Mary Stephens widdow late of Uffculme in this County deceased taken & apprized the 21th day of Aprill

1692 by Robert Burrow & Thomas Dunne as followeth

	£	s	d
Imp^s her appell	02	10	00
Item five Cowes	07	10	00
Item two yerlins	01	00	00
Item one mare	01	10	00
Item sixteene sheep & 8 lambs	02	10	00
Item two swine poggs	00	10	00
Item Tenn[?] puter dishes	00	07	00
Item six brass panns	01	00	00
Item three brass caldrons	00	07	00
Item three Candlesticks	00	00	06
Item two spitts & one pottcrooke	00	02	00
Item one brandice & one fryinge pann	00	01	06
Item three brass potts	00	15	00
Item two table boards	00	05	00
Item 4 tubbs 3 barrills & one Trendle	00	10	00
Item one brewinge pann	00	05	00
Item four beds performed	04	00	00
Item corne in barne	00	05	00
Item Corne in ground	02	05	00
Item in hay	00	10	00
Item in draggs & harrows	00	05	00
Item horse tacklinge	00	03	00
Item one chest & two boxes	00	04	00
Item one wynnow shett	00	03	00
Item table lininge	00	02	00
Item in provision butter & cheese &c	00	15	00
Item in lumber goods not seen or befor apprized	01	00	00
	£27	15	00

[£1 short?]

[Will 19 Jan 1690/1 of Mary Stephens of Uffculme, widow: residue to s Henry Stephens, exec; 12d to s Arthur Stephens; 10s each to s Augustin & dr Mary Bray; 20s to grandch John Stephens; best suit to grandch Edith Bray; 2s 6d each to rest of grandchn; bed to chn of s Arthur Stephens, or 5s each from Arthur if he keeps the bed; marked by Mary Stephens & signed by Jno Grantland, Shelah(?) Grantland, & Will: Grantland as witn.]

210 WILLIAM MOGFORD 1693 (PU)

[Husbandman (/miller?) with mill, "dwelling house" & room over, & buttery; wheat, 5 horses, 3 cattle, 3 pigs; total, including debts both ways, £15.]

An Inventary of all & Singluar the Goods of William Mogford late of Uffculme in ye County of Devon deceased taken & appraized by James Frey & Baptist Andro both of Uffculme Aforesaid the sixteenth daye of December in the yeare of our Lord God one thousand six hundred ninty & three as Folloeth -

	lî	*s*	*d*
Imp His Waring Apparall & Money in Purce	02	00	03
It In the Chamber over the dweellinghouse one bed filled with flocks & one pillow of the same three beds & three pillows filled with dost three halfheded bedsteads one truckell beadstead fower Cords & fower Matts too Ruggs & too Coverlets on payre of Blunckets three payre of sheets one Chest on Coffer one boxe three sheelfs fifteen Cheeses	05	00	05
It In the Buttrey too fletches of bacon one Trundell three old barrells one littell Standerd	01	07	11
It In The dweellinghouse too Keittells one Brass pott one Iron pott three puter dishes one brass scumer one Ladell one Brass Chaffin dish six small brass panns too paills one old Cupbord one forme one old Cheeswringe one Grud-Iron two pottooks one Saltbox one payre of Andoggs	02	03	01
It In The Mill one old fatt & fife old tubs eight baggs one Winowingsheet	00	19	07
It Three Horses with theire tacklin & one Mare & Coult	07	00	00
It two Cows one Chalfe	06	00	00
It Three small swines	00	18	06

	lî	*s*	*d*
It Wheatt in Ground	02	10	00
It Hay	02	00	00
The Sum is	29	19	09
It In debts desparate	05	01	00
It In things unseen & out of Mind	00	05	00
The Hole Sum is	[35	05	09]
Debts due & oweing by the sd William Mogford at the time of his death ware asfolloeth			
Imp for Rent	14	10	00
It Debts on Credit	05	00	00
the Sum	19	10	00

Jã Fry: Bap Andro

[Exhibited by Anne Mogford, widow & admin, 18 May 1694 (sic).]

[Admon 18 May 1693(?4) names Anne Mogford as widow & admin, & also Baptist Andrew of Uffculme, genm; marked by Anne Mogford & signed by Bap: Andro in presence of Bernard Byrd & Geo: Woodford.]

211 MARGERET BARNFIELD 1694 (PU)

[Widow of John 193; household items & £3 owed to her; £14.]

A true & perfecte Inventory of all & Singuler the goods Chattles & Creditts of Margeret Barnfield Late of Uffculme in the County of Devon widdow deceased taken & apprized by Jn° Grantland & Edward Wine the 10th day of Aprill 1694 as followeth;

	£	*s*	*d*
Imp^s her Appell	01	05	00
Item in money due to her	03	04	04
Item four bedsteed	01	10	00
Item bedinge	01	10	00
Item one brewinge Chettell	01	00	00
Item four brass panns	01	00	00
Item two Caldrons	01	00	00
Item six puter dishes	00	06	08
Item three brass potts	00	15	00
Item a table board in ye new chamber	00	05	00
Item two other boards	00	05	00
Item three hogsheads	00	10	00
Item one old Cubboard	00	03	04
Item five tubbs	00	07	06
Item three old Chests	00	13	04
Item in lumber goods not befor apprized	00	13	04
the Totall is	£14	08	06

Jn° Grantland
the [E] marke of Edward Wyne

[Will 16 Mar 1693/4 (sic) of Margeret Barnfeild of Uffculme, widow, sworn before Mr Byrd 18 May 94: residue to s William Barnfeild, exec; 20s to s John Barnfeild within 3 months after his return home "from being a soldier", & 10s between his 3 chn; 20s to dr Elizabeth; 10s to dr Mary Hutchens; a little chest to grandch Agnes Pullen; marked by Margret Barnfeild in presence of John Grantland, Nicholas Boobere (B mark), & John Hollill (J mark).]

212 JOHN BUTSON 1694 (PU)

[Weaver (cf.182, admon) with looms, spinning gear, & cloth; no stock; shop, hall, & two other rooms; 3 bibles & 5 other books; total, including £3 chattel lease & £15 owed to him, £34.]

An Inventory of the goods and Chattles of John Butson of Uffculme in the County of Devon deceased taken by Sam: Bonifant, Phill Fulford, Franc: Butson & John Thomas this 25th day of June: 1694

	£	*s*	*d*
Imp^rs: his Purse & girdle and wearing Apparrell	1	0	0
Item: In the hall 3 Brasse kittles 3 Brasse Crockes one Brasse pan: one Brasse Skillett & one Bellmettle Skillett	2	10	0
Item Eight Puter dishes one Butter puter stand	0	16	0
Item one table Board, one forme & side table	0	8	0
Item Two Chaires one Glasscaige Fower stooles and Bacon Rack seaven shelves one planke one Buckett & dish rack	0	5	0
Item one Frying pan three pot			

	£	s	d
crookes one paire of Dogs one Brandice one toster one fire pan and tonges three paire of Pothanges one Ax one hattchett one reephooke one hand saw & two Iron wadges	0	10	2
Item one Gridiron & Iron pot Three Bibles & five other Bookes	0	2	6
Item In the Backe Shopp: one old Coffer one trindle one Cand[l?]e mould two Gibbs one doughtub: eight shilves one old frying pan	0	16	6
Item In the hall Chamber one halfe head Bedstead dust Bed Bolster & feather pillow two Rugs	1	0	0
Item one Chest: one Hutch Sideboard two Boxes one Beame & Scales ten Baggs 3 pair of Harnise staves	1	0	0
Item In the Inner Chamber one Chest one halfe head Bed stead dust Bed feather Bolster & two Feather pillowes one Coorlet one old Coffer	2	0	0
Item one trukle Bestead dust Bed & Bolster one Rugg two pair of Blanketts	0	15	3
Item fower y^{r}ds of Kersey & two y^{r}ds of Cotton Cloath	0	10	0
[subtotal]	11	13	5
Item two paire of sheets five pillow drawers two Bolser Cloathes fower shirts & one tablecloath	1	05	6
Item In Bills and bonds & desperate debts	15	0	0
Item In mony	1	0	0
Item: one Chattle Lease	3	0	0
Item the Shopp: one Loome Slea & Harnis one Spiñing turne & Queeling turne two tubbs one pair of Brasse Scales & other Lumber in the shopp	1	0	0
Item In the wood house in wood and furse & other lumber	1	0	6
Item Earthen ware & nine spoones two Brusshes one Iron Box three Barrells	0	5	0
Item Things unthought of and unappraised	0	5	0
	22	16	0
	11	13	5
Apprayed by us	34	09	5

Phillip Fullford Franc: [F? mk] Butson
Sam: Bonifant Jo Thomas

[Will 16? Jun 1694 does not name testator but was sworn to by exec, John Foweracres, before Mr Bernard Byrd 24 Aug 1694: to John Buttson, s of Amose Buttson, the house for the remainder of the lease from Mr Walrond; £20 to s Amose Buttson (who owes £13 & collects £7 more from James Babesh); £20 to John Foweracres (who owes £7 & collects £13 more from James Babesh); household goods, wood, & furze between 3 chn, with conditional help from Francis Butson sen^{r} & jun^{r} & Samuel Bonifant sen^{r}; money to be invested for chn until grandch Elianor Butson, dr of John Butson decd, can inherit by age or by choice of new guardian; no signature or witn.]

213 JAMES TIDBURY 1695 (PU)

[Prosperous; hall & milkhouse, with other rooms; 2 horses, 2 cattle, 23 sheep; cider press; total, including £15 owed to him & £80 + £9 chattel leases, £136.]

An Inventorie of all ye Goods & Chattles of James Tidbury late of Uffculme deceased Taken This Twenty eighth day of Januarii Anoqz dm 1694[/5] as follow by John Garnesey John Hurley & Edmund Bishop

	lî	s	d
Imp his waring Apparrill	02	00	00
It on bond fifeteine pounds	15	00	00
It Goods in ye hall	02	18	00
It in ye milkehouse in brasse & pewter	03	10	00
It Goods in ye hall Chamber & ye milkehouse Chamber	07	02	00
It A Cheese wring	00	04	00
It A Cyder wring & Engine	01	10	00
It Two hogsheads	00	08	00

	lî	*s*	*d*
It in horse Tackling	00	03	00
It A mare & Colt	02	10	00
It A Cow & heifer	06	00	00
It Twenty Three sheep	05	02	00
It in hay	00	10	00
It A Swaine hog	00	06	00
It boardes & plankes in ye barn	00	10	04
It ye home Tenem^{t}	80	00	00
It ye hill Close	09	00	00
It for Goods seen & unseen	00	03	08
Sum Tottall	136	17	00

Jo: Garnsey Edmond Bishop John Hurly

[Admon 14 Feb 1695(?) names Elizabeth Tidbury of Uffculme as widow & exec, & also Edmund Bishop of Dungswill (Dunkeswell?) & Thomas Hurley of Uffculme, yeoman; marked T by Elizabeth Tidbury & signed by Thomas Hurley & Edmund Bishop in presence of Bernard Byrd & Antho Merson.]

214 THOMAS SALKIELD 1695 (DS)

[Prosperous yeoman; hall with room over, parlour, & buttery; corn, 3 horses, 13 sheep, 1 pig; no clothmaking gear; total, including £23 owed to him, £54.]

A true and perfect Inventorey of all and singular the goods of Thomas Salkield of the perish of Uffcullme in the County Devon youmon decesed taken and Apraized the thirtyeth of January 1694[/5] by Philip Fulford Thomas Donne and Henrey Bryant as Followeth

	lî	*s*	*d*
Imprimis his wearing apparell	02	00	00
Item in the hall 2 Iron potees and the setell	00	10	00
Item in the buterey on hogshead on barell on amorey		12	00
Item in the parler on tabell board in the parler	00	10	00
Item two pewter dishes	00	02	00
Item in the hall Chamber 4 bedsteds one ould Feather bed 2 coverlets 2 sheets one boulster and two pilowes one Cheare one coufer one box	02	15	00
Item one Mill tow grind Mault	00	12	00
Item in wood	01	10	00
Item one yeating Fate one ould huch	00	10	00
Item 13 sheep	04	00	00
Item one swine heg	00	12	00
Item one horse and two coltes	08	00	00
Item corn in barne	03	00	00
Item in Mault	01	04	00
Item corne in ground	04	00	00
Item 3 Chears and one littell board	00	12	00
Item one pot Crooke one pare of hangings	00	01	06
Item one pack sadell and on hagny sadell	00	08	00
Item in desprut debts	23	00	00
Item in lumber stuffe & goods not seen	00	05	00
	54	03	06

Thomas Dunne Henry Brient

[Admon 4 May 1695 names Richard Salkeld ("maulster"? "minister"?), Susanna Frank, & Elionor Dunne, wife of farmer ("agricola") John Dunne, all of Uffculme, as bro & sisters & admin^{s} of the goods of Thomas Salkeld, intestate. Signed by Rich. Salkeld & John Dune & marked by Susanna Frank & Thomas Northam in presence of witn Geo: Frome jun^{r} & Geo: Frome sen^{r}.]

215 HENRY SALKIELD 1695 (DS)

[Worsted comber (see will) with £30 annuity; £32.]

A true and parfect Inventory of the Goods and Chatills of Henry Salkield of the pish of Uffculme Taken this 28 Day of March 1695 Taken and Appraized by us under

	lî	*s*	*d*
Imprimis his wareing apparrell	01	00	00
Item one bead pformed	01	05	00
Item for one anuety of a rent			

	lî	*s*	*d*
Charge	30	00	00
	32	5	0

John Jutsum Will: Ston

[Will 21 Sep 1690 of Henry Salkeld of Uffculme, "westerdcomber": residue to Humphry Marsh, exec; bed to bro Thomas Salkeld; to sister Anne Melhuish £10 p.a. annuity from Smithencott farm (given to him by his father John Salkeld), & £4 p.a. for life; apparel shared by bros & sisters; attested to by David Webber sen[r] & David Webber jun[r], & later (3 Jan 1694/5) sworn to by them and (23 Mar 1694) by Humphry Marsh before Mr. Bernard Byrd. The Admon of 17 May 1693, which names Thomas Salkeld as bro & admin of the goods of Henry Salkeld of Uffculme, "intestate", (signed by Thomas & marked by George Checke & Hugh Northam in the presence of Bern: Byrd & John Grantland), was presumably overruled when the above will turned up.]

216 JOHN CUNNANT 1695 (DS)

[Miller: inner & outer rooms, buttery, kitchen, & mill; wheat, barley, malt, 4 horses, 3 pigs; no clothmaking gear; £43.]

A True & p[r]fict Inventorie of all y[e] Goods & Chattles of John Cunnant late of Uffculme deceased Taken & Apprised this Third day of May Anoq~ dm 1695 by Antho Merson Will Croyden As followeth

	lî	*s*	*d*
Imp his waring Apparrill	02	00	00
It mony in purse	07	03	03
It fower horsis & mares	10	00	00
It on sow & two swain hogs	03	00	00
It in ye kitching fower kittles	01	15	00
Thertein pewter dishes Two sawsers A butter plate	01	05	00
fower brass potts & A skillet	01	10	00
A paire of Andogs A paire of Andirons Two potthangings Three hanging Crookes on spit	00	04	00
A fryeng pan An old Gridiren A saving Iron & fire pan	00	01	06
Two stiling[?] Irons	00	01	00
A table boarde A settle A furme & Chaire	00	10	00
Seaven Tubbs & Two bucketts	00	11	00
It in bacon & porke	02	00	00
A Range searge dish Racke A dosen of Trenchers A Lanthorne	00	02	00
A pewter flaggon A bole A dish & saltseller	00	01	08
It in y[e] Inner Roome & buttery seaven barrills A sillting standish A Gibb & stoole	00	15	00
Two potts of mortt on butter pott	00	06	00
An old presse A Gibb An old standish An Iron musterd bowle	00	06	00
Two sawes Three barrills Two Chessels & A Goodge	00	02	06
It in y[e] Inner Chamber on feather bed A feather bolester Three feather pillowes	02	05	00
Two dust bed ties A Rugge A paire of blanketts A Coverlett & A flocke bolster	00	15	00
It Two bedsteads A chest A box	00	12	00
Two paire of sheets A boarde cloath Three pillputies[?] & A flaske	00	07	00
It in y[e] outter Chamber A feather bed A feather bolester & Three feather pillowes	02	10	00
Two Ruggs A blanckett A dust bed tie & bolester	00	10	00
Two bedsteads	00	05	00
A law nett	00	10	00
It in wheate	00	05	00
in barley	00	02	00
in mault	01	10	00
It Three packe saddles & Gursis	00	12	00
It in ye mill A Trundell A draught fatte Two peckes A half pecke & A quarter A pecke	00	05	00
A hackney saddle Gambadoes			

	lî	*s*	*d*
& bridell	00	02	06
Two paire of Crookes	00	01	00
A fann & six baggs	00	10	00
& for things seen & unseen in & About ye house	00	05	00
Sum Tot	43	00	05

Antho Merson Will Croyden

[Will 12 Sep 1693 of John Connet of Uffculme, miller: residue to dr Sara Connet, exec; 40s to sister Agnes Connet; 20s to Grase Modgredge; 12d each to Thomas Modgredge, Elizabeth Hart, Mary Modgredge, & Illean Modgredge; ovsrs Fyllep Fulford & Zakrey Connet to hold residue in trust for dr Sara, but if she dies before age 21 the residue to be divided between Zackrey, Sara, & Agnes Connet & Mary Osmond's 2 chn; marked by John Connet & signed by William Croyden & Joseph Tuckins as witn.]

217 SAMUELL BISHOP 1695 (PU)

[Bur: "Samuell Bishop" 26 Jun 1695. Prosperous (bachelor) yeoman with hall & other rooms, milkhouse, drink-house, & shop; corn, hay, 2 cows, 1 pig, & poultry; total, including £40 part chattel lease, £79.]

The Inventorey Indented of all and singuler the goods and Chatells of Samuell Bishop of Uffculem in the county of Devon yeoman deseased made and praised the Furstt daye of July in the yeare of our lord god on thousand six Hundred ninty and five By Robeart Gill Gilles bishop and William Waldron

	lî	*s*	*d*
Imprimes his waring apparill and money in pockett and four silver spounes	6	0	0
Itt part of A Chatill Lease	40	0	0
Itt in the hall on Tabell Borde on Cubed seventeene puter dishes to Chares with other things in the sd rume	2	10	0
Itt in the Chambers to bedsteds and furnitude theareunto Belonging with other things in the sd Chambers	5	0	0
Itt in the millhowse six brass panes to brass pots and other things in the Rume	2	1	0
Itt in the Drinkhouse Four barills and on Hoxids [hogshead] with other things	1	0	0
Item in the backes on hutch on Cheesewring on Vate to tubes with oather things in the rume	1	2	0
Itt in the shop for his working tooles and timber with oather things In the Rume	1	4	1
Itt Corne in growne and in house	9	10	0
Itt to Cows on swine and haye	8	9	11
Itt on wood [voood?] vine standing in the court	1	5	0
Itt pultrey and oather things about the house seen and not seen and not befor perticallary praised	1	10	1
The Sum is	79	12	1

[Will 13 Jun 1695 of Samuell Bishop of Uffculme, bachelor, sworn before Mr Bernard Byrd 13 Jun 96 (signed Geo: Woodford Regr): residue to sister Elizabeth Bishop, exec; 10s to sister Katherine Caddy; tools to bro Giles Bishop; 10s to sister An Cole; to cousin Samuell Bishop, s of Giles Bishop, a silver spoon marked with 1st 2 letters of his name; box to Elizabeth Pearse, dr of sister An Cole; signed & sealed by Samuell Bishop in presence of Grac(e) Gill, John Bishop, & Nic: Tucker.]

218 HENREY STEVENS 1696 (PU)

[Bur: "Henry Stephens" 4 Jan 1695/6. The inventory has no introduction & appears to be in three sketchy parts, all of which are attached to the admon. The 2nd & 3rd parts may be notes made during the assessment by John Bray & Arthur Stevens, both of whom are named as admins. Yeoman? 1

mare, 2 (4?) cows; total, including £15 for house, £35 (or £51?).]

jaenurey the 8 - 1695[/6] then take the Inventory of Henrey Stevens his goodes

	[£	*s*	*d]*
for his weareing aparil	1	15	0
for to bordes and to formes	1	00	00
for bed and beding	3	00	00
for on Chest	00	6	00
for on bedsted	00	15	00
for 3 bras panes on Cetel	1	10	00
for on stole on barile	00	4	00
for on mare and sadel	3	00	00
for to Calving cowes	8	00	00
for the dweling hose	15	00	00
for lumber godes	00	10	00
	35	00	00

the [R] marke of robert tosere
the [m?] marke of Jose Dave [Davie?]

John Bray for [o]n Covelete 2 blankes	0	11	0
to pole[?] draares [drawers?]	00	1	0
for the bedsted	1?	11	0
for on barel	00	3	0
for on shole [shovel?]	00	2	0
for bedtie and bolster	1	16	5
for waring aparil	1	8	0
for on Ches wereng	00	10	0
for to lomes [lambs?]	1	15	0
for to Couese [cows?]	8	0	0
the some is	15	17	5

Arther Stevenes for on Chest	0	7	0
for wheles and a fote [vat?]	0	8	0
for on Chene	0	1	3
for borers Cheseles	0	1	10
for on Colter and toubele[?] and gam bades [gambadoes?]	0	3	1
for a sadel and briadel	0	3	6
[Incomplete, but sum so far is	1	4	8]

[Admon 13 Jun 1696 names Augustine & Arthur Steevens, yeomen, & John Bray, weaver, all of Uffculme, as bros & bro-in-law & admins, & also Christopher Bussell, woolcomber; signed by Augustine & Arthur Stevens & Christopher Bussell & marked J by John Bray in presence of Bernard Byrd & Geo: Woodford.]

219 JUSTIN DUNNE 1697 (PU)

[Bur: "Justin Dunn" 15 Jan 1696/7. Widow (of John No. 197) & grandmother. Entry, parlour, buttery, kitchen, & 2 other rooms; 1 yearling; no clothmaking gear; £29.]

Devon//A true and perfect Inventory of all and Singuler the goods Chattles & Creditts of Justin Dunne late of Uffculme taken and apprized the 10th day of May j697 by Jno Grantland & Humfy Welch as folloeth

	£	s	d
Imp^{r}s her appell	02	10	00
Item in p^{r}sent money	00	12	00
Item in the parler			
One table board one Carpett & Furme	01	06	08
One Cubboard	01	05	00
One Chaire two Stooles	00	03	06
Four puter Dishes	00	10	00
Four Cushions	00	03	00
Item in the buttery			
One tryndle & one jebb	00	06	08
Item in the Entry			
one Cheese press & lyd Sisterne	00	10	00
Item in the Kitchen			
one table board & Furme	00	06	08
one old Cubboard & 9 puter dishes	01	00	00
one pessell & morter & puter Chambr pott	00	05	00
six brass potts & seven brass panns	04	15	00
Four Caldrons and one pease pann	02	11	04
One Chaire Settle & baken rack	00	07	06
Item in ye old Chamber			
one old bed pformed	01	00	00
Item three other beds pformed	07	10	00
Item in the buttery Chamber			
One bed pformed	01	10	00
one Chest one Chaire	00	14	10
Item one Yerlynge	01	00	00
Item Lumber goods not			

	£	s	d
befor apprized	01	10	00
	29	16	06
			[8d short?]

Jno Grantland Humphry Welsh

[Will 17 Sep 1696 of Justin Dunne of Uffculme, widow, pr before Mr Bernard Byrd 12 May 1697: residue to 2 grandchn, John & Thomas, 2 oldest ss of Thomas Dunn dec^d, exec^s; 20s & bed, chair, &c to s John Dunn; bed &c to grandch Rebecka Dunne; brass pan each to drs Florence & Dorothy; cauldron & 40s to grandson Wm, s of Wm Dunne; pans to grandchn Dorothy & Sarah Dunne; 1s to dr-in-law Joane Dunne; 5s each to grandchn Henry, Robert, Margret, & Joane, chn of Thomas Dunne, & John, Henry, William, Anne, & Hannah, chn of John Dunne; marked by Justin Dunne in presence of John & Sarah Grantland.]

220 SARAH JAMES 1698 (DS)

[Bur: "Sarah James" 14 Jan 1697/8. Few items; spinning turn; total, including £15 for house, £28.]

January the 16th 1697 then thooe a ture Illmotarey of Sarah Jamesis Goods Latly Desesed

	£	s	d
for here wearing apparel	02	10	00
in money	05	00	00
on bed performed	02	15	00
on box on cofer on Spinning turn	00	08	00
on pottidg pot to cettels on colet	00	15	00
6 putter Dishes 2 candel-sticks	00	08	00
on tabel board on chest on coberd	01	00	00
on forme on tube	00	02	06
for the Dwling house	15	00	00
for Lomber Goods	00	04	06
	28	03	00

Arther Stevens
the [G or C?] Marke of Gorge Copp
the [S] Marke of Agosten Stevens

[Will 25 Nov 1697 of Sarah James of Uffulme: residue to k James Pearcy of Uffculme, exec; £4, a rug, & a bed tie to bro James Pearcy of Cullompton, & a cupboard to his s John Pearcy; 20s to Sarah wife of George Copp of Temple, & a pewter dish to her s Richard; 10s to Margaret Pearcy, & table, form, cauldron, & pewter dish to her dr Mary Pearcy; a chest to Richard, s, & 2 pewter dishes to 2 drs of James Pearcy; pewter dish to Anna, wife of Ames Mors of Cullompton; apparel to Margaret Pearcy & her dr Mary, & to Sarah Copp & Anna Mors; old clothes to wife of Peeter Tozer of Uffculme; marked by Sarah James & signed by John Dunne & Humphry Bowden & marked by Narbor(?) Strang as witn.]

221 RICHARD ROSE 1698 (PU)

[Bur: "Richard Rose of Craddock" 15 Dec 1697. Mar: "Richard Rose junr & Margaret Lannam" 16 Apr 1676. Husbandman; corn, hay, 1 horse, 4 cows, 1 pig; no clothmaking gear; £26.]

An Inventory of all & Singuler the Goods & Chatles of Richard Rose deseased taken and Apprаysed the twenty fowerth day of March Anno 1697[/8] by Richard Gill and Baptist Andro as folloeth _ _ _

	£	s	d
Impri For His wearing Apparell And Money in purse	05	00	00
It Corne in barne	04	00	00
It Hay	01	00	00
It fower Cows	08	00	00
It one Crepled Horse & his tacklin	01	00	00
It A Swine	00	08	06
It in the iner Chamber one bed & bedsted performed	01	10	00
It in the outter Chamber one bed & bedsted performed	01	10	00
It one Chest & one Coffer	00	05	00
It Halfe A Doz of Chaires & one little bord	00	05	06
It Six puter dishes	00	10	04
It in Brass	01	08	00
It A Table bord & forme	00	08	06
It for Timber Stuffe &			

	£	s	d
other Lumber Goods	00	09	04
It for things unseen & out of minde	00	05	00
The Sum is	26	00	02

Richard Gill Bap Andro

[Will 13 Nov 1697 of Richard Rose of Uffculme, husbandman, sworn before Mr Bernard Byrd 22 May 99: residue to wife Margaret, exec; £5 each to ss Henry & Thomas Rose at age 21; £10 to dr Mary Rose at age 21; marked R by Richard Rose in presence of James Gill, Wm Balston, & Will(?) Hill.]

222 JANE WELSH 1698 (PU)

[Inventory undated, but will 1698. Prosperous widow of Simon 189; hall, parlour, milkhouse, malthouse, & 2 other rooms; 2 gold rings & £25 in purse; no clothmaking gear; mostly domestic items; £61.]

An Inventary of ye Goods & Chattels of Jane Welsh Widdow of Ufculmbe in ye County of Devon Late deseced taken & Appraised by Edwarde Marshall Frances Butson & Samuell Bonnifant is as Followeth

	£	s	d
Imprimes her waring Apparell	09	15	6
Item tw[o] Gold Rings	01	18	0
Item mony in purse	25	13	5
Item her lining	02	07	6
Item in the Inner Chamber			
one Bed performed	01	15	0
one Chest one Trunke three Coffers one plank to bords	00	18	7
Item in the hall chamber			
one Olde mald huch	00	02	9
to Old Bedsteds	00	06	11
one Old tabell	00	02	3
Item in the Palar Chamber			
one Bed performed	02	19	4
one spryse Chist	02	13	8
one old Bedsted and bede	00	09	0
one Forme one Coffer to old Fats one old Trendell one Chare one Joynstoole	00	10	6
Item in ye Parlor one Cobberd	00	13	8
Item ye milkhuse fouer Barels five shelfes	00	13	4
Item in ye wreng house one Trendell to Fats[slats?] one Old Chest wreng	00	15	6
Item in ye Hall one Tabell bord & Forme	00	07	5
one Carpet	00	05	7
one settell to Chares	00	03	2
three spits to pothoocks three pot hangings one pare of hanirnes	00	08	3
Item ye Brass fower pots one scallet	01	05	9
Item Eight Brass pans to Kittels	04	08	5
Item one pessell morter to Candellstecks one Brass Chafing desh one old warming pan	00	07	10
ye pater [pewter] ten platters one fluging [flagon?] one bedpan three tening Candelsticks one plate	01	04	0
Item in ye malt house one Uting Fate	00	05	0
Item Tooles of Husbantry	00	12	3
Item lumber stuffe & things forgoten	00	13	4
	61	15	11

This is a true Inventory to ye best of our Knoledg
Wittnes our hands
Edward Marshall
the [f] mark of Franci Butson
Sam: Bonifant

[Will 2 Dec 1698 Of Jane Welsh of Uffculme, widow: residue to John Marshall sen^r ("thath now liveth with me"), exec; 10s each to Francis & Henry Butson, ss of bro Francis Butson; 5s each to Amos Butson, Jane Ide, & Amy Foweracres, chn of bro John Butson; marked by Jane Welsh in presence of Mary Lee, Edw Southwood (mark), & Sam: Bonifant.]

223 W[ILLIAM] WOOD 1699 (PU)

[Mar: "William Wood & Elizabeth Golsworthy/Gouldsworthy" 1 May 1663, Exminster or Exeter St Peter Cathedral. Inventory undated and partly missing at right. Husbandman. (Paper mills mentioned in will.) Largely the £30 chattel estate; 2 horses & domestic items; £45.]

The Inventory of Wm Wood goods

	£	s	*[d]*
The Chattle Estate in the house & mils	30	00	
his appell	01	10	
one horse & one mare	03	10	
Item 3 beds performed	03	00	
9 little puter dishes	00	09	
5 brass panns	00	12	6
2 brass potts	00	10	
2 old Cubbords	00	06	[8]
2 table boards	00	06	[8]
2 tyndles	00	05	
3 barrills	00	7	6
1 hogsheade	00	4	0
1 Chesse press	00	2	6
1 settle board	00	3	0
2 Chests	00	8	0
Item in bro [brown?] paper	02	0	0
It a curinge [?] pan	00	4	0
It 2 Caldrons	01	0	0
Item old lumber goods	00	10	0
	45	8	10

[Will 24 Oct 1697 of William Wood of Uffculme, husbandman, sworn before Mr Bernard Byrd 22 May 1699: residue to wife Elizabeth Wood, exec; to ss Humfry & John house, gardens, & paper mills after death of wife, for remainder of lease, from profits of which they pay £15 p.a. for 4 years to s Wm, £10 to dr Elizabeth, £10 to s James, & £5 to dr Mary; 1s to dr Sarah; feather bed & bolster to s Wm & flock beds to dr Elizabeth & s John after death of wife; signed by William Wood in presence of John Grantland, Anthony Bale, & John Bale.]

224 WILLIAM ESCOTT/ ARSCOTT 1700 (PU)

[Inventory undated. Tailor; largely £24 estate value; barley, hay, 2 cows; 1 bible; spinning turn; £36.]

an Enventory of the Goods of William Escott Taken by us hereunder named

	£	s	d
for wearing aparill		13	4
for Tow Cows	5	0	0
for barlly	0	11	0
for hai	0	5	0
for on bedstead and beding therunto belonging	1	14	0
for Tow bedseads	0	6	0
for Tow Coffers and a Trunk	0	5	0
for puetter	0	9	0
for bras	0	18	0
for Too bras pots	0	5	0
for Too Tabell boards and form		6	0
for a bibell	0	2	0
for six Tubs and a paill	0	8	0
for Too boards and 2 Chees fats	0	3	0
for frying pan pot hooks hangings and broatch and brandice	0	4	0
for baggs	0	1	6
for Too hooks Ax presing Iron and shears and hacknine [?]	0	3	0
for a spining turn	0	1	0
for Too barrells and Tuner [turner?]	0	2	0
for a peck and half peck	0	1	0
for Too Laders and a wheellbara	0	5	0
for Lumber		5	0
for Right in The Estate	24	10	0
	36	17	10

Richard Thomas
The [G] mark of George Hill

[Will 1 Mar 1698/9 (sic) of William Arscott of Uffculme, tailor: residue to s William Arscott, exec; to wife Grace Arscott the estate & tenement & necessary goods for life; to dr Joane Arscott best kettle & 10s p.a. out of estate after wife's death; to dr Joyce Godbeere part of house, linhay, &

garden where Allice Burgess lives; to s George Arscott church park close, furse close, 2 acres of great meadow, & part of house, barn, mowplot, gardens, & orchard, paying £3 10s rent to exec; marked by William Arscott in presence of Matthew Deere, George Hill (G mark), & Ann Hill (O mark).]

225 HUMFRY WELCH 1700 (PU)

[Bur: "Humphry Welch" 8 Jun 1700. Mar: "Humphry Welsh & Dorothy Dunn" 23 Dec 1696, Exeter St Petrock. Yeoman; 6 cattle, 2 horses, 1 pig, corn; 2 bibles; plough tackle; no clothmaking gear; £62.]

A true and perfecte Inventorie of all and singuler the goods Chattles and Creditts of Humfry Welch late of Uffculme in this County deceased taken & appraised the 11th day of June Annoqz Dom^{i} 1700 by Jno Grantland & Peter Parsons

	£	*s*	*d*
Imp^{s} his apparrell	003	00	00
Item in p^{r}sent money	003	00	00
Item two milch Cows	007	00	00
Item two Calves	002	00	00
Item a Yoake of Steers	005	10	00
Item two horses	004	10	00
Item one swinehogg	001	05	00
Item corne in ground	018	00	00
Item in fagott wood	001	00	00
Item in reede	000	10	00
Item two brass potts	001	00	00
Item three brass pans	000	16	00
Item six puter dishes	000	12	00
Item in wheate and mault	001	00	00
Item two table boards & dresser	001	13	04
Item three barri[l]s & two Tubbs	000	10	00
Item plough Tacklinge	001	00	00
Item two bedsteeds	000	15	00
Item one bedtie & three shitts two bolsters & one pillow	001	10	00
Item Dunge & soyle	002	10	00
Item One Coverlett & two blanketts	001	00	00
Item One Chest	000	10	00
Item One Trunk & one box &c	000	10	00
Item in butter & Cheese	000	13	04
Item 4 planks	000	06	08
Item a packing saddle brydle and gambadoes	000	05	00
Item one winnow sheet	000	10	00
Item horse tacklinge	001	00	00
Item two bibles	000	03	00
Item in Lumber goods not apprized	000	13	04
	062	12	08

Jno Grantland Peter Parsons

[Will 23 May 1700 of Humphery Welsh of Uffculme, yeoman: residue to wife Dorothy Welsh, exec; £10 (p.a?) to mother Mary Welsh after 7 years; £30 (p.a?) after 8.5 years to uncle Robert Welsh as trustee for John Welsh, s of Robert Welsh; marked H by Henry Welsh in presence of Peter Pason, Tho: Donn, & John Burrows.]

226 MARGRET GAY 1700 (DS)

[Bur: "Wid. Guy, of Yancott" 18 Jul 1700 (no first name). Very prosperous widow; entry, hall, & rooms off them; no clothmaking gear; largely £125 in bonds & money owed to her & £20 for cottage in Yondercott; £163.]

A true and perfect Inventory of all and singular the goods Chattles & credits of Margret Gay latte of .....[v faint] taken and prized on the 21th day of July Annoqz Domini 1700

	£	*s*	*d*
Imp^{r}mis her appell	003	00	00
Item in money upon upon accompt of Trade	019	00	00
Item in money due [to her] upon bond	100	00	00
Item other debts standing out	006	00	00
Item her Cottage house in Yondercott	020	00	00
Item In the entery Chamber three beds performed	005	00	00
Item in ye same chamber two old Coffers	000	06	08
Item in the hall Chamber two Chests & a Trunke	000	15	00

	£	s	d
Item in the Hall one Table board & Furme	000	05	00
Item one old Cubboard	000	05	00
Item thyrteene puter dishes & one plate	001	00	00
Item two Caldrons & three brass panns	001	10	00
Item four brass potts	001	03	04
Item two old table boards & one Furme	000	05	00
Item two joyn stooles & two Chaires	000	02	06
Item one hogshead & four barrills	000	06	08
Item one Cley Furnass & washing pann	003	00	00
Item one Cloth press	000	15	00
Item four old Tubbs	000	10	00
Item in Lumber goods not befor apprized	000	10	00
	163	14	02

Jno Grantland }
Leonard Poake} Appraizers

[Will 24 Aug 1699 of Margret Gay of Uffculme, widow: residue to dr Mary Gange, exec; 20s in apparel to bro John Poake; £10 to bro Leonard Poake to manage for dr Mary Gange; cottages, outhouses, gardens, &c to grandch James Gange after decease of his parents James & Mary Gange, the inheritance to pass to his bro Henry's line if he has no chn, & thence to his sister Elizabeth's line if Henry has no chn; marked by Margret Gay & signed by Jno Grantland, Wm Grantland, & Sarah Grantland as witn.]

227 JOHN MARSHALL 1702 (PU)

[Bur: "John Martiall of Bradfield" 18 Jul 1702. 3 spinning turns; 4 cattle, 1 pig; books; total, including £22 for house, £56.]

An Inventory of the Goods Chattels of John Marshall of Ufculmbe in the County of Devon late deceased taken & Apprayased ye ninteenth day of Auguste 1702 by John Churly Samuell Bonifant Francis Butson as Followeth

	£	s	d
Imp^{r} his waring Apparrell	02	00	00
Itt the Brass 6 Brass Pots 8 Brass panes too Posnets 4 kettels 1 pessele & mortar 2 Candell stecks 1 warming pan	06	02	00
Itt ye Puter 21 Platters one Flagone 3 tening Candelsticks 1 plat 1 Chamber pot one Bedpan	01	04	00
Itt one spruce Chist	01	10	00
Itt one Bedstede & Bede performed	02	10	00
Itt for fower Bedsteds & bedding	02	4	
one chest five Coffers one Boxe & one Forme	01	04	06
Itt one Coberd & two Table bords	00	17	03
Itt one Carpet	00	05	07
Itt one settell two Chairs one forme one Frame of shilfs	00	06	00
Itt five pair of Pootcrooks three Iron Crooks fower spits one pair of fier Tongs	00	09	00
Itt one paire of Andogs one driping pan one pair of dogirons one Gridiron & brandece	00	05	03
Itt two glasscages one dishcage	00	01	00
Itt his Boocks	00	02	06
Itt a Stile Iron & a Brush	00	01	00
Itt five Barrels & five shilves	00	13	04
Itt one trundell two fatts & one old Chiswreng	00	15	06
Itt one Chiswreng	00	06	00
Itt for Woolcombs & wrench	00	10	00
Itt for seven Tubs & three spining Turns	00	16	06
Itt for two Cows two yearlengs & one swine	11	00	00
Itt his House	22	10	00
Itt For Tooles of husbandrie & things forgote	01	00	00
	56	13	05

[Admon 10 Oct 1702 names Ann Marshall as widow & admin, & also Christopher Bussell & George Cheeke of Uffculme, yeomen; marked + by

Ann Marshall & George Cheeke & signed by Christopher Bussell in presence of Bernard Byrd.]

228 ROBBERTT HELLINGS 1703 (DS)

[Bur: "Robert Hellens of Gaddon down" 14 Jun 1702. Mostly household items; 1 cow; £5 chattel lease (?); £15.]

A True and pfitt Inventory of all the Goods and Chattles of Robbertt Hellings of Uffculme in the County of Devon Deceased made prized and Taken this Three and Twentyeth Day of September And In the yeare of our Lord God One Thousand Seaven Hundred and Three <u>1703</u>

Imprimis	*£*	*s*	*d*
For his Waring Apparill And money In his Purse	01	10	00
Item For his Chattles	05	00	00
Item For one Cow	02	05	00
Item For one Furnice	01	00	00
Item For 2 Bras pans & 1 Coldren	00	14	00
Item For 3 Bras porridg pots	00	09	06
Item For 6 puter Dishes	00	06	09
Item For one paire of Bras weights And one scillet & one sceamer	00	02	06
Item For 2 Frine pans one teening Bowll & spoone	00	03	03
Item For one Bed pfformed and Two Bedsteeds	01	10	00
Item For two Chists	00	10	00
Item For 1 Amery & 1 Box	00	02	00
Item For 7 Barrills & 1 Ferken	00	08	06
Item For 3 hogsheds	00	10	00
Item For 4 Tubbs	00	05	00
Item For 1 sarge & 2 Ranges	00	01	00
Item For 1 paire of panniers	00	01	06
Item For 1 Long saw and his working tools	00	10	00
Item 2 Bar Croockes 2 Iron dogs And one Grid Iron	00	03	00
Item 1 Cheeswring 1 trendle And one Wheeall Barrow	00	06	00
Item For Lumber and all other things out of sight not seen & Forgotten	<u>00</u>	<u>01</u>	<u>06</u>
The Sume is	<u>15</u>	<u>18</u>	<u>09</u>

John Goard [9d short?]

The [R] marke of Robertt Tozer

noe coppy written

229 HUMFREY BISHOPP 1704 (PU)

[Bur: "old Gaffer Bishopp" (no forename) 7 Sep 1704. Mar: "Humphrey Bishoppe & Mary Palmer" 26 May 1659. Prosperous yeoman (retired?); higher, inner, outer, wring, & milk houses mentioned, & several rooms; no stock or clothmaking gear, but £150 chattel estate; £172.]

A True and pfect Inventory of the goods & Chattles of Humfrey Bishopp late of Uffculme in the County of Devon yeoman Deceased taken and apprised this twentyeth day of September Anno Dom 1704 By John Mills and Giles Bishopp both of the sd pish of Uffculme as Followeth

	£	*s*	*d*
Imp^{r}ms his weareing apparrell	05	00	00
Itm money in Purse	03	00	00
In the Inner Chamber of the higher house			
Itm one Dust bed pformed one Chest one Trunck one Stoole one Chair	02	00	00
In the other Chamber			
Itm one Dust bed and half headed bedsteed pformed & one Chest	01	00	00
Itm In the Inner house one Table board three Stooles and other Small things	00	10	00
Itm In Lynnen	01	00	00
Itm In pewter 12 Dishes & 8 Spoones	00	10	00
In the outer house			
Itm one Tableboard one Cupboard one Chaire and other Small things	00	05	00
Itm three brasse Crocks one Brasse Skillett and one Brasse Caldron	01	02	00
Itm three Small Silver			

	£	s	d
Spoones	00	04	06
In the wring house			
Itm one fate one Barrell	00	02	06
In the milke house			
Itm foure barrells & one Jebb	00	03	06
Itm two old Tubbs in the Shopp	00	01	06
Itm two old fates in the bakes	00	02	00
In the higher paurlour			
Itm one Tableboard one forme one Chair one Cupboard one side Table and three Joyned Stooles	01	01	00
In the Hall			
Itm one Side Table one Tableboard one Settle one Great Crocke	01	05	06
Itm In the lower Buttery one Trundle one Salter and one hogshead	00	10	00
In the milke house			
Itm Six Brasse pans one Kittle one furme	01	10	06
In the Buttery Chamber			
Itm one Tester bedsteed & feathrbed pformed	02	00	00
In the paurlor Chamber			
Itm one Tester bedsteed	00	10	00
Itm one Chattle Estate	150	00	00
Itm Things out of Sight & forgotten	00	10	00
In toto	172	08	00

[Will 9 Feb 1702/3 (sic) of Humfrey Bishopp of Uffculme, yeoman: most to wife Mary for life, exec; to s John Bishopp great & little Stuphill, great & little Loameleare, great Morecroft, Winkey wood meadow, little ham, pit & old orchard, old mowplot, new house & garden (lately enclosed), shop by garden of old house, & several other specified items, all after death of wife Mary; to s Samuell rest of estate &c after death of Mary; to dr Mary a bed & £20 from each of the 2 bros after death of wife Mary; s John Bishopp to pay 40s to grandson Humfrey; to grandchn John Bishopp, Mary Bishopp, & May Codridge 10s p.a; marked H by Humfrey Bishopp in presence of Wm(?) Mills & John Smith.]

230 MARY SPEED 1709 (PU)

[Bur: "Mary Speede" 6 Jan 1708/9. Spinster; shopkeeper? Household items & £40 in shop goods; £52.]

A True and perfect Inventory of all and Singular ye goods Chattles and Creditts of Mary Speed late of Uffculme in ye County of Devon Spinster Deced taken and appraized the 18th day of June 1709° by John Grantland and John Howe as Followeth /

	£	s	d
Imp^r^mis Her apparrell	03	00	00
Item In p^r^sent money	03	00	00
Item one Bedstead & bed pformed	04	00	00
Item In Shop Goods	40	00	00
Item one Brass pott	00	05	00
Item Two Pewter dishes	00	05	00
Item a Little brass Caldron	00	03	00
Item a Little tableboard	00	06	08
Item a Trunk	00	06	08
Item six Chaires made Witheys	00	06	00
Item Three little Barrells	00	04	06
Item Goods not Seen nor before appraized	00	05	00
Sume totall	52	0j	j0

Jn° Grantland Jo^n^ How

[Will 10 Dec 1708 of Mary Speed of Uffculme: residue to cousin Alis Churly, exec; £5, gown, & coat to sister Hannah Hallett; £10 to bro Philip Speed; £5 to sister Margaret Speed at age 21; 1s & rest of apparel (except scarf to cousin Alis Churly) to sister Elizabeth Speed; £5 to bro John Speed at age 21; signed by Mary Speed in presence of Robert Churly & Jo^n^ How (all sign).]

231 GYLES BISHOPP 1709 (DS)

[Bur: "Giles Bishop" 15 Jul 1709. Mar: "Giles Bishop & Sarah Bishop" 13 Nov 1673. Prosperous yeoman; hall & kitchen with rooms off, buttery, & milkhouse; £20 in corn; 2 horses, 14 cattle (including 2 oxen), 5 pigs, 40 sheep; plough tackle; clock; no cloth-making gear; no books; total, including £285 for 2 estates (at Leigh & Ashill?), £439.]

A true and perfect Inven^{tr}y of all and singular the Goods & Chattles of Gyles Bishopp late of Uffculme in the County of Devon Yeoman taken and apprized by Samuel Bishopp and Robert Westron ye 16 day of July Annoqz Domini 1709 as followeth

	£	*s*	*d*
Imp^{r}mis his Wearing Apparrell	5	0	0
Item in p^{r}sent Money	5	0	0
Item in Bills Bonds & other Securities	5	0	0
Item his right in ye home Estate	120	0	0
Item his right in Wollecy Estate att Lee	165	0	0
Item in ye Kitchen Chamber on feather Bed & bedsteed pformed	5	0	0
Item One Dust bed pformed	1	5	0
Item two Chests & two boxes	1	10	0
In the Hall Chamber			
Item One feather bed & bedsteed pformed	4	0	0
Item two other beds performed	2	10	0
Item two Chests & two Coffers	1	12	0
Item two Trounks & two Chares	0	6	4
Item Lumber Goods in little Chamber	1	1	6
Item two board Cloathes & one dozn of Naptkins	1	0	0
In the Hall			
Item One table board and furme	1	0	0
Item One Cupboard & Settle & side table & two Joynt Stooles	1	0	0
Item One Clock	1	0	0
Item One Warming Pann	0	6	8
Item three spitts	0	4	0
Item One Pair of Andirons	0	2	6
Item two Glass Cages	0	3	0
Item One Pestle and Mortar Chaffendish and two brass Candlesticks	0	6	4
Item five Chaires	0	7	0
Item seventeene Pewter dishes	1	10	0
Item Holland Clome	0	5	0
In the Milkhouse			
Item twelve brass Panns	3	0	0
Item two Trendles	0	16	0
Item four Standards	0	8	0
Item other things in Milkhouse	0	5	0
In the Buttery			
Item thirteene barrells	1	1	0
Item for Woole	1	17	6
Item One frame of shelves	0	6	0
Item four hogsheads & three halfe hogsheads	1	15	0
In the Kitchen			
Item One table board and furme	0	6	4
Item four brass Potts & One Posnett	3	0	0
Item two brass Caldrons	1	0	0
Item One brass Furnace	1	0	0
Item One sideboard & one Amory & a salt barrell	0	10	0
Item One Frying Pann & Juggs	0	5	0
Item three Pott Crookes & one pair of Andirons	0	5	0
Item One Malt Mill	2	0	0
Item two Cheese Presses	0	10	0
Item six uting Vates & one brewing Vate	2	0	0
Item Seven Tubbs & 3 Pailes	1	0	0
Item twenty Cheeses & Bacon	3	10	0
Item in barne two Corne Hutches	1	10	0
Item six Cowes	18	0	0
Item five Swine Hoggs	4	0	0
Item two Oxen	9	0	0
Item three Heifers	4	10	0
Item three Calfes	3	0	0
Item one white Mare	3	0	0
Item One bay Horse	6	0	0
Item in Wood and browse	2	0	0
Item forty sheep	10	0	0
Item One pair of Harrows			

	£	s	d
& draggs	2	0	0
Item in horse tackling	1	0	0
Item Corne in Ground	20	0	0
Item in plow tackling	0	10	0
Item a Bittle Wedges & Sawe	0	15	0
Item Lumber Goods not seene or before apprised	2	0	0
Sum totall	439	9	10
[£3 0s 8d too much?]			

Robert Westron Sam^ll^: Bishopp

[Will 5 May 1708 of Giles Byshop of Uffculme, yeoman: residue to exec Sarah Bishop "now" wife, who retains the following bequeathed items for life; specified furniture to k Samuell Byshop & his s Samuell; to cousin Mary, wife of Marmaduke Edwards, (& later to their ss John & William Edwards) the tenement at Leigh in Uffculme; to cousin Giles Byshop of Ashill, a bed, chest, harrows, a suit, plough gear &c (shared with cousin Samuell Byshop); suits &c to cousin John Byshop of Leigh; 40s a year to sister Ann Guterige; truckle bed to Samuell Evance; brass & pewter to cousin Mary Dotheridge & to Katherine Caddey, Ann Cole, Elizabeth Holley, & Fides Evance; ovsrs Samuell Byshop, William Byshop, & Nicholas Cawley; marked by Giles Byshop in presence of John Maning, John Evens, & Nicholas Cawley (all signed).]

232 JOHN BLACKALLER 1713 (PU)

[Tradesman who went to prison? Mostly household items; hall & shop mentioned & other rooms; £5.]

A true & perfecte Inventory of all and Singular the goods of Jno Blackaller Late of Uffculme in this County deceased taken and apprized this 2^d^ day of March Annoqz Domini 1712[/3]

	[£	s	d]
Imp^s^ his appell lost in prison	00	00	00
in money	00	00	00
In the Hall Chamber			
One testerd bedsteede	00	10	00
A Canvas bedtie filled with dust	00	03	00
an old rugge	00	03	06
one old blankett & old sheet	00	02	06
one old dust bolster	00	02	00
It in the same chamber a truckell bedsteede & bedtie of dust filled and an old rugg	00	06	08
in the same chamber one Chest	00	08	6
one sideboard	00	02	6
an old Coffer & chaire	00	02	0
In the Shop chamber			
One halfheaded bedsteede	00	08	0
a flock bedtie very old	00	04	0
an old board	00	02	6
three old Coffers	00	05	0
In the hall			
One table board	00	05	00
one Cubboard	00	08	00
three puter dishes about six pound	00	03	06
three tyn candlesticks	00	01	08
[Missing item at join in copy	00	02	00]
One little brass pott	00	04	00
a little Caldron	00	05	00
one Furme & old chaire	00	02	06
Item in barly	00	08	00
It in goods of Lumber and of little value	00	05	00
	05	04	10

Jno Grantland John Dunne

[Admon 26 Jul 1715 names Mary Blackaller as widow & admin, & also Samuel Dunn of Uffculme, clothworker; sworn by Mary & marked by both in the presence of Bernard Byrd, surrogate.]

233 RICHARD GILL 1713 (DS)

[Bur: "Richard Gill" 6 Jun 1713. Yeoman? Entry, hall, kitchen, & rooms off; shop, milk-, plump-, malt-, pound-, & crook-house mentioned; corn, 3 horses, 1 heiffer, 1 pig; hourglass, virginals; £3 from deceased sister, Thomasin Southwood; £57.]

Where margins are indented before inventory items there were 3 stamps, one bearing the words "Seven Pence p Quire" in a circle with a crown on top.]

A true and perfect Inventory of all the Goods and Chattells of Richard Gill of the pish of Uffculme in ye County of Devon Lately deceased taken and Apprized by Mr Henry Chury and Mr Robert Marshall both of the same pish and County Abovesaid on the fourth day of June 1713

	lî	*s*	*d*
Imprimis his wearing Cloaths	01	00	00
Item Six Silver Spoons	02	00	00
In the Kitchen			
Item Seven Brass potts	02	05	00
Item Nineteen putter dishes	02	05	00
Item Three postnets	00	06	00
Item Two Kittles	00	06	00
Item Fower Spitts	00	03	06
Item Three back Crooks	00	02	06
Item Two pair of hangings	00	00	06
Item One Gridiron	00	00	04
Item one pair of Brandice	00	00	08
Item one pair of fire doggs	00	00	06
Item one Chaping Knife	00	00	01
Item one Pestle and Morter	00	01	00
Item one Skeem^{r} and brass weight	00	00	09
Item one Stilling box	00	00	09
Item Eight Cloam Bassons	00	02	00
Item one Table board & Furm	00	02	00
Item one Backon Rack & two Shelves	00	02	00
Item one Little Side board	00	02	00
Item frame of Shelves	00	02	06
Item one dish Cage & on Trancher Cage	00	01	00
Item one dursen of Tranchers	00	00	06
Item on Suttle on Chare & on board	00	02	00
Item one Houre Glass	00	00	04
Item one piece of Leather & a box and a Old pair of bellows	00	01	00
Item Backon and pork	01	00	00
Item on fleshpick troll & Reaphook	00	00	06
Item Goods in ye Shoop being marchandse	01	15	02
Item a pair of Brass Scalls & Stones	00	01	06
Item one board and Sheelfs	00	01	00
Item Goods in y^{o} Milk house eight brass pans	01	15	00
Item one frame of Shelfs & Salt box	00	02	00
Item Goods in ye Hall one Table board	00	07	00
Item on Suttle & three Joynt Stools	00	05	00
Item one Warming pan	00	04	00
Item Two pair of Andoggs	00	03	06
Item a hamer and pincees	00	00	06
Item a pair of Virginells & frame	00	15	00
Item one flask and Straw hatt	00	02	00
Goods in the Hall Chambr			
Item one Beadsteed Cortins & Vallants	00	10	00
Item one Rugge and two Sheets	00	08	00
Item Two feather pillows	00	03	06
Item one Chest	00	10	00
Item One Table board	00	02	00
Item a bead and beading	00	10	00
Item in ye Little Chamber a Bead pformed	01	00	00
Goods in the Little Chamber			
Item one Beadstead Six pills on bolster	00	15	00
Item one bagge and piece of Cloath	00	01	00
Item Lumbr Stuffe & one Chair	00	03	00
Goods in the Entry Chamb^{r}			
Item one Bead pformed	00	15	00
Item one Truckle Bead pformed	00	10	00
Item one Chest	00	06	00
Item two Coffers	00	02	00
Item one Cubbard	00	05	00
Goods in ye Kitchen Chamb^{r}			
Item one Bead pformed	01	00	00
Item Two Coffers	00	04	00
Item two Joynt Stoolls on trunk & two boxes	00	02	00
Item two Boards	00	00	06

	lî	*s*	*d*
Item one Lookinglass	00	02	00
Item in ye Cockloaft a Cradle & Lumbr stuffe	00	05	00
Item Goods in ye Malthouse on brass kittle	00	06	00
Item Two Fates	00	05	00
Item three tubs and a Standerd	00	03	00
Item other Lumber	00	02	06
Item Goods in ye Old Milkhouse	00	02	00
Item in the plumphouse a Cheesewring	00	02	00
Item one Standerd two barrells on tube	00	04	06
Item on woodbittle on Shoule on Sparknife and on Maddick	00	01	06
Item other Lumber	00	01	06
Goods in the Poundhouse			
Item The Engin and Press	06	00	00
Item Fourteen Hogsheads	01	10	00
Item one pair of harrows & a Soule	00	12	00
Item Lumbr Goods in the pownhouse and Sider house	00	12	00
Item the Wood in ye Kitchen Orchard	02	00	00
Item Goods in ye Crookhouse two Soules	00	05	00
Item one bulocks yook & a Laddr	00	02	06
Item five bundls of Lafts	00	02	00
Item Lumber Goods	00	05	00
In ye Mow plott			
Item one mow Stadle and Lumbr wood	00	10	00
Item in ye fore Court & Liney Lumbr Stuffe	00	05	00
Item in ye Barn Corn and Reed	01	15	00
Item one Heffer	02	15	00
Item one Coult	02	15	00
Item one Mare and Coalt	01	00	00
Item one Close of Wheat	02	10	00
Item one Gray horse	02	10	00
Item a Old Wheell	00	02	06
Item on Sow	00	12	00
Item on Hogshead & two Andoggs and a old Standerd	00	05	00
Item for debts due	03	00	00
Item for his devidend belonging to him out of ye Affects of his sister Thomasin Southwood deceased	03	00	00
It might be more the Account being not made up	57	03	07
	[6s 6d short?]		

Henry Churly   Robt Marshall

234 JOANE PIPRILL 1713 (PU)

[Bur: "Joane Pepprell, single woman" 28 Dec 1713. Spinster; total, including £6 owed to her, £8.]

An Inventory of the Goods and Chattles of Joane Piprill of Uffculme Decd Appraysed and taken the Twenty Ninth Day of Decembr 1713 by Samuell Bishop and John Hayne as Followeth -

	£	*s*	*d*
Imprs her Wearing Apparell	00	12	06
It her bed and beding thereunto belonging	01	02	06
It Three old Boxes one old Trunk and one old Coffer	00	05	00
It a little Cupboard and 2 putter [pewter] Sausers	00	01	06
It in Debts owing If Recoverable	06	00	00
It for Things Unseen and out of Mind	00	05	00
	£	*s*	*d*
Sum tot	08	06	06

The [S] Marke of Samll Bishop
the [J] mark of John Hayne

[Exhibited at Uffculme before Bernard Byrd, cleric, by Henry Piperell, admin, 21 Jul 1714. Latin endorsement signed G. Frome Regr.

Nuncupative will 25 Dec 1713 of Joane Piprell of Uffculme, single woman, witn 25 Dec 1714 & pr at Uffculme 21 Jul 1714; all to the owner of the house where she died, her cousin Henry Piprell, forgiving 1s debt to her by her cousin William Piperell; marked by George Leaman, Anne Leaman, Jane Greedy, John Goard, Sam Bishop, & Bap Andro.

Admon 21 Jul 1714 names Henry Piperell of Uffulme, weaver, as cousin & admin, & also George Leaman of Uffculme, farmer (agricola); signed by Henery Peperel & marked by Georgy Leman in presence of Mr Bernard Byrd & Tho: Frome n.p.]

235 WILLIAM DAVY 1714 (PU)

[Bur: at Spiceland (quaker) 2 Apr 1714. Prosperous husbandman; parlour, middle room, & kitchen, & 2 other rooms; £40 in corn; 6 horses, 18 cattle, 4 sheep, 5 hogs; plough; no cloth-making gear; total, including £5 owed to him, £151.]

An Inventary of all and Singular the Goods Chattles & Credits of William Davy late of Uffculme in the County of Devon husbandman deced taken & appraised the 19th day of Aprill Anno Dm 1714 by Us whose names are hereunder written

	£	*s*	*d*
Imprimis debts due to the decêd	02	10	0
More due to the deceased	03	0	0
Item Six Steers & two Oxen	27	0	0
Item Five Cowes one Heifer and two Yearlings	26	5	0
Item two Horses and one Mare	12	0	0
Item one old Mare & 2 Colts	06	17	6
Item two Yews and two Lambs	01	1	0
Item five Hoggs	02	10	0
Item two Sucking Calves	00	10	6
Item in the Inner Chamber four Beds and Bedsteeds & other goods valued at	10	2	6
Item in the outer Chamber 2 beds & bedsteeds & other Goods valued at	04	1	0
Item in the Parlour one Cupboard one Tableboard & forme & Seven pewter dishes valued at	02	0	0
Item in the Middle Roome Some Tubs and Barrells	00	15	0
Item in the Kitchin 5 Cauldrons	02	0	0
Item Twelve brasse pans	02	12	6
Item Seven pewter dishes three Crocks 2 Skillets one Skimmer & other goods valued at	02	10	0
Item Corne in Mows & in the Barne	20	0	0
Item Corne in Ground	20	0	0
Item Horse Tackling & Plough tackling & other Lumber	03	0	0
Item Wearing apparel & money in Pockett	03	0	0
The totall	151	15	0

Roger Row Henry Rugge Appraisors

[Exhibited at Uffculme 21 Jul 1714 before Bernard Byrd, cleric, for the Prebendary of Uffculme. Latin endorsement signed by G Frome Regrius.

Will 23 Jan 1713/4 of William Davy of Uffculme, husbandman, pr before Bernard Byrd 21 Jul 1714: residue to wife Honner Davy, exec; after death of wife, legacies as follows - to s William Davy "middle & ancient house", stable, & garden at Hillturner, Uffculme, now in possession of Atwill Parkhouse; west part of above house, &c, to dr Honner, wife of Thomas Tozer; east part, now in possession of John Gillard, to dr Hannah, wife of John Welland; to dr Mary Davy a house near Uffculme town, now in possession of John Davy; £5 each to s William Davy & drs Honner, Dorothy (wife of John Bray), Mary, & Hannah; 50s to grandson William Tozer; marked by William Davy in presence of Henry Rugge, Roger Row, & Nich Sommers (all sign).]

236 JOHN QUICKE the elder 1714 (PU)

[Bur: "John Quick" 23 Nov 1714. Mar: "John Quicke & Mary Bussell" 22 Sep 1677. Mason (retired?); domestic items, & houses valued at £8; £13.]

A true & perfecte Inventory of all & Singuler the good & Chattles of John Quicke thelder Late of Uffculme in the

A true & perfect Inventory of all & singular the goods & chattells of John Quick the elder late of Uffculme in the County of Devon Mason taken & appraised the 28th of November 1714 by John Gilliford sen Henry Russell & Jn Grantland as followeth

	li	s	d
Imps his apparell	02	00	00
Item one brass pott	00	07	00
Item one Iron pott	00	03	00
Item seaven puter dishes	00	09	00
Item one porrenger	00	00	06
Item one puter paint	00	01	00
Item his Estate in the fronte house	03	00	00
Item his Estate in the middle house called patter noster lane	05	00	00
Item one little brass pan	00	02	06
Item a skillett	00	01	00
Item six earthen platts	00	01	00
Item a candlesticke	00	00	03
Item one paire of fire doggs	00	02	00
Item a brewing pann & the stuff of ye kill	01	01	00
Item a syndle	00	06	00
Item an old barrill	00	00	06
Item a table board	00	04	00
Item two old tubbs	00	02	00
Item a little brewing fatt	00	02	00
Item a ringe bittle	00	01	00
Item old implements of iron	00	00	06
Item a screene of shelves	00	02	06
Item for old lumber goods	00	06	00
Totall	13	12	09

The inventory of John Quick the elder 1714 [236]

County of Devon Mason taken & appraised the 28th of November 1714 by John Culliford sen[r] Henry Russell & Jn[o] Grantland as followeth./

	£	s	d
Imp[s] his appell	02	00	00
Item one brass pot	00	07	00
Item one Iron pot	00	03	00
Item Seven puter dishes	00	09	00
Item one porrenger	00	00	06
Item one puter paint	00	01	00
Item his Estate in Frenches House	03	00	00
Item his Estate in the middle house called Patternoster Lane	05	00	00
Item one little brass pan	00	02	06
Item a skillett	00	01	00
Item six earthen platts	00	01	00
Item a candlesticke	00	00	03
Item one paire of firedoggs	00	02	00
Item a breweinge pann & irestuffe of y[e] kill	01	01	00
Item a Tryndle	00	06	00
Item an old barrill	00	00	06
Item a Table board	00	04	00
Item two old tubbs	00	02	00
Item a little brewinge Fatt	00	02	00
Item a ringe bittle	00	01	00
Item old implem[s] of iron &c	00	00	06
Item a Frame of Shelves	00	02	06
Item for old Lumber goods	00	06	00
Totall	13	12	09

[Will 1 Aug 1714 of John Quicke the elder of Uffculme, mason, pr 26 Jul 1715 at Uffculme before Bernard Byrd, cleric: residue to s John Quicke, exec: to wife Mary (while she remains unmarried) the house & garden, & the house where widow Poole lives, & 2 houses in Paternoster Row for remainder of 99-year lease, & use of bed & other specified domestic items; after death of wife all houses to s John Quicke on condition that £5 is paid to dr Mary Patch; marked in presence of John Were, Mary Were, John Were jn[r] (all sign), & Robert Manning (mark).]

237 RICHARD RUGGE junior 1719 (DS)

[Bur: "Richard Rugg" 22 May 1719. Son of Richard Rugg sen[r]; household goods & poultry; although he only marks documents with "R" he has 7 books & 10 sheets of stamped paper valued at 15s; £15.]

A true and p[r]fect Inventory of all and Singular the Goods and Chattells of Richard Rugge ...n[r] [unclear: not "Sen[r]" since "Jun[r]" clearly in the will] of the pish of Uffculme in y[e] County of Devon Latly Deceased taken and Apprized by Mr Robert Marshall and Mr John Bishop the Twenty Seventh day of May 1719 as Followeth -

	£	s	d
Imprimis his Waring Apparrell and Money in Pockett	10	00	00
Five Pewter dishes & one plate	00	10	00
One Chest	00	10	00
Three Silver Spoons	00	10	00
Fower pair of Cock Spurs	00	03	00
Seven Books	00	10	00
Tenn Sheetts of Stampt Papp[r]	00	15	00
Fifteen Cocks and Hens	00	05	00
one Wimsheet and Bagge	00	08	00
Coops for feeding of Cocks	00	02	03
One Fether Bead and Goods out of Sight	02	00	00
[Total not given	15	13	03]

Robt Marshall John Bishop

[Exhibited at Lyme Regis 30 May 1719 before the Rev. Tho: Henchman, cleric M.A., surrogate for the Dean of Salisbury, by Nicholas Rugg, exec. Latin endorsement signed Geo: Frome Reg[r] D.

Will 2 May 1719 of Richard Rugg junior of Uffculme, pr 30 May 1719 at Lyme Regis before Rev Tho: Henchman: residue to father Richard Rugg & bro Nicholas Rugg, exec[s]; to bro William Rugg the money he holds; £5 to be invested & shared between Theophilus, James, & John, chn of Theophilus Rugg, & Prudance, dr of

James Rugg, when John Rugg reaches 21; £10 (plus £3 mentioned later?) to bro James Rugg; 2 guineas plus 10s a year for life to sister Mary Tucker to be paid out of inheritance of field called Milleate, recently purchased & now bequeathed to father Richard Rugg &, after his death, to bro Nicholas Rugg, he then paying also £1 per year to bro James Rugg; after the death of Nicholas Milleate to pass to Richard Rugg, s of William & Ellenor Rugg, & then, if he has no heirs, successively to Theophilus jun^r^, James, & John Rugg on same condition, with obligation to pay £5 each to bros Theophilus & James or their families; £3 to bro Theophilus Rugg; apparel, books, toys, & pewter to bros; 3 silver spoons to father; marked R by Richard Rugg in presence of William Southwood, Samuel Bishop, & John Bishop, who all sign. In a codicil a "particular book entitled Saint osten" is given to sister Mary & after her death to John Rugg, s of Theophilus, & a bed in the custody of bro William is given to the execs.]

238 CHRISTOPHER BISHOP 1719 (PU)

[Prosperous yeoman; Willands estate (Bodmiscombe) £70; hall, parlour, & kitchen, & 3 rooms adjoining; corn, hay, 2 horses, 11 cattle, 71 sheep, 3 pigs; plough; gun; clock; no books or clothmaking gear; £252.]

A true and perfect Inventory of All and singular the Goods and Chattles of Christopher Bishop Late of Uffculme In the County of Deavon yeoman taken and Appraised by Mr Thomas North & John Bishop & Tho: Bishop the 5th day of December Annoqz Domini 1719 As Followeth -

	£	s	d
Imp^s^ his Waring Apparrell	10	00	0
Item In present Money In pockett	05	00	0
Item his Right In Willands Estate	70	00	0
Item for Eight Cowes	24	00	0
Item for 71 Sheep	19	10	6
Item for two oxen	05	10	0
Item for five yearlens	05	05	0
Item for on fat Cow	03	10	0
Item for two heafers & on bull	05	00	0
Item for on horse & on Mare	05	05	0
Item for three piggs	01	00	0
Item for five Ackers of Wheat in Ground	10	00	0
Item for on hayreek	10	00	0
Item for hay In ye tallots [haylofts]	06	00	0
Item for Corne In barne & Reed	02	00	0
Item for the fackett wood & fewell	02	10	0
Item for plow tacklen	01	00	0
Item for packhorse tacklen	01	01	0
Item for two hackney sadles & other tacklen	01	10	0
Item for on Clock & Case	02	05	0
Item for two table boards & forme in ye paller	01	00	0
Item for two Joyen Stooles & Cubard in ye paller	01	00	0
Item for on warming pan	00	06	8
Item for pare of Andoggs In ye hall	00	05	0
Item for two tables boards In ye hall	00	17	0
Item for A Dresser In ye hall	01	10	0
Item for on backen Rack in ye hall	00	02	6
Item for on Settle in ye hall	00	02	6
Item for six Chares in ye under Rooms	00	05	0
Item for back Crooks & two fier Doggs In ye hall	00	05	0
Item for on Dozen of putter Dishes	02	00	0
Item for two Dozen of plates	00	16	0
Item for seaven tining Dishes	00	03	6
Item for A pessell Morter & A brass Candlestick	00	05	0
Item for two tining Candle sticks two Saltes & A Mustard pott	00	03	0
Item for three brass pottage			

	£	s	d
poots	01	10	0
Item for fower brass Kittles	02	05	0
Item for three brass Scillets	0	06	6
Item for two pye plates & scruate[?] & on flagon	00	04	0
Item for on box and Ires	0	02	6
Item for thirteene brass panes	05	10	0
Item for on fowlling Gune	00	10	0
Item for A Driping pan & Saving Ire	00	02	0
Item for two Spites	00	02	0
Item for tonges & fier pan & on Dozen of Rosting scuers	00	02	0
Item for on Clever one scemer & A Shriding Knife	00	01	6
Item for two Cheese preeses	00	10	0
Item for three vates to ute and brew	00	08	0
Item for teen tubs	01	05	0
Item for Seaven pailes A Cheese Range & tuner[?]	00	07	0
Item for on peck & halfe peck	00	01	6
Item for two pare of brandis	00	03	0
Item for on sawe on Iron bare & A bittell & three wages	00	05	0
Item for All ye Rest of ye husbandry Goods	00	10	0
Item for three trundels	01	05	0
Item for on pare of brass Wights	00	03	6
Item for three hogesheeds	00	15	0
Item for teen barills	01	00	0
Item for Cheese fats and follyers [?]	01	01	0
Item for Cheese	05	00	0
Item for Malt	05	00	0
Item for butter	03	10	0
Item for bakeen	01	11	0
Item for Wooll	00	10	0
Item for A bed performed In ye Kitchen Chamber	00	10	0
Item for two Cheese Racks and boards	01	10	0
Item for on Malt hutch A Coffer & hogsheeds to put Corne in	01	04	0
Item for boards & other things In ye Kitchen Chamber	00	10	0
Item for on bedd In ye Entry Chamber performed	01	15	0
Item for A Chare & settle & box in ye Same Chamber	00	05	0
Item for A Chest and A trunck In ye hall Chamber	00	05	0
Item for two beds performd In ye hall Chamber	01	18	0
Item for on bed performd In ye pallor Chamber	04	00	0
Item for on Chest & three trunks	00	15	0
Item for seaven Chares In ye pallor Chamber	00	06	0
Item for A hanging press & on Cofer In y^{t} Chamber	01	03	6
Item for six silver Spoons	01	05	0
Item for on Furniss	00	15	0
Item for three Dozen of tranchers	00	03	0
Item for Lumber Goods and Goods Unseen	03	00	0
	£	s	d
Sume totall	252	12	8

Tho: North Thomas:Bishop

[Exhihited at Uffculme 20 Jul 1720 before the Rev John Windsor by Eliza, relict & exec. Latin endorsement signed Geo: Frome Reg^{rius}.

Will 18 Nov 1719 of Christopher Bishop of Uffculme, yeoman, pr at Uffculme 20 Jul 1720 before Rev John Windsor & Rev Francis Eyre: "now" wife Elizabeth Bishop, exec, to have use of all goods &c in trust for s John Bishop while he remains unmarried; to s John Bishop all goods &c & the tenement of Wellands in the Manor of Bodmescombe after decease of wife Elizabeth, during life of bro Thomas Bishop; friend John Garnsey, wife Elizabeth, & Justinion Maning of Culmstock to be trustees during s's minority; signed by Chr:Bishop in presence of John Bishop & Bap Andro (both sign).]

239 ROBERT PERSEY 1720 (PU)

[Bur: "Robt Persey" 10 Jan 1719/20. Husbandman (retired?) Household items only; no clothmaking gear; total,

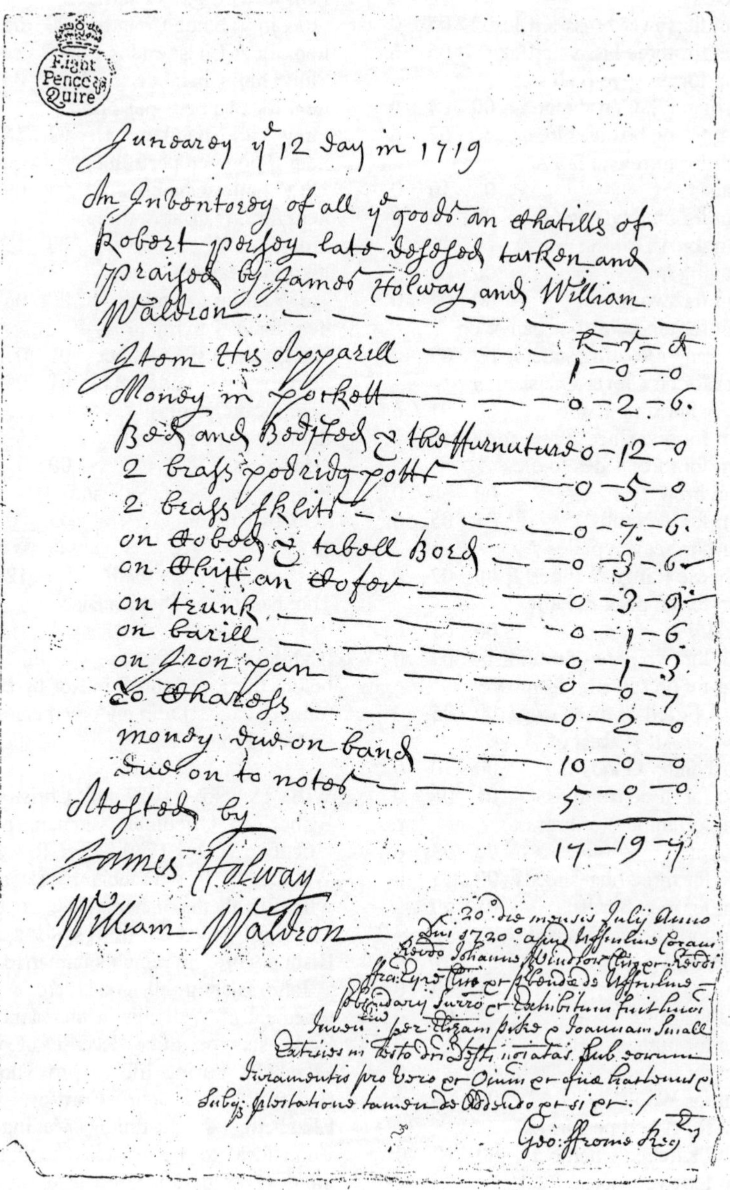

Januarey yᵉ 12 day in 1719

An Inventorey of all yᵉ goods an chatills of Robert persey late desesed tarken and praised by James Holway and William Waldron

	£–s–d
Item His Apparill	1–0–0
Mondy in pockett	0–2–6
Bed and Bedsted & the furnuture	0–12–0
2 brass podridg pott	0–5–0
2 brass skitts	0–7–6
on cobord & taboll bord	0–3–6
on chist an cofor	0–3–9
on trunk	0–1–6
on barill	0–1–3
on Iron pan	0–0–7
20 charcols	0–2–0
mondy due on band	10–0–0
due on to notes	5–0–0
	17–19–7

Atested by
James Holway
William Waldron

20° die mensis Julij Anno Dni 1720° apud Uffculme Coram Revdo Johanne Windsor Clico Revdi Fra: Eyre Clici et Prebendae de Uffculme Prebendary Surro et Exhibitum fuit hoc Invent. per Elizam Pike et Joannam Small Extrices in Testo dci Defti nominatas sub forma Juramentis pro Vero et [illegible] et [illegible] Subj. protestatione tamen de Addendo et si etc. /

Geo: ffrome Regr

The inventory of Robert Persey 1720 [239]

including £15 on bond & notes, £17.]

Janearey ye 12 day in 1719 [/20]

An Inventorey of all ye goods an Chatills of Robert Persey late desesed tacken and praised by James Holway and William Waldron _

	£	s	d
Item His Apparill	1	0	0
Money in pockett	0	2	6
Bed and Bedsted & the Furnuture	0	12	0
2 brass podridg potts	0	5	0
2 brass sklits	0	7	6
on Cobed & tabell Bord	0	3	6
on Chist an Cofer	0	3	9
on trunk	0	1	6
on barill	0	1	3
on Iron pan	0	0	7
To Charess	0	2	0
money Due on band	10	0	0
Due on to notes	5	0	0
	17	19	7

Atested by James Holway
William Waldron

[Exhibited at Uffculme 20 Jul 1720 before the Rev. John Windsor, cleric, by Elizabeth Pike & Joan Small, exec^s. Latin endorsement signed Geo: Frome Reg^r.

Will 4 Jun 1709 of Robert Persey of Uffculme, husbandman, pr at Uffculme 20 Jul 1720 before Rev John Windsor & Rev Fran Eyre: residue to drs Elizabeth Pike & Joan Small, exec^s; £10 to s Richard Persey if he returns to Uffculme within 4 years, otherwise to grandson Richard Persey, s of Robert Persey, plus s Richard Persey's coffer; 1s to s Robert Persey, & all the money he owes his father; 5s to s Humprey (sic) if he claims it; ovsrs ks William Waldron & Giles Bishop; marked in presence of Nich Sommers, Bap Andro (sign), & Richard How (mark).]

240 JOHN CADDY 1720 (PU)

[Bur: "John Caddy of Ashill" 31 Jan 1719. Mar: "John Caddy & Catherine Turner" 15 Dec 1678, Buckland Brewer. Woolbroker; looms & quill turn; brewing gear; 1 horse; total, including £5 lease, £18.]

A true and perfect Inventory of all and singular the Goods and Chattles of John Caddy Late of Uffculme In the County of Devon wool Breker taken and Appraised by George Manning and John Bishope the 16th Day of July Anno Domany 1720 As followeth.-

	ll	s	d
Imp^r for waring Apparrill and Money In Pockett	03	00	00
Item for his Right In the house and orchard	05	00	00
Item for nine Puter dishess	00	13	00
Item for three brass Pottage Potts	00	15	00
Item for two brass Kettels	00	10	00
Item for one table boord two Joynstools & two Chars	00	08	00
Item for two back Crocks and fier dogs fierpan & tongs	00	06	00
Item for one brewing fate and on tube	00	04	00
Item for three barrills one hoggs-hed & halfe hogsheed	00	14	00
Item for one pare of searge Loombs and quill turne	00	18	00
Item for a Malt Hutch and a pare of whights	00	07	00
Item for two Cobards and two Chests	01	00	00
Item for three Coffers and three boxes	00	08	00
Item for three dowst beeds and beedsteds	02	00	00
Item for two frames of shellfes	00	02	06
Item for A dish Rack	00	00	06
Item for A baken Rack	00	01	00
Item for Lumber Goods and Goods unseen	00	10	00
Item for one horse	01	10	00
Sume totle	18	07	00

George Manning John Bishop

[Exhibited 20 Jul 1720 at Uffulme before Rev John Windsor & Rev Francis Eyre, prebendary of Uffculme, by John Caddy, s & exec. Latin endorsement signed Geo: Frome Reg^r.

Will 14 Jan 1719/20 (sic) of John Caddy, "Wooll Breaker", pr at Uffculme 20 Jul 1720 before Rev John Windsor & Rev Francis Eyre: residue & house & garden to s John Caddy exec; best bed, 1 potage pot, & 1 pewter dish to wife Catherine; 1 potage pot to s Abraham; pair of serge looms to s Samuel; 1s each to drs Thomasin Manning & Anne How alias Tanner; marked in presence of Richard Cole, Jacob Leaman, & James Hill (all sign).]

241 WILLIAM MILLS 1725 (DS)

[Retired? Cottage lease & debts £6; total £9.]

A True and perfect Invertory of the Goods and Chatteles of William Mills Latly Deceased of the parrish of Uffculme Taken and appraised by us Whose names are under written the First day of June 1725./

	ll	*s*	*d*
Imp^rs for Waring Apparrill and Money In pockett	02	05	2
Itme for Working tooles	00	03	6
Itme two poridge poots	00	04	10
Itme one Chest and Settle	00	06	4
Itme two tubes [tubs] and one Vate	00	03	2
Itme one bede performed	00	05	2
Itme A Coffer and two boxes	00	01	8
Itme one Chare a buckett and two stoles	00	00	10
Itme for other Lumber Goods seen and not seen	00	06	2
Itme one Cottage house for on old Life	04	10	0
Itme for Deptes Goode and bad	01	10	0
	9	16	10

John Bishop James Hollway
John Tozer } Appraisors

[Exhibited 1 Jun 1725 by Abraham Mills, s & admin. Latin endorsement signed by Tho: Baden.]

242 ANN MARSHALL 1731 (DS)

[No farming or clothmaking gear; detailed kitchen items; £8 for house on the Waste (?); £14.]

A True Inventory of the Goods of Ann Marshall lately deceased taken by Thomas Cross & [space] the 26° February 1730/31 ~ whose names are hereafter subscribed

	[£	*s*	*d]*
Imprimis.			
In the Kitchin.			
1 Table board and form	0	3	6
1 Culberd	0	2	0
1 dresser & Howthorn[?]	0	7	6
1 picture	0	0	2
1 Looking glass	0	0	2
2 brass panns	0	10	0
1 feather ped	0	0	6
1 dyaper board cloth	0	5	0
1 Canvas board cloth	0	1	0
! box and Irons [?box iron]	0	1	6
1 pair bellows	0	0	10
1 hour Glass	0	0	2
1 Timber Bowl	0	0	1
18 Cloming Plates &c	0	2	0
1 Pestle & Mortar	0	3	0
1 spitt.	0	0	6
1 Candlesticks Iron	0	0	1
1 schoomer	0	0	2
1 flesh peck.	0	0	2
1 driping Ladle	0	0	6
2 Timber Chairs	0	0	2
16 Timber Tranchers	0	0	4
0 fire pan	0	0	0
2 pot hangings	0	0	2
2 pot Crooks	0	1	6
1 frying pan	0	0	6
1 pair hand Irons	0	0	9
1 Gridle	0	0	6
1 pewter plate	0	0	6
4 pewter dishes	0	5	0
1 pye plate	0	0	8
In the Buttery			
2 Empty hogsheads	0	6	0
1 brass pan	0	2	0
2 brass Kittles	0	10	0
2 barrell	0	1	6
1 Empty half hogshead	0	2	6
1 bell mettle Skillett	0	1	6
2 bell mettle Crocks	0	10	0

	[£	s	d]
& Some other Lumber			
Goods	0	1	0
A house on the weast	8	0	0
In the outer Chamber			
2 boxes	0	2	0
2 Coffers	0	9	0
1 bed performed.	0	15	0
1 furm	0	1	0
Spoon 3/- 12 napkins 3/-			
Table cloth 6[d]	0	6	6
In the Inn. Chamber			
1 bed performed	0	15	0
1 Chest	0	7	6
Sum Total	14	13	6
	[5s 11d short?]		

Taken and apprizd by us Thomas Cross Thomas Cross Jun[r]

[Will 24 Dec 1730 with no name mentioned in text, pr 21 Jun 1731 at Uffculme before Joh: Talman Sur[o]: house to s Richard Marshall, exec; 20s a year each to drs Jone Starke & Ann Rowland to be "paid out of my house"; a pewter dish each to Amos Starke's chn & Ann Rowland's chn; residue divided among her 3 chn; marked by Ann Marshall in presence of Henry Bryant & Susanna Night (mark).]

243 HENRY CALLOW 1731 (PU)

[Mar: "Henry Callo & Mary Southard" 21 Jul 1689. Sergeweaver; chamber, kitchen, buttery, & shop; loom; total, including £9 lease, £19.]

A True Inventory of the Goods and Chatles of Henry Callow late of the parish of Ufculme deced taken and appraised by us whose names are hear under subscribed this twenty first day of July 1731./

	£	s	d
Imprîs Waring apparel and			
Mony in purs	1	10	0
One Cott House	9	00	0
In the Chamber			
two Dust beds performed	1	15	0
two Chests	1	0	0
one Coffer and five litle			
boxes	0	5	0
five barrels	0	7	6
one dozen of Hupe [?]	0	1	6
In the Ching			
A Rasing Nife and spade	0	1	0
One Table Board and five			
Join Stools	0	12	6
One old Cupboard and			
ten putter Dishes	0	12	6
Holland Clome	0	1	3
one Settle and three			
Cheers	0	2	6
two Brass pots and one Cetle			
and a Selet	1	1	0
Bacon Rack Spet frying pan			
2 back Crooks Grid Iron belles			
pot hanging flesh fork	0	5	0
one pail fire pan and tonge	0	1	0
In the Butery			
one Hoxhead one Barrel			
and one Dish Rack	0	7	6
four toubes and one			
Tunner	0	8	0
Six Glass Bottels three Iron			
Wages	0	2	0
In the Shop			
two peckes hammer and			
penses	0	1	0
one weving Lumb	0	15	0
a ladder and hard wood	0	5	0
one wood Reek and poles	0	15	0
other small things not yet			
valued	0	3	4
	[19	12	7]

Will 13 Oct 1728 of Henry Callow of Uffculme, sergeweaver, pr at Uffculme 16 Mar 1737/8 before Rev Benjamin Hope, surrogate of the Prebendary of Uffculme: residue to wife Mary Callow, exec; to s Henry Callow after death of wife the house & garden he now occupies, & also a pair of serge looms; to s Joseph Callow the house & orchard where the testator now lives, & his tester bed; marked H by Henry Callow in presence of William Cooke & John Aplin (sign), & John Hurley (mark).]

244 NICHOLAS TUCKER 1731 (PU)

[Bur: "Nicholas Tucker" 7 Aug 1731. Mar: "Nicholas Tucker & Joanna Scoble" 29 Dec 1702, Slapton. Entry, parlour, kitchen, & rooms off, milk- & wash-house, cheese room; wheat, barley, hay, 1 horse, 3 colts, 7 cattle, 5 sheep, 14 pigs; plough, gun; no books or clothmaking gear; £108.]

A True & perfict Inventory of ye Goods & Chattells of Nicholas Tucker of ye pish of Uffculme in ye County of Devon Lately Deceased Taken & Apprized by Mr James Hollway & Mr Robert Marshall the 21th Day of August 1731 As Followeth

	£	s	d
Imprimas his Wereing Apparrell & in Pockett	10	00	00
Four Milch Cows & one Ill Cow	15	05	00
One Erelin [yearling]	02	00	00
One Calf	01	01	00
Two Colts on a Sucker ye Other one Yeare Old	03	02	06
One horse Saddle & Tackling	04	00	00
Five Sheep	01	15	00
One Sow & Nine Sucking Piggs	03	00	00
Four Store Piggs	02	04	00
Wheat & Barly in Barn & One Wheat Mow	10	00	00
Hay in the Tallatt	03	10	00
One Hundred of Reed	00	15	00
Goods in ye Parlour Chamb^r^			
One Beed pformed	03	03	00
One Chest Two Trunks & one Box	00	12	00
One Side Board one furm & Three Chairs	00	08	00
Goods in ye Kitchen Chamb^r^			
Three Beeds pformed	05	02	06
one Hanging Press & Two Chests	01	02	06
one Little Box and on Little Trunk	00	02	00
Goods in the Entry Chamb^r^, One Beed pformd	00	19	06
Goods in the Cheese Chamb^r^			
40 Cheeses	02	02	06
Goods in the Parlour Two Table Bords & one Furm	00	17	06
One Settle & four Chairs	00	08	06
one Side Board & ye Fine Cloam Standing Thereon	00	10	06
Goods in the Kitchen 13 Peuter Dishes & 15 peuter plates	03	15	00
One Dresser & 5 pieces of fine Cloam	01	01	06
one Warming Pan & Tea Kittle	00	12	06
one Table Board & furm	00	04	00
And other Lumber Goods & Cloam	00	05	06
One Fowling Piece	00	10	06
Goods in ye Milkhouse			
12 Brass Pans	03	01	06
one Trundle	00	12	06
and other Lumbr Goods	00	10	00
Goods in the Wash house			
Lumb^r^ goods	00	02	06
Two Brass pottage poots & one Boyler	01	15	00
Two Spitts 4 back Crooks 2 pair of fire Doggs 2 pair of Tongs & a fire pan	00	10	00
Three and Twenty Hogsheads	05	15	00
Five Halfe Hogsheads	00	17	06
Eight Barriells	00	16	06
Two Cheese Wrings	00	10	06
Two Utting Vates	01	01	06
One Malt Mill	00	15	00
One Copper Furness	02	02	00
Seven Tubbs & 4 Bucketts	00	18	00
Three Brass Kittles & Two pair of Brass Scalls	01	15	00
One Skillett	00	01	06
Wood Furze & Brouse	03	10	00
One Grinding Stone and Turnner	00	07	06
Plow Tackling Two Soules a pair of Draggs a pair of harrows on Chain	02	02	06
Thre Ladders	00	04	00
Dung in Both Courts	01	15	00
Two While Barrows & Two pair of Crooks	00	05	00
Goods out of Sight and out of Mind	00	10	06
Robert Marshall	108	09	00
James Hollway	[6d too much?]		

[Admon 14 Jun 1732 names Joan Tucker as widow & admin, & also James Hill, schoolmaster, & John Wills, innholder, both of Uffculme; marked by Joan Tucker & signed by James Hill & J Wills in presence of Tho:Baden n.p.]

245 MARY GANGE 1732 (PU)

[Household items only; no clothmaking gear or books; total, including £10 for houses, £19.]

A true and Parfect Inventary of all and singgular the Goods and Credats of Mary Gange Late of Uffculme in the County of Devon Deceased taken Vallued and apraised the 16 Day of February 1731-2 by Will Peparel and Jams Gange

	£	*s*	*d*
Iprimis her wearing aparel boath Lining and woolling	0	12	6
Item on table board and furm	0	5	0
Item on Litle table board	0	1	0
Item 4 Chairs	0	2	0
Item 2 Joyn Stools	0	1	0
Item 3 Brass Pots	1	0	0
Item 3 Brass pans	0	15	0
Item 3 Kettels	1	10	0
Item a Little Skellet a Skemer and two Driping Ladls	0	2	6
Item 8 puter Dishes six puter plats	1	0	0
Item in Cloome	0	0	6
Item 9 trancher	0	0	6
Item a Litle tineing Tanket	0	0	3
Item a flesh pike, tongs fire Dogs old Spit 2 Backe Crooks	0	4	0
Item a Litle Looking Glass	0	0	3
Item a old Box and Irons	0	0	3
Item 3 Barels	0	2	6
Item a old Cobbord	0	3	0
Item a old Baking tub Sereg [?] and Rang[e?]	0	2	0
Item on bed performd	1	10	0
Item on old Bed sted with som Beding	0	5	0
Item 2 Cheests	0	7	0
Item 2 Coffers	0	3	6
Item 2 old Boxs	0	0	6
Item a old trookel Bedsted	0	2	0
Item on board Cloath and 2 table Napkins	0	2	6
Item a grater and Collender	0	0	2
Item a old Geb	0	0	3
Item old Billows	0	0	6
Item old paire of wights	0	0	4
Item old friing pan	0	0	3
Item in money	0	5	0
Item ye Estate in houses	10	10	0
	19	7	3

[Will 21 Sep 1731 of Mary Gange of Uffculme, widow, pr at Uffculme 14 Jul 1732: exec^s^ George Pecock of Kentisbeare & John Dunn of Uffculme, trustees to dispose of or hold all for benefit of her chn; to dr Elizabeth Gange at age 21 the house where Joane Rugg now lives & half the garden rented by Will:Parsons; to s Henry Gange at age 21 the house & garden where Rich Sanders lives, & all the orchards; to dr Mary Gange at age 21 the present house & half the garden rented by Will:Parsons; to s Richard Gange at age 21 the house & garden where James Gange lives; signed(?) Mary Gange in presence of Mary Gange jn^r^ & Marg:Rice (mark).]

246 WILLIAM HOLWAY 1733 (DS)

[Bur: "William Hollway" 22 Dec 1733. Mason with £7 in purse or due for labour; kitchen, buttery, shop, & 2 other rooms implied; household items only; no clothmaking gear or books; total, despite mention of 6 houses in will, £16.
Halfway down the inventory, on the left, the paper is stamped with a crown above the words "Eight Pence p Quire" in a circle. The same device in 1713 (No. 227) showed the value at 7d per quire.]

A true and perfect Inventory of all the goods Chattles and Creadits of William Holway late of Uffculme in the County of Devon Mason Decease taken and appraised this Seven and Twentieth day of December in the year of our Lord One thousand Seven hundred & thirtythree by John Grantland of Uffculme aforesaid Yeoman and William Ware of the Same Parish of Uffculme Yeoman

as Followeth

	£	s	d
Imprimis: his Wearing Apparrell	01	17	00
Money in Purse and due for Labour	07	02	04
In the Kitchen: Eight Chairs	00	04	06
one round Tableboard	00	10	00
one pair of andirons backcrook and bellows	00	03	00
one Spet one Fleshpike and one Skimer	00	01	00
Two brass potts and one Skellett	00	18	00
one Brass Kettle	00	05	00
one Iron pottage pot & hangings	00	03	00
one Sconce	00	00	09
Five puter dishes and one plate	00	10	00
All his Earthen Vesells	00	01	00
one puter half paint	00	00	06
In the Buttery one Board and Form	00	02	00
one Tub	00	02	00
one Cupboard	00	04	06
one Barrill	00	01	06
In the Kitchen Chamber: one bedsteat, matt cord and rugg	00	10	00
one Chest	00	05	00
In the Shop Chamber: one Bed performed	01	10	00
one Sheet and one Blankett	00	07	00
Dowlas not made up	00	04	00
one Chest	00	07	00
one old box and two trunks	00	03	00
one Flask	00	00	06
one barrell	00	02	00
one Half hogshead and one barrell	00	05	00
Carsey not made up	00	15	00
Goods out of Sight and not Appraized	00	01	06
	£16	16	1

Appraized by us the day and year above mentioned John Grantland

[Will 15 Dec 1733 of William Holway of Uffculme, mason, pr 19 Jun 1734 at Uffculme before Mr John Talman surrogate: residue to exec, sister Joane, wife of John Cotton, who also inherits for life his present dwelling & garden & the house next door in Mill Street, Uffculme town, where Thomisin Hooper lives, & also the house in Mill St where Joseph Kinge lives, all to pass at her death to sister Susanna, wife of Robert Wyatt, who also inherits the house next door occupied by James Forward; to sister Elizabeth, wife of John Griffin, the 2 houses where Roger Whittinhow & Thomas Critchett live, lying on the south side of the house in Mill St where James Forward lives; marked by William Holway in presence of Jo: Were, Wm Shaddock, & Edward Harris, who all sign.]

247 MARY JERWOOD 1743 (DS)

[Widow; household items; £18.]

A True and Perfict Illventory of all the Goods and Ready Moneys of Mary Jerwood Lately Deseased.

	£	s	d
one Bed performed	1	1	0
one Round Table	0	8	0
one Brass Kittel	0	5	0
one Brass pott	0	3	0
one Bellmetle Skellet	0	1	6
2 Silver spouns	0	10	0
one Chest	0	4	0
one Coffer	0	3	0
2 Boxes	0	1	6
1 Barrcrook	0	1	0
Waring aparril	2	0	0
1 Iron pott	0	2	0
2 Tubs	0	1	6
1 Barrel	0	0	8
1 Leather Chare	0	1	6
one Gold Ring	0	10	0
Money purse and pocket	12	10	0
Lumber forgott	0	1	0
	£18	4	8

This is a True and a perfect Illventory of all ye Good Moneys and affects appaised By us this 24th Day of March 1742/3 as Wittnes our hands

John Parsons Thoms Smyth

[Will 16 Jan 1742 of Mary Jerwood of Uffculme, widow, pr at Uffculme before Benj: Hope, surrogate, 28 Mar 1743: residue to exec, Sarah Whetten, wife of John Whetten of Culmstock; 1s each to ss Thomas, Peter, & Anthony Jerwood; to s James Jerwood bedstead, brass pot, bellmetal skilett, & ban? crooke; £4 & round table to dr Elizabeth Jurden; £4, gowns, coats, ½hogshead to dr Mary Channing; a silver spoon each to Robert, s of Robert Jurden, & Robert, s of Robert Channing; chest to John, s of Thomas Jerwood; a box each to Thomazin & Ann, drs of Peter Jerwood; a coffer to John, s of Anthony Jerwood; marked by Mary Jerwood & witn John Green (signed) & Humphry Green (marked H).]

248 GILES BROOK 1754 (PU)

[Husbandman; household items; £6.]

A True and perfect Inventory and Appraisement of all and Singular the Goods Chattles and personal Estate of Giles Brook of Uffculm in the County of Devon Deceased as Taken and Appraised on the Seven and Twentieth day of September one Thousand Seven Hundred Fifty and Four By us whose Names are hereunto Subscribed as Appraisers therof That is to Say

	£	*s*	*d*
Cash Money at his Death	0	17	0
Four old Hogsheads	0	5	0
a Malt Mill	0	2	6
one old Board	0	0	6
Four Gebbs	0	1	0
Wearing Apparil	0	5	0
one Clock and Case	1	1	0
one Table Board	0	1	6
Two Chairs	0	1	0
one Iron Barr	0	3	0
Three Pewter Dishes	0	3	0
Three pewter plates	0	1	6
one Brass pan	0	1	6
Two old Barrels	0	1	0
one Bed performed	0	7	6
Debts	0	15	0
Desperate Debts	1	10	0
Six Wedges of Iron	0	3	0
one old Standard	0	0	6
one Coffer	0	1	0
a Corn fan	0	1	0
one Box one Trunk	0	2	0
Total Sum	6	4	6

The mark of John + Dercy }
George Southey [signature]}Appraisers

[Will 25 Apr 1754 of Giles Brook of Uffculme, husbandman, pr at Uffculme 4 Sep 1754 before Rev Ben Hope, surrogate of the Prebendary of Uffculme: residue to k & exec William Cotterel the elder (with whom he now lives); 1s each to bro Thomas Brook, to nephew & niece Giles & Elizabeth Brook (chn of bro Thomas Brook), & to nieces Mary Gillard & Sarah Brook; marked by Giles Brook in presence of Henry Bryant & Geo:Southey (both sign).]

249 APPENDIX: re JOHN TOSER prebendary, c 1553 (PU)

[The first two fragments are undated & anonymous & may relate to a clothier, but they clearly involve the Toser family.]

Fragment (a): a detached Inventory

[This inventory is completely crossed out & the reference to "Cant" (Kent) as well as Uffculme could be puzzling (though it is confirmed unequivocally in the following fragment), since the inventory would then be expected to be in the PCC group. Perhaps this was a copy lodged with the prebendary, or (like fragment (c)?) it may have been in his possession because of the Toser family connexion. The use of "my" in the tenth item even suggests that the list was drawn up during the owner's lifetime. Section total £16 11s.]

The Inventarye of Cant~.

Itm~ In p^r^mis. iiij fetherbedds *xlvj^s^*
Itm~ iij bolsters *iiij^s^*
Itm~ a gowme of murrey fyrryd *xxxiij^s^ iiij^d^*

Itm~ v cov^{r}letts xl^{s}
Itm~ ij ioyned beddsteyds x^{s}
It~ ij ?eosers $iiij^{s}$
Itm~ vj pere of shets $xxvj^{s}$ $viij^{d}$
Itm~ λ[?] iiij shepe at the barton v^{s}
It~ ij testers iij^{s}
It~ my hangyns of my cham~s [chambers?] vj^{s} $viij^{d}$
It~ a short gowne $xiij^{s}$ $iiij^{d}$
It~ a longe syngle blacke gowne xij^{s}
It~ a gowne furryd xvj^{s}
It~ iiij cherys [chairs] ij^{s} $viij^{d}$
It~ a carpytt $viij^{d}$
It~ a iakett vj^{s}
It~ napkyns & other stufe xx^{d}
It~ ix silv^{r} sponys $xxxiij^{s}$ $iiij^{d}$
It~ iij drynkyñ cups of silv^{r} iij^{li} vj^{s} $viij^{d}$ one doble gylt

Fragment (b): a detached Inventory

[This fragment is separated from the former but has been attached here since it is clearly related and could well be a continuation. There is a very clear reference to Ruckinge in Kent, where Mr Toser's sister appears to have lived, & probably to Faversham also. Again the use of "y owe" is unexpected & suggests that the list was drawn up during the owner's lifetime. He was probably a clothier & had a house at Uffculme with a hall, parlour, kitchen, "chapel" chamber (& chapel too?), & one other room, which would be substantial for the middle of the 16th century.]

The Inventarye of ufcombe

p[ar]ler

It~ In p^{r}mis a fetherbed $xiij^{s}$ $iiij^{d}$
It~ a bolster ij^{s}
It~ ij pillowis of downe ij^{s} vj^{d}
It~ a cov^{r}lett of doxnes[?] v^{s}
It~ iiij cushyns v^{s}
It~ a cheyste ij^{s} $viij^{d}$
It~ a presse iij^{s}
It~ a bason & ewer ij^{s} $iiij^{d}$
It~ a tester iij^{s} $iiij^{d}$
It~ the hangyns there iij^{s} $iiij^{d}$
It~ iij gownys l^{s}

The chapell cham^{r}

It~ a fetherbedd x^{s}
It~ a bolster ij^{s}
It~ a cov^{r}lett v^{s}
It~ a tester xx^{d}
It~ a pere of harnys vj^{s} $viij^{d}$

The next cham^{r}

Itm~ a fetherbed x^{s}
It~ a bolster ij^{s}
It~ small [?severall] pillowis ij^{s}
It~ iiij pere of sheytts $xiij^{s}$ $iiij^{d}$

The hall & the kichyn

Itm~ xvj platters xj potengs vj sawsers & iij chargers xxx^{s}
It~ ij brasse potts ix^{s}
It~ a chafer ij^{s} $iiij^{d}$
It~ a chafer w^{t} a beyle v^{s}
It~ posnett xx^{d}
It~ a lytle spytt $viij^{d}$
It~ a greydyron vj^{d}
It~ iij tubbs $iiij^{s}$
It~ iij pãnys x^{s}
It~ the hangyns of the hall vj^{s} $viij^{d}$
It~ iij tableclots iij^{s}
It~ iij towells xx^{d}
It~ iij pewt~ potts xx^{d}

It~ In corne vij^{li}
It~ in haye xx^{s}
It~ ij [iij with line through first i] colts v^{li}
It~ vj key [cattle] iij^{li} vj^{s} $viij^{d}$
It~ a steyre $xiij^{s}$ $iiij^{d}$
It~ iij hoggs iij^{s} $iiij^{d}$
[It~ iij pultrey (whole line crossed out) vj^{s} $viij^{d}$]

[The following lists seem to belong to the same inventory but these sections are completely crossed out, twice at some points (*italicised*) where a correction was made at the time of the original drafting.]

Detts which y do owe

It~ to thom~s p[er]cye alš Whitt xx^{s}
It~ for a pece of vestements vj^{s} $viij^{d}$
It~ for a scytt x^{s}
It~ for a salt of sylv^{r} coñ xiij unc[e]s at iij^{s} iiij^{d} the unce $xliij^{s}$ $iiij^{d}$

Sm~ $iiij^{li}$

Itm~ to [my lady phelyppe xij^{s} ix^{d}]
It~ to mye ladye for a gowne cloth xx^{s}[$ij^{s}viij^{d}$]
Itm~ to my ladye for deynge of the same cloth $iiij^{s}$
Itm~ for a cov^{r}lett & a bankar $xxiij^{d}$

It~ my lady apon a silv^r salt *xl^s*
at ufcombe
It~ to willm Skynñ[er] *xx^s*
It~ to Salters wedowe *xv^s*
Detts y^t y do owe a^o m^o v^o *xx*
[*xx* erased, followed by *xl*--?]
Itm~ to thom~s p[er]cye [*x^s*] *vj^s*
Itm~ to m^r Danyson *xv^s*
Itm~ to maistres francys for canvas *x^s*
Itm~ to maistres bartholomew *v^s*
cant~
Itm~ to trott *xl^s*
It~ to henrye salt^r *xxxiij^s iiij^d*
ufcombe
unto s[ir = Rev here probably]
Willm *xvj^s viij^d*
unto Walys my s[er]vant
unto Roger & bowdon
unto m^r tosers systers *xl^s vj^li*
It~ the bayly of fev^rsha~ [Faversham in Kent?] hath of myne a geldynge w^t sadell and brydell p'ce *xxvj^s viij^d*
[The following item is not crossed out & is significant in fixing the Kent connexion & showing that Mr Toser had a sister there.]
Itm~ the p[ar]son of Ruckynge in Kentt oweth me *xlvj^s viij^d* for a velvytt coyte which moneye m^r tosers syster muste have

Fragment (c): tinworks settlement (in Latin) involving the Toser family 1553

[Reference is made to the Chagford Stannary jurisdiction over a tin works in the parish of (Lower?) Morton, called "Buckydbeine Casen"(?), a twelfth part of which seems to have been a legacy to Symone Toser junior. Richard Senthyll & Richard Toser of North Bovey were involved in the case and John Toser, rector of Uffculme, officiated on 6 Jun 1553.]

THE INVENTORIES

(b) Canterbury (PCC) Jurisdiction

A few Uffculme inventories (mostly for the second half of the 17th century) have survived amongst the probate documents of the Prerogative Court of Canterbury held at the Public Record Office in London, and they are reproduced below. There are, however, many PCC wills without surviving inventories and abstracts of 166 of those up to the year 1700 are printed in the companion volume, *Uffculme: a Peculiar Parish*, where their reference numbers are preceded by the letters LW, for London Will.

Editorial policy and abbreviations are explained on page xxxi-xxxii [?].

L1 THOMAS JERMAN yeoman 1661

PROB 4/ 11157: figures mostly clear. [Bur: "Thomas Jerman" 17 Jan 1660/1. Mar: "Thomas German & Mary Santer" 22 June 1625. Rich; Uffculme & Burlescombe leases, oxen, 7 cows, 100 sheep, 3 horses, 3 pigs, wheat & rye, bible & other books; £997.]

An Inventory of the goods and Chattells of Thomas Jerman late of Uffculme Deceased taken the twenty second day of January 1660 by Peter Snow James [-l---] and John Lowdwell

	£	*s*	*d*
Imprimis [his wearing] Apparrell	08	00	00
Two feather [beds & bed]steads pformed	14	00	00
One chest and one little boxe	00	13	00
one Flocke bed wth a bedsteed pformed	02	10	00
three Coffers one mault hutch one Cupboard	01	00	00
one tableboard 4 Joynt stooles one forme one Carpett & Cushings & one Chaire	03	00	00
one Cubboad one Chest one Glasscage	02	00	00
one Silver bowle Eleven silver spoons	06	10	00
sixteene yards of Kersy cloath	04	00	00
one paire of hand Irons one paire of dogg[s] one warming pan	00	10	00
on tableboard one Cupboard one forme one livery table & other small implents	01	10	00
Thirty pewter dishes six saucers two Flagons two saults	04	00	00
Five Brasse potts two Cauldrons one posnett one skillet	04	00	00
two barrells of Salte[?] 6 pothangers two potcrookes two brandIrons one GridIron & two tosters	01	00	00
Three spitts one driping pan one Saving Iron and some other smale implents	00	10	00
Sixteene Cheeses Apples and Shilfes	06	10	00
Two dust beds wth bedsteeds pformed	05	00	00
one hundred & forty Fleeces of Wooll	14	00	00
two Sawes[?] two bages wth some hopes	01	10	00
one peece of tinne two bittles and 9 wedges	02	10	00
one Coffer wth some tooles for Carpentry and some other smale implemts	01	05	00
one bed wth bedsteed pformed	03	00	00
one livery table 2 Coffers one Amery one Standerd	01	05	00
three tablecloaths & twelve Napkins	02	00	00
one great Bible and other smale books	01	00	00
Fower Flutches of bacon & other meate in salte	06	00	00
one trendle one standerd one Jeb 10 beare barrells	03	00	00

	£	s	d
one Limbecke and one holbert	00	15	00
Ten brasse panes 3 brasse Candlestickes one pestle morter	08	10	00
For butter seame and tallow	01	10	00
one Gorner[?] and one Cheese wringe	01	10	00
ten bagges 1 mill 1 trendle 2 Coffers 6 tubes wth some feathers two turnes 1 saw 10 pitcheforkes	04	00	00
one Coffer one bed pformed	02	00	00
(one Coffer one bed pformed) [*not included in total]	02	00	00*
Fower hogesheads full of Syder and one of beare	06	00	00
Fower Emty hogsheads	01	00	00
one Brasse Furnice and two bruing Vates	03	10	00
one Fire pike one cowle 2 tubbes one brake stocke and two old hogsheads	00	10	00
one grinding stone wth the turners belonging	00	04	00
one pounding wringe wth the trow & implents belonging	02	00	00
one Sullow one paire of Harrowes wth thames and other plowstufe	02	10	00
three packe saddles 3 paire of long Crookes 3 paire of short Crooks 3 pair of dungpotts wth packe girts & other furniture belonging	01	10	00
one hackney saddle one paire of Gambadowes 2 bridles	01	00	00
for Corne & hay in the barne & hay loftes	26	00	00
three woodrickes and one furze ricke	20	00	00
one hundred sheepe	32	00	00
one yoake of Fat Oxen	16	00	00
Five Cowes & two Heifers	24	00	00
two naggs & one Mare	10	00	00
three swine hoggs	03	00	00
three acres of wheat in ground	08	00	00
one acre and halfe of Rye in ye ground	03	00	00
For his estate in Broke tenemt	100	00	00
For his estate in Dowdines tenemt	150	00	00
For his estate in the tenemt of Chackerell	080	00	00
for debts due uppon bond	288	00	00
more due uppon bond wch is desperate	100	00	00
For goods forgotten and unprized	00	10	00
[ ]sume is	997	02	00

[Signed] Jo.Clements

[Exhibited by John Clements for the exec, 11 May 1661

Will 22 Dec 1660, pr London 11 [?] May 1661: William Merrick named. Use of *tenement where I now live* to wife Mary, then to grandson Thomas Croydon, with £50; reversion of tenement at Stenhold *where John Dowdney lives* to grandson John Croydon, then to Thomas; 1/2 household goods at death of wife to Alice, 1/2 to Thomas & John; £100 to granddr Mary Croydon; use of tenement called Chackerell in Burlescombe to Alice, then to John, then to grandson William Croydon; 20 guineas to poor of Uffculme in bread; £1 to kinsman John Lowdwill; residue to dr Alice Croydon, exec; ovsrs: friends Henry Hart & William Jerman, who both witn.
(PROB 11/304 - 74, pp.153-4)]

L2 JOHN MILLS yeoman 1670

PROB 4/ 10078: top badly worn, some figures obliterated.
[Bur: "John Mills" 12 Nov 1669. Rich yeoman; house with hall, parlour & chamber, study, middle & men's chamber, inner & outer buttery, new house with chamber, drink-, milk-, cider-, bake-, & malt-houses; 160 sheep, 9 pigs, corn, 20 books, clock, gold ring; leases at Rill, Umbrooke, & Craddock; £1481.]

An Inventorie of all & singular [the] goods chattels & debts of John Mills late of Ufculme in the County of Devon yeoman deceased taken & praised the three & twentieth day of November the year of our Lord one thousand six hundred sixty and nyne by William Eveleigh Francis Pratt and Henry Dowdney as followeth

[	£	*s*	*d*]
--primis ----------pparell			

Item ---------------dettes			

Item one hundred sixty sheep	61		
It nyne swine hogg	15		
It Corne in the barnes in house and Mowes		70	00
It corne in ---------	24		
It two paire of------------- one sider wringe in the wood house & other plough tackling ---tymber there	21	00	00
It packe Sadd[l]es & his horse tackling		3	
It tooles for husbandry		3	
It hay in house & in rickes	25	00	00
It tymber & wood in rickes	06	00	00
It wooll shorne the last yeare	16	00	00
It his weapons & Armour	2	10	
It one Silver Salt two Silver boales and twelve Silver Spoones	12	00	00
It Cheese & Butter	12[s?]		
It Bacon & other victualls	4[s?]		
It a lease for yeares in a tenemt called Rill	300		
It a lease for yeares in a tenemt called Umbrooke	200		
It two chattle leases at Craddocke	180	00	00
It in the parlour two table boards one livery table on Cupboard fower chaires a doozen of ioyned stooles seaven brasse candlestickes two Andirons one doozen of Cushions fower Carpetts a paire of tables & other small things there		12[s?]	
It one bason & ewer sixe & forty pewter dishes, one other bason halfe a doozen of pottage dishes three Flaggons one butter sawcer & other smale pewter wth two chamber potts a bed panne and a Lymbicke	09[£ or s?]		
It in the Inner butterie one table board seaven barrels one forme one Ammorie one glasse cage & other smale goodes there	03[s?]		
It in the utter butterie one tableboard one forme one hogshead two barrells one coffer & other smale things there	02	10	
It in the hall one tableboard one forme one Settle one Ammorie one Jacke two drippinge pannes three spittes two Bacon rackes three chairs & other small things there		4[s?]	
It in the drinke house two Cheese wringes five ferkinges two tubbes & other smale things there		01	10
It in the milke house seaventeen brasse pannes two Caldrons one bason one Chaffinge dish one trendle on Standerd a warming pan & other smale thinges there		07	00
It eight brasse pottes & two posnettes	04	05	00
It in the new house & new house chamber one Corne Hutch two trendles fower Standerdes three Coffers a workinge board one Truckle bedsteede one cradle & other smale thinges about the said roomes	02	10	00
It in the Syder house three hogsheads two barrells & other smale thinges there	01	10	00
It in the Bakehouse one brewinge furnace one yeatinge fate nyne tubbes one brake board wth other smale thinges there	04	00	0
It in the malt house & malt house chamber sixe hogsheads three barrells two cheese tubbes			

[*£ s d*]
one butter tubbe a mill to cleanse corne two turnes & other smale things there 04 00 00
It in the two bakehouse chambers sixe tubbes one Corne hutch & other smale thinges there 01 00
It in the Parlour Chamber one standinge bedsteede & featherbed pformed one trundle bedsteede & featherbed pformed one Chest three Chaires two Andirons one greate truncke & other smale thinges there 15 0
It in the middle Chamber two Standinge Bedsteeds & featherbeds pformed two costes two coffers & other small thinges there 12 00

[on 2nd roll, wrapped inside the 1st:]
In the hall chamber one standinge bedsteede & featherbed pformed one other standinge bedsteede & dust bed pformed two trundle bedsteeds & one dust bed & one flocke bed pformed one presse two coffers one truncke & other smale thinges there 12 00 00
It in the study twenty bookes a Clocke & other smale thins there 3[£ or s?]
It in the mens chamber three standinge Bedsteeds & three dust beds pformed one old coffer & other small thinges there 06
It one Gold ringe & deske 2 10
It one diaper table cloth one doozen of diaper table napkins three other table clothes & other lyninge 5 00
It in Umbrooke house two table boards one forme one cupboard one standinge bedsteede one Trundle Bedsteede & other smale things there 7
It goods seene & unseen not before in this Inventorie vallued 3 [s?]
Suma totalis 1,481 02 02
[Signed] J.Horne[?]

[No Latin endorsement.

Will 4 Nov 1669, pr 1 Dec 1669 "in y[e] Strand, London" names Robert Mills as exec: 6s "towards the reparation of Uffculme Church"; 40s to the poor. "Messuage & tenement wherein I now live" also that at Umbrook and use of household goods to Elizabeth "my now wife", also 3 kyne 21 horse & 10 ewes, 2 sacks of wheat & 2 sacks of malt. £200 each to drs Elizabeth & Rebeccah Mills, also £5 each to these and to married drs Frances Pratt & Anne Dowdney; his desk & gold ring to dr-in-law Grace Mills; £40 to grandson John Mills; 40s to each of other grand-chn; 20s to each of living-in servants; residue to s Robert Mills, exec. £5 each to ovsrs Francis Pratt & Henry Dowdney, ss-in-law; signed by John Mills; "Memorandum that these words (and two sacks of wheate an two sacks of Malte) were underlined"; witn: William Eveleigh & Simon Pratt. (PROB 11/332 -24, p 189)]

L3 GERVAS RANISFORD husbandman 1671

PROB 4/ 10063: figures clear.
[Bur: "Jarvis Ransford" 21 Dec 1670; wife Barbara buried 1 Dec 1670. Mar: "Jarvis Ransford & Barbara Woodrow" 17 Feb 1643/4. Husbandman; £47 in bills & bonds, otherwise household goods & tools listed; £58.]

An Inventory of all the Goods Chattels and Creditts of Gervas Ranisford late of Uffculme in the County of Devon husbandman[?] duly taken and Appraized by Humphrey Bowden and Adrian Ayshelford Yeomen the 19th day of December Anno Domini 167[0]

	£	*s*	*d*
Imprimis his Weareing Apparell and money in Howse	003	00	00
Item in Bills and Bonds	047	00	00
Item in Bedding Sheetes Ruggs and Bedd Tyes	001	10	00
Item two Beddsteads two Chayres tableBord and foarme	1	00	00

	£	s	d
Item two Chests an Armory and Coffer	1	2	6
Item three brasse Caldrons and three brasse potts	2		
Item eleaven Porrengers two brasse panns and sawsers and other pewter	1		
Item Pott cronkes[?] Andirons Spitt panns and other Iron stuffe		3	0
Item in Gardiance, A Rack Betell Wedges Stoole and Mattock, Hooke and Axe and other small stuffe		3	0
Item three Barrells a Tubb and Steane[?] and other old timber stuffe, Bayes[?] and other small things		10	0
Item other small Trifelling things - Ladders [blank] and other things		10	0
Item in wood		5	0
	58	3	0

[Signed] Jo.Deely [6d short]
Signed Humphrey Bowden
The marke of Adrian Ayshelford
The marke of Arthur Stevens

[Exhibited 21 Jul 1671 by John Deely for exec.

Will 2 Dec 1670, pr *in le Strand* 28 July 1671, names Joan Clarke wife of Robert Clarke as exec: Jarvase *being aged* to be buried *in the parish church of Ufcolm*; £15 & *best wearing apparell* to bro Josias[?] Ransford in Monghton (or if dead, £5 to wife); £10 to cousin Barbara [or Barbary] Clarke dr of Robert Clarke; Residue, bonds, money to Cozen Joan Clarke, wife of Robert Clarke, exec; ovsr Humphrey Bowden to look after Barbara's money so *it may not be brazled away*; mark of Gervase Ransford; witn: Humphrey Bowden, William Clarke[?] James P--. (PROB 11/336-99, p 100)]

L4 ELLEN SAMES, 1672

PROB 4 18301
[Bonds & apparel; £31.]

An Inventary of all & Singular the goods Chettles and creditts of Ellen S[ames] late of Uffculme in the County of Devon deceased taken the Nine and Twenty day of January in the yeare of our Lord God 1672 as Followeth

[	£	s	d]
Inprimis her wearing Apparell			*xx*
Item two bonds	*xxx*		
Suma total	*xxxj*		

(Signed) Franc.Nixon

[Exhibited by Francis Nixon for the admin, 18 Feb 1672; Latin endorsement signed by Marcus Cottle

Admon Feb 1672 names Nicholas and John Lake (nephews? minors?) but connexion is unclear. (PROB 6/ 48-173)]

L5 JOHN BROOKE 1673

PROB 4/19467: figures uncertain.
[Mostly lease, bonds, & debt; £39.]

An Inventory of [ ] singular ye goods chattles & debpts of John Brooke late of Uffculme in the County of Devon h-- d Decd taken & apprised the 12th day of July A Dmi 1673[?] by Simon Gill, Chas[?] Godfry & Baptist And[ro]

[	£	s	d]
Inpris his weareing apparell	*ij*	*ij*	
Item one Chattle lease	*xvj*	[?]	
Item money upon Bond & Desperate Depts	*xij*		
Item things forgotten & out of Mind		*v*	[?]
Sum'tot hujus In.	*xxxix*	*x*	[?]

[signed] John Thomas & admin[?]

[Exhibited 20 Mar 167[ ] by John Thomas (Curatt)[?] and/for admin.]

Admon 21 Feb 1673 names Simon Brookes]

L6 RICHARD HOLWAY alš ANDRO widow 1659 & 1675

PROB 4/ 4911: figures uncertain.
[Bur: "Richord ye wife of Nicholas Hollway" 26 Jan 1658/9. Mar:

"Nicholas Hollway & Richord Androw widdow" 30 Sep 1658: see L7. Widow; house with entry, hall, room within & chamber over, kitchen & chamber over, malt- & pound-house; household goods; £18.]

An Inventary of all the goods chittles of Richard Holway alš Andro late of Uffculme in the County of Devon widdow Deced taken and appraized by Simon Merson and William Bertlet both of Uffculme aforesaid the 10th Day of May in the yeare of our Lord God 1675 as followeth

[	£	s	d]
In the Chamber over the hall one Tester Bedstead		*vj*	[?]
In the Hall one Cupboard			*xx*
In the Roome wthin the hall one old Sideboard		*j*	*vj*
In the Entry one Trendle			*viij*
In the Parlour one tableboard 5 Chayres 5 Joynt stooles and one furme			*xxv*
In the Chamber over the parler two Coffers two boxes 3 old Barrells one hodshead one little Chaire one Jebb 7 brasse[s] pans 4 brasse potts on Chaffing dish -- one warming pan one payre of tongs one fire pann 3 pre of Andirons one payre of fire dogs, on pr of pothookes one Iron Barr one Iron Wedge 2 brasse kittles 2 little Joynt stooles one tray		*v*	[?]
In the Kitchin one old Cupboard			*iij vj*[?]
In the Chamber over the Kitchin one Chest two Coffers one tester Bedstead one truckle Bedstead 4 feather Beds & feather bolsters one feather pillow 4 old Coverlidds 2 pre[?] of Blanketts 10 pewter Dishes 2 brasse dishes two Brasse Candle stikes one Skillet		*v*	*x*
In the Malt house One[?] yeating fate			*x*
In the pound house two halfe hogshead fatts one hogshead fate and two other fates one Brewing fate one sider wring and the trough		*iiij*	[?]
Other things forgotten and not seene the Sum of			*x*
Suma totalis Inventary		*xviij*	*xviij*
	[£1 14s short?]		

[Signed] Rob.Chapman

[Exhibited 18 May 1675 by Robert Chapman for admin.

Admon 9 Feb 1658/9 to Baptist Baseleigh as guardian of Baptist & Penelope Andro, minors, chn of her first husband William Andro [LW134]; a second admon 17 May 1675 to Baptist Andro, now of full age. (PROB 6/ 50-152)]

L7 NICHOLAS HOLWAY 1666 & 1675

PROB/4 10000: figures uncertain.
[Bur: "Mr Nicholas Hollway" 23 Oct 1665; see L6. Debts only; £46.]

An inventary of all and singular the Goods [C]hattells and credetts of Nicholas Holway late of Ufculme in the County of Devon decea[sed] --------------------Holway the sonne[?] & --dafter of the said decead---------followeth viz

[	£	s	d]
Imprimis due & owing to the said decceased from one John Burden being sperate the sume of	*xxij*	*xvj*	*iiij*
Item from Zachary Gardiner being desperate		*vj*	
Item from Peter Cole decd despate		*ix*	
Item from George Rookes desperate		*viij*	*ix*
Suma totalis hujus Invy est	*xxxvij*	*vij*	

[Signed] Mary Hollway [£46 5s 4d]

[Testification in June 1675 by Mary Holway alš Rowe to the truth of this inventory. Signed "Char. Lawes"[?]

Exhibited 5 Jun 1675 by F-- Cole for the admin. Note at the end reads: *this to be signed & sworne to by Mrs Holway & if need require it may be rectified but if made to 40 Li shee need not sweare.*

Admon 13 Feb 1665/6 to Peter Hollway, son of Nicholas; a second admon 5 Jun 1675 to Maria Holway alš Rowe, 1st cousin on mother's side to Nicholas, Peter having died. (PROB 6/ 50-152)]

L8 ALEXANDER MELHUISH clothier 1695[1681?]

PROB 4/ 3935: figures faint; on outside, "Dorset" crossed out.
[Bur: "Alexander Melhuish" 8 Apr 1681. Rich clothier; barley, wheat, cider, peas, 16 cattle, 3 horses, 12 pigs, 48 sheep; leases in Uffculme, Burlescombe, & Wellington; £937.]

A true and perfect Inventary of all & singular ---goods-------------and credits ----------er Melhuish late of --------- County of Devon------------valued & appraised the twelfth Day of April An- ---1681 by ---[John Rowe?] Jno.Westbeere[?] follows viz

[	£	s	d]
Impris his wearing apparell	*xj*		
Item in money in purse	*xxx*		
Item for barley in the barne and tallet	*viij*		
Item for Corne in pt of B--mell P-ing Mesling[?]	*iij*		
Item for wt corne is left of a little Mow of Barley		*xx*	
Item for 1000 of wood & wallet[?]	*iij*	*vj*	*viij*
Item for the rook of barly --in-- Medborow	*xij*		
Item for the Corne in Ground in Medborow	*viij*		
Item for the sider ring and Cloath Press	*ij*	*ij*	
Item for two Andirons		*x*	
Item for the trendle		*iij*	*iiij*
Item for one pr of curtains & Vallens		*v*	
Item for one cupboard & a Tableboard	*j*	*vj*	*viij*
Item for things out of sight		*v*	
Item for ye lease in Longfurse hill [?]Prescott[?]	*j*	*x*	
Item for one acre & half of Pease	*j*	*x*	
Item for the wheat in Culming[?] [?]Fiveford[?]	*vij*	*x*	
Item for wheat growing	*v*		
Item for one acre and half of Pease growing	*j*	*x*	
Item for sheat barley & Pease in house and in Mow	*j*		
Item for two Oxen & 2 steers	*xiij*		
Item for five young Pullocks and one heifer	*viij*	*xiij*	*iiij*
Item for two horses and one mare	*viij*	*v*	
Item in Hay		*x*	
Item for five swines of the greater sort and six of the lesser	*v*		
Item for four milk Cows and two milke heifers	*xix*	*vj*	*vj*
Item for one Fat Sow	*v*	*xv*	
Item for twenty seaven fat sheep	*xvij*	*xj*	
Item for seaventeen Ewes & hogs and four Lambes	*v*	*xiij*	*iiij*
Item for the Chattle estate in the Pish of Burlescombe called Oats	*CCL*		
Item for a lease in Hart for Mills	*Lxxx*		
Item for the Chattle estate in Prescott	*Lxxx*		
Item for ye Lease in Culm meadow	*xv*		
Item for the Lease in Wealches house	*Lx*	*x*	
Item for Debts Sperate & desperate	*C*		
Item for ye furniture in the house called Fivefords and the goods therein	*L*	*xvj*	
Item for a Lease in the mills at Fivefords	*Lx*		
Item for the Chattel estate in Wellington	*x*		

[	£	s	d]
Item for things out of sight		x	
Suma totalis	DCCCC	vj	iiij
[11s 6d too much?]			

Omitted to be Inventaryed by the Appraizors

A lease of two Closes of Pasture called Brook hams and Lea[r]e hams wherein the Testator had an estate-- determinable on the Death of one Parson Worth	*xxxv*		
Item a house in Uffculme called Oatways house	*ij*	*x*	
Suma totalis hujus Inventariy	*DCCCCxxxvij*	*xv*	*iiij*

[Exhibited 23 Nov 1695 by Robert Peirson [for?] John Lovell, exec. Latin endorsement signed by R.Peirson.

Will 29 Mar 1681, pr London May 1681 names John Dyer & John Lovell as execs; former wills revoked; 50s to poor; household goods in Fivefords to *now wife* Dorothy for life if unmarried, then to s Thomas; £700 to dr Margaret, (or £500, and £500 to Dorothy's poss. unborn ch); £300 to s Thomas; residue to exec^s^: John Dyer, mercer & Uncle John Lovell of Uplowman, yeoman, to pay for chn's upbringing; witn: Tho. Marke, John Watson, & Edward Rowland. (PROB 11/336-76, pp 225-6)]

L9 EDWARD CALLOW, 1683

PROB 4/ 4792: figures reasonably clear.
[Bur: "Edward Callow" 10 Mar 1683/4. Prosperous; hall & chamber, buttery & chamber; largely £300 for Broadhembury tenement; £340.]

An Inventorie of the Goods Chattles & Debts of Edward Callowe late of Uffculm & in the County of Devon deceased taken & aprised the Eleaventh day of March 1683 by Peter Symons James Callow Peter Pringe John Garnsey & Robert Mills as followeth

	£	s	d
Imprimis his Apparell	*vj*	*xiij*	*iv*
Item money in purse	*00*	*xj*	*ix*
Item in good debts	*xiiij*	*00*	*00*
Item in the Hall six brasse panns two pottage potts thirteen pewter Dishes one Flaggon two Kooles [booles?] a kittle & two Skillets with other small things there	*0v*	*00*	*00*
Item in the Butterie Eight Barrells two Standards Five Tubbs a fryeinge pann Two halfe pecks wth sevrall shelves & boards & other small things there	*ij*	*xiij*	*iv*
Item in the Butterie Chamber one standinge Bedstead & Dust bedd pformed one Truckle bedstead & Dust bed pformed Two Coffers vessell [?] Tymber & hoops with other small things there	*ov*	*ox*	*oo*
Item in the Hall Chamber one standinge Bedstead & Dust bed pformed one Chest one Box & Fower Aishen planks wth other small things there	*ij*	*xiij*	*iv*
Item Carpentry & husbandry Tools	*ij*	*ox*	*v*[?]
Item a lease for yeares in a Tenemt called Stowford in the pish of Broadhembury	*CCC*	*oo*	*oo*
Item goods seene & unseene & not before in this Inventory vallued	*oj*	*oo*	*oo*
Suma total	*CCCxl*	*xj*	*ix*

Signo J[ ] [5d short?]
[Signed] Franc.Nixon

[Exhibited 23 Oct 1684 by Francis Nixon for admin.

Admon Oct 1684 available but not found. (PROB 6/ 59-192)]

L10 JAMES BATT clothier 1691

PROB 4/ 5286: most figures reasonably clear.
[Rich clothier; cloth stocks, corn, hay, 3 horses, 8 cows, pigs; total, largely

due to payment for goods in Tiverton, Bristol, London, & Flanders, £1182.]

A true & perfect Inventory of all and singular the goods chells & creditts of James Batt late of Ufculme in the county of Devon Clothier deceased taken & appraized the 6 day of [?] A D 1690 by Wm.How, John Grantland Tho.Pooke as foll. viz.

[	£	*s*	*d*]
Impris his apparell	*x*		
Item in prsent money	*xx*		
It in ye hands of Tiverton merchnts	*CCiiij*	*xviij*	
It in ye hands of the merchts of London as by ye accompt of Mr.Phillip Bickter, Factor dated ye 4 Day of May 1690 appeareth	*CCCx*	*v*	*xj*
It 12 broads in the Factors hands unsold	*Lx*		
It 3 bills due from persons in Bristoll	*xxvij*	*vij*	*x*
It 5 packs of cloth shipt for Flanders	*Cxx*		
It wool in house not dyed	*xxiiij*	*x*	
It yarne in house for making cloth	*xxvij*	[s?]	
It serges in house	*xlviiij*		
It cloth serges	*x*	*xij*	[?]
1 double Carsey	*v*		
3 single Carseys	*vj*		
lysting yarne	*iiij*		
24 broads in house	*Cxx*		
in --[r]uffe dyed wool	*ij*		
in dyed clothing wool	*ix*		
in short course wool & white pinnions		*xij*	*vj*
in white slyvered wool		*xiiij*	*viij*
in worsted yarne		*xviij*	
in other dyed clothing wool		*vij*	
in superfine wool for mixtures	*iij*		
in Gingerlyne & blew wool	j	*iiij*	
in Oyle	*iij*	*x*	
in dyed druggett wool		*vij*	*viij*
in dye stuffe	*ij*	*viij*	
in dyed combing wool	*v*		
in ye wool in hand for making of cloth	*vij*	*x*	
It. the deceds. estate in the Tenement where his father now liveth	*xxx*		
It corne in the barne	*ij*		
It hay in ricks	*v*		
It corne in ground	*vj*		
It wood & furze	*vj*	*x*	
It three horses	*ix*		
It [8] milch cowes	*xiij*		
It swine hoggs	*ij*		
It in Clover seed	*iij*		
It two feather beds performed & two other beds	*x*		
It 6 brasse pans	*j*	*vj*	*viij*
It 2 brasse Coldrons		*x*	
It j brasse kettle & j brasse pott	*ij*	*x*	
It j dozen & halfe of pewter	j	*xvj*	
It in plate	*vj*		
It j chest of drawers		*xv*	
It 5 truncks	*j*		
It in table linnen	*j*	*x*	
It victualls butter & cheese etc	*iiij*		
It in beer & syder	*iij*		
It in mault	*iij*		
It three keeping presses	*iij*		
It in Armor	*iij*		
It in barrils tubbs & fatts	*j*	*x*	
It wheat winnowed	*j*	*xvj*	
It chairs formes & stools	*j*		
It j furnace & implements of the clothing trade	*xx*		
It horse tackling	*j*		
It debts upon book sperate & desperate		*x*	
It goods seen & not seen & not before appraized	*iij*		
The sum totall of this Invry is	*MD[/C]LXXX11*	*iij*	*ij*
	£1182	3	2

(Signed) Jo.Hungerford [3s 11d high?]

[Exhibited by John Hungerford for the admin 21 Apr 1691.

Admon April 31 Mar 1691 names Prudence Batt as widow & admin. (PROB 6 / 67 - 231, p 66)]

L11 JOHN DYER 1695

PROB 4/ 19031: some figures uncertain; roll appears to have been burnt down the left hand side.

[Rich; hall & chamber, buttery & chamber; total, largely debts & estates, £970.]

------------------true and
perfect Iny of all and
--ngular the goods chattles
--d Creditts of John Dyer
of Uffculme in the [this?]
------Devon [deceas]ed
------valued & appraised
---[Twen]tieth day of Appril
--nno Dmi 1695[/6?] by John
--reenway Tho. Wilhi[--]
Abram ----rd and Jno. Grantland f[--]

	LL	*s*
---------------apparrell	*ij*	
----ey in his chest	*lxx*	
---due upon bills		
---er securities	*DCCLXX*	
---------	*vj*	*vj*
---estate in Hewish		
-----a Good estate	*C*	
--in his dwelling	*iiij*	
---erate Debts	*v*	
---ne Chamber---med--	*iiij*	*x*
----Table and one ---	*j*	
----Chairs one Closestool		
---ass and around------		*xiij*
Linnen	*j*	
[In the H]all Chamber		
----d -----	*iij*	*x*
[In the B]uttery Chamber ----		
and other lumber -----	*j*	
----Hall fourteen-----		
six plates five -----		
a Table board	*j*	*x*
--brass pots one -----		
[s]killet -- warming		
---- & Chafing dish	*ij*	
---[th]ree spits and -----		*x*
---Buttery two ----ns one brass		
---- [b]arrells one ----mber		
goods	*ij*	
Due upon ------	*iiij*	
----not seen neither		
[prais]ed ----		*v*
-talis	*DCCCCLXXij*	*j*

[£7 3s short?]

[No Latin endorsement.

Admon 25 May 1696 names Margaret Dyer widow & admin. Note in margin gives 8 May 1696. The card index states that this admon is missing, but it exists on microfilm. (PROB 6/ 71-229)]

L12 ROBERT BURROW 1695

PROB 4/ 4915: figures very faint.
[Bur: "Robert Burrough" 24 Sep 1695. Hall & chamber, parlour & chamber, wring- & milk-houses; wheat, barley, hay, 1 mare, 4 cows, 8 pigs, 12 sheep; £1088?]

A true and perfect Invent[ory of all] and singular the goods [cha]ttells and cred[its] of Robert [Bur]row late of the parish of Uffculme in the County of Devon ---- deceased ---- taken -----------[of the raigne of our] Sovereigne Lord King William Ann dmi 1695 --by------ Ballyman ------ ----- and Anthony Crosse as followeth viz.

[	£	s	d]
Imprimis the decd wearing appare		*vj*[*xj*?]	
---[mo]ney in his [purse]	*iij*		
In the Hall Chamber			
Item one standing bedsted with the curtains & vallins & furniture thereunto belonging	*v*		
Item j halfe bedstead with a feather bed ---	*iij*		
Item 2 sheets		*xij*[?]	
Item one pillion & Covering cloth		*v*[?]	
Item 2 boxes		*ij*	
In the parlor Chamber			
It one halfe head[ed] bedstead & one bed [tye--]	*v*[?]		
It 8 coffers		*vij*	*vj*
It j mault hutch		*v*	
It in mault	*j*	*viij*	
In the parlour			
Item one table-board		*iiij*[?]	
Item on chaire		*j*	
In the hall			
Item one table board and furme		*iij*	
Item one cupboard		*iij*	
It --- little side table		*ij*	
It 3 chairs		*vj*	
It 8 crooks & a pair of Brandice 1 pair of tongs			

[£ s d]
& 2 pair of Iron Doggs *vij vj*
Ir j frying pan *j*
It 2 bras[se] potts *xij*
It 12 pewter dishes *j x*
It 1 pewter flaggon *j vj*
It one pestle morter *j vj*
It 1 fowling peice *vj*
In the hall
Item 1 spitt *j*
Item j hourglasse *vj*[?]
In the wring house
It one brasse pan *xv*
It one cheese wring *v*
It 3 small barrels *v*
It 5 tubbs & one butter bole *xij*
It --- pair of weights *ij*
It 2 par-les [?] *iij*
In the milke house
It j trendle *viij*
It j standard *iij*
It 2 brasse kettles *xiiij*
It 5 brasse panns *xv*
It 6 crockes of butter *j x*
It a cheese *ij*
It one brasse skillett *j*
It 3 acres of wheat & 3 acres of barly *xij*
It [8?] acres of Hay *iiij*
It one old mare *iij*
It 4 milch cowes *xij*[?]
It 8 hoggs *ij*
It 12 sheepe [?] ----
In the stable
It one pack saddle ----
It j pare of Harrows ----
It one shovell ----
It j hackney saddle & stirrups ----
It one shovell ij
It j Dung pike ij
It j pair of long crookes ----
dung potts [1 sheafe] ----
It in hard wood & faggotts --- ----
It j small chattell lease -------
It goods unseen & unappraised v
Item due upon bond [-]*liij*[?]

The sum total of this Iny [?] *Mlxxxviij* [?]

[No Latin endorsement.

Admon 23 Oct 1695 names Lucia[?] Burrow as widow & admin. (PROB 6/ 71-229)]

L13 THOMAS DUNNE 1697

PROB 4/ 8935: figures resonably clear. [Bur. "Thomas Dunn & wife" 15 Apr 1697 or "Thomas Dunn" 6 May 1697. Prosperous; several leases; corn, 8 cows, 3 horses, 33 sheep, 3 pigs; £608.]

A true and perfect Inventary of all and singular the goods chetles and credits of Thomas Dunne late of Uffculme in the County of Devon decd taken valued and appraized the Fourth day of M[arch] Anno Domini 1696/7 by virtue of a Comicon of appraisers arising out of the Prerogative Court of Canterbury by Joh[n] D-------------wife of James Pratt who ------------wth Dorothy the eldest daughter------------and John ---al---John Grantland on ye pt of F-------- by the said decesd

[£ s d]
Impris his wearing apparrell both linnen and woollen *ij*
Item in debts due to him upon book *Clxxvj xix*
Item in ready money *x*
Item on Estate in Smithincot Tenemt upon which was a life upon each halfendeale *Cx* [?]
Item three lives on his estate of Stedyards *C*
Item one other estate of two lives in the Towne Tenement *Cxxx*
In the dye house
Inpris one old dye Furnace *j v*
Item one brewing panne *xiij iiij*
Item one washing panne and wrench *xiij*
Item one paire of warping barre[s] *vj*
In the Parlour Chamber
Item one bed performed *iij*
Item one other bedstead *j x*
Item one Table board *xv*
Item one Chest *x*
Item one Coffer and one Settle *v*
In the Hall Chamber

[	*£*	*s*	*d*]
Item two beds performed	*iiij*		
Item one Coffer		*v*	
In the wool chamber			
Item one bed performed		*x*	
In the Parlour			
Item one Table board an forme	*j*		
Item one Carpett		*x*	
Item one livery Table board		*ij*	*vj*
Item one Settle		*vj*	*viij*
Item Six Chaires		*xij*	
Item one other great Chaire		*ij*	*vj*
Item one Cupboard		*xv*	
Item three pewter dishes		*xij*	
Item one glass Cage with two little pewter dishes		*iij*	*vj*
Item one pair of Andirons			[6?]
In the Hall			
Item one Table board and forme		*vj*	*viij*
Item Six pewter dishes		*ix*	
Item two brasse pots and one Iron Pott	*j*		
Item one brasse Cauldron		*x*	
Item one little Cauldron pestle and mortar and two Oyle pans		*viij*	*vij*
Item one box and Irons one pr of brass scales one Cheese press one Set of Selves and one Settle	*j*		
In the Milke house			
Item Six brass Pans	*j*	*v*	
Item one Salting Standard		*ij*	
In the Drinke house			
Impris one Trindle old barrels Tubs three empty hogsheads two old pails one Corne Hutch Plough stuffe and horse Tacking	*iiij*	[s?]	
Item in Lumber goods and other goods not before appraized	*j*		
Item Corne in the ground	*x*		
Item Corne in the Barne	*iiij*	*x*	
Item foure milch Cowes	*xv*		
Item one heifer and three yearlings	*viij*	*viij*	
Item three Horses	*vj*	*x*	
Item three and thirty Sheepe	*xiij*		
Item three Swine hogs	*ij*	*xv*	

[	*£*	*s*	*d*]
Sume totall	*DCviij*	*xj*	*iij*
			[6d short?]

Besides this wee the s^d Commissioners upon examinacon and accounts of John Dunne eldest son of the said before deceased Thomas Dunne (before and in the presence of ye aforesaid John Pratt and the rest of the Infants -- Do find s[evra]ll debts due and owing from the said deced paid by the said John Dunne on ye behalfe of the rest, in ye whole amouting to *Lx* [or *Lj*] Li, *xvij*s. A Particular whereof the said John Dunne is ready to give wh[en] thereunto required
[Signed] R.Peirson

[Exhibited 12 Mar 1696 (Stilo Anglia) by Robert Peirson for the admin.

Admon, 15 Jul 1700, very hard to read, names s John; Florence Dunn, Dorothea Welch alš Dunn & Humphrey Welch; John, Thomas, Margaret & Joan; Rebe[ccah?] and Henry Dunn; and Dorothy and John Pratt. Evidently a family dispute.]

L14 EDWARD MARSHALL junior, mercer 1699

PROB 4/ 1655: figures very faint.
[Bur. "Edward Martiall Jun" 15 Feb 1698/9. Rich mercer; trade & household goods, corn, 3 horses, 20 sheep, 2 pigs, 1 ox, horse & plough; chattel leases; £770.]

A true and perfect Invenry of all and singular [the] goods chattels and credits of Edwd Mars[hall] Junr late of Uffculme in the County of Devon deced taken valued and appraized the Third daye of March Anno [Dmi] 1698/9 by John Grantland and Edward Marshall----------[len] followes

	Li	[*s*	*d*]
Impris the deceaseds wearing apparrell	*iiij*		
Item in ready money	*v*		
Item the decd estate in T[owne] tenemt	---		

	Li	[*s*	*d*]
Item the decd estate in Craddock	*C*		
Item his Reverction in Halften Tenemt	*Lx*[*D*?]		
Item in mercery goods	*C*[?]		
Item corne in barne and [house]	*x*		
Item three horses	*x*		
Item twenty sheepe	*v*		
Item two Swine hoggs	*j*		
Item one Ox	*iij*		
Item five beds performed	*xij*		
Item ten pewter dishes	*j*	*vj*	*vj*
Item three brass potts	*j*	*v*	
Item two brass kettles		*x*[£?]	
Item one brewing pann		*x*	
Item Six leather chaires	*j*	*x*	
Item one round Table board		*x*	
Item three chests	*j*		
Item a dozen of old leather chairs		*x*	
Item two old brewing Vatts		*iij*	*iiij*
Item in the Kitchen an old table board		---	
Item in Table Linnen		*x*	
Item in hogsheads and barrells and Tubbs	*ij*[?]		
Item in plough and horse tackling		*v*	
Item debts due on the Shop booke	*x*	*viij*	*vj*
Item desperate debts	*xiij*		
Item goods unseen	*j*	*vj*	*viij*
Summa totalis	*DCClxx*----		

Sig R.Peirson [values incomplete]

[Exhibited -7[?] Mar 169[?] by Robert Peirson for the exec.

Will 10 Jan 1698/9, pr 7 Mar 1698[/9] names Alice Marshall widow as exec: *that tenement wherein I now live commonly called my Town Tenemt* to wife Alice for life, then to dr Elianor Marshall, (otherwise to William s of Henry Hopper of Cullompton,[?]) thence to William & John, ss of John Kent of Uffculme; reversion of *Halften* tenement *now in possession of Uncle Edward Marshall by Copy of Courtroll* to Elianor; Craddiocke tenement to (Elianor? & then to) Kinsmen John & Robert Bow ss of John Bow of Crewkerne; *gray hackney nagg* to Uncle Edward Marshall & 1gn to Aunt Margaret; £5 to poor; residue to wife Alice, exec; 1gn each to friends Edward Ellis & John Chorley to be Elianor's guardians; witn: John & William Grantland, marks of John Tozer & Anne [D]owdney. (PROB 11/450-45, p 4)]

L15 MARK WESTRON yeoman 1699

PROB 4/ 9997: figures resonably clear. [Bur: "Mr.Mark Westron" 16 Nov 1699. Rich: hall & chamber, parlour & chamber, brewhouse & chamber; 3 cows, 4 horses, 100 sheep, 4 pigs, corn, hay; £502.]

A true and perfect Inventary of all and singular the goods chattels and credits of Mark Westron late of the parish of Ufculme in the county of Devon decd taken valued and appraised on the twenty second day of November 1699 by James Cadbury John Westron Thomas Townsend and John Grantland as followeth viz.

[	£	*s*	*d*]
Impris the deceds wearing apparel	*x*		
Item ready money bills bonds & other Securities	*CCC*		
Item in plate	*ij*	*x*	
Item three Cows	*x*		
Item Four horses	*xij*	*x*	
Item One hundred sheep	*xx*		
It Corn in ye barn & Mowes	*xxij*		
It Four swine hogs	*vj*	*x*	
In the parler			
It one table board & Seven joynt stools	*j*	*v*	
It one Cupboard one livery table & one table board		*xv*	
It six pewter dishes eight pewter plates two brass candlesticks, one warming pan One chafing dish one flaggon of pewter one pewter quart and one pint	*ij*	*x*	
In the Hall			
Item One old table board and			

[£ *s* *d*]
Frame two Settles One Cupboard and one Salt Mill *j*
It fifteen pewter dishes two pewter saucers two pewter porringers two Salts one tin chamber pott & bedpan *j* *x*
In the milke house
It 5 brass pots 18 brass pans four brass Caldrons one bell mettle skillett one brass Skillet and brass weights *x*
It one Jack two Spits two pothooks three pothangers two pair of bellows one toaster two gridirons one frying pan *j* *x*
It 8 chairs *x*
In ye parlor chamber
It two beds pformed & one truckle bedsted *xij*
It one hanging press *iij*
It four chests and one coffer *j*
In ye hall chamber
It two beds pformed *xv*
It one table board and a livery table *x*
It one coffer three boxes & a desk *x* *vj*
It three turky cushions *iiij* *vj*
In ye brew house chamber
Item One bed pformed *ij*
It 6 Hogsheds and nine barrels *ij*[?]
In the little parlo[r]
It one table board *v*
It three Standers & a trendle x
It One Saw & one Cupboard *v*
It a brewing Furnace *ij*
It 3 brewing Fats two cheese presses seven cheese Fatts one cheese tub one washing tub three payls two butter tubs *xv* *vj*
It in Hay *iij*
It one dripping pan and a Saving iron *v*
It in horse tackling & seed butt *ij* *x*
It in wood & timber *x*
It in table Linnen *ij*
It in Lumber goods not seen neither before appraised *ij*
tot *Dij*^{li} *v*^{s}

[Signed] [E] Shaw [£40 item missing?]
[Exhibited 21 Feb 1699 (stilo Anglia) (1700?) by Edward Shaw for exec.

Will 4 Nov 1699, pr 21 Feb 1699/1700, names Robert Westron as exec: £60 to dr Thomasin Cadberry; £10 each to her ss James, Marke, John & Robert; £80 to dr Jane Townsend on surviving husband; £10 each to her chn Thomas & Mary; 1s to s-in-law Thomas Townsend; 1 gn. to s-in-law James Cadberry; *2 peices of broad gold* to dr-in-law Temperance Westron; £20 to grson Marke Westron; £10 to grson Henry Westron; 40s to Thomas Westron of Kentisbeare; 40s to Anastice Ellicott of Cullompton; 20s to servant Charity Channon; 20s to servant John Marke; 40s to Uffculme poor; 40s to Sheldon poor; residue to s Robert, exec; mark of Mark Westron; witn: John Grantland, James Heallings, Wm. Grantland, James Cadbury.
(PROB 11/ 454-33, pp 262-3)]

L16 ROBERT BATT senior, clothier 1702/3

PROB 4/22529: figures reasonably clear.
[Bur: "old Mr Robt Batt" 11 Mar 1702/3. Mar: "Robert Batt & Joane Lane, both of Uffculm" 3 Jan 1699/1700. Rich clothier; hall, parlour, & buttery, all with chambers, back court, wood house; household goods, bills, & bonds; £696.]

A true and perfect Inventary of all and sngular the goods chattels and credetts of Robert Batt the elder late of Uffculme in [the] County of Devon decd taken valued and appraised on the 25th day of Feby the year of our Lord 1702 by Thomas Drew, John Caddy and ---da/Sa--morly----as followeth viz.
[£ *s* *d*]
Inpris It[m h]is wearring Apparrel valued at *ix*
In the parlor
Item bords chairs joint stools and other small things valued at *iij* *ij*

[	£	s	d]
In the Hall			
Item a board and settle and brasse and pewter and Clock valued att	*x*		
In the Buttery			
Item a hutch and malt and tubbs and barrells valued at	*v*	*vj*	*vj*
In the Buttery Chamber			
Item three beds and three bedsteads and a presse and a Chest and coffer and Boxes	*v*	*x*	*vj*
In the Hall Chamber			
Item two beds and bedsteads and a board and barrells valued att	*v*	*iv*	*vj*
In the Parlor Chamber			
Item three bedsteads and 3 beds a chair and trunks valued att	*v*	*x*	
In the Kitchen			
Item a brewing Furniss and tubs and malt in the flower valued att	*ij*	*xvj*	*vj*
In the back Court and wood house			
Itm wood and Furse valued att	*x*	*xv*	
All things in sight and out of sight not yet appraised being forgotten and valued att		*iij*	*iv*[?]
Sume hitherto	*lvij*	*xj*	*iv*
		[3s too much?]	
Item money in pockett and bills and bonds and one life on the [moite] part of an estate and money otherwise owing to the said deceased valued	*DCxxxix*[?]	*xv*	*vj*
		[no final total given]	

[Signed] Mar.Sayer

[Exhibited 27 Mar 170[?] by Mark Sayer for exec.

Will 15 Jul 1701, no probate details: to be buried *in the middle Alley of the parish church under the tombe of my first wife*; £60, best feather bed & brass pan to wife Joan; £40 to dr Sarah, wife of John Dowdney; £40 to dr Mary wife of Thomas Thomas; 1s to dr-in-law Patience Batt; *my instrument of music, commonly called virginalls* to grdr Dorothy, dr of James Batt; 5s each to servants William Dunnett, John Woodberry & Symon Hunt[?]; residue to s Robert Butt of Burrington [?]; made mark; witn: John Grantland, Nicholas Pringe (mark), ---- Shepherd. (PROB 11/ 22529)]

L17 MARY COOMBE spinster 1762

XL5544 PROB 31/470/737: very clear. [Spinster; clothing, chest, gold ring, & books only; intriguing details of dealings with the Walrond family & larger sums mentioned, not included in total; c £1 only?]

Inventory bro[t] in by Com~ with Clause 15 Nov 1762.

A true and perfect Inventory of all and singular the Goods Chattles and Credits of Mary Coombe late of Uffculme in the County of Devon Spinster deceased which since her death have come to the hands possession or knowledge of Agnes Frost (wife of John Frost) one of the Executrixes named in the Last Will and Testament of the said Deceased follows (to wit)

The following Goods were taken Valued and appraised by Robert Ellicott and John Frost (the younger) appraisers the fifth day of November one thousand Seven Hundred and Sixtytwo -

	£	s	d
One Coat and Jacket Converted into Pettycoat	0	5	0
One apron	0	1	6
One Gold Ring	0	5	0
One Deal Box	0	1	6
One little Trunk	0	1	0
Appraised by us	0	14	0

Rob[t] Ellicott of Cullompton Sergemaker

John Frost Junr of Uffculme Woolcomber

Also this Exhibitant declares that since the death of thesaid Deceased She has possessed herself over and besides the Cloaths and things herein before mentioned of one pair of stays two aprons two Pocket Handkerchiefs one Silk Hendkerchief and one Pettycoat other part of the Cloaths of the said deceased which have been since worn out and this Exhibitant believes the value of them to amount to the Sum of One pound Eight Shillings and Sixpence and not more

Also this Exhibitant declares that She has now in her Custody one Promisory Note of hand dated sometime in the year of our Lord one thousand Seven hundred and forty three Given to the said deceased by Courtnay Walrond Esquire also deceased late Husband of Elizabeth Walrond widow the other Executrix in the said Will named for the Sum of Six pounds and ten Shillings

Also this Exhibitant declares that she does in her Conscience verily believe thatall and Singular the Goods Chattles and Credits of the s^d deceased save as aforesaid have Since her death come to the hands and possession of the said Elizabeth Walrond and are now in her Custody possession or power or by her disposed of as she also verily believes

Lastly this Exhibitant believes that no further or other Goods Chattles or Credits of the said deceased have or hath at any time Since the said deceaseds Death come to this Exhibitants hands possession or knowledge

Agnes Frost [signed]

On the fifth day of November 1762 the said Agnes Frost was Sworn to the truth of the above Inventory before me

Robert Wight a Commissioner

Present Tho: Furlong Notary Publick

A true and perfect Inventory of All & Singular the goods Chattles Rights Creditts & Effects of Mary Coombe late of Bradfield in the parish of Uffculme in the County of Devon Spinster decêd, wch Since her Death have come to the hands posŝion & knowledge of Elizabeth Walrond wid^o one of the Executrixes named in the last Will and Testament of the said decêd, and are as follows (to Witt).

One old slan [stand? flan?]	0	1	0
One old Cookery Book	0	0	9
One other Book part of Tom Browns Works	0	2	0
One other Book of Jests	0	2	0

The s^d Elizabeth Walrond the Exhibitant Sets worth [*sic* - forth?] that some time after the Death of the s^d Mary Coombe decêd She together wth Agnes Frost wife of John Frost the other Executrix in ye s^d will named examined into what Effects the s^d decêd had left at her Death when they found in her Trunk or Boxes in money to the amount of One hundred pounds & no more as she beleives but what particular peices it consisted of she cannot at this distance of time recollect, but beleives there was in ye s^d money wch was then found One five Moidore piece, One old Broad piece of ab^t twenty five Shillings Value and one Moidore, and no other particular or uncommon piece of money amongst it as she beleives - She further Sets forth that there were three Gold Rings left at the decêds Death and no more as she beleives - One a Stone Ring wch ye s^d Agnes Frost took into her Custody, One other Ring belonging to Courtenay Walrond Esqr now decêd and came to him upon the Death of his Uncle Edm^d Walrond - the other Ring being a plain one as this Exhibitant beleives came into the hands of Agnes Frost - She further sets forth all the decêds Cloaks and Wearing Apparell left at her death were as she beleives partly given away among the Serv^ts then at Bradfield and Several other persons by the s^d Agnes Frost wth the consent & Approbacõn of the s^d Exhibitant and the remainder was kept by the s^d Agnes Frost as she beleives - She further Sets forth that ye s^d Courtenay Walrond decêd was indebted to ye s^d Mary Coombe decêd by his Note for Six pounds and no more as she beleives wch Note the s^d Agnes Frost hath Shown to the s^d Exhibitant and she beleives it to be now in her Custody - That upon inspecting the Boxes and Trunk of the s^d Mary Coombe decêd wth the s^d

Agnes Frost they found five promisory Notes from Stephen Saunders of Bradninch in the s^{d} County of Devon Soap Boiler to the s^{d} Mary Coombe decêd for the Several Sums and of the Several Dates following (to Witt) One for Fifteen pounds wth Interest dated April 3^{d} 1739 - The Second for Ten pounds dated 19th June 1740 - The Third for Seven pounds dated 16th December 1740 - The Fourth for Eight pounds & Eight Shillings dated the 8th May 1743 - The Fifth for Twenty pounds wth Interest dated Seventh of April 1744, All wch Several Notes were Satisfyed and paid by the s^{d} Stephen Saunders or by his Order to the s^{d} Mary Coombe in her lifetime as the s^{d} Exhibitant verily beleives, she haveing heard the s^{d} Mary Coombe to Say in her lifetime that the afores^{d} Notes were all Satisfyed & paid - The s^{d} Exhibitant further Sets forth that she never went to or examined into any Trunks or Boxes of the s^{d} Decêds after her Death without the s^{d} Agnes Frost being present wth her, and that sometime after the Death of the s^{d} Mary Coombe, she did by the Interposition and express order of the afores^{d} Courtenay Walrond her late husband decêd, and in Compulsive manner, insisted that she sh^{d} deliver up the Keys of the Trunks & Boxes with all the Effects of the s^{d} Mary Coombe decêd to the s^{d} Agnes Frost, wch for particular reasons best known to her self she Complyed therewth and delivered the Keys and all the Effects of the s^{d} Mary Coombe decêd to the said Agnes Frost except as afores^{d} , and w^{t} is now become of ye same, she knows not, but beleives they are in the Custody of the s^{d} Agnes Frost, or applyed to her use - The s^{d} Exhibitant further declares that no other goods Chattles Creditts of Effects of the s^{d} Mary Coombe decêd other than those Comprized in the foregoing Inventory have Since her Death come to her hands posšion or knowledge./Eliz: Walrond [signed]

11th day of October 1762 the s^{d} Elizth Walrond was Sworn to the truth of the s^{d} Inventory Before me

Ja^{s} Wilkins a Commissioner

In the Presence of

Tho: Furlong Notary Publick

ABSTRACTS OF WILLS & LETTERS OF ADMINSTRATION WITHOUT SURVIVING INVENTORIES

Salisbury Jurisdiction.

The documents abstracted here are all deposited at the Wiltshire Record Office at Trowbridge. As with the inventories, they were either in the list of the Prebendary of Uffculme (PU) or of the Dean of Salisbury (DS), though a few copies occur in both groups. Taken together with the inventories, these summaries virtually cover all the wills and letters of administration held at Trowbridge up to 1800, though strays can always turn up mixed with other papers, or from private collections. Some from the Dean's list for the early 19th century are also included.

The corresponding abstracts of the PCC wills without inventories (up to 1700) are printed in the companion volume, *Uffculme: a Peculiar Parish*, where their reference numbers are preceded by the letters LW, for London Will.

In the admons, where the description of the deceased as *intestate* and *of Uffculme* is to be understood unless otherwise stated, the Latin paragraphs distinguish between "yeoman", which is not Latinised, and "agricola", which is therefore assumed here to denote "husbandman". Occasionally the same man in described as a yeoman or a husbandman in different documents. The word "farmer" also begins to appear in the wills and admons in 1726.

Editorial policy and abbreviations are explained on pp xlv-xlvi.

W1 JOHN DOWDNYE the elder of Foxhill 1545 (PU)

[Bur: "John Dowdney of Foxhill" 22 May 1545.]

Will 12 May 1541 of John Dowdnye the elder of Foxhill, pr 25 Jun 1545 before Mr John Toser, prebendary: residue to wife Margery, exec; 6s 8d to the Brotherhood of Uffculme; £6 13s 4d ea to 5 unmarried chn named as John the younger, Elyn, Jne (Jo/ane?), Agnys, & Elyn (Glyn?); £10, including the value of a furnace, vat, & cupboard, to s John Dowdnye "the elder" (*sic*, of a former marriage?); 20d ea to ovsrs John Goodrych of Rull & John Olande; witn: John Toser, parson of Uffculme, James Burman, & John Calowe; inventory value £8 13s 4d.

W2 JOHN DOWDNYE husbandman 1545 (PU)

[Bur: "John Dowdney alš Genkins" 13 May 1545.]

Will 16 Apr 1545 of John Dowdnye, husbandman (of Smithincott in index), pr 25 Jun 1545 before Mr John Toser, prebendary: residue to wife Elizabeth, exec; 20d to Brotherhood of Uffculme; £1 for wax (candles?); items to Robert Dowdnye, bro, and John Chelcoytt; witn: William & John Woodroffe & Edmonde Gervys(?); inventory value £10 2s 11d.

W3 ALSE LONDON widow 1546 (PU)

[Bur: "Alice London" 29 Jan 1545/6.]

Will 29 Oct 1545 of Alse (Alys in index) London, widow, pr 6 Sep 1546 at Uffculme: residue to chn Robert & John Westbere, Elizabeth Helyer, Margarett Assenford, & Alson Helyer, execs; a gown(?) to the Brotherhood of Uffculme for prayers & 20d for rood light; specified furniture & clothing to above chn, to s-in-law Wm Assenford, & to grchn (John, Robt, & Richd Assenford, Agnes Westbere); ovsrs John Woodroffe & John Mandon; witn: Wm Woodroffe, curate, John Woodroffe, John Mandon, & Thomas Hughe.

W4 JOHN SKYNNER of Hurste 1546 (PU)

[Bur: "John Skinner" 10 May 1546.]

Will 8 May 1546 of John Skynner of Hurste(?), pr 6 Sep 1546 before John Toser, prebendary of Uffculme: residue to wife Gelion, exec; 20d ea for the rood light & the Brotherhood; furnace, 2 looms(?), brass pan, & bullock to s John; best gown to s Wm; mare to s-in-law Thomas Huff; witn: Wm Woodrofe, curate, John Atwood, John Woodrofe, & Thomas Coterell.

W5 EDMUND GERVYS 1546 (PU)

[Bur: "Edmund Jervice" 26 Aug 1546. Mar: "Edmund Jervise & Jone Marshall" 22 Nov 1545.]

Admon 6 Sep 1546 names widow Johan admin; granted by John Toser, prebendary.

W6 JOHN CAMPENY clothier 1546 (PU)

[Bur: "John Champeney" 1 Aug 1546.]

Will 2 Aug 1546 of John Campeny, clothier, pr 6 Sep 1546 before Mr John Toser, prebendary of Uffculme: residue to wife Jone, exec; 6s 8d to church; £20 ea at age 20 to 5 chn, Elzabeth, Jone, Ketheren, Agnes, & Marye; 20s ea to Jone Rolle & Elen Dowdnye; 3s 4d to curate William Woodroffe; 20s to Edmond Gervys, clerk; 5s ea to ovsrs, Mr John Toser, parson, & Mr John Syddename; witn: William Woodroffe, John Snyght, & William Dowdenaye.

W7 RICHARD MORELL 1547 (PU)

[Bur: "Richard Morrell" 22 May 1547.]

Will 16 May 1547 of Richard Morell , pr 31 May 1547 before Mr John Toser, prebendary: residue plus house at "Pylten" to bro John Morell, exec; 6s 8d to church; 40s to mother-in-law Elyzabeth Dowdnye; 3s 4d ea to Crystian Rugge, John Rugge, & a servant Alys; 6s 8d to Rev Thomas Dale to pray for him; £3 to William Manley of Sampford; 20s to Robert Dowdnye as ovsr; witn: Thomas Dale, curate, Robert Dyble, John Rugge, & Robert Dowdnye.

W8 JOHN MANDEN 1547 (PU)

[Bur: "John Manndon" 31 Aug 1547.]

Will 8 Jun 1547 of John Manden, pr 29 Sep 1547 before John Toser, prebendary: residue to the poor; 20d ea to the churches of Uffculme & Welland; 20s & household items to servant Alys Phellipps; £4 (in Umfrye Skinner's hands) & household items to nephew Thomas Mandan at age 21 or, if he should die, for prayers or, failing that, to John Bynford's & Alsy Losemory's chn; 20d ea to ovsrs (administrators here) John Bynford & John Buttyston; witn John Toser, parson of Uffculme, William Woodrofe, parson, & John Buttyston.

W9 ROBERT KARSWELL alš COLL 1547 (PU)

[Bur: "Robart Cole" 15 Oct 1547.]

Will 16 Sep 1547 of Robt Karswell alš Coll, pr - Apr 1549 (day blank) before John Toser, prebendary of Uffculme: residue to wife Katryn, exec; 20d to Brotherhood; 40s & best shears to s Thomas; sheep shared between 2 ss; 20(s ?) to dr Ane(?); (5th best?) pan to Jone Erle(?); ovsrs John & William Woodrofe; witn: Thomas Dale, curate, John Karswyll, & William Marshall.

W10 JOHN CARSWELL alš COLLE 1549 (PU)

[Bur: "John Carswill" 10 Apr 1548.]

Will 23 Mar 1548/9 of John Carswell alias Colle, pr 16 Apr 1549 before John Toser, prebendary of Uffculme: residue to wife Elizabeth, exec; furniture to s Robert; 8s to s John; 24s to s Thomas, from which 10s to dr Jo(h)an; witn: Thomas Dale, curate, Robert Dowdnye, Robert Myll, William Rede, & William Skynner.

W11 KATEN COLL alš CARSWELL 1549 (PU)

[Bur: "Katherine Carswell alš Cole" 3 Apr 1549.]
Will 18 Mar 1549 of Katen Coll alias Carswell, pr 16 Apr 1549 before John Toser, prebendary: residue to chn, John, Thomas, Elzabeth, & An[m?]e, execs, to whom also specified household items, clothes, & money; similar to Alys Eston the younger; Alys Eston the elder & John Serdle to share the money owed by bro-in-law Cuthbert; ovsrs bro John Woodrofe & bro-in-law William Reydd; witn: Thomas Dale, curate, Robert Dowdnye, John Pococke, & William Skynner.

W12 UMFRYE CROSSE 1549 (PU)

[Bur: "Humfry Crosse" 16 Sep 1549.]
Will 13 Sep 1549 of Umfrye Crosse, pr 2 Oct 1549 before John Toser, prebendary: residue conditionally to Margerett Gold & George Crosse, exec^{s}; 35 sheep given to Henry & Joan Skynner, godson Roland, dr Brydgytt Roche, Marye Serell, bro Edmund's chn, Roger & Jone, bro Robert's 8 chn, Umfrye Tawton, Jone Rygge, William Medylton, Edward Shale, John Dowdnye, John Rygge's 3 chn, Henry Tawton, Agnes Tawton; 4 cattle to Antonye Wotway's chn, Katey & John, & to Joan & Agnys Goodrygge; fleeces to Roger & Joan Crosse, Alys Rygge, & Joan Goodrygge; wheat mow to servant Alys; rye to Antonye Wotway; hay to John Goodrygge the elder; to an unnamed person a secret donation of 20s; ovsrs John Goodrygge of Rull & Antony Wotway; witn: John Toser, parson, John Goodrygge the elder, Antony Wotway, Alys Goodrygge, Margerett Gold.

W13 JOHN WOODROF the elder 1550 (PU)

[Bur: "John Woodroffe" 1 Apr 1550. Mar: "John Woodroffe & Mary Tilley, gentlewoman" 29 Oct 1542.]
Will 29 Mar 1550 of John Woodrof the elder, pr 12 Apr 1550 before John Toser, prebendary: residue to wife Marye, exec; 6s 8d for [church?] window glazing; £20 ea to 5 chn, 2 drs + James, Henry, & John, with provision for their custody & apprenticeship if wife remarries; 40s at age 20 to [servant?] boy John Prowe; 10 ewes to sister Dorothy Telye; 4d ea to godchn; 6s 8d ea to maidservants & 3s 4d ea to menservants; 40s to (friend?) Henry Norwood; 13s 4d to Marye Hill; ovsrs Mr James Telye Esq, John Toser, parson, & s Wm Woodrofe; witn: James Telye, John Toser, & Dorothy Telye.

W14 ROBERT MYLL of Craddock 1550 (PU)

[Bur: "Robart Mille" 29 Apr 1550.]
Will 5 Apr 1550 of Robert Myll of Cradock, pr 23 Jun 1550 before John Toser, prebendary: residue to wife, exec; occupation gear to s John & (son?) Richard; £5 ea to drs Alys & Gelion; £3 6s 8d ea to (sons?) Richard & William; 20 groats to 20 poor; witn: John Toser, Mr Leonard Kelwaye, John Coll, & John Myll the elder; inventory value £38 16s.

W15 ELZABETH MEFLYNGE widow 1551 (PU)

[Bur: "Elizabeth Meffelinge" 15 Sep 1550.]
Will 1 Sep 1550 of Elzabeth Meflynge, widow, pr 22 Jan 1550/1 before John Danger for John Toser, prebendary: residue to John Coyk, exec; 4 pewter dishes, girdle, pair of beds, & brooch to Elizabeth Holwyll; witn: John Segar, curate, Richard Myll, Thomas Davye, & John Skynner.

W16 JOHN HELMAN 1551 (PU)

[Bur: "John Helman" 4 Jan 1549/50.]
Will 15 Jan 1549/50 of John Helman, pr 22 Jan 1550/1 before John Danger for John Toser: all to wife Mawytt, exec; witn: John Segar, curate, John Marshall, & William Skynner.

W17 WYLMOTT SQUYRE widow 1551 (PU)

[Bur: "Wilmote Squyer" 9 Jul 1550.]
Will 28 Mar 1550 of Wylmott Squyre, widow, pr 22 Jan 1550/1 before John Danger for John Toser: residue to dr Jone, exec; 8d for glazing church windows; 1 sheep ea to John & Joan Crosse; 12d ea to godchn, John Cadberye, Harrye Gaydon, & Jone Hogge; a bushel of rye to Gelion Crosse; ovsrs John Sherlonde & Thomas Gaydon; witn: John Segar, curate, Thomas Gaydon & John Skynner(?).

W18 ELZABETH DOWDNYE widow 1551 (PU)

[Bur: "Elizabeth Dowdney widdow" 7 Jul 1551.]
Will 2 Jul 1551 of Elzabeth Dowdnye, widow [cf W2], pr 7 Dec 1551 before Nicholas Mason for John Toser: residue to k Thomsyn Barons, exec; petticoats to Jone Woodrofe, Elzabeth & Alys Reed, & Jone Lawerence; 12d ea to all godchn except those who are chn of Richard Crugge who get 3s 4d ea, like the chn of Robert Dowdney & of Hugh Hurford; utensils & coffers to John Morell, Richard Crugge of Ottery, John Woodrofe, Jone Hurford, Thomsyn Coyse, Richard Crost's wife, & to the chn of Hugh Barons, Richard Crost, Richard Crugge, & William Crugge; kerchiefs &c to sister, & to Jone Dowdney; cheese(?) to the poor; ovsrs Hugh Hurford, Richard Seruge of Ottery, & William Serugge (Crugge & Serugge are possibly the same name, but the initial letters are quite distinct in the manuscript); witn: John Toser, parson, John Woodrofe the elder, William Reed, & John Skynner.

W19 WILLIAM LEYMAN of Ashill 1551 (PU)

Will 29 Oct 1551 of William Leyman of Ashill, pr 7 Dec 1551 before Nicholas Mason for John Toser: residue to wife Margerett, exec; 13s 4d ea to chn, John, Robert, William, Umfrye, & Nycholas Leyman; a heiffer ea to s Nycholas & to Elzabeth Percye, who gets 20d a year until married from wife Margerett in lieu of the heiffer; to William(?) Eston a wether & 26s 8d if he completes his apprenticeship; 4d ea to godchn, to Agnys Baylye, & to Robert Layman's chn; witn: John Toser, John Done the elder, John Hogge, William Reed, & John Broyke.

W20 RICHARD PERHOWSSE 1551 (PU)

[Bur: "Richard Phurs(-)e", 5 Aug 1551 (at the height of the Stupgallant plague).]
Will -Aug 1551 of Richerd Perhowsse, young man, pr 7 Dec 1551 before Nicholas Mason: residue to Am[n?]e Dowdnye, exec; hat(?) to Jone Myll; witn: John Gregorye the elder, Wm Myll, Jone Myll, & Elyn Dowdnye.

W21 ROBERT DOWDNYE the elder 1552 (PU)

[Bur: "Robte Dowdney of Cradocke" 8 Mar 1551/2.]
Will 20 Feb 1551/2 of Robert Dowdnye the elder, pr 28 Jun 1552 before Giles Hilling: residue to wife Elyn, exec; to wife conditionally & to s Austen 15 sheep; to ss John & John (elder & younger) 45 sheep; 6s 8d to s Robert; 2 pairs of shears ea to ss Lauerence & John the elder; to dr Jone conditionally £6 13s 4d to be repaid in 5 years (at 4 nobles p.a.) by John Marten; folding table to s John the younger & cupboard to (son?) Thomas; furnace conditionally to ss Robert & John the elder; a lamb ea to Robert's chn; best gown to John the elder; witn: Christofer Hudson, curate, Thomas Prynge, & John Coll.

W22 JOHN HOWE 1552 (PU)

[Bur: "John Howe" 12 May 1552.]
Will 23 Jul 1551 of John Howe, pr 27 Jun 1552 before Giles Hilling for John Toser: residue to wife Jone & s Thomas Howe, exec^{s}; unspecified sums to poor; 6s 8d ea to drs Alys & Julyan Baker; 12d ea to chn of 2 drs;

further 13s 4d to Julyan & her husband Robert Baker, conditionally upon their making no more claim on estate, otherwise to s John Howe of London; witn: John Howe of London, gent, & Henry Howe, clerk.; marked with a cross by John Howe junior.

W23 WILLIAM SKYNNER the elder 1552 (PU)

[Bur: "William Skinner" (9-13) Mar 1551/2.]

Will 3 Dec 1550 of William Skynner the elder, pr 27 Jun 1552 before Giles Hilling for John Toser: residue to s Umfrye, exec; 6s 8d to poor; best gown & 2 sheep to s John; rest of sheep to Umfrye; witn: John Toser, John Segar, & Umfrye Skinner.

W24 JOHN BROYKE 1552 (PU)

[Bur: "John Browke" 28 Jan 1551/2.]

Will of John Broyke 20 Nov 1551, pr 27 Jun 1552 before Giles Hilling for John Toser: several items to remain with wife Alys, exec, until death or marriage of chn; pan to s John & successively to his bros; heiffer to [drs?] Alys & Julyan; 2 sheep ea & half the lambs to ss Robert, Jamys, John, & John [*sic*]; mare already sold through need to s John for 33s[?] 4d to remain with wife Alys for life; witn: Christofer Hudson, curate, John - [?], John Down[i?]e [=Dowdney?], & Wm Reed.

W25 WILLIAM MARSHALL the elder of Craddock 1553 (PU)

[Bur: "Williã Marshall" 18 Oct 1552.]

Will 11 Jul 1552 of William Marshall the elder of Craddock, pr 18 Apr 1553 before Nicholas Mason for John Toser: retention of most willed items for life & residue to wife Jone, exec; 6d to poor; crockery to 4 chn, Elyn, Jone the younger, Syble, & Nicholas, & a heiffer ea to all except Elyn, to whom £3 6s 8d; 4 marks ea to drs Jone & Syble(?) & brass pots to all 3 drs; a pan & a steer to s Nicholas; a ewe to Wilmotte(?); table to Jone Gervys; 4d ea to godchn; witn: John Toser, Parson, Thomas Prynge, & John Pococke. Inventory value £35 5s 2d.

W26 JOHN GOODRYGGE of Northcott 1553 (PU)

[Bur: "John Goodridge of Norcote" 31 Mar 1553.]

Will 31 Mar 1552 of John Goodrygge of Northcott, pr 18 Apr 1553 before Nicholas Mason for John Toser: residue to wife Kat[er]en, exec; to dr Jone utensils, cow, calf, & 15s in lieu of a sold cow; heiffer to dr Agnys; debts to Richard Baker 26s, Nycolas Baker 6s, John Mychell 10s, & George Welche 4s; s Robt owes "a Ryall of gold & a angelytt"; witn: Nycolas Baker & Alexander Beuse(?). Inventory value £11 5s 8d.

W27 JOHN WOOD 1553 (PU)

Will 15 Aug 1552 of John Wood, pr 18 Apr 1553 before Nicholas Mason for John Toser: residue to wife Mawytt, exec; lands & goods half ea to wife & s John; 4d ea to grchn & godchn & chn of Edward Wood; witn: Crystofer Hudson, curate, John Cheyl(?), & Edwarde Wood. Inventory value £19 3s 6d.

W28 ANNYS CHOWNE 1553 (PU)

Will 12 Aug 1553 of Annys (Agnes in probate) Chowne, pr 25 Oct 1553 before John Uly for John Toser: Robert (Pole?) exec (Robert Pole's minority apparently affected the probate & John Rowland may have been called upon); residue to bros & sisters; a steer to Phelippe Rowland; 4s to bro Gregorye Chown's 4 chn; clothing to Joane Phylpott & sister Joane Rowland; to Robert Pole a silver spoon & £5 if he reaches age 16, otherwise 26s 8d to Gregory Chown's 4 chn & the rest shared between bros & sisters; witn: Richard Mitt(??-)lynge John Myller, & Henrye Osmonde. Inventory value £6 11s 8d.

W29 RICHARD MARSHALL of Umbrooke 1553 (PU)

[Bur: "Rich~ Marshall of Umbroke" 23 Apr 1553.]

Will 20 Apr 1553 of Richard Marshall of Umbrook, pr 25 Oct 1553 before John Uly for John Toser: exec s John Marshall, to whom everything is left if he provides for his sister Joane; witn: (Rev?) John Rondele, Robert Baker, & Richard Kerswell. Inventory value £18.

W30 RICHARD CRUGGE of Smithincott 1553 (PU)

[Bur: "Richard Crudge of Smithencote" 16 May 1553.]

Will 5 May 1553 of Richard Crugge of Smithincott, pr 25 Oct 1553 before John Uly: residue to wife Christen & s John, exec[s]; (her own!) cow & calf conditionally to maid Elzabeth Freer; 3s 4d to poor; ovsrs Mr Thomas Beere, John Broy(ke?) of Five Fords, & John Goodrygge the elder of Rull; witn: John Toser, parson, John Barnarde the elder, & John Woodrofe of Smithincott. Inventory value £17 15s.

W31 WILLIAM TURNER alš PYTT 1563 (DS)

[Bur: "William Pitte alš Turñ" 28 Dec 1552.]

Admon 12 Jan 1562/3 names widow Agnes Turner alš Pytt as admin.

W32 JOHN MARSHALL 1563 (DS) & 1567 (PCC)

[Bur: "John Marshall of Norcote" 18 Oct 1563. Mar: "John Marshall & Alice Rudge" 26 Jun 1552.]

Admon 30 Oct 1563 names widow Alice Marshall as admin; but evidently referred to the PCC, where another admon was granted to widow Alice Marshall in London on 23 Aug 1567.

W33 AGNES CROSSE widow 1564 (DS)

[Bur: "Agnes Crosse widdow" 5 Mar 1563/4.]

Will 27 Feb 1563/4 of Agnes Crosse of Uffculme, widow, pr before John James, surr, 16 Mar 1563/4: residue to Nicholas Leyman & John Downey[*sic*], exec[s]; 6s 8d to church; 6s 8d to 20 households of the parish; 12d ea to godchn; 2 bushels of wheat to Alson Noriter; to Agnes Baylye & Elizabeth Holwill the £20 20d (Robert Goodridgg's debt) in the hands of John Goodridgg & Rychard Baker; to Agnes Baylye a pan, cow, gown, coffer, coste, vats, & a pair of beds, plus on her marriage the 6s 8d in the hands of Hûfray Leyman; great pan to Nicholas Leyman; 2 bushels of wheat to John Badcoke & 3 pewter dishes to his 3 chn; 6s 8d to Elyzabeth Persye; to sister Marge Leyman a girdle, a silver spoon, a yewne[ewe?], & contents of coffer; a pan ea to George Leyman & Elyzabeth Leyman.

W34 JOHN MYLL 1564 (DS)

[Bur: "John Mill" 14 Mar 1563/4. Mar: "John Mill & Jone Halse" 31 Aug 1550? (but cf 7).]

Will 9 March 1563/4 of John Myll of Uffculme, pr before John James 9 May 1564: residue to wife Jone, exec; 20d to church; "Goodlyford" tenement in Kentisbeare (indenture granted 18 March 1558 [1 Eliz 1] by John Fursse of Kentisbeare, gent) to wife Jone for life, (but John Herden to have first "his whole covenant") & after her to John & Humfry Myll jointly; to [son?] John Myll an anvil, bellowes, "sleye", harness, pincers, & vice to be given him at age 21 by bro Rychard Myll; bro Rychard to pay to wife John £7 for all the stuff of the shop & grinding stones; hose to bro Robert; fustian doublet to bro Will[m]; coat to Nicholas Halse; witn: vicar John Segar, John Norhamton, John Saunder, Hue Gauntlove, & John Colle.

W35 JOHN ORNGE 1564 (DS)

Will 28 Jun 1557 of John Ornge of Uffculme, pr 10 Aug 1564 before Will[m] Bradbrydge; residue to wife

Agnes, exec; 12d to church; £6 13s 4d ea to drs, Agnes & Marye at their marriage or age 21; 4d ea to godchn; ovsrs Mr John Champneyes, John Peperell, & John Woodrow; witn: vicar John Segar, Mr John Champneyes, John Peperell, & John Lawrence.

W36 JOHANNE HOWE widow 1564 (DS)

[Bur: "Jone Howe alš Tanner" 28 Mar 1562.]
Will 26 Mar 1562 of Johanne Howe of Uffculme, pr 28 Aug 1564 before Willm Bradbrydge: residue to s Thomas Howe, exec; to parish use 6s 8d; to church 3s 4d; clothes & sheets to drs Julyañ Baker & Alyce Walshe, & to dr-in-law Anstyce Howe, wife of s Thomas; clothes, beds, &c to Amie Howe (dr of s John Howe), Marye Howe (dr of s Thomas Howe), Elizabeth & Elynor Walshe, Jone & Elizabeth Baker, Jone Stephens, Payschall Broke, & Jone, wife of Robert Peperell; 20s to give 4d ea to godchn, 8d ea to any grchn not already mentioned, & the rest to the poor; 40s to Robert Walshe for service done; heifer calf to John Walshe; 3s 4d to ovsr Robt Baker; witn: vicar John Segar, John Howe of London, gent, & Robt Baker.

W37 RICHARD ROCHE 1564 (DS)

[Bur: "Richard Roache" 8 Nov 1563.]
Will 2 Nov 1563 of Richard Roche of Uffculme, pr 28 Aug 1564 before Willm Bradbrydge: residue to wife Jone, exec; debts of 20s to Mr Champenys of Smithincott, 5s 8d to Alice Litlejohn of Cullompton, & 3s 4d to John Bagstar; to eldest s Harry cupboard, coat, hose, & cupboard & bedlinen after wife's death; to second s Wylliam 10s [20s?] at age 21; to youngest s John 26s 8d at age 21; to eldest dr Elizabeth 20s on marriage; to dr Agnes on marriage a 3-gallon pan, platter, & saucer; 4d ea to godchn; 4d ea to ovsrs Thomas Smythe & Hughe Grantland, who also witn.

W38 NICHOLAS MARSHALL 1567 (DS)

Admon 19 Jan 1566/7 names sisters Joan & Sibyll as admin^s^.

W39 HUMFREY SKYNNER 1567 (DS)

[Bur: "Humfry Skinner" 13 Dec 1566. Mar. "Humfrey Skinner & Wilmote Ballam" 6 Feb 1559.]
Will 29 Nov 1566 of Humfrey Skynner of Uffculme, pr 20 Jan 1566/7 before John James: residue to Wylmott, exec; 12d to church; to dr Katheryn 3 silver spoons, 4 pans "of the middle sort", 1 candlestick, & 4 pewter dishes; to dr M^r^gery 3 silver spoons, 4 pans, 1 candlestick, & 4 pewter dishes; witn: vicar John Segar, Wm Woodrow, & Peter Facy.

W40 THOMAS PRINGE 1567 (DS)

[Bur: "Thomas Pringe" 2 Apr 1566.]
Will 29 Mar 1565 of Thomas Pringe of Uffculme, pr before John James 2 Jun 1567: residue to dr Julyañ & ss Richarde & Thomas, exec^s^; table & cow to s John; ewe[?] to Jone Payne; witn: vicar John Segar, Anstece Downey, Richard Pringe, & Thomas Pringe.

W41 RICHARD COLE 1567 (DS)

[Bur: "Richard Cole" 6 Mar 1566/7.]
Will 2 Mar ["May" in Dean's copy] 1567 of Richard Cole of Uffculme, pr before John James 2 Jun 1567: residue to Elizabeth Please, exec; the "backs", & his things in the shop, between the elder & younger John Cole, also a trendle to John the elder & a bed to John the younger; to dr Jone Pringe a standard; a heifer between Anstie, dr of John Cole, & Elizabeth, dr of Richard Please; best coat to Thomas Facye; 2d to Jone Cole, dr of William; ovsrs John Hogg & John Baker: witn: vicar John Segar, William Reade, & the ovsrs.

W42 JOHN WHITE 1567 (DS)

Will 28 Feb 1566/7 of John White of Uffculme, pr before John James 2 Jun 1567: residue to s Richard White, exec; to Jone Knolman a 6-gallon pan & 2 dishes; to Alice Hayley 26s in wages; 5s to Bridgett Dollyñ; to the "p̲[er/ro]cters of tithing urne"[?] 7s; a dish ea to ss Thomas & John White; witn: vicar John Segar, John Norhampton, Richard Mill, & John Pringe.

W43 NYCHOLAS GOODRIDGE 1567 (DS)

[Bur: "Nicholas Goodridge" 1 Mar 1564/5.]
Will 3 Feb 1564/5 of Nycholas Goodridge of Uffculme, pr before John James 3 Jun 1567: residue to bro Edward Goodridge, exec; contents of coffer to sister Agnes Goodridge; 20s ea to bros John & Willm & to godson Willm Facy, who also has a sheep; a sheep ea to sister Jone Facy & to all her chn, & to goddr Jone Myddletoñ & to James Enoy[?]; to Agnes Baylye £4 at her marriage; 20s to k Agnes Goodridge; 6s 8d to poor; witn: vicar John Segar, John Goodridge, & John Rugge.

W44 JOHN PERCYE 1567 (DS)

[Bur: "John Persy" 22 Mar 1565/6. His s John was buried the same day.]
Will 18 Mar 1565/6 of John P̲cye of Uffculme, pr before John James 3 Jun 1567: residue to wife Jone, exec; 12d to poor; 40s & 4 ewes to s John; 12d to Richard Broke's household; coat to Richard Percye; 4d ea to John Ayshelford, John Clotham, & John Will^{m}s; 1 ewe to godson Peter Percye; witn: John Stanbacke & Richard Percye.

W45 ALICE GOODRIDGE widow 1567(DS)

[Bur: "Alice Goodridge widdow" 2 Sep 1567.]
Will 31 Aug 1567 of Alice Goodridge of Uffculme, pr before John James 24 Nov 1567, when described as widow: residue to s John, exec; 20d to church; 20d to poor; £6 13s 4d to dr Agnes Goodridge; 26s 8d ea to ss Wm & Edward; a sheep ea to Peter Facy's chn; 4d ea to her [god?]chn; 20s ea to Agnes Goodridge & Thomasyne Knyght; 12d to Willm Myddletoñ; witn: vicar John Segar, John Rugge, & Robert Rugge. Debts owed to her: £4 13s 4d by Robert Leyman & 3s 4d by M^{r}gery Dowdney. Debts owed by her from husband's bequests: £3 6s 8d to dr Agnes, & 26s 8d ea to ss Wm & Edward.

W46 MARGARETT LEYMAN widow 1568 (DS) & 1570 (PCC)

[Bur: "Margeret Leaman widdow" 23 Jun 1567.]
Will 28 May 1567 of Margarett Leyman of Uffculme, widow, pr 12 Jan 1567/8 before John James: residue to ss Hû[m]fry & Nicholas Leyman, exec^{s}; 12d to church; 12d to poor; "Syldoñ Grange" in parish of Syldoñ [Sheldon?], & remainder of term in "Rocke" in Uffculme, to s Nicholas; to s John a mare colt, sack of rye, & 2 bushels of oats; to s Willm a pair of looms, 2 pans, & a cow; £6 13s 4d, a pewter dish, & a saucer to servant Isabell Percy; 4d ea to godchn; 1 bushel of rye to John Hogg & Margaret his wife; a store to John, s of Robert Leyman, & a sheep ea to the rest of Robert's chn; a sheep ea to William Leyman's chn, & to Agnes Reade & Margaret Baker; 12d ea to John Williams, Willm Sorell, & Willm Norwood; witn: vicar John Segar, Robert Leyman, & Willm Reade.
A copy at the PRO shows that the will was referred to the PCC where a further probate was obtained for the same execs in London 28 Nov 1570.

W47 JOHN HASELDEN 1570 (DS)

Will of John Haseldeñ [undated & with *no mention of Uffculme* in deposited copy], pr before John James 13 Sep 1570: residue to wife Margaret, exec; coats, pots, plates, & chests to ss Stephen & Willm; feather bed, cauldron, plate, pot, & chest to dr Jone;

An example of a will copy in a 16th century register from which some abstracts were made: Nycholas Goodridge 1567 [W43]

sackcloth doublet to John Warreñ; James the horseman owes 12d; witn: John Westover, Willm Whiterowe, Willm Jervys, & Gyles Welshe.

W48 JOHN HALSE 1570 (DS)

[Bur: "John Halse" 21 Aug 1570.]
Will 17 Dec 1568 of John Halse of Uffculme, pr 14 Sep 1570: residue to s Nicholas Halse, exec; to Robert Halse, s of s Nicholas, coffer, crock, broche, & silver spoon after death of Nicholas; to Jone Halse, dr of Nicholas, 5 pots & 4 plates of pewter, & cupboard after death of Nicholas; witn: Richd Halse, Thomas Cotterell, & John Sander.

W49 JOHN CROSSE 1570 (DS)

[Bur: "John Crosse" 3 Dec 1569. Mar: "John Crosse & Jone Brooke alš Butson" 18 Aug 1550.]
Will 30 Nov 1569 of John Crosse of Uffculme, pr before John James 14 Sep 1570: residue to wife Jone, exec; after death of wife, house contents shared between drs Christian & Alson, who also ea have a heifer & 3 ewes; ovsr bro Nicholas Crosse; witn: Richard Walshe, Thomas Cotterell, John Davy, John Sander.

W50 THOMAS DAVY 1570 (DS)

[Bur: "Thomas Davy" 16 Apr 1570.]
Will 14 Apr 1570 of Thomas Davy of Uffculme, pr before John James 14 Sep 1570: residue to eldest s John, exec; to s Robert (conditionally on compliance with the will) 10s, tin platter, potager, & candlestick; 4d ea to Robert Davy's chn; pans to dr-in-law Ede & niece Mary; 4d ea to godchn & to Jone Persye's chn; 6s 8d ea to Humfry, William, John, & Dorathe, chn of s John; witn: Humfry Skynner & Hughe Gantloo.

W51 JOHN TOSER 1570 (DS)

[Bur: "John Toser the sonne of William Toser" 16 Jun 1570.]
Will 1570 of John Toser of Uffculme, pr 14 Sep 1570 before John James: residue to father William Toser, exec; £6 13s 4d ea to bros William & Robert Toser, & to bro-in-law Thomas Membrye; 40s to sister Mary; witn: Roger Stone, Edmunde Crosse, Richard London, Agnes Lane, Agnes Farland, & Jone Franke.

W52 JOHN PERSSE 1570 (DS)

[Bur: "John Pearse" 17 Aug 1570.]
Will 14 Jun 1570 of John Persse of Uffculme, pr before John James 14 Sep 1570: residue to wife Agnes & dr Christian, exec^{s}; to s John half the standing rye; 12d to church; 1 bushel of wheat to goddr Jone Facy; witn: vicar John Segar, Thomas Cotterell, & John Davye.

W53 ALSON BROKE widow 1570 (DS)

[Bur: "Alice Browke widdow" 17 Sep 1570.]
Will 4 Jul 1562 of Alsoñ Broke, widow of Uffculme, pr 16 Oct 1570 at Salisbury before John James: residue & a bed ea to Jone Webber, Marye Saunder, & Margery Walker, exec^{ces}; cow to godson John Saunder; furnace, heifer, & 2 sheep to s Humfrey; 40s to Christian Saunder; 4d ea to godchn; 6s 8d to the poor; 1 sheep ea to John Saunder's chn, to Richard Broke s of Thomas Broke, & to Margarett & Edithe drs of John Webber; vat to s Thomas; ovsrs John Segar, vicar, John Saunder, & Humfrey Skynner.

W54 WILLIAM TOSER the younger 1571 (DS)

[Bur: "William Toser" 24 Feb 1570/1. Mar: "William Toser & Elizabeth London" 15 Sep 1566.]
Will 21 Feb 1570/1 of William Toser the younger of Uffculme, pr 22 May 1571 before John James: residue to wife Elizabeth, exec; £3 6s 8d ea to ss Thomas & Harrye; he owed 10s 8d to widow Jone Owde & 30s to Thomas Memberye, & was owed 22s 8d by John Cadburye, 9s 8d by Willm Hoge, 8s by father Willm Toser (who also

owes s Harrye 6s 8d & s Thomas 2s 6d of their godfather's bequest), & £3 10s by mother-in-law; witn: vicar John Segar & John Lundon.

W55 DEANES RIGGE widow 1572 (DS)

[Bur: "Dewnes Rudge widdow" 8 Oct 1572.]
Will 5 Oct 1572 of Deanes Rigge of Uffculme, widow, pr 25 Oct 1572 before John James: residue to s Thomas Rigge, exec; 12d to poor; to s Roberte Rigge 5 silver spoons, vat, 2 pans, 8 pewter dishes, & 40 "stetches" of wheat; to s John Rigge 1 yearling, heifer; to dr Alson Marshall mantle, side-saddle, & a pan; to dr Johan Facy petticoat & best cassock; to Alson & Mary Rigge kerchiefs, & neckerchief; to Johan Facye a fleece; to grchn a sheep each; to godchn 4d each; ovsrs vicar John Segar & John Goodrydge; witn: ovsrs & Robert Rigge.

W56 JOHN WHITE 1573 (DS)

[Bur: "John Whyet" 26 Apr 1572.]
Will 18 Apr 1572 of John White of Uffculme, pr 13 Jan 1572/3: residue to "my master" John Norhampton, exec; 20s, best hose, jerkin, & hat to bro [*sic*] John White; 6s 8d, dish, & saucer to bro Robert White; 6s 8d ea to bro Willm White & sister Jone Pike; 20s, coffer, & chest to Elizabeth Pulman; 20s to Mary Norhampton; 12d ea to Jone Norwood & Jane Golde; hose & canvas shirt to John Horne; witn: Richarde Baker & John Norhampton.

W57 ELIZABETH MYLL widow 1573 (DS)

[Bur: "Elizabeth Mill widdow" 28 Jun 1573.]
Will 24 Jun 1573 of Elizabeth Myll of Uffculme, widow of Robert Myll, pr at Uffculme 10 Sep 1573: residue to s Willm Myll, exec; 20d to poor; to dr Alice Skynner 1 close of wheat called *barly croft*, 1 close of oats called *the furse close*, 1 heifer (at s Wm Myll's at Kentisbeare), bed & bedclothes, pan, crock, plates, saucer, barrel & a tub for dough; clothes & linen shared by drs Alica Skynner & Julian Salter; to s Robert Myll 1 close of oats called *the foote land*, pan, barrel, tub to make dough, planks, & wooden vessels in the "bakehouse"; to dr Julian Salter a barrel & a tub to make dough; to servant Mary Gregory 6s 8d, petticoat, & bed in 4th chamber; 1 ewe ea to grchn; 4d ea to godchn; wring to Robert, s of s Richard Myll; brewing furnace (if consistent with late husband's will) to Henry, s of s Robert Myll; witn: Thomas Wyne, Robert Borowe, Mary Gregory, & Dalye.

W58 ALSON NORHAMPTON 1573 (DS)

[Bur: "Alice Northampton the dr of William Northampton" 13 Aug 1570; her sister Helen was buried 24 Aug.]
Will 10 Aug 1570 of Alson Norhampton of Uffculme, pr 11 Sep 1573 before John James: residue to bro John Norhampton, exec; felt hat to mother; to bro John the 4s owed her by Robert Peperell; to bros John & Willm & sister Ellyn Norhampton £1 ea of the £3 owed her by Willm Myll of Kynnesbury [Kentisbeare]; witn: Richard Rugg & Alexander Hardman.

W59 WILLIAM RAWLYNS 1573 (DS)

[Bur: "William Rawlings" 24 Oct 1571.]
Admon 11 Sep 1573 names s William Rawlyns as admin.

W60 WILLIAM TAUNTON 1573 (DS)

[Bur: "William Tawton" 29 Mar 1573.]
Admon 11 Sep 1573 names relict Joan as admin.

W61 JOHN DOWDENEY 1573 (DS)

[Bur: "John Dowdney" 30 Mar 1573. Mar: "John Dowdney & Alice Merye" 25 Sep 1553.]
Admon 11 Sep 1573 names relict Alice as admin.

The admon for the goods of John Stabacke 1575 [W63]

W62 HUGHE GRANTLAND 1574 (DS)

[Bur: "Hugh Grantland" 20 Jan 1573/4. Mar: "Hugh Grantland & Alice Bourrowe" 13 Oct 1560.]

Will, 30 Nov 1573, of Hughe Grantland of Uffculme, pr before John James 22 Feb 1573/4: residue to wife Alice, exec; 12d to poor & to church; 4d ea to godchn; £18 each, tables, pots, pans, crocks, &c to drs Mary & Thomasyñ (& possibly an unborn ch) at age 22 or marriage, the £18 to be augmented to £26 6s 8d if wife remarries; ovsrs ["rulers"] bro John Grantlande & John Saunders; witn: vicar John Segar, Humfrey Skynner, Edward Pawleñ, & Willm Grantlande.

W63 JOHN STABACKE 1575 (DS)

[Bur: "John Stabacke" 29 Jan 1574/5.]

Admon 19 Mar 1575 [Eliz 18] names widow Fortune Stabacke & also Humfry Woodroff of Uffculme, clothier, & binds Fortune Stabacke to bring up the s William Stabacke properly & to pay him the lagacies from his father at 21.

W64 JOHANE MYDDLETON widow 1576 (DS)

[Bur: "Jone Middledon" 14 Apr 1576.]

Admon 16 May 1576 names s Robert Myddleton , husbandman, as admin & also John Rawlyns, yeoman, & Richard Pearcye, weaver, all of Uffculme.

W65 WILLIAM & JOHANE NORMAN 1578 (DS)

[Bur: "William Norman of Norcote" 3 Mar 1576/7, "Jane Norman widdow" 26 Mar 1577.]

Admon of Willm & Johê Norman of Burcott in Uffculme, 26 Mar [?*M^r cij*] 1577[8?] names s Paul Norman as admin.

W66 ARTHUR CANWORTHE 1589 (DS) &1590 (PCC)

Admon (Salisbury) 24 Jun 1589 names bro John Canworthe as admin during minority of Chr[ist]ofer Canworthe, s of dec^d; but the will was evidently referred to the PCC and pr there the following Feb.]

PCC Will of Arthur Canwarthie of Uffculme, 4 Jun 1589: all to wife while unmarried, otherwise £5 for my ch to John Gregory, who may keep half the increase for his own use; if wife dies, John Gregory to bring up oh; if ch dies, £10 to bro Philip & residue to John Gregory exec; witn: Philip Canworthie, John Gregory & Wm Sankie. Probate obtained for John Gregory exec, London 7 Feb 1589[/90].

W67 ELIZABETH NORMAN alš PEYRS 1600 (DS)

[Mar: "John Pearse & Elizabeth Norman" 21 Nov 1575.]

Admon 23 Jul 1600 names bro Paul Norman & also husband[?] John Peyrs & makes reference to the minority, possibly of the chn William (the elder & younger?), Peter, & also Nathaniel, Humfrey, & John Norman. [Unusual complications not easy to read.]

W68 ROBERT RIDGE husbandman of Blewits 1619 (DS)

Will 6 Jul 1619 of Robt Ridge of Rilewith, Uffculme, husbandman, pr 25 Aug 1619 before Ven John Gordon (inventory value £4 16s 8d); residue to mother Alice Ridge, exec; apparel & a nag to bro Richard; 11s to sister Joane Collee; ovsrs Thomas Middleton & Moyses Purchase, who also mark as witn.

W69 WILLIAM HURLEY 1619 (DS)

Admon 25 Aug 1619 for William Hurley of Uffculme names father Thomas Hurley as admin & quotes inventory value as £15 6s 8d.

W70 CHARITY DOWDNEY widow 1625 (DS)

[Bur: "Charitie Dowdny widdow" - Feb 1624/5.]

Admon 23 Feb 1624/5 names s Henry Dowdney as admin (who marks) & also Ambrose Purnett (who signs); signed by James Hill, not[y] pub.

W71 JOHN CADBURY 1625 (PU)

[Bur: "John Cadbery" 13 Feb 1624/5.]
Admon 29 Feb 1624/5 names s Matthew Cadbury of Uffculme, yeoman, as admin and also John Cheeke, yeoman; both sign.

W72 MARGARET MINIFY spinster 1630 (PU)

Admon 8 Jun 1630 names Humfrey Clash of Bradninch, yeoman, as admin, who signs as Humfry Clashe.

W73 ROBERT MARSHALL yeoman 1630 (DS)

[Bur: "Robert Marshall" 26 Sep 1630. Mar: "Robert Marshall & Anne Pringe widowe" 5 Jul 1627.]
Will 13 Sep 1630 of Robert Marshall of Umbrocke, yeoman, pr at Salisbury before Edmund Mason, Dean, 30 Sep 1630: residue to James Butson, exec; 10s to parish church & 30s to poor; £30 to wife Anne plus "household stuff she brought with her"; 16s 8d ea to 2 drs of wife; suit, cloak, & 20s to bro John Marshall; 5s to bro's dr Joane Marshall & 3s 4d ea to rest of his chn; 20 sheep & mare colt to Joane Marshall's s William Marshall; bed & bedclothes to goddr Margarett Marshall; 6d ea to Joane Marshall's chn John & Robert Marshall; 6d ea to godchn; crock to Robert s of Christopher Knolman; 3s 4d ea to ovsrs Humfry Butson & Robert Bishopp; marked by Robert Marshall; witn: Humfry Butson, Robert Bishopp (marked), & John Mills.

W74 JOHN CHEEKE bachelor 1635 (DS)

[Bur: "John Cheeke" 6 Sep 1635.]
Will 12 Jul 1633 of John Cheeke of Cradocke, bachelor, pr at Uffculme before John Gandy, 18 Sep 1635: residue to bro-in-law Simon Merson, exec; 40s to sister Susanna; 5s ea to godsons Richard Gill & Henry Poockocke; 10s to goddr Johan Androw; 12d ea to chn of John Mills & Edward Androw; 12d ea to youngest dr of John Cheeke the elder & to the chn of John Cheeke the younger; 10s to preacher for sermon at burial; 15s to be "bestowed in my shrode & Coffen"; 3s to 2 bellringers; 4s to 8 coffin-bearers; 4s to women layers-out; 2s to woman servant; 5s to dr of uncle George Cheeke; £4 invested for the poor at Easter; box & blankets to servant Ame Brooke; witn: John Beare & William Reed (marked).

W75 JOANE WILLIAMS 1642 (PU)

[Bur: "Johane Williams widdow" 5 Apr 1642.]
Nuncupative Will 2 Feb 1641/2 of Joane Williams of Uffculme, pr before Mr Steare 18 Apr 1642: all to dr-in-law Tomson Williams, exec; marked by Thomson Boweman & Elizabeth Pringe.

W76 MATTHEW WOODRUFFE, husbandman 1646 (PU)

Admon 28 Nov 1646 names s Humfrey Woodruffe, weaver, of Uffculme as administrator and also Baptist Baselie, yeoman; signed by Baptist Baselie in presence of Fran. Roberts, not[y] public.

W77 MARY STEARE 1647 (PU)

[Bur: "Mary Steare" 1 May 1647.]
Will 31 Mar 1647 of Mary Steare of Holcombe Rogus: 30s ea to Aaron Atkins & Lydia his sister; remainder to bro Thomas Steare; 27s ea to execs Humfry & Richard Steare, uncles; signed by witn Tho. Cadwalladoe, Wm Palmer, Christopher Roach[?].

W78 PRUDENCE BURROWE 1649 (PU) [?]

[Bur: "Prudence Burrow" 28 May 1649.]

Will 23 Apr 1649 of Prudence Burrowe of Uffculme, widow, pr at Uffculme before Mr Humfrey Steare 4 Aug 1649: residue to dr Willmot Burrowe, exec; 40s to s Jonathan Burrowe to discharge his debt to Richard Patch of Uffculme; mare, best cow, & £40 bond to s James Burrowe, to be paid (?) to exec after providing 1 year's board & lodging to his bro Jonathan; James Burrowe to allow exec access to & storage of all the corn in the barn for 1 year; marked by Prudence Burrowe; witn: Thomas Moulton & Humfrey Mill (both sign).

W79 JOHN STEPHEN yeoman 1671 (DS)

[Bur: "John Steevens" 4 Jan 1670/1.]
Will 6 Mar 1668/9 of John Stephen of Uffculme, yeoman, pr 6 May 1671: residue to dr Mary Godfree, exec; house, garden, orchard, & other land adjoining to wife for life, then to pass to exec; £40 to dr Joane Bennett; conditional bequest after death of wife to dr Joane of *Brode* [broad?] *Meadow* (in possession of Thomas Coliar) for remaining term of years; £10 after wife's death to be shared by An Chereton & her chn; to John Maning, s of dr Joane, the house where Barnard Prince lives, together with garden & adjoining fields; £3 ea after wife's death to the 5 other chn of dr Joane; £40 between 4 chn of dr Mary Godfree; to Ambrusse Stephen, s of s John, the house called "Three Keayse" with orchard, garden, & field; to John Stephen, s of s John, all Frogstreet house, orchard, garden, & 2 meadows adjoining; signed John Stephen; witn: Jno[?] Sowthey (signs) & Georg Parker (P mark).

W80 ANSTICE BOWERMAN 1673 (PU)

[Bur: "Anastice Bowerman widdow" 21 Oct 1672.]
Admon 13 May 1673 names John Greene of Uffculme, weaver, as admin; marked J by John Greene & signed by John Ball in presence of Robt Russell.

W81 MARIE ELLIS 1677 (PU)

[Bur: "Mary Ellis widow" 14 Feb 1676/7.]
Nuncupative Will 6 Dec 1676 of Marie Ellis, widow, of Uffculme: £10 & a bowl worth £10 to Jane, wife of Nicholas Rowe,; 10s to Marie Baker; 5s to Edward Walrond; her land to William Rowe, exec; rest divided between Wm Rowe & his 2 sisters, Jane & Marie; witn: John Ballaman (signed), John Borrowe, & Nicholas Rowe (both marked). John Borrowe said that as far as he could remember Marie Ellis said that she would give a further £10 ea to Jane & Marie.

W82 MARGARET PRINCE 1678 (PU)

[Bur: "Margaret Prince widow" 19 Dec 1677.]
Admon 22 Apr 1678 names Bernard Prince as admin and also Edward Cole of Uffculme, weaver.

W83 JOANE SNOW 1678 (PU)

[Bur: "Joane Snow widow" 14 Apr 1678.]
Will 22 Feb 1677/8 of Joane Snow, widow: to dr Joane Croyden apparel & 5s; to grch Mary Croyden box & contents, brass pan, brass crock, ½-headed bedstead bought by Phillip Rowland; residue to s John Snow, exec; marked J by John Snow in presence of Wm Cotterell, John Dowdney (D mark), & Agnes Cotterell (A mark).

W84 ANDREW BURROW alš BARBY 1681 (PU)

[Bur: "Andrew Burrow" 28 Feb 1680/1.]
Admon 11 March 1680/1 names bro-in-law John Lovell of Uplowman, yeoman, as admin and also John Stone of Uffculme, shoemaker (crepidarius); marked JL by John Lovell & signed by

John Stone in presence of Mary Salter sen^r & Mary Salter jun^r (both mark).

W85 JOHN LONEY 1681 (PU)

[Bur: "John Loney" 22 Jan 1680/1. Mar: "John Loney & Alice Rabbets" 26 Jun 1676.]

Admon 5 Feb 1680/1 names widow Alice Loney as admin and also Robert Salter of Kentisbeare & Henry Briant of Uffculme, yeoman; marked by Alice Loney & Robert Salter and signed by Hen(e)ry Briant, in presence of Thos Salkeld & Mary (M mark) Salter.

W86 AMOS FRANCK 1681 (PU)

[Bur: "Amoz Francke" 21 Feb 1680/1. Mar: "Ames Frank & Susan the dr of John Salkield Gent" 5 Jun 1667. See W99.]

Admon 9 Jul 1681 names Susanna Franck, relict, as admin and also Richd Salkeld of Halberton, gent, & Thos Salkeld, gent; marked by Susanna Franck & signed by Rich^d & Thos Salkeld in presence of James Hollway & Fran St Barbe.

W87 EDWARD MANNING 1682 (DS)

Admon 11 May 1682 names s Edward Manning, fuller, as admin & also John Grantland, yeoman, both of Uffculme; both sign in presence of Geo Frome, not^y pub.

W88 JOHN GAY 1685 (PU)

[Bur: "John Guy junr" 20 Jun 1685. Mar: "John Guy junr & Elianor Wood" 31 Jul 1675.]

Admon 31 Jul 1685 names widow Elinor Gay as admin and also Henry Gay, sergemaker, & John Grantland, yeoman, both of Uffculme; marked E by Ellen (*sic*) Gay & HG by Henry Gay and signed by John Grantland in presence of Mary Russell & Judith Miller (marked).

W89 THOMAS LEE 1685 (PU)

[Bur: "Thomas Liegh" 28 Dec 1684. Mar: "Thomas Leigh & Mary Middleton" 20 Aug 1666.]

Admon 16 Oct 1685 names Mary Batting, now wife of Thos Batting of Uffculme, as relict & admin and also Thos Batting of Uffculme & John Daggle of North Wootton in Dorset, yeoman; marked B(?) by Thos Batting & signed by John Daggle in presence of Geo Woodford, not^y pub.

W90 JOANE STARKE, widow 1686 (PU)

[Bur: "Joane Starke" 9 Jun 1686.]

Admon 2 Jul 1686 names Thomas Hollwill of Honiton, "wostardmaker", as admin and also Robert Shoobrooke of Uffculme, weaver; signed by Thomas Hollwill & marked by Robert Shoobrooke in presence of John Grantland & Dorothy Baker (mark).

W91 RICHARD COLE sen^r, yeoman 1687 (PU)

[Bur: "Richard Cole" 11 Jun 1686.]

Admon 28 Jan 1686/7 names s Richard Cole, yeoman, & dr Mary Cole, spinster, as admins and also Ambrose Bayliff of Uffculme; marked by Richard & Mary Cole and signed by Androse Brayly (*sic*) in presence of John Goard, Ben Byrd, & Philip Starke (P mark).

Also Nuncupative Will 16 Jun 1686 of Richard Cole sen^r of Uffculme, yeoman: to dr Florence a cow called Gentle; to s George a cow called Jaffe; residue to s Richard & dr Mary; signed 16 Aug 1686 by Ambrose Brayly & Deborah Brayly, and marked by Mary Prince & Joyce Carswell.

W92 JOANE BURROUGH 1690 (PU)

[Bur: "Joane Burrough" 1 Nov 1689.]

Admon 30 May 1690 names s Robert Burrough of Uffculme, yeoman, as admin & also Christopher Bussell of Uffculme, woodworker; signed by Robert Burrow & Christopher Bussell in presence of Bernard Byrd & Geo Woodford.

W93 ROBERT JOHNSLING 1691 (PU)

Admon 15 May 1691 names friend John Rowe of Uffculme, weaver, as admin & also John Grantland, yeoman; marked JR by John Rowe & signed by John Grantland in presence of Geo Woodford, not^{y} pub.

W94 WILLIAM FORWARD 1692 (DS)

Admon 29 Apr 1692, before Robert Woodward, names James Forward, yeoman of Culmstock, bro & principal creditor, as admin & also Samuel Downe (Donn?), mercer of Uffculme; both sign in presence George Frome, not^{y} pub, & George Frome jun^{r}.

W95 SAMUEL DOWNE 1693 (PU)

[Mar: "Samuel Dunne & Mary Holwill" 25 Aug 1677.]

Admon 10 Oct 1693 names widow Mary Downe as admin & also Richard Goodridge of Uffculme; marked by Mary Downe & Richard Goodridge in presence of Bernard Byrd.

W96 NICHOLAS WREFFORD 1693 (PU)

Admon 22 May 1693 names widow Mary Wrefford of Uffculme as admin and also Henry Jeffery alš Langden of Uffculme, yeoman; marked W by Mary Wrefford & J by Henry Jeffery in presence of Bernard Byrd & Geo Woodford, not^{y} pub.

W97 MARY DUNN 1695 (PU)

Admon 29 Nov 1695 names mother Joane Dunn, widow, as admin and also John Fowler, weaver; signed by Joane Dunn & John Fowler in presence of Bernard Byrd & Bernard Byrd jun^{r}.

W98 THOMAS DUNN 1696 (PU)

[Bur: "Thomas Dunn" 6 May 1696.]

Admon 13 Jul 1696 names Justin Dunn, widow, as grandmother (*sic*) & John Dunn as s, both of Uffculme, and also Richard Cole of Uffculme, yeoman, & Thomas Dunn of Burlescombe, yeoman; marked by Justin Dunn & Richard Cole and signed by John Done & Thomas Dunne in presence of Bernard Byrd, John Grantland, & Florence Dunn (mark).

W99 SUSANNAH FRANKE 1697 (PU)

[Bur: "wid Susanna Frank" 17 Nov 1695. See W86.]

Admon 12 May 1697 names bro Richard Salkeild of Uffculme, maltster, as admin and also Robert Dunston of Uffculme, weaver; signed by Rich Salkeld and marked X by Robert Dunston in presence of Bernard Byrd & Geo Woodford.

W100 HENNERY BRYANT sergeweaver 1698 (DS)

Will 21 Nov 1696 of Hennery Bryant of Uffculme, sergeweaver, pr 4 Jun 1698: residue to exec, wife Margreat subject to no remarriage; to s John apparel, chest, & bed, & right & title in Fasies house, Uffculme town, & 1/3 of proceeds from O[?]pescotes estate at Smithincott, &, after death of his mother, right & title in overland, called Magers ground, Cullompton, paying therefrom for the remainder of the lease 20s a year to his sisters Mary & Ellinor Bryant; to dr Mary Bryant bed, chest, & pair of looms out for hire, & right & title to Scoiers House, Gaddon Down, & 1/3 of Opescotes proceeds, & 10s a year from profits from Thomas Roges house; to dr Ellinor Bryant table, chair, cupboard, swift(?) & queel turn, & at age 20 right & title in house at Stenhill, where sister Jane Bryant is to be allowed to remain in her present part for life, & 1/3 of Opescotes proceeds, & right & title in Thomas Roges house; the said John, Mary, & Ellinor Bryant to share the proceeds from the sale of 6 cows & 3 horses & to pay 2s ea a year to their aunt Jane Bryant; if those lives "upon my estate", Anthony

Merson sen^r & jun^r , should die before wife Margreat Bryant, John, Mary, & Ellinor to pay £1 10s a year ea to their mother Margreat for life; signed Henery Bryant & witn Symon Coles jun^r, Joseph T(?)uching, & William Martin (all sign).

W101 JOHN HOLT 1700 (PU)

[Bur: "old Holt the Quaker" 9 May 1700.]

Admon 14 Nov 1700 names Joan Brooke, wife of husbandman William Brooke & dr of John Holt, as admin and also Peter Parsons of Uffculme & John Belleme of Willand, both yeomen; before perebendary Abraham Brooksbank; signed William Brook, Peter Parson, Jo Belleme, in presence of Edward Cooke & Peter Cooke (both sign).

W102 MARY BALLIMAN, widow 1703 (PU)

Will 19 Oct 1703, pr at Exeter (no inventory exhibited) 10 Dec 1703, sworn by Robert Kerslake: 1s ea to ss John & Thomas Balliman; residue to execs bro-in-law Mr Benjamin Heath of Exeter, fuller, & Mr Robert Kerslake of Holcombe Burnell, Devon, in trust for education in Exeter of her chn, & to recover all debts & invest for use of dr Mary Balliman at age 21; signed by Mary Balliman in presence of Jno Harris & Jno Irish. On 10 Dec 1703 Mr Benjamin Heath renounced all interest in the will & named Mr Robert Kerslake as sole exec; signed by Benj Heath in presence of John Clarke & Peter Cooke.

W103 JOHN SEARLE 1704 (DS)

Admon 9 Jun 1704 names widow Sarah Searle as admin & also John Clarke of Uffculme, gent, who signs while Sarah makes her + mark in presence of Geo Frome, not^y pub & Tho Frome.

W104 HUGH SMYTH, yeoman 1706 (PU)

[Bur: "Hugh Smith yeoman yeoman (*sic*)" 17 Jun 1705.]

Will 12 Jun 1705 of Hugh Smyth of Uffculme, yeoman, pr 15 Apr 1706: residue to dr Elizabeth Smyth, exec; house & estate & £50 to wife Elizabeth Smyth; signed by Hugh Smyth in presence of John Grantland & Elizabeth Maninge (M mark).

W105 WILLIAM HAWKYER 1706 (PU)

[Bur: "Hawker the Taylour" 1(?) Nov 1705.]

Will 23 Oct 1705 of William Hawkyer of Uffculme, pr 15 Apr 1706: residue to wife Agnes, exec; best suit to James Brook; pottage pot to dr-in-law [step-dr?] Sarah Hake; 1 coat ea to Will Brook, Phillip Hake, & John Brook; black & white coat & green waistcoat to bro John Hawkyer; marked by Wm Hawkyer in presence of Henry Rugg & John Burrows (both sign).

W106 LEONARD POCOCK bachelor 1707 (DS)

Will 22 Mar 1705/6 of Leonard Pocock of Uffculme, bachelor, pr 27 Aug 1707 before Hum Henchman: residue to k George Pocock, exec; to k James Row the cottage & garden in Craddock where he lives & the weaving shop, & also 5s a year for life of himself & his "now" wife Mary Row ; to k George Pocock the house, cottage, & garden in possession of Thomas Rose; £7 ea to Leonard, George, & Joane, ss & drs of George Pocock, & to John, Ann, & Thomasin, ss & drs of James Row; £5, bed, & gold piece to Margaret, dr of James Gange; 2s 6d & brass crock to William, s of James Gange; silver spoon ea to Joane, dr of George Pocock, & Thomasin, dr of James Row; 5s ea to James Gange & his "now" wife Mary; 2s 6d ea to James, Henry, & Elizabeth, ss & drs of James Gange; marked by Leonard Pocock;

witn: John Pears, Roger Row, & Nicholas Sommers (all sign).

W107 JOHN BURROW yeoman 1707 (DS)

[Bur: "John Burrough" 3 Feb 1706/7. Mar: "John Burrow & Ann Cross" 30 Dec 1684, Willand.]
Will 1 May 1706 of John Burrow of Uffculme, yeoman, pr 29 Aug 1707 before Humfrey Henchman: residue & right & title to Whitmore estate to s James Burrow, exec; 5s to *now wife* Anne Burrow; ; 5s ea to ovsrs John Clarke, gent, & James Dowdney, yeoman, both of Uffculme; witn: Thomas Hake, William Richards, & Anthony Crosse.

W108 JOHN GOARD yeoman 1707 (DS)

[Bur: "John Goard" 9 Apr 1707.]
Will 5 Apr 1707 of John Goard of Uffculme, yeoman, pr 29 Aug 1707 before Humfrey Henchman: residue to wife Martha Goard, exec, but only £10 a year if she remarries; £20 to dr Pricilla Goard; to ss John & Robert Goard, after the death of their mother, the "Sowell" estate to share, except the meadow by the river near Coldharbour & the Yencott houses, which go to s Richard Goard at age 21; £20 ea at age 21 to drs Martha, Mary, Elizabeth, & Jone; if wife dies within 10 years, ss John & Robert Goard are to pay the 5 drs an extra £10 each; ovsrs bros-in-law Rich Locke & John Hitchcock; signed John Goard; witn: John Davie & John Tozer (sign), & Robert Tozer (mark).

W109 ROBERT GILL yeoman of Holcombe Rogus 1707 (DS)

[Bur: "Robert Gill" 9 Jun 1705.]
Will 12 Oct 1704 of Robert Gill of Holcombe Rogus, yeoman, pr 17 Oct 1707 before Bernard Byrd: residue for her own (not her husband's) use to exec, k Grace Southey, wife of Robert Southey of Holcombe Rogus; to the chn of k Robert Southey, brass pan to Mary, his bed, coverlet, & bolster to Elizabeth, chest to John, & 2 chairs & a pewter dish to Grace; marked by Robert Gill; witn: Pet: Kerslake (signs), Joane Hancock & George Twechens (both mark).

W110 ELIZABETH LEE widow 1708 (PU)

[Bur: "wid Leigh of Bradfield" 12 Feb 1707/8.]
Will 25 Jun 1707 of Elizabeth Lee of Uffculme, widow, pr 29 Apr 1708: residue to ss & drs, Thomas, Mary, Henry, Hannah, & Susanna, joint exec^{s}; linen & woollen apparel to drs; bed to Hannah; kettle, brass pan, & barrels to Mary; 10s to ch of Thomas; 20s ea to Mary's chn; £5 out of his part share to pay for Henry to learn a trade; friend Mr Anthony Heathfeild, tanner of Cullompton, & his bro Mr William Heathfeild of Tiverton as ovsrs, expenses to be paid by exec^{s}; marked by Elizabeth Lee & Will Coombe & signed by Sam Bonifant & George Hunt.

W111 EDWARD MARSHALL yeoman 1708 (PU)

[Mar: "Edward Marshall & Mary Corp" 29 Mar 1703.]
Will 11 Dec 1703 of Edward Marshall of Uffculme, yeoman, pr 29 Apr 1708: residue to wife Mary Marshall; apparel to Thomas Corke & 2s 6d to Christopher Bustle to sing a psalm, both trustees; marked by Edward Marshall, Simon Tozer, John Tozer, & John Aplin.

W112 ANN DOWDNEY 1709 (PU)

[Bur: "Mrs Ann Dowdny" 10 Feb 1708/9. Mar: "Henry Dowdney & Anne Mills the dr of Mr John Mills" 26 May 1661. See LW159.]
Will 17 Nov 1708 of Ann Dowdney of Uffculme, widow: residue to dr Temperance Westron, exec, & residence for life at house at Foxhill; 40s to poor; £10, brass pan, & iron mill to dr Elizabeth, wife of Edward Cross; £30

to grdr Allice wife of Robert Parsons; £5 & a silver spoon ea at age 21 to grchn Mark, Henry, Ann, Robert, & William Westron; £5 ea to grchn James, Ann, & Joane Cross, plus a coffer marked AD to Ann; 40s at 21 to Ann, dr of Robert Parsons; wearing apparel between drs Elizabeth Cross & Temperance Westron; 20s ea to Francis Pratt, Thomasin West, & Mary Pratt, s & drs of Francis Pratt; 5s ea to servants; 20s ea to ovsrs, bro-in-law Thomas Helmore, ss-in-law Edward Cross & Francis Waldron, & k Robert Parsons; signed by Ann Dowdney; witn: Nicholas Sommers, Tho Bishopp, & John Westron (all sign).

W113 PETER PASSONS 1709 (PU)

[Bur: "Peter Parsons of Towne" 8 Aug 1708. Mar: "Peter Parson & Florence Dunn" 24 Feb 1697. See W132.]
Admon 20 Jun 1709 names wife Florence Passons as admin & also John Dunn, yeoman, & Christopher Bussell, husbandman; before Abraham Brooksbanke, prebendary of Uffculme; marked F by Florence Passons & signed John Dunne & Christopher Bussle in presence of Peter Cooke.

W114 EDWARD PLEASE 1709 (PU)

[Bur: "Young -Plaice" 18 Mar 1708/9.]
Admon 25 Mar 1709 names Elizabeth Moore, spinster, as admin & also James Bray, husbandman; marked by Elizabeth Moore & James Bray & signed by Williams Addams in presence of Peter Cooke, not^{y} pub.
Nuncupative Will 13 Mar 1709 of Edward Please of Uffculme, pr 25 Mar 1709 before John Lome: residue to Elizabeth Moore of Uffculme, spinster; 10s & apparel to father; witn: James Bray (marks) & Wm Addams (signs).

W115 JOHN BISHOP sen^{r}, yeoman 1710 (DS)

Will 14 Jan 1708 of John Bishop of Uffculme, yeoman, pr before Hum Henchman 4 Sep 1710: residue to dr Mary Edwards, exec; to s Christopher Bishop messuage & tenement of Goodleigh for remainder of term of years, & table, cupboard, clock, chairs, pots, pans, &c, & to pay £5 as heriot; to s John Bishop bed, chair, pots, & pans; to s Thomas Bishop messuage & tenement at Luppitt, lately in possession of Richard Burrow or his assigns, for remainder of term of years, & table, cupboard, silver spoon, &c at Luppitt, but to pay the heriot due there; £20 ea at 21 to grsons John & William Edwards; ovsrs friends Robert Westron of Uffculme, yeoman, & William Bishop of Churchstanton, yeoman; witn: John Dinster, Thomas Pulman, & James Hill (all sign).

W116 ROBERT HILL yeoman of Goodleigh 1711 (PU)

Will 22 Jul 1711 of Robert Hill of Goodleigh, Uffculme, yeoman, pr 14 Nov 1711 (signed by G Frome, Reg^{r}): residue to wife Joane Hill, exec; to s John £20 at age 21; lands at Clayhanger, called Bonday, to s John but to be mortgaged to pay £100 debt to Edward Ellis & Robert Sowthey, which they held in trust for the use of Elizabeth, late wife of Hugh Poole; signed & sealed by Robert Hill in presence of John Grantland, Jacob Wesbear, & Ann Knowman (K mark).

W117 GEORGE HILL, yeoman 1712 (PU)

[Bur: "Old Gaffer Hill by Culliford" 24 Mar 1711/2.]
Will 13 Mar 1711/12 [*sic*] of George Hill of Uffculme, yeoman, pr 8 Jul 1712 (signed by G Frome, Reg^{r}): tenement & estate & residue to wife Ann, exec; interest on £110 owed to Edward Ellis of Uffculme to be paid out of estate, or whole sum to be repaid if required, by mortgaging property up to value not exceeding £110; after death of wife & of s-in-law John Westbere, property to pass to John Westbere's ss, Isaac & John

Westbere, but if they die without issue then to Henry Hill, s of cousin George Hill of Holcombe Rogus, who then pays £30 to John James, s of Richard James of Sampford Arundel, & £30 to Anne Hill, dr of John Hill of Culmstock, s of Henry Hill of Holcombe Rogus; 5s to John Westbere, s-in-law; marked by George Hill in presence of Jas Cooke, Robert Webber (R mark), & Mary Webber (M mark).

W118 SAMMUELL BONIFANT 1712 (PU)

[Mar: "Samuel Bonifant & Tacey the dr of Richard Marshall" 6 Jun 1667.]

Will 8 May 1708 of Sammuell Bonifant, pr 8 Jul 1712 (signed by G Frome, Reg^r): residue to grson Sammuell, exec; to wife Dacye Bonifant half the dwelling house, gerden, & goods for life; the other part where s Richard Bonifant lived to grson Sammuell Bonifant, who also pays for upkeep of whole house; on death of wife all to pass to grson Sammuell, who then pays 20s p.a. to grson Edward Bonifant or, if he dies, to grson John Bonifant; clock to Isack Bonifant; chest of drawers to grdr Jane Bonifant; best chest to Ann Bonifant; silver spoon ea to 4 grchn, Edward, John, Mary, & Anes[?] Bonifant; marked S by Sammuell Bonifant in presence of John Wescott, Mary Cross, & George Hunt (all sign).

W119 JAMES DOWDNEY, husbandman 1712 (DS)

[Bur: "James Dowdny" 30 Apr 1713.]

Will 2 Nov 1712 of James Dowdney of Uffculme, husbandman, pr 4 Sep 1713 before Tho Henchman: residue to wife Jane Dowdney, exec: £20 ea to drs Joane (crossed out?), Jane, Mary, & Elizabeth; cottage & garden at Stenaller (*during my terme & Estate therein*) after death of exec to drs Joane & Jane; if exec remarries she pays £30 ea to drs Mary & Elizabeth & £15 ea to 2 elder drs Joane & Jane; signed James Dowdney; witn: John Grantland & Anne Coombe (C mark).

W120 SARAH BISHOP widow 1713 (DS)

Will 5 Nov 1711 of Sarah Bishop of Uffculme, widow, pr 4 Sep 1713 before Tho Henchman surr: residue (apart from legacies in husband's will) to exec^s, John & Thomas Bishop, ss of bro(-in-law) John Bishop, dec^d; red coats to Jane Hurly, wife of John Hurly of Kentisbeare, & to Joan Shackle of Holcombe Rogus, widow; a coat, hood, napkin, & a "change" ea to the 3 drs of Amos Tozer; coats & pewter dishes to k Mary Byrd, wife of Thomas Byrd of Uffculme; 10s ea at age 21 to cousins John & William Edwards; 10s ea to cousin Christopher Bishop & his s John; also a cow & pewter dishes to Christopher Bishop; 20s ea to 3 chn of cousin Nicholas Cawley of Sidmouth; marked by Sarah Bishop; witn: William Wood & Nicholas Cawley (both sign), Mary Leaman & Thomas Uptol alš Stone (both mark).

W121 JOHN SMITH woolcomber 1713 (DS)

[Bur: "Smith the Quaker" 14 Jun 1712.]

Nuncupative will 12 Jun 1712 of John Smith of Uffculme, woolcomber, (died 8 Jun 1712), pr 4 Sep 1713 before Tho Henchman, surr: all to exec, wife Joan Smith, except for specified clothes & his sister Marge's box to k Robert Smith of Uffculme; marked by Elizabeth Smith & George Leaman sen^r, & signed by Henerey Peperell, in the presence of Robert Westron (signs) & George Leaman (jun^r?, who, like his father, surprisingly marks with an H).

W122 THOMAS PEARCY woolcomber 1715 (PU)

[Bur: "old Pierce" 10 Mar 1714/5

This will gives details of the relative dispositions of the houses & gardens owned at Northcott and also specific

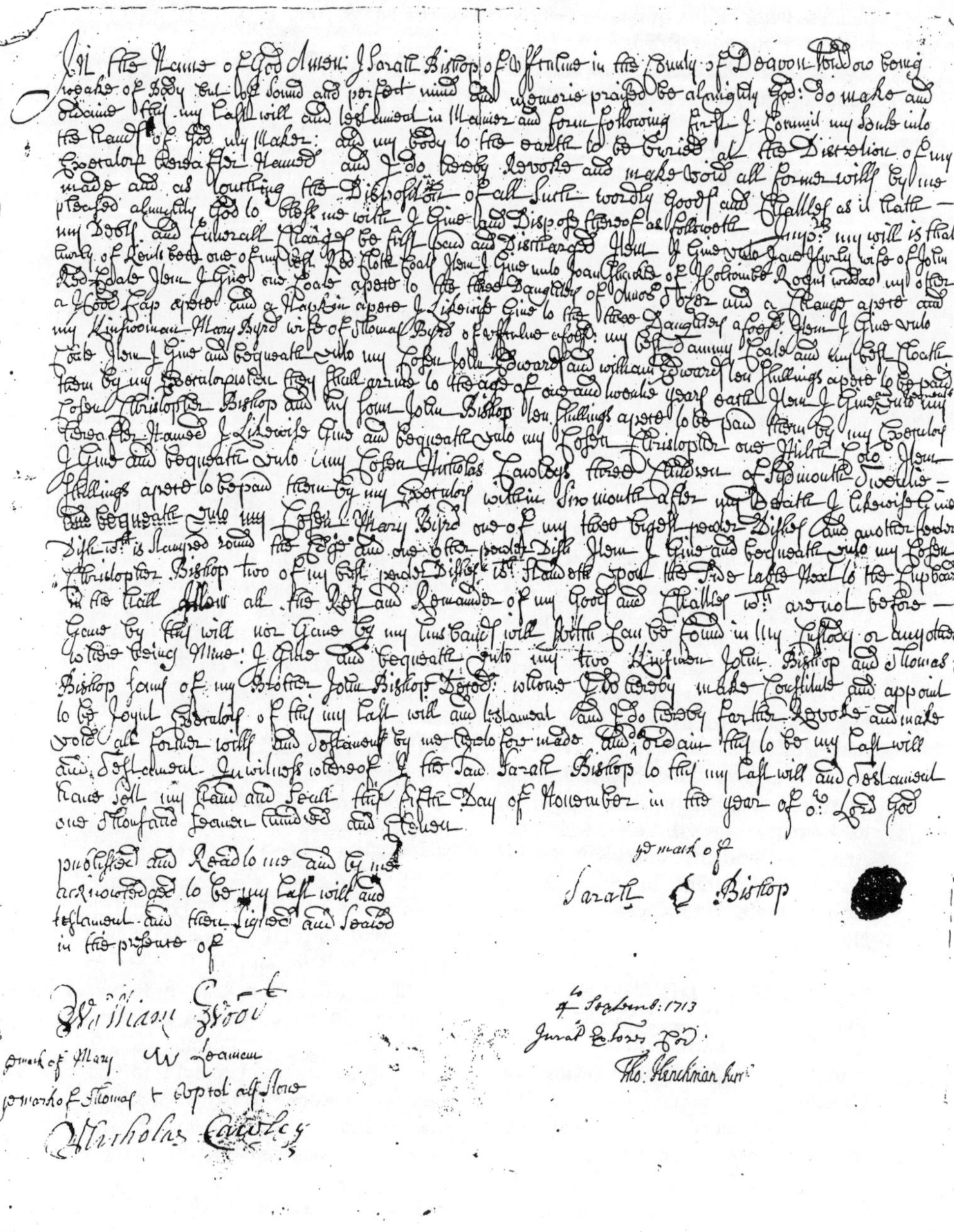

In the Name of God Amen I Sarah Bishop of Uffculme in the County of Devon widdow being
weake of body but of sound and perfect mind and memorie praised be almighty God: do make and
ordaine this my last will and testament in manner and form following first I commit my soule into
the hands of God my Maker: and my body to the earth to be buried at the discretion of my
Executors hereafter named and I do hereby revoke and make void all former wills by me
made and as touching the disposition of all such worldly goods and chattles as it hath
pleased almighty God to bless me with I give and dispose thereof as followeth Imps: my will is that
my debts and funerall charges be first paid and discharged Item I give unto Jane Hurly wife of John
[illegible] one of my best red [illegible] coate Item I give unto Joan [illegible] of Holcombe Rogus widdow my other
[illegible] Item I give one [illegible] apeece to the three Daughters of Amos [illegible] and a [illegible] apeece and
a hood cap apeece and a napkin apeece I likewise give to the three Daughters aforesd. Item I give unto
my kinswoman Mary Byrd wife of Thomas Byrd of Uffculme aforesd: my best [illegible] coate and my best cloake
[illegible] Item I give and bequeath unto my cosen John Edward and William Edward ten shillings apeece to be paid
them by my Executors when they shall arrive to the age of one and twenty years each Item I give unto my
cosen Christopher Bishop and my cosen John Bishop ten shillings apeece to be paid them by my Executors
hereafter named I likewise give and bequeath unto my cosen Christopher one [illegible]
I give and bequeath unto my cosen Nicholas Cawley three children of Sydmouth twelve
shillings apeece to be paid them by my Executors within six months after my death I likewise give
and bequeath unto my cosen Mary Byrd one of my two biggest pewter dishes and another pewter
dish wch is stamped round the edge and one other pewter dish Item I give and bequeath unto my cosen
Christopher Bishop two of my best pewter dishes wch standeth upon the side table next to the cupboard
in the hall Allso all the rest and remainder of my goods and chattles wch are not before
given by this will nor given by my husbands will which can be found in my custody or any other
where being mine: I give and bequeath unto my two kinsmen John Bishop and Thomas
Bishop sons of my brother John Bishop decesd: whome I do hereby make constitute and appoint
to be joynt Executors of this my last will and testament and I do hereby farther revoke and make
void all former wills and testaments by me heretofore made and ordaine this to be my last will
and testament In witness whereof I the said Sarah Bishop to this my last will and testament
have sett my hand and seale this fifth Day of November in the year of our Lord God
one thousand seaven hundred and eleven

published and Read to me and by me acknowledged to be my last will and testament and then signed and sealed in the presence of

William Grant

the mark of Mary W Leaman

the mark of Thomas + Upton alias Stone

Nicholas Cawley

the mark of Sarah S Bishop

4to Septemb: 1713
Jurat Exores Cor:
Tho: Hinchman Sur

The will of Sarah Bishop 1713 [W120]

instructions about the succession to the various legacies in case of death.]
Will 5 Feb 1711/2 of Thomas Pearcy of Uffculme, woolcomber, pr before Bernard Byrd 26 Jul 1715: residue to nephews Richard, Thomas, & Humphry Pearcy, exec^{s}: the testator owned several dwellings and the surrounding ½-acre at Northcott, formerly the property of Hackpen Manor, and left the houses (with 2 or 3 rooms downstairs and 2 rooms above) and gardens to his nephews, Richard (weaver), Thomas, Humphry, John, & James Pearcy, - (a) to Richard the one in which he lives, (bordering on land of Henry Churley, sergemaker, & of James Gill, yeoman of Culmstock), (b) to Thomas the one occupied by k John Lake, weaver, (c) to Humphry the one occupied by Nicholas Woodroffe, (d) to John for his life only (after which it goes to James the s of nephew James Pearcy, who pays respectively 4s & 2s a year for life to his bros William & John Pearcy) the one occupied by John Brooke, sergeweaver, and (e) to James, s of nephew James Pearcy, the one occupied by John Piprell, woolcomber; -(f) a further cottage at Northcott Moor, with garden & orchard, (occupied by bro-in-law Wm Hookway for life & lives of his ss John & Wm Hookway) to sister Julian for life & then to nephew William Hookway; £7 shared by drs of nephew Richard; nephew John to pay £3 to sister Mary, wife of John Lake; nephew Thomas to pay £5 to Mary & Jane, drs of John Pearcy; specified household goods & looms to drs (Elizabeth, Mary, Jone, & Julian) & ss (John & Wm) of William Hookway, to sister Julian, & to ss of Pearcy nephews; marked by Thomas Pearcy; witn: (marked) George Collier sen^{r} & jun^{r} & George Cooke.

W123 JACOB MANNING 1715 (PU)

[Bur: "Jacob Manning" 24 Jul 1715.]
Admon 26 Jul 1715 names bro Robert Manning of Hemyock, miller, as admin & also Christopher Bussell of Uffculme; both sign in presence of G Frome & Bernard Byrd (both sign).

W124 ROBERT POOKE miller 1715 (PU)

[Bur: "old Gaffer Pook ye Miller" 5 May 1715. Mar: "Robert Weekes & Mary Brailie" 23 Jun 1673 possibly, since "Pooke alš Weekes" does occur.]
Will 26 Apr 1715 of Robert Pooke of Uffculme, miller, pr at Uffculme before Rev Bernard Byrd 26 Jul 1715: residue to wife Mary Pooke, exec; £15 to s Robert Pooke; £5 at age 21 to Elizabeth, dr of s Robert Pooke; the £15 & £5 to be paid in 10 years' time; marked by Robert Pooke; witn: Edward Pooke & John Pratt (both sign), & John Carpenter (mark).

W125 JOSEPH FRANCK 1715 (PU)

[Bur: "Joseph Franck" 27 Sep 1714.]
Admon 27 Jul 1715 names (son?) Amos Franck of Uffculme, woolcomber, and also Christopher Bussell, clerk; both sign in presence of G Frome, not^{y} pub, & Bernard Byrd.

W126 WILLIAM BALSTER yeoman 1715 (PU)

Will 2 Feb 1714/15 of William Balster of Uffculme, yeoman, pr at Uffculme before Bernard Byrd 26 Jul 1715: residue to exec, servant Mary Knowman, wife of Christopher Knowman; apparel to bro Abraham Balster; 40s to Anne, dr of bro Abraham Balster; £5, a silver spoon, & a bed each, all after 21, to Robert & Samuel Knowman, ss of Christopher; signed by Wm Balster; witn: Jo Were & Richard Clarke.

W127 AUGUSTUS STEPHENS senior 1717 (PU)

[Bur: "Augustine Stephens" 20 Jun 1717.]
Will 8 Feb1715/6 [*sic*] of Augustus Stephens sen^{r} of Uffculme, pr 2 July 1717 at Uffculme before Bernard Byrd: residue to s Arthur Stephens,

exec; bed, pot, & hangings to dr Joane; armory & great chest; to s John Stephens the house where John Loney lives if he pays the £4 bond with interest to John Colliford; if not, house goes to s Arthur & 20s to John Stephens; to dr Mary Stephens the house where Henry Bray's family lived, but if she dies without issue to pass to Ann Job for life, thereafter to Joane Stephens for life; to dr Mary his bed, brass pot & hangings, & little chest; table linen divided between 2 drs Mary & Joane; to ss John & Augustus 1s each; 1s to dr Ann; marked by Augustus Stephens in presence of Sam[l] Godfrey, Wm Kent, Edmond Lucane[Lemene?].

W128 HENRY DODGE weaver 1717(PU)

Will 20 Nov 1710 of Henry Dodge of Uffculme, weaver, pr 6[?] Sep 1717 at Uffculme before Bernard Byrd, surr for Rev Francis Eyre, prebendary: residue to exec[s], drs Alice, wife of William Combe, & Jane, wife of Marke Brook; £5 to wife Jane Dodge; 1s & mortgage on William Lemon's house to only s Henry Dodge; cauldron to eldest dr Alice Combe; loom & accessories to grch Marke Brook, s of Marke Brook & Jane; marked HD by Henry Dodge; witn: George & John Manning (both sign).

W129 FRANCIS PERRY 1717 (PU)

[Bur: "old Francis Pearsy" 21 May 1717.]

Will 8 May 1717, pr 2 Jul 1717 before Bernard Byrd: 40s ea to 2 ss James & Francis, who share his apparel; £4 to Ann, dr of Will Richards; residue to dr Ann, exec; marked by Francis Perry in presence of Thomzine Tarlow [Carlow?] & Peter Oland (both mark).

W130 PETER HOLLWAY strawjoiner 1718 (PU)

[In the short probate note Peter Hollway's name is spelt in that way while his s's name is written as Henry Hollwell.]

Will 13 Jan 1717/8 of Peter Hollway of Uffculme, strawjoiner, pr 24 Jun 1718 at Uffculme before Rev J Windsor for Rev Francis Eyre, prebendary, signed by Geo Frome, Reg[r]: residue & woollen & linen apparel to s Henry Holway of Hemyock, exec, who also has houses & gardens called Pearseys Houses for 3 years, & use of household goods owned before present marriage, which after Henry's death pass to his 3 chn, Henry, William, & Elizabeth, who also inherit, for the remainder of their term, the Pearseys Houses; to wife Susan Hollway for life the present estate of houses at Madgelake plus all the goods she owned before marriage; bed & settle in shop chamber, press & coffer in hall chamber, table, brass pot, & kettle in hall, sergeloom & dresser in shop, all to s James Hollway if he returns from beyond the seas, otherwise all to go to James's dr Susan or, if she dies unmarried before 20, then to Henry's chn; houses & estate at Madgelake to Susan Holway [*sic*], dr of s James Holway, but if she dies to chn of s Henry; marked P by Peter Hoilway; witn: John Grantland (signs) & Mary Luttley (M mark).

W131 BERNARD BYRD 1718 (PU)

[Bur: "y[e] Rever[nd] Bernard Bird Vic. of this Parish" 24 Mar 1717/8. A note of a family dispute].

The will of Rev Bernard Byrd, who died in 1718, made s Bernard exec, to whom was bequeathed a leasehold estate at Combe Raleigh for life, thereafter to pass to grson William, with the condition that he paid to Bernard, another grson, £40 plus £5 p.a. during William's life. Bernard the exec died in 1746 making his s Thomas exec & William a trustee; but William, now in possession of estate on death of his father, refuses to pay legacy or annuity & Thomas & Willm, having suppressed the will, are told that it must be produced or probate will not be granted on the complaint of Bernard the legatee.

W132 FLORENCE PARSONS 1720 (PU)

[Bur: "Florence Parsons" 16 Feb 1719. See W113.]
Will 14 Nov 1718 of Florence Parsons of Uffculme, pr 20 Jul 1720 before Rev J Windsor: residue & Venners tenement to sister Dorothy Welsh, exec: 1s ea to bro John Dunne, bro-in-law William Brooke, & sister-in-law Anne Hill; 40s to Henry, s of bro John Dunne; £5 to Dorothy Tucker, dr of k Nicholas Tucker; £5 at 21 to William Dunne, s of nephew William Dunne; marked by Florence Parsons; witn: John Churly, George Collier jun^r^, & Elizabeth Langman (all sign).

W133 JAMES WOODBURY 1724 (PU)

[Mar: "James Woodberry & Joane Mogford, both of this parish" 11 Oct 1701.]
Admon 8 Jul 1724 names widow Joan Woodbury as admin & also John Land of Uffculme, husbandman, & John Doe; before J Windsor; marked by Joanne Woodbury & John Land & signed by R S Wyche.

W134 JOHN MANNING maltster 1724 (PU)

Will 27 Apr 1723 of John Manning of Uffculme, maltster, pr 8 Jul 1724 before Rev Jn Windsor, surr: residue & messuage & tenement where John lived to s George Manning, exec; £10 p.a for life to wife Elizabeth Manning; £5 to s James Manning & 5s to ea of his chn; £2 10s to dr Elizabeth Southey, wife of Robert Southey, & 5s to ea of her chn; signed John Manning; witn: Nich Sommers & Edward Skinner (both sign).

W135 JOHN GRANTLAND the elder, yeoman 1725 (DS)

[Bur: "old John Grantland was putt into Ground without Xtian bur~" 24 Jul 1723. Mar: "John Grantland of Uffculme & Sarah Manly of Sampford Peverell" 12 Mar 1671/2.]
Will, 4 Feb 1723 of John Grantland the elder of Uffculme, yeoman, pr at Uffculme 1 Jun 1725 before Hen: Fisher, surr: residue to s John Grantland, exec, (but modified by codicil 16 Jun 1724 in view of illness of s John, making wife, Mark Westron, Robert Dunn, & Thomas Dunn trustees & co-exec^s^ with s John: signature of John Grantland witn by Zachary Turner, Joseph Howe, & George Marling); £10 a year during widowhood, bed, & sufficient household goods to wife Sarah; fee simple & inheritance of *Tanners Tenement* to s John Grantland; £60 to s-in-law Robert Dunne & his chn; £10 ea to dr Elizabeth Roach & to her chn, at age 21, Sarah, Elizabeth, & James Roach; to dr Elizabeth Roach the profits from house & garden where Thomas Land & others live, for her life & that of her next ch; to dr Sarah Stephens 40s a year during her husband's life & then £20 for the use of her chn; £20 ea at age 21 to grchn Sarah & William Grantland, & £10 a year ea while they remain under their grandmother's tuition before being placed out in apprenticeships; signed John Grantland sen^r^; witn: Hugh Ellis, Joseph Howe, & George Marling.

W136 JOAN COOMBE widow 1725 (DS)

Admon 10 Jul 1725 names Augustine Stevens farmer, & Stephen Peirce, both of Cullompton; both sign, as does Joh: Talman, surr.

W137 ROBERT WESCOMB yeoman 1725 (DS)

[Bur: "Robt Westcombe of Uffculme Town" 20 Nov 1724.]
Will 8 May 1723 of Robert Wescomb of Uffculme, yeoman, pr 12 Jul 1725

before Rev John Talman: residue to s Robert Wescomb, exec; houses, orchards, & gardens called *Patches*, *Meldiches Field* (now *Amurferry*[?]), 2 acres on other side of river against nursery, & a field called *the old hill firse close*, all in Uffculme, to friend Urial Churly of Burlescombe & s Robt Wescomb in trust for rent & issues to pay debts & funeral expenses & then all (except the old hill furse close) to go to dr Kathrine Talbut for life (not for Richard Talbut her husband's use or influence) & then divided amongst her chn at 21, & if none to s Robert & heirs, or if no heirs to grson John Garnsy; to s John Wescomb the old hill furse close, which passes, if no heirs, to s Robert & heirs, or to dr Kathrine or John Garnsy as before; Uffculme estate called *Godfrys* to same trustees to pass to s Robert & his wife for life, then to their heirs or s John &c as before; to dr Sarah *one broad piece of gold*; 1 guinea to grson John Garnsey; 1s ea to s Wm's widow & her 3 chn; to s Robert freedom for 4 years to tend apple trees & carry away from *Meldiches* nursery; 1 guinea ea & expenses to trustees; signed Robert Wescombe; witn: Joseph How, Richd Gange jun^{r}, & Tho Gapper (all sign).

W138 HENRY RUGG farmer of Yandecott 1726 (PU)

[Bur: "Henry Rugg was put in ye ground like a dog" 1 Oct 1725. Mar: "Henry Rugg & Joane Radford" 21 May 1702.]

Will 2 Nov 1717 of Henry Rugg of Yandecott, *farmer*, pr 25 Jun 1726 before Benjamin Hope: all to wife Joane, exec, but if she die without issue then to nephews Hugh & Thomas Northam; signed Henry Rugg; witn: Sam Godfrey, John Hale, & Thomas Jeffery.

W139 ROBERT WELSH tallow chandler 1726 (PU)

[Bur: "Robert Welsh Jnr" 16 Sep 1725. Mar: "Robt. Welch & Elizabeth Goard both of Uffculme" 16 May 1722.]

Will 2 Jun 1725 of Robert Welsh of Uffculme, tallow chandler, pr 25 Jun 1726 before Benjamine Hope, surr: residue to wife Elizabeth, exec; £20 ea at age 21 to s John Welsh & to unborn ch of wife, these amounts to be invested by trustees, friend John Salter of Croyell in Kentisbeare parish, & Ambrose Pring of Uffculme, yeoman; a further £20 shared by the chn if wife remarries; signed Robert Welsh; witn: John May & Will Sellecke (both sign).

W140 NICHOLAS JOB 1727 (PU)

[Bur: "Nicholas Job" 19 Nov 1726. Mar: "Nicholas Job & Ann Stephens both of o pish" 12 Nov 1703.]

Will 20 Oct 1726 of Nicholas Job of Uffculme, pr 12 Jun 1727 at Uffculme before Benj Hope, surr: residue to wife Anne Job & ss Nicholas & John Job, she to relinquish her part if she remarries, retaining only £10; to wife Anne Job right, title, & interest in house at Coldharbour where his sister-in-law Mary Stevens lives; £30, bed, & pot to dr Anne Job; £30 at 21 to ss Richard, William, & Robert Job; younger ss Richd & Wm to be kept & clothed to age 21 by exec^{s}; signed Nicholas Job; witn: Elizabeth Ballyman, W[?] Parks, & James Parsons (all sign).

W141 JOHN DOWDNEY 1727 (PU)

[Bur: "John Dowdney" 3 Oct 1726.]

Admon 12 Jun 1727 names widow Joanne Dowdney as admin & also Mark Westron, gent; before Rev Benj Hope, surr, & signed by Ri Sam Wyche, Reg^{r}; marked X by Joanne Dowdney & signed by Mark Westron.

W142 NICHOLAS RUGGE 1727 (PU)

[Bur: "Nickolas Rugg" 3 Jul 1727. Mar: "Nichol. Rugg & Ann Hurly both of Uffculme" 27 Nov 1722.]

Will 12 Sep 1726 of Nicholas Rugge of Uffculme, pr 25 Jul 1727 before

Benj Hope: residue, including rights, titles, & interest in houses & land between Hillturner & Gaddon Down at present occupied by bro William Rugge, to wife Anne Rugge, exec; 1s ea to father Richard Rugge, bros William & Theophilus, sister Mary Tucker, & bro James Rugge; marked R by Nicholas Rugge; witn: Edward & Grace Churly, & James Hill (all sign).

W143 JOHN CULLIFORD innholder 1728 (DS)

[Bur: "John Cullyford" 22 Apr 1728. Mar: "John Culliford & Jane Clark of Culmstock" 5 Mar 1712/3.]

Will 17 Aug 1725 of John Culliford of Uffculme, innholder, pr 20 Jul 1728 before Benj Hope, surr: residue to dr Mary Culliford, exec; 40s annuity out of *Babbidges* estate to s John Culliford; £5 ea to grchn Edward, Thomazine, Anne, & Jane, chn of s John Culliford; crockery to *now wife* & Anthony Bale in trust for dr Mary; brass & pewter between dr Mary & grson John Culliford & apparel to the latter; to s John (with provision for succession) the rights in 99-year lease (determinable on lives of grchn Edward & Anne Culliford) on house occupied by William Loudwell & his wife; to dr Mary (with provision for succession) the lands lately purchased from Courtnay Babbage & the lease for the house occupied by Nicholas Jones, which passes after her to grson Edward Culliford; fee simple of the "Rainbow" inn to grson John Culliford & heirs (or, if none, to his bro William), but wife Jane to live there for the rest of her life if she does not remarry; to Elizabeth, *now wife* of grson John, a £40s annuity after his death if she does not remarry; further specified fields & closes distributed to descendants; 40s ea to wife Jane & Anthony Bale, sergemaker, to be guardians/trustees during minority of exec; marked by John Culliford; witn: Ja[s] Cooke, Edm[d] Merson, Rich[d] Keule[?] (all sign).

Admon 20 Jul 1728 names Anthony Bale, sergemaker, & John Land, yeoman, both of Uffculme; signed by Anthony Bale & marked by Jane Culliford & John Land before Benj Hope, surr.

W144 RICHARD RUGGE yeoman 1728 (DS)

[Bur: "Rich Rugg" 15 Mar 1727/8.]

Will 27 Jun 1727 of Richard Rugge of Uffculme, yeoman, pr at Uffculme 20 Jul 1728 before Benj Hope, surr: tenement (where he lived, part of manor of Hackpen) & all residue to ss Theophillis & James Rugge, exec[s]; 5s to s William Rugge; £10 & brass pan to dr Mary Tucker, & a pewter dish to her dr Grace Tucker; brass pot to grson Richard Rugge, s of James; pewter dish to grdr Prudence Rugge, dr of James; marked RR by Richard Rugge; witn: Will Southwood & John Bishop (sign) & John Row (mark?).

W145 PETER HOLWAY yeoman 1728 (DS)

[Bur: "Peter Hollway" 26 Apr 1728.]

Will 15 Apr 1728 of Peter Holway of Uffculme, yeoman, pr at Uffculme 20 Jul 1728 before Benj Hope, surr: residue to ss John & William Holway, exec[s]; 40s ea to 6 drs, Elizabeth Morish, Sarah Reedwod, & Mary, Beaton, June, & Joan Holway; signed Peter Hollway; witn: William Cape & Bap Andro (both sign).

W146 ANTHONY BALE sen[r], sergemaker 1723 (PU)

[Mar: "Anthony Bale & Anne Ayshelford" 14 Jan 1679. See W156. Positioned here because of proximity to the will of John Lake (1730), but no date of probate for either.]

Will 21 Feb 1722/3 of Anthony Bale sen[r] of Uffculme, sergemaker: residue to s Anthony Bale, exec; £200 (as £20 a year) to wife Anne; household goods divided equally between wife Anne & s Anthony; to s Anthony dyeing furnace, brass kettle, chittle for washing wool, & all other implements & materials of serge trade; £5 at 21 to Elizabeth Bale, dr of s John; £8 ea at 21 to Jane & Mary Bale, drs of s John, & to Anne & Sarah Bale, drs of s Anthony; witn: William Deynan & Jo Were.

W147 JOHN LAKE butcher 1730 (PU)

[Bur: "John Lake" 6 Aug 1730. Mar: "John Lake & Widow Wrayford, butcher" 25 Mar 1705.]
Will 17 Jan 1729/30 of John Lake of Uffculme, butcher: residue to *now wife* Mary Lake, exec; 1s ea to Henry Dowdney sen^{r}, tailor, & John Lake sen^{r}, sergeweaver, both of Uffculme; 5s to John Lake jun^{r} of Uffculme, sergeweaver, & also 5s after death of wife Mary, to be paid out of *my House every year so long as Thomas Cross jun^{r} shall live*; marked JL; witn: Richard Langhm & Elizabeth Parsons (both sign), & Mary Babbage (MB mark).

W148 JOANE FULFORD widow of Stenhill 1731 (DS)

Will 14 Dec 1729 of Joane Fulford, widow of Stenhill, Uffculme, pr 21 Jun 1731 at Uffculme before John Talman, surr: to be buried beside husband at Bradninch; residue to exec, nephew (?) Mary Murch, dr of Joseph Dolman of Cullompton; 1s a week for life to bro John Reed of Butterly; £20 ea at age 21 to 2 ss of John Reed (the elder being John);£50 to Joseph, s of Joseph Dolman, or, if he dies within 1 year, to John Murch, s of Mary Murch; second best suit to Susanna, *now wife* of John Reed; a gold ring ea to Mrs Mary Walrond & Mrs Hester Carwithen, *now wife* of John Carwithen; funeral to have cake, wine, & roast beef, & 4 bearers to have hat bands & gloves; marked by Joan Fulford; witn: Francis Cross & Henry Bryant (both sign).

W149 EDWARD SKINNER quaker of Plymtree, sergemaker 1731 (DS)

Will, 13 Feb 1729/30, of Edward Skinner of Plymtree, sergemaker, pr 21 Jun 1731: to be buried as a quaker; proceeds of sale by trust of Uffculme property & residue of estate to wife Mary Skinner, exec; trustees (*viz* wife Mary Skinner, Benjamin Colbrath of North Currie in Somerset, mercer, Anthony Bale of Uffculme, sergemaker, & Thomas Skinner of Plymtree, sergemaker) to sell house, outhouses, & garden in Uffculme town (in possession of subtenant Joseph Colbrath, woolcomber) & all other property in Uffculme & elsewhere (except *Wills's* in Plymtree where father lives) & proceeds for wife & for settling debts, especially a £26 bond to exec^{s} of Edward Ellis, late of Uffculme, to discharge father's obligation; signed Edward Skinner; witn: Will Sellicke, John Sidwell, Wm Pannell, & Paul Hitchcock (all sign).

W150 JOHN MARSHALL 1731 (DS)

[Bur: "John Marshall" 31 Oct 1729.]
Admon 21 Jun 1731 names John Marshall, gen[t], as s & admin of the goods &c of the intestate John Marshall, & also John Dunn & John Grantland; all signed & sealed in presence of John Talman sur^{o}.

W151 THOMAS ROOKLEY 1732 (PU)

Admon 14 Jun 1732 names sister Elizabeth Ellworthy of Cullompton as admin & also John Dunn of Uffculme, yeoman, & John Penny of Blandford, Dorset; marked Elizabeth Ellworthy & signed by John Donn & J Penny.

W152 THOMAS MARSH 1733 (DS)

[Mar: "Thomas Marsh & Elizabeth Eveleigh" 28 Apr 1730, Tiverton. See W249, W255.]

A will (missing) of Thomas Marsh was sworn 20 Aug 1733 by his widow Elizabeth, exec, before Benj Hope.

W153 ALICE CHURLY widow 1733 (PU)

[Bur: "Alice Churley" 19 Mar 1732/3.] Will 18 Jan 1732[/3?] of Allice (sic) Churly of Uffculme, widow, pr 20 Aug 1733 before Rev Benj Hope, & signed by Ri Sam Wyche, Reg^r: residue & silk garments & gold ring to cousin Elizabeth Marsh, wife of Thomas Marsh, exec; to friend & k (cousin) John Churly, presbyterian minister, as trustee for investment, the bond dated 7 May 1729, held by Sarah Ford of Halberton & her s John Ford, for £60 with condition for payment of £30 with lawful interest to pay late husband's bequests; £3 to John Thomas, s-in-law of sister Elizabeth Langwell, in trust for his mother-in-law's use not her husband's (!) or, at her death, for her dr Anne Thomas; *duroy gown, popling coat, & callaminco mantle* to Elizabeth Langwell; 1 guinea ea to cousins Anne Thomas & Mary Pattin; to wife of cousin Thomas Howe 2 guineas, woollen & linen clothes, silk handkerchief, & a bed, to be conveyed by cousin Joseph for 5s; to cousin Mary Jeffery 2 guineas & 2 suits of linen, not for husband's use (!); a gold ring ea to wives of cousins John & Joseph Howe; silk garments, gold ring, silver spoon & buckles, & 2 leather chairs to Sarah, dr of Joseph Howe; coat, silver spoon, & 2 leather chairs to Elizabeth, dr of Joseph Howe; oak chest & 2 leather chairs to John, s of Joseph Howe; ½ guinea ea to Joseph Howe's 3 chn; 30s ea to 5 young chn of John Howe; 1s ea to cousins Robert & Thomas How[e]; 1 guinea to Margaret Flood; Mr Ambrose's book to cousin John How[e], a book of Mr Flavil's ea to cousins Robert & Edward Pattin, & Mr Burkit's book to cousin Edward Pattin; signed Alice Churly; witn: Margaret Flood & Tho Gapper (both sign).

W154 ANTHONY BALE sergemaker 1733 (PU)

Will 18 Mar 1732/3 of Anthony Bale of Uffculme, sergemaker: all (including land, &c) in trust for exec^s, 2 drs Anne & Sarah Bale; if either should marry, husband can be tenant for life at house where John Wescombe lives, & lawful issue to own after his death; signed Anthony Bale; witn: Jno Wescombe & Tho: Gapper.

Admon 20 Aug 1733 names Sarah Bale, quaker, as admin during minority of Ann & Sarah Bale, chn of Anthony Bale, exec^s, & also William Evans, woolcomber, & John Tucker, tailor, both of Uffculme; before Benj Hope, surr.; all sign in presence of William Boucher, not^y pub.

W155 THOMAS JERWOOD joiner 1733 (PU)

Will 21 Apr 1733 of Thomas Jerwood of Uffculme, joiner, pr 20 Aug 1733 before Benj Hope, surr: residue to wife Elizabeth, exec; after death or remarriage of wife, house & garden to s Thomas Jerwood, if he pays £5 to his mother within 3 months of testator's death, & 20s ea to testator's drs, Mary wife of Wm Carter, Elizabeth wife of Robert Parsons, Thomasin wife of Wm Fry, Anne wife of James Tozer, & Alice widow of Thomas Ward within 6 months of mother's death; if s Thomas defaults, all to go to husband of dr Anne Johane, James Tozer of Kentisbeare, butcher, with same provision; iron vice to grson John Jerwood, s of Thomas; rest of tools to apprentice John Norman if he marries dr Alice Ward; signed Thomas Jerwood; witn: John Jerwood, William Rugge, & James Hills (all sign).

W156 ANNE BALE widow 1734 (DS)

[See W146.]

Will 8 Oct 1733 of Anne Bale of Uffculme, widow, pr 11 Jan 1733/4 before Benj Hope, surr: residue to Jane Evans, exec; 1 guinea ea to Anne &

Sarah Bale, drs of dec[d] s Anthony Bale; 5s ea to Elizabeth & Mary Bale, drs of dec[d] s John Bale; 1 guinea & warming pan to Jane Brooks, dr of s John Bale; all sums to be paid after receipt of money (over £100) due from late husband Anthony Bale of Uffculme; marked by Anne Bale; witn: Mathw Cooke, George Marling, & Richard Langham (all sign).

W157 JOHN CULLYFORD jun[r], innholder 1734 (DS)

[Bur: "John Cullyford" 14 Jun 1734. Mar: "John Cullyford & Jane Hawker" 22 Apr 1731.]
Nuncupative will 7 Jun 1734 of John Cullyford jun[r] of Uffculme, innholder, pr at Uffculme 19 Jun 1734 before John Talman, surr: specifies interment near graves of his ch & his grandmother Ann Cullyford; most to wife Jane, exec, including rights in *Hames Meadow* (described in will of grandfather John Cullyford), which passes to father John Cullyford if she dies first but otherwise to bro Edward Cull[e]yford, who then pays from the proceeds £20 to Sarah, dr of deceased bro Wm Cull[e]yford; if bro Edward dies without issue before wife Jane, value of Meadow to be divided between sisters Thomasin, Jane, & Ann (who also receive 5s each), after £20 paid to niece Sarah; best suit to bro Edward; 5s ea to Marmaduke & John, ss of sister Jane; everyday suit with stockings, shoes, & hat to John Dunster; witn: George & Catherine Russell, (both sign), & John Dunster (mark).

W158 THOMASIN MARSHALL spinster 1734 (DS)

[Bur: "Thomasin Marshall" 12 Aug 1732.]
Will 28 Apr 1732 of Thomasin Marshall of Uffculme, spinster, pr at Uffculme 20 Jun 1734 before John Talman, surr: residue to bro-in-law Henry Westron, exec; £100 (mentioned in relation to a bequest of £350 from Thomasin's late father, Robert Marshall) to sister Agnes, wife of Henry Westron, gent of Uffulme; to nephew Robert Westron 6 *septer Jacobesies* [James I coins?]; £100 to sister Elizabeth, wife of Samuel Bishopp jun[r], yeoman of Uffculme; £17 10s to niece Betty Bishopp, dr of Samuel; £5 ea to bro Robert Marshall & his wife Joane; £5 & a 1-guinea mourning ring to Robert Manley, gent of Uffculme; 1 guinea ea to k James Gill jun[r], & to the ss of William Southwood sen[r] of Uffculme, James & William jun[r]; clothes shared between sisters Agnes & Elizabeth; £5 & a 1-guinea mourning ring ea to ks Ann Searle of Otterton & Joane Southwood, dr of William Southwood sen[r]; signed Thomasin Marshall; witn: Jo Were & Henry Cadbury (both sign).

W159 THOMAS SHOOBROOK 1735 (PU)

[Bur: "Thomas Shoobrook" 13(?) Apr 1735. Mar: "Tho. Shoebrook & Jane Seymour of Uffculme" 29 Apr 1720.]
Admon 8 May 1735 names widow Jane Shoobrook as admin & also Mark & Henry Westron, both gents of Uffculme, before Benj Hope, surr; marked by Jane Shoobrook & signed by the Westrons in presence of Tho Martin, not[y] pub,

W160 HENRY RUSSELL tailor 1735 (PU)

[Bur: "Henry Russell" 2 Jan 1734/5.]
Will 6 Sep 1732 of Henry Russell of Uffculme, tailor, pr 8 May 1735 before Benj Hope, surr: residue & houses & gardens where testator, Honor Toser, Abraham Tapscott, & Nicholas Boyle live, to grson Henry Russell (s of s James decd.) but, if he dies without issue, all to go to grsons James & Henry Russell (sons of s Henry decd.), except the pair of houses occupied by Abraham Tapscott & Nicholas Boyle, which go to 2 grsons James & John Russell (ss of James decd.), who also receive, with their sister Anne Russell, 20s each; to grdr Sarah (dr of Henry

decd.) for life, house & garden to SW of where testator lives, thereafter to grson Henry Russell (s of James decd.); £20 ea to grsons James & Henry (ss of Henry decd.); signed Henry Russell; witn: Jo Were, John Wills, & Mary Wills (all sign).

W161 HUMFRY PEARCY 1735 (PU)

[Bur: "Humphrey Peircy" 2 Jan 1734/5. Mar: "Humphry Peircy & Jane James" 24 Apr 1718.]
Admon 8 May 1735 names widow Jane Pearcy admin, & also Henry James, weaver, & William Evans, woolcomber, both of Uffculme: before Benj Hope, surr for prebendary Francis Eyre; marked by Jane Pearcy & signed Henry James & William Evenes (*sic*).

W162 JAMES ROACH the elder, blacksmith 1736 (PU)

[Bur: "James Roach" 12 Jul 1736. Mar: "James Roach & Agnis Westcomb of Kentisbeere" 4 May 1716. See plaque on 2 & 4 Coldharbour "E Roach 1720".]
Will 12 Jan 1733[/4?] of James Roach the elder of Uffculme, blacksmith, pr 14 Aug 1736 before Benj Hope, surr: residue to wife Agnes Roach, exec; all rents & profits from Uffculme property to wife for life, thereafter as follows: (a) Twenty Acres (2 dwellings, garden & orchard) to grson William Kent, if he pays 20s p.a. for life to his bro John Kent; (b) to grson James Roach, house, garden, 2 shops, &c where his mother lives, plus a further garden; (c) to grdr Anne Kent, the house called the Bakes where Thomas Mildy[?] lives, plus adjacent plot by paper mills; (d) to grdr Sarah Whitcomb, the higher house *lately erected out of the Anabaptist meeting-house* next to Henry Davis[?] house; (e) to grson John Roach, 2 houses & garden lately in possession of Edward Seatherd & William Cotterall, but to pay 5s ea p.a. for life to grdrs Agnis & Joan Roach; (f) to grdr Mary Stark, wife of John Stark, lower part of the meeting-house, subject to payment of 10s p.a. to grdr Sarah Kent; (g) to grson James Roach, the Little Meadow, subject to payment of 5s p.a. for life to grdr Elizabeth Kent & 10s p.a. for life to dr-in-law Elizabeth Maning; marked JR by James Roach; witn: John & Jane Grantland & Tho Gapper (all sign).

W163 AMOS BUTSON yeoman 1737 (DS)

Will 26 May 1732 of Amos Butson of Uffculme, yeoman "aged & infirm", pr 2 Jul 1737: residue, if she does not remarry, to wife (unnamed), exec: 1s ea to s John Butson, dr Jane Byrd, widow, & to grchn Ann Ellis, wife of John Ellis, & Samuell Byrd, s.of Jane Byrd; signed by Amos Butson; witn: Francis Hurleigh, Henry Bryant, Joan Bryant (all sign).

W164 JAMES RUGGE 1737 (DS)

[Bur: "Jam(es) Rugg" 20 Feb 1736.]
Admon 2 Jul 1737 names widow Grace Rugge as admin & also William Brooke, miller, & John Tucker, tailor, both of Uffculme (both men sign & Grace Rugge marks).

W165 GEORGE WALL 1737 (DS)

[Mar: "George Wall & Priscilla Woodberry 2 Jul 1733, Burlescombe.]
Admon 2 Jul 1737 names widow Priscilla Wall as admin & also Wm Evans, woolcomber, & Henry Davy, weaver, all of Uffculme [clearly Uffculme but described as in Dorset!]; Priscilla Wall marks but others sign.

W166 HENRY RUSSELL 1737 (PU)

Admon 2 Nov 1737 names widow Jane Russell as admin, & also James Russell of Uffculme, tailor, & John Oatway of Culmstock, yeoman; before Benj Hope, surr; all sign in presence of John Deyman. The bond of admin^{n} of the same date (signed by Henry Hearst,

Reg[r]) has *Henry* Russell correctly on the cover but *John* Russell (with widow Jane) within the note; but *John* must be an error & hence only one deceased Russell is involved here.

W167 SAMUEL SHORT 1737 (PU)

[Mar: "Samuel Short & Agnes Payge" 8 Jun 1709, Exeter St David. See W186.]

Will 24 Feb 1720[/1?] of Samuel Short of Uffculme, pr 24 Nov 1737 before Benj Hope: residue to wife Agnes, exec; books to s Samuel & dr Agnes; 1s ea to James & Thomas, ss of sister Anna Willy, decd; Peter Dunnet & his wife mentioned; signed Samuel Short.

W168 FRYDISWED PAGE widow 1737 (PU)

Will 9 Jul 1729 of Frydiswed Page of Uffculme, widow, pr 24 Nov 1737 before Benj Hope: residue, including house & garden, to dr Agnis Short; 20s at 21 & 2 silver spoons to grson Sammuell Short; 20s at 21 to grdr Agnis Short; marked F by Frydiswed Page; witn: John Churly, Elizabeth Eveleigh, & Tho Gapper (all sign).

W169 JOAN MOORE widow 1738 (PU)

[Bur: "Joan Moore" 14 Dec 1738.]

Admon 9 Dec 1738 names next of kin George Bright of Bickly [*sic*], husbandman, as admin, & also George Bright the younger of Bickly & James Row of Uffculme; before Benj Hope; all 3 mark in presence of Christopher Baker (CB mark) & .?.Parke (signs).

W170 ROBERT PIPPERELL carpenter 1739 (PU)

[Mar: "Robt Pipperell & Mary Milton of Uffculme & Culmestock" 25 Feb 1722/3.]

Will 7 May 1738 of Robert Pipperell of Uffculme, carpenter, pr 3 Jul 1739: residue to dr Ann Pipperell, exec; 1s ea to ss Robert & William & to wife Mary; marked by Robert Pipperell.

W171 RICHARD MARSHALL woolcomber 1739 (PU)

Will 7 Feb 1738/9 of Richard Marshall of Uffculme, woolcomber, pr 24 Jul 1739 before Benj Hope: residue to *now wife* Mary Marshall, exec, thereafter to 2 grchn, Margaret & Robert Marshall, who also receive £5 & 50s respectively at age 21; signed Richard Marshall; witn: Margaret Butson (signs), & Anne Rowland & Richard Rowland (both mark).

W172 JOHN CULLIFORD 1740 (DS)

Will 3 Mar 1739[/40?] of John Culliford of Uffculme, pr 12 Jul 1740: residue to dr Ann Culliford, exec; to wife Elizabeth the house, garden, & stable where s William lives, to pass to exec after wife's death; to s William the Rainbow House & field & most of apparel; 40s annuity to dr Thomasin James; 30s annuity to dr Jane Edwards; coat & pewter dish to grson Marmaduke Edwards; signed John Culliford; witn: Hugh Seatham & Humphry Culliford (both sign).

W173 LAWRENCE PALMER gent 1741 (PU)

Will 9 Sep 1741 of Lawrence Palmer of Uffculme, gent, pr 31 Oct 1741 before Rev Benj Hope: all property & residue to John Cross of Halberton, John Dunn of Uffculme, & John Denham of Holcombe Rogus, all sergemakers, in trust for exec, niece Martha Bird (& not for her husband, John Bird of Uffculme, sergemaker); £20 at 21 to niece Mary Marshall, dr of John Marshall of Uffculme; £10 to servant Catherine Bale if still with him; signed Laurens Palmer; witn: Tho Dunn, John Dunnett, & Robert Pearcy (all sign).

W174 JOHN BLACKMORE sergemaker 1742 (PU)

[Mar: "John Blackmore & Mary Moore 1720, Sheldon.]

Will 18 May 1739 of John Blackmore of Uffculme, sergemaker, pr at Salis-

In the name of God Amen I John Culliford of the Parish of Uffculme in the County of Devon being sick & weak of Body but of sound & perfect mind & memory Blessed be almighty God for ye same calling to mind the uncertainty of this mortal Life and that it is appointed for all men once to dye when it shall please almighty God to call do hereby make this my last will & Testament, first being sorry for all my sins most humbly desiring forgiveness of the same I Commend my soul to almighty God my Creator & to Jesus Christ my saviour & Redeemer in whome and by whose merits I trust and believe to be saved, & to receive full pardon of all my sins, and my Body I commit to the Earth to be Decently Buried at the discression of my Executrix hereafter named & as Tuching such worldly goods & Chattles as it hath pleased God in his goodness to bestow upon me I give and Dispose thereof in manner and form following, Item I give & bequeath unto Elizabeth my Wife the House my son William Culliford now lives in with the Garden platt and Stabling adjoyning thereunto during the Lives I have on it now, if my Wife shall so long live. but if she should dye before ye sd lives then my will is that ye sd House Garden platt & Stabling Shall Return to my Executrix, Item I give and bequeath unto William Culliford my son all the Right & title of Reversion that I have or shall have in ye Rainbow House & field after my death, and likewise I give to my son William all my wearing apparell Except one light Colour Coat to be delivered by my executrix in one month after my Decease, Item I give unto my Daughter Thomazin James one annuity of fforty shillings a year and to Commence one year after my decease Item I give unto my Daughter Jane Edwards thirty shilling a year to be paid her Quarterly to Commence in one year after my Decease, both annuitys to be paid by my Executrix and for nonpayment of ye same, I do give my Daughters full power to take distress on the sd premises, but in Case my Children to whome I have gave Legacys should be troublesome or cause a law sute in any way, my will is that in any such default by any of them that ye Legacy by me given shall Remain to my Executrix, Item I give to Marmaduke Edwards my Granson one light Colour Coate which I excepted out of my apparell, and likewise I give to my Granson Marmaduke one pewter dish to be delivered by my Executrix in one Month after my Decease, Item all the Rest of my goods and Chattles not before given or bequeathed I give and bequeath unto my Daughter Ann Culliford whome I make Constitute and ordain my whole & sole Executrix of this my last will and Testament, hereby Revoking all former wills by me made declaring this to be my last will & Testament. In witness hereof I have hereunto sett my hand and seal this third day of March in ye year of our Lord one thousand seven hundred and thirty nine

Further my will is in Case any accident of fire should happen in the sd House that my Legacys here given to be void until ye Charges of Rebuilding the same fully paid Item one more I give unto [illegible]

Signed sealed & delivered to be the last will and Testament of John Culliford in ye presents of us

William Scott
Hugh Gresaham
Humphry Culliford

John Culliford

The will of John Culliford 1740 [W172]

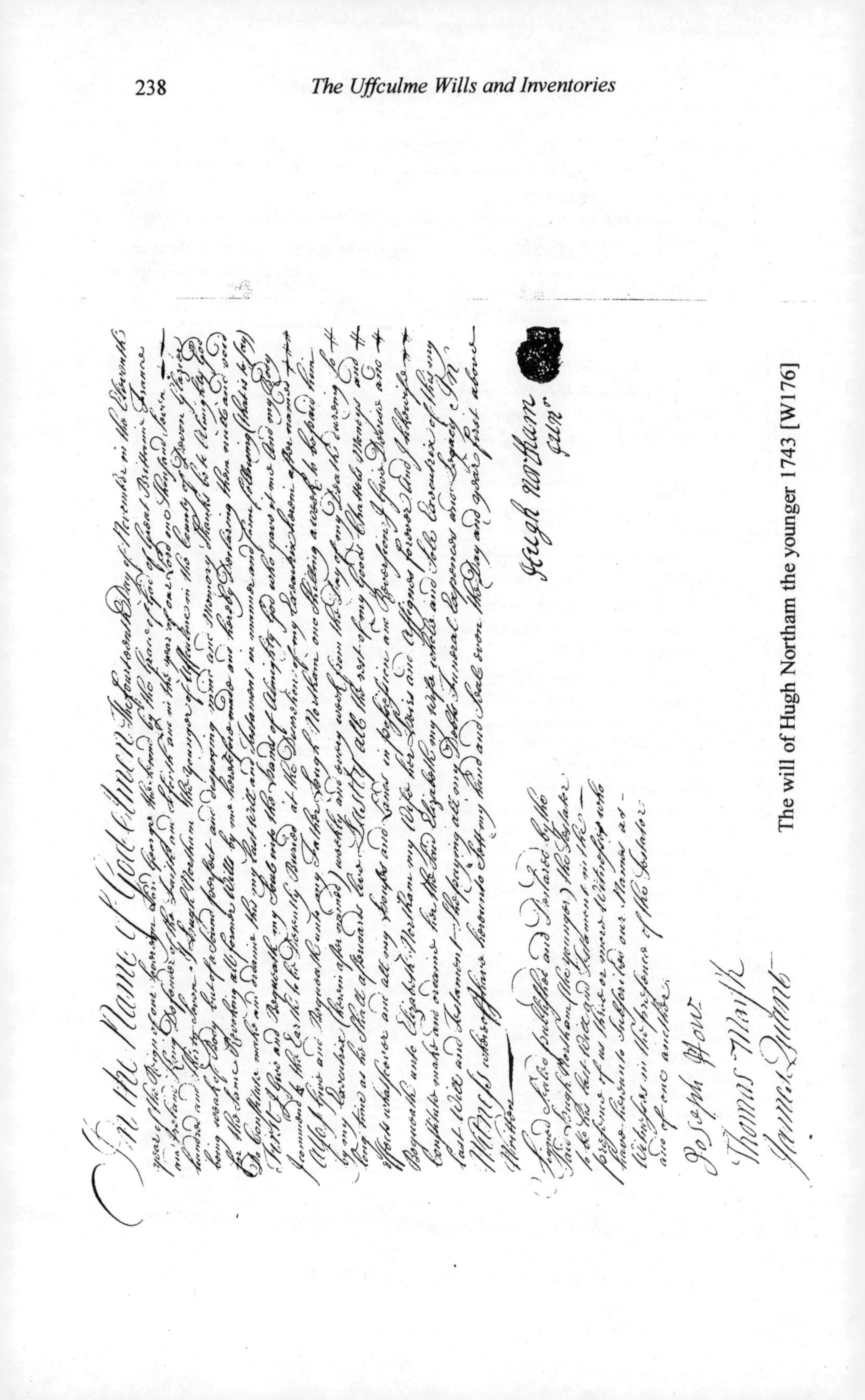

The will of Hugh Northam the younger 1743 [W176]

bury 1 Jun 1742 before Rev John Talman, surr: residue to wife Mary, exec; £120 to be invested by trustees Joseph Ellis of Bradninch & bro-in-law John Frayne of Okehampton for s John Blackmore at age 21, interest meanwhile for his education & maintenance, to pass if he dies to dr Mary at 21 or marriage (if with consent of her mother & trustees); similarly £100 in trust for dr Mary Blackmore, or s John if she dies, or wife Mary if both die; signed John Blackmore; witn: William & Anthony Saunders & Jno Frayne the younger (all sign). [In the probate the widow Mary Blackmore is described as a quaker.]

W175 NICHOLAS JONES 1742 (DS)

Will 8 Sep 1742 of Nicholas Jones of Uffculme, pr 1742: residue to dr Hannah Pringe, exec; best coat, waistcoat, & breeches to s-in-law John Pringe; rest of apparel to s Edward Jones; 2s ea to nephews Nicholas & William Gange; 1s to Thomas Crow; signed [shakily] Nicholas Jones; witn: Elie Northam & Wm Escott (both sign).

W176 HUGH NORTHAM jun^{r}, glazier 1743 (DS)

Will 14 Nov 1737 of Hugh Northam the younger of Uffculme, glazier, pr 19 Apr 1743: apart from 1s a week for life to father, Hugh Northam, houses, lands & all else to wife Elizabeth Northam, exec; signed Hugh Northam; witn: Joseph Howe, Thomas Marsh, & James Quant (all sign).

W177 JOHN DUNNE 1743 (DS)

[Mar: "John Dunne & Mary Parkhouse of Halberton" 25 Jul 1711.]
Admon 12 Jul 1743, before Rev Richard Younger, surr, names widow Mary Dunne as admin & also John Dunster, weaver, & Henry Watts, shoemaker, all of Uffculme; all make marks in presence of Willm Boucher, not^{y} pub.

W178 DAVID ERWIN 1743 (DS)

Admon 12 Jul 1743, before Rev Richard Younger, surr, names widow Joan Erwin as admin & also John Dunn, yeoman, & John Gay, woolcomber, all of Uffculme: all sign in presence of Willm Boucher, not^{y} pub.

W179 JOSEPH HOWE 1743 (DS)

[Mar: "Joseph Howe & Sarah Marshall" 14 Jul 1715, Tiverton. See W250.]
Admon 17 Jul 1743, before Willm Boucher not^{y} pub, names widow Sarah How as admin & also John Donne, yeoman, & Nicholas Wrayford, butcher, all of Uffculme; sign as Sarah How, John Dunn, & Nicholas Wreford.

W180 JOAN SOWTHEY widow of Northcott 1744 (PU)

Will 10 Dec 1741 of Joan Sowthey of Northcott, widow, pr 16 Apr 1744 before Benj Hope, surr: residue & all rents, household goods, &c between s Thomas Sowthey & dr Elenor Gill, execs; 5s to s George Sowthey; £10 (if recoverable from exec^{s} of dec^{d} bro Nicholas Churly) or a bed to grdr Elizabeth Trickey; marked by Joan Sowthey; witn: William Hitchcock & Rob: Fry (both sign).

W181 ROBERT POOKE yeoman 1744 (PU)

[Bur: "Robert Pook" 28 Sep 1744. Mar: "Robert Pooke & Rachell Wood of Willan" 14 Sep 1715.]
Will 26 Jan 1743[/4?] of Robert Pooke of Uffculme, yeoman, pr 8 Nov 1744 before Benj Hope, surr: residue to wife Rachael, exec; *Carters* tenement at Hackpen, *Mitchells* & *Walronds* at Ashill, & any other fee simple &c in Uffculme to James Holway of Ashill, yeoman, & Thomas Stone of Cullompton, in trust to provide rents to wife Rachael for life (if no remarriage) & by lease, mortgage, &c to raise £600 to be equally divided between 3 drs,

Elizabeth, Rachael, & Mary; then *Carters* to go to s John Pooke, *Mitchells & Walronds* to s Jacob Pooke; signed Robert Pooke; witn: Margeret & Wm Flower & Tho Gore (all sign).

W182 RICHARD GILL sergemaker of Craddock 1744 (PU)

[Bur: "Richard Gill" 29 Mar 1744.]

Will 17 Mar 1743[/4?] of Richard Gill of Craddock, sergemaker, pr 8 Nov 1744 before Benj Hope, surr: all to wife Sarah & drs Dorithey & Sarah, execs; signed Richard Gill; witn: William Southwood, John Tozer, & Anthony Jerwood (all sign).

W183 JOHN HURLEY 1744 (PU)

[Mar: "John Hurley & Bridget Manning" 6 Mar 1700/1.]

Admon 8 Nov 1744 names s John Hurley, yeoman, as admin (after renunciation by his mother the widow, Bridgett Cooke, now wife of William Cooke, woolcomber) & also Samuell Evans, miller, Richard Babidge, labourer, all of Uffculme; John Hurley & Richard Babidge sign, but Samuell Evans marks. [Surprisingly, the labourer signs but not the miller.]

W184 MARTHA GOARD widow 1744 (PU)

[Bur: "Martha Goard" 14 Oct 1744.]

Will 14 Sep 1734 of Martha Goard of Uffculme, widow, pr 8 Nov 1744 before Benj Hope: residue to exec^s^, 3 drs Mary Holway, Elizabeth Welsh, & Joane Fouracres; 1s ea to ss John, Robert, & Richard Goard; £5 at 21 to grson William Brooks, s of William Brooks the younger of Uffculme by dr Martha; 5s ea to grchn John, Sarah, Ann, Martha, Elizabeth, Joane, Abraham, Mary, & Robert Manley (chn of Abraham Manley of Kentisbeare, dec^d^); marked by Martha Goard; witn: Edward Davie & James Quant (both sign), & William Cotterell (marked C).

W185 HUGH SWEETLAND maltster 1744(PU)

[Bur: "Hugh Sweetland Senr." 13 Nov 1742.]

Will 7 Oct 1739 of Hugh Sweetland of Uffculme, maltster, pr 8 Nov 1744 before Benj Hope, surr: residue to ss Hugh & William Sweetland, exec^s^; house & garden where he lived to s William Sweetland, together with all malt mills and malt-making gear; £5 to grson Hugh Sweetland, together with hanging press (in parlour chamber); £5 ea at age 14 to grchn Prudence & Ralph Sweetland, & to (chn of s Hugh) Henry, John, Thomas, David, & Charles Sweetland, & also to unborn ch of Hugh & his wife Margarett; John Drew to be forgiven £10 of his debt if he pays remainder to exec^s^; signed Hugh Sweetland; witn: Jas Skinner (signs), Sarah Weeks alš Pook (X mark), & Mary Hosegod (H mark).

W186 AGNES SHORT widow 1745 (PU)

[See W167.]

Will 24 Aug 1743 of Agnes Short of Uffculme, widow, pr 15 Jan 1745 before Benj Hope: residue to trustees John Churly of Uffculme, clerk, & Richard Clark of Halberton, gent, execs, to trustees house, garden, &c at Bodmiscombe (on 99-year lease terminable on own & dr Agnes's death) for s Samuel Short & heirs; to trustees house, &c in Uffculme (where testatrix lived) in trust for dr Agnes Dunn, wife of Robert Dunn (not for her husband's use) & her heirs; to trustees £40 ea to be invested for s Samuel Short & dr Agnes Dunn; signed Agnes Short; witn: E Manley, John Pring, & John Gage (all sign).

W187 HENRY TRICKEY sergemaker 1745 (PU)

Will 6 Feb 1744[/5?] of Henry Trickey of Uffculme, sergemaker, pr 9 Sep 1745 before Benj Hope, surr: residue to s William Trickey, exec; 1s 6d a week to wife [unnamed] for life from s

John Trickey for as long as his debt lasts, then from s William; bed, potage pot, & cottle to wife; mare to s John Trickey; 1 pewter dish ea to 2 ss of s John; signed [shakily] Henry Trickey; witn: Robert Evans, Francis Cross, & W[?] Byrd (all sign).

W188 HENRY DUNN woolcomber 1745 (PU)

Will 8 May 1745 of Henry Dunn of Uffculme, woolcomber, pr 9 Sep 1745 before Benj Hope: residue to bros John & Thomas Dunn, exec[s]; £5 to sister Dorothy Pratt; 1 guinea to sister Margaret Rugg; 4 guineas to bro Robert Dunn; to chn of bro John Dunn, £10 ea to Jane & John, £12 to Mary, & £10 to Elizabeth Dunn; 1 guinea ea to Thomas Grantland & k Dorothy Pratt; signed Henry Dunn; witn: Bernard Byrd (signs) & Elizabeth Woland (marks).

W189 WILLIAM HOOKWAY husbandman 1745 (PU)

Will 28 Aug 1739 of William Hookway of Uffculme, husbandman, pr 9 Sep 1745 before Benj Hope: *Petty Croft* (part of the manor of Hackpen, in testator's possession) for remainder of 99-year lease & residue to grson William Hookway, exec; 1s to wife Julian; 1s ea to 2 ss John & William, & to 4 drs Elizabeth, Mary, Joan, & Julian; marked by William Hookway; witn: Tho: Tucker & James Townsend (both sign).

W190 SARAH GARNSEY widow 1746 (DS)

[Bur: "Sarah Garnsey" 3 May 1746. Mar: "Robt Garnsey & Sarah Wescomb" Whitsunday (May) 1705.]
Will 4 Feb 1745/6 of Sarah Garnsey of Uffculme, widow, pr 1 Jul 1746: residue to s John Garnsey, exec; £50 (with interest) at age 21 to grdr Sarah Garnsey, who also has a chest & contents, oval table, cupboard, & still; £20 ea at age 21 & gold rings to grdrs Mary & Jone Garnsey; 1 guinea ea at age 21 to grsons Robert & John Garnsey; signed Sarath [*sic*] Garnsey; witn: Mary Holway & Simon Cullon (both sign).

W191 WILLIAM DUNN yeoman 1747 (PU)

[Bur: "William Dunne" 8 Apr 1747 - before will!]
Will 25 May [Mar?] 1747 of William Dunn of Uffculme, yeoman, pr 16 Dec 1747 before Benj Hope, surr: residue to s Henry Dunn, exec; £30 to s John Dunn; £20 to dr Dorothy Tamas; £30 to dr Mary Dunn; 1 guinea ea to grdrs Sarah & Elizabeth at 21; *Venners* tenement to s Henry Dunn & heirs; signed [shakily] William Dunn; witn: Richard Langham, Rich: Gange, & Fran[s] Beer (all sign).

W192 JACOB POOK yeoman 1749 (DS)

[Bur: "Jacob Pook" 22 Aug 1746.]
Will 9 Aug 1746 of Jacob Pook of Uffculme, pr 21 Jun 1749 before Rev John Talman, surr: residue to Richard Langham in trust for bro John Pooke, exec; £20 ea to sisters Elizabeth Pooke, Rachall Pullman, & Mary Pooke; £10 to Iset Eveleigh; £5 to tenant Edward Hitchcock; 40s to aunt Rebaca Backer; 40s to William Starke, s of Amos Starke of Uffculme, woolcomber; if any of these die before the legacies are due, the sums pass to the exec; marked J by Jacob Pook; witn: Jonathan Burrow, John Stark, & Joan Haskings (all sign).

W193 ELIZABETH WALROND widow 1749 (DS)

[Bur: "Mrs Elizabeth Walrond" 29 May 1749. Mar: (1st) "James Hollway & Elizabeth Bishopp" 27 May 1696.]
Will 25 Jan 1747 of Elizabeth Walrond of Uffculme, widow, pr 21 Jun 1749: residue to dr Anna Windsor, exec; *to be decently Interred in a private manner in the Vault of Uffculme Church by my Dear Husband James Holway deceased*; 6 guineas for a mourning suit to grson Henry Blackmore; £100 to grson Humphry Black-

more; £10 for a mourning suit to grdr Dorothy Baker; £100 to grson John Windsor; £5 to k John Floyer in trust for nephew Anthony Floyer; gold watch & chain & £10 for mourning suit to grdr Elizabeth Westron; 5 guineas ea to nieces Elizabeth & Eleanor Floyer; 1-guinea mourning gold ring ea to nephew John Floyer Esq, & to 3 nieces Sarah Young, Mergaret Floyer, & Katherine, wife of Charles Jennings; to k James Holway a "Scepter peice or Broad peice of Gold"; signed Eliz Walrond; witn: Edwd Manley & Hugh Radford (both sign).

W194 GILES BISHOP yeoman 1749 (DS)

[Bur: "Giles Byshop" 11 Mar 1747/8.] Will 31 Dec 1745 of Giles Bishop of Uffculme, yeoman, pr 21 Jun 1749: residue & all messuages, lands, & tenements in Uffculme (*Hydons*, &c) to s Humphry Bishop, exec; £5 to dr Eleanor, wife of Richard Goard, yeoman of Uffculme, or shared by her drs Elizabeth, Mary, & Martha Goard if she should die; £15 ea to these grdrs & to Richard Goard in trust for grdr Eleanor, wife of Robert Pearsey of Uffculme, blacksmith (but not for his use); 1s ea to Richard Goard & Joan Bishop, widow of late s Samuel Bishop; £15 to grson William, & 1 guinea ea to grsons Samuel & Giles, all ss of Samuel Bishop; pewter, brass, settle, & hogshead to dr Eleanor; trunk to Elizabeth Goard; marked by Giles Bishop; witn: Thomas Ogenes(?), Robeart Manley, James Quant (all sign).

W195 WILLIAM BROOKE the elder, miller 1749 (DS)

[Bur: "William Brook Senr" 26 Jun 1747.] Will 12 Jun 1747 of William Brooke the elder of Uffculme, miller, pr 21 Jun 1749: residue to exec, s William Brooke; 40s to dr Mary, wife of Richard Boobeer; after the death of s Wm, their father, 20s to William & Ann Brooke (& 40s to Marke Brooke?), & to John Brooke, their bro, the house in Uffculme town occupied by James Cadbury, from the proceeds of which these legacies are to be paid; 10s ea to Joan, Mary, Hannah, Ellenor, & Elizabeth Boobeer, chn of s-in-law Richard Boobeer, & to Richard Boobeer, their bro, the house occupied by Mark Brooks, from the proceeds of which these legadies are to be paid; signed Willm Brook; witn: James Brooks, Henry Davey, & Calbreath (all sign).

W196 JOHN NORMAN gunsmith 1749 (DS)

[Bur: "John Norman" 15 Aug 1748. Mar: "John Norman & Alice Ward" 26 Sep 1733.] Will 9 Aug 1748 of John Norman of Uffculme, gunsmith, pr 21 Jun 1749: residue to be sold by exec^{s}/trustees, bro Lawrence Norman & friend James Tozer of Kentisbeare, butcher, & proceeds to be invested , 30s a year of the interest to maintain s John Norman from age 15 in apprenticeship to a trade & the remainder to wife Allice for life, then to s John; bedding & 1 of every sort of household article to wife, to whom also the yearly proceeds from property till s John is 15; all lands of inheritance to s John (& heirs) at 15 but, if he should die without issue before 21, all to pass to bro Lawrence, to pay £10 ea to all bros & sisters & £20 to Elizabeth Ward, dr of wife; clock case to be disposed of by trustees & *wife to have nothing to do therewith*; signed John Norman; witn: Jno Hill, John Rugge, & E Manley (all sign).

W197 JOHN RADFORD woolcomber 1750 (PU)

[Bur: "John Radford" 17 Jun 1750. Mar: "John Radford & Eliz. Pocock" 15 Feb 1742/3.] Will 1 May 1750 of John Radford of Uffculme, woolcomber, pr 10 Sep 1750 before Benj Hope, surr: residue to wife Bettey Radford, exec; £10 ea to dr Elizabeth & s John Radford; (a codicil also assigns a ring to Elizabeth &

puts the s's £10 in the hands of Nicholas Farr for management); signed John Radford; witn: Richard Row & Anthony Jerwood (both sign).

W198 ELIZABETH JARMAN widow 1751 (PU)

[Bur: "Elizabeth Jarman" 12 Sep 1751.]

Will 15 Aug 1751 of Elizabeth Jarman of Uffculme, widow, pr 21 Nov 1751 before Benj Hope, surr: refers to terms of husband's will (Francis Jarman of c 3 Feb 1749), giving £100 ea to 3 chn Francis, Elizabeth, & Catherine, which will now be paid as directed; 6d a week to aunt Mary Westron; all goods, chattels, &c to exec[s], bro Nicholas Wreford & bro-in-law John How, to be sold up & proceeds invested for interest to maintain 2 drs, Elizabeth & Catherine to age 21, when they inherit the principal; marked EJ by Elizabeth Jarman; witn: Edw[d] Manley & Robert Lock (both sign).

W199 SAMUEL COLE yeoman 1751 (PU)

[Bur: "Samuel Coles" 21 Sep 1749.]

Will 18 Aug 1749 of Samuel Cole of Uffculme, yeoman, pr 12 Jul 1751 before Benj Hope: *Picks houses* at Ashill & residue of estate to bro Richard Cole, exec; joint interest in *How's* tenement at Craddock & *Hackpen Mills* (with houses, &c) to [mother & ?] bro Richard Cole; marked SC by Samuel Cole; witn: Will Cape, Humphry Bishop, & James Quant (3 sign).

W200 JOHN BISHOP gent 1751 (PU)

[Bur: "Mr John Byshop" 2 Jan 1749/50.]

Will 14 Oct 1748 of John Bishop of Uffculme, gent, pr 12 Jul 1751 before Benj Hope, surr: residue to dr Mary Wyat (wife of John Wyat of Uffculme, gent), exec; bed, 6 chairs in parlour chamber, chest & hanging press in hall chamber, clock & case in kitchen, malt mill, bell-metal potage pot, & large brass pan (all to stay in house according to marriage settelment) to dr Mary for life, then to grson John Wyat jun[r], who also has a gold ring at 21; *Langlands & part of Welches* (purchased from James Gill the elder and/or the younger) tenements to Samuel Coles of Uffculme, yeoman, & John Barnfield of Sheldon in trust for life for dr Mary (not for her husband) & then as willed by her; signed John Bishop; witn: Robert Clarke & James Townsend (who sign) & Sarah Knight (who both makes an S mark and signs shakily).

W201 FRANCIS JARMAN miller 1751 (PU)

[Bur: "Francis Jarman" 22 Apr 1750.]

Will 3 Feb 1749[/50?] of Francis Jarman of Uffculme, miller, pr 12 Jul 1751 before Benj Hope, surr: residue to wife Elizabeth, exec; tenement & mills in Langford Budville, Somerset, (recently purchased from M[r] Bernard Byrd) to wife Elizabeth for life, then to s Francis Jarman; messuage, malthouse, &c, (recently purchased from M[r] John Grantland) to trustees, bro Wm Jarman of Broadclist, yeoman, & bro-in-law Nicholas Wreford of Uffculme, butcher, in trust for wife until death or remarriage (then to s Francis), to be mortgaged sufficiently to pay £100 ea at age 21 to drs & s, Elizabeth, Francis, & Catherine (method of payment to depend upon value of inventory to be drawn up by wife); £1 a year to sister Mary Jarman; signed Fran[s] Jarman; witn: Edw[d] Manley, Ambrose Pring, & Joseph Bennett (all sign).

W202 HUMPHREY BISHOP 1751 (PU)

[Bur: "Humhery Byshop" 22 Jun 1750.]

Will 30 May 1750 of Humphrey Bishop of Uffculme, pr 12 Jul 1752 before Benj Hope, surr: tenement, *part of Hidons*, at Ashill to James Hollway sen[r], exec; £30 to Mary Goard & £20 ea to Elizabeth & Marthew (*sic*) Goard, drs of Richard & Elinor Goard; £10 to Elinor Hollway, dr of James Hollway; £5 ea to John Green, husbandman of Uffculme, & James & Wm James, ss of Robert & Elizabeth James; apparel to Robert Manly of Bradninch, husbandman; signed Humphry Bishop; witn: Will Hocker, Thomas Fry, & John Rugge (all sign).

W203 JACOB RIDGE husbandman 1751 (PU)

Will 13 Oct 1749 of Jacob Ridge of Uffculme, husbandman, pr 12 Jul 1752 before Benj Hope, surr: residue to wife Sarah, exec; 1s ea to bros John & James Ridge; if wife remarries, half of goods to go to chn of bros & sister; if wife dies without remarriage, half of goods as before & other half to wife's relatives; marked R by Jacob Ridge; witn: James Halway (signed thus) & Mary Hilleker (marks).

W204 ANN CULLYFORD spinster 1752 (DS)

Admon 27 Jun 1752, before Benj Hope, surr, names sister Thomasine, wife of John James, as admin, & also Mr Edward Manly, gent, & William Sweatland & Thomas Marsh, sergemakers, all of Uffculme; 3 latter all sign in presence of Willm Boucher, not^{y} pub. On 21 May 1752 Elizabeth Cullyford, mother of Ann Culliford of Uffculme, single woman, intestate, renounces admin^{n} in favour of sister Thomazin, wife of John James, innkeeper of Caldicott, Mon., & appoints as proctor on her behalf William Boucher, proctor of the Ecclesiastical Court of Sarum; marked by Elizabeth Culliford in presence of Susanna Hoopper & William Escott (both sign).

W205 ELIZABETH HURFORD spinster 1752 (DS)

Will 25 Mar 1752 of Elizabeth Hurford of Uffculme, spinster, pr at Uffculme 27 Jun 1752 before Benj Hope: 1 guinea ea to friends Robert Dunne, soapboiler, & John Hill, sadler, both of Uffculme & appointed trustees to pay 1 guinea to the members of the Anabaptist Meeting House in Uffculme, & to manage all the rest of the property (after expenses paid) for the sole benefit of mother Anne, wife of yeoman Nicholas Weslake, & not of her husband; signed Elizabeth Hurford; witn: Nich^{s} Wreford & James Rugg (both sign).

W206 ANNE WESLAKE, wife of Nicholas, yeoman 1753 (PU)

[Mar: "Nicholas Weslake & Ann Lane" 30 Apr 1745.]

Will 15 May 1752 of Anne Weslake of Uffculme, wife of yeoman Nicholas Weslake, pr 9 Jan 1752[/3] before Benj Hope: residue to exec, Thomas Musgrave the younger, s of Thomas Musgrave the elder; (reference is made to conditions of marriage settlement with Nicholas Weslake & to will of dec^{d} dr Elizabeth Hurford); 2 guineas to trustees, friends Robert Dunn, tallow chandler, & John Hill, sadler, (both of Uffculme), for the Anabaptist meeting house in Uffculme; 1 guinea to bro baptist Frank; £5 to cousin baptist Frank the younger; 2 guineas to s of bro baptist Frank by his present wife; 3 & 2 guineas respectively to Elizabeth Mills & Agnes Baker, drs of baptist Frank the elder; 2 guineas to Anne, wife of Edward Parkhouse of Uffculme; 1 guinea ea to Thomas Musgrave the elder of Culmstock & to his 2 drs Elizabeth & Rebecca Musgrave, & £5 5s to his s John Musgrave; 1 guinea to sister Mary Milton & ½ guinea ea to her chn; 2 guineas to cousin Anne Frank, dr of Wm Frank; 1 guinea to Anne, wife of James Parkhouse of Uffculme, woolcomber; marked Ann Weslake; witn: Nich^{s} Wreford, James Rugg, & Thomas Northam (all sign).

W207 FRANCIS EVELEIGH gent 1754 (PU)

[Bur: "Francis Eveleigh" 16 Feb 1754. Mar: "Francis Eveleigh & Mary Wind"

1 May 1718, Halberton.]
Will 16 Mar 1750[/1] of Francis Eveleigh of Uffculme, gent, pr 27 Sep 1754 before Benj Hope, surr: residue to exec dr Isat Eveleigh, who also has the proceeds from *Crowdens* estate until 25 Mar 1752 (*sic*); to wife Mary all money in house or out at interest; to trustees John Dunn the younger of Halberton & John Wyne of Culmstock, gents, moiety of *Crowdens* (where testator dwelt) in Uffculme in trust for life for dr Mary Cockram (after 25 Mar 1752) - not for husband's use; other moiety of *Crowdens* to wife, who also gets the first moiety if dr Mary dies; *Epswood* meadow in Uffculme to dr Elizabeth Haddon for life (who pays £40 to wife on 25 Mar 1752), & after her to be put in trust for grson John Haddon, or successively in absence of heirs, for John's bros Christopher & Thomas Haddon; signed Francis Eveleigh; witn: Isaac Westbear, Thomas Cross, & Jo^s Mill (all sign).

W208 RICHARD LAUGHAM yeoman 1754 (PU)

[Bur: "Richard Laugham" 8 Nov 1753. Mar: "Richard Laughan & Ann Potter" 13 Aug 1714. See W254.]
Will 10 Sep 1753 of Richard Laugham of Uffculme, yeoman, pr 27 Sep 1754 before Benj Hope, surr: residue to wife Ann, exec; to wife *Kitchells* tenement at Hayne, & money owed by s-in-law James Callow, in trust for dr Elizabeth Callow, wife of James Callow (but not for her husband's use); to wife Ann all his houses at Coldharbour (lately purchased of William Shaddick) for life & then to dr Joanna, wife of William Derham, & her chn, but if she has no issue then to grdr Joanna Callow & her heirs; board & lodging for life to father-in-law Samuel Potter; £20 ea at age 21 to grchn Elizabeth, James, Joanna, Richard, Samuel, & Ann Callow; these legacies charged to *Whitmore* estate which goes to wife Ann for life & then to chn or grchn, as willed by her; signed Richard Laugham; witn: Thomas Laugham, John Trickey, & James Quant (all sign).

W209 ROBERT PRING 1754 (PU)

[Bur: "Robert Pring" 10 Jul 1752.]
Admon 27 Sep 1754, at Uffculme before Benj Hope, surr, names widow Mary Pring as admin & also Henry Davy, yeoman, & William Grantland, woolcomber; Mary Pring marks, the other 2 sign.

W210 JACOB MOONE husbandman 1756 (PU)

[Mar: "Jacob Moon & Sarah Bayley" 4 Apr 1743. See W219.]
Will 3 Feb 1753 of Jacob Moone of Uffculme, husbandman, pr 24 Feb 1756 before John Fox, surrogate for John Fountain, Prebendary: residue to wife Sarah Moone, exec; 10s ea to cousins (sons & dr of dec^d uncle John Moone) Robert, John, & Thomas Moone, & Mary Wide; 10s, a loom, 5s, & 5s respectively to cousins Mary Tozer & Ann Hooper, & Joan & Simon Woodrow, drs & s of Mary Woodrow, sister of uncle Jacob Moone; signed Jacob Moon; witn: James Thomas (signs) & Bridget Dodge (B mark).

W211 MARTIN SALTER husbandman 1755 (PU)

Will 3 Jan 1753 of Martin Salter of Uffculme, husbandman, pr 7 Jun 1755; Father's house (in possession of James Selway) after mother's death to exec, bro Jeptha Salter (who, living in Middlesex, appointed his mother Joyce Salter to act for him), or if he dies to bro John Salter; £5 to Ann Pring, wife of William Pring; 1s to mother; clothes to bros Isaac & John Salter; house (in possession of John Dinster) to bro John Salter & sister Ann Pring; 1s to bro George Salter; signed Marten Salter; witn: Charles Knight (signs), Humphery Pring & Samuel Blackmore (both mark).

W212 JOHN HUTCHINGS sergeweaver 1755 (DS)
[Mar: "John Hutchins & Joan Oatway" 2 Jul 1718.]
Will 28 Dec 1754 of John Hutchings of Uffculme, sergeweaver, pr before John Leach 14 Jun 1755: residue to wife Joan Hutchings, exec; to s John Hutchings apparel, plus loom after death of wife; marked by John Hutchings; witn: Nich[s] Farr, J [?] Sweatland, & William Quick (all sign).

W213 WILLIAM HOLWAY 1755(DS)
Admon 14 Jun 1755 names father James Holway, yeoman, as admin & also Edmund Brome/Broom of Cullompton, yeoman, & Robert James of Kentisbear, yeoman; all sign.

W214 GRACE CHURLY spinster 1755 (DS)
Will 7 Oct 1754 of Grace Churly of Uffculme, spinster, pr 14 Jun 1755: residue, including lands, tenements, &c., in trust to bro-in-law Edward Hitchcock, yeoman, & k Edward Manley, gent, both of Uffculme, exec[s], all apart from the further legacies & annuities specified, to be invested for the maintenance & education of nephews Nicholas Churly (s of bro George) & Nicholas Churly (son of dec[d] bro Nicholas) until age 21, when they share the inheritance; £50 ea plus annuity of 40s at age 21 to Elizabeth & Joan Hitchcock, drs of sister Joan, together with a bed, chest, silver cup & spoon, & a gold ring (one marked GC) ea & residue of clothing; to niece Joan Churly best common prayer book &, at 21, chest marked JC & silver spoon; to Joan, dr of k Edward Churly, best bible & silver spoon marked GC JC 1713; to servant Elizabeth Coles £5 & clothing; to bro-in-law Edward Hitchcock her grey mare; her mother's box, silver buckles & clasps to niece Ann; signed Grace Churly; witn: Tho: Fannell[?], Samuel Green, John Parsons (all sign).

W215 AMOS STARK victualler 1756 (PU)
[Bur: "Amos Starke" 21 Feb 1756. Mar: "Amos Stark & Dorothy Cooke" 2 Jun 1740, Culmstock.]
Will 12 Nov 1755 of Amos Stark of Uffculme, victualler, pr 25 Feb 1756 before John Fox, surr: residue to wife Dorothy, exec; clothes between bros John & Humphry Stark; marked AM by Amos Stark; witn: E Manley, Tho[s] Marsh, & Henry Dewey (all sign).

W216 JANE JERWOOD widow 1756 (PU)
[Bur: "Jane Jerwood" 29 Nov 1755.]
Will 23 Nov 1755 of Jane Jerwood of Uffculme, widow, pr 25 Oct 1756 before John Windsor, surr: residue to dr Elizabeth Jerwood, exec; s John Jerwood to retain the £50 he owes and to receive £50 more; £100 to s Thomas Jerwood; marked by Jane Jerwood; witn: Laurance Norman & James Quant (both sign).

W217 JOHN HILL yeoman 1756 (PU)
[Mar: "John Hill & Dorothy Richards" 26 Apr 1740, Thorverton.]
Will 23 Nov 1754 of John Hill of Uffculme, yeoman, pr 25 Oct 1756 before John Windsor: wife Dorothy Hill named as exec in probate notice; part of *Redhill* estate (where s lives) in Holcombe Rogus to s John Hill; part of *Broadwells* estate in Holcombe Rogus in trust to Richard Manning of Culmstock, gent, for dr Mary, *now wife* of Ephraim Baker (not for his use), for 99-years or life, then to grson, her s John Baker; £100 in trust to Richard Manning & Robert Bicknell of West Buckland in Somerset, yeoman, for education & final shared inheritance of chn of dr Mary; signed John Hill; witn: James Quant, James Snook, & John Bale (all sign).

W218 GEORGE COLE yeoman 1756 (PU)
[Bur: "George Coles" 20 Feb 1756.]

Will 21 May 1754 of George Cole of Uffculme, yeoman, pr 25 Oct 1756 before John Windsor, surr: residue to dr Mary Fry, exec; £40 to friends James Holway & John Wyatt of Uffculme, & Samuel Byshop, gents, in trust to invest for maintenance & education of grchn Elizabeth & Thomas Fry until 21, when ea receives £20; £10 to grdr Ann James if she does not dispute the testator's ownership of the *farmering business* of his late ss Richard & Samule Cole, otherwise the £10 goes to the exec & Ann James gets only 1s; to Elizabeth Fry *the Bed hang'd with paper now in the Chamber over the Parlour*; marked C by George Cole; witn: Elinor Fry & Tho Pannell (both sign).

W219 SARAH MOONE widow 1756 (PU)

[See W210.]
Will 22 Jan 1756 of Sarah Moone of Uffculme, widow, pr 25 Oct 1756 before John Windsor, surr: residue to Ann Govier of Tiverton, exec; 1 guinea shared at age 21 by cousins John, James, Elizabeth, & Hester Meadow, s & drs of George Meadow of Broadclist, yeoman; 10s 6d ea at 21 to Sarah & Mary Meadow, drs of George Meadow; 10s to k Robert Moon; 3 guineas for her own & separate use to Joan ("Govier" crossed out), wife of Roger Pitt of Tiverton, tucker; marked S by Sarah Moone; witn: Henry & Robert Westron (both sign).

W220 MATTHEW HILL woolcomber 1756 (PU)

Will 18 Nov 1755 of Matthew Hill of Uffculme, woolcomber, pr 25 Oct 1756 before John Windsor, surr: residue to *father-in-law* (step-father) Robert Dunn of Uffculme, tallow chandler, exec; £80 for her sole use to mother Bathsheba Dunn, wife of Robert Dunn; £10 ea at 21 to mother's chn Thomas, Joan, Mary, & Bathsheba (Dunn); £5 ea at 21 to Joseph, James, & John Hill, ss of cousin John Hill; £20 to *father-in-law* Robert Dunn in trust for Anabaptist meeting-house in Uffculme; signed (shakily) Matthew Hill; witn: John Parkhouse & James Quant (both sign).

W221 JOHN HURLEY yeoman 1757 (PU)

[Bur: "John Hurley" 14 Jul 1757. Mar: "John Hurley & Thomasin Gill" 9 Dec 1725.]
Will 5 Jul 1757 of John Hurley of Uffculme, yeoman, 13 Oct 1757 before John Windsor, surr: residue to exec^s^, dr Betty Fowler, wife of Edward Fowler, & grdr Jenny Callow, dr of Jos Callow; 5s to dr Bridget Callow; brass crock to Jenny Callow; £5 a year for life to wife Tamsin Hurley out of estate so long as the exec^s^ possess it (but intention that s-in-law Edward Fowler should be *Entirely Cutt off*!), whence put in hands of trustee, friend John Corke of Uffculme; signed John Hurley; witn: Jos Merson (signs) & John Corke (X mark).

W222 JAMES BROOKE tailor 1758 (DS)

[Bur: "James Brook Senr" 4 Aug 1758. Mar: "James Brooke & Wid. Dun's dr called Susanna Taylour" 24 Jan 1705/6. See plaque on 15 Fore St "James & Susanna Brooks 1732".]
Will 3 Feb 1758 of James Brooke of Uffculme, tailor, pr 7 Sep 1758 before Rev John Windsor: residue to wife Susanna, exec, who also inherits the house where he lived & the houses lately purchased from Robert Westcombe & occupied by James Rugg, widow Alice Gange (these to pass after death of wife to dr Sarah, wife of James Rugg, & then to grson William Rugg), & those occupied by widow Joan Green, & Mary Pepperel (these to pass after death of wife to dr Alice, wife of Henry Dickinson), & 5 houses lately purchased from James Hellings & in possession of himself & John Dodge (these to pass to dr Sarah, & then to grchn Susanna, Sarah, & James

Rugg), & houses called *Kitwell* in possession of Wm Tozer & Wm Bently (these to pass to drs Joan Besley[*sic*] & Alice Dickinson); to s James Brooke annuities of 50s & 10s for life from the estate after his mother's death, plus 3 houses, called *Tanners*, in possession of himself, Henry Woodrowffe, & Ann Bray, plus halfendale in garden of *Stevens's*, but after James's death all to pass to grdr Joan Rugg, dr of James & Sarah Rugg; 10s annuity to grdr Susanna Rugg; marked IB by James Brooke; witn: Edwd Manley, James Quant, & Joseph Motley (all sign).

W223 HENRY PARSONS 1758 (DS)

[Bur: "Henry Parsons" 21 May 1758.]
Admon 7 Sep 1758 names s Henry Parsons, thatcher, as admin & also John Kent, woolcomber, both of Uffculme, & John Parsons of Culmstock, weaver (only Henry Parsons signs, the others mark).

W224 JOHN DOWDNEY husbandman 1759 (PU)

[Bur: "John Dowdney" 17 Dec 1758.]
Will 13 Dec 1758 of John Dowdney of Uffculme, husbandman, pr 8 Jan 1759 before John Windsor: residue (including *messuages, lands, tenements, & hereditaments*) to niece Joan Fry, exec; £5 ea to Joan Dowdney, dr of bro Robert Dowdney, to sister Mary Veals, & to sister's dr Sarah Mare; 1s to sister Ruth Palmer; coats to bros-in-law Christover Bray & Jacob Veals; marked by John Dowdney; witn: John Lockyer, George Salter, & Wm Stark (all sign).

W225 EDWARD HITCHCOCK 1759 (PU)

[Bur: "Edward Hitchcock" 23 Mar 1759 or "Edward Hitchcock Junr" 3 Jul 1759. Mar: "Edward Hitchcock & Ann Charley" 26 Feb 1746/7, Exeter St Sidwell.]
Admon 9 Jul 1759 names widow Ann Hitchcock admin & also Mary Clark, spinster, & Edward Manley, gent, both of Uffculme; all sign in presence of John Windsor & William Stark.

W226 WILLIAM SMALL blacksmith 1759 (PU)

[Bur: "William Small" 18 Feb 1759. Mar: "William Small & Elizabeth Hobbs" 28 Mar 1714, Whitestone. See W241.]
Will 22 Jan 1759 of William Small of Uffculme, blacksmith, pr 29 Sep 1759, with related paper 5 Mar 1759 (announcing dispute by creditor Wm Stone): working tools, ½-ton of iron, & 10 seams of coal at 21 to s William, exec; residue to wife Elizabeth until chn of full age; £5 & house at 21 to dr Elizabeth or, if without heirs, to dr Ester; £10 at 21 to dr Ester; signed Wm Small; witn: Robert Brabham, Henry Tozer, & Thomas Hutchings (all sign).
Admon 29 Sep 1759 names *widow* Elizabeth Small as admin & also John Bale of Halberton & Henry Davy of Uffculme, both yeomen; all sign in presence of Wm Boucher, not^{y} pub.

W227 JOHN BAKER carpenter 1760 (PU)

[Bur: "John Baker" 27 Apr 1760.]
Will 21 Apr 1760 of John Baker of Uffculme, carpenter, pr 25 Jun 1760 before John Windsor, surr: all to wife exec, but to distribute working tools to 3 eldest ss Christopher, John, & Robert; signed (shakily) John Baker; witn: Edwd Manley. Thos Marsh jun^{r}, & Thomas Binford (all sign).
[A letter is attached to this will:
"*Sir! Inclosed you'll receive ye Will of John Baker; you'll be so good as to send ye Probate as soon as possible with ye Charges; The Apparitor has rec^{d} his Fee of 2s 6d already. - A poor old Fellow y^{t} receives Pay from ye Parish has desired me to send to you for a Copy of y^{t} Part of Thomas Percy's Will which relates to ye Hookway's family; It was proved about ye Year 1714. As his Circumstances are*

very mean, He hopes you'll be as easy in your Charges as you can, He tells me y[t] my Father got him a Copy of it which he has now lost, as he remembers it cost him 6s 8d, if you cou'd send it for less 'twou'd be an Act of Charity: - Be so good to let me know whether we shall have any Visitation this Year & about what Time & you'll oblige S[r] Y[r] Humble Serv[t] John Windsor
Uffculme 25th June 1760"]

W228 JAMES HOLLWAY the younger, yeoman of Lowmore 1760 (PU)

[Bur: "James Holway Jnr" 5 May 1760.]

Will 6 Jan 1760 (with codicil 26 Apr 1760) of James Hollway the younger of Lowmore, yeoman, pr 12 Sep 1760 at Uffculme before John Windsor, surr: all tenements &c to exec, k James James of Uffculme, yeoman, who pays bequests & annuities; £5 ea to Thomas, John, James, Philip, Henry, Mary, & Elizabeth Broome, chn of Edmond Broome & his wife's aunt Jane; £5 ea to William, Robert, Henry, John, Elizabeth, Eleanor, & Sarah James, chn of Robert James & his wife's aunt Elizabeth; £10 to half-sister Elizabeth Hollway at 21, & also 1s a week until 14 (from Wm Matthew the elder, yeoman, in trust for her); £5 to aunt Eleanor Green & 1s a week for life (from Thomas Fry the elder, yeoman, in trust for her), not for her husband John Green's use; £10 to aunt Beatton Hollway & £7 10s a year for life; £10 to k Wm Broome; signed James Hollway jun[r]; witn: Edw[d] Manley, Robert Matthew, & Henry Parsons (all sign). The codicil 26 Apr 1760 revokes the sections giving £5 ea to the chn of Edmond Broome & of James James, & £10 to k Wm Broom(e), & replaces them by £5 ea to Wm Broom, Thomas Broom, & Wm James; exec , residue, & main legatee as before; signed (more shakily) James Hollway jun[r]; witn: Edw[d] Manley, Jn[o][?] Marsh, & William Stark (all sign).

W229 ELIZABETH BYSHOP widow 1761 (DS)

[Bur: "Elizabeth Bishop" 19 May 1758.]

Will 31 Dec 1757 of Elizabeth Byshop of Uffculme, widow, pr 19 Aug 1761: residue to grdr Betty Scadding, exec; to Grace Byshop, widow of late s John Byshop, the Wollands estate (part of the manor of Bodmiscombe, on lease granted by Sir William Portman, dec[d]), & after her death to pass to grdr Betty Scadding, for her own use & control & not for debts of her husband Bernard Scadding; money from the estate to be used to extend the Wollands lease to 3 lives, by adding that of great-grson John Scadding (son of Bernard), who will then ultimately inherit; £5 at age 21 & £4 annuity from estate to Anna Scadding, sister of John; also to John Scadding £1 7s, cider press, & 11 hogsheads (parents to have use of these provided mother does not die & father Bernard remarry); ovsrs/trustees Samuel Byshop of Culmstock, gent, John Garnsey of Uffculme, gent, & Grace Byshop; marked b by Elizabeth Byshop; witn: Eliz Callow, John Eldon, & George Southey (all sign).

W230 RICHARD RUGG 1762 (PU)

[Bur: "Richard Rugg" 16 Nov 1761. Mar: "Richard Rugg & Elizabeth Radford" 17 Oct 1751.]

Admon 20 Sep 1762 names widow Elizabeth Rugg as admin & also William Stark, sergemaker, & Henry Davy, clerk, all of Uffculme.

W231 JOHN DUNN the elder, yeoman 1762 (PU)

Will 13 Feb 1762 of John Dunn the elder of Uffculme, yeoman, pr 20 Sep 1762 before John Windsor, surr: residue of goods & of estates in Uffculme & Burlescombe to s John

Dunn, exec; Uffculme estates called *Aplins houses & Cuniger Hill* to 3 drs Jane, Mary, & Elizabeth Dunn, plus £105, a bed, & a brass pan each; also clock, chest, looking-glass, new square table, & all her own goods to Jane, black chest of drawers to Mary, & hanging-press & warming-pan to Elizabeth (entry-, middle-, & inner-chambers mentioned); 3 drs to continue to live where testator lived & to receive food & either a hogshead of cider or 20s a year ea from the exec; shaky signature of John Dunn described as his mark; witn: Robert Dunn, James Quant, & Jane Parkhouse (all sign).

W232 ROBERT SANDERS gent of Sampford Peverell 1762 (PU)

[Mar: "Robert Sanders of Sampford Peverell & Allice Mrs Dobny" 7 Mar 1754, Uplowman.]
Admon 23 Apr 1762 names widow Alice Sanders as admin & also John Ley & John Jones, both gents of Exeter; signed by all 3. In a separate document, reference is made to the purchase of an estate in Uffculme, by the father of the present testator (with the same name) and legally transfers ownership to the testator's widow. The estate was purchased 15 Nov 1726 from William Walrond of Bradfield, Esq, with 99-year lease commencing after death of Joanna Rowe (then called Joanna Sanders & wife of Robert Sanders) & Robert Sanders, & determinable on the death of William Ballyman, s of Richard Ballyman of Sampford Peverell, weaver, under yearly rent of 12s & the best beast of occupier as heriot, or £3 6s 8d in lieu thereof. But Robert Sanders died intestate, leaving Joanna his widow, Robert Sanders his only s, & Mary & Joanna Sanders, his 2 drs, & the estate was distributed amongst these. Then Joanna died leaving will 14 May 1738, appointing Peter Kerslake, William Were, & George Wood as trustees (pr at PCC), & dr Joanna having married Francis Surrage (alš Hagley) & dr Mary having married George Wood (surviving trustee), this estate and others were assigned to s Robert Sanders by indenture of 18 Feb 1754. Then s Robert Sanders died, leaving widow Alice Sanders, now authorised to take over the property.

W233 SARAH CALBREATH widow 1763 (PU)

Will 27 Feb 1762 of Sarah Calbreath of Uffculme, widow, pr 19 Sep 1763 at Uffculme before John Windsor, surr: residue to be sold up by exec[s]/trustees, friends William Byrd & Stevenson Dunsford, both sergemakers of Uffculme; all goods & furniture in his possession to s Benjamin Calbreath; to grdr (Benjamin's dr) Sarah Calbreath 1 guinea, bed, 2 best coats, warming-pan, skimmer, butter-melter, brass grater, flower box, & copper, all at 21 or marriage, but if she dies to be shared by her bros Joseph, William, & Benjamin Calbreath at 21; sums in trust to trustees to pay grson 2 guineas for apprenticeship, & grdr Mary (dr of Benjamin Calbreath) ½ guinea at 21; pewter dish to grson John (son of s Joseph Calbreath); marked S by Sarah Calbreath; witn: Robert Dunn, Samuel Caddy, & James Quant (all sign).

W234 ANNA WINDSOR widow 1764 (DS)

[Bur: "Mrs Anna Windsor" 25 Nov 1763. Mar: "The Revd John Windsor & Anna Downes" 16 Oct 1720.]
Will 24 Oct 1758 of Anna Windsor of Uffculme, widow, pr 14 Sep 1764; residue, including lands, tenements, &c, to s Rev John Windsor, exec; £10 for mourning clothes & 2 mourning rings to dr Elizabeth, wife of George Greenway of Uffculme, Clerk; diamond earrings before age 18 to grdr Anna Windsor, dr of s John; £50 with interest at 21 to grson James Windsor; signed Anna Windsor; witn: Edw[d] Manley, John [?T,P]ratt, & Henry Mathew (all sign).

W235 JOHN DUNN gent of Halberton 1764 (PU)

[Mar: "John Dunn & Elizabeth Curry" 23 Sep 1756, Exeter St Sidwell.]

Will 4 Jun 1763 of John Dunn of Halberton, gent, pr 14 Sep 1764 before John Windsor: residue to s John Dunn, exec; to wife Elizabeth (subject to release of her rights of dower) 6 cows, 2 plough bullocks, 2 heifers, 1 mare, 1 gelding, half the pigs, pork, & bacon, all the household goods & cider, 30 bushels of malt, plus the *Langlands* tenement where he lived, subject to payment of 1s a week until age 25 to drs Mary, Elizabeth, & Margaret; to these 3 drs also at age 25 £80 ea & a further 1s a week; to Richard Clarke Esq. & Henry Pullin, both of Halberton, in trust for s Henry, £20 at 14 for apprenticeship to a trade, & *Hales's* messuage & tenement in Uffculme (to go to s John if Henry dies before 21), subject to the £20 payments to the 3 drs; to s John the *Newton's* messuage & tenement in Uffculme, subject to the £80 payments &1s a week to the 3 drs; signed Jn° Dunn; witn: Jane Dunn, Mary Dunn, Ja^{s} Huish (all sign).

W236 WILLIAM JOB gardener 1764 (DS)

[Bur: "William Job" 10 Nov 1763. Mar: "William Job & Eliz Wakely" 26 Dec 1739.]

Will 29 Oct 1763 of William Job of Uffculme, gardener, pr at Uffculme 14 Sep 1764 before John Windsor: residue to sister Ann Trickey, widow of Uffculme, exec; best suit to Daniel Henson, yeoman of Burlescombe, & watch & chain to his wife Ann; 1 guinea ea to wife Elizabeth, to bros Richard & Robert Job, & to Ann Hookway, dr of late bro John; £3 & a crown piece to niece Jane Colman; £5 to Francis Jarman, sadler of Uffculme; 40s to Susanna Coram, widow of Burlescombe; 10s to Thomas Fry, yeoman of Ashill; 15s to Thomas Coles; signed [shakily] Will Job; witn: Bern^{d} Byrd, John Dumett [Dunnett?], & James Quant (all sign).

W237 JOHN GRANTLAND 1764 (PU)

Admon 14 Sep 1764 names widow Sarah Grantland admin & also Henry & Thomas Davies [*sic*], all of Uffculme; marked by Sarah Grantland & signed Henry Davy & Thomas Davy [*sic*].

W238 ELIZABETH JOHNSLIN widow 1765 (PU)

Admon 29 Apr 1765 names s Roger Johnslin, yeoman, as admin & also George Russell, sergemaker, & John Holland, victualler, all of Uffculme; Roger Johnslin marks & others sign.

W239 JOHN HILL saddler 1765 (PU)

[Mar: "John Hill & Sarah Dunne" 14 Jun 1744.]

Will 26 Nov 1764 of John Hill of Uffculme, saddler, pr 27 Sep 1765 before John Windsor, surr: residue to wife Sarah, exec; £20, saddle trees, & working tools to s John Hill at age 22; signed Jn° Hill; witn: James Quant, Bathsheba Dunn, & Sarah Parsons (all sign).

W240 JOHN BAKER tailor 1765 (PU)

Will 18 Feb 1765 of John Baker of Uffculme, tailor, pr 18 Aug 1766 before John Windsor, surr: no bells at funeral; residue to s John Baker, exec, who also inherits the house where the testator lives, that where Edward Hardy lives, & that where Wm Kent lives (all in Uffculme town & freehold in fee simple), subject to payment of 10s a year to dr Joan Rookley for life; 2 stone houses occupied by Lawrence Norman & John Jerwood (in Uffculme town & freehold in fee simple) to s James Baker & his wife Margarett, subject to payment of 10s a year to Joan Rookley for life, but after their deaths to go to s Robert Baker & his heirs; to s Thomas Baker the house where he lives & the house where Robert Job lives (both freehold in Uffculme), subject to 10s a year to Joan Rookley for life; various specified plates, dishes, & furniture to ss John & Thomas, & to grchn Wm, Thomas, John, & James Rookley (sons of John Rookley), & John, Thomas, Margarett, Mary, Ann, Joan, & James Baker, & Ann Gillard; 5s to dr Sarah Gillard; signed John Baker; witn: Lawrence & John Norman & Geo Wood (all sign).

W241 ELIZABETH SMALL widow 1766 (PU)

[Bur: "Elizabeth Small" 12 Aug 1766.]
Admon 30 Aug 1766 names s William Small, blacksmith, as admin & also Thomas Baker, cordwainer, & John Baker, woolcomber, all of Uffculme; all sign in presence of John Windsor & Edwd Manley jun^{r}.

W242 HUGH RADFORD yeoman 1766 (PU)

[Bur: "Hugh Radford" 10 Jan 1767.]
Will 23 Aug 1765 of Hugh Radford of Uffculme, yeoman, pr 13 Sep 1766 before John Windsor, surr: residue to wife Joan, exec; 1s ea to sister Alice Parsons, nephew John Parsons, & niece Sarah Parsons; marked H by Hugh Radford; witn: John Windsor, James Quant, & William Trickey (all sign).

W243 JOAN RADFORD widow 1767 (DS)

[Bur: "Joan Radford" 1 Jul 1767.]
Will 8 Jun 1767 of Joan Radford of Uffculme, widow, pr 10 Jul 1767: residue to exec, nephew William Mundy, s of bro Wm Mundy; 50s to bro Thomas Mundy; 5s to bro Wm Mundy; 1 guinea to nephew John Mundy (lately servant to Rev George Greenway); 10s to niece Mary Austin; 5s ea to nieces Joan Austin & Mary Martin, & to ea ch of bro Thomas Mundy by his present wife Patience; 10s to nephew Edmund Mundy; 5s to nephew Thomas Mundy, s of bro Wm; 1s to nephew Thomas, *now in the Workhouse at Uffculme*; marked by Joan Radford; witn: Mark Cadbury, William Trickey, & James Quant (all sign).

W244 JAMES BAKER 1767 (DS)

[Bur: "James Baker" 20 May 1767. Mar: "James Baker & Margaret Byrd" 23 Oct 1741. See W252.]
Will 20 Jun 1763 of James Baker of Uffculme, pr 22 Sep 1767: residue to wife, exec; £60 ea at age 24 to drs Margaret, Joan, Ann, & Mary; signed James Baker; witn: Amos Langdon & James Holway (both sign).
Admon **(PU)** 10 years later, 6 Jan 1773 (with obligation 22 Jan 1773), grants admin^{n} to drs, Joan Southey, Margaret Broom, & Anne & Mary Baker, since widow Margaret Baker (exec, unnamed, in the will) died before admin^{n} (see W256); signed Margaret Broom, Joan Southey, Anne Baker, & Mary Baker in presence of John Windsor, Thomas Southey, & Henry Broom (all sign).

W245 JOHN KENT the elder, woolcomber 1767 (DS)

[Bur: "John Kent" 25 Jan 1767. Mar: "John Kent & Agnis Curram" 9 Apr 1721.]
Will 23 Feb 1761 of John Kent the elder of Uffculme, woolcomber, pr 22 Sep 1767 before John Windsor: residue to wife Agnes, exec; *Twenty Acres* estate to wife Agnes for life, & thereafter to John Kent, s of dec^{d} bro William; 5s ea to nephew Willam Kent, & to nieces Mary (wife of John Starke), Elizabeth Jarman, & Ann Kent; marked by John Kent; witn: Samuel Caddy, Richard Babbidge, & James Quant (all sign).

W246 BEATON HOLWAY spinster 1768 (PU)

Admon 26 Dec 1768 names sisters Jane (wife of Edmund Broom of Cullompton, yeoman) & Eleonor (wife of John Green of Kentisbeare, yeoman) as admin[s] & also William Broom of Kentisbeare, yeoman; signed by Edmond & William Broom & marked by John Green, in presence of Joseph Taylor.

W247 THOMAS FRY 1769 (PU)

[Bur: "Thomas Fry" 19 Feb 1768. Mar: "Thomas Fry of Columbton & Mary Maugridge of Uffculme" 25 Aug 1721, or "Tho. Fry & Mary Cole" 4 Apr 1743.]
Admon 1 Feb 1769 names widow Mary Fry as admin & also William Starke, sergemaker, both of Uffculme; signed Mary Fry & Willliam Starke in presence of William Fouraker.

W248 JAMES CHANNON 1769 (PU)

[Mar: "James Channon & Friswell Shallis" 31 Mar 1744, Tiverton.]
Will 12 Nov 1762 of James Channon of Uffculme, pr 2 Feb 1769 before John Windsor, surr: residue to wife Frizwell, exec; apparel to bros William, Joseph, & John Channon; 5s ea to bro Thomas & sisters Frizwell (wife of John Bowden), Elizabeth, Mary, & Alice Channon; signed James Channon; witn: R Sweetland, James Quant, & Susanna Yare (all sign).

W249 ELIZABETH MARSH wife of Thomas the elder 1771 (PU)

[See W255.]
Will 20 Feb 1771 of Elizabeth Marsh of Uffculme, wife of Thomas Marsh the elder, pr 9 Oct 1771 before John Windsor, surr: residue to husband Thomas Marsh sen[r], exec; quotes indenture of 19 Aug 1747 before marriage to Thomas Marsh; to trustees/ execs, *son-in-law* (stepson) Thomas Marsh & k John How, both sergemakers of Uffculme, £30 to be raised out of houses (near Uffculme market place) occupied by Ambrose Pring the younger, M[rs] Cutliffe, widow, & John Holland, woolcomber, within 3 years of death of husband (Thomas Marsh sen[r]) to be paid to the Presbyterians at Croslands (or wherever they worship) for their use; to nephew John Croyden, after husband's death, the house &c near the market place occupied by Simon Fry Baker, & the adjoining house in possession of M[r] Hugh Ellis; £5 ea to nephew Jeremiah Croyden & to k Mary How, wife of John How; £10 to *son-in-law* Thomas Marsh; the houses (occupied by Pring, Cutliffe, & Holland) after death of husband to be managed by the trustees for payment of legacies & then sold & proceeds divided between *son & drs-in-law*, Thomas Marsh jun[r], Jane Lamprey, & Ann Marsh, & nephews John & Jeremiah Croyden, 2 parts to Thomas Marsh & 1 part ea to the others; bureau to nephew John Croyden; chest of drawers & gown ea to Ann Marsh & Jane Lamprey; gowns to Priscilla Cornelius & Susanna Price; quilted coat to sister Lucretia Croyden; £12 shared by chn of nephew William Woolcott, after husband's death; to husband's grdr Elizabeth Marsh 1 guinea & gold ring marked TM EN 1747; Bishop Burkitt's *Exposition of the New Testament* to M[r] Thomas Turner; Henry on *the four Evangelists & the Acts of the Apostles* & bible to Tho[s] Marsh jun[r]; silver tea tongs to Mary wife of John How; marked Eliz M by Elizabeth Marsh.

W250 SARAH HOW widow, sergemaker 1771 (PU)

[See W179.]
Will 20 Mar 1770 of Sarah How widow of Uffculme, sergemaker, pr 9 Oct 1771 before John Windsor, surr: residue to dr Elizabeth How, exec; £5 to s John How; 2 guineas to dr Mary Drewer; signed (shakily) Mary How; witn: John Sanders & Mary Parsons (both sign).

W251 WILLIAM BROOK 1772 (PU)

[Bur: "William Brook" 13 Apr 1772.]
Admon 30 May 1772 names s Mark Brook, tailor, as admin & also John Sanders & James Brook, all of Uffculme; all sign in presence of Anna Windsor.

W252 MARGARET BAKER widow 1773 (PU)&(DS)

[Bur: "Margaret Baker" 9 Apr 1770. Widow of James Baker W244.]
Admon 6 Jan 1773, granted by Rev John Windsor as surr., names Joan, wife of Thomas Southey, Marg^{t}, wife of Henry Broom, & Ann & Mary Baker, drs; all signed in presence of John Windsor; further letter signed Hen: Hearst Reg^{r}.

W253 SARAH DUNNETT widow 1773 (PU) & (DS)

[Bur: "Sarah Dummett" 5 Mar 1767.]
Admon 19 Jan 1773, granted by Rev John Windsor as surr., names s John Dunnett, blacksmith, as admin & also Benjamin Donne, officer of excise, & Thomas Dunn, tallow chandler, all of Uffculme; all signed in the presence of John Windsor & Mary Donne; further letter signed Hen: Hearst Reg^{r}.

W254 ANNE LAUGHAM 1773 (PU) & (DS)

[Bur: "Ann Laugham" 2 Aug 1769. See W208.]
Will 17 Oct 1768 of Anne Laugham of Uffculme, pr at Uffculme 6 Mar 1773 before John Windsor, surr: estate & interest in "Haying" in parish of Uffculme (not for her husband's use) & residue to dr Elizabeth Callow, exec; £5 & all the goods in her custody to grdr Elizabeth Hope; £100 to grson James Callow; £5, yellow bed, & gold ring to grdr Johanna Callow; £5 ea to grsons Richard & Samuel Callow; £5, silver & china tea things, & a gold ring to grdr Ann Callow; witn: John Saunders, John & Sarah Tozer.
[*Laugham* could be read as *Langham*, but the admon of 6 Mar 1773 actually has the *n* corrected to a *u*.]

W255 THOMAS MARSH sergemaker 1773 (DS)

[Mar: "Thomas Marsh & Eliz. Northam" 1 Sep 1747. See W152, W249, & plaque on 6, Fore St "T.M. 1746".]
Will 2 Mar 1773 of Thomas Marsh of Uffculme, sergemaker, pr 6 Sep 1773 before Thomas Windsor, surr: residue to s Thomas Marsh, exec; £3 a year for life to dr Jane, *now wife* of Nicholas Lamprey, (not for his use); £5 a year for life to dr Ann Marsh; £5 ea at age 24 to grdrs Elizabeth, dr of dec^{d} s John Marsh, & Betty, dr of s Thomas Marsh; £1 1s at age 24 to 3 drs of dr Jane Lamprey; signed Thomas Marsh; witn: John Holland & Henry Howett sen^{r} (both sign).

W256 JOHN MANLEY 1773 (DS)

Will 2 May 1771 of John Manley of Uffculme, pr 6 Sep 1773: apart from 5s ea to ss John & Robert, all to wife [unnamed], exec, & after her death to be divided amongst 7 of his chn, *viz* William, Edward, Mary, Elizabeth, Ann, Jane, & Sarah; marked by John Manley; witn: William Stark & Tho Byrd (both sign).

W257 MARY BYSHOP spinster 1774 (PU)

Will 24 Mar 1774 of Mary Byshop of Uffculme, spinster, pr 1 Jun 1774 before John Windsor, surr: all to sister Thomasin Byshop, exec; signed Mary Byshop; witn: Elizabeth Byshop, Thomasin & Mark Westron (all sign).

W258 HENRY DUNN of Uffculme but living in Bristol 1774 (PU)

[Mar: "Henry Dunne & Ann Hodge" 13 Dec 1753.]
Will 15 Jul 1773 of Henry Dunn of Uffculme, living in Bristol, pr 16 Jun

1774 before John Windsor, surr: residue to wife Ann Dunn, exec; £25 ea at 21 to drs Ann, Sarah, Elizabeth, & Mary, wife to have interest meanwhile; trustees Mr Edwd Manley & Mr Nicholas Wreford; marked by Henry Dunn; witn: Edmund Burcher, William Critchett, & Robert Jordan (all sign).

W259 THOMASIN BYSHOP spinster 1775 (PU)

Will 23 May 1775 of Thomasin Byshop of Uffculme, spinster, pr 26 Oct 1775 before John Windsor, surr: *all* for investment in trust to pay legacies &c, (funeral not more than £20), to exec^s^ John Wyatt the younger of Uffculme, gent, & Edward Davie of Kentisbeare, gent, who also receive £10 ea for themselves; £100 to Henry Pyle the younger of Payhembury, yeoman; £10 to Christopher Mountstephen of Cullompton, gent, in trust for his dr Mary Mountstephen at 21 or marriage; 1 guinea to bro Samuel Byshop; all dividends for life to mother Elizabeth Byshop & then £200 to be invested for sister Betty Pook, wife of John Pook of Uffculme, gent, for herself alone & after her for her chn; remainder of estate to be invested for these 3 chn of Betty Pook, *viz.* John, Thomas, & the dr (born 20 May 1775) not yet christened, at 21 or marriage, the dr to have £50 more than the others; signed Thomasin Byshop; witn: Charles Leigh, Peter Hollway, & Thomas North (all sign).

W260 PHILLIP CORKE cordwinder 1776 (DS)

[Bur: "Philip Cork" 31 Jan 1771.]

Will 24 Jan 1771 of Phillip Corke of Uffculme, cordwinder[*sic*], pr 19 Sep 1776 before John Windsor, surr: residue in trust (with expenses allowed) to exec^s^, Mr George Wood of Halberton, gent, & bro John Corke of Uffculme, for s John Corke, dr Martha being maintained & clothed until 21, when she receives £10 (if enough left!); 20s ea to ss & drs Grace Alford, Joane Harding, Hannah Potter, Phillip Corke, Elizabeth Corke, Sarah Sheers, Susanna Corke, & Patience Corke (to whom also her feather bed), & to grdr Sarah Night Corke; marked by Phillip Corke; witn: John Marsh & John Dunn (both sign).

W261 AMOS LANGDON shopkeeper 1776 (DS)

[Bur: "Amos Langdon" 15 Oct 1773. Mar: "Amos Langdon & Joan Wyatt" 30 Jun 1742. See W263.]

Will 29 Jul 1772 of Amos Langdon of Uffculme, shopkeeper, pr 19 Sep 1776 at Uffculme before James Windsor, surr: residue to wife Joan Langdon, exec, with provisions for extra bequests in trust for his chn if she should remarry; part of *Holways* houses in Mill Street (in possession of James Mills) to s Joseph Langdon & Thomas Marsh jun^r^, sergemaker, for term of 80 years in trust for dr Sarah Norman (not for her husband) for life, therafter to pass to s Joseph Langdon & heirs; similarly £80 in same trust for Sarah's chn; £50 to s Joseph Langdon; part of *Holways* estate (in possession of Henry Tremlett, Elizabeth Knight, Ann Parkhouse, Mary Martin, & Henry Dunn), plus *Greens Cottage* for rest of term, to wife Joan till her death or marriage, when it passes to s Joseph; signed Amos Langd^on^; witn: Jno How sen^r^, Dalbey Parrock, & Ja^s^ Huish (all sign).

W262 WILLIAM SANDERS 1778 (PU)

Admon 27 Aug 1778 names s John Sanders, cordwainer, as admin & also William Sanders, woolcomber, & John Sanders, cordwainer; all sign as Saunders in presence of Anna & John Windsor.

W263 JOAN LANGDON widow 1779 (DS)

[Widow of Amos, W261.]

Will 13 Mar 1777 of Joan Langdon of Uffculme, widow, pr at Uffculme 6

Sep 1779 before John Windsor, surr: residue to s Joseph Langdon, exec; £80 & goods (bed, gold ring, 6 chairs, brass pot, copper kettle, pewter, washing kettle, warming pan, chest, box, & her father's silver sleeve buttons) to s Joseph & John Fickars of Taunton St Mary Magdalene, Somerset, tobacconist, in trust for dr Sarah Norman (not for her husband John Norman) & after her death any residue to pass to s Joseph; marked by Joan Langdon; witn: Robert Wilcocks & Ja^{s} Huish (both sign).

W264 WILLIAM HOCKER whitebread baker 1779 (PU)

[Mar: "William Hooker & Elizabeth Melhuish" 6 Apr 1761, Crediton. See W265.]

Will 16 Jun 1777 of William Hocker of Uffculme, whitebread baker, pr 4 Nov 1779: residue of tenements, grounds, &c to wife Elizabeth, exec; present house & 2 gardens (purchased from James Leamon) & orchard/close (purchased from Mr Nicholas Churly), all near Ashill Green, to wife for life, then to nephew John Middleton of Kentisbeare (*sic*), yeoman; signed Wm Hocker; witn: Elizth Leigh, J Mounstephen How, & Thos North (all sign).

Wife Elizabeth died before executing this will & the admon 4 Nov 1779 then names John Middleton of Broadhembury (*sic*) as admin & also Edward Davies of Kentisbeare & James James of Uffculme, all yeoman; marked + by John Middleton & signed by Edwd Davies & James James in presence of Anna & John Windsor.

W265 ELIZABETH HOCKER 1779 (PU)

[Widow of William, W264]

Will 18 Mar 1779 of Elizabeth Hocker of Uffculme, pr 4 Nov 1779 before John Windsor, surr: residue of lands, tenements, goods, & securities to sister Ann Saunders of Uffculme, widow, cousin Ann Madge, wife of John Madge of Payhembury, & servant Ann Cullyford of Uffculme; late husband William Hocker's clothes & £5 to k John Midleton of Payhembury; gold ring ea to late servant Elizabeth Johnslen, dr of William Johnslen of Uffculme, & to Elizabeth Midleton, dr of John Midleton; marked by Elizabeth Hocker; witn: Richard Rugg, Robert Pring, & James James (all sign).

W266 JANE CORKE wife of John Corke 1780 (PU)

Will 20 Jan 1765 of Jane Corke of Uffculme, wife of John Corke, yeoman, pr 2 Feb 1780: marriage settlement referred to; residue to dr Rebecca Dunn, exec; 2 guineas ea to sisters Mary Dunn & Elizabeth Dunn; 1 guinea to *cousin* Mary Dunn, dr of bro John Dunn; *Aplin's House* & third of *Cunnegar Hill* close to dr Rebecca Dunn, these to be shared by Rebecca's chn as *common not joint tenants* but, if no issue, to pass to sisters Mary & Elizabeth Dunn; signed Jane Corke; witn: Ann Allen, Temperance Westron Ballyman, & James Parkhouse (all sign).

Rebecca Dunn died before executing this will & on 2 Feb 1780 John Corke the husband agreed that in her place Rebecca's husband John Dunn should be exec; marked ‡ by John Corke in presence of Charles Leigh & Henry Crosse. Admon 2 Feb 1780 names John Dunn, yeoman, as admin & also Charles Leigh, gent, & Thomas North, yeoman, all of Uffculme; signed Jno Dunn, Charles Leigh, & Thos North In presence of John Windsor.

W267 REBECCA DUNN wife of John Dunn 1780 (PU)

Admon 2 Feb 1780 names husband John Dunn, yeoman, as admin & also Charles Leigh, gent, & Thomas North, yeoman, all of Uffculme (all sign).

W268 ELIZABETH DUNN spinster 1782 (DS)

Will 19 Jul 1781 of Elizabeth Dunn of Uffculme, spinster, pr 3 Aug 1782 before James Windsor: exec[s] John Cork & Thomas Bidle, yeomen of Uffculme; £10 to John Cork of Uffculme, yeoman, who is also to hold in trust the residue & the estates, *viz.* 1/3 ea of *Aplins Houses*, *The Plump*, & a field on *Cuniger Hill*, for John & Mary Dunn, s & dr of nephew John Dunn of Uffculme, at 21; 5 guineas ea to nephews & nieces Mary Skinner, wife of yeoman John Skinner of Tiverton, Elizabeth Bidle, wife of yeoman Thomas Bidle of Uffculme, Henry Dunn of Halberton, & Margret Dunn of Halberton; 1 guinea to sister-in-law Elizabeth Dunn, widow of Halberton; signed Eliz[th] Dunn; witn: James Row & W Garnsey (both sign). On 25 May 1782 Thomas Beedle [*sic*] was named as the surviving exec in a note signed at Salisbury by Will[m] Boucher, Reg[r].

W269 NICHOLAS FARR haberdasher 1782 (DS)

[Mar: "Nicholas Farr & Prudence Sweatland" 5 May 1743. See W285.] Will 13 Oct 1777 of Nicholas Farr of Uffculme, haberdasher, pr 23 Aug 1782 before John Harrington: effectively all to wife Prudence Farr, exec; £1 1s ea to buy a mourning ring to ss William & Henry & to dr Catherine Farr; signed Nich[s] Farr; witn: Matt[w] Miller & Mary Churly (both sign).

W270 WILLAM SWEETLAND 1782 (DS)

Will 1781 of William Sweetland of Uffculme, pr 23 Aug 1782 before John Harrington: residue to s Ralph Sweetland, exec; to dr Prudence Farr the house where she lives in Uffculme town if she gives £5 to grson Henry Farr; £5 ea to grdr Margaret Holland, wife of William Holland, & grson William Sweetland; £20 to grdr Betty Sweetland; £5 ea to grson Thomas Sweetland & grdrs Prudence & Mary Sweetland; 2s a week for life to dr-in-law Mary Sweetland, wife of s Ralph Sweetland, if he dies first, to be paid out of estate at Coldharbour bought from Stephen Maunder; signed William Sweetland; witn: Richard Taylor, W[m] Gay, & John Saunders jun[r] (all sign).

W271 NICHOLAS CHURLY gent 1784 (PU)

[Bur: "Nicholas Churly" 4 Aug 1783.] Will 25 Apr 1783 of Nicholas Churly of Uffculme, gent, pr 1 Sep 1784 before John Windsor, surr: all household goods & furniture to wife Sarah & all residue of estate in trust to exec[s], wife Sarah Churly, Christopher Mounstephen of Cullompton, gent, & Henry Melhuish of Cullompton, linen draper; trustees empowered to invest, sell, or mortgage property to pay debts &c (including £300 bond on marriage to wife Sarah & funeral expenses, not more than £20) & to maintain & educate s Nicholas Churly till 21 or marriage (or to wife Sarah if s dies); signed Nicholas Churly; witn: R[t] Baker, Alice Baker, & Joseph Tayler (all sign).

W272 RALPH SWEETLAND 1785 (DS)

[Bur: "Ralph Sweetland" 4 Aug 1785.] Will 24 Oct 1783 of Ralph Sweetland of Uffculme, pr 19 Sep 1785 before Ja[s] Windsor: residue to s Wm Sweetland, exec, who also inherits all houses & estates, subject to payment of legacies; £100 to s Thomas Sweetland; £5 ea to drs Prudence Sweetland & Margaret Holland (wife of Wm Holland); 1s to dr Betty Chaplain (wife of John Chaplain); £1 1s at 21 to dr Mary Sweetland, to be maintained & placed as an apprentice by exec; 6d a week to wife Mary Sweetland, in addition to the 2s a week left by his father [Wm 1782]; signed R Sweetland; witn: John Saunders, sen[r] & jun[r], & W Saunders (all sign).

W273 SIMON WOODDROW clockmaker 1785 (DS)

[Bur: "Simon Woodrow" 23 Feb 1785.] Will 25 May 1784 of Simon Wooddrow of Uffculme, clockmaker, pr 19

Sep 1785: house & garden where teatator lived & others (in possesion of tenants Robert Green, weaver, Rachael Hooper -now untenanted, Elizabeth Loney, widow, & all others not given below) & all residue of estate to niece Ann Cotterell of Uffculme, widow (residing with testator), exec; house, garden, & orchard (in possession of testator) & meadow alongside (in possession of tenant Samuel Norton, innholder), all near Smithincott bridge, to nephew Nicholas Hooper of Uffculme, weaver; house & garden at Coldharbour (in possession of tenant Henry Tozer, woolcomber) to Richard Hook alš Graves of Uffculme, carpenter; another house & garden at Coldharbour (in possession of tenant Solomon Cotterell, woolcomber) to Solomon Cotterell; signed [shakily] by Simon Wooddrow; witn: Charles Leigh, Wm Holland, & Wm Fry (all sign).

W274 JOHN RUCKLY yeoman 1785 (DS)

[Bur: "John Ruckly" 29 Aug 1784.]

Will 25 Aug 1784 of John Ruckly of Uffculme, yeoman, pr before Rev James Windsor 19 Sep 1785, signed Willm Boucher Reg^{r}: all to wife Elizabeth Ruckly, exec, for maintenance of their chn, but if she remarries then all to trustees for the chn; trustees Wm Munday of Halberton, yeoman, & John Baker, shopkeeper; marked by John Baker & trustees.

W275 LAWRENCE NORMAN gunsmith 1787 (PU)

[Bur: "Lawrence Norman" 19 Aug 1786.]

Will 4 Jan 1780 of Lawrence Norman of Uffculme, gunsmith, pr 24 Jan 1787 before John Windsor, surr: all estates in Uffculme, Culmstock, or elsewhere & all residue to exec^{s}/trustees, Joseph Langdon & Richard Boobier, both of Uffculme, in trust for grson Lawrence Norman at age 21; marked & signed shakily by Lawrence Norman (*The Mark or Name of the Testator Being Ill in the Gout*); witn: Jno Windsor, John Rugg, & Mary Windsor (all sign).

W276 WILLIAM SNOW farmer 1790 (PU)

Will 29 Apr 1786 of William Snow of Uffculme, farmer, pr 30 Oct 1790 before John Windsor, surr: residue to exec, wife Elizabeth Snow, for life & then to dr Mary Cottman in trust for s John Snow, Ann Vinnicombe, Joan Snow, & Sarah Cottner (dr of Mary Cottner), to be shared between them; apparel to John Snow; bacon hutch & New Testament to Joan Snow; signed William Snow; witn: John Melhuish & John Pulman (both sign).

W277 NICHOLAS WREFORD 1792 (DS)

Will 19 Jan 1782 of Nicholas Wreford of Uffculme, [Devon misread as Dorset by the Salisbury copyist] pr 20 Aug 1791 before Rev John Harrington DD; £10 a year to maintain 2 ss to age 21 [& residue?] to wife Betty Wreford, exec; drs Mary Skinner & Elizabeth Willcocks to share all effects in Tiverton, paying *head rents & incumbrances* & receiving rents from tenants; s Nicholas to have James Smyth's Tenement after death of his mother & Brabham's House at 21; Wm Wreford [son] to have house where Dr Dinness lives & Turner's Tenement at 21; witn: Thos Marsh, Thos Hutchengs jun^{r}, & John Dunn (all probably signed, but not clear from copy)..

W278 HENRY PARSONS thatcher 1794 (DS)

Will 24 Jan 1773 of Henry Parsons of Craddock, thatcher, pr 25 Aug 1794: residue to wife Sarah & s Henry Parsons, exec^{s}; 3 houses at Yondercott (lately purchased from Madam Vaun & in possession of tenants Thomas Ayres, Ann Cork, & Jacob Davey) to wife Sarah & James James, yeoman of Uffculme, as trustees for s John until

21, when he inherits; 3 houses at Coldharbour (in possession of tenants William Hitchcock, Susanna Langdon, & Richard Furber) in same trust for s James until 21, when he inherits; 3 houses at Yondercott (in possession of tenants Peter Spurway, James Tanner, & John Dunster) in same trust for s Henry until 21, when he inherits; £20 ea to drs Frances & Sarah Parsons; marked by Henry Parsons; witn: Thomas Norton, Mary James, (both sign), & Sarah Furber (marks).

W279 ELIZABETH OXENHAM widow 1794 (DS)

Will 20 Jan 1791 of Elizabeth Oxenham of Uffculme, widow, pr at Uffculme 25 Aug 1794 before Jno Harrington DD, but subsequently re-examined at the PCC because of significant property interests outside Uffculme: residue to exec, dr Dorothy, wife of William Dickinson; to be buried for not more than £20 beside husband at Oakford; mother's wedding ring & 1 guinea for mourning ring to sister Susanna Lawrence; satin christening garment to s William Oxenham; bed with fittings, table, 6 silver teaspoons, & cedar chest to grdr Susanna Dickinson; bible & 2 silver tablespoons to grson Henry Dickinson; silver shoe buckles to godson William, s of Wm Oxenham; £10 ea to ss Roger Broughton Oxenham, & Thomas, Robert, & John Oxenham; £5 to s Hugh Oxenham; £10 ea to s William Oxenham & s-in-law Wm Dickinson; £5 to goddr Elizabeth Oxenham, dr of William; 1 guinea ea to goddrs Mary Abraham & Elizabeth Maunder & to grdr Dorothy Oxenham, all drs of Roger Broughton Oxenham; armchair, table, dressing box to dr Dorothy for life, then to her dr Susanna Dickinson; £6 to fit out s Arthur Oxenham in decent mourning & also to William Dickinson, in trust for maintenance of Arthur, the proceeds from the recent sale of Westbrook Wood in the parish of Bampton (£40 already received); if s Hugh dead or not heard of in 5 years, his £5 to augment the annuity for Arthur; witn: Robert Crout & N^s^ Spencer [from a copy authorized with probate by Willm Boucher, not^y^ pub, & his clerk Tho^s^Lush].

W280 JOHN DENNING 1795 (PU)

[A note on the admon states that John Denning died on 15 Jan 1795.]
Admon 25 Feb 1795 names 1 of the ss, Francis Denning, yeoman, as admin & also Richard John Marker, gent, & Wm Trickey, yeoman, all of Uffculme; all sign in presence of Ja^s^ Windsor.

W281 HENRY GREEN 1797 (DS)

[Bur: not found but cf "Hannah Green" 14 Mar 1797. Mar: "Henry Green & Ann Pulman 7 Oct 1780, Willand.]
Will 20 May 1783 of Henry Green of Uffculme, pr 29 Aug 1797: house, garden, & all other residue to be shared by execs, s William Green & dr Jane Cottrell, wife of Charles Cottrell; mare or £4 4s to s Wm; 1s to wife Ann Green *in full discharge of her dower*; marked Henry Green; witn: Jno Holland, & John Saunders sen^r^ & jun^r^ (all sign).

W282 JOHN HOLLAND 1797 (DS)

[Bur: "John Holland of Asshill" 26 Nov 1797.]
Will 23 Aug 1785, of John Holland of Uffculme who died in Feb 1797, pr at Uffculme 29 Aug 1797: all houses, &c to exec^s^, wife Susanna, & 2 ss William & James Holland, apart from £5 ea to ss George & Mich-ael, 1s ea to ss Thomas & John, & £1 1s to s Joseph Holland; signed Jno Holland; witn: John Dunn, Samuel Green, & John Saunders (all sign): "under £100".

W283 SARAH DINNHAM widow 1797 (DS)

[Mar: "Thomas Dinnham & Sarah Dyer" 19 Aug 1734, Exeter St David.]

Will 19 Nov 1795 of Sarah Dinnham of Uffculme, widow, pr 29 Aug 1797: to be buried near late husband Thomas Dinnham at Burlescombe churchyard; ¼ part of *Eastbrook* estate, Burlescombe, (another ¼ having been willed by husband to s Peter) to ss-in-law William Sweetland & John Fry, exec[s]; £25 to dr Sarah, wife of John Fry (qualified by a loan or mortgage complication); marked by Sarah Dinham; witn: Jos[h] Langdon, A Langdon, & John Chilcote (all sign).

W284 THOMAS GORE surgeon 1798 (PU) & 1830 (DS)

[Bur: "Thomas Gore" 14 Dec 1797; a note on the admon gives the date of death as 4 Dec 1797.]

Admon 19 Apr 1798 names Thomas George Maddock of Staple Inn London, gent, (a principal creditor) as admin & also Richard John Marker, gent, & Giles Bowman[?], scrivener, both of Uffculme; all sign in presence of Ja[s] Windsor. The document 24 Mar 1798 transferring admin[n] to T G Maddock names Jane Gore as widow and Ellen Maddock (wife of Thomas George Maddock of Staple Hill London, gent), Ann Gore, spinster, Ellis Button Gore, & John Escott Gore as chn of the intestate dec[d] Thomas Gore; all sign in presence of Rob[t] Manley, Giles Bowerman, & Th[o] Jagg.

Admon 14 Jul 1830 before Edm[d] Benson, surr, names Rob[t] Farrant of New Sarum as admin & accompanying papers relate to land holdings which were not assigned when Thomas Gore died intestate. The 1830 papers refer to the original admon 19 Apr 1798 of Thomas Gore of Uffculme, surgeon, & report that the original admin, Thomas George Maddock, a principal creditor appointed on the renunciation of the widow, had also died intestate & had not assigned the property in question, *viz*. houses & gardens (including *Easter House*, where J Maunder rebuilt, *Wester* Houses, & *Vowler's House*) in North Street, Uffculme, bought (for the remainder of the 1000-year term) by Thomas Gore by the agreement of 13 Sep 1776 with Edward Manley sen[r], William Bird, William Hellings, Henry Barham Harris, Stevenson Dunsford & his wife Ann, & Charles Leigh, gent. Since Stevenson Dunsford had allegedly not paid a £600 sum agreed earlier (17 Jul 1775) when the property was transferred to Edward Manley, the remainder of the 1000-year term was assigned in 1830 to Edward Manley Leigh. In 1775 Vowler's House was in the possession of William Brook and other parts of this property, which was bounded to the north by Edward Ellis's land, were in the possession of Philip Cook & others as tenants of William Bird.

W285 PRUDENCE FARR widow 1798 (PU)

[Bur: "Prudence Farr" 9 Jan 1797; oath 1 Jun 1798 (sworn by Edward Crosse & Hugh Sweetland before Ja[s] Windsor) carries a note that Prudence Farr died on 3 Jan 1797. Widow of Nicholas W269.]

Will 22 Apr 1793 of Prudence Farr of Uffculme, widow, pr 28 Jun 1798 before Ja[s] Windsor, surr: clothes to dr Catherine, wife of Edward Davies, clerk; all estates (*both real and Freeholde and Leasehold and Chattlehold*) to execs/trustees, Edward Crosse of Woodcocks Hayes, Halberton, gent, & Hugh Sweetland the younger of Topsham, baker, to be sold to pay funeral expenses & remainder to be divided in two; one part invested for dr Catherine Davies (not for husband's use) & her chn after her (with detailed arrangements for disposal in case of death); other part to s Henry Farr; signed Prudence Farr; witn: Anna Marker, Rich J Marker, & Giles Bowerman (all sign).

Codicil 24 Oct 1796; silver pint cup to s Henry Farr to be given to either of his chn at his choice; wedding ring & silver spoon marked EN-NF to grdr Mary Farr; mother's mourning ring to dr Catherine Davies; silver spoon marked IT-NF to s Henry Farr, plus books she has written his name in; signed Prudence Farr; witn: Rich J Marker & William White (both sign).

W286 PETER HOLWAY 1799 (PU)

[Bur: "Peter Holway" 19 Aug 1798. The admon carries a note that Peter Holway died on 12 Sep 1799, but this must be wrong. No other burial of that name occurs around then and it was much too late in the century for Feb 1799 in the admon to mean 1800.]
Admon 1 Feb 1799 names widow Elizabeth Holway as admin & also Richard John Marker, gent, & Richard James, yeoman, both of Uffculme; marked E by Elizabeth Holway signed by R J Marker & Richd James in presence of Ja^{s} Windsor.

W287 JAMES BRAY yeoman 1800 (DS)

[Bur: "James Bray" 22 Dec 1799.]
Will 8 Dec 1799 of James Bray of Uffculme, yeoman, pr 6 Jun 1800 before Rev John Windsor: execs friends William Blackmore & Robert Trott; £21 to dr Elizabeth Bray; £15 ea to ss James, John, & Thomas, & to dr Mary Bray; £20 to dr Jane Bray; £15 to s William; £20 at age 21 to s Richard Bray; residue to be divided between these chn; marked by James Bray; witn: Ann Melhuish & William Byrd (both sign).

W288 SAMUEL CALLOW yeoman 1800 (DS)

[Bur: "Samuel Callow" 29 Mar 1799.]
Will 5 Mar 1799 of Samuel Callow of Uffculme, yeoman, pr before Ja^{s} Windsor 28 Aug 1800: all (in control of trustee Thomas Garnsey of Uffculme, gent) to go to wife Joyse, exec, or, if she remarries, just £50 and remainder to drs Elizabeth & Mary Callow at 21; signed Samuel Callow; witn: Catherine Barne[s?] & Wm Hurley (both sign).

W289 WILLIAM BISHOP woolcomber 1800 (DS)

[Bur: "William Bishop" 27 Jul 1800.]
Will 31 Jan 1797 of William Bishop of Uffculme, woolcomber, pr 18 Aug 1800: residue to ss Samuel & John Bishop, exec^{s}; to s Samuel Bishop the houses in his possession as tenant; to s John Bishop the house lately in possession of Thomas Hookway as tenant, plus the house of the dec^{d}; £15 ea to drs Elizabeth, wife of Michael Wiet, Ann, wife of Thomas Tratt, & Eleaner, wife of James Graves; £5 to grch Mary Graves; orchard to be sold to pay these legacies; marked by William Bishop; witn: Thos Marsh, Robert Rugg, & William Saunders (all aign).

W290 WILLIAM GRANTLAND yeoman 1800 (DS)

Will 4 Aug 1794 of William Grantland of Uffculme, yeoman, pr 28 Aug 1800: residue to John Hewett, exec; 2s a week ea for life to half-bro John Grantland & to cousin George Adams, butcher of Uffculme; all property in trust (with provision for his expenses) to exec, John Hewett of Uffculme, yeoman (with whom WG lived), for sale & investment to meet the following bequests; interest on £30 for life to half-sister Rachel, wife of John Turner, & after her to her chn at age 21; £30 ea to half-bros & sisters James, Sarah, Elizabeth, & Joseph Ford; £15 ea to 3 drs of late uncle Thomas Grantland, Lucy, Jane or Jenny, & Ann or Nancy (of whom 2 are married); £15 ea at age 21 to 6 chn of late uncle Thomas Standerwick; £10 ea to cousin Henry Baker of Sherbourne & his s at age 21; £20 ea to cousin Thomas Hobbs of Portsmouth & his sister Elizabeth (now married or a widow); £10 to James Turner & at age 21 to Thomas Turner, ss of aunt Hannah, widow of James Turner; signed William Grantland; witn: Rich^{d} J Marker, Giles Bowerman, & William Veals (all sign).

W291 ELIZABETH PERCY widow 1800 (DS)

[Bur: "Elizabeth Pearcey" 11 Jan 1799.] Will 31 Dec 1798 of Elizabeth Percy of Uffculme, widow, pr 28 Aug 1800: residue to s John Pearcy [*sic*], exec; £5 ea to ss & drs, William (with 5 bushels of wheat), Robert (with clock & case), Elizabeth Sweetand (with her father's oak box & gold ring), James & Thomas (with her bed), & Mary Pearcy (with feather bed, tea-kettle, & weights); 2 drs share her clothes; £5 ea to 2 grsons John & James Saunders at age 21; signed [shakily] by Elisa Percy; witn: Ann Melhuish & W[J?] Byrd (both sign).

W292 JOHN BROOM thatcher 1800 (DS)

[Bur: "John Broom" 29 Aug 1798.] Will 8 Apr 1797 of John Broom of Uffculme, thatcher (died 22 Aug 1798), pr 20 Oct 1800: house for the rmaining term of years & residue to wife Agnes (unless she remarries) & s Simon Broom, exec^{s}; 2 guineas to dr Mary (wife of Simon Churly); 12 guineas to s Henry; 2 guineas ea to drs & ss, Elizabeth (wife of William Fair), Margarett Elworthy, Edward, William, Grizzel Broom, &, at age 21, Sarah Broom, who is also given 5 guineas towards an apprenticeship in a trade of her choosing; signed John Broom; witn: Deborah Dennis, Mary Farley, & Geo Dennis (all sign).

W293 JOHN BLACKMORE miller 1803 (DS)

[Bur: "John Blackmore" 25 Jul 1803.] Will 11 Apr 1802 of John Blackmore of Uffculme, miller, pr 27 Aug 1803 before Rev Mr Hetley (value under £300): residue to s Thomas Blackmore, exec; sale for £245 confirmed of fee simple of Hackpen Grist Mills & appurtenances to Charles Leigh of Uffculme, gent, (5 guinea deposit already rec^{d}) to be carried through by trustee Richard Hellings of Holcombe Rogus, gent, £130 of the proceeds to be used to pay off the mortgage on the property to Thomas Hellings of Tiverton, gent; to present wife (Mary Coombe, spinster, before her marriage) £100 (or 3s a week for life in lieu) agreed at marriage, & bed, brass pot, chest, oak boxes, & saucepan, but if she dies all these to go to dr Sarah Blackmore, who also has a legacy of £5; after death of wife 1 guinea ea to eldest s John Blackmore, to dr Jane, wife of Ephraim Elworthy, to s William Blackmore, & to dr Anna, wife of William Richards; marked by John Blackmore; witn: John Wyatt, James Gillard, & Ch^{s} Trishe(?) (all sign).

W294 JOHN NORTON carpenter 1803 (DS)

[Bur: "John Norton" 11 Sep 1803.] Will 19 Jun 1802 of John Norton of Uffculme, carpenter, pr 1803: residue in trust to exec, s John Norton, for sale & equal division of proceeds amongst ss John & Richard, drs Mary & Jane, & s Thomas; £10 extra to dr Jane; 5s ea at 21 to grdr Mary Norton & to 2 grsons, chn of dr Catherine Dilbridge; 1 guinea at age 21 to grson William Norton, s of dr Mary; 5s to grdr Elizabeth Norton, dr of s John; signed John Norton; witn: Franncis Dening, Agnes Matthews, & Richd James (all sign).

W295 JOAN HURLEY widow 1806 (DS)

[Bur: "Joan Hurley" 29 Jun 1806.] Will 10 Apr 1806 of Joan Hurley of Uffculme, widow, pr 1806: residue of money securities (after debts & expenses) equally to exec^{s}, grdrs Elizabeth Ware alš Cross & Jane, wife John Hewett jun^{r} of Uffculme; "Ratts-Ash" (2 houses with gardens, orchard, &c near road from Five Fords Water to Hillturner), plus household goods, furniture, & clothes, to grdr Elizabeth Ware alš Cross; marked Joan Hurley; witn: John Hewett & Giles Bowerman (both sign).

W296 JOHN POOK of Ashill, gent 1809 (DS)

[Bur: "John Pook" 25 Jun 1809. Mar: "John Pook & Betty Farrant" 31 May 1734, Hemyock.]

Will 6 May 1809 of John Pook of Ashill, gent, pr (with value put at under £450) at Uffculme 26 Aug 1809 before Robt Morres: residue to wife Betty Pook, exec; *Mitchells* tenement, together with closes *Standbridge & Standbridge Meadow*, at Ashill (where he lived) to trustees William Thomas of West Buckland, Somerset, Robert Farr-ant of Culmpine, Clayhidon, & James Gillham of Culliford, Culm-stock, gents, in trust for use for life of wife Betty & for £20 annuity to bro Thomas Pook; after death of wife to pass to nephew John Pook & his heirs; the same trustees also to sell *Umbrook* tenement, together with 3 closes of ground of *Waldrons* tenement, partly to pay off any mortgage on *Mitchells* & partly for a £300 fund in trust for nieces Elizabeth, Mary, & Sarah Pook, drs of bro Thomas Pook, but if all die before age 21 to pass to nephew John Pook; trustees to have expenses paid; signed John Pook; witn: Samuel & Elizabeth Glanvill & Giles Bowerman (all sign).

W297 NICHOLAS HOOPER alš COOKE yeoman 1809 (DS)

[Bur: "Nicholas Hooper" 12 Jun 1809.]

Will 22 May 1809 of Nicholas Hooper alš Cooke of Uffculme, yeoman, pr 1809: all messuages, lands, goods, & chattels divided equally between execs, wife Joan, ss John, Nicholas, William, Thomas, James, & Samuel, & dr Mary, wife of William Owens, as tenants in common, not joint tenants; a codicil states that a cow & best bed had already been given to wife; marked N by Nicholas Hooper alias Cooke; witn: Robt & John Skinner & Wm Hurley (all sign).

W298 AMOS LANGDON shopkeeper 1812 (DS)

[Bur: "Amos Langdon" 31 Jan 1812, age 78. Mar: "Amos Langdon & Sarah Norman" by licence 10 Oct 1786.]

Will 24 Jan 1812 of Amos Langdon of Uffculme, shopkeeper, pr at Uffculme 19 Aug 1812 before Ja^{s} Windsor, surr: residue to wife Sarah Langdon, exec; 2 houses at Coldharbour (in possession of tenants Thomas Jordan & Ellen Greaves) to wife Sarah for life, then to pass to Joseph Wood, yeoman of Uffculme, who also has all the clothes; signed A Langdon; witn: Robert Drew, John Nott, & Giles Bowerman (all sign).

W299 ELIZABETH NORTHAM widow 1812 (DS)

[Bur: "Elizabeth Northam" 16 Dec 1814, age 78.]

Will 24 Feb 1812 of Elizabeth Northam of Uffculme, widow, possibly pr 1815[?]: residue to bro Philip Stark, exec; picture of *Abelard & Louisa* to John Hill of Uffculme, painter; to niece Mary Louch, widow, (dr of bro Philip Stark) gold ring, 2-guinea piece, silver spoon, silver shoe buckles & stay-hook set with stones, & specified garments of silk, linen, & muslin; to niece Ann Stark (dr of bro Philip) muslin shawl handkerchief; marked X by Elizabeth Northam; witn: Mary Howe & Giles Bowerman (both sign, the first shakily).

W300 GEORGE MARSH 1818 (DS)

[Bur: "George Marsh" of Smithincott 19 Apr 1816, age 36.]

Admon 19 Sep 1818 before Ja^{s} Windsor, names widow Grace Marsh as admin & also Samuel Radford & Thomas Fry, both yeomen of Uff-culme; marked by Grace Marsh & Samuel Radford & signed by Thos Fry.

W301 RUTH JAMES widow 1818 (DS)

Will 17 Sep 1808 of Ruth James of Uffculme, widow, pr 1818: all to dr Anna Maria James, exec; signed Ruth James; witn: R J Marker & Giles Bowerman (both sign).

W302 THOMAS HELLIER yeoman 1818 (DS)

[Bur: "Thomas Hellier" of Uffculme Town 18 Oct 1817, age 78. Mar: "Thomas Hellier & Elizabeth Minefy" by licence 7 Mar 1803.]

Will 24 Oct 1816 of Thomas Hellier of Uffculme, yeoman, pr 1818: residue to wife Elizabeth Hellier, exec, plus all the property which, after her death is bequeathed as follows: *bushes orchard* to s Thomas; *Peperals houses* to s John; to s Nicholas part of *Woodrows* (2 houses occupied by William Knight & Nicholas Hellier); the other part of *Woodrows* (occupied by Henry Bodgers & Henry Lockyer) to s John & s-in-law Thomas Dunn alš Melhuish in trust for dr Mary Dodge, wife of James Dodge, for her own use & to inherit if she predeceases him, or otherwise to pass to her chn; part of *Shaddocks* to dr Elizabeth Dunn alš Melhuish; common land on Uffculme Down allotted to him to pass to ss John & Nicholas; marked H by Thomas Hellier; witn: W^m^, Thos & Sarah Sweetand (all sign).

W303 WILLIAM HOLWAY 1821 (DS)

[Bur: "William Holway" of Penslade 30 Apr 1820, age 55.]

Will 2 Mar 1820 of William Holway of Uffculme, pr 11 Apr 1821 at Uffculme before Ja^s^ Windsor, surr: residue to wife Elizabeth Holway, exec; £20 ea to bro James Holway & sister Sarah Mull[^t^?]; signed William Holway; witn: Mary Cundick, Joseph Hill jun^r^, & Wm Sweetland (all sign).

W304 HENRY DUNN gent 1821 (DS)

Will 28 Sep 1820, with codicil 4 Feb 1821, of Henry Dunn of Uffculme, gent, pr 1821: residue to sister Margaret Bromfield (wife of John Bromfield), exec; £40 to be invested by a trust set up to augment the salary of the Officiating Minister at the Coldharbour Meeting, power to elect replacements being vested in the 11 trustees (*viz* Richard Hall Clarke Esq of Bridwell, Halberton, John Bromfield, yeoman of Uffculme, John Skinner, yeoman of Tiverton, James Baker, shopkeeper of Uffculme, John How the younger, umbrella manufacturer of Bristol, William How, shopman of Bristol, William Parkhouse, yeoman of Halberton, James Hussey & his s William, both yeomen of Uffculme, John Fry & his s John Fry the younger, both yeomen of Uffculme); to bro-in-law John Bromfield, nephew John Skinner, & William Parkhouse *Hales's* tenement & *Venner's Meadow* (now in testator's occupation) in trust for an annuity of £10 to nephew John Dunn for life, the premises to be for the use of sister Margaret (with prohibition on ploughing areas other than *Poolclose*, *Great Close*, *Pook's Close*, *Tinker's Close*, & *The Nursery*); £10 annuity to John Bromfield; £10 ea to niece Elizabeth Jarman, wife of Willm Jarman of Tiverton, & to great-nephews Henry Dunn Skinner & John Dunn Skinner, ss of nephew John Skinner, at age 21; £5 ea to great-nephew Richard Skinner of Tiverton, schoolmaster, s of Richard Skinner late of Thorverton, & to Ann Melhuish alš Dunn, & to Betty Billing (of dec^d^'s address); signed Henry Dunn; witn: James Holland, William Bowerman, & Giles Bowerman (all sign). The codicil modifies succession to *Venners Meadow* if sister Margaret should die before her husband; Sarah Babb signs in place of James Holland as witn.

W305 THOMAS GARNSEY gent of Bodmiscombe 1821 (DS)

[Mar: "Thomas Garnsey batchelor & Elizabeth Hurley" by licence 31 May 1798.]

Will 25 Jun 1814 of Thomas Garnsey of Bodmiscombe in Uffculme parish, gent, pr 17 Oct 1821, after renunciation by original trustees in bond of 28 Aug 1821 (which all 3 signed): the testator's intention was to put all his property in trust for his s John Garnsey during his minority, to allow his wife Elizabeth £40 a year (if no remarriage), and to provide £1500 ea at age 21 for his drs Mary & Elizabeth, they to be supported until then by the interest from those sums; the original execs, bros-in-law William (gent) & Richard Hurley (surgeon) & k William Mountstephen (gent of Bristol), were to assist wife Elizabeth Garnsey in this administration, but they renounced all such duties in her favour; signed Thos Garnsey; witn: R^d^ Manning, Wm Moore Ayshford, & John Cork (all sign).

W306 HENRY HEWETT yeoman 1824 (DS)

[Bur: "Henry Hewett" 4? Feb 1823, age 44.]

Will 7? Feb 1823 of Henry Hewett of Uffculme, yeoman, pr 13 Aug 1824 before Ja^s^ Windsor, surr: residue to bro Thomas Hewett, exec; £50 due from bro John to be shared by bros John & William; signed [shakily] H Hewett; witn: R J Marker, Wm Parkhouse, & James Baker (all sign).

W307 NICHOLAS WREFORD yeoman 1824 (DS)

[Bur: "Nicholas Wreford" 16 Jul 1824, age 53.]

Will 10 May 1824 of Nicholas Wreford of Uffculme, yeoman, pr 26 Aug 1824 before Rev Edm^d^ Benson, surr: all property & money to friend John Hellings of Tiverton, gent, exec, in trust, using interest for maintenance of s Robert Wreford during minority & yielding all to him (& his heirs) at age 21; £30 to housekeeper Ann Scadding; signed Nicholas Wreford; witn: Wm Bennett, Wm Bowerman, & R^t^ Loosemore (all sign).

W308 MARY TRICKEY widow 1827(DS)

Will 13 Jun 1825 of Mary Trickey of Uffculme, widow, pr at Uffculme before Rev Ja^s^ Windsor, surr, 11 Aug 1827, when the exec, Samuel Henson, made a *solemn affirmation* rather than an oath, *being of the people called Quakers*: residue to nephew Samuel Henson of Uffculme, exec; all apparel, warming-pan, pestle & mortar, & £30 (for her own use, not her husband's) to niece Ann Morgan, wife of John Morgan of Landcocks in Wellington; £10 ea to *niece* Mary Baker (dr of dr-in-law Ann Baker dec^d^, late of Tiverton), & to nephews John Trickey (son of late bro-in-law John Trickey of Culmstock), & Richard Fry (of Woodgate in Culmstock); £5 & £10 respectively to nephews John & Samuel Henson of Uffculme; signed Mary Trickey; witn: Benjamin & Eliz^th^ Hussey (both sign).

W309 JOHN WERE of Craddock 1827 (DS)

[Mar: "John Were jnr & Mary Were" 12 Oct 1827.]

Admon 11 Aug 1827 names widow Mary Were as admin & also John Were of Halberton, yeoman, & Samuel Henson of Uffculme, yeoman; Mary Were marks & the others sign.

W310 SARAH BOWERMAN widow 1827 (DS)

[Mar: "Giles Bowerman & Sarah Were" 4 Jun 1792.]

Admon 15 Sep 1827 names husband Giles Bowerman of Tiverton, scrivener, as admin & also William Dickinson & William Sweetland, both gents of Uffculme; all three sign before Rev Ja^s^ Windsor, surr.

W311 JOHN PRING the elder, gent of Ashill 1830 (DS)
[Bur: "John Pring" 8 Apr 1830, age 88.]
Will 19 Sep 1825 of John Pring the elder of Uffculme, pr 28 Apr 1830 at Uffculme (exec^{s} sworn 24 Apr 1830 before Ja^{s} Windsor): £100 to trustees/ execs William Wyatt of Uffculme, gent, & Samuel Henson of Burlescombe, builder, to be invested in trust for chn of s Robert Pring at age 21; to same trustees *Welshes* houses at Ashill (occupied by himself & s John Pring), houses at Hillturner (occupied by William Pursey, John Spurway, & Sarah Dimond), & all other freehold or leasehold estates, in trust for s John Pring for life, then for grson Thomas Pring (& heirs), who pays £200 to his bro John Pring; household goods & furniture, cider press, apple engine, hogsheads, pipes, & other vessels all to same trustees for use of s John & then grson Thomas; all securities & residue of estate to same trustees for payment of legacies, debts, & expenses; £50 to dr Mary Voisey, widow; £100 to dr Jane, wife of Thomas Cook of Tiverton, linen draper; signed John Pring; witn: Harriet Stoddon Rendell, & Giles & Ann Bowerman (all sign).

W312 JOSEPH HILL 1830 (DS)
Will 1 Nov 1826 of Joseph Hill of Uffculme, pr 1830: all legacies after death of wife, when residue, including all property not otherwise specified, to exec^{s}, s John & dr Sarah; to s Joseph £516 in trust for his chn, £156 being for his dr Mary (who has the interest for her own use during the life of her husband but the capital at his death if she outlives him) and £360 for his other chn; £2 to trustees of Particular Baptist Chapel in Coneygar Lane, from proceeds of *Greens ground* adjoining Coneygar Lane; signed [shakily] by Jos Hill; witn: John Wood, William & Sarah Welland.

W313 THOMAS PARR thatcher 1833 (DS)
[Bur: "Thomas Parr" 25 Mar 1833, age 53. Mar: "Thomas Parr & Elizabeth Woodrow" 25 Dec 1818, Halberton; Uffculme banns.]
Will 15 Mar 1833 of Thomas Parr if Uffculme, thatcher, pr 1833: all to wife, Elizabeth Parr, exec; signed Th^{o} Parr; witn: Charles Leigh, att^{y} at law, & Edward White (both sign).

W314 ROBERT HAWKINS 1833 (DS)
[Mar: "Robert Hawkins & Harriett Chown" 5 Jun 1828, Exeter St Thomas.]
Admon 9 Sep 1833 before Henry Manley, surr., names widow Harriett Hawkins as admin & also Charles Cottrell, lacemaker, & Robert Hill, gent, all of Uffculme (all sign). Effects said to be under £200.

W315 ROBERT RADFORD yeoman 1836 (DS)
[Mar: "Robert Radford & Joanna May" 22 May 1794.]
Will 15 Nov 1835 of Robert Radford of Uffculme, yeoman, pr 11 May 1836: all household goods, farming stock, chattels & effects to execs, John Trott & Richard May the younger, to be sold & proceeds to be in trust for use of wife Joanna for life, except for the following; £7 ea to bro Edmund Radford, & sisters Ann Radford (spinster), & Rosanna Radford (wife of William Radford); if any residue after death of wife, half to go to bro & sisters & half to wife's kin; signed Robert Radford; witn: R A Bevan & Mary Radford (both sign).

W316 ELIZABETH GRANGER of Milverton 1836 (DS)
[Mar: "Robert Granger & Elizabeth Jacobs" 10 Sep 1787, Exeter St Thomas.]
Admon 11 May 1836 (of effects at Uffculme, sworn before George T

Smith, surr, to be worth less than £100) of Elizabeth Granger of Milverton names husband Robert Granger of Milverton, accountant, as admin, & also Giles Bowerman, gent, & Richard Bowerman, scrivener, both of Uffculme; all sign in presence of George T Smith.

W317 WILLIAM DICKINSON gent 1836 (DS)

[Bur: "William Dickinson" 5 Apr 1836, age 80. Mar: "William Dickinson & Dorothy Oxenham" 17 May 1779, Holcombe Rogus. See W279.]
Will 27 Oct 1826 of William Dickinson of Uffculme, gent, pr at Uffculme 29 Apr 1836 before George T Smith, surr: residue to s Benjamin Dickinson, exec; ratified settlement of 24 Mar 1779 at marriage to *now wife* Dorothy (née Oxenham) & disposes property accordingly, with provision for wife to remain for life & use household goods &c; *White Hele* freehold close in Uffculme to (incapable) s William, but to be managed by s Benjamin; several closes called *Three Grattons*, *Easter Ham*, *& Staple Hill* in Uffculme to s Benjamin (&his heirs for the residue of 2000 years!), & also *Long Acre* in Uffculme, which wife Dorothy has for life; £16 annuity to Benjamin for care of William, in addition to provision made for the latter in his grandfather's will; signed Wm Dickinson; witn: Wm Gillard & T Oxenham (both sign).

W318 JAMES HUSSEY yeoman of Culmstock 1836 (DS)

Will 4 Aug 1829 of James Hussey of Nicholashayne Pond, Culmstock, yeoman, pr 15 Oct 1836 before George T Smith, surr: all to exec, wife Ann Hussey, including amongst properties *part of Kent's* in Uffculme, comprising certain houses & gardens & a smith's shop, stable, & meadow close; signed James Hussey; witn: Harriet Stoddon Rendell, & Ann & Giles Bowerman (all sign).

W319 SUSANNAH SOUTHWOOD widow 1842 (DS)

Admon 27 Jun 1842 names s William Southwood, carpenter & joiner, as admin & also Richard Bowerman, gent, & Richard Dunstanne Bevan, surveyor, all of Uffculme; all sign in presence of George T Smith.

W320 GRACE WYATT spinster 1845 (DS)

[Bur: "Grace Wyatt of Yondercot" aged 82, 8 Jul 1845.]
Will 18 Feb 1837 of Grace Wyatt of Uffculme, spinster, pr (sworn before George T Smith, surr, goods less than £200) 28 Jun 1845: all residue to exec^{s}, George Berry & Mary Wyatt, in trust for Martha Wyatt at age 23, or, if she dies, to pass to Mary Wyatt; £2 to niece Jane Wyatt; £3 to William, eldest s of nephew Edward Wyatt, £2 ea to Edward & John, ss of Edward Wyatt, & to 3 chn of niece Sarah Potter; £4 to [unnamed] sister if living; all clothes to be boxed up by George Berry for Martha Wyatt (at Taunton with Mrs Voysey, upholsterer) at age 23; marked by Grace Wyatt; witn: R J Marker & Richd Bowerman (both sign).

W321 WILLIAM BOWERMAN blacksmith 1845 (DS)

[Bur: "William Bowerman of Town" aged 65, 2 Mar 1842. Mar: "William Bowerman living in this parish and Hannah Duckham of this parish" 4 Oct 1801.]
Will 20 Feb 1839 of William Bowerman of Uffculme, blacksmith, pr at Uffculme 30 Aug 1845 before George Smith, surr: apparel & watch to James Duckham, s of John Duckham of Shirehampton, Glos., everything else to wife Hannah Bowerman, exec, if she does not remarry, but trustees (Benjamin Hussey, of the Lamb Inn, & Richard Dunnstanne Bevan, schoolmaster, both of Uffculme) to oversee

the proceeds from the property formerly bought from Thomas Hellier & Richard Milward, *viz*. 5 houses with gardens, outhouses & workshop, called *late Mary Northams* and in possession of himself, James Cotterell, William Williams, William Parr, & James Duckham; at wife's death or remarriage, all to pass to James Duckham & then, if he has no issue, to surviving chn of Fanny Braddon, wife of Samuel Braddon & dr of George & Elizabeth Wood; signed William Bowerman; witn: William Welland, James Welland, & Mary Rice (all sign).

W322 GEORGE SOUTHEY miller 1845 (DS)

[Bur: at Spicelands?]
Will 23 Dec 1842 of George Southey of Uffculme, miller, pr 30 Aug 1845 before George T Smith, surr: residue to 3 chn Anne, George, & James Southey, exec[s]; 4 cottages & gardens in Kitwell Street, Uffculme, (occupied by William Williams, William Parr, [blank] Wyatt, & James Braddick) to dr Anne Southey & heirs or, if she dies without issue, 2 to the east to s George & 2 to the west to s James; signed George Southey; witn: R J Marker & Rich[d] Bowerman (both sign).

A GLOSSARY OF 16 TO 18th CENTURY WORDS

The following are put forward as likely, though not always certain, meanings of words found in the archive documents or in the text. Where no definition is given, the reference to the inventory or will number where the word occurs may help readers to deduce possible meanings. Some words may have been incorrectly transcribed. The 16/18th centuries secretary's hand is not always easy to decipher and spelling was erratic and frequently phonetic. Thus some words can best be identified if they are spoken out loud, but for this it helps if one is familiar with Devonshire speech.

The context can sometimes help. The room or building in which the items were listed can give a clue, but as things were kept in different places in the 16/17th centuries, it is not always helpful.

By no means every spelling variation is given and sometimes variations are given in brackets, e.g. be(e)d(e) = bed, beed, bede or beede.

This glossary was first compiled by Peter Newton for *Uffculme: a Peculiar Parish*, with help from joint authors, but has since been revised at some points by Mary Fraser. The main books consulted were:

Dictionary of the English Language, Samuel Johnson, 1755.

Lloyd's Encyclopaedic Dictionary, Edward Lloyd Limited, Fleet Street, London, 1895.

The English Dialect Dictionary, Joseph Wright, 1898-1905.

The Shorter Oxford English Dictionary on Historical Principles, Clarendon Press, 3rd ed., 1980.

Devon Inventories of the 16th and 17th Centuries, Margaret Cash, Devon & Cornwall Record Society, New Series, Vol.11, 1966.

The Woollen Industry of South-West England, Kenneth G Ponting, Adams & Dart, 1971.

C Willett Cunnington, *A Dictionary of English Costume*, Black, 1660.

C.Willett Cunnington and Phillis Cunnington, *Handbook of English Costume in the 16th Century*, Faber 1954, (revised ed.1970); *Handbook of English Costume in the 17th Century*, Faber, 1955.

C.Willett Cunnington, *Handbook of English Costume in the 18th Century*, Faber, 1957.

The Century Dictionary, The Times, 1899.

Chambers Encyclopaedia.

Ackauntinge knife: from the context a slaughterer's knife [17]

Admon: "administration" abbreviated.

Almen, Almein, Alamain Rivets: a cheap off-the-peg type of armour providing an adjustable form of arm protection, originating from Germany in the 16th century.

Almerye: [49] a variant of ambry

Ambry, amery, armore: a cupboard in which to keep meat, victuals and bread.

Andier dog, andogg: one of a pair of horizontal bars, supported on legs, with an upright in front, used for supporting a spit or logs in a fireplace. "Head like an apple, neck like a swan, back like a long dog and dree legs to stan." - old riddle.

Andiers, andirons: a pair of movable iron plates to contract the fire grate.

Angelytt: [W26] probably a corruption of *angelot*, a coin containing two penny-weights of gold, then worth 10 shillings. Struck at Paris in 1431 when held by the English.

Annige: [9] listed with a pail and a tub. Meaning not known

Appell wring: a crush for apples.

Apprentice: a young man or woman, bound by indentures to serve a particular master or mistress for a term of years, in return for which they are taught the trade or profession of the master/mistress.

Arme zawe: carpenter's hand saw.

Arquebus: an old handgun, longer and larger than a musket and hooked onto a rest fastened to the barrel.
Arsse: possibly harness (armour).
Astell pane: a board or plank [26]; or possibly a steel pan.

Back crook: iron hook hanging in a hearth [245].
Bakes: [122] possibly 'backs' - ie outbuildings
Bankett: a wooden bench.
Bands: the collars that superseded ruffs as men's neckwear, or specifically preaching bands, prescribed by Queen Elizabeth for Anglican clergy.
Bandstrings: tasselled ties.
Barraty: (not certain) possibly *barras*, a coarse linen fabric from the Low Countries, or *baratine*, a silk fabric, or *borato*, a light wool/silk mixture [187].
Battell and wedge: a mallet or hammer and wedge for splitting wood; (see beetle)
Bayes, bays, baize: [French *baie*] a cheap cloth made of worsted warp and woollen weft, fulled, but only finished on one side.
Beam: a yard arm, a circular shaft on to which the warp is wound.
Bearinge sheet: mantle or cloth used to cover an infant when carried for baptism. "Thy scarlet robes, as a child's bearing cloth I'll use." Shakespeare, Henry VI pt.I i,3.
Be(a)d(e): the mattress rather than the bedstead.
Be(e)d(e) tye: the ticking or case enclosing the filling of a mattress. "Yü can't use barley-doust vur bedties, 'cuz tha iles wid urn intü 'e". Devon peasant speech - Hewitt 1892.
Beetle, bittel, bittle: A heavy wooden club or mallet. "Plaize tü vatch in tha bittel an' wadges, I wan'th tü slat these moots". Devon peasant speech - Hewitt 1892.
Bell metal: an alloy of copper and tin, sometimes zinc and lead.
Beydds, a pair of: a string of beads or a rosary (suspended from a girdle).
Bigge: a coarse kind of barley, Hordeum hexastichum, that thrived on poorest soils and was used for malting. It attracted less duty than good barley. In [*88*], however, possibly *biggin*, a small wooden vessel.
Blew/blue: the colour blue or a blue woollen cloth of which servants' and apprentices' clothes were made.
Bodyes, pair of: the top part of a dress made separately from the kirtle and attached to it.
Booes: [3]
Bo(a)rde clothe: a table cloth.
Bosting iron: possibly a heavy smoothing iron.
Botelin: [175] bottles?
Botts: wooden mallets later used inbreaking flax, except that flax was not then grown. Maybe an alternative spelling of butts.
Bow dye: scarlet, from the "new" (1643) dye-house at Bow in East London.
Br(e)akeboard, brakinge board: according to Johnson a brake is a baker's kneading trough, so this could be a surface upon which the baker rolled out his dough.
Brake(n)stocke, brakinge stocke: in the same context as the above, i.e. in a bakehouse or kitchen- a piece of baking equipment. Or it could be an implement for clearing rough ground, (especially bracken?).
Brandi(e)s, brandyse: a trivet or grid iron.
Brandiron: a brand is a piece of firewood 3 feet long: this supports those brands.
Brase, brasen: brass.
Brazled away: frittered away [L3]
Breache: probably a spit [49]
Brichandize: (by association) a piece of hearth equipment.
Broads, brode, broadcloth: originally a cloth made in a broad loom, but later a fine cloth woven in a plain weave.
Broake buttons: Maybe broken or brocade buttons.
Broach, broche: a spit.
Browse: brushwood, young furze, etc used for kindling. "A vaggot o' browse thit were there ready vor th'oven". Passmore 1892.
Buckram: cloth stiffened with gum [187].
Bugle: a glass bead, usually black.
Burding pece (pice): a shotgun or fowling piece.
Burling: the removal of vegetable matter and the rectification of certain cloth faults in woollen and worsted fabrics, but not including mending.
Burrier: a device for picking and burling woollen cloth.
Butt: a heavy farm cart on two or three wheels.
Buttes of bees: hives of bees.
Byll: possibly a mattock, billhook, or a weapon [2].

Cabby & Shiff: [187]
Caffer: coffer
Cage: a cupboard for storage of utensils.
Calico, callacow: a cloth of cotton weft and linen warp until the 1770s, thereafter an all-cotton cloth.
Calamanco/callaminco: [*W153*] a glossy woollen satin-twilled stuff, checked or brocaded.
Cambric: fine linen, originally from Cambray in France.
Candellmolde: a pewter or tin mould for making candles. [121]

Canmas, canmy: [191] lists canmy -sheets as part of a bed, probably canvas or coarse linen sheets.
Carchieff, charcher: kerchief.
Card: an instrument used in pairs for preparing wool for spinning (carding).
Carme: context suggests cart [53] maybe carine misspelt.
Carpet: a table covering rather than a floor covering. [191] "It: 1 side table and 2 coverings the one linnen, and the other Kiderminster."
Carsey: = kersey.
Catheren: = katheren: listed with kitchen equipment it is probably the device to support pots in front of the fire.
Cattle, cattell: originally a man's wealth was measured by the number of cattle he possessed and the word 'cattle' came to mean a man's 'chattels', ie livestock as opposed to goods.
Cauldron: large cooking pot with three legs.
Cauvnes, sokinge: calves, presumably suckling. [13]
Chafendish, chaf(f)er: a vessel to make anything hot in, a portable grate for coals. Can be made of brass. [17]
Chain (harrow): cultivating equipment, possibly a part of a plough.
Chain (weaving): alternative name for the warp.
Cha(y)re, chear, cheere: chair.
Chamber: a room, usually a bedroom.
Chaping knife: chopping knife.
Charger: a large, flat dish [49]
Chattels: any kind of movable property, wealth, goods without life (see cattles above)
Chattell lease: the unexpired amount of any lease enjoyed by the deceased.
Cheesefatt: vessel used in turning curds into cheese.
Cheesewring(e): a press in which the curds are compressed in cheese-making.
Cheseles: chisels. [218]
Chimney crane: iron brackets fixed on the back wall of the fireplace and made to swing over the fire to support a vessel.
Chitell, chyttle: a kettle or covered brewing vessel. [193]
Chop stuff: either shop stuff or firewood [9].
Chufes: [85] possibly a chafing dish.
Chusen dishe: probably synonymous with a chafing dish. [42]
Citherne or **Cittern**: a musical instrument, resembling a guitar, but strung with wire instead of gut. [78]
Cley furnass: probably a furnace made of clay for heating up a copper. [226]
Cloam, clome: earthenware.
Clocke: [33] probably cloak.
Cloming: made of earthenware.
Cloth press: a press used in the finishing processes of woollen cloth.
Clowtinge leather: leather used for patching an article of dress: coarse leather. [5]
Clyant: any dependent: a person under the protection or patronage of another [LW103]
Cockloaft: attic or garret. [233]
Colet: [220]
Colter: coulter, part of plough [218].
Combs and **combing**: tools and process for preparing long staple wool for spinning.
Coast, co(o)ste, coust: a measure of nine gallons: associated with barrels and brewing and made of wood, it is also possibly a stand.
Copcase: cupboard for cups. [49]
Copyhold: a tenure, for which the tenanthas nothing to shew but the copy of the rolls made by the steward of his lord's court, also called *base tenure*.
Cornehutch: corn bin. [178]
Corslet, costlet(te furnished): piece of body armour (complete with strappings, etc) worn by foot soldiers of the late 15th to early 17th centuries.
Costatie: context suggests 'custody' [46]
Cotterells: associated with hearth equipment, they could be hooks used to support pots: see [27] "ij potthangeinges iij peere of Cotterolls wth the Reste of the Iron stufe".
Cottninge boxes: boxes associated with the fulling process, use not known.
Coule, cowle: either a cover to put over the fire embers for safety, or a tub with ears for carrying water.
Crok(e), croke: a cooking pot with three legs and a handle.
Crokes: by the yard in the stock of a shop-keeper [187] crocus/crokers - a yellowish-brown linen dyed with saffron.
Crockes, crookes, crucks: hooks of iron or wood associated with pack saddles or hearths.
Crooke: a crochet, a small hook suspended from the girdle to carry a purse.
Crookhouse: the inventory [233] suggests it is a building in which agricultural equipment was stored.
Cubet: cupboard [217].
Cubett board: a shelf for a cupboard.

Desperate debt: a debt unlikely to be recovered.
Diaper: a linen with a small repeated pattern, used for table cloths/napkins [173].
Diascordiall, dyescordyell: diascordium, a medicinal powder [188].
Dishcage: a cupboard for dishes.
Distaff: the cleft stick that holds the carded wool for a hand turn/spinning wheel.
Douse: dust/chaff for a bed.

Dowlace, dowlas, dowlis: a kind of linen used by the poor for sheets, shirts, smocks, etc. (Falstaff, about shirts given him by Dame Partlet - "Dowlas, filthy dowlas: I have given them away to bakers' wives, and they have made bolters of them". Henry IV III iii 18).
Dozens: a form of kersey cloth.
Draares, pele: pillowcases.
Drab: a thick woollen cloth of a dun colour.
Draftror: a cart (carin draught), or a dragger, a scoop for removing loose soil [88].
Drags, a pair of: a piece of ploughing equipment.
Dressing board: a board on which cloth is laid to raise the nap.
Druggett: a coarse woollen fabric felted or woven, self-coloured or printed one side. Swift refers to being "in druggets drest, of thirteen pence a yard".
Dryhorll: unknown meaning, but listed along with brewing and cheesemaking equipment.
D(o)ung(e) pots: panniers with bottom opening doors in which dung was taken out onto the fields.
Duroys: a common quality of woollen serge.
Dustbedd, duste bedde: a bed mattress stuffed with chaff

Eared tub: a tub with handles.
Ell(e)s: cloth 45 inches wide or a 1¼ yard length of cloth.
Enkle: see inkle.
Estemenes: a type of woollen cloth.

Farsse: [119] probably furze.
Fat, fate, fatte: a vat or cask.
Feestal timber, in the garden: [147] meaning unknown; fair poles?
Ferkinge: firkin, contained 9 gal.
Firevote: probably firewood; possibly *frewte*?.
Flaming: red flannel, used for underclothes & bedding.
Flesh pick, pike: a long fork for handling hot meat.
Flock: very short lengths of wool obtained during processing into cloth, and used for stuffing bed mattresses.
Follyers: listed along with cheese vats [238], meaning unknown
Foslet(t): a piece of furniture, type not known.
Freeze: context [42] suggests it is a piece of material, a coarse woollen cloth having a rough or shaggy nap on one side, originating in Ireland.
Freith: brushwood or wattle for fencing.
Frine pan: frying pan, either having handles or rings.
Fuller: one who fulls cloth, shrinking and milling it: known as a tucker in Devon, hence Tuckers Hall in Exeter.
Fuller's earth: a clay used for degreasing woollens.
Furnace, furnisse: a boiler or cauldron.
Furnished: an adjective applied to items such as beds, guns, looms, harness, etc. meaning all that goes with it, sometimes called the furniture.
Furse: furze that was cut, dried and used as a fuel for cooking.
Fustian, fustin: a coarse twilled cloth with a cotton weft and a linen warp and a pile like velvet.

Gallowses, gelloses: braces used for supporting the breeches.
Gambadans, gambadoes: boot-like attachments to the saddle to protect the rider's legs.
Gardiance: context suggests a location possibly the gardens or a locked outhouse [L3]
Gauginge: probably a measuring container.
Gebb, gibb, gybb: a stand for a barrel.
Gerses, gersey, gesses, gurses, gyrses: the leather strap around the belly of a horse that holds the saddle or pack in place.
Gimp: coarse lace on a wire or twine foundation, used for trimming wearing apparel.
Gingerline: see gyngerline below.
Girses: girths
Glasse box, cage, keadge: a wooden cupboard for glasses.
Goodge, goudge: context suggests a gouge.
Goodloom: listed together with lace in a shop, the context suggests 'galloon', a narrow ribbon or braid.
Gooespane: a dripping pan or a large cooking pan.
Gossip: 1. a sponsor in baptism, 2. a friend or neighbour, 3. tittle-tattle.
Greninge, grinying stone: grinding stone.
Grediron, gridiron, gridyre: a grated iron utensil on which flesh and fowl were cooked.
Gresse: grease
Groat: a silver coin worth 4d.
Grogram, grograyne: a thick coarse taffeta of mohair, silk or worsted, stiffened with gum.
Guisses, gyrses: horse girths.
Gyngerlyne: an adjective meaning a reddish-violet colour from the French *zinzolin*.

Halfendeale: a half share or moiety, usually in an estate. [88] refers to the "moitye or halfendett" of all goods & chattels, in will.

Hamborough: a fine woollen cloth originating in Hamburg.
Hanyburrows: the collar of a draught horse.
Harknine: found in the inventory of a tailor [224] along with pressing iron and shears.
Harnise, hurns: the parts of a loom that raise and lower the warp to form the shed.
Harratings, a pair of: in the inventory of a carpenter [164], meaning not clear.
Heriot(e), heriott: a fine, such as the best beast, payable to the lord of the manor upon the decease of the tenant. It is always personal and is no charge upon the lands, but merely upon the goods and chattels.
Hieran pot: an iron pot.
Hogside: hogshead.
Holbert: listed along with a limbecke [L1], together worth 15s: meaning not apparent (halberd?).
Holland, hulland: a closely woven linen fabric from Holland.
Holland cloam: earthenware imported from the Low Countries.
Hoolldisshes: [16].
Houpes quart: listed in [80] along with pewter dishes, salts and candle sticks. Possibly a quart pot bound round with hoops like a barrel.
Howst, implements of: [39] possibly household equipment.
Howthorn: listed in [236] along with a dresser: meaning not apparent (Hawthorn pattern china?).
Hupps and hupp timber: [LW85] context suggests timber used by a cooper.
Hutch: a box, bin, chest, coffer or other moveable receptacle.
Hutt apron: a common apron made of tow; or *huck* (= *huckaback*) misheard.

Inkle: coarse linen tape used for girdles, garters, apron strings and cheap binding, or the thread or yarn from which it is made.
Intermeddle: to meddle or interfere officiously in the affairs of others in which one has no concern.
Ireish cloth: a cloth of wool or linen.
Ironfoot: [173] possibly an anvil for nailing on the soles of boots.

Jack(e): a device for turning a roasting spit using weights [191]. Also cheap armour, especially for an archer, of steel plates sewn onto a leather or canvas jerkin.
Jeb, jebbe, jibb: wooden stand for a barrel.
Joyned, joynt, ioyned: an adjective used to describe furniture joined by mortices and tenons, instead of by nails or screws.
Justes: context suggests dialect pronunciation of joists.

Karin draught: listed in [132] along with farm wagons (probably "carrying").
Katherins: trivetts [82].
Kee, k(i)ene, key(ne): cattle.
Kene meat: cow meat, beef.
Kercher, kerchyff: kerchief.
Kersey, kersie: an important coarse woollen cloth, originally made in Kersey in East Anglia: known locally as Devonshire dozens.
Kertell: the skirt of a dress (strictly a half-kirtle) later called a petticoat.
Kettle: an open pot.
Kever: a cover for a dish.
Kytle butter: [28] cream? Or "kettle, butter" in a list?

Laces: ties or braids.
Laddersheeds: listed in [119] along with ladders and harrows.
Lafts: thin strips of wood, laths.
Lade pail: a lead bucket.
Lanthdend: [187] a lantern
Larnder: a wooden trough [36].
Lattine, latten: a metal alloy like brass.
Law nett, layer net: a net for catching game.
Legese, debts of: [46].
Ley sword: the beating up apparatus in a loom.
Limbecke, lymbicke: [L1] a contraction of alembic - a still. ("What potions have I drunk of Siren tears, distill'd from limbecks, foul as hell within" - Shakespeare: sonnet 119).
Lime waightis: appear among the weaving gear of [52] and were the weights to tension the warp in a vertical loom at which the weaver stood.
Linhay, linry: a shed open at the front for carts and cattle.
List: selvidge.
Lister: woollen equipment [51].
Locks: the short wool from a fleece.
Lommes, lumbes, a pair of: looms.
Longbow: a traditional "English" weapon - a six foot bow stave and yard long arrows, that could be fired at six per minute.
Lyd Sisterne: listed in [219] with a cheese press (lead cistern?).
Lysten, lysting yarn: a coarse cloth or yarn.
Lyverye tabell: a sideboard or side table.

Mail pillion: a leather or wooden saddle for carrying luggage, usually behind a servant.
Maltewhitche: malt hutch - a bin for storing malt.
Mark: a coin worth 13s 4d.
Massige, messuage: a dwelling house with the adjacent buildings and curtilage appropriate to the use of the building, a manor house.

Maties servis: majesty's service - appears in connection with arms in [13] and [16].
Mattcord and rugg: presumably table coverings.
Melting burrow: a heap of barley.
Milke borde: a shelf for milking utensils.
Morchadue: [1] mockado, a mock velvet of silk & wool or silk & linen.
Morrion, muryon: a steel helmet
Morte, morde: lard or fat.
Mortuary: a fee paid to a parson of a parish on the death of a parishioner - a sort of ecclesiastical heriot.
Moulding board: a bench where loaves of bread were shaped.
Mow: a rick or stack of corn or hay.
Mow stadle: a stand for a mow to keep it off the ground and away from vermin.
Muxpotts: a synonym for dung pots.

Napkin: a handkerchief, or table napkin.
Napre, nap(e)rye: household linen especially of the table.
Napron: an apron.
Nightcap: a male skull cap with close upturned brim worn indoors.
Noble: a gold coin struck by Edward III originally worth about 6s 8d.
Noil: the short fibre from the worsted combing.

On: one.
Overland: land held by a particular tenure in the West of England. [LW165]

Packe: a bundle of anything tied or bound up: the staves of a cask hooped up in a compact bundle: about 240 lb of wool.
Pale, payle, peel(e): a baker's shovel: a vertical timber in a fence.
Pangers: context suggests panniers.
Partlet: a fill-in of transparent gauze for a low neckline.
Peale, pele, pe(e)ll: a pillow.
Peater: pewter.
Peeson: [188] listed along with bacon, probably peason/pease, i.e. peas.
Pe(y)ck(e), pick, pike: a fireside poker or a pointed weapon, depending on the context.
Pediron: an implement of the hearth [24].
Pele draare, pellitye: pillow cases.
Performed, pformed: an adjective used to describe a bed (or musket) made up.
Perpetuanas: (end of 16th century) one of the "New Draperies", a glossy-surfaced woollen fabric, the warp of combing wool, the weft of carding wool: (cf. "The sober perpetuana-suited Puritans", 1606).
Petticoat, petycoytt: *m* an underdoublet [191]; *f* a skirt or underskirt.
Pieboard, pyeboard: listed along with barrels and tubs.
Piece: a length of finished cloth.
Pigstroos: probably pig's troughs.
Pikes: long spears (12/18 feet long) carried by infantry soldiers, usually in a square.
Pillowdrawer(tie), pellitye: a pillowcase.
Pillyan, pyllion: a low saddle: the part of a saddle that rests on the horse's back: a cushion for a woman to ride on behind the horseman: a pouffe; see also *mail pillion*.
Pinnions, pynnions: the short wool left in the comb when preparing worsted wool, known as noil.
Pirn: an alternative name for the weft spool.
Pish: short for parish.
Planchent: described as over the hall it is probably flooring, from the French *plancher*.
Plongs: planks.
Plowe stuffe: ploughing equipment.
Poddish dishes: possibly earthenware dishes.
Podinger, podger, poger: a porringer.
Points: laces or ribbons with metal tags for joining such as breeches to doublet. ("Their points being broken, down fell their hose" - Shakespeare, 1 Henry IV, ii.4.)
Pooledavis wimsheet: a coarse canvas used for sailcloth, formerly made at Poldavide, Douarnenez Bay, Brittany.
Posnet, po(r)snet, porsnut, posselet: a cooking pot with three feet and a long handle.
Pothangings: devices for suspending pots over a fire.
Pottager, pottinger: a soup bowl or a porringer.
Pown house: cider barn.
Poyt: [4] pewter.
Praise: appraise, value.
Presse: a large cupboard for holding clothes, often shelved.
Pruce cheast: a chest made of spruce from Scandinavia or a chest made in Prussia.
Putt: [132] in this context a cart: elsewhere a cask.
Putter, puyter: two of the many spellings of pewter.

Queel: an alternative name for the warp in weaving.
Que(e)lturne, queeling turne: a device for winding the warp.
Querte: quart.
Quickestuffe, quickstofe: livestock.
Quietus est: literally "he is quit" an acquittance given on payment of sums due or the clearance of outstanding accounts (accomptes).
Quill: an alternative name for the weft in weaving.
Quilturne, quylturne: a device for winding the weft.
Quuk pots: probably dung pots.

Rack(e)s: frames for hanging out the fulled cloth on tenterhooks to stretch and dry.
Rack tarrows: in the inventory of a fuller's widow [84] whose rack was indoors and was probably a warping frame, unbeknownst to the assessors, and the tarrows were the pegs round which the warp was wound.
Rang(e): sieve or strainer.
Rath(e): a rake like instrument used in weaving.
Reasons of the sun: sun-dried grapes, raisins.
Reed: the name given to the part of the loom that controls the set of the warp.
Remlet(t): remnant.
Ringe bittle: a heavy wooden mallet with an iron band round its head.
Rosom: probably rosin.
Roving: the name given to the sliver in the last stage of worsted drawing immediately before it is spun.
Ruffeband: a large collar of muslin or linen plaited, crimped, or fluted, worn by both sexes [LW98]
Russet: a coarse cloth or homespun of brown or grey: a dark brown colour.

Safeguard: a riding-skirt: a large outerpetticoat worn by females when riding to protect them from the dirt - Elizabeth Farthing [LW58] in 1609.
Safferon: [188] presumably saffron from a crocus.
Sagathes: a type of worsted cloth in the range of fabrics known as the New Draperies.
Sallet: a dish for salads or raw vegetables: a light helmet.
Salting standard: a measuring vessel for salt.
Sarcenet: a thin kind of silk used for linings.
Sar(d)ge: listed with kitchen equipment, searce
Saucer, sawcer: a receptacle, usually metal, for holding the condiments and sauces at a meal.
Sav(er)inge iron: an iron plate to protect the cook from the heat of the fire.
Sayes: relatively cheap worsted cloth, possibly used as a wall hanging.
Schoomer: scummer or skimmer.
Scouring: one of two processes of washing the wool or washing the woven cloth.
Scribling: the first part of the carding process when carried out by a machine.
Scruate: listed amongst kitchen equipment in [238].
Seame: fat, grease, hog's lard.
Searce: sieve [191].
Seasie: [238]
Secatreny: [188] listed along with safferon and dyescordyell, meaning not known.
Seedlip: a basket in which the seed to be sown is carried by the sower
Seeleinge, selyng, siling: the wainscotting, belonging to the tenant/householder.
Segard: safeguard.
Sellope: seedlip.
Semmett, semott: separator [19] & [5].
Serge: a cloth with a worsted warp and a woollen weft.
Shagg: a thick-piled long-haired cloth of worsted or silk.
Shalloon: an early worsted cloth.
Shaves: sheaves.
Sh(e)ares: heavy implements used to produce the required nap on the woollen cloth, not to be confused with sheep shearing.
Shed: the opening of the warp threads so that the weft can be passed through.
Shefe, sheaf, of arrows: storage for 24 arrows in separate compartments, to be placed in the quiver.
Shiff: [*187*]
Shool, show(r)le, showell: shovel.
Shopstuffe: stock-in-trade.
Shuttle: the spool carrier for the weft thread.
Sie(th): scythe.
Siling, sylinge: see seelinge above.
Sisors, sises: scissors.
Sines: [113] possibly sieves.
Sisterne, lyd: probably a lead cistern.
Skayner, skeemer, skeeml, skeymer: a scummer, skimmer, perforated spoon.
Skeys of sherops: cloth making tools.
Skillet, skellett: a metal vessel with a long handle, used for boiling and stewing.
Skranes: listed in [78] with shearing equipment, meaning not known (screens?).
Slaye, slea, sley, slia: an alternative name for the reed of a loom.
Slubbing: removing lumpy imperfections from slyvered wool.
Slyvered wool: a continuous strand of wool in a loose untwisted condition, ready for slubbing and roving preparatory to spinning.
Snappe for a mouse: a mouse trap.
Soale, soole, sowell, sowle: the ploughshare or sole of a plough.
Sokinge cauvnes: sucking calves.
Solar, soller: a loft or upper chamber.
Sparknife: a knife for cutting thatching spars.
Specialty, specialltie: a sealed obligation or bond: these are "sperate" debts owed to the deceased, as opposed to "desperate" debts which are not likely to be honoured.
Specketmaker: [169] the trade of Homephery Ashelford: possibly spectacle maker: "specks" is a long standing abbreviation for spectacles.
Sperate debts: see specialty.

Spill press: a press for finishing cloth employing interleaved papers (spills)
Spindle: the earliest device for spinning wool. It put the twist in the yarn and carried it wound on its shank. Also called a "turn" in earlier inventories.
Spindle whorl: the small round weight that fitted on the lower end of the spindle and acted as a flywheel.
Splintes: (pair of splints) overlapping metal plates of armour for the outer arms & elbows.
Spruce chest: a chest made from spruce imported from Scandinavia.
Spyninge turne: see spindle.
Stadel, stadle: a platform for a rick, raised on staddle stones.
Staffhooke: a hook or sickle with a long handle.
Stamen: the warp thread in an upright loom.
Stamen cloth: light woollen cloth.
Stammel: used in LW58 and LW74 as an adjective: made of stammel, a kind of woollen cloth, usually red in colour. "I'll not quarrel with this gentleman for wearing stammel breeches" - Beaumont and Fletcher - Little French Lawyer.
Stampt paper: paper, vellum, and parchment on which has been paid the duty levied in 1694.
Standard: a measuring vessel.
Stander, standish: a stand.
Standing presse: a wardrobe.
Standynge bedsted: a large high bedstead on legs.
Staple: thread of wool.
Stayned, stened clothes: decorative wall hangings, usually canvas.
Ste(a)ne: a drinking vessel made of stone (German steinern)
Steeche: stooks: 10 or 12 sheaves of cut cereal stood up in the field.
Sterling box: listed in [191] with irons, as is styleing box below.
Stile/steel cap: a simple steel skull cap packed with rags, used by foot soldiers to protect their heads.
Stile iron: an iron for pressing clothes.
Still: [133] & [191].
Stilling box: stand for a cask or distillation gear [233].
Stock: the part of a plough or other implement to which the irons are attached: the wooden frame that supports the wheel: a frame of a spinning wheel: a collective name for farm animals.
Stockyns: tailored or knitted leg coverings, worn with breeches.
Stoneinge, stonynge: stoneware.
Stowels: stools.
Styleing box: stilling-box [173].
Succingle: surcingle: a strap used to fasten the saddle.
Sullow: a plough.
Sweetmort: listed with foods in [173] it could be a kind of lard.
Swoule and hanginge: sword and scabbard.
Sylinge: ceiling or wainscotting.

Table board: a trestle table which was common at the time (no separate mention is made of the trestles).
Taches, targes: clasps, broaches, buckles or hooks.
Tacklen, tackling(e): tackle, equipment associated with a plough, saddle, etc.
Tallet(t): a hay loft with an open front.
Tammy: a worsted weft / cotton warp cloth in fancy colours, usually with a highly glazed finish; or a glossy silk fabric (tamine/estamine).
Teeck: a commodity (food?) in the inventory of a shopkeeper [129].
Tenter hook: a "nail" fixed in a frame on which cloth is stretched to dry to the right size and shape, without creases.
Tester: a wooden canopy over a four-poster bed.
Teening. teyninge, tyninge: an adjective to describe anything made of tin.
Tenement: any species of permanent property such as an abode, habitation, house or dwelling, which is held of another by any tenure.
Thames: the hames, part of the collar of a draught horse.
Thelder: the elder.
Thrum(b)(e)s: the surplus ends of cloth or warp thread arising out of weaving.
Thurt zaw, thwart saw: crosscut saw.
Ting(e)s, tynges: part of the harness of a packhorse.
Tong(e)ing(e) axe: from the context a slaughterer's tool.
Tops: the slivers of wool fibre produced by the comb in the manufacture of worsted cloth.
To, tow: two.
Torne: a spinning turne.
Toubele, twobill: a double-bladed mattock, with one blade parallel with the handle like an axe and the other at right angles.
Trancher cage: a trencher cupboard.
Treen, treing, treyng: wooden.
Trencher, tranche(r): a wooden platter.
Trendell, trundle, tryndell: a small truck on wheels.
Tresses: part of the ploughing gear.
Trillet, trylett: possibly a trivet.
Trining tools: listed in the inventory of a weaver [82], probably the tools of his trade.
Troll: [233].
Trowses: male garment worn under breeches.

Truckle/trundle/trokel bed: a low bed that was kept under a higher one, to be slid out. According to his diary (1667) Pepys and his wife slept on the high bed, whilst their maid, Willet, slept on the trundle bed.
Tuchcock: a 'touch-wood' or tinder box listed with a musket [43]. Touch-wood was a soft white substance into which wood was converted by the action of a fungus. It was easily ignited and continued to burn for a long time like tinder.
Tucker: an alternative name for a fuller, *vide* Tuckers Hall.
Tunne(r), tunnell: a funnel.
Turkey: red.
Turky cushions: cushions covered with wool with cross stitching.
Turn(e): a spinning turn.
Tyninge, tynnynge: made of tin.

Urinal: a night-pot.
Uster, usterd: worsted.
Ut(t)ing vate: a yeasting vat used in brewing.

Va(i)ntage: advantage, gain, profit; or surplus, excess.
Valines, vallants: valances, probably of a bed.
Vates, vatts: large tubs or vessels used for many purposes, often connected with brewing.
Verkins, virkinges: firkins.
Vesselstaves: strips of wood forming the sides of a barrel or vat.
Virginal: a stringed instrument like a harpsichord.

Wagges, waggets, wadges: wedges.
Waine: waggon.
Wallett, wood and: firewood.
Warp: the threads that run lengthwise in the cloth.
Warpin barrs, warpinge fra(r)mes: frames fixed to the wall and the pegs that are fixed into them, on which the warp or chain is prepared.
Warpinge pynes: the pegs which are stuck into the warping frame, around which the warp is threaded.
Waynebody and wheels: a wagon.
Weathers (of sheep): castrated rams, wethers.
Weats, woats: wheat or oats.
Weaving: forming the fabric by crossing the weft and the warp.
Week yarn: listed in the stock of a shop [187] at 6d per lb; wick yarn for candles?.
Weft: the threads that run across the woven fabric.
Wellturns: queelturns.
Whish: listed in the stock of a shop [187]; whisk, a small brush?
Whissels: sold in boxes along with hooks and eyes [187].
White cloth: undyed cloth.
Whitteells: possibly victuals as pronounced by Sam Weller.
W(h)ittells: large white shawls, usually of Welsh flannel, worn by country women and by mothers carrying babies [167] [LW162].
Whombe living: the lease on the house lived in by the deceased [135].
Whorres: [188]
Whyte candlesticks: silver candlesticks.
Widge beasts: horses.
Wimsheet, wemshett, wemshite, wymsheete: a winnowing sheet.
Window lid: possibly a shutter.
Witheys (of chairs): willow.
Woates: oats.
Woodrick, woodvine: a stack of timber.
Wool sorting: the separation and grading of wool from a fleece according to quality.
Woollens: cloth made from carded short staple wool.
Worsted: cloth made from combed long staple wool.
Wrench: [227] [L3] a tool associated with wool.
Wring(e): a press.
Wytt: corruption of *weed* (garment)?

Yeartubs: tubs with handles.
Yeating, yowtinge fatt(e): a vat used in the brewing of beer.
Yeild yewes: barren ewes.
Yolde yeawes: possibly excessive use of letter Y - old ewes [16].

NAME INDEX

References are to inventory and will numbers and are in bold print if the name is that of the deceased. Other occurrences of the name in inventories or wills are indicated by ordinary print, except when they refer to assessors or official signatories, when they are in italics. Ranges then show frequent (though not usually continuous) service. However, except for obvious witnesses, italics are not used for occurrences in administrations because it is not always easy to distinguish relatives and friends from overseers. Roman numerals refer to the Introduction. Some spelling variants are omitted here.

For reasons of space, the London Wills without surviving inventories were incorporated into the companion volume, *Uffculme: a Peculiar Parish*, which must therefore be consulted for all items beginning with LW. (Since all such cross-references can easily be recognized in this way, italics are not used for this purpose here, as was done in the other volume.)

PLACE INDEX

References are to inventory and will numbers. It is often clear from the context when names refer to fields or tenements in Uffculme, or are variant spellings of Uffculme hamlets or places in other counties; but in some cases the location has not yet been identified. Salisbury and London are not indexed where they occur as places where wills were proved.

References beginning with LW are to items in the companion volume, *Uffculme: a Peculiar Parish*. (Since all such cross-references can easily be recognized in this way, italics are not used for this purpose here, as was done in the other volume.)

Places in or near Uffculme

Places elsewhere in Devon

Places further afield

THE DEVON AND CORNWALL RECORD SOCIETY

(Founded 1904)

The Devon and Cornwall Record Society (founded 1904) promotes the study of history in the South West of England through publishing and transcribing original records. In return for the annual subscription members receive the volumes as published (normally annually) and the use of the Society's library, housed in the Westcountry Studies Library, Exeter. The library includes transcripts of parish registers relating to Devon and Cornwall as well as useful genealogical works.

Applications to join the Society or to purchase volumes should be sent to the Assistant Secretary, Devon and Cornwall Record Society, c/o Devon and Exeter Institution, 7 Cathedral Close, Exeter EX1 1EZ. New series volumes 7, 10, 13, 16 and 18, however, should normally be obtained from the Treasurer of the Canterbury and York Society, St Anthony's Hall, York YO1 2PW.

PUBLISHED VOLUMES, NEW SERIES

(Volumes starred are only available in complete sets)

1. *Devon Monastic Lands: Calendar of Particulars for Grants, 1536-1558*, edited by Joyce Youings (1955).
2. *Exeter in the Seventeenth Century: Tax and Rate Assessments, 1602-1699*, edited by W.G. Hoskins (1957, reprinted 1973).

*3. *The Diocese of Exeter in 1821: Bishop Carey's replies to Queries before Visitation*, edited by Michael Cook. Vol. I, Cornwall (1958).

*4. *The Diocese of Exeter in 1821: Bishop Carey's replies to Queries beforeVisitation*, edited by Michael Cook. Vol. II, Devon (1960).

*5. *Cartulary of St. Michael's Mount, Cornwall*, edited by P.L. Hull (1962).

6. *The Exeter Assembly: The Minutes of the Assemblies of the United Brethren of Devon and Cornwall, 1691-1717, as transcribed by the Reverend Isaac Gilling*, edited by Allan Brockett (1963).
7. *The Register of Edmund Lacy, Bishop of Exeter, 1420-1455: Registrum Commune*, Vol. I, edited by G.R. Dunstan (1963).

*8 *The Cartulary of Canonsleigh Abbey*, calendared and edited by Vera C.M. London (1965).

*9 *Benjamin Donn's Map of Devon, 1765*, with an introduction by W.L.D. Ravenhill (1965).

10. *The Register of Edmund Lacy, Bishop of Exeter, 1420-1455: Registrum Commune*, Vol. II, edited by G.R. Dunstan (1966).

*11. *Devon Inventories of the Sixteenth and Seventeenth Centuries*, edited by Margaret Cash (1966).

*12. *Plymouth Building Accounts of the Sixteenth and Seventeenth Centuries*, edited by Edwin Welch (1967).

13. *The Register of Edmund Lacy, Bishop of Exeter, 1420-1455: Registrum Commune*, Vol. III, edited by G.R. Dunstan (1968).
14. *The Devonshire Lay Subsidy of 1332*, edited by Audrey M. Erskine (1969).
15. *Churchwardens' Accounts of Ashburton, 1479-1580*, edited by Alison Hanham (1970).
16. *The Register of Edmund Lacy, Bishop of Exeter, 1420-1455: Registrum Commune*, Vol. IV, edited by G.R. Dunstan (1971).
17. *The Capture of Seisin of the Duchy of Cornwall (1337)*, edited by P.L. Hull (1971).
18. *The Register of Edmund Lacy, Bishop of Exeter, 1420-1455: Registrum Commune*, Vol. V, edited by G.R. Dunstan (1972).
19. *Cornish Glebe Terriers, 1673-1735, a calendar*, edited by Richard Potts (1974).
20. *John Lydford's Book*, edited by Dorothy M. Owen (1975).
21. *A Calendar of Early Chancery Proceedings Relating to West Country Shipping, 1388-1493*, edited by Dorothy A. Gardiner (1976).
22. *Tudor Exeter: Tax Assessments 1489-1595, including the Military Survey, 1522*, edited by Margery M. Rowe (1977).
23. *The Devon Cloth Industry in the Eighteenth Century: Sun Fire Office Inventories, 1726-1770*, edited by Stanley D. Chapman (1978).
24. *The Accounts of the Fabric of Exeter Cathedral, 1279-1353, Part I 1279-1326*, edited by Audrey M. Erskine (1981).
25. *The Parliamentary Survey of the Duchy of Cornwall, Part I: (Austell Prior-Saltash)*, edited by Norman J.G. Pounds (1982).
26. *The Accounts of the Fabric of Exeter Cathedral, 1279-1353, Part II 1328-1353*, edited by Audrey M. Erskine (1983).
27. *The Parliamentary Survey of the Duchy of Cornwall, Part II: (Isles of Scilly-West Antony and Manors in Devon)*, edited by Norman J.G. Pounds (1984).

28. *Crown Pleas of the Devon Eyre of 1238*, edited by Henry Summerson (1985).
29. *Georgian Tiverton: the Political Memoranda of Beavis Wood, 1768-98*, edited by John Bourne (1986).
30. *The Cartulary of Launceston Priory*, edited by P.L. Hull (1987).
31. *Shipbuilding on the Exe: the Memoranda Book of Daniel Bishop Davy (1794-1874)*, edited by Clive N. Ponsford (1988).
32. *The Receivers' Accounts of the City of Exeter, 1304-53*, edited by Margery M. Rowe and John M. Draisey (1989).
33. *Early-Stuart Mariners and Shipping: the Maritime Surveys of Devon and Cornwall 1619-1635*, edited by Todd Gray (1990).
34. *Joel Gascoyne's Map of Cornwall, 1699*, with an introduction by W.L.D. Ravenhill and Oliver Padel (1991).
35. *Nicholas Roscarrock's Lives of the Saints: Cornwall and Devon*, edited by Nicholas Orme (1992).
36. *The Local Customs Accounts of the Port of Exeter, 1266-1321*, edited by Maryanne Kowaleski (1993).
37. *Charters of the Redvers Family and the Earldom of Devon, 1090-1217*, edited by Robert Bearman (1994).
38. *Devon Household Accounts, 1627-1659, Part I*, edited by Todd Gray (1995)
38. *Devon Household Accounts, 1627-1659, Part II*, edited by Todd Gray (1996)
40. *The Uffculme Wills and Inventories*, edited by Peter Wyatt, with an introduction by Robin Stanes (1997).

FORTHCOMING VOLUMES

41. *The Cornish Estate of the Arundell Family, Fourteenth to Eighteenth Centuries*, edited by H.S.A. Fox and Oliver Padel (1998).

In the course of the next few years, the Society hopes to publish a volume on 19th century Cornish politics, an edition of John Hooker's *Synopsis Chorographicall of the County of Devon*, a new edition of Carew's *Cornwall* and an updated edition of the *Guide to the Parish and Non-Parochial Registers of Devon and Cornwall.*

EXTRA SERIES

I. *Exeter Freemen, 1266-1967*, edited by Margery M. Rowe and Andrew M. Jackson (1973).

II. *Guide to the Parish and Non-Parochial Registers of Devon and Cornwall, 1538-1837*, compiled by Hugh Peskett (1979).